Nellie Bly

Nellie Bly

Daredevil, Reporter, Feminist

Brooke Kroeger

TIMES T BOOKS

RANDOM HOUSE

Copyright © 1994 by Brooke Kroeger

All rights reserved under International and Pan-American Copyright Conventions.
Published in the United States by Times Books, a division of Random House, Inc., New York,
and simultaneously in Canada by Random House of Canada Limited, Toronto.

Library of Congress Cataloging-in-Publication Data

Kroeger, Brooke
   Nellie Bly: daredevil, reporter, feminist / Brooke
Kroeger. — 1st ed.
     p. cm.
   Includes bibliographical references (p.) and index.
   ISBN 0-8129-1973-4
   1. Bly, Nellie, 1864–1922. 2. Women journalists—United States—
Biography. I. Title.
PN4874.C59K76 1994
070'.92—dc20
[B]   93-30656

Manufactured in the United States of America

9 8 7 6 5 4 3 2

FIRST EDITION

Design by Laura Hough

*Endpapers: Nellie Bly ephemera, 1890–1901. Largely game
boards and promotional material resulting from Bly's
victorious globe-girdling race in which she circled the
world in the fastest time ever achieved. Photograph
by Starr Ockenga.*

For Alex

CONTENTS

✤ ✤

Contents

LIST OF ILLUSTRATIONS

❧ ❧

INTRODUCTION

❧ ❧

NELLIE BLY WAS ONE OF THE MOST ROUSING CHARACTERS OF the late nineteenth and early twentieth centuries. In the 1880s, she pioneered the development of "detective" or "stunt" journalism, the acknowledged forerunner of full-scale investigative reporting. While she was still in her early twenties, the example of her fearless success helped open the profession to coming generations of women journalists clamoring to write hard news.

Bly performed feats for the record books. She feigned insanity and engineered her own commitment to a mental asylum, then exposed its horrid conditions. She circled the globe faster than any living or fictional soul. She designed, manufactured, and marketed the first successful steel barrel produced in the United States. She owned and operated factories as a model of social welfare for her 1,500 employees. She was the first woman to report from the Eastern Front in World War I. She journeyed to Paris to argue the case of a defeated nation. She wrote a widely read advice column while devoting herself to the plight of the unfortunate, most notably unwed and indigent mothers and their offspring.

Bly's life—1864 to 1922—spanned Reconstruction, the Victorian and Progressive eras, the Great War and its aftermath. She grew up without privilege or higher education, knowing that her greatest asset was the force of her own will. Bly executed the extraordinary as a matter of routine. Even well into middle age, she saw herself as Miss Push-and-Get-There, the living example of what, in her time, was "That New American Girl." To admirers, she was Will Indomitable, the Best Reporter in America, the Personification of Pluck. *Amazing* was the adjective that always came to mind. As the most famous woman journalist of her day, as an early woman industrialist, as a humanitarian, even as a beleaguered litigant, Bly kept the same formula for success: Determine Right. Decide Fast. Apply Energy. Act with Conviction. Fight to the Finish. Accept the Consequences. Move on.

It is baffling that a life of such purpose and accomplishment—still daunting, even by the contemporary standard—did not incite the passions of any number of serious authors over the years. Even if none of the more commercially successful biographers sensed the essential universality of Bly's dramatic story, at least it should have snared the imagination of a feminist scholar or two, a doctoral candidate, perhaps. And yet, the Library of Congress catalog is without one documented biography of Nellie Bly. There isn't a single doctoral dissertation about her listed in any of the national computer registries. More disturbing is the puny place she occupies in journalism histories, which dismiss her with a sentence, maybe a paragraph.

Biographical sketches still appear in academic works and in literary and women's biographical dictionaries, however, and Bly's exemplary story has inspired over the past half-century at least a score of juvenile books. As a girl of ten, I happened to read one of them. Bly's story had greater impact on my life than that of any other nonfiction heroine.

I hadn't thought about Bly in years, but when my daughter, Brett, turned ten in 1986, I wanted to introduce her to the real-life character who had affected me so deeply. We had moved to New York two years before, and I thought a book-length encounter with Mother's patron saint would help her make sense of the hopscotch childhood she had been subjected to between the ages of three weeks and eight years. In that time, Brett had lived in Brussels, London, Tel Aviv (with weekends in the occupied Gaza Strip), and London again.

It suddenly became very important to locate that book and share it with her.

That is when I first became conscious of Bly's near invisibility. Judging from what was available in the bookstores, nothing had come along to replace those early biographies. From the reference librarians at the Library of Congress, I learned of the two Bly biographies that had been published in the 1950s in addition to the one I had read as a child, and that numerous others had come out since.

Through a search firm, I obtained a 1971 reprint of Mignon Rittenhouse's *The Amazing Nellie Bly* and Jason Marks's *The Story of Nellie Bly*. In the main branch of the public library in Kansas City, I found the other two from the 1950s, Iris Noble's incorrectly titled *Nellie Bly: First Woman Reporter* and Nina Brown Baker's *Nellie Bly*. I also found two fairly extensive juvenile biographies written as recently as 1989: *Making Headlines: A Biography of Nellie Bly* by Kathy Lynn Emerson and *Nellie Bly* by Elizabeth Ehrlich.

Brett and I read the books. She grew interested enough to turn Bly into a research project for school a few years later. We found that though all these books covered much the same ground, none of them agreed on any of the most basic facts of Bly's life, right down to the dates, ages, and spellings of important names, including hers. None seemed to have been based on much primary material. I began to think there wasn't much primary material. Brett thought I should find out.

She finished her project, a clever board game based on one of Bly's trips around the world, although Brett's version tracked Bly's whole life history with dice, markers, and squares ("*The Pittsburg Dispatch* offers you a job at $5 a week—advance two spaces!"). I began mine.

In the years since women's studies emerged as an academic discipline in the 1970s, specialists have scrambled to create a comprehensive feminine historical record, seizing on the most remarkable characters in history as their subjects. Hundreds of women's lives have been reclaimed in this period to fill what was an unconscionable void—what the historians refer to as the marginalization of women's achievements. Literary and other major luminaries whose fame endured, understandably, have turned up as subjects again and again. But the shelves of libraries and feminist bookstores also include fully researched works on the lives of the less well-known: obscure painters and composers, authors and orators, abolitionists and feminists, educators and actors, humanitarians and adventurers—even some of the women journalists (Margaret Fuller, Fanny Fern) who preceded Bly by several decades. The deterrent to Bly getting her due, then, does not appear to have resulted from deflation in the magnitude of her achievements with the escaping helium of passing time.

Bly's error seems to have been not leaving behind a substantial written record to which there would be ready access. Given her circumstances at the end of her life, this probably was not by design. But the fact is, no diaries or journals of hers have surfaced. When I began this project, there were only seven known letters of hers—six at the Carnegie Library in Pittsburgh and one in the Sophia Smith Collection at Smith College. The only family memorabilia, assembled by her grandnephew, James Agey, disappeared after his death in 1981.

The sheer volume of Bly's newspaper writing—long stories, always in the first person—could have helped make up for this deficit. In spurts over nearly four decades, Bly produced hundreds of newspaper articles for her three newspaper homes: *The Pittsburg Dispatch, The New York World,* and *The New York Evening Journal.* Unfortunately, none of the publishers of these newspapers had the foresight to provide an annual subject or writer index to their publications, in the wise manner of, say, *The New York Times* or *The Wall Street Journal.* To compile a comprehensive file of Nellie Bly's work required months in libraries in three cities, wading through more than 100,000 pages of infinitesimal typeface on what used to be crumbling pages of yellowed newsprint. These have been reproduced on scratchy reels of microfilm, which must be viewed on eye-straining mechanical readers that break down or refuse to print with exasperating regularity. Other historical figures have warranted such tedium over the years, but apparently, without the guarantee of a substantial body of additional available resource material, not Bly.

The result of this situation has been that whenever the known details of Bly's life have been summoned for those passing references in journalism histories or for sketchy biographical profiles, they have always derived from the same anorexic body of sources:

- the relatively few known newspaper stories by or about her clipped by libraries in Pennsylvania, where she grew up; or those retrieved and mentioned by previous researchers. These include brief biographical sketches by *The New York World* and *The Pittsburg Commercial Gazette* in 1890, and by *The World* in 1895
- the three nonfiction books she wrote: on her assignment to Mexico, her madhouse exposé, and her round-the-world race
- the entry on Bly in the 1893 encyclopedia *A Woman of the Century* by Frances Willard and Mary Livermore
- whatever articles appear under her name or her company's name in *The New York Times Index*
- her obituaries in various newspapers
- the seven known letters, available since the 1960s
- personality sketches of Bly included in Ishbel Ross's 1936 tome, *Ladies of the Press,* and in her 1965 book of profiles called *Charmers and Cranks*—largely based on the previously named sources
- a brief but informative text about Bly prepared by Jason Marks as a promotional gift from the American Flange Manufacturing Company in 1951
- the three undocumented biographies of Bly written in the 1950s for juvenile readers, all partly fictionalized
- glimpses of her in interviews conducted long ago with people who still remembered Bly.

The problem with Bly's legacy, then, was poor planning for posterity. Guaranteeing a place in history, it seems, takes more than living a phenomenal life. In most cases, it takes careful attention to creating a documented record of that life that isn't too hard to retrieve. Something like: I squirreled; therefore I was.

It began to make sense why the life of Nellie Bly had been relegated to the fascination of little girls—and fewer and fewer of them as time passed, with the limited circulation of those juvenile books. Bly's was an amazing story, but as a subject of serious inquiry, simply not cost-effective. Scholarship, then, was not going to be the impetus for her historical rescue. Alternative motivation was required: a quirky, even maniacal devotion to her memory, perhaps; and an intuitive belief that, in the end, she would turn out to have been worth the bother.

By tracing Bly's life trail backward through the layers of accepted lore and faulty secondary information, drilling for the closest primary source, I attempted to eliminate all the confusing "factoids" about her. Most of these had emerged from incorrect information in books and newspaper and magazine articles over the years, which had gained credence through repetition. Some came from fictions the early biographers supplied to fill in gaps. Census records helped clarify dates and family circumstances, as did old county and family histories, however flawed. I found enlightening paragraphs about Bly in the memoirs of some of her colleagues and in biographies of them.

Combing through all those old newspapers on microfilm, page by page by page, I have compiled as complete a record as possible of Nellie Bly, Working Reporter, and have copies of all those stories. This effort was ably supplemented by dogged helpers in Washington, Austin, Chicago, and Harrisburg, who receive more fitting tribute in the acknowledgments.

Several hunches paid off: For example, I located Bly's baptismal record, which put the confusion Bly herself had caused on the question of her birth date to permanent rest. Thankfully, she was highly litigious. There was court testimony of hers on record from the time she was fourteen years old and records of lawsuits filed into her final years. National, county, and municipal archives in all the places she lived, including Vienna, Austria, yielded information I only dreamed I would find, as did libraries, special collections, and historical societies all over the United States.

Although the numerous books on journalism and newspaper history tend to slight her, many have provided or confirmed important background information or inspired new ways of looking at Bly's life, as have biographies of editors and publishers such as Joseph Pulitzer and William Randolph Hearst, John Cockerill and Arthur Brisbane.

I traveled to all the key locations. I met and got to know just about everyone alive who has expressed serious interest at any time in

Bly's life. Several of these people, whose names appear in the acknowledgments, made indispensable contributions to this work.

Of the traditional sources on Bly, I have used only a few: the 1890 and 1895 biographical sketches that appeared in the newspapers, because she was likely the source for them; a 1936 profile in *The Pittsburgh Press* based on interviews with people who knew her growing up; the 1893 sketch in Willard and Livermore, again because she was a likely source; and Bly's three nonfiction books, plus her one novel. In addition, I amassed reams of court and archival documents, relevant birth, military, military intelligence, and death records, more than 600 newspaper or magazine articles by Bly and 1,000 others either about her or of direct relevance to her story. From the original 7 pieces of personal correspondence, my collection has grown to 130. I have interviewed her few last living links, some, by this point, frustratingly tangential, others of great assistance.

I realize that, compared with the collections most biographers work with, what was assembled for this effort may sound paltry. The story may not be as complete as I would have liked, but it is infinitely more complete than I thought would be possible when I began. Given what was available when I started, I rest pleased.

Some cautionary notes:

Throughout the text, the use of qualifiers will alert the reader to places where some informed speculation supplements the facts available, facts being what they are in the writing of a life. I have notated this work heavily so that the sources of information about Bly can be known and evaluated on merit, once and for all.

The city of Pittsburgh underwent several decades of confusion with reference to the spelling of its name. According to the Carnegie Library, from 1758 to 1890, *Pittsburgh* was spelled with an *h* at the end, as it is today. In 1890, the U.S. Board of Geographic Names decreed that every city keeping an *h* at the end of *burg* had to drop it. Pittsburgh, however, kept the *h* anyway and in 1911 petitioned to have it officially reinstated. That request was granted on July 22, 1911. During Bly's period there, 1880–1887, the newspapers spelled *Pittsburg* without the final *h*. I have handled this by spelling the city's name with the *h* everywhere except in the titles of the newspapers or in quoted references where it is spelled the other way.

My account of Bly's long legal entanglement is re-created from a combination of court records, transcripts where available, and reports carried in several New York newspapers during high points in the proceedings. If the result leaves a few slight unclarities in the text, my apologies.

Where information is sketchy—about her love life and her marriage, for example, as well as about the five years in Pittsburgh before she went to work for *The Dispatch*—it has not been for want of trying to obtain it.

Ishbel Ross's *Ladies of the Press* is the most complete reference on American women in journalism up to 1936, and I have referred to it several times for information on other women reporters of the era. Ross let most of the old saws about Bly stand uncorrected, however—which opens the question of how reliable her accounts of other early women reporters may be.

As for the weekly magazines *The Journalist* and *Town Topics,* they are quoted often enough in this book to give them an authoritative standing in Bly's life I am sure they do not deserve. Both were essentially gossip publications, largely reflecting the commercial and editorial biases of their proprietors. They were, however, well-regarded and well-read publications in their time and appeared without interruption during relevant periods in Bly's life. They provide, I believe, a reasonably fair representation, a baseline indication, of how Bly's glib journalistic colleagues and social peers perceived her life as she was living it. They also make for wonderful reading. Given the paucity of reliable, surviving, contemporaneous information about Bly, I made full use of these magazines' every reference to her. Although neither publication was indexed, it was possible to go through them for the relevant years from complete sets of neatly bound volumes. The Library of Congress has a full collection of *The Journalist* and the New-York Historical Society, *Town Topics.* Again, the same story: Whoever keeps the best and most accessible records gets the last word.

Now that the work is done, I remain convinced that Nellie Bly was worth the effort. She is an example of possibility, even still. Bly viewed every situation as an opportunity to make a significant difference in other people's lives as well as her own. Not wealth or connections or position or beauty or outstanding intellect eased her way to greatness. She never dwelled on inadequacy or defeat. Bly just harnessed her pluck, her power to decide, and then did as she saw fit, to both impressive and disastrous ends.

My immersion in Bly's life has triggered a dozen reactions—from delight to distaste. Her story is fascinating. She deserves a full and lasting legacy. I hope this book renews her license to provoke and to inspire.

Part One

❧ ❧

1864–1887

ARMSTRONG DEMOCRAT
AND FARMER'S AND MECHANICS ADVERTISER.

KITTANNING, PA. THURSDAY, AUGUST 10, 1843.

endeavored to be a consistent politician—I hold my principles as sacred, and I would not move to the right or left for the sake of office. For the truth of what I have here asserted, I would refer the public to my neighbors.

M. COCHRAN.

Warren, August 3, 1843.

The Armstrong Democrat and Farmer's and Mechanic's Advertiser,

August 10, 1843

(Don Toy)

I

❦ ❧

Childhood

ON MAY 5, 1864, IN THE WESTERN PENNSYLVANIA HAMLET OF Cochran's Mills, Mary Jane Cochran gave birth to the daughter the world would one day know as Nellie Bly.

Mary Jane was the second wife of Judge Michael Cochran, and Bly was his thirteenth child. He was a man of great standing in Armstrong County, born into a family of its early-nineteenth-century Irish settlers. Still, he made his own way to prominence and financial success. From the age of four, after his own father's death, he lived in the town of Apollo, bound out by his mother to learn the trade of blacksmith and cutler. By the time he was nineteen, he had a shop on Main Street, taking in his own indentured apprentices.

He married Catherine Murphy, and they started their family in a log house at what is now 217 South Second Street, having ten children in all, one about every two years. Michael was active in county politics. An avowed Democrat, he was elected justice of the peace in 1840, but three years later, his bitter campaign for the Pennsylvania State Assembly failed.

By 1845, he was buying up the property known as Pitts' Mills on the banks of Crooked Creek, eight miles from Apollo. There, he established a general store and took over a four-story gristmill, powered by the creek and modernized at his expense. He prospered quickly, augmenting his fortune with the profits of real estate speculation. In 1850, he was elected to the esteemed position of associate justice of Armstrong County. In his honor, Pitts' Mills became Cochran's Mills in 1855, at the end of his five-year term of office. After that, Michael Cochran would always be known as Judge.

The Cochran homestead was a large, functional box built on property Michael had acquired at Cherry Run, along the creek's winding banks. The year after Bly was born, a rattly covered wooden bridge was anchored onto stone piers, traversing the waterway near the mill site. No experience was more harrowing than getting caught inside that bridge when a horse thundered through. Legend held that a hair from a horse's tail slipped into the bridge's watering trough would turn into a snake. As for the creek, it boasted some of the region's best fishing: spoonfish, carp as large as fourteen pounds, and the finest bass.

Catherine died in 1857, and a year later, Michael Cochran married the widow Mary Jane Cummings. She had been born a Kennedy in nearby Somerset, Pennsylvania, the great-granddaughter of that county's first sheriff, Thomas Kennedy, a saddler and innkeeper by trade. Already fifty when the Civil War broke out, the judge was too old to join the Pennsylvania volunteers, although two of his sons by Catherine, John Michael and George Washington, mustered into Company C of the 103rd Regiment on September 16, 1861. Both were back home with honorable discharges before Bly was born or the war had ended. John reached the rank of captain.

With the two returning veterans, six of Catherine's children were at home when Mary Jane joined the household: Thomas Jefferson; Juliana; William Worth, who would run away to enlist before he turned fifteen; and seven-year-old Mildred. Catherine's three older daughters, Mary Ann, Angeline, and Isabelle, had long since married and left home, as had her oldest son, Robert Scott, who was raising his family in nearby Apollo.

Bly came along in the early spring of 1864, the day the Battle of the Wilderness began 300 miles south in the dense northern Virginia woods. But in western Pennsylvania, all was calm. The season brought noisy towhees, wild turkeys, and frogs. The woods hosted

Cochran's Mills, Pennsylvania, late 1800s
(Courtesy of Suzanne Myers)

yellow coltsfoot, mayapples, bluets, and violets. Skunk cabbage shot up dense in the swamps. Full brothers Albert Paul, born in 1859, was already five years old when Bly was born, and Charles Metzgar was three.

The Reverend J. S. Lemon at the local Methodist Episcopal Church christened the scrawny Cochran daughter Elizabeth Jane, but the name never took. While the other mothers of Cochran's Mills dressed their daughters in traditional gray calico and drab brown merino cloth, Mary Jane chose a starched, stand-out pink for her little girl, set off by frilly white challis and long white stockings instead of the standard utilitarian black. The soft colors brought blush to the child's pale cheeks, gave definition to the wishy-washy hazel of her eyes, and probably occasioned the nickname Pink, which stuck. From the very start, Mary Jane groomed her daughter to know how to attract attention and revel in it. The lessons would never be lost.

Albert, Charles, and Pink had ready playmates in their half nieces, half nephews, and numerous cousins, some of whom were their own ages and slightly older. Half sister Mary Ann was about the

The Cochran home in Cochran's Mills, Pennsylvania, late 1800s
(Carnegie Library of Pittsburgh)

same age as her stepmother. The twin daughters of half sister Juliana and her husband, David Shoemaker, could have called their playmate Aunt Pink even though the three little girls were separated in age by only five months—and Pink was younger.

Just before Christmas in 1866, when Pink was two and a half, Mary Jane bore another daughter and named her Catherine May. The last child, a boy she named Harry Cummings, came three years later. Pink doted on them both. Cummings, oddly, was the family name of Mary Jane's deceased first husband.

Although Judge Cochran had been prosperous by the local standard for some time, his wealth burgeoned after his marriage to Mary Jane. By his own reckoning, in the period between 1850 and 1860, his assets in personal property and real estate amounted to between

$3,000 and $5,500, at a time when an acre of Cochran's Mills land sold for about $30. Eleven years into his second marriage, Michael Cochran evaluated his own holdings at $57,000, a very substantial sum for 1870.

Burrell Township, where Cochran's Mills was located, counted some 950 residents in 350 households during this period, nearly half in Cochran's Mills, the township's only important settlement. They were laborers and farmers raising corn, oats, rye, and buckwheat—all grist for the judge's mill, which produced the highest quality buckwheat around at a dollar per fifty-pound sack or a barter of winter wheat in lieu of cash. Although farming was the major occupation, miners had begun to exploit the area's mineral wealth in bituminous coal, limestone, iron ore, and salt.

By 1869, the hamlet of Cochran's Mills had grown from the juncture of a few farms into a thriving community with a school, churches, a wagon maker, a shoemaker, a salt manufacturer, six blacksmiths, a huckster, a miller, a stonemason, two resident teachers, a minister, a dentist, a doctor, and another physician in training.

Little is recorded about life in the village during the 1860s, although Pink herself provided a glimpse in an article she wrote in 1888. She described her weakness for chewing gum, fine horses, letters, and, by implication, older men. She told a tale from the time she was a four-year-old, "still in bibs" in 1868, and how her passion for correspondence began:

> The seed which implanted this mania was the receipt of a letter addressed to my full Christian name which crossed the envelope twice. The writer was a boy of 12, so I have been told. I had formed his acquaintance while he was visiting his grandmother's in the country. We got up the flirtation by peeping at each other through the crevices in the back fence. He soon called, and many long summer days we spent "keeping house" under the east piazza. Cupid's cousin, Miss Sudden Fancy, made a dent in our baby hearts. So my little lover wrote me many misspelled love letters after cherry time when he had been taken home.

"Piazza" was a rather fanciful description for the yard beyond the plain, unpainted country porch attached to the Cochran house.

The judge was nearing sixty at about this time and, with his young second family, decided on another change. He sold off some of his real estate—but not the Cochran's Mills property—and purchased three acres of prime land in Apollo for the move back to the town he really considered home. The four adjoining lots formed a neat square on Wood Street, later called Terrace Avenue but always known as Mansion Row. On this acreage a grand two-and-a-half-story frame house was built for Mary Jane. There was enough surrounding land to graze the family cow and horse and give the two dogs plenty of running ground; a pleasure carriage stood parked outside.

The Cochran children who moved into the new house in 1869 were all Mary Jane's. William Worth died during the Battle of Plymouth, and all Catherine's other children had grown and moved on. Mildred, the only one of Catherine's children young enough to have developed a strong attachment to her stepmother, had married R. M. McLaughlin, of fine Apollo stock, and moved with her husband to a house a few streets away from her father's handsome new manse. Mildred always maintained a loving relationship with Mary Jane, and so did the McLaughlin children.

Years later, when reporters would ask, the family let it be understood that Judge Cochran had been a lawyer, even though his training was never more than avocational and self-styled. An associate justice was not required to be "learned in the law," since he participated only in the minor details of court business, such as appointing township officials, taking bail, selecting guardians for minors in Orphans' Court, and approving sureties in recognizance. Only the "president judge" was required to have an exacting education and examination in law and the classics before he could assume his post.

In published information only Pink or her mother could have supplied, the judge was described as "broad-minded and high-principled, a gentleman, cultured and polished." He was credited with "appreciating all the advantages of education," giving his children every possible academic boost. It was, at best, a loving embellishment; at worst, an attempt to fabricate a more sophisticated background for the Cochrans once they determined this was an advantageous thing to do.

If any of the judge's fifteen children pursued higher studies, there is no known record of it. None of them, for example, entered law or any other profession, although several demonstrated their father's appetite for entrepreneurial risk—Pink being not the least of them. Although the judge apparently kept a library, from which Pink liked to take his medical book and amaze her playmates with its titillating contents, the only other evidence of his reported passion for learning was a contribution of twenty-five dollars recorded in 1848 as an "endorsement" of Allegheny College in Meadville, Pennsylvania, at the behest of the regional conference of the Methodist Episcopal Church. This contribution entitled him and his descendants to "perpetual scholarship" at the college, that is, free tuition after payment of room and board. The college has no record of any of Michael Cochran's family members ever attending.

Whatever influence the judge had on Pink "in the direction of study" would soon be consigned to her deepest imaginings. Within a year of the move to Apollo and the beautiful new house, four months after Harry's birth and just two months after Pink turned six, Judge Cochran was stricken with a crippling, dumbing paralysis and quickly died.

If Michael Cochran had intentions for the disbursement of his estate, they would never be known. The former associate justice of Armstrong County had never bothered to make out a will.

❦

The seminal event in the young life of Pink Elizabeth Jane Cochran, the one that irrevocably changed the course of everything that was to come, was the loss of her beloved father. More to the point, it was the loss of a beloved and wealthy father who had made no specific provisions for the security of her mother, her siblings, or herself. It would not be long before Pink would begin to see herself as the one responsible for everyone else's well-being, the one who could right this seeming injustice and every other one she ever encountered.

The judge was dead not quite seven weeks when Robert Scott Cochran, his oldest son by Catherine, filed a petition in Armstrong County Orphans' Court at Kittanning, demanding an inquest to determine the appropriate partition of the estate among the judge's many heirs. The nature of the property made it impossible to divide, so under provisions of Pennsylvania state intestate law, it was appraised for sale at public auction. The four allotments included Mary Jane's beautiful new home.

Although no direct record has survived, it is impossible to imagine that the decision to sell Mary Jane's house out from under her did not cause a severe breach in whatever relations existed between Michael Cochran's older children and their stepmother. It is likewise impossible to imagine that the judge did not intend for his wife and five minor children to be able to keep their home in the event of his death. And yet, it was not unusual in 1870 for a man of Michael Cochran's means, especially in his particular circumstances, to die intestate. The difficulty in making equitable distribution between children of two mothers was pervasive.

Within a year of the judge's passing, all his property had been sold off. The Apollo house and acreage, for example, was appraised at well over $3,000 but sold at auction for $2,650 to the town banker, Colonel Samuel Jackson, and his brother, James. The mill and surrounding fourteen acres went to John Schwalm and W. H. Carnahan for $17,000. Two other parcels sold for a total of $250, bringing the full value of the judge's real estate to nearly $20,000. Under Pennsylvania law, Mary Jane was entitled to the customary dower, the portion of the estate known commonly as "the widow's third." This was effectively a stipend from the estate representing the interest on a third of its total value paid in twice-yearly installments until her death. At that point her husband's heirs could divide up the principal. That left the other two-thirds of the proceeds of these sales to be divided equally among the children. Of course, in this case there were fourteen children. Catherine's surviving nine, all adults, got their portions outright, amounting to about $1,000, a modest but not inconsequential stake. Colonel Samuel Jackson, the town banker and now the new owner of the house, was appointed guardian to

The Cochran mansion in Apollo, Pennsylvania, 1993
(Don Toy)

administer the funds of Mary Jane's minor children until each came of age.

What all this meant was that Judge Michael Cochran's wealth came very quickly to mean a measure of disappointment to his family. Mary Jane ended up with her furniture and other household possessions, the horse and carriage, the cow and one of the dogs, and very little money. Her dower from the proceeds of her husband's estate amounted to some $400 to $500 each year. In addition, she could claim, and did, a yearly allowance from the children's money while they lived at home to help defray the cost of their room and board. This amounted to another $400. In other words, in addition to whatever other monies she may have had, Mary Jane could count on an income of roughly $16 a week until the children were out of the house. After that, it would be a little less than $10 a week—a bit more than the wage of a well-paid factory worker of the time. Not poverty, to be sure, but a dramatic comedown even by 1870 standards. For one of Apollo's most prominent families, it was a disaster.

✧

Apollo had 764 inhabitants in 1870, nearly twice its population of ten years earlier. All but two were white. In October of that year, when it was clear Mary Jane would have to give up her home, she paid $200 for a modest two-story frame house on a lot two streets away, into which she transferred what furniture would fit. When the grand house was sold, she and the children moved into their new residence. The contrast between the two dwellings was as profound as the drop in standard of living it symbolized. The Mansion Row residence had more than 10,000 square feet of space for the children to roam; the new house, with its narrow stairwells and four stone fireplaces, was five rooms in one-tenth the area.

Albert, Charles, and Pink, and later Catherine and Harry, all went to school a short walk from home and to Sunday School at the nearby Methodist Episcopal Church. Pink's classmates remembered her as a skinny, sickly, plain brunette, whom the boys called Lizzie— a name she would detest for the rest of her life—and her family and all the girls called Pinkey or Pink. She was already quick with repartee. Lillie Elliott Myers, one of Pink's childhood friends, told her grandchildren how much she had envied Pink's long white stockings and that she had often told her so. Pink would always reply that she wished they were black.

Despite their reduced economic circumstances, Mary Jane made sure her daughter learned to play the piano and organ, a parlor skill she enjoyed into adulthood. Horseback riding was another great pleasure. Even in this troubled period, Pink already was demonstrating her independence. Years later, she liked to tell the story of her first attempt, with no adult supervision, to make tea when she was just "a small tot." She put the entire contents of a five-pound canister into one pot and covered the tea with water. Then, as she recounted, in a short while it had grown—Jack and the Beanstalk wasn't a marker. I tried to hold down the lid—it simply grew off. After it had covered the stove and commenced to grow on the floor, I tried to pick it up. It grew too fast.

Finally, I was rescued by my family when the tea had carpeted the kitchen.

It would be her last attempt at tea making until World War I.

School was a two-story white frame building, forty-eight by forty-five feet, with rooms adapted to accommodate separate primary and high school departments. It was built just before Pink was born and furnished with comfortable, unpainted white pine desks and seats. There were two teachers. William Davis taught the older children upstairs, and a succession of young women conducted the downstairs primary. His salary was twenty-five dollars a month; theirs, eleven dollars less. A total of 120 "scholars" studied the customary four months a year.

By the time Pink entered school, the new desks had all been grooved with curves of "railroad tracks," carved by boys using both prongs of a broken pen point. The pen points would then be set into them to run as trains. For punishment, there were willow rods, usually cracked off trees up the ravine in Owens' Woods. Mr. Davis would send the boys out to cut the switches—which, on the advice of the oldest boys, would be notched at the joints for easy breakage before they got to the teacher's hands.

Pink was not an outstanding student. Although she later claimed to have been a voracious reader in childhood, favoring travel books, her schoolmate (later her half nephew-in-law) Dr. T. J. Henry remembered her years afterward as one who "acquired more conspicuous notice for riotous conduct than profound scholarship." In other depictions, he said simply that she was "rather wild." Given the combination of her youth, grief, and unsettling changes at home, it is not surprising that school would become the place for Pink to act out.

Her own recollections of childhood, supplied years later to reporters as they tried to fathom the sources of her spunk and daring initiative, painted a slightly different picture:

When [she was] a very little girl, she wrote love and fairy stories by the score. On the flyleaves of books and on loose scraps of paper. For whole hours at night she lay in bed unable to go to sleep because of the tirelessness of her imagination, weaving tales and creating heroes and heroines simply for her own delight or the gratification of the young companions to whom she would relate them. It was her wont to get the girls of the town together and tell them these stories; it was easier to make up some story to tell them than to repeat an old story. So active was the child's brain and so strongly her faculties eluded sleep that her condition became alarming and she had to be placed under the care of physicians.

After school, the children helped with chores and then would head out to play. The girls enjoyed rag dolls, mussel shells, broken dishes, and whatever else they scavenged. The boys favored mumbletypeg, marbles, I Spy in the graveyard, football with an air-inflated pig's bladder, and paddleball with a flat paddle instead of a bat. There was fishing, sledding, skating, and rolling barrel hoops down the hills. Monotony was broken by the sheep and cattle that passed through the town's streets on drives to the East Liberty Stockyards. Entertainment was provided by such characters as the storekeeper, John Bair, who would buy frogs caught by the older boys, conk their heads to stun them, hack off their hind legs, and ship the severed appendages off to Pittsburgh while the poor maimed creatures were left, half-dead, to flounder in the alley behind Bair's store. Everyone was appalled, but no one did anything about it.

The town was almost fully self-sufficient. Farmers raised the grain that the millers ground into flour and feed. They raised cattle for butchering and for hides that were fashioned locally into boots, shoes, harnesses, and saddles. The crocker turned out crocks and canning jars on Maple Street, and Mr. Mills in his tin shop made the containers for canning fruit. Even a coffin could be built overnight upon demand. Lime was burned up at Lime Quarry Hill, and just outside the town limits were carpet weavers and cradle makers who also fashioned hickory chairs and split brooms of shaved hickory saplings.

By January of 1873, when Pink was nine and the judge had been dead two and a half years, Mary Jane Cochran took her third set of wedding vows at home in the presence of her children and William Henry, the justice of the peace. She married John Jackson Ford, known as Jack, whose wife, Henrietta, had died six months before. Mary Jane was at least forty-three at the time, twice widowed, and raising five children alone on a modest fixed income in a small western Pennsylvania town. Any partner for a woman in that place and situation was better than none; and what she had to pick from offered not much more selection than that. This may be all the explanation there is for Mary Jane's disastrous choice.

Ford was a Civil War veteran, a member of Company G, 6th Artillery, 212th Regiment of the Pennsylvania Volunteers, a sometime cooper and sometime laborer who had tried his hand at gold panning out west in the 1850s. He was a couple of years younger than Mary Jane, and childless, since his and Henrietta's only offspring had died in infancy. At the time of the marriage, his taxable assets were worth $400. Parts of two Apollo lots he owned were soon forfeited to debts and "bad company." Plainly, he was no match for the memory or the person of Judge Michael Cochran, not as stepfather, not as provider, not as a husband, not as a man. More ominously for Mary Jane and her children, he was a mean and abusive drunk.

Ford moved into Mary Jane's little house right after the wedding. By then, she had given up the horse and carriage and the cow.

During that time Pink's oldest brother, Albert, had come of age and was in need of a position. It seems that none of the many Cochran relatives in Apollo was willing to help the widow's son get established. His respected half brother Robert Scott Cochran, later referred to in newspaper articles as "squire," had moved from clerking to being Apollo's toll collector on the Pennsylvania Main Line Canal to postmaster out of the cigar and stationery store he ran in town. Cousin Thomas A. Cochran was the local pharmacist and, as brother-in-law of Colonel Jackson, a member of nearly every prominent board. Neither, with numerous sons of his own to look out for,

had any place for Mary Jane's oldest boy. Albert's own retelling of his
employment history had him working at age twelve as a newsboy on
the Pennsylvania Railroad for sixteen months before going to Parker,
at the northern tip of Armstrong County, for nine months to pump
oil during its very short-lived boom. In 1875, he claimed to have
clerked for two years for the Burtis House, a hotel in Davenport,
Iowa, where his half brother George had settled. But he returned to
Apollo in 1877 to work as a clerk for the iron firm of Rogers and
Burchfield. In 1878–79, he said, he opened the DuBois House, a
hotel established by the millionaire lumberman John DuBois in the
Pennsylvania town that carried his name northeast of Apollo.

The dates and job descriptions were included on the curriculum
vitae that Albert had supplied for a gushy collection of prose and
verse portraits titled *All Sorts of Pittsburgers* that appeared in book
form in 1892, indicating the measure of prominence he was to attain
in his own right as a local distributor of rubber goods. Mary Jane
added some details in a sworn statement delivered in 1879. In 1874,
Mary Jane said, she decided to set Albert up in the grocery and confectionery business with his stepfather. She herself made and sold the
ice cream. It turned out to have been a terrible idea. Hostilities flared
constantly, exacerbated by Ford's intemperance. In March 1875,
Ford, in a drunken rage, had threatened Albert at gunpoint. Soon
after, they closed the business down, and Ford went back to cooper-
ing. It would have been at this point that Albert left for Iowa. In
1878, Ford tried grocering again—this time without Mary Jane's
help—but he gave it up almost immediately.

Pink was an impressionable age eleven in 1875, when life for
her mother was in monstrous disarray and the women's rights movement in Pennsylvania, indeed across the nation, was just starting to
take root. The status of women had started to change in Pennsylvania in all areas except politics. So-called normal schools had opened
throughout the state to train young women as well as men for careers
in teaching and business; the state's first women's medical college
had been established; a progressive married women's property law
had been passed; and *Godey's Lady's Book,* the most widely circulated
women's magazine, no doubt a favorite in many Apollo households,
was advocating advances for women on all fronts except suffrage.

The most immediate example of possibility for Pink was Jennie Stentz, the woman who in 1875 established a weekly newspaper called *The Kiskiminetas Review.* Stentz sold the paper within two years, then left town for unknown destinations. If she had a special relationship with Pink during her time in Apollo, no record of it has survived. Yet it stands to reason that in a community the size of Apollo, Pink was well aware of the lady newspaper publisher and the model of new initiative she represented.

Life in town, except whatever went on behind closed curtains, was mostly uneventful, save the terrifying fire of 1876. All lighting was provided by kerosene in this period, dangerous in a town with no fire department. On January 19, a lamp overturned in the shoe store of H. A. Rudolph. Flames, whipped along by an unfortunately timed gust of high wind, destroyed three square blocks in the center of Apollo, including twenty-four buildings above the canal. Townspeople fought back with common household buckets filled with water, their only weapon. Property loss was set at $32,000, only $12,000 worth of which was insured. Miraculously, no one was killed.

The town appealed to Albert, now eighteen, as a place to settle down and plan his future. He saw himself as a man of leadership and great potential, although he already was developing a reputation for too much fondness for alcohol. A year after the fire, when he was working for the iron concern, he led his school chums in forming a club called the Muggins Family, choosing a star and crescent for their emblem and cardinal red for their color. Albert took the club name of Dudley, as father of this oddly constituted group of unknown purpose. Among its members was Michael Hermond Cochran, a contemporary of Albert and the son of his half brother Robert Scott. Of Pink's other siblings—Charles, Catherine, and Harry—in this period, nothing is known.

꧁ꕥ꧂

New Year's Eve, 1878. Against her husband's wishes, Mary Jane Ford went with her children to the holiday celebration of the Methodist Episcopal Church. The church had taken over the Odd Fellows' Hall for the occasion, setting up tables on the upper floor of the small two-story building on Main Street. As neighbors in festive mood chatted happily, Jack Ford, drunk and muttering, burst into the hall, stomped up behind Mary Jane, jerked a loaded pistol out of his pocket, and announced that he would kill her if she were "the last woman on earth." Albert, aided by two townsmen, subdued Ford while Mary Jane fled down the stairs and out the door. Breathless, hysterical, she ran to the home of her friends Millie and John G. King. She stayed with them for several days while Ford cooled off and Mary Jane regained composure.

The couple would reconcile, but only for nine more months. On September 30, things fell apart again.

That evening, the family sat down to dinner and an argument erupted. Ford went wild. He swore at Mary Jane and the children, broke furniture, slammed into the plaster walls until they cracked, knocked down and broke the hanging baskets, and kicked a hole in a rocking chair. His rage continued into the next day, when he came home shouting and carrying on, took Mary Jane's freshly ironed clothes off a chair, threw them on the floor, then dumped whatever clothes remained in the laundry basket into the backyard, where he drenched them with water.

At the table, Ford flung his coffee to the floor, then carved the meat. He picked up the bone and hurled it at Mary Jane. She threw it back. Ford jumped up, took a loaded pistol out of his pocket, and lunged at his wife. Pink and Albert jumped between them and blocked him while Mary Jane escaped out the front door. Albert followed, and the two ran over to the home of Mary Jane's stepdaughter Mildred Cochran McLaughlin. Even the neighbors claimed to hear the pistol snap and ran to the windows to see Mary Jane and Albert tearing down the street. The younger children quickly followed.

Ford nailed the doors and windows shut and used a ladder to an upper window to enter and leave the house. It was a week before Mary Jane could get in to remove her furniture. The house was a wreck. She rented another home and moved her family into it. Ford left town.

On October 14, 1878, Mary Jane Kennedy Cummings Cochran Ford, in the beady, gossipy, small-town gaze of all Apollo, took the momentous step of suing Jack Ford for divorce in the Armstrong

County Court of Common Pleas. Amid a total county population of some 40,000 people, Mary Jane's was one of only fifteen divorce actions that year, one of only five in which the wife was the plaintiff. Explained differently, although the number of divorces in Armstrong County doubled in the 1870s against the previous decade, just eighty-four divorces were granted in that ten-year period.

For Mary Jane's case, two of her five children, Albert and Pink, offered testimony, along with eleven of the Fords' friends and neighbors, who, under oath, bore colorful witness to the truth of Mary Jane's charges on ten counts of "cruel and barbarous treatment." To wit: drunkenness; neglecting to provide her the "necessaries of life"; chiding, swearing at, and cursing her; threatening to do her bodily harm; carrying a gun and keeping it loaded under the bed at night; ungovernable temper; making "pugilistic demonstrations," kicking the household furniture, and breaking and destroying things; calling her all kinds of vile names and doing violence to her person; threatening to shoot her and pulling and driving her out of her own house and his presence; and putting her in fear and dread so that she had been forced to withdraw from her house and family. If Ford ever responded in his own defense, there is no record.

Almost all the witnesses added graphic details to Mary Jane's moving account. Albert, by then nineteen, testified that Ford was vulgar and referred to his mother almost daily as "whore" or "bitch," words Mary Jane could not bring herself to utter. He threatened to kill her on more than one occasion, Albert said, and charged that Ford had tried to extort money from her numerous times and never provided her with any kind of a living.

Phoebe Stitt said there was no way she would risk her life with the likes of J. J. Ford. Margaret James swore she heard Ford tell little Harry to call his mother a "black-eyed devil." Phoebe Smith said her neighbor Mary Jane was a good and tidy housekeeper who tended to all her wifely duties. Lizzie Small said to her knowledge Ford was never sober.

John King described Mary Jane's state the night of New Year's Eve, when she ran to his house for safety. "Mrs. Ford was so frightened that she went behind the chimney for fear that Ford would shoot her through the window," he said. "Afterwards she went upstairs and all that night she was in constant fear that Ford would break into the house and kill her." He added in her defense that he knew for a fact she had always washed and ironed Ford's shirts, bought and paid for his underwear out of her own money, and was never cross or ugly to him, despite how he treated her.

Colonel Samuel Jackson, the children's court-appointed guardian, said that Jack Ford had been "quarrelsome" for the twenty years he had known him and that since his marriage to Mary Jane he had been drunk at least half the time.

Pink was between the ages of nine and fourteen during this miserable marriage, a time of extreme sensitivity in her development. This was her testimony:

> My age is 14 years. I live with my mother. I was present when mother was married to J. J. Ford. I [have] seen them married about six years ago. Ford has been generally drunk since they were married. When drunk, he is very cross and cross when sober. [I have] heard him scold mother often and heard him use profane language towards her often and call her names: a whore and a bitch. [I have] seen mother vexed on account of his swearing and bad names and [I've] seen her cry. Ford threatened to do mother harm. Mother was afraid of him. [I've] seen Ford throw the clothes after being washed and ironed on the floor and throw water on them and seen him upset the table. The first time I seen [*sic*] Ford take hold of mother in an angry manner, he attempted to choke her. This was sometime after they were married. The next time was in the Oddfellows Hall New Years Night 1878.

Pink went on to detail Ford's abuses, her mother's long-suffering domestic care for him, his habit of keeping ale and sometimes liquor in the house and that he fought often with Mary Jane about money. The name she signed to the court reporter's rough transcription was Pinkey E. J. Cochran.

Pink came of age in the heat of that domestic turmoil while the early rumblings of revolutionary change in the role of women caused their own temblors outside. Very soon, she would begin to exhibit an unflagging devotion toward her mother. Its origins seem obvious. The specter of Mary Jane's willful helplessness in the face of Ford's brutality no doubt loomed. Pink, despite having two active and devoted older brothers, took upon herself the role of Mary Jane's champion and protector, a position Mary Jane accorded her without hesitation.

At the same time, Pink understood with precocity the power of unflinching self-reliance, and would come to grasp the necessity of being prepared to provide for her own financial and emotional security. She had seen firsthand that a commitment of dutiful service to family and husband—three husbands, in her mother's case—carried no lifetime guarantees.

On June 3, 1879, the court granted Mary Jane her divorce from J. J. Ford. No one could have blamed her for taking a course so drastic and shameful for its time, but that did not make the result any less demeaning for the once-venerated family. Mary Jane handed her elaborately decorated marriage certificate back to the Armstrong County authorities in Kittanning, where the clerk, not knowing what to do with it, stuck it in her divorce file. She dropped the name Ford and with that, moved quickly to eradicate the painful episode from family memory. Immediately, she resumed her more comfortable station as the widow Cochran. Ford was never mentioned again. Pink, by then fifteen and no doubt afflicted by the sting of these disgraceful events, thought the time was right to move on. Given her determination to be able to support her mother and herself, it made sense to use the opportunity to train for a career. She was a girl. Teaching seemed a logical choice. At her age and station, the only reasonable avenue of escape was boarding school.

❧

If Pink were going to take the daring step of going away to school, the obvious choice was the State Normal School at Indiana, fifteen miles due east of Apollo. The school had opened its doors only four years earlier, on May 17, 1875, in accordance with the Pennsylvania General Assembly's decision nineteen years before to accredit twelve private "normal schools," each in a different district. Their main purpose was to train young men and women for careers in teaching and business.

Indiana's normal school was the pride of Indiana County. Its twelve-acre campus with three school buildings cost nearly a quarter of a million dollars and was "conceded to be the best of its kind in the United States." It had a first-rate teaching staff and state-of-the-art facilities: gas lighting, steam heating, hot and cold running water, bathrooms, lavatories, water closets, laundry, bakery, cooking department, engine room, workshops, reading room, reception room, reference library, gymnasium, 1,000-seat chapel, book shop, and carpet on the floors of the women's dorms. For Pink, the only question was whether she had enough money to go.

Since Judge Cochran's death nine years earlier, Apollo's banker and most distinguished citizen, Colonel Samuel Jackson, had administered the funds set aside by the court from Judge Cochran's estate for Mary Jane's children. Although Jackson was given the appointment because of his position as cashier and later head of the nine-year-old Apollo Savings Bank, his sister's marriage to one of the nephews of the late Judge Cochran coincidentally had made him kin.

Colonel Jackson made frequent disbursements from each of the children's accounts, the largest amounts going to Mary Jane to defray the cost of their board. According to Jackson's accounting sheets, Mary Jane claimed about $100 each year from Pink's account, as well as from each of the other children's. Other specific entries on Pink's ledger sheets over ten years include three doctor visits, clothes, a sixty-eight-dollar organ, sheet music, tuition by "Professor French"—presumably John H. French, the highly cultured principal of the normal school, for music lessons—a few books, cash to visit Saltsburg, and three dollars cash another time to attend an exposition. On at least two occasions, Jackson petitioned the court to release funds early for the children's use and comfort.

In the summer after her mother's divorce, Pink walked over to the bank to discuss her finances with Colonel Jackson. Expenses at the Indiana State Normal School would run about $75 per term for "tuition, board, lights, heat and washing up to 10 pieces." The total, including travel and spending money, would amount to well over $400 to complete the three-year teacher's curriculum, which she had

COL. SAMUEL McCARTNEY JACKSON.

Colonel Samuel M. Jackson, Bly's court-
appointed guardian, circa 1890
(Carnegie Library of Pittsburgh)

decided to pursue. Jackson, who happened to be a state-appointed member of the normal school's board of trustees, told her she would have enough money to graduate. With that understanding, Pink enrolled for the fall term on September 8, 1879. Jackson signed her registration as guardian.

To be accepted at the normal school, a student had to be of "good moral character" and more than fourteen years of age, unless the school made an exception. Pink was already fifteen the year she applied with 124 other girls and 146 boys. Each was expected to rise at 6:00 A.M. and be asleep by 10:00 P.M., sweep his or her own room, and be punctual to meals or forfeit the right to eat. "In the intercourse of the sexes, the utmost decorum is required," a school pamphlet explained, "without, however, oppressive interference, or the hindrance of that mutual influence which is deemed so beneficial in the coeducation of the sexes." It continued, "Hence, while a due degree of intercourse is allowed in daily recitations and amusements, the bounds of strictest propriety are never transgressed, and the dormitories are as completely separated and guarded as though they were two distinct buildings."

In a childish, penciled script, Pink wrote to her brother Charles two weeks after she arrived to describe her exciting new surroundings. She told of her room on the fourth floor of John Sutton Hall and of her roommate, Kit Beower, who had been at the Orphan's School at Dayton. She mentioned how expensive the school was going to be—about $200 a year—and she urged Charles to be "upright" and not to follow the path Albert had started to slide down into unemployment and drunkenness. Her mother, back in Apollo, was much on her mind. She asked Charles to send money to Mary Jane. Charles apparently had already left to seek his fortune in Pittsburgh. "I teach in model school," she wrote, with appalling punctuation. "Ain't I a young teacher. Be a good boy and remember me in your prayers."

Pink apparently viewed this adventure as her opportunity for a fresh start, away from all the unhappiness and embarrassment in Apollo. Only six months before, she had signed "Pinkey E. J.

Indiana State Normal School, Indiana, Pennsylvania (now part of Indiana University of Pennsylvania), circa 1875
(Stapleton Library, Indiana University of Pennsylvania)

Cochran" to the transcription of her testimony at Mary Jane's divorce hearing. At Indiana State Normal School, she enrolled as "Elizabeth J. Cochrane," abandoning the childish Pink and adorning *Cochran* with a silent, final *e* for sophistication and flourish. This spelling also, perhaps coincidentally, created some convenient confusion with Apollo's other well-known Cochranes, a family of respected attorneys who did not happen to be related. Albert and Charles affected the same change in spelling, although Pink appears to have acted first. It was in this way that Mary Jane's older children erased the awful Jack Ford episode and moved to reinvent themselves. Mary Jane, too, after a few years, gave her Cochran the final *e,* quietly acquiescing to whatever her children proposed in the pattern she would establish for the next half century.

The teacher's program at Indiana State Normal School involved two years in the "junior studies" division and one year as a "senior." Miss Cochrane enrolled in the "preparatory" class, signing up for required courses in arithmetic, grammar, reading, writing, drawing, composition, and spelling. Colonel Jackson paid Pink's school costs that first term directly from her trust account and during that period sent her two checks for ten dollars each for spending money. Mary Jane gave her another five dollars in cash before Pink left for Indiana. Pink later claimed to have received no other funds. Finances were much on her mind, and when the term was nearly over, Pink wrote to Colonel Jackson to arrange to come home. Jackson sent her another ten-dollar check but advised her to be very careful because her money was running low.

Once at home, she went over her accounts only to find that there was not enough money for her to return to school. There was no other source of financial help. Mary Jane was barely scraping by. Albert and Charles had yet to establish themselves. Jackson, as her guardian, the man responsible for her finances, a trustee of the school, and a wealthy relation to boot, might have found a way to help out but apparently felt neither the inclination nor the obligation to do so.

Pink felt wronged, certain that Colonel Jackson had let her down, that the money should have been in her account as he had led her to believe. If it wasn't, the responsibility was his. Seven years later, in 1886, at her first opportunity, having reached the legal age of twenty-one, Pink sued the colonel in Armstrong County Court, charging the powerful Jackson with mismanaging her trust.

But at the end of 1879, perhaps dejected by the news that she would have to leave school, perhaps too distracted to study, Pink dropped out of Indiana State Normal School without taking the examinations to complete the term. No grades for the fall semester 1879 appear on the school record of Elizabeth J. Cochrane. Under the words "date of leaving," a check mark was entered without further elaboration. She did not return. Her formal schooling ended abruptly, as did her plans to teach. She was going to have to find some other way to make a living.

The Dispatch.

Lonely Orphan Girl.

If the writer of the communication signed "Lonely Orphan Girl" will send her name and address to this office, merely as a guarantee of good faith, she will confer a favor and receive the information she desires.

The Pittsburg Dispatch, *January 17, 1885*

(Library of Congress)

2

The Dispatch

PINK RETURNED TO APOLLO BUT SOON LEFT ON A VISIT TO WHAT was known as "the oil country," the area around Oil City, sixty miles north of Apollo. She stopped in Pittsburgh for some time on her way back.

For Pink, confessing to her friends and neighbors the actual reason for her leaving school on top of the sordid business that had preceded her departure must have been an unbearable prospect. Another explanation began to take shape. By the time she had become a legend ten years later, this is how it read in a newspaper account derived from information either she or her mother must have provided:

> When Miss Cochrane was old enough to leave home, she was sent to a boarding school at Indiana, Pa., where she remained from 1879–1881. She was obliged to leave the institution on account of threatening heart disease and later when arrangements were nearly complete to send her to the Blairsville Seminary, the doctor said one year's study would probably cost the girl her life. She was anxious to continue her studies but she did not want to die. She remained at home and her waking hours not given to books were devoted to horseback

riding and light outdoor exercise which greatly improved
her health. She became so skilled in equestrianism that she
soon had the reputation of being the best horsewoman in
Armstrong County.

Both Indiana State Normal School records and Pink's own testimony show clearly that her tenure at the school was the one incomplete fall term of 1879 and not the two full years later reported. In
her 1886 testimony about these events in connection with her suit
against Colonel Jackson, she made no mention of any stymied plan to
transfer to the ladies' seminary at Blairsville.

Nor did she mention any illness. Further, Colonel Jackson's
accounts of his administration of Pink's money for all of 1879 and
1880 show her visiting a physician only once, on January 22, 1880.
The doctor's bill was two dollars, whereas her two much earlier
recorded doctor visits—and there were only three in ten years—had
been billed at twice and three times that amount.

The equestrian claims could be true, but in light of the other
fabrications, maybe not. Given that by December the whole family
had moved to Pittsburgh, it seems doubtful. In any event, it is of little consequence. She did pose for a photograph many years later, on
March 2, 1913, riding in Washington as a herald in the historic Suffragists Parade and expressing her passion for the sport in the accompanying text. More than that is anyone's guess.

༚ཚ

Pink's oldest full brother, Albert, left Apollo to start his new life in
Pittsburgh on February 4, 1880, after Pink had returned from boarding school. He took up residence in the as yet unincorporated part of
town known as Allegheny City, which was Pennsylvania's third
largest city in its own right. Charles appears to have arrived several
months earlier, working briefly as a painter. Albert at first went to
work as a corresponding clerk for Bailey, Farrell and Co. but left the
firm after only a year to set up the short-lived Cochrane and Co. with
Charles. The city directory lists Cochrane and Co. as the Pittsburgh
agent for the Akron Rubber Co. and as dealers in Wickersham steam

Albert Paul Cochrane, circa 1892
(Carnegie Library of Pittsburgh)

and hydraulic and locomotive packing as well as plumbing and machinists' supplies. A few years later, without his brother, Albert became manager of the Revere Rubber Company, for which he would work for more than a decade.

By December of that first year, Mary Jane had arrived to set up a proper home for her two grown boys, with the three younger children in tow. Harry, by now, was ten; Catherine had just turned fourteen, and Pink, at sixteen, was of marriageable age but, perhaps still reeling from her mother's unhappy experience, almost defiantly uninterested in getting married. Mary Jane held on to the small house in Apollo. Whether this was for security's sake or because there was no buyer is unclear. It finally sold for $300 at sheriff's auction nearly a decade later. The purchaser was none other than Pink's court-appointed guardian, Colonel Samuel Jackson.

In Allegheny, the Cochranes first took up residence in a small frame row house at 50 Miller Street, in the unremarkable industrial neighborhood known as Manchester. Within a year, Charles and Albert appear to have parted ways in business. The 1882–83 City Directory still lists both young men as living on Miller Street with their mother and younger siblings. Although Albert proudly lists his occupation as proprietor of Cochrane and Co., Charles is listed as a laborer in 1882 and then as a clerk every year thereafter until 1886, when he appears as a laborer again.

On May 16, 1881, Charles, over twenty-one and employed, wrote the parents of Sarah Gillis, the girl he had left behind, to ask for her hand in marriage. The Gillises lived in West Valley, another Armstrong County town not far from Apollo.

"I venture to hope that you will call all your friendly feelings to my assistance in considering a proposal I am about to make," the letter began. Not one punctuation mark followed:

> For a long time past your daughter Sarah has had a strong hold over my affections and I have r[e]asons to beli[e]ve I am not indifferent to her[.] I believe I am able to support her and as to regards to my character I trust I am sufficiently well known to you to give your confidence in the prospect of your child's happiness[.] anxiously awaiting the result of your consideration on this important and interesting subject
>
> I remain Sir your most faithful and obedient servant.

The wedding took place soon after. Sarah then joined the closely knit Cochranes in their various joint and separate living arrangements in several Allegheny locations, a few details of which survive, thanks to old city planning maps and directory listings.

The houses were all of the more modest row-house variety, but from the first addresses at 50 and 52 Miller Street to 246 Chartiers Street in 1884 and then 195 Arch Street in 1885, the neighborhoods got steadily better. Arch Street, for example, was a very respectable part of Allegheny, with gracious streets and fair-sized brick homes. To afford the better neighborhood, the Cochranes appear to have taken in as boarders a couple of young men working on the Baltimore and Ohio Railroad.

Catherine May, sometimes called Kate, turned sixteen and soon married a railroad sleeping car conductor named John Elmer Kountze—perhaps one of Mary Jane's boarders or one of her boarders' friends, but certainly not the kind of man her older sister would have considered a suitable mate. As it turned out, neither did Catherine. The marriage ended in divorce. While in Pittsburgh, the Kountzes lived with the Cochranes.

In April of 1885, Albert married Jane Hartley, daughter of Susan and the late William T. Hartley, at the home of the bride's mother in the town of Tarentum outside Pittsburgh. The Reverend W. J. Holland officiated. Soon after the marriage, the newlyweds took a house at the corner of Dithridge and Fillmore in Pittsburgh proper and lived for several years in that comfortable middle-class neighborhood.

Over the next five years, Mary Jane would become a grandmother three times. Kate, a week after her seventeenth birthday, had a daughter she named Beatrice Cochrane Kountze. One year later, Sarah and Charles had a son, whom they called Charles Grant, and three years later, in 1888, a daughter they named Gertrude. Beatrice, Charles, and Gertrude would be Mary Jane's only grandchildren. Not Albert, Harry, or the woman all three would come to know as their Aunt Pink ever had children. Perhaps for this reason, Pink accepted her position as aunt with great seriousness. Her nieces and nephew, in turn, adored her.

⁓ఞ⁓

For the four years in Allegheny City, nothing is known for certain about the occupation of Mary Jane Cochrane's older daughter. She was between the ages of sixteen and twenty, unmarried, financially strapped, and frustrated by her inability to find suitable employment. There are indications she tried her hand at tutoring, nannying, maybe even housekeeping, while her brothers, with less education, were able to land acceptable white-collar positions. Her sense of the injustice awaiting any woman who needed a good job and tried to get one in fast-industrializing Pittsburgh no doubt grew with every disappointment.

One can easily see her at this point deciding to augment her educational background with the claim of two full years at the Indiana State Normal School instead of the one unimpressive, incomplete semester she actually attended. No one was likely to check, and such a story could well have enhanced her job prospects. The completion of two-thirds of a three-year course cut short by sympathy-producing heart disease would show serious training at a prestige institution while providing a reasonable explanation for the lack of a diploma.

⌘

As much as a decade before the Cochranes arrived, Pittsburgh had earned the reputation of the "blackest, dirtiest, grimiest city in the United States," a place where the value put on river trade and the manufacture of iron, glass, and refined petroleum surpassed by far the importance of Stephen Foster's songs and the paintings of David Blythe. Its geography destined the city for industrial capitalhood, situated as it was where the Allegheny and Monongahela rivers joined to form the Ohio. By 1843, both the Pennsylvania Canal and the Portage Railroad had been completed, opening the way to better trade and shipping. For the people of Pittsburgh, the importance of arts and letters lay simply in their place as a "distraction from the all-absorbing business of making a living." The city spawned some phenomenal fortunes, most evident in the lifestyles honed in steel (Andrew Carnegie, B. F. Jones, James Laughlin, and Henry Oliver), in glass (J. B. Ford), in oil (Charles Lockhart, James M. Guffey, and Captain Jacob Vandergrift), in ships (William Thaw), and in merchandise (John Wanamaker).

The newspaper industry grew at an equivalent pace. Although the population of Pennsylvania's second largest city in this period hovered in the 60,000 range, Pittsburgh managed to support seven rival daily newspapers for fifty years after the end of the Civil War.

The Republican *Pittsburg Gazette* was established first. Its main competition in the morning field came from the Democratic *Pittsburg Post* and *The Pittsburg Dispatch,* considered to be "independent Republican" in its editorial viewpoint. Probably more significant for the growth of *The Dispatch*'s circulation since 1882 was its position as editorial home to the city's most revered newspaper columnist, Erasmus Wilson, who began writing his "Quiet Observations" column on July 23, 1884. Wilson was a man of humility, homespun wit, "homely wisdom and keen human sympathy," and his columns, later carried in book form were given such titles as "Light Words from Heavy Hearts," "Why the Good Die Early," "Graveyard Timidity," and "Umbrellas and Morals," reflect these qualities. As he described his own intent, it was to "pose the same old topics so they may be seen at different angles than those from which they are usually viewed. This gives them a new aspect without rendering them strange or unfamiliar."

His "Quiet Observations" ran regularly for more than three decades, first on the editorial page of *The Dispatch* and, from the end of 1887, in *The Pittsburg Commercial Gazette.*

Pink Elizabeth Jane Cochrane, now twenty, was an avid reader of *The Dispatch,* following closely the work of "The Quiet Observer" as well as that of the newspaper's one featured woman columnist, Elizabeth Wilkinson Wade, whom readers knew as Bessie Bramble, the byline that always appeared in oversized type above her columns. Wade's work was "terse, breezy, yet full of weighty argument," especially on subjects that inflamed her passions. A strong proponent of women's advancement, Bessie Bramble was the doyenne of newspaperwomen in Pittsburgh, precious few though they were, and had been for a decade. Before that, she had written anonymously as a highly regarded music critic.

Wilson had been writing as Q.O. for half a year when 1885 rolled around. For several weeks, he fixed on the subject of the role of women, presenting a staunchly traditional view. So unreconstructed were his attitudes, even by the not-so-yielding standards of the Victorian era, that Pink began to picture the Quiet Observer as a little "gray-haired, sharp-nosed sour-visaged chap who could look clean through you." This was hardly an apt description of the tall, avuncular country gentleman who was about to come into her life as a true and respected admirer, advocate, and friend.

In a column he later entitled "Woman's Sphere," Wilson railed against "those restless dissatisfied females who think they are out of their spheres and go around giving everybody fits for not helping them to find them." Women were forever "on the lookout for gnats and are constantly swallowing camels," he harped, admonishing every member of the fair sex to "let up on this sphere business" and make "her home a little paradise, herself playing the part of angel."

"Her sphere," he concluded with a slap, "is defined and located by a single word—home."

Even more provocative for Pink Cochrane and dozens of other readers was his advice to "Anxious Father," who wrote to Wilson about his unmarried daughters, ages eighteen to twenty-six and not particularly accomplished at anything. "I have five of them on hand, and am at a loss how to get them off, or what use to make of them." Wilson had no advice for the father. Instead, he lamented a society in which parents no longer had the time to rear their children properly so that boys would emerge as exemplars of honor and industry, and girls would grow into women who could spin, sew, cook, and clean house to perfection. He then waxed facetious about what the future might hold:

> In China and other of the old countries, they kill girl babies or sell them as slaves, because they can make no good use of them. Who knows but this country may have to resort to this sometime—say a few thousand years hence? Girls say they would sooner die than live to be old maids, and young men claim they cannot afford to marry until they get rich because wives are such expensive luxuries.

Wilson's views were so outrageous that even Bessie Bramble had to respond. In her column, she declared that whatever Q.O.'s hankerings, "the women of a century ago couldn't hold a candle to those of today."

> It is true they do not spin. Machinery has done away with that. Neither do they quilt bed quilts, except in the country, because it does not pay. The sewing machine has played havoc with what used to be woman's chief weapon, the needle. Cooking and housework are drudgery—so why should they do that unless they are compelled to, anymore than the brethren should all go out and hew logs and carry hods? Does it never occur to them that in insisting that all women should do housework they would consign them to the ranks of a dollar a day laborer on the railroad?

Bramble's advice to Anxious Father was to train his girls as "fiddlers and preachers," even if they weren't prodigies, and forget about finding them husbands.

The father wrote to Q.O. again, complaining his daughters simply did not have the talent for such vocations. Wilson obliged with a response, this time summoning even more reactionary force on the subject of women unfit to be housewives. Any woman found "outside her sphere" in the place of a man is, he asserted, "a monstrosity . . . Women who have an insatiate desire to rush into the breaches under the guise of defending their rights, but which is in reality an effort to wrest from man certain prerogatives bequeathed him by heaven, are usually to a degree disgusting to womanly women and manly men . . . There is no greater abnormity than a woman in breeches, unless it is a man in petticoats."

His rant crashed like cymbals in the ears of young women all over town. One, calling herself Becky Briarly, addressed him snidely as "Queer Observer," and taunted,

> In our Eastern cities there are more women than men. What are you going to do with the surplus? Change Horace Greeley's famous advice to young men to suit the case: Go West, young woman, Go West? Perhaps you could get up a cheap excursion and send a lot of us out on a husband-hunting expedition, or send us on consignment to a marriage broker. The cars might be labeled: "Perishable freight; Western Bound Maidens; Hurry up: Keep on Ice."

Another, calling herself Fatima, told the editor of *The Dispatch* that she had always liked the Quiet Observer, "but since he got onto this woman question he is just as crazy as the rest of the men." She continued,

> I am old enough to vote, if selfish man would give me a chance, yet not so old but what I may reasonably hope to see the day when women will march to the polls in a solid phalanx and assert their rights. I have had plenty of opportunities to marry, and, if so disposed, can go out now and pick up

any one of a half dozen good men and be at the head of a domestic establishment, but I don't want to.

The response that most intrigued the managing editor came from a young woman who could easily have been one of Anxious Father's five hapless daughters, except that her own father was long dead. Q.O. had certainly overlooked the plight of young women in her predicament. This one had spent four years in a succession of Allegheny row houses, most in working-class neighborhoods. She had heard the hard-luck tales of poor young women boarders and had experienced for herself the frustration of needing a good job and not being able to find it. She was not about to let the Quiet Observer go unchallenged in his myopia.

She drafted a brisk but lengthy rebuttal to Q.O.'s column, addressed to the editor of *The Pittsburg Dispatch*. Following the pseudonymous custom of the day, this ward of the Armstrong County Court signed herself "Lonely Orphan Girl." She did not provide a return address.

Erasmus Wilson remembered well the day a letter written on a large sheet of paper "with no style about it" landed on the desk of George Madden, *The Dispatch*'s recently named managing editor. Madden, originally from Newburg, Ontario, had bounced around the various Pittsburgh newspapers since the 1870s in every capacity from assistant foreman in the composing room to telegraph editor to local reporter. This was his third stint on *The Dispatch*.

Judged by appearance alone, Wilson said, the letter, signed "Lonely Orphan Girl," would have ended up in the trash. But Madden happened to look it over himself. He was struck by the earnestness of the writer's approach and the spirit she conveyed.

He tossed it onto Wilson's desk. "She isn't much for style," Wilson recalled Madden as saying, "but what she has to say she says it right out regardless of paragraphs or punctuation. She knocks it off and it is just right, too." With guidance, Madden thought, the girl could learn the newspaper craft quickly. He was no doubt looking to bring something fresh to the new Sunday edition, and perhaps this "orphan" could help provide it.

Wilson suggested putting a note in the "Mail Pouch," *The Dispatch*'s letters to the editor column, to ask the writer to come forward. Madden did. "If the writer of the communication signed 'Lonely Orphan Girl' will send her name and address to this office, merely as a guarantee of good faith, she will confer a favor and receive the information she desires." That announcement appeared in *The Pittsburg Dispatch* on Saturday, January 17, 1885.

The next day, what Wilson described as "a shy little girl," breathless from climbing four flights of *Dispatch* building stairs, arrived in the newsroom dressed in a floor-length black silk Russian circular and an unpretentious fur turban. Terrified, her voice abandoned in the climb, she asked in a hyperventilated whisper where she might find the editor. Willie the office boy pointed to Madden, who was sitting within earshot. Wilson went on: "The girl's countenance brightened, and she smiled for the first time, showing a

George Madden, managing editor,
The Pittsburg Dispatch, *circa 1892*
(Carnegie Library of Pittsburgh)

Erasmus Wilson, the Quiet Observer
(Carnegie Library of Pittsburgh)

beautiful set of teeth. 'Oh! Is it?' she exclaimed. 'I expected to see an old, cross man.' "

Later, Bly herself recalled that first meeting. Madden, she had imagined as a "great big man with a bushy beard who would look over the top of his specs and snap, 'What do you want?' " Instead she found a "mild-mannered, pleasant-faced boy." Q.O., she said, turned out to be "a great big good-natured fellow who wouldn't even kill the nasty roaches that crawled over his desk. There wasn't an old cross man about the place."

Madden did not print her letter but instead asked her to compose an article on "the woman's sphere." He edited it personally, paid her for it, and asked for a second piece. The next subject she picked was divorce. Again, Madden edited the story himself. Although her grammar was still "rocky," Wilson recalled, she did manage to get her facts straight.

Her first piece was "The Girl Puzzle," published on January 25, and prominently placed at the top of page 11 of the paper's new and successful Sunday edition. In it, she asked the reader to consider Anxious Father's question carefully, not in terms of privileged women, such as Bessie Bramble or the late revered writer Jane Grey Swisshelm, but with respect to those "without talent, without beauty, without money." She was especially sensitive to the plight of widows.

> The schools are overrun with teachers, the stores with clerks, the factories with employees. There are more cooks, chambermaids and washerwomen than can find employment. In fact, all places that are filled by women are overrun, and still there are idle girls, some that have aged parents depending on them. We cannot let them starve. Can they that have full and plenty of this world's goods realize what it is to be a poor working woman, abiding in one or two bare rooms, without fire enough to keep warm, while her threadbare clothes refuse to protect her from the wind and cold, and denying herself necessary food that her little ones may not go hungry; fearing the landlord's frown and threat to cast her out and sell what little she has, begging for employment of any kind that she may earn enough to pay for the bare rooms she calls home, no one to speak kindly to or encourage her, nothing to make life worth the living?

She went on: "If sin in the form of man comes forward with a wily smile and says, 'Fear no more, your debts shall be paid,' she cannot let her children freeze or starve, and so falls. Well, who shall blame her? Will it be you that have a comfortable home, a loving husband, sturdy, healthy children, fond friends—shall you cast the first stone?" She assailed the rich for their lack of concern for the female poor, hard at work in low-paying or health-imperiling jobs: "They read of what your last pug dog cost and think of what that vast sum would have done for them—paid father's doctor bill, bought mother a new dress, shoes for the little ones, and imagine how nice it would be could baby have the beef tea that is made for your favorite pug, or the care and kindness that is bestowed upon it."

She had suggestions as to what could be done. Ambitious young men could start as errand boys and work their way up to good positions. Why not girls? "Just as smart and a great deal quicker to learn; why, then, can they not do the same?"

She proposed allowing young girls to be employed as messengers or office "boys" instead of as workers in airless factories. Better yet, she suggested, how about making a girl a conductor on the Pullman Palace car?

She had advice for leaders of the women's rights movement, too: "Here would be a good field for believers in women's rights. Let them forego their lecturing and writing and go to work; more work and less talk. Take some girls that have the ability, procure for them situations, start them on their way and by so doing accomplish more than by years of talking."

"Orphan Girl" was the signature Madden affixed to the polemic.

Divorce was an awkward theme to pick, but she happened to know a good deal about it. She felt that the divorce laws should be abolished and marriage laws redrafted to prevent drunkards and ne'er-do-wells, men unlikely to make good husbands and providers, or women unable to master the skills of homemaker, from getting married without first making full disclosure of their inadequacies. She proposed it be made a crime for either prospective husband or wife to swear falsely to his or her personal history. In her words, "Let the young girl know that her intended is cross, surly, uncouth; let the young man know that his affianced is anything that is directly opposite to an angel. Tell all their faults, then if they marry, so be it; they cannot say, 'I did not know,' but the world can say, 'I told you so.' "

She commended Governor Robert E. Pattison's recent proposal for divorce law reform, under which the husband or wife of a spouse convicted of forgery or other "infamous" crimes had the right to sue for divorce. She preferred, however, that Pennsylvania follow the lead of Bavaria, which had recently passed a law forbidding anyone to marry who had received public charity within three years, who had not paid taxes, or who "by means of dissolute habits, laziness or poverty, are likely to make home wretched."

One highly specific example in the piece sounded as if it came out of her own experience, with a fast poke at her ever-irritating brother Albert, who was soon to be married:

> A young man drawing a comfortable income has a widowed mother, who has doubtless worked hard to give him a start in life, and helpless sisters. He lets his aged mother work, and allows his sisters to support themselves where and how they will, never has five cents or a kind word to give at home, dresses in the height of fashion, has every enjoyment, gives his lady friends costly presents, takes them to places of amusement, tries to keep it a secret that his mother and sisters work. If the fact becomes known, he will assert positively that it is against his most urgent desire. Will he make a good husband, think you?

The article, published under the headline "Mad Marriages," was controversial enough to attract wide attention, and, according to Bly's own later recollection, even "contributed to causing the salutary change which was made shortly after in the marriage laws of Pennsylvania," although this could not be documented.

When she proposed her next idea, a series on the factory girls of Pittsburgh, Madden decided to make her a permanent member of the *Dispatch* staff. Starting salary: five dollars a week—slightly higher than that of the factory girls she would be interviewing.

As he edited the divorce piece, Madden decided to choose a byline for his newest staff member. Orphan Girl had served well enough for her Anxious Father rebuttal, but now he wanted a name "neat and catchy." Her own name was out of the question since the custom, in this period, was for ladies who deigned to write for newspapers to do so without making their true identities public. He called out to the newsroom for suggestions. Several writers and editors offered up ideas, "Nelly Bly" among them. Madden pondered for a moment, Wilson recalled, but cut his deliberations short with "the howl from above for copy." Without further consideration, Nellie Bly it became.

In his haste, Madden had not been faithful to the spelling of that name made famous thirty-five years earlier in a song written by one of Pittsburgh's favorite sons, Stephen Collins Foster. Foster's "Nelly Bly" was the "comely colored servant" of Henry Woods, the daughter of a former slave in the Woods household. Foster, the story went, was playing piano at the Woodses' home when this young Nelly "poked her head out of the cellar door to hear the music." Asked who the pretty girl was, Foster was told. She was invited into the room to listen. At that, the composer was seized with a "flash of inspiration," and he improvised the words and tune for the song "Nelly Bly," almost exactly as they would later be published:

> *Nelly Bly, Nelly Bly,*
> *bring de broom along*
> *We'll sweep de kitchen clean, my dear,*
> *and hab a little song.*
>
> *Poke de wood, my lady lub*
> *And make the fire burn,*
> *And while I take de banjo down*
> *Just gib de mush a turn.*
>
> *Heigh! Nelly, Ho! Nelly,*
> *Listen lub, to me*
> *I'll sing for you, play for you*
> *A dulcem melody.*

"Nelly Bly" the song and Nellie Bly the reporter both sprang from inspiration in Pittsburgh, and, thanks to each, the name has been casting in and out of history for more than a century, creating for its more recent hearers an often vague but no less pleasant association. Other than that, the two have no connection.

∽✿∾

The plight of Pittsburgh's poor working girls was Bly's first theme in print. Instinctively, she understood how to tell the story that needed telling. Her ability to attract and hold the reader's attention masked her deficiencies as a thinker or wordsmith. Her work exuded energy and confidence; her weaknesses simply did not get in her way. Readers responded. This was how she excelled.

To explain what life was like for the female working poor, Bly approached the subject from a clever sidetrack. Instead of focusing on the obvious—the drudgery of the workday—she wrote about these women's lives after hours. In gossipy detail, she explained "catching a mash," a practice sure to have raised more than a few Victorian eyebrows. The idea was for a woman to meet a man casually on the streetcar, for example, accompany him to a bar, get drunk with him, and sometimes, in the euphemistic sexual parlance of the day, "fall."

Over the course of her career, the talent that set Bly apart as a reporter was her total lack of compunction in asking the question that would elicit the telling detail. This was already evident in her early work. Of one "man-masher," she asked, "Why do you risk your reputation in such a way?" The response told the whole story and gave Bly her angle:

> "Risk my reputation!" and she gave a little short laugh. "I don't think I ever had one to risk. I work hard all day, week after week, for a mere pittance. I go home at night tired of labor and longing for something new, anything good or bad to break the monotony of my existence. I have no pleasure, no books to read. I cannot go to places of amusement for want of clothes and money, and no one cares what becomes of me."

Although Bly found the experiences of these women degrading ("I drink, my weary feelings leave me, my cheeks flush, my eyes sparkle and I am a new being"), her years among the working poor had taught her not to be too quick to judge: "If no amusement is offered them they will seek it and accept the first presented. No excuse can be offered for girls with pleasant homes and kind friends; no excuse for the men who can seek amusement elsewhere. But for the poor working girl, without friends, without money, with the ceaseless monotony of hard work, who shall condemn and who shall defend?"

The second part of the piece ran through some inane and point-less gossip Bly had overheard on the streetcar about which she was able to make no discernible point. She showed no early promise as a columnist of the caliber of Q.O. or Bessie Bramble.

Perhaps on the strength of what she had learned from the man-mashers, Bly suggested to Madden that she go into the factories and investigate conditions for working women. Madden agreed, even sending an illustrator with her. She produced eight articles, detailing life in the factories for the city's growing female workforce. The series ran over two months of Sundays, featured under a special illus-trated logo with the words "Our Workshop Girls: Women's Labor in Pittsburg" worked into the design.

It is amusing to note that in personality sketches and juvenile biographies of Bly published long after her death, this early series is remembered as her indignant crusade to unmask the desperate con-ditions under which Pittsburgh's poor women were forced to labor. Yet the series had no such intent. Judged by the current standard, the articles read like a Chamber of Commerce booster pamphlet, free from any criticism of the eight factories she toured. The only nega-tive comments came from the women she interviewed in speaking about what had happened to them on their last jobs—at factories Bly neither named nor visited in her subsequent reports.

In piece after piece, she extolled the cleanliness of the work environment, the excellent lighting, the untaxing labor, the well-supplied bathrooms, the kind and caring foremen and owners, the gentility and competence of the women workers, and the complete satisfaction they expressed in their work. She reported everything at face value, describing in minute detail all aspects of the female laborer's workday.

In the first installments, she did at least touch on the contro-versial subject of child labor. In the workrooms set apart for "female toilers" at the nut and bolt works of Oliver Brothers and Phillips, she asked a little girl why she was not in school:

> "I'm through school, and father don't make enough money to keep us all."
> "How old are you?"

> ## THE GIRL PUZZLE.
>
> Some Suggestions on What to Do With the
> Daughters of Mother Eve.
>
> ### THE OLD FIELDS OF LABOR OVERCROWDED
>
> How the Average Employer Discriminates Against
> Petticoated Workers.
>
> ### THE ROAD AS SAFE AS THE FACTORY.
>
> For the Dispatch.
>
> What shall we do with our girls?
>
> Not our Madame Nellisons; nor our Mary
> Andersons; not our Bessie Brambles nor
> Maggie Mitchells; not our beauty or our
> heiress; not any of these, but those without
> talent, without beauty, without money.
>
> What shall we do with them?
>
> The anxious father still wants to know
> what to do with his five daughters. Well
> indeed may he inquire and wonder. Girls,
> since the existence of Eve, have been a
> source of worriment, to themselves as well
> as to their parents, as to what shall be done
> with them. They cannot, or will not, as
> the case may be, all marry. Few, very
> few, possess the mighty pen of the late Jane
> Grey Swisshelm, and even writers, lecturers,
> doctors, preachers and editors must have
> money as well as ability to fit them to be
> such. What is to be done with the poor
> ones?

The logo on Bly's working girl series for
The Dispatch, *1885*
(Library of Congress)

"I don't know just how old I am."

"Well, you look to be eight or ten."

"I don't know; maybe I am."

Two weeks later, in her report on female workers at the McKinney Manufacturing Company, a producer of hinges, she presented the issue in a light wholly sympathetic to management:

The "helpers" are the smallest girls in the works. The foreman states that it is not their custom to take such young girls, but mothers come with tears in their eyes and beg work for them to help along at home. Upon investigation, if their story is found to be correct, the firm employs the little ones. This is undoubtedly an act of kindness and charity, and if this rule was

lived up to by all employers of child labor in the two cities
[Pittsburgh and Allegheny City], many a home would be
cheered and to many worthy ones extended a helping hand.

Bly had yet to develop the skepticism her craft, at its best,
demanded. For this series, she lacked both the evidence to refute
what she had witnessed and the skill to figure out how to get it. It is
possible the factories she visited were all exemplary facilities, though
one wonders. Bly seems to have done what most cub reporters would
do under the circumstances. She followed her editor's instructions to
report faithfully what she saw and heard.

Viewed from a later perspective, it is important to remember
that newspapers, as a whole, had yet to see investigation and exposé
as intrinsic to their mandate in the way they would a few years hence.
Although Bly showed the promise to help raise the curtain on this
new era, her first big series did not even qualify as a dress rehearsal.

All the same, the stories pulse with vivid detail about poor
working women, their style, their job performance, and the manufacturing processes at which they worked. Bly later claimed that the
series was so successful, newspapers around the country hastened to
imitate it. Indeed, within two years the pacesetting *New York World*
had standardized this type of reporting.

If nothing else, the series may have provided Bly's first lesson in
how difficult it can be for a reporter to extract the truth that he or she
suspects. It is one thing for a factory-working man-masher to gossip
in a boardinghouse parlor without fear of identification. It is quite
another for a factory manager, or a female worker who is dependent
on that man for her next meal, to speak candidly for quotation in *The
Pittsburg Dispatch.* Ultimately, to tell the stories that would put the
name of Nellie Bly on the nation's lips, a more inventive reportorial
approach would have to be devised. For now, she was just a junior
trainee with spunk.

After the eight-part series ran, Madden moved Bly to women's
interest news: fashion, society, gardening, and the arts. Perhaps it was
his idea of a compliment. In those days, it was almost unthinkable
for a woman on the staff of a mainstream newspaper—half-severed
appendage in the best of cases—to be covering anything else.

⌒᪑᪐

Even before the last piece in the "Workshop Girls" series had been published, Bly dug into garden reporting with a prescient admonition to Pennsylvanians to start planting trees or risk deforestation of their woodsy state. She praised Governor Pattison's decision to declare April 16 Arbor Day but pointed out that this was the state's only official act regarding trees since 1681, when William Penn started requiring the preservation of one acre of forest for every five acres cleared.

The next week Bly shared with her readers the latest in selections for spring planting, following up with three days of lively coverage of the annual flower show, staged to benefit Pittsburgh's Library Association. In a list of distinguished guests spotted at the exhibition, she included both her mother and brother Albert. Albert, who was about to be married, she mentioned two days running.

While still giving garden advice, she tried her hand at fashion reporting, detailing the prices and latest styles in shoes, dresses, hosiery, lace, evening wraps, jewelry, kerchiefs, collars, and even hairstyles. By the end of May 1885, she had convinced Madden to let her attempt some more general interest features. Her first was a report on the Economites, a thrifty sect living in a town called Economy, Pennsylvania.

At the end of the month, Bly had added culture reporting to her journalistic repertoire, offering under the headline "A Plucky Woman" an enlightening profile of E. H. Ober, whom she described as the first woman to own and run an opera company. She followed the next week with an intimate look at the life of a chorus girl in which she dispelled the prevailing notion of what someone who would pursue such an occupation was like. In Bly's words, the stereotype was "a big, loud-voiced, flashily dressed, ill-bred woman who would rather be dressed in pink tights than petticoats—a woman devoid of all principle, who lived but for show." Instead, she found "a pretty, dark-eyed, golden-haired lass of probably 21 summers; a slender, girlish form clad in a light blue house dress with a plain white lined collar around her throat, the golden hair brushed smoothly back, dressed in two braids, displaying an intelligent forehead."

Straight out, Bly asked her: "Do men ever make love to you?" (the words *make love* had a less explicit connotation in this nineteenth-century context):

How can you, being a girl, ask such a question. Of course they do; on every occasion members of the company make love to one another, and then in every new town they make "mashes" who wait for them at the door and take us out to supper. Some of the girls would ask the fellows for money and they always got it, with lots of presents, jewelry, flowers and candy, which always lead in the gift line. And the love letters; if you could only see some you would be amused. Men get "mashed" at first sight and write long letters declaring their undying love and such rubbish. The girls get lots of proposals.

The same day, she reported on a musical prodigy named Clara Oehmler, who played piano by ear. As part of the story, and in describing Miss Oehmler, Bly gave her own definition of a "true woman"—"innocent, unaffected and frank; what some say is hard to find of late years." Only sketchy details survive of what Bly herself was like at this time, though "innocent, unaffected and frank" were three virtues she always liked to project.

In word portraits of Pittsburgh's "gifted women" for a book entitled *The Social Mirror* written at this time, the entry for "Miss 'Pink' Elizabeth Cochrane" reads in part: "In person 'Nellie Bly' is slender, quick in her movements, a brunette with a bright, coquettish face. Animated in conversation and quick in *repartée,* she is quite a favorite among the gentlemen."

Two young men working on the Baltimore and Ohio Railroad project, Tom Smiley and Tony Orr, were boarding with Mary Jane Cochrane in the family's Allegheny City home. Bly, who was said to prefer the company of men, befriended the young railroaders and sometimes would join them when they went out for the evening. At other times, the two would think up ways to pull pranks on Bly, who never found their antics funny.

Smiley, years later, recalled once stringing a number of chairs together in the hallway while he and Orr hid behind the upstairs door to await Bly's arrival. She walked in with her "usual deep stride," then bumped into one chair and tumbled over another. Sprawled on the floor, unamused, she called out for her mother. Although she gradually got accustomed to the two young men and their sense of humor, Smiley said she never laughed at the jokes they played on her or took them good-naturedly.

She liked—and would later be chided for—making revealing, sometimes flattering references to herself in her stories. This tendency was first seen in a piece about the difficulty florists have in pleasing customers who range from "mourners to lovers to blooming brides." Bly quoted one florist as asking her if she knew the language of flowers. When she told him she had never bothered to learn it, he responded, "Well, you never have been very much in love with any particular man." One can imagine the impact of this little aside on whoever was courting her at the time.

As summer approached, Bly attempted to explain to the readers of *The Dispatch* the probable causes of a relatively new malady known as hay fever. She based her story on an interview with Dr. W. H. Winslow, a severe sufferer of "grasp, gasp, cough and asphyxiate" who was having a yacht built for the sea voyage he considered the only possible cure. Winslow was convinced that the debility of the nervous system known as neurasthenia was the prime inviter of hay fever. Although neurasthenia was sometimes congenital, he said, it was "oftener [sic] a result of excessive action and is recognized by morbid irritability, irregularity of emotion and thought, and great depression after sustained effort." Bly gave him forum to explain a thoroughly modern viewpoint:

> Many people in towns and cities shut out from fresh air and sunlight by massive walls, walking and working upon heated pavements and floors, smelling the foul odors of sewers, streets and cellars, inhaling the dirty dust of the streets and the poisonous gases of home and workshop, carrying the heavy burdens of the busy day far into the night, turning

night into day by the pernicious gas and electric lights, eating irregularly and hastily, sleeping fitfully between the roars of commerce, taking few holidays (and those at lightning speed), taxing the nervous system in every way possible and at last "dying as the dog dieth." Is it any wonder that with this environment and these habits, diseases are becoming more developed and typical?

Some of Bly's ideas sprang from conversations in the dining room at home with her mother's adventuresome boarders, or with her friends. Others she simply overheard in the streets. A poor woman complaining about how rudely a clerk had behaved while she was trying to buy a carpet gave Bly the idea of finding out from clerks all over town how they treated their customers. This was Bly's advice: "In this age of wonders, one can entertain an angel unawares; they may be poor today, tomorrow they may strike oil or work out a patent. Then they will remember who treated them well."

She rounded out her summer reporting with a story on the Schenley mansion, a thirty-room brick pile set on 150 manicured acres in the Oakland section of Pittsburgh and uninhabited because the Schenleys preferred to spend their time in England. Bly got access to the house and grounds and interviewed the servants, one of whom had once been an undermaid in service to Queen Victoria.

August found her back in Armstrong County, where she profiled the ailing Civil War Colonel William Sirwell, Armstrong's most revered war hero. Sirwell died twelve days after her story appeared. Another local war hero fared less well against the feisty newspaperwoman on this visit. Now that she had turned twenty-one, Bly started preparing a suit in Armstrong County Court against her former guardian, Colonel Samuel Jackson, for mismanaging her inheritance.

By the time she returned to Pittsburgh, Bly seems to have convinced Madden to let her write a weekly column under her own name. She detested writing women's interest news and angled fast to create an alternative niche for herself on the staff. The first column, which actually ran a column and a half, appeared on September 6, 1885, just seven months after she had joined *The Dispatch* staff. It was a rapid elevation, even though the headline "Nellie Bly" appeared in type no larger than the text itself. For her debut as a columnist, Bly had compiled a diary of metropolitan vignettes in which she made fun of the way city folk gawk, witnessed a drunken husband's behavior coming home to his devoted wife, and described an organized dogfight. Her execution was decidedly flat.

By the next week, her name appeared over the column in larger, bolder type, followed by four distinct subheads, identifying the subject matter of her vignettes. Although the column was well set off on the page, the vignettes themselves were not much, the best item being the story of a man who purchased two large bouquets from the florist every week to be distributed anonymously to the sick by his minister at the Methodist Episcopal Church. By the third week, her space was cut back by two-thirds and only one vignette appeared, an amusing description of the behavior of the increasing numbers of ladies going to baseball games.

A week later, she praised the work of the Young Men's Christian Association and called for a similar organization for women in Pittsburgh. This time the column had the essential element of excellence: Bly's distinct voice expressing a clear point of view. And it provoked response. A wealthy woman offered to assist in establishing a sanctuary for working girls. A second woman, who signed herself "A Mother," wrote that just at the point where young women "need protection, care and guidance, we leave them to be buffeted on the waves of fate, to fight temptation as best they can." She went on to praise Bly's work: "I watch for your articles always, and turn from the chronic growlers and heavy writers to your happy, cheery way with a sense of relief. Now, Nellie Bly, please keep up this association idea you have started and receive the thanks of not only the poor girls, but of women with daughters and sisters."

Bessie Bramble was quick to correct "Sister Bly" about the Woman's Christian Association of Pittsburgh. "That they have no elegant building like the Y.M.C.A. is from the lack of means, not of will and deed," Bramble replied in her column. Further:

> Women in general have no money to speak of. It is doled out
> to them for family use, but they have little or none to bestow
> as they please on other purposes . . . Still, the Woman's

Bly, circa 1886
(*The Pittsburgh Post-Gazette*)

Christian Association of Pittsburg is a large institution and its members have a home of their own, though a modest one, on Penn Avenue. And they have besides established homes in both Pittsburg and Allegheny to aid destitute women and to hold out help to friendless girls and orphan children. That they are so quiet and silent about their good works, that Sister Bly did not know such an association was in existence, shows how well they have been taught the silence and submission theory, so long held and enforced by the church. Still . . . they are fast outgrowing it.

In her own column, Bly respectfully told Bramble she had missed the point. "If Pittsburg and Allegheny have homes for destitute women and friendless girls, what of their work? In all the rounds among the working girls, there is yet the first to tell of being aided by any benevolent society. The facts are pretty conclusive." What was needed was "a place where poor girls will find inducements to spend their leisure time, especially evenings—a place that will offer and give assistance." And it needn't be grand. She went on, "While not daring to offer our humble opinion against that of a talented writer and learned lady like B.B., yet the belief infuses our soul that one girl saved—put on a sure footing, and given a lift on life's rough road— is more creditable and will receive a brighter reward than a lifetime spent in prayer."

By the following Saturday, Bly had become the Pittsburgh working girl's patron saint. One young woman proposed that Bly get a reading room established so she could visit it "instead of going to the skating rink tonight . . . If we had more people like Nellie Bly to think of something for the good of the working girls, it would be better for us."

Despite the strong reader response to her working girl suggestions, Madden put Bly back on the fashion beat almost at once, with a piece on the advent of rubber raincoats. Maybe Bessie Bramble objected to the competition. Maybe Pittsburgh's embarrassed if benevolent Christian women had exerted some pressure. For whatever reason, the "Nellie Bly" column never appeared again. Bly finished out November with boilerplate stories on tree grafts obtained from garden nurseries, almost two full columns on a Pittsburgh minister with a collection of 50,000 butterflies, and a piece on ladies and hair care. And she hated it.

Nothing with Bly's signature appeared in December. Miffed over her killed column, sick of writing women's page goop, Bly quit as a member of *The Dispatch*'s permanent staff, although she was careful to maintain her good relations with Madden and Erasmus Wilson. A seemingly conciliatory piece under her name appeared on January 24, 1886, in which the paper devoted nearly four columns to Bly's report on the noble charitable work of Pittsburgh's "self-sacrificing Christian ladies."

Most likely, this story was produced on a freelance basis for payment by the word. Bly most certainly was in need of extra cash. At the end of January, she had left Pittsburgh with her mother as chaperon. But on February 21, she was back in print in *The Dispatch* on her own terms. In a deft maneuver, she had forced Madden to put her name over the column again, this time in tall, bold type with an unexpected geographic twist. More than thirty times over the next six months, the same headline, or a near variation, would get prominent display in the pages of *The Dispatch* and in other papers around the country that picked up her reports. "NELLIE," those headlines read, "IN MEXICO."

NELLIE IN MEXICO.

She Finds a Great Many Odd Things to Write About.

THE FATE OF FEMALE CORRESPONDENTS.

Scanty Dress the Prevailing Style in the Country and Small Towns.

MARRYING INTO PERPETUAL SLAVERY

Special Correspondence of the Dispatch.

CITY OF MEXICO, February 12.—Journalists from the States are not regarded with much favor by the people of Mexico, the many have been those who were unable to speak the language, and an overflow of truth, they misrepresented everything.

Even now Mexicans are imagining about a lady who came here to represent some New York magazine. Renting rooms out from the city, she retired with banks on Mexico she had obtained at different stores, and without making an observation or caring to know the truth, she wrote from the books and sent the articles back to the States. A railroad conductor found much amusement in watching her.

Male writers are as much at fault as the women, but at the present day there are no less than six widows of the crankest type, writing up Mexico, each expecting to become a second Humboldt and have their...

3

❦ ❦

Travel

B LY LEFT *THE DISPATCH* BECAUSE AT AGE TWENTY-ONE, AFTER only nine months in journalism, she was, in her words, "too impatient to work along at the usual duties assigned women on newspapers." She was determined to return on her own terms. By distinguishing herself at foreign reporting, she reasoned, she could explode the ossified mind-set of editors who had relegated her for no good reason to work she considered dull, meaningless, and without the potential for promotion.

Why Mexico? Her brief experience as a member of the entertainment committee for a visiting Mexican delegation had a lot to do with it. Although she spoke no Spanish and the Mexicans, very little English, she managed to get "a lot of good stuff," including an invitation to visit their country. The conversations she overheard of the young railroad men who roomed at her mother's house were a factor, and she appropriated their dreams of following the tracks from Pittsburgh south to the far side of the border. Erasmus Wilson said later that Bly's editors tried hard to dissuade her from going, but she was resolute, set on doing "something that no other girl had ever done."

Mexico was mysterious, exotic, dangerous, and, by this point, accessible. Both the Mexican Central Railroad Company and the

Mexican National Railroad Company had laid thousands of miles of track since the first inauguration of Porfirio Díaz in 1877, opening the country's inhospitable terrain to travel and investment. A six-month reporting stint from the land of sombreros, tortillas, and political repression was certainly a better advancement strategy than a score more Sunday features on feathers and butterflies.

Concerned about appearances, Bly convinced Mary Jane to accompany her as chaperon. From the railroad companies, she secured train passes, presumably free, for both of them. Mother and daughter set off on the four-day journey to the border, crossing into Mexico at Paso del Norte with Bly making note of the sights en route to the City of Mexico, as it was then known, the dateline which started most of her dispatches.

The scenes from the train, she said, were "beautiful in the extreme." Pear cacti, which she had only seen nursed in greenhouses, grew wild to heights of twenty feet. Century plants, used in the making of pulque, the local beer, were everywhere. She was amazed that farmers were able to plant a new crop as soon as they had harvested the last. They yanked wheat and barley out of the ground by the roots, without benefit of machinery. Haystacks were shaped like those north of the border but upside down, with the points at the bottom. Strawberries and tomatoes could be bought only a day's distance from the big city, from peddlers who were as wily as any she had encountered in Pittsburgh.

The country had just passed through a terrible winter, with the first snowfall in a quarter of a century. Even in Veracruz, Mexico's warm land, the people had been "frozen out," Bly said.

The City of Mexico, she found, gave an appearance of great prosperity:

> New buildings are rapidly going up, old ones being repaired, and Eastern people opening up stores. Everything has a brisk look as if money were plenty. President Díaz has been having plans made by which the city may be drained better. The streets are swept daily and no garbage is permitted to collect on them. Men are employed by the authorities to call at houses every morning and collect all the refuse, so no

Bly, circa 1886
(*The Pittsburgh Post-Gazette*)

unhealthiness will arise from decaying matter in the courts. All this has a tendency to show the city is growing and is being bettered by growth.

She was determined not to let the usual journalistic quicksand swallow her, thereby attracting the disdain of both the Mexican and the expatriate intelligentsia. Although both sexes of foreign correspondent were equally at issue, Bly singled out women reporters for especially withering rebuke: "So many have come here who were unable to speak the language and so careless of truth, that they misrepresented everything."

On her arrival, she learned immediately of "no less than six widows of the crankest type writing up Mexico, each expecting to become a second Humboldt and have their statues erected on the public square." Her sarcasm may have had more to do with her unhappiness at finding she had been beaten to the assignment of female foreign correspondent than with the quality of her competitors' work.

As evidence of the incompetence of these other women, Bly recounted the tall tale that a train conductor had told a visiting woman reporter in jest. It was about how Mexicans roast whole hogs—uncleaned, "heads and all"—and serve them at table. The journalist reported the story as fact. That was not all: According to Bly, that woman reporter spent little time in the country, saw nothing of Mexican life, never entered the homes of any Mexican families, and yet, Bly said, "she is still contributing articles on Mexico to the Eastern press."

Bly had loftier aims. She quickly made it her business to befriend the best English-speaking analysts in the capital, including diplomats and expatriate editors such as Theo Gestefeld of *Two Republics,* formerly of *The Chicago Tribune.* Although she did not speak Spanish and was unlikely to learn the language during such a brief tenure, Bly was determined to report on the country in a bold, factual, and colorful manner, emphasizing the people, their families, habits, customs, style, and, later, their politics. She would make this assignment her catapult to prominence. "Maybe I'll not be more fortunate than other female correspondents in getting at the characteristics of Mexican life," she mused in print, "but if I fail to find enough to write about, instead of going to the guide books, you can look for me to come home."

⌇

The Mexico Bly was about to discover was well into the second presidential term—with one four-year term off in between—of Porfirio Díaz, who would ultimately rule Mexico for a total of thirty years. Díaz adorned his administration with the trappings of democracy and was generous with foreign buyers interested in Mexican land. Over the years, he cultivated an excellent international image. His tenure, known as the Porfiriato, was considered Mexico's golden age of prosperity until it collapsed in 1910, exposing some of its more questionable aspects. At the height of his power more than a decade after Bly's assignment, Díaz was being widely extolled abroad by industrialists such as Andrew Carnegie, by American statesmen from William Jennings Bryan to Theodore Roosevelt and President William Howard Taft, even by Leo Tolstoy, who admired him as a "prodigy of nature." The American Peace Society had made him an honorary vice president.

For Bly, however, her Mexican sojourn was a source of enlightenment on the nuances of expatriate life under an authoritarian regime with a muzzled press. She learned the dubious art of self-censorship, of gratuitously emphasizing the positive, of slipping the plain truth into her work wherever she could while being careful to avoid jail or expulsion for what she wrote.

Bly sought to write about subjects that would cut against the prevailing stereotypes of the country and its people. For example, she advised the women of Pittsburgh, her readers, to hire Mexicans as servants because they would find them clean (except in the preparation of food, which could be taught), industrious, honest, and uncommonly hardworking, if a bit slow. The common perception held otherwise on all counts. She detailed the sordid living conditions of the poor and the opulence of the wealthy; she dined in a Mexican home, eating "nauseating" and "detestable" cold meats, salad, red pepper, and pickled beans. She reported the activities of prominent members of the expatriate community and celebrity visitors from the United States—the landscape painter Frederick Church and writers Joaquin Miller and Charles Dudley Warner among them. She produced something akin to a social column replete with items about well-known Mexicans and visitors whose comings and goings might be of interest to readers abroad. When President Díaz and his very young wife attended a performance by the controversial French performer Madame Judie every night, despite gossip that the show was immoral, Bly reported it.

Bly made it a point to praise the obvious "mental capacity" of the large unschooled Indian population, evident in their fine sculpture, music, and paintings. She applauded the governor of Chiapas, José Maria Ramírez, for proposing a $10 million appropriation for schools throughout Mexico, dedicated to ending Indian illiteracy.

Bly liked writing about whatever struck her as weird and even ghoulish. Workmen excavating to plant trees in front of a cathedral unearthed "great heaps of human bones," she reported in an early dispatch. The "grinning skulls" baked in the sun half a day before workmen hauled them off and deposited them on level land as fertilizer. Bly and other expatriates who witnessed the transfer were astonished by the unsentimental handling of human remains. "Some claim the bones are of priests or victims of the Inquisition while others say they are of a more ancient origin," she wrote. "They would certainly have furnished a study for Eastern people but they caused hardly a second thought to the Mexicans."

She was moved by the reverence that Mexican children displayed for their parents. She decried the lotteries, "a curse to the poor," whom she witnessed pawning their clothes to buy the usually fruitless chances.

By February 18, she had seen the Mexican bureaucracy at its most hardened in a case of interest to her western Pennsylvania readers. She reported the death of a poor Indian fireman and the engineer Jacob Heiney of Allegheny County, Pennsylvania, who was the only support of his aged father. She described the funeral in much detail, including why it was so long delayed by difficulties in trying to get the body released from the Mexican Government Office of Deputation. Apparently, the bureaucrat entrusted with the release had left the office. No one else would take responsibility for it.

The Americans organized an "indignation committee" to present U.S. Legation Minister Henry R. Jackson with the facts of the case. Jackson sent the legation secretary to the deputation office to expedite the release, but the Mexican bureaucrats held on to the body for another five hours. Bly went on, "After the burial, a sensation was created by a leak that the body had been taken from its coffin and when officials went to replace it they found it had swollen until it was too large to go in. So the arms and legs were cut off and the breast split open so it could be doubled up." This so enraged the Americans, Bly said, that a second indignation meeting was held and an apology demanded from the Mexican government. She never reported whether this apology was obtained.

Bly had an eye for small detail, a way of answering for readers questions they would not think to ask. She took pains to explain the intricacies of bullfighting; how people behaved at intermission at the theater; how smoking cigarettes was the national pastime for rich and poor alike; how the women tortilla makers on the streets always "spit on their hands to keep the dough from sticking" before they threw their little flat breads into greased pans for cooking over small charcoal fires. "Rich and poor buy them," Bly said, "apparently unmindful of the way they are made."

The small kindnesses the Mexicans displayed toward their brethren moved Bly to deep respect: how every man paused and bowed his head when a father passed shouldering the tiny coffin of his dead child; how laborers covered the body of a co-worker in a white cloth and prayed as police ordered removal of the corpse.

> As a people, they do not seem malicious, quarrelsome, unkind or evil disposed. Drunkenness does not seem to be frequent and the men in their uncouth way, are more thoughtful of the women than many who belong to a higher class. The women, like other women, sometimes cry, doubtless for very good cause, and then the men stop to console them, patting them on the head, smoothing back their hair, gently wrapping them tighter in their rebozo.

She wrote about the observance of the Sabbath, of the finely dressed women and the paseo promenades of tallyho coaches, elegant dogcarts, English gigs, handsome coupés and carriages that would have put a similar Pittsburgh showcase to shame. She described everything from Lent to the customs of love and courtship—which she personally experienced to her great amusement and wrote about in detail. She liked letting her readers know how interesting men found her and how detached, even mocking, she was about their pursuit. Every explanation involved the same crisp detail she had given to her descriptions of the factories of Pittsburgh. She even claimed to have determined the true value of the sombrero: how effective the hat's wide brim was in shading the spinal column and thereby preventing sunstroke. (When she wore her little round hat horseback riding, she became dizzy and had to stop. A companion chivalrously offered her his sombrero, forcing him to ride bare headed. She suffered no further complaint, but the heat then overcame him, cutting short the ride.)

In a dispatch dated March 22, she protested the incarceration of a local journalist, editor of a Spanish-language newspaper, whose sole crime was writing an editorial critical of the government.

Bly sometimes would try to affect a worldly, ironic humor in her writing, not always with perfect success. In explaining the Mexican passion for dueling, she said, "Men are seldom killed. They are good marksmen but they generally just graze one another and pronounce their honor satisfied, but the other day two fought fatally. We hope their honor was satisfied."

⸜⸝

Her articles churned enough stir in Pittsburgh for gossip about them to swirl around the city and right back to Mexico City. Bly, not yet twenty-two though a worldly ingenue, was as self-absorbed as she was self-important. She was sensitive to criticism. Gossip about her in a letter received by a colleague moved her immediately to set the record straight. Her missive to the editor, which *The Dispatch* reprinted in full, is telling on several counts: It states her intent as a woman in a man's business, her sense of achievement, her debts of gratitude for her opportunities, and her fury that even the casual speculation of readers would credit one of her brothers with any part of her very personal success:

> For the last year I have been engaged on the staff of your paper and have endeavored, in my humble way, to perform my duties faithfully, careful not to take advantage of my being a woman, and yet without the least desire to be mannish. During my short newspaper career, I have experienced nothing but kindness not only from acquaintances I have formed, but from your managing editor and Quiet Observer, to whom I owe everything. I came to Mexico with the intention of doing as well as was in my power, in the way of news for the paper. So far I have received but favorable comments from those I left behind.
>
> The newly found friends here have endeavored to extend every kindness and courtesy to me and I, feeling my inability to do justice to their beautiful country, have refused all requests to see my letters. Some very anxious ones have written to private parties in Pittsburg and obtained the *Dispatch* containing my communications. The other day, a gentleman received a letter from which I make this extract: "Nellie Bly is quite a scribe, but envious people hereabouts do say that it is not she, but a brother who writes the articles signed by her name. However, I believe this report to be false."
>
> With the desire not to appear in a false light to my friends here, I have written this, which I hope you will favor me by publishing. Although they know that I am here alone with my mother, I desire that they may also know that Nellie Bly has no brother, and never had, to whom she was indebted for one item or suggestion in her newspaper efforts.

In the same issue of *The Dispatch,* she lashed out at a visiting "Roosevelt," whom she identified only as "the banker." This man and three lady companions toured Mexico, according to Bly, all the time "flaunting tales of their riches in the faces of the inhabitants yet spending less than any who have yet come here." She was appalled that these wealthy tourists had left "neither the hotel keeper nor guide the better for their coming."

Bly bragged to brother Charles in a letter dated April 3, 1886, that in the two and a half months she and her mother had been in Mexico, they had only managed to spend fifty-five dollars.

She struck up a flirtation with Joaquin Miller, whom she mentioned repeatedly in her stories. In one piece, she described him as "a bear one day; a blue-eyed angel the next." On an "angel" day, Bly discovered a street in the city on which every doorway led to a coffin maker. She shared her discovery with Miller, who flattered her by saying, "Little Nell, you are a second Columbus. You have discovered a street that has no like in the world and I have been over the world twice." Clearly delighted with both the accolade and the diminutive, Bly shared his words with her readers, verbatim.

Enamored as she was with the crusty adventurer, she declined to heed Miller's warning not to destroy the myth of Mexico's famous "floating gardens" at La Viga. Miller confided to Bly that the gardens do not actually float, but he implored her not to share this information with the public. In Bly's words, "Either our respect for the truth or a desire to do just the opposite of what others wish has made me tell just what the floating gardens really are. At the very least, they repay one's trouble for the journey."

She traveled the countryside—to Zocala, Guadelupe, Veracruz, and Jalapa—and sent detailed travelogues back to Pittsburgh. On the train to Jalapa, she and her mother refused to pay a dollar to have their satchels carried because Bly knew very well the going rate was only a quarter. Her fellow travelers were amazed when she and Mary Jane picked up their own bags, especially since Mexican women almost never traveled without male escort and were certainly not in the habit of doing their own hauling. She reveled in the chance to demonstrate the power of the new woman: "The Mexicans surveyed myself and my chaperon in amazement," Bly wrote proudly, not mentioning that the chaperon was her mother. "But I defied their gaze and showed them that a free American girl can accommodate herself to circumstances without the aid of a man."

Bly's original plan was to remain in Mexico the full six months, until July 1. In fact, by May 6, she was counting the days until her departure, dreaming of her escape from the unending diet of boiled cheese, chili-stuffed meat, fried pumpkin sprinkled with chilies, and poorly slept nights on her iron-bottomed bed. She told readers how she longed to head back to Pittsburgh and "try once again the pests which inflict [sic] mortals there."

Fear of impending arrest, however, precipitated a change in schedule, and Bly and her mother were back in Pittsburgh, stepping off the Panhandle Express after a week's travel on June 22. A *Dispatch* reporter awaited their arrival on the platform. Now safely home, Bly began unloading a harsher set of reflections than those that had appeared in print while she was within foreign boundaries. Mexicans she now described as generally cruel, not very highly civilized, and harboring "a sort of horror for everything that comes from the States." She told of how frequently editors and newspaper writers found themselves in jail for expressing sentiments too freely.

The Mexican press she described as "tools of the organized ring" whose only capability was "deceiving the outsider." The twenty-five newspapers, she said, were held in such disregard that no one even used them "as a subterfuge to hide behind in a street car when some woman with a dozen bundles, three children and two baskets is looking for a seat."

"To say libelous things is as dangerous as to write them," she wrote, adding that this applied to foreigners as well. "I had some regard for my health," she explained, "and a Mexican jail is the least desirable abode on the face of the earth, so some care was exercised in the selection of topics while we were inside their gates."

While in Mexico City, she said, she had quite innocently decided to report the story of an editor who had been arrested for writing antigovernment editorials. This must have been the report that appeared in *The Dispatch* of March 22. *The St. Louis Globe-Democrat* had picked up the story, and a copy of the St. Louis newspaper for that day made its way back to Mexico City and into the hands of authorities. Bly said, "The subsidized sheets [newspapers which accept government subsidies] threatened to denounce me and said in Spanish, 'One button was enough,' meaning from one article the officials could see what my others were like, but by means of a little bravado I convinced them that I had the upper hand and they left me unhurt."

On arrival in Pittsburgh, Bly explained that Theo Gestefeld of *Two Republics* had come to her aid with the authorities. "I did a good deal of what is commonly called 'bluffing' in regard to the power of the American government to protect the freedom of her citizens and the press," she said. The effort must have been convincing, she said, for the arrest was never carried out.

Once safely back in Pittsburgh, Bly spared nothing in her indictment of Díaz and his administration. With these words, she began her series of revelations in *The Dispatch:*

> My residence in Mexico of five months did not give me ample time to see all these things personally, but I have the very best authority for all statements. Men whom I know to be honorable have given me a true statement of facts which have heretofore never reached the public prints. That such things missed the public press will rather astonish Americans who are used to a free press; but the Mexican papers never publish one word against the government or officials and the people who are at their mercy dare not breathe one word against them, as those in position are more able than the most tyrannical czar to make their lives miserable. When this is finished the worst is yet untold by half, so the readers can form some idea about the government of Mexico.

Mexico, she said, though a republic in name was actually "the worst monarchy in existence," despite what, on paper, was an excellent constitution. President Díaz, she said, had the confidence of the people when he first took office, but soon lost it. Since a Mexican president cannot succeed himself, Bly reported, Díaz arranged for Manuel González to succeed him with the understanding he would return the presidency to Díaz after his term, which he did. González,

No. 1324.   20 Cents.

Lovell's Library.

A TRI-WEEKLY PUBLICATION OF THE BEST CURRENT & STANDARD LITERATURE

No. 1324. Annual Subscription $30. Entered at the Post Office, New York, as second class matter, Jan. 3, 1889.

Six Months in Mexico

BY

NELLIE BLY,
AUTHOR OF "TEN DAYS IN A MAD HOUSE." .C.

NEW YORK
JOHN·W·LOVELL COMPANY
14 & 16 VESEY STREET

The cover of the 1889 edition of Bly's Six Months in Mexico
(Library of Congress)

she said, milked the national treasury for more than $25 million and even bought a lottery ticket and demanded from lottery administrators that it be declared the winner. "President Díaz has two years from next December to serve," she said, "that is, providing a revolution does not cut his term short. The people will not say much about his going out, as one just as bad will replace him."

She reported on the prospects of war with the United States, of how Díaz had assembled a standing army of 40,000 men or more, composed of officers of the highest classes leading a rank and file of "half-breeds and Indians" who are "nearly all convicts."

> The Mexicans have a good deal of suppressed wrath bothering them at the present day. They know that Díaz is a tyrannical czar and want to overthrow him. It may be readily believed that Díaz knows they are bound to get rid of this superfluous feeling, and he would much rather have them rent [sic] its strength on America than on himself. Thus he stands on the war question. He is a good general and has many good tough old soldiers, the best of whom is President González, to aid him, beside the convict soldiers and rurales.

She did not supply attribution for her information, nor did she back up what she wrote with verifiable examples. Her reporting on these sensitive topics was more in the nature of gossip and hearsay than the stuff of hard-nosed inquiry—not uncommon for the time. However unsubstantiated, what she wrote was lively and attention demanding. Maybe even true.

Erasmus Wilson, for one, gave an enthusiastic if somewhat ambiguous evaluation of the very young lady's achievement. "There was little in Mexico she didn't see or write about," he said, but complained bitterly about the eye-straining sheets of blue-glazed paper scripted in lead pencil—"bad pencil at that"—which he had so painstakingly edited for his colleague and friend. "Her copy," he moaned, "—the thought of it almost causes tears to start."

⸴⸜⸝⸞

By mid-September of 1886, Bly had emptied her notebook of stories about Mexico, the last, headlined "Mexican Manners," appeared in *The Dispatch* on Sunday, September 19. She was almost ready to resume full-time employment on the newspaper. But first, she headed to Kittanning, seat of Armstrong County, to testify in the suit she had filed against her former guardian, town banker Samuel Jackson, who, she charged, had mismanaged her modest trust.

Since Judge Michael Cochran's death, Colonel Jackson had administered the total $5,000 left to the judge's five minor heirs. In addition, Jackson had purchased for $2,650 the judge's home on Mansion Row. For that, he was paying in twice-yearly installments to Mary Jane, as part of her widow's dower, the interest on one-third of the purchase price.

Because of Jackson's complicated financial arrangements with the Cochran heirs, he told the court he found it more convenient to keep record of these various deposits, credits, interest, and debits on paper. The actual funds he deposited in his personal account. That way, he said, he was able to make the small, relatively frequent disbursements that Mary Jane favored with ease. He said he credited the Cochrans' monies with interest payment of 6 percent until January of 1876 and 4 percent after that—regardless of the rate of interest he received personally.

Jackson was negligent on several counts: He commingled the Cochran money with his own and kept faulty records. He misled Pink about the money she had available to enroll in normal school, and his account sheet showed that she had attended the boarding school for two terms instead of one. He sealed Pink's enmity on making final settlement to each of the children after the family had moved to Pittsburgh: To close out her account, Pink was offered three dollars, which she refused to accept, while each of her siblings received several hundred dollars.

In the course of testimony, Mary Jane, Pink, brother Charles, and sister Kate all disputed the signatures on the receipts that Jackson produced for the court. They also charged that the colonel had inappropriately released funds from their trust accounts to their former stepfather, Jack Ford, who had put the money to his own use. Matters were further complicated by Mary Jane's ignorance of the fact that Jackson had been paying her money for boarding the children directly out of the children's trusts. She was under the impression that that money was part of the dower he owed her as a result of having purchased the Mansion Row residence.

The accounts were a mess. The esteemed Colonel Jackson, if nothing else, was guilty of very sloppy handling. The court appointed a second auditor to review the books, but by the time his report was in and Jackson had taken legal exception to his findings, nearly two more years had passed. Pink Elizabeth J. Cochran/Cochrane, by that time much better known as Nellie Bly, had lost interest in pursuing a couple of hundred dollars. The nuisance she had created for Jackson was apparently victory enough.

❧

Now that she was back at *The Dispatch*, Madden, Bly's mentor at the paper, got her more involved in theater and arts reporting. This was not exactly what she had envisioned as a fitting reward for her gutsy freelance performance from Mexico, but grudgingly she accepted the new tasks. The fact was, she needed work. If she were going to stay in newspapering, this was as good a job as a woman could expect. It was true that the new "free American girl" had become a popular topic in the pages of *The Dispatch*. The impact of this discussion on personnel decisions in the newsroom, however, was nil.

Bly made her theater coverage debut at the end of October with two pieces, one titled "In Stage Circles," and the other, "Some Stage Secrets," both about prominent theatrical personalities who had recently visited Pittsburgh. She submitted a few inconsequential features on other topics to round out her year's work, and, by January 1887, she was the newspaper's reluctant lead culture writer.

Although she continued writing longer, timeless features on everything from the history of visiting cards and the origins of wedding rings to the rituals of marriage in various cultures, she also started two columns which she regularly signed. One, entitled "Footlight Gossip," gave backstage insights into the theatrical presentations appearing in Pittsburgh and the artists who performed them. She also sometimes used her new forum to give the "Bly take" on what she had observed. In one column, she laid down the definitive theater etiquette, a reaction to all the bad manners she had witnessed as a member of so many audiences. In another, obviously annoyed by the view-blocking hats then in fashion among theater-going women, Bly devoted two columns to the history of women's headwear.

Bly's other column, "Among the Artists," followed the progress of Pittsburgh's own community of painters and sculptors. She bemoaned the philistine tastes of even the city's most sophisticated residents. "It is certainly time for people to wake up to the fact that there is beauty in other things than the face of a dollar," she wrote, "and that, as they now have money, it is time to cultivate taste." She wrote of the man who had commissioned a series of ancestral portraits—of ancestors not his own—and of "Mr. Money," who visited an artist's studio, sat rapt for many minutes staring at the painter's work, and then emoted, "That's truly a beautiful frame: wonder what it cost?" She repeatedly urged the opening of a place where the city's artists could show their work. From this, there was apparent impact. Soon, discussions were under way for the city's first gallery for exhibiting local work.

Still, she was not satisfied. In the recollection of her good friend Erasmus Wilson, Bly in this period, still flush from the novelty and pace of her Mexican adventure, simply found her old newspaper routine too dull. "The city editor couldn't find anything to her taste," Wilson recalled, "and they jarred and fussed a good deal."

Her last piece as a full-time staff member of *The Pittsburg Dispatch* appeared on March 20, 1887. Her career as a culture writer lasted not even three months. Soon after, Bly simply did not show up for work. Wilson remembered the day well: "No one knew where she was," he said, "until the following note was discovered:

DEAR Q.O.—*I am off for New York. Look out for me.*

BLY.

Part Two

❦ ❦

1887–1893

INSIDE THE MADHOUSE.

Nellie Bly's Experience in the Rockwell's Island Asylum.

Continuation of the Story of Ten Days With Lunatics.

How the City's Unfortunate Wards Are Fed and Treated.

The Terrors of Cold Baths and Cruel, Unsympathetic Nurses.

Attendants Who Harass and Abuse Patients and Laugh at Their Miseries.

INSIDE THE MADHOUSE.

Nellie Bly's Experience in the Rockwell's Island Asylum.

Continuation of the Story of Ten Days With Lunatics.

How the City's Unfortunate Wards Are Fed and Treated.

The Terrors of Cold Baths and Cruel, Unsympathetic Nurses.

Attendants Who Harass and Abuse Patients and Laugh at Their Miseries.

THE VIOLENT PATIENTS.

INSANE HALL NO. 6.

IN THE BATH.

Scrubbed with Soft Soap and Put to Bed in a Wet Gown.

THE FIRST MORNING.

Combed with a Public Comb, the Breakfast and the Uniform.

BAD FOOD AND WORSE HELP.

4

⚜ ⚜

The World

T HE DRUMROLL PINK COCHRANE COUNTED ON TO HERALD HER debut in the capital of newspaperdom turned out to be nothing but a long, loud, flat thud. She arrived in May 1887, hell-bent on swift hire at one of the city's major dailies. But as May stretched into June, and June into August, her forays down the one-sided crush of newspaper offices angling from Ann Street and Broadway into Printing House Square, known as Park Row, proved ever more futile. Her Pittsburgh portfolio meant little to the surly nay-sayers at the office doors of *The Sun, The World, The Herald, The Tribune, The Times,* and *The Mail and Express,* the guards who stood sentry in the shadow of City Hall. She, like so many hopeful provincial reporters, couldn't get past them. It began to seem that the small furnished room overlooking a dark back alley at 15 West Ninety-sixth Street might be home forever.

Although she would have accepted any opportunity, *The World* was where she wanted to work. In the four years since Joseph Pulitzer had bought the ailing newspaper from financier Jay Gould, he had fashioned it into the most successful, most imitated newspaper in the country by combining a taste for the lurid and grisly sensations and scandals of the day, captured in provocative headlines, with top-notch reporting of all the day's news, strong use of illustrations, crusades and contests, and an editorial page renowned for its excellence. As an immigrant himself, Pulitzer instinctively understood the need to appeal to the diverse pool of potential readership represented by the masses of new Americans settling in the city. He took up their causes, appealed to their interests, confronted in newsprint the issues they faced, and commanded their attention. The catapult in circulation *The World* experienced between 1883 and 1887—from 20,000 to 200,000 on Sundays alone—generously affirmed the wisdom of his approach.

The longtime leaders in the field, the sophisticated *New York Sun* and the elitist *New York Herald,* were soon forced to play catch-up. This was all the more galling because *The Sun* had long enjoyed its reputation as the best reported and best written of all the country's dailies and the most sought after place to work, and *The Herald,* which had pioneered in the use of illustrations, had led the field in amassing advertising revenue. *The New York Times* and *The New York Tribune,* lacking strong editorial direction in this period, were second tier, and the others, too small to offer real competition.

Park Row, known as "Newspaper Row," circa 1887
(The Bettmann Archive)

Then as now, New York was the nation's publishing capital, a city of more than a million and a half residents poised for a population surge. The talented tended to gravitate to the metropolis and angle for jobs under outstanding editors. As the saying goes, knives sharpen knives. The great reputations of reporters in this day— Julian Ralph, Richard Harding Davis, Jacob Riis, for example— were being made in New York.

Upon her arrival, Bly must have found fortuitous the announcement in *The World* of May 1 that the newspaper planned to send up a hot-air balloon in St. Louis, home of Pulitzer's other newspaper, *The St. Louis Post-Dispatch.* The manned balloon was to travel west with the two newspapers chronicling its journey day by day. Bly, seeing her opening, immediately offered in a letter to be the reporter on board. She enclosed a note of introduction from a Pittsburgh acquaintance, Edward Dulzer. The rejection pointed out that the undertaking was too dangerous for a lady. In any event, the assignment already had gone to another reporter, Edward Duffy. Weather delayed the liftoff until June 17, when, to much fanfare, the ropes were cut and the balloon ascended. But the journey sputtered out long before its expected completion date, as did the story.

By mid-July, with no prospect of a local job, Bly brought in some money writing women's features sent back for publication in her alma mater, *The Pittsburg Dispatch,* alongside the reporting of George N. McCain, the paper's regular New York correspondent, who could not have taken kindly to this incursion onto his turf. She stayed out of his way for the most part, directing her attention to the very subjects she had fled Pittsburgh to escape. There were Sunday pieces on what fashionable New York women were wearing—puffed sleeves, women's hats worn hind-end front, hair tresses knotted Grecian-style at the neck—and some unrelated, oddly recounted tales of the sometimes strange turns of city life.

The second week in August, Bly told the readers of *The Dispatch* that she had received a letter from an ambitious young lady who longed to become a journalist, replete with "empty glory and poor pay," which was Bly's snide depiction of the profession's finest hallmarks. The woman asked Bly if she thought New York was the best place to get a start. Rather than answer herself, Bly got the idea to use this excuse to put the question to the city's most powerful journalistic personalities, the men she described with a knowing air as "the newspaper gods of Gotham." Her *Dispatch* credentials were all the entrée she needed, and she visited them all: Charles A. Dana of *The Sun;* Dr. George H. Hepworth of *The Herald;* Colonel John A. Cockerill, Pulitzer's chief editor at *The World;* Foster Coates of *The Mail and Express;* Robert G. Morris of *The Telegram;* and Charles Ransom Miller of *The Times.* The story that resulted, though it was not much more than the editors' verbatim quotes, read like a feminist's lament. Getting past their editorial mind-set and into the city room was going to be some trick for Bly or the young female aspirant, who might well have been one and the same.

Bly found Dana of *The Sun* twirling his gold-rimmed glasses while seated behind his tidy desk in a cozy, homelike office. "His intelligent face, framed by silvery hair and beard, had a look of kindness which half dispelled the fear of interviewing so great a man," she wrote. He denied any prejudice against women reporters but said they were "not regarded with editorial favor in New York" and, as a class, were worse than men in the matter of accuracy, a journalist's most important asset. In parentheses, she quipped, "Here I groaned mentally for the fate of this interview."

Honing what would become her signature technique, Bly "posed" as a job applicant when she went to see the strikingly intellectual-looking Dr. Hepworth of *The Herald,* a man "with the manners of a Chesterfield." He asked her what she could do. The answer and the way she reported it were vintage Nellie Bly: " 'Anything,' I replied with a candor that was probably about as startling as it was true . . . 'Do you object to women entering newspaper life?' " He said he did not, but then at the same time could not imagine sending a woman to cover the police or criminal courts since the officials in those posts would give her "as little information as they could to get rid of her." And further, given the sensations and scandals demanded by "the present popular taste, a gentleman could not in delicacy ask a woman to have anything to do with that class of news."

Colonel Cockerill of *The World,* of whom she ventured no description, was even more disheartening. What women were fit for in newspaper work—society coverage, for example—they didn't want to do. "A man," he said, "is of far greater service." Gratuitously, the mustachioed Cockerill added that there actually were two women on staff at *The World*, "So you see we do not object personally."

Whatever the circumstances that led to Bly's story, her requesting the interviews on behalf of her old Pittsburgh paper was a slick and enterprising maneuver through the phalanx of bodyguards and bouncers who had blocked her entrance on Newspaper Row all spring and summer. It certainly made it unnecessary for her to burst into any private office in a job-demanding frenzy, as the apocrypha on Bly has long held. Besides, given the attitude toward women reporters disclosed by "the gods," such an escapade would have made her look ridiculous.

The story Bly wrote, published in *The Pittsburg Dispatch,* proved a better showcase for her ability than any stunt or letter of introduction. The statements of these editors proved so out of touch—women had started to elbow their way into city rooms across the country—that the story ricocheted from Pittsburgh to New York to Boston over the next two months and then out to the rest of the nation's journalistic community through the trade magazine, *The Journalist.*

More important for Bly, it got her in personal contact with the men who held the power to hire and showed her how to position herself for the New York market, pathetic as it was for women reporters. The responses she elicited from these men let her know exactly what she was up against. "We have more women now than we want" was the way Bly would later summarize her first reception by New York's editors. "Women are no good, anyway."

Bly's story caused Joseph Howard, Jr., to react in one of his syndicated "Howard Letter" columns. The well-known New York newspaperman had lost his job at *The World* after coming to blows, literally, with Pulitzer himself. In his column, Howard criticized the "lamentable ignorance of Sunday newspaper editors . . . on the subject of women in journalism. One would imagine that there are no successful women in the metropolitan field, but the editors are mistaken." *The Journalist* reprinted Howard's remarks, as carried by *The Boston Globe,* as well as his long list of successful women correspondents, topped by "Miss Nellie Bly [who] came here from Pittsburg where she made name and fame and cash. She writes for *The Mail* most readable matter and is as bright as a new pin."

The editors in New York were clearly resistant to seeing women take their place in the field. Ida M. Tarbell, writing earlier that year, was of the same mind as Howard in her piece for *The Chautauquan,* a magazine that would later deign to name her managing editor. The field was "wide open," Tarbell said, for any woman in good physical condition who would ask no special dispensations on the basis of her sex, pull no feminine tricks, and be willing to undertake any assignment. "The standard it raises is high," Tarbell acknowledged. "But the opportunity is as great as her ability. Any woman who can do as strong and finished work as a man will find a position."

Excerpts from Bly's interviews with New York's top editors were reprinted in *The Mail and Express* on August 27, 1887. That article described Bly as a "bright and talented young woman who has done a great deal of good writing for the newspapers." This must have been gratifying, but it still did not produce an offer of a full-time job. She was nearly four months into her New York foray by that time, and the issue of finding a steady way to make a living could no longer be avoided. Bly was running out of money. On top of that, she had the utter misfortune to lose her purse containing the little money that remained. "I was penniless," she wrote of the experience a year later. "I was too proud to return to the position I had left in search of new worlds to conquer. Indeed, I cannot say the thought ever presented itself to me, for I never in my life turned back from a course I had started upon."

✦

Bly borrowed carfare from her landlady, rode down to Park Row, and, with classic flair, turned her predicament into the propulsion to finally land a job. That and "a great deal of talking" got her past the guards at the doors of *The New York World* and up the elevator to Cockerill's private office. Given the number of barriers between the entrance and Cockerill's office aimed at keeping down intrusions, this was an achievement in itself. "I really think," she recalled, "I at

Colonel John Cockerill, managing editor of
The New York World
(Courtesy of The New-York
Historical Society)

last gained admission by saying that I had an important subject to propose, and if the editor-in-chief would not see me, I would go to some other paper."

This was her maxim: "Energy rightly applied and directed will accomplish anything."

Ushered into Cockerill's "sacred precincts," Bly wasted no time. She presented her story ideas, suggestions "as desperate as they were startling to carry out." Cockerill looked them over but declined to give her an immediate response. Instead, to keep her from going elsewhere, presumably until he could speak with Pulitzer, he handed her twenty-five dollars to retain her services until a decision could be made.

She called him at the appointed time and by September 22, had her chance. Her idea to travel to Europe and return steerage class, so she could report firsthand the experiences of an immigrant, was rejected as too far-flung for a newcomer. Instead, Cockerill commissioned her to feign insanity and get herself committed to the Women's Lunatic Asylum, set amid the prisons, charity hospitals, almshouses, workhouses, and "other cancer spots of modern Manhattan" on the 120-acre sliver of land in the East River then known as Blackwell's Island. It was a harrowing demand to make of a gentlewoman only trying out for a position, but to Bly it was far more appealing than the prospect of starvation. Cockerill knew what he was asking. "You can try," he told her. "But if you can do it, it's more than anyone would believe."

Even without the impetus of penury, it would have been like Bly to see the potential of an attention-getting first assignment, no matter how dangerous, and then seize whatever opportunity presented itself without thought to the risks. She liked risks, in fact. For Cockerill's part, it would have been like him to ask her to take them. It was the way *The World* pushed the edges of creativity. It was the sort of thing that made *The World* the newspaper to beat.

Whose idea was it? According to a *World* biography of Bly, it came from Pulitzer himself, who, having turned down her idea to travel steerage from Europe, "preferred that she should try a local story at first and he personally suggested the Insane Asylum exposé." Bly's first recounting of the episode said merely that she was "asked by *The World*" to have herself committed "with a view to writing a plain and unvarnished narrative." Her later telling was more ambiguous on the issue of credit for the idea that catalyzed a new journalistic movement. Bly left the impression that the insane asylum exposé was among the "desperate" and "startling" suggestions she had reeled off in Cockerill's office that late summer day.

The next year, in 1888, a member of *The World*'s staff made a careful handwritten listing of every "Conspicuous Feature" the newspaper had published since 1885, who wrote it, and who suggested it. Next to "Nellie Bly and the Madhouse," in this private memo, credit for the idea went to Cockerill. Two months after the story ran, Pulitzer received a note marked "private" from a tipster at *The Sunday Argus* in Washington, D.C. "A good while ago we gave you a tip to investigate Insane Asylum—you remember—and we suppose that 'Nellie Bly' is the result—"

With the benefit of hindsight, *The World* retold the story of how Nellie Bly ended up an inmate on Blackwell's Island, in the newspaper's tenth-anniversary issue, May 7, 1893. This time the paper said, without specifying the originator of the idea, that it directed Bly to investigate the asylum after "frequent reports of shocking abuses . . . but no direct evidence on the subject had been given out to the public."

In fact, in the two months before attendants carted Nellie Bly away to Bellevue Hospital and then to the dreaded island, all the newspapers were full of stories of asylum abuses at the city's various institutions. *The World* itself ran two editorials, July 3 and July 9, demanding investigation of alleged maltreatment of patients at the charitable and penal institutions on Ward's Island, also in the East River, just north of Blackwell's. Meanwhile, two keepers of the Ward's Island facility were indicted for manslaughter in the killing of a "lunatic," prompting *The World* to call for an overhaul of the "disgracefully overcrowded" facility.

The New York Times ran frequent stories. In August, two nurses, ages seventeen and twenty-eight, leveled what the prim *Times* would only describe as "charges seriously affecting the character" of two Blackwell's Island physicians, resulting in the suspensions from duty of all four. An editorial in the newspaper on August 18 decried the "very ugly and painful stories" circulating about brutality and neglect of the island's inmates. "It would be as much a mistake to assume that there is nothing in these stories as to assume that they are all literally true," the newspaper wrote.

The asylum cried out for independent investigation, which newspapers by this point in their evolution saw as part of their domain. Thanks to *The World*'s revival of the shocking as daily newspaper fare, the subject of ill-treated lunatics was a natural. And women in journalism had only one hope of escaping work on the dreary society pages: the new, wild-side genre of "stunt" or "detective" reporting with which Bly's name would fast become synonymous. Although such exploits had been attempted before by male reporters in the name of public service and, more important, wider newspaper circulation, this one launched the decade of Girl Reporter Derring-Do.

Stunt reporting, in the opinion of historian Frank Luther Mott, best exemplifies the mood and method of what became known as Pulitzer's "New Journalism." The notion of combining the exploitation of crime, scandal, or shocking circumstance with the spirit of a crusade, delivered into words by a clever and talented writer who donned a disguise to get the story was sensationalist in character and something altogether new in the field.

By the time *The Journalist* reprinted Joseph Howard's column damning the New York editors for shortchanging women, Bly was back from the asylum, in print, and the talk of New York in ways a woman reporter had never been discussed before. Cockerill rewarded her with a place on *The World*'s permanent staff.

"Behind Asylum Bars" was the headline of the first installment of the illustrated two-part series, which *The World* started running October 9, 1887. The newcomer was permitted to sign her story at the end of the two entire pages of newsprint it occupied as the lead of the Sunday feature section, another Pulitzer innovation. As rare as bylines were for veterans on the pages of *The World,* other than stars like Bill Nye or a guest columnist like the poet Ella Wheeler Wilcox, they were almost unheard of for a new hire, no matter how impressive his or her feat.

By the time the second installment ran one week later—with the same sensational display, lead feature on two successive pages—Nellie Bly was no longer just a byline, that line above or below a newspaper story that gives the name of the writer. Even though so little time had elapsed, *Nellie Bly* meant enough to be part of the headline, the large type atop a story aimed to attract the reader's eye:

INSIDE THE MADHOUSE

Nellie Bly's Experience in the Blackwell's Island Asylum

Continuation of the Story of Ten Days with Lunatics

How the City's Unfortunate Wards Are Fed and Treated

The Terrors of Cold Baths and Cruel, Unsympathetic Nurses

Attendants Who Harass and Abuse Patients

and Laugh at Their Miseries

Bill Nye, the columnist, in a letter to his pal and co-lecturer the poet James Whitcomb Riley, mentioned that Cockerill had snapped up for the Sunday *World* a "pome" Riley had written privately to Nye's wife, Catalpa. "But so far," Nye whined, his shorthand indicating just how far word of Bly's exploit had spread, "the Insane Asylum and the Bacon-Shakespeare controversy have crowded out everything else but the advertisements."

Two months later, Nellie Bly's *Ten Days in a Mad-House* was out in book form, slightly embellished with Bly's afterthoughts on her adventure, along with reprints of two subsequent stunts that appeared in *The World* to fill the work out to book length.

In a matter of days, Nellie Bly had caused the New York sensation she hoped for and, in the process, become one herself. Her name appeared in the headline of that story and virtually every other story she wrote for the rest of her newspaper life. To succeed at feigning insanity and live to write about it was an extraordinary feat. As the achievement of a woman journalist in this period, its brilliance was blinding. The acclaim Bly won was as much of a sensation as the achievement itself. Fame ignited and spread fast and far.

The girl who looked like an East Coast Annie Oakley may not have burst into any office on Newspaper Row with her reportorial guns drawn, but she might as well have. The effect was the same. In a seeming instant, Nellie Bly became, and remained through several more incarnations, an explosive national presence.

༈

The strategy for getting into the Blackwell's Island Insane Asylum for Women was Bly's concoction. Cockerill gave her no more instruction than to use the name Nellie Brown, so that she could be identified by her monogram no matter what, and to try to suppress her chronic smile. He promised to find a way to get her out when the time came.

For hours, she practiced looking like a lunatic in front of a mirror. Always meticulously groomed, she put on her idea of old clothes, later described by the reporters she duped as stylish. She left behind her soap and toothbrush. Faraway expressions look crazy, she decided. She wandered the streets in a daze.

For legal advice, she called on Assistant District Attorney Henry D. Macdona. "I looked at the little woman with amazement," he later recalled. "I learned that she had obliterated every vestige of her identity and would go into the asylum absolutely leaving no trace behind. At first I declined to have anything to do with the matter and cautioned her as to the danger. I expressed the opinion that she did not possess sufficient bodily strength to enable her to pass harmless through the threatened ordeal."

Although writers as early as the 1840s, notably Charles Dickens in his *American Notes* and Margaret Fuller in *The New York Tribune,* had gone to Blackwell's Island and reported on conditions, no one before Bly had assumed the guise of the deranged for the assignment. Macdona earnestly advised Bly to give up the idea, but she jumped from her chair, stamped her foot defiantly, and declared that no asylum keeper or anyone else was going to frighten her off. "That settled the question in my mind," Macdona said, and he agreed to give her immunity from prosecution for the ruse.

Giving her name as Nellie Brown, Bly checked into Matron Irene Stenard's Temporary Home for Women at 84 Second Avenue, a working-class boardinghouse. There, after two meals and a few irrational conversations, she would contrive to lose her mind. Her performance was convincing enough that by bedtime one woman was heard to say, "I'm afraid to stay with such a crazy being in the house." Added another, "She will murder us before morning."

"But how I tortured all of them!" Bly wrote later. "One of them dreamed of me—as a nightmare." She herself would stay up all night—standing "face to face with self!"—engulfed in the melodrama of the adventure that was about to alter the course of her life.

> How strange it all seems! One incident, if never [*sic*] so trifling, is but a link more to chain us to our unchangeable fate. I began at the beginning, and lived again the story of my life. Old friends were recalled with a pleasurable thrill; old enmities, old heartaches, old joys were once again present. The turned-down pages of my life were turned up, and the past was present.

"It was," she would write later, "the greatest night of my existence."

By morning, the assistant matron tried to get Bly out of the house, but she refused, keeping up a refrain about looking for her missing trunks. One woman left and returned with two police officers, who escorted her to the station house. From there she was taken into the Essex Market police courtroom of the kindly Judge Patrick G. Duffy, who offered in compassion that he was sure this well-dressed, well-spoken lady was "somebody's darling."

Bly covered her face with a handkerchief so the laughter he provoked would not betray her. Judge Duffy concluded she had been drugged and brought to the city. "Make out papers and we will send her to Bellevue for examination," he ordered. In the meantime, trying to determine the origin of her odd accent, he asked her if she were from Cuba. She said yes and at that, putting the fruits of her Mexican sojourn to good use, took to calling herself Nellie Moreno (Spanish for Brown, misspelled by all the reporters). Duffy called in reporters, hoping publicity about the case would help in locating the family to whom the pretty 112-pound, five-foot five-inch young woman with the size two and a half shoe belonged.

The Sun played the story as a mystery, placing it in the lead right-hand column of the front page on September 25 under the headline "Who Is This Insane Girl?" The newspaper described the modest, comely girl of nineteen with the low, mild voice and cultivated manner, handsomely dressed in a brown-trimmed frock of gray flannel with sleeves cut in the latest style, accessorized by brown silk gloves and a black straw sailor's hat trimmed in brown and veiled in thin gray illusion. It reported the contradictions in the story of her background, her apparent disorientation. The doctors, confounded, called hers "the most peculiar case that ever came into the hospital."

The examining physicians at Bellevue ruled out belladonna, or deadly nightshade poisoning with its attendant delirium and hallucinations, as the cause of her apparent dementia. Dr. William C. Braisted, head of the insane pavilion at Bellevue, repeated his diagnosis to *The New York Herald*: "She never seems to be restless. Her delusions, her dull apathetic condition, the muscular twitching of her hands and arms and her loss of memory, all indicate hysteria."

To *The Evening Telegram* the next day, he said she was "undoubtedly insane." Only Bellevue's warden, William B. O'Rourke, was suspicious. He told *The Sun* reporter he considered the girl "a humbug." No one listened.

If Bly could fool the doctors, it is no surprise that she hoodwinked her new colleagues from *The Sun, The Herald, The Evening Telegram,* and *The Times.* On Monday, September 26, *The Times* wrote movingly of the "mysterious waif" at Bellevue with the "wild, hunted look in her eyes," describing her plaintive whisper, her incoherence, and the despair in her oft-repeated cry, "I can't remember. I can't remember."

In her wordy series, Bly elaborated on every sensation, every detail. There was the filthy ferry that carted her across to Blackwell's Island; the "coarse, massive" female attendants who "expectorated tobacco juice about on the floor in a manner more skillful than charming"; and the foreign women, wholly sane, who were committed simply because they could not make themselves understood. She wrote about the wretched food, the lack of salt, too little warm clothing, and the freezing cold baths:

> My teeth chattered and my limbs were goose-fleshed and blue with cold. Suddenly I got, one after the other, three buckets of water over my head—ice-cold water, too—into my eyes, my ears, my nose and my mouth. I think I experienced the sensation of a drowning person as they dragged me, gasping, shivering and quaking, from the tub. For once I did look insane.

She told in detail of witchy, vicious nurses who choked, beat, and harassed their deluded patients; of fire hazards; of having to share towels with "crazy patients who had the most dangerous eruptions all over their faces"; of oblivious doctors, and of sitting idle all day long after a brief, morning walk.

> What, excepting torture, would produce insanity quicker than this treatment? Here is a class of women sent to be cured. I would like the expert physicians who are condemning me for my action, which has proven their ability, to take

a perfectly sane and healthy woman, shut her up and make her sit from 6 a.m. to 8 p.m. on straight-back benches, do not allow her to talk or move during these hours, give her no reading and let her know nothing of the world or its doings, give her bad food and harsh treatment, and see how long it will take to make her insane. Two months would make her a mental and physical wreck.

Near the end of her stay, Bly barely escaped exposure. A reporter she had known for years was sent by his newspaper to eyeball the mysterious patient, himself posing as a man in search of a lost loved one. In a desperate whisper, Bly begged her stunned colleague not to give her away. Much to her relief, he obliged. "No," he told the nurse. "This is not the young lady I came in search of."

After ten days, on Tuesday, October 4, *The World* sent attorney Peter A. Hendricks to arrange for Miss Moreno's release, ostensibly to the care of friends willing to take responsibility for her.

The World's cartoonist, Walt McDougall, accompanied Hendricks. Left alone in the inner courtyard for a few minutes, McDougall recalled years later almost having his clothes ripped off by "a raging crowd of female maniacs, idiots and plain bugs. The way the mob rushed me, one would have thought I was the first train out after a subway hold-up."

The Sun reported the mysterious waif's release in a brief paragraph on October 7. *The Times* provided a longer account, concluding that her treatment for mental depression had achieved "gratifying results" and with further care, her reason could be restored. The facts of her case, however, remained a mystery.

Two days later, imagine the editorial fury, not to mention embarrassment, along Newspaper Row when the first installment of Bly's report appeared in *The World*. *The Times* dropped the story entirely, but Dana's staff at *The Sun* did its best to recoup. A good yarn is a good yarn, and *The Sun* cleverly undertook to make the story its own. Before Bly could get into print with the continuation of her account, the part of her saga that dealt with her actual stay on Blackwell's Island, *The Sun* produced its own quite comprehensive version of those events, gleaned by an unnamed *Sun* reporter from medical reports and interviews with the asylum's staff. It was published on the Friday before Bly's second Sunday piece.

The World may have been scooped on half of its scoop, but it was all the better for Bly, who, in the process, got her first boost into legend. In tall, heavy black type, *The Sun* led its front page with a blaring headline:

PLAYING MAD WOMAN

--

Nellie Bly Too Sharp for the Island Doctors

--

Nine Days' Life in Calico

--

The Sun Finishes Up its Story of the "Pretty Crazy Girl."

In six columns of type, *The World*'s rival newspaper recounted the entire saga. *The Sun* included rumors which had circulated at the asylum after Bly's release that Nellie Brown actually was a pretender. Speculation as to her identity, *The Sun* said, ultimately settled on "a young woman known as Nellie Bly as the heroine of the adventure." And who was Nellie Bly?

> She has been doing newspaper work in New York for several months and is the metropolitan correspondent of a Pittsburgh newspaper. Her mother is the widow of a Pittsburgh lawyer [*sic*]. She is intelligent, capable and self-reliant, and, except for the matter of changing her name to Nellie Bly, has gone about the business of maintaining herself in journalism in a practical, business-like way.

The story detailed the reactions of physicians and staff as they tried to explain how so many professionals could have gone so wrong. *The World* cribbed from the piece and reprinted or re-reported whole sections of it under a gloating headline the next day:

94

ALL THE DOCTORS FOOLED

THEY TRY TO EXPLAIN NELLIE BLY'S STAY IN THE INSANE ASYLUM

Six Columns of Excuses, Apologies, Defenses—Somebody Ought to Have Found Out that the Plucky Representative of "The World" Was Not Insane, of Course, but Nobody Is to Blame, as Usual.

Bly refuted most of the excuses of doctors, nurses, and administrators in a subsequent story. And the doctors and administrators, in turn, denied her charges.

News of the young reporter's exploit traveled well beyond the city. Papers all over North America lauded her achievement. *The World* carried excerpts from as many as it could. Most of the comments focused on how frightening it was that so many experts could be taken in by a girl with no special training or rehearsal performing a lunatic charade. "We all know that in times not so very remote men and women were sent to insane asylums on the certificates of doctors who were in collusion with relatives interested in having them put out of the way" was the ominous comment of *The Hamilton Times* of Ontario.

Shortly after the story appeared, Pulitzer was traveling back to New York by rail after a visit to his St. Louis staff. On a brief stopover at Pittsburgh's Union Station, a *Pittsburg Dispatch* reporter asked the publisher for his assessment of Bly's feat. Pulitzer remarked on how pleased he was with the performance of his "very bright" and "very plucky" new staff member, whom, he said, he had rewarded with a "handsome check." He went on, "She is well-educated and thoroughly understands the profession which she has chosen. She has a great future before her."

Probably the sweetest tribute came from Bessie Bramble, the venerable lady columnist whom Bly did not manage to unseat during her Pittsburgh reporting days. Bramble compared her former colleague with Ada Bittenbender, the woman who had just been nominated for judge in Nebraska. Bramble was bemused by the reactionary comment Bittenbender's nomination had provoked from U.S. Senator John James Ingalls, a Republican from Kansas. "Even the most passionate pleaders for equality," Bramble quoted him as saying, "had never affirmed that a woman would make a valuable judge." As if the senator's stupidity was not enough,

> now even the great editors of New York have been caught. They had scarcely got done saying that women could not cross the "great gulf" that separated them from reporters of the first order of enterprise, or words to that effect, when behold! Nelly [sic] Bly steps in and performs a feat of journalism that very few of the men of the profession have more than equaled. She has shown that cool courage, consummate craft and investigating ability are not monopolized by the brethren of the profession. By her clever woman's wit she has shown how easily men can be humbugged and imposed upon—and men hitherto deemed smart and experts at their business at that.

The World did its own vaunting. "The World Their Savior" the headline read. "How Nellie Bly's World Will Help the City's Insane." The story was about the appearance on October 27 before the Board of Estimate and Apportionment of commissioners for the Department of Public Charities and Corrections. The men appealed for a $1 million increase in their appropriation for the department. Mayor Abram S. Hewitt, noting Bly's exposé, recommended appropriating the full amount. Bly's own report on the impact of her investigation served as the last paragraph of her book, published immediately after the series ran. She wrote, "I have one consolation for my work—on the strength of my story the committee of appropriation provides $1 million more than was ever before given, for the benefit of the insane."

The actual sequence of events was somewhat different. Before Bly's exploit, the Board of Estimate already was considering its budgetary provisions for 1888, as required by law. On October 5, four days before Bly's first report appeared, requests were submitted for substantial increases in the budgets of all the facilities under the jurisdiction of the Department of Public Charities and Corrections, including the prisons, hospitals, workhouse, and almshouse, as well as the asylums. The request would increase the department's budget from nearly $1.50 million in 1887 to more than $2.64 million in 1888. The commissioners acknowledged how "overcrowded and entirely inadequate" these facilities had become, reaching a point "where relief has become imperative." For the Lunatic Asylum, they requested funds for a new building to accommodate staff so they would not have to share living quarters with the inmates. They asked for new bathrooms, a double oven for the kitchen, and funds to remodel the "Old Lodge," the building "for many years containing the most violent maniacs" now "unfit for habitation." They wanted to turn it into workshops and an amusement hall.

On October 25, Dr. Charles Simmons, head of the charities and corrections board, invited Mayor Hewitt and the rest of the Board of Estimate to visit the island and see for themselves how deplorable conditions were. Two days later, the department's commissioners appealed to the board in person, as reported in *The World*.

Two weeks after Bly's report appeared, Assistant District Attorney Vernon M. Davis led the October grand jury in an investigation of conditions at the asylum, which *The World* said was prompted solely by Bly's report. She was invited to accompany the panel. In her book, Bly reported that by the time she and the grand jury made their island tour, many of the abuses she had reported had been corrected, the foreign patients she named had been transferred away, the food service and sanitary conditions had been improved, and the hateful nurses and attendants she described had disappeared.

Still, when the jury members filed into the General Sessions courtroom of Judge Henry A. Gildersleeve on November 2, they immediately recommended approval of the larger appropriation of funds for care of the insane, specifically calling for improvement in the quality of staff members and food service, appointment of several women physicians to oversee nurses and attendants, relief of the overcrowding, and a change in the existing system of individual locks on each ward door because of the obvious fire hazard it created.

On December 18, the Board of Estimate took up the commissioners' invitation to visit the various facilities, even causing an

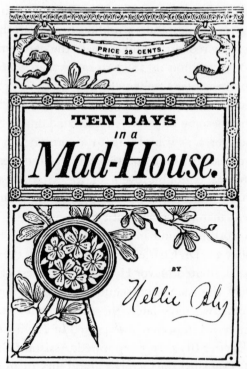

The cover of Bly's Ten Days in a Mad-House,
1887
(Library of Congress)

uproar at the Lunatic Asylum among the most violent inmates. The grim tour further convinced them of the department's need for more money. By December 29, the board made a few trims, then voted to approve an increase in the department's appropriation of $850,000 over the previous year—a 57 percent raise and the largest appropriation increase by far granted any department. The total amount of $2.34 million was only 10 percent under the department's total original request for all the facilities under its control. Of this amount, some $50,000 of $60,000 requested was earmarked for the Blackwell's Island asylum.

In light of the adverse publicity that preceded Bly's exposé, it is clear that a consensus had been forming for some time to increase funding to the city's jails, hospitals, almshouses, workhouses, and asylums. Given the sensation her report caused, however, it is an allowable lapse into hyperbole to claim as she did that the additional funds came "on the strength of my story." She certainly had added valuable heft.

⚬ॐ⚬

For a reporter's first assignment in a new city to outclass the competition so dramatically, and at the same time help encourage the city fathers to enact vital reforms for the "poor unfortunates" was the stuff of sweet fantasy. If Bly hadn't predated the phrase "hit the ground running," it might have gotten its currency among editors from her.

In just a few months, she had become a player, a personality with standing on the staff of the most revolutionary, most imitated newspaper in the country's most prestigious metropolis. With galling effortlessness, Bly had insinuated herself into a station of worth, hearing her pen name among those of *The World*'s best-known personalities: Nym Crinkle, Bill Nye, Henry Guy Carleton, Sol Pringle. More than anything else, Bly's ability to conjure impact, to seize attention, was her greatest gift. A tender good-heartedness came second.

A letter arrived from her Pittsburgh mentor and beloved friend, Erasmus Wilson, whom she still called Q.O. Her affection for him was immense, and she wrote back at once, on November 13, surprised to learn he had left *The Dispatch* and had been writing for *The Bulletin.* She adored his farewell column "to the roaches"—she could just picture it, she said—and told him of her plans to be in Pittsburgh soon; a reception was being planned in her honor by "Mrs. Mellon of the East End." She urged him to attend. She caught him up on her news. She had yet to meet Wilson's old friend Bill Nye, the renowned humorist on *The World* staff, but she had run into the venerable Ella Wheeler Wilcox in a less than satisfactory encounter. "Rather patronizing of Mrs. Wilcox to think that I had 'something in me,' " Bly snapped.

She told Wilson she had "buried the hatchet" with George McCain, *The Dispatch*'s correspondent in New York, and had thanked him "for not betraying my secret." McCain was almost certainly the reporter who came calling on Blackwell's Island and almost gave her away. They had parted good friends, she said. This he demonstrated in the items on her he included in his report from New York of November 20:

> That a streak of good luck favored Nellie Bly in conjunction with her own ready wit, in her recent insane asylum adventure, is evidenced in the fact that she escaped detection in one instance by a very remarkable circumstance. There is at present engaged on one of the Press News Associations in this city as reporter a young gentleman named Louis T. Golding, who was for a year, almost, on the local staff of several of the Pittsburg evening papers. During the week of Nellie Bly's evolutions from sanity to alleged insanity, and from the station house to the asylum, Golding was doing the police headquarters for the syndicate. On the day that Nellie Bly in the role of the pretty Cuban imbecile was examined by the police authorities, by a fortuitous chain of circumstances the reporter got left on this one item. Had he been at the police station house when she was marshaled before the assembled moguls, he would have recognized her, for he knew her personally, her identity would have been betrayed and the history of the abuses at Blackwell's Island would doubtless have never been written.

McCain did not mention his own encounter with Bly but did choose to note that as her fame had increased, so had the volume of her mail, from all parts of the country—"letters of commendation and congratulations; pathetic stories from people who have themselves looked out on the world at one time from behind iron bars and the embrace of a straight jacket; letters from cranks, downright crazy people and dudes." And then he plugged her new book on the adventure, for which, he said, she had received "a good round sum."

To Erasmus Wilson, she reported numerous offers to lecture or to go onstage as an actress, having now demonstrated her considerable talent, but she said she had turned them down. She planned to stick with the newspapers, "so long as this pays. They are very good to me in the *World* office and no one but Col. Cockerill dare say a word to me. Somehow they treat me as if I was a pretty big girl." She signed her letter to Wilson, as became her habit with him, "Your naughty kid, Nellie Bly."

By the time Q.O. received her letter, Bly was in print with her next two exposés, one for which she pretended to be a maid in order to report on the unscrupulous practices of employment agencies for domestic help and another on clandestine trafficking in newborns, an idea that came from one of her readers. Bly, posing as an unwed mother with a child to give up, answered several "suggestive" medical and manicure ads in the newspaper.

In recent years, posing as something other than a reporter in an effort to get better information has fallen into disfavor among print journalists, although television reporters still employ the device from time to time. The editorial handbooks of several respected newspapers ban the method outright on ethical grounds. In Bly's day, there was no such edict. Reporters considered any method of getting information out of their subjects, particularly those engaged in wrongdoing, fair game.

By the time *The World* printed on November 27 Bly's report on the arduous labors of the female "white slaves" who worked in paper box factories, the newspaper had already redeployed another of its new women reporters to produce work in a similar vein. She was Fannie B. Merrill, a Boston native, about Bly's age, who had married at the age of eighteen, but only briefly, then struck out on her own to be a writer.

By the age of twenty, Merrill was making a little money writing letters to out-of-town newspapers, but to survive she had to supplement that income with private tutoring, music lessons, local newspaper work at two dollars a column, clerking at the Bureau of Statistics, and secretarial work paid at twenty-five cents an hour. She refused to take money from her family.

Finally she landed a position on a fledgling, understaffed Boston daily newspaper, where she put in sixteen-hour days for a poor, irregularly paid salary. Soon the paper was driven out of business. By the time sheriff's deputies came to take possession of the premises, Merrill had been subsisting for three days on five cents' worth of pilot bread and a sandwich. The proprietor and city editor had gone off "to find surcease in a way refused by society to women" when the paper's two green but earnest young reporters rushed in with report of a gory and atrocious murder. Merrill convinced the sheriff's men to let her put out one more issue, which she did by herself.

In March of 1885, Merrill arrived in New York with two dollars in her pocket and the promise of regular work on *The Graphic*, where she stayed two years before *The World* hired her in the spring of 1887, several months before Bly joined the staff.

The Sunday before Bly's paper box factory investigation appeared in *The World*, Merrill produced an informative look at the hardworking girls who rolled tobacco for cigarettes. Merrill wrote her piece in the third person, however, and her style lacked the personal investigative flair that Bly, in a matter of weeks, had made a *World* staple. Although Merrill had more experience than Bly, and had been with the newspaper several months longer, her name did not appear in the headline.

For the following Sunday, Bly toured the city's matrimonial agencies, posing as an applicant, and by the next week, December 11, she had another competitor for stunt space: Viola Roseboro, whose story was signed at the end, but also without her name in the headline. Roseboro's piece had a Bly-like ring: "I went begging. I don't mean I got contributions to buy red flannels for the wild Africans, or sold tickets for a benefit to be given in aid of the widows and orphans of deceased messenger boys, but that I went begging on the street in rags."

Bly's smear of success across New York gained new readership for *The World* and popularity for Bly but, understandably, not much goodwill among her colleagues. They were jealous of the way she had captured the city's imagination. Word of mouth was vicious; the green-eyed monster flailed. *The Journalist* gave her very pointed short shrift. Perhaps it was the personal vendetta of the magazine's editor, Allan Forman. Perhaps it was his reading of the prevailing attitude among Bly's colleagues that made him single her out for disregard. In either event, Forman, since he founded the magazine three years earlier, had developed a reputation for using his publication's columns to praise his friends and financial supporters and scorn his enemies. Evenhanded he was not.

The publication, whose editorial mainstay was news of the achievements of publishers, reporters, and editors, seemed to make a point of ignoring Bly's first burst of New York glory. In fact, Forman picked this period to produce a lengthy and flattering profile of Fannie B. Merrill under a glamorizing three-column line sketch. The magazine described Merrill, a five-year veteran, as "at once handsome and brainy, a woman still young who has won distinction in the arduous field of journalism through her own unaided pen and pluck." A week later, *The Journalist* followed with a valentine to Viola Roseboro, slobbering over her stint as a raggedy beggar as a demonstration of "considerable literary ability as well as praiseworthy courage and dramatic power."

In the meantime, Bly produced a light reading feature titled "Learning Ballet Dancing" ("Nellie Bly in Short Gauze Skirts Kicks at a Mark"), to which *The World* devoted three full columns. And *The Journalist* ended the year with an entire issue devoted to "Our Women Journalists" in which the by now very illustrious Bly was not mentioned once.

꧁꧂

With her induction into the contentious fraternity that was Joseph Pulitzer's *New York World,* Bly became not only part of, but a key force in, the creation of the "New Journalism." In that city room, the combined force of talent, energy, and product was so overwhelming, it moved *The Journalist* to comment jokingly that *The World's* only defect was its practice of giving too much for the money. *The Sun* and *The Herald* resisted the more base aspects of Pulitzer's approach, but at the peril of their revenues. The demands of competition forced all the papers to adjust in some measure. Joseph Pulitzer ran his newspaper without apology for the masses and saw it shunned by the elite whom he otherwise cultivated so assiduously for his own social elevation.

Soon after Bly joined the staff, Pulitzer's failing eyesight and hypersensitivity to noise forced him out of the newsroom. He began directing the enterprise by remote control through his editors, led by John Cockerill. There is no indication that Bly ever got to know him very well. Yet for most of Pulitzer's objectives, Bly's talents were custom-made, including the way her stories lent themselves to illustration, often by the newspaper's revered cartoonist, Walt McDougall, who accompanied her on stories and knew her as well as any colleague. It was McDougall's opinion that in terms of "mere acclaim," Bly's reputation, among all those that *The World* spawned, was by far the most brilliant and far-reaching.

> Her appearance was at the precise moment when sensations were coming so fast and so plentiful as to begin to pall and a fillip was needed. This was supplied by femininity. A voyage through the Minetta sewer or a fake bomb attack on a British man-of-war no longer stirred the jaded sense, but done by a girl with a name like Nellie Bly . . . any live story was bound to register.

This was true, but her reach was more profound, likely because her assignments so often had the aura of mission, embracing the needs of the helpless or laying bare the schemes of scam artists and hucksters, from fortune-tellers to powerful lobbyists. What set her apart was the force of her personality and the way she wove it without apology or humility into everything she wrote. It was not the opinions she injected into stories. These she often seemed to fashion on the moment to *épater les bourgeois*, to suit her take on a given subject, or to offer to her readers what she perceived to be the sophisticated response. It was more the way her own voice, her personality, her essential self penetrated the page in spite of whatever she actually had to say.

Bly would assay the universe through a special lens with her own peculiar tint, and the reader, seeing her name in the headline, knew he or she would be in for an excruciatingly detailed account of whatever she had encountered. How she approached the subject and how she felt about anything that came into her mind at the time, even the most extraneous details, were as essential to the telling as why she had reported the story in the first place. Unlike her unwitting heirs of the 1960s and 1970s, when the phrase "New Journalism" would come around again, it was not her wit or sarcasm or counterculture stream-of-consciousness that delivered a ripe audience. It was her compassion and social conscience, buttressed by a disarming bluntness. There was no mind-splitting intellectual insight or noteworthy literary finesse. Bly simply produced, week after week, an uninhibited display of her delight in being female and fearless and her joy in having such an attention-getting place to strut her stuff. It was "gonzo" journalism cloaked in Victoriana. *The Journalist* notwithstanding, even detractors found her too astounding to ignore.

Bly was a perfect vehicle for the objectives of Pulitzer and Cockerill, and *The World* was ideal for the advancement of Nellie Bly. That other girl stunt reporters were brought on staff alongside her was part of another Pulitzer managerial tactic—his ill-considered habit of pitting talent against talent in the same job, a technique he claimed was meant not to foment competition among the staff but to "enhance suggestiveness," to incite each of them to do the most for the paper. Although this was mostly applied against his editors, and ultimately helped drive Cockerill and Julius Chambers away, it also explains why so soon on the heels of Bly's every success came challengers such as Viola Roseboro, Fannie B. Merrill, and Nell Nelson, fighting her for feature space. And it makes obvious why *The World* was such a nerve-racking place to work. Walt McDougall said the level of suspicion, jealousy, and hatred became so intense it drove "at least two editors to drink, one into suicide, a fourth into insanity and another into banking." Even staff members of ordinarily kind and generous instincts resorted to dirty tricks in self-defense.

Pulitzer constantly egged his staff on to brighter ideas and greater activity while ever wary that any editor should become overzealous. " 'Activity and accuracy' were two words most frequently upon his lips," onetime managing editor Julius Chambers recalled, "and yet he seemed to fear men who were too full of energy." The paradoxes drove his managers to distraction.

At the same time, his newspaper was a cauldron of great vision and superb talent, steaming up a mist of larger purpose and high romance. In 1924, *World* editorialist Edward S. Van Zile wrote to

congratulate Don C. Seitz on the publication of his biography of
Pulitzer, Seitz's longtime boss. The book moved Van Zile to verse:

To Don Seitz
Am I the last survivor? To me your volume seems
A wonderland of memories, fantastical as dreams
The old years pass before me. Again I know the truth
That Romance ruled our council-board who quaffed the wine of youth

II
Who had a vision made it real
Behold a new crusade!
The master-mind that guided us pushed forward unafraid
A wrong that should be righted, a tyrant swept away—
Ah, those are epic tales you tell in your impressive way.

III
Let me, who knew the spirit of that Round Table where
The Press, in shining armor, went forth to do and dare.
Freed from its ancient shackles, chivalric, earnest, bold,
Give thanks that I have lived to read the story you have told.

By 1888, with a steady income from the well-paying newspaper,
Mary Jane Cochrane and her daughter, Pink, moved into an apartment at 202 West Seventy-fourth Street, about where Broadway now
triangles between Amsterdam and West End avenues. The infight-
ing of Pulitzer's editors had little impact on Bly's production, and
through the first three months of the year, she kept a steady balance
between wielding the sword of social conscience and some lighter
side silliness.

She produced nothing during January, but in February and
March investigated the Magdalen Home for Unfortunate Women,
posing as a sinner in need of reform to learn how seldom the requisite six-month stay in these pleasant surroundings did wayward
women any good. The futility of trying to reform fallen women or
outright criminals became a recurring theme in her reportage. She

went onstage in a helmet and tights as a part of the chorus line in the "Amazon March." She exposed a sham mesmerist and learned how to fence.

McDougall recalled her at the time as a shapely young woman with "gray-blue eyes in a pointed eager face, her voice with that indescribable rising inflection peculiar to West Pennsylvanians . . . Her sole assets were courage, persistence and a modest unassuming self-confidence. She was sprightly, yet not frivolous; like [Bill] Nye, everybody knew her but she had very few familiars. Not a deep mind but a warm and sensitive heart."

Not much is known of her private life then, and likely there was not much to it. It was certainly at about this time that James Stetson Metcalfe came into her life. The Yale-educated Buffalo native took over drama criticism at the humor magazine *Life* in 1888 and quickly became known in the field as a controversial "treader upon tender toes." His name would weave through Bly's life for some time,

James Stetson Metcalfe, June 6, 1909,
caricature by Jim Flagg
(Picture Collection, The New York Public
Library)

as would that of Dr. Frank G. Ingram, who had been the assistant superintendent of the Blackwell's Island Lunatic Asylum during Bly's brief sojourn. Keeping her true identity as quiet as possible, the city directory listed only her mother's name until years later. *The World* did what it could to keep her real name secret, and it probably worked in her favor that *The Journalist* ignored her for most of her first year in New York.

Her major assignment of 1888 came the last week in March. By Bly's account, she had received several letters charging bribery in Albany and suggested to Cockerill that she go to the capital and determine if the charges were true. The short list of "Conspicuous Features" in *The World*, 1885–1888, on which Bly's madhouse investigation also appeared, gave Cockerill credit for the idea. Nevertheless, it was with the editor's say-so that Bly decided to try to expose the powerful Albany lobbyist Edward R. Phelps for the "briber and boodler" he was reputed to be. What better way for *The World* to bring this off than to have its premier stunt girl shed her tights, drop her foil, and suit up again to turn a feature stunt in the first person into front page news?

The Great Blizzard of '88 happened March 12 and lasted three days. The Bly blizzard went on all that year and into the next. And then the next.

༺๑๖༻

Bly took the train up to Albany and went to Phelps's office at the Kenmore Hotel, posing as the wife of a patent medicine manufacturer who wanted to block proposed legislation affecting her husband's industry, Assembly Bill No. 191. Bly knew before she arrived that the bill already was effectively dead. In her story, which ran April Fool's Day, Bly recounted word for word her entire conversation with Phelps, claiming he asked her to put up $1,000 to pay off six assemblymen in order to get the bill killed. He not only named them but ticked their names off on a printed list of the relevant committee's members, which Bly took with her. *The World* printed a facsimile. Phelps, she said, also asked for $250 in expense money. The bill indeed died in committee before Bly met Phelps at his office in

New York to arrange for the payment. It was then Phelps declared that he had hastened to get the job done on her behalf, she said. "I have control of the House and can pass or kill any bill that so pleases me," Bly quoted him as bragging. "Next week, I am going to pass some bills and I'll get $10,000 for it. I often get that and more to pass or kill a bill."

Bly then arranged to meet Phelps at the St. James Hotel to hand him a check but instead took a cab by roundabout route to *The World* office to write her story. *The World* quickly dispatched another reporter to the St. James, where Phelps and his son came and went for the next two hours, awaiting the would-be patent medicine dealer's wife, who, of course, never appeared.

Bly's story filled the front page of the Sunday feature section, and the next day, April 2, Phelps's lame explanation filled the right-hand column of the front page and ran onto the next page. *The World* led this story by saying,

> The remarkable narrative that Nellie Bly presented to the readers of *The World* yesterday of her visit to the headquarters of Ed Phelps, the "King of the Albany Lobby" and her exposure of how legislation is promoted or destroyed was a startling revelation to the honest citizens of New York. From time to time, *The World* has heard rumors of an organized lobby at Albany, but tangible proof of its existence has been difficult to secure. To Nellie Bly was entrusted the by no means easy task of not only discovering who was at the head of the "Third House" but of receiving detailed and exact evidence of how bills are killed or forced through the Legislature. This mission Nellie Bly undertook and carried through with success at every point.

Phelps replied in a letter to *The World,* which the newspaper printed in full:

> I have read with some amusement from time to time the remarkable stories got up by your smart female confidence correspondent, Nellie Bly, who must be admitted to be the

champion story-teller of the age. I have no objection to the attention she has now paid to me, but I do object to her resort to groundless statements that affect other people in her efforts to concoct a sensational romance such as you seem to suppose that your readers relish.

He went on to say that he knew Bly to be "a blackmailer or a newspaper imposter" from the start, that his intention was to teach her a lesson, that it was "positively a whole-cloth lie" that he ever named a single assemblyman or even hinted at " 'buying' anybody," something he would never do. He said while poking fun at the "bogus lunatic," he gave her a list of the members on the relevant committee and told her to go see each of them, but she declined, saying she preferred to deal through him. He said he only made the subsequent appointment with her in New York because he intended to expose her at that time and had his son on hand for the anticipated entrapment.

The Times also printed a letter from Phelps, in which he declared the *World* article about him "a romance, with the single exception that a female scribbler, signing herself Nellie Bly, did call on me in Albany in reference to killing a patent medicine bill in the Assembly . . . I do not deny that I am a legislative agent in which I do legitimate work for pay, but do unequivocally deny that I have ever said to any one that I could purchase any member of the Legislature. I am not quite fool enough for that and no one who knows me will take me to be such an idiot as this sensation-monger has painted me."

The World stood by its stunt girl, issuing a point-by-point rebuttal to every assertion in Phelps's letter of complaint. The newspaper also carried the comments of legislators reached in Albany, such as Senator William H. Robertson, who referred to Bly as a "wonderful little woman." Only a woman could succeed in tricking a character as notorious and shrewd as Phelps, he said, and Bly had performed admirably.

Newspapers in Albany were quick to put their own spin on the story. *The Albany Times* was blasé about Bly's revelations, harkening to several previous but ineffectual exposures of the power of the lobby in influencing legislation in the state capitol. "The place to expose the lobby is in the precincts of a court room," *The Times* said, adding that even there "the exposure amounts to but little." Phelps it described as "this veteran dealer in legislation, who has grown rich in the service and has been on the ragged edges of several court trials." The paper scoffed at Phelps's contention that he actually had intended to expose Bly: "Highly virtuous in Mr. Phelps, indeed, but ruinous to business."

In the legislature the next day, the six lawmakers named in Bly's article all rose to proclaim their innocence for the record and distanced themselves from the charges by demanding an investigation. On April 5, Representative Ernest H. Crosby presented a resolution calling for a vigorous investigation of the lobby and its methods. The Assembly Judiciary Committee agreed to take up the matter at once and referred it to the district attorney of Albany County for a separate probe.

The World produced a second exposé, not by Bly, on April 4, this time charging that Phelps had offered bribes of $500 and $1,000 respectively to Senators George Langbein and Eugene Ives on March 19, to get them to introduce a bill in the state senate concerning the seizure of property for an elevated railway without adequate compensation to the city. The senators, according the *The World,* had "indignantly spurned the offer." By Friday, April 6, the buzz all over Albany was that Phelps had left town. The lobbyist had boarded a train headed south to avoid inquiries.

The Albany Argus was cynical about the prospects for the kind of investigation that was really needed to clean house in the legislature, predicting instead that

> there will be a great deal of dust kicked up about outsiders, in order, likely, to throw the same dust in the eyes of the public in regard to the chief lobbyists on the floor, the members themselves. It is not an agreeable sight for the people to see their representatives in agony of terror over charges from a disreputable source, which should not receive any attention from a reputable body. The investigating committee will,

likely, provide themselves with a goodly supply of white-wash, so that all foul spots within the sacred precincts of the house will be provided with immaculate coats, laid on thick and hard.

By April 11, a grand jury had been called to investigate, and Assistant District Attorney Andrew Hamilton spent a day interrogating the two state senators under oath regarding the second alleged bribery incident *The World* had exposed. The next day, the Assembly Judiciary Committee began its own investigation, of which *The Albany Argus* reported in apparent disgust:

> The assembly judiciary committee began, yesterday afternoon, its investigation into the lobby. In turn, Assemblymen Tallmadge, Gallagher, Hagan, Prime, DeWitt and McLaughlin appeared before the committee and, for lack of a Bible on which to be sworn, affirmed that they had never been approached by lobbyists and had only a remote acquaintance by sight with lobbyists. They testified that the cities committee never had had the patent medicine bill before it, as did Index Clerk Cyrus Lawrence. Then, after sucking its several thumbs for half an hour, and waiting for some lobbyist or a victim to turn up, the committee postponed its investigation until next week.

The grand jury concluded its investigation the next week, deciding that, in the senate matter, there was insufficient evidence on which to base an indictment. As for Bly's report, the grand jury decided to await the result of the Judiciary Committee investigation before proceeding further. According to a report on its proceedings, "In the opinion of the Grand Jury, the gratitude of the people of this State, and more particularly of the county of Albany, is due to the *New York World* for its diligent effort to suppress the legislative lobby, and express the hope that further evidence may be obtained sufficient to indict and convict the guilty parties."

Two days later, Bly appeared before the Assembly Judiciary Committee to tell her story in detail. Phelps testified as well and, according to *The World*'s report, was put to shame by Bly's complete believability. *The Albany Argus* reported that the giggling, "rather pretty" witness attracted more interest than anything else that had occurred in the assembly all winter.

> She proved to be a slender woman of perhaps 22 or 23 years of age, clad in a dark blue cloth dress with a corsage bouquet of red roses, a somewhat stunning hat with a big gilt arrow at the side crowned a face of some regularity of feature, and from under the hat to the rear projected that arrangement of women's hair technically known as the "Psyche twist."
>
> Nellie Bly, or Pink Cochrane, as she subsequently announced her name, evinced an uncontrollable desire to laugh all through her testimony. She swore to the story as related in *The New York World,* producing in corroboration the committee list which she said Phelps had marked. She added nothing to her story except that personally she knew nothing to the discredit of members of the cities committee.

With that, the committee's investigation concluded; the grand jury had nothing more on which to proceed. *The Albany Morning Express* offered this in summation:

> The "crash" had come and gone, and no one was hurt. The spectators had been highly amused, and all united in expressing their satisfaction with the entertainment. If *The New York World* had entered into an agreement with Mr. Phelps to have this "investigation" take place for the purpose of advertising itself, things could not have worked more smoothly. All that was wanting was the presence of Bill Nye, the humorist, to do justice to the occasion. Of course the committee acted in good faith and did its duty, and so far as the innocence of the accused assemblymen is concerned, that is certainly established.
>
> *The World* is great at building bonfires out of straw and this is one of them.

Although Bly's exposé did not result in a formal indictment, its force did achieve the objective of "de-throning the Lobby king." Phelps left Albany and did not return the following winter.

⚘

In the course of her testimony, Bly revealed a habit that apparently posed no problem for her editors. During her interrogation by the Assembly Judiciary Committee, she was asked if she had made "any memorandum" of her conversation with Phelps:

A: Yes sir.

Q: Did you write out any portion of this article there?

A: Oh, no.

Q: Just made a memorandum?

A: Just made notes so that I could get it exactly correct.

Q: Have you got those notes with you?

A: No, I haven't.

Q: Can you tell me where they are?

A: Yes, or I can tell where they were; I tore them up after I had written my article, as I do all my notes.

Q: Did you preserve them?

A: No sir, I never do.

The World reported the exchange verbatim and without comment as part of its story of Bly's testimony, indicating that this was not a matter of embarrassment for the newspaper, nor did it urge reporters to keep their notes after publication of their work. The newspapers in Albany, which covered the hearing in some detail, also seemed to find nothing unusual in Bly's revelation. Since libel suits were as unwelcome a hundred years ago as at present, one would have thought the keeping of records of conversations later repeated in newspapers would have been essential. Apparently not. The legislators did not question her further on the subject. Not once was it suggested that she might have destroyed her notes because they did not corroborate her published account. Her disclosure prompted no one connected with the incident to question Bly's integrity. And Phelps wasn't about to sue.

⁓⚬⁓

It is not surprising that by the end of May 1888, for her first story since the Phelps exposé, both Bly's confidence and her stature on the paper were such that she could fill a column of *The World* sharing some of her "odd" fan mail.

With the level of Bly's acclaim on the rise, *The Journalist* felt compelled to rehash in an item its earlier profile of *The World*'s Fannie B. Merrill, now calling her "the most beautiful reporter in this city" and repeating what may not even have been a non sequitur at the time, that "she comes from Boston, but does not wear eyeglasses." The publication followed with a gossipy item on the state of play among Pulitzer's ever-shifting editorial staff: Ballard Smith had been sent to Washington to cover his "warm, personal friend" President Grover Cleveland. J. C. Graham had been named city editor of *The Morning World,* replacing E. A. Grozier, who moved to managing editorship of *The Evening World.*

June and July brought Bly to police court, where she interviewed women prisoners about why they did not reform; to a "mind healer" who taught her how to think her way out of difficulties and discomforts; and to Colonel Bill Cody's Wild West Show, where she got to know the women riders, who, she decided, made far more interesting copy than the cowboys.

In the meantime, the publisher of *Ten Days in a Mad-House,* Norman L. Munro, issued the compilation of her Mexico travel reports in a book entitled *Six Months in Mexico,* edited to reflect her growing maturity as a journalist. For example, in one of the earliest of her dispatches from Mexico City, Bly had scoffed at the New York woman magazine writer who had written up as fact the false story told her by a railway conductor about Mexicans eating uncleaned hogs whole. Yet in the same piece, Bly repeated the same conductor's tale of a *laguna* in the state of Chihuahua with crystal-clear water that tempted a group of Americans working on the railroad to shed their clothes and jump in for a bath only to find the water so alkaline it burned their skin and forced them to scurry out like "scalding pigs." In the book version, she repeated the scalding pigs story, this time with a disclaimer about the conductor's tales: "I give his stories for what they are worth," she wrote. "I did not investigate to prove their truth."

Fame was starting to mean new opportunities, which, in turn, meant extra money. Bly's next big piece, on August 5, became the seed for her only novel, *The Mystery of Central Park,* published a year later to a fair amount of derision and no known literary acclaim. It apparently had been envisaged as the first of many, since the cover bore the tag line "The Nellie Bly Series." But it was the first and the last. For the story in *The World,* Bly reported the case of Charles Cleveland, a stable foreman who had plied the policemen in Central Park with beer so they would look the other way while he rode around in a carriage picking up girls who were new to the city, in an effort to lure them into prostitution. He would prey on their innocence, taking them for buggy rides to uptown saloons. Bly, armed with a description of Cleveland and his method, disguised herself as a country girl and waited for him alone on a bench until she could let him entice her into his cab. He did. The police looked the other way as she drove off with him. Her story appeared in *The World* soon after.

Bly's popularity grew and, with it, a curiosity about who she really was. It was not until mid-August of 1888, when a reader of the society gossip sheet *Town Topics* asked to know Nellie Bly's real name, that an answer, almost right, was supplied:

A fair reader who confesses to an honorable admiration for the intrepid and energetic Nellie Bly of *The World,* writes to inquire if this is the real name of that enterprising young woman. *The World's* Nellie Bly is, I believe, in private life, a Miss Pink Jane Elizabeth Cochran. She is the daughter of a country judge in western Pennsylvania, who is now dead, and began her career in journalism on a Pittsburg paper.

THE "NELLIE BLY" SERIES

The Mystery of Central Park

Bly's only published novel, The Mystery of Central Park, *1888*
(Library of Congress)

By any standard, but certainly for an ingenue from western Pennsylvania with little formal education and no formal training, Nellie Bly's first year as a New York reporter was an unqualified triumph.

❦

The fall of 1888 was presidential campaign season, and Bly did her part to round out *The World's* election-related coverage, always with a woman's take on events. She first interviewed Belva Lockwood to learn more about the feminist attorney who was running for president a good thirty-two years before women would win the right to vote. Lockwood had studied law at National University Law School from 1871 to 1873, the year she was admitted to the bar of the District of Columbia. She was the first woman admitted to practice before the Supreme Court, requiring an act of Congress in 1879.

Bly was never a really polished writer, which her critics took no end of pleasure in pointing out. But she was masterful at framing questions in ways that elicited powerful quotes. Of Lockwood, she asked: "What class of women support you in your equal rights ideas?" The candidate replied, "Thinking women and working women. Society women never go outside society. It is all in all to them, so they give us no support, and the very poor—the masses—are no better. One is the slave, the other the doll and equally useless to us."

Bly followed the Lockwood interview with an intriguing report on her encounter with New York's famous "VouDoo Knave," Dr. James A. Bass. But throughout September and October she was back on the campaign trail, although she did spend one week among the men and women she described as the "fun-loving hop-pickers" of Oneida County's Sangerford Center [actually Sangerfield]. In her merry portrait of this dance-happy group, the issues surrounding the subject of migrant labor escaped her notice. Everyone seemed quite pleased with the working and living arrangements.

Political coverage was the real focus during this period. Bly interviewed all the presidential candidates' wives and, later, all the former and present living first ladies.

For the latter assignment, she began at Oak View, or Red Top, the home President Cleveland kept to escape the public crush of the White House. It was declared off-limits to reporters, who were wildly interested in his young, beautiful, and stylish wife, Frances, who, as the daughter of a deceased law partner, had been his much-doted-upon ward before the couple married at the White House in 1886. Frances Cleveland, whom the press dubbed Frankie, was a source of endless popular scrutiny and intense public interest. She was considered the president's greatest political asset, even giving weekend receptions at the White House for women of all walks of life. This openness, however, did not extend to the press.

Armed with a letter of introduction explaining her purpose, Bly went calling at Oak View. She was ushered into the front hall, presented her letter, then stood waiting for what seemed an interminable period before an aide returned with a note, referring her to the president's secretary and primary aide, Colonel Daniel S. Lamont.

Bly felt afterwards that on the strength of the introduction she carried, she would certainly have been received had she not revealed her actual purpose. However, she said, "it being one of my first rules never to obtain an interview without the knowledge and comment of the party interviewed," that was not possible. (She clearly did not apply the same knowledge-and-comment rule when disguising herself to interview charlatans of various stripes.)

Undeterred by her failure, Bly fulfilled the assignment. She described the house and grounds in detail and made much of her fleeting glimpse of the first lady, who, seeing Bly's carriage approach, sprang out of a hammock on the veranda and hurried inside the house. Although Mrs. Cleveland's friends were uncooperative, Bly managed to glean some insight into the first lady's life. She angled her story on the disadvantages of life aside the highest office in the country for someone of Mrs. Cleveland's beauty, charm, and intelligence. The White House had completely isolated the first lady, Bly wrote. She had no close friends, could not engage in gossip, fashion chat, or other favored female pastimes. Even shopping was out "for fear of the crowds which gather and stare her out of countenance."

Still, Bly was dismayed at her own inability to break convention at the president's household and come away with the interview she had set out to get. "I hated to allow anyone to say, 'I told you so,' " she confessed in her story, adding by way of excuse that she later learned that even the wives of senators and cabinet officers who wished to see Mrs. Cleveland had to notify her in advance. "Had I used my ordinary ingenuity as a newsgatherer and not relied on common report that Mrs. Cleveland was accessible and democratic and tactful and kindly," Bly groused, "I could have told the readers of *The World* more about her appearance and her history."

Neither a popular wife nor the editorial support of Pulitzer's Democratic *World* was enough to ensure Cleveland's reelection. Republican Benjamin Harrison won the presidency in 1888 with an electoral college victory despite his loss of the popular vote. The Clevelands would return to the White House, however, on the next presidential ballot, four years later.

Pulitzer, as usual, was making changes in *The World's* leadership, too. Soon after Harrison's election, Pulitzer installed Julius Chambers as news editor. Another woman, known in print as Nell Nelson, was soon added to the stable of feature writers. Nelson weighed in with a hard-hitting series on the "White Slave Girls" of various industries, originally written for *The Chicago Times* but reprinted in *The World.* To get her story each time, Nelson posed as a worker in what was already the Bly tradition. By the third installment of *The World* reprint, Nelson's name, too, rated mention in the headline.

The Journalist, on October 13, 1888, produced a two-column piece on Chicago's best-known women reporters, which included Nelson, whose real name was Nell Cusak. Chicago, the trade magazine said, had generally been regarded as "a most unpromising field for women of journalistic ambition"; however, a small but growing number had prevailed anyway. Nelson was described as "very pretty" with her brown hair and brown eyes and as having "exceedingly affable manners . . . Her work has been in the general domains of society and fashion, in which her nimble thought and piquant style are displayed to advantage, but she has also written much on general themes," *The Journalist* said, favorably noting her "highly interesting" slave girl series.

A month earlier, *The Journalist* had carried an item praising Viola Roseboro as "a charming little lady with a wonderful love for the bright side of Bohemia and one of the cleverest and daintiest writers in New York journalism." Bly, with her women's angled campaign coverage consuming whole pages of the Sunday *World,* got no notice from *The Journalist* at all.

On Sunday, November 4, 1888, *The World* published what amounted to a "reporter's notebook" of Bly's campaign travels, a story made up of all those disparate but interesting items she had not yet found a way to get into print. Bly led the piece with word of the undisputed "belle of Nashville," Miss Saidee Polk Fall, whom the vain Miss Bly—whose own waist was so tiny it was always part of her caricature in illustrations—thus described: "Miss Falls [*sic*] is above the medium height and dresses in perfect taste. Her waist would break a New York girl's heart, it is so wide. Of course, it is very noticeable in these days of curving waists, and would cause many heads to turn for a second look, but after the first glance of surprise one rather admires it."

In the same article, Bly mentioned an encounter with the poet James Whitcomb Riley, a great chum of her pal Erasmus Wilson. Riley asked her if she wanted to succeed in life. "I do," she reported herself saying and added revealingly, "with an earnestness that might have been felt a block."

About this time even *The Journalist* had to relent and give Bly some notice, however backhanded. It carried one item on November 10, 1888, reprinted from the magazine *Puck:* "When a charming young lady comes into your office and smilingly announces she wants to ask you a few questions regarding the possibility of improving New York's moral tone, don't stop to parley. Just say, 'Excuse me, Nellie Bly,' and shin down the fire escape."

Nell Nelson finished out the calendar year with several more "White Slave" installments, a look at New York's young opera singers, the fitful disorders of actors and actresses, and a report on a week getting sick at "Dr. Cooley's Cure Factory."

Bly, with leap year almost at an end, wrote for three weeks in a row on whether women should propose marriage to men, a feature that sparked an enormous write-in response. Opinions varied, but hers was clear from the opening salvo: "In this day of almost equal rights, when women fill the same positions—yes, and ably too— which were considered man's and man's alone, is it just that women shall not have the right to propose?"

Before Christmas, Bly had time for one stunt, joining the "throngs of poor invalids" as a charity patient in the Throat, Skin and Ear infirmaries, where, the headline blazed, "Nellie Bly Narrowly Escapes Having Her Tonsils Amputated." And *The Journalist,* ever fickle, did not fail to note yet another woman to pay attention to on the staff of *The World,* Elizabeth Bisland, a native of New Orleans, who was doing book reviews for the newspaper. Apparently, Forman forgot he had crowned Fannie Merrill the city's "most beautiful" reporter seven months earlier and declared Bisland "undoubtedly the most beautiful woman in metropolitan journalism." Bisland had been literary and society editor of *The New Orleans Times-Democrat.* "Her great beauty and aegis of powerful friends give her ready entrance into New York society and her talents have realized for her that recognition of publishers which gladdens the heart and burdens the purse," *The Journalist* said.

By the middle of January 1889, Bly was steam propelled, producing one arduous stunt after another at a near rate of once a week and making enough money to move her and her mother downtown to a "cozy little flat" at 120 West Thirty-fifth Street in fashionable Murray Hill. At the end of the month, *The Journalist* published its annual issue devoted to women reporters, in which Nell Nelson, now settled in New York, rated half a column under a portrait, which included the declaration "If there is a brighter newspaper woman on the face of the earth we do not know her habitation." It went on,

> Nell Nelson's work on the *Chicago Times* was not only phenomenal in its journalistic excellence, but bore the most important results in a practical way. Her articles, illustrating the hard-ships of women wage-workers, and the cruel straits to which they are sometimes subjected by rapacious task-maskers [*sic*], revolutionized the methods of unscrupulous employers and put women working in the trades and in various forms of business on a much-improved footing. This good work of Nell Nelson attracted attention, and when she came to New York she had no difficulty in securing a most satisfactory position on the staff of the *New York World,* where she is highly esteemed.

Although Bly was by no means featured, she did, this time at least, get passing notice:

> The *New York World* has called to its staff a number of clever newspaper women whose brainy work has done not a little toward the rapid growth of that phenomenal paper. A portrait and brief sketch of "Nell Nelson" appears in another column. Of Mrs. Fannie B. Merrill, *The Journalist* has already honestly and appreciatively written. Miss Bisland, who reviews books for the *World* and conducts the literary department of that most excellent among the younger magazines, *The Cosmopolitan,* Mrs. Julia Hayes Percy, a brilliant and

graceful writer and Nellie Bly, the audacious investigator of
abuses, are among the women who make the *World*'s columns
sparkle and hold the enthusiastic friendship and support of
two millions of readers a week.

Soon after, *The Epoch,* another New York magazine, provided a
word sketch of Bly, frank about her limitations but highly flattering
nonetheless. It described her as "quite pretty and gifted with an
indomitable pluck and nerve."

Her real name is Elizabeth Cochrane and she lives with her
mother and sister, whom she supports, in a cozy little flat in
West 37th Street [*sic*] in this city. Nelly [*sic*] Bly, although
neither highly educated, cultured nor accomplished, is a
woman of intellectual power, high aims and a pure and
unblemished career. She will, one day, I think, make a greater
and better mark in the world of letters than she has in that of
journalism.

The Epoch made much of Bly's apparent disinterest in social climbing.
"She eschews all the literary 'sets' of society," it said, "and is to be
found neither in the parlors of Bohemia nor in the drawing rooms of
the wealthy and lion-hunting." This is also the only known reference
to her sister Kate, by then divorced and caring for little Beatrice,
having become Bly's dependent.

Added appraisal of Bly at this time came from *World* illustrator
Walt McDougall, who recalled that, more than once, she had to be
held back from undertaking too dangerous a venture. "Nothing was
too strenuous nor too perilous for her if it promised results," he said,
adding that she also "suffered the penalty paid by all sensation-
writers of being compelled to hazard more and more theatric feats."
He remembered twelve long, miserable nights before flashlights
were invented when the two of them moved through a roundup of
Connecticut's most notorious haunted houses looking for ghouls and
ghosts. "This trip was a dreadful fizzle," he said.

Forman of *The Journalist* used the occasion of publishing the
1889 "women's issue" to dispel any lingering notion that women in

journalism were not utterly mainstream—a complete turnabout from the opinions expressed by New York's top newspapermen to Bly only two years earlier. This was testament to how quickly the atmosphere for women in the business was changing. However, the personal hesitancy Forman described told more about the ambivalence of the times than he probably realized. He wrote, "I knew in a vague way that there were a good many clever women engaged in newspaper work, I knew that their number was constantly increasing and that their work was each day being more highly appreciated. But I did not know, as I do now, that I might publish a volume the size of Webster's Unabridged Dictionary and then not half cover the field." Yet, Forman wrote, inadvertently demonstrating how far there was yet to go, he left some women journalists out who should have been included, simply because "for a modest man, I have found it a matter of no little difficulty to write to a lady who is an utter stranger and demand her photograph."

Flora McDonald contributed to the same issue a frank description of the unique difficulties women experienced as members of this male profession, even when their male counterparts generously treated them as " 'one of the gang,' with extra privileges accorded for femininity." Except for the tell-tale examples that date the essay before the turn of the century, its sentiments could as easily have been expressed by any number of McDonald's female successors in the field over the next hundred years.

> The privilege of being the receptacle of all the love affairs of the "Salad" reporters, of being solemnly consulted about the cloth and cut of their occasional (very occasional) new trousers, of hearing both sides of opposing factions, of being admitted, with odds in her favor, to pools on election, of losing money by "tips" on the races that the sporting editor "wouldn't give to any man but her," and of having some of the number go no more than a block out of his way to see that she gets home safe when the day's work is done and the crowd has "fed" and discussed and settled the affairs of the nation at some chop house between 2 and 3 o'clock in the morning— she may enjoy all this and still the fact remains that she is a

woman, still she suffers in a greater or less degree the uneasy sensations of a fish out of water. Not, mind you, that her discomfort is occasioned by the men who are companions—not a bit of it; the reason lies only in the natural order of things.

If Bly felt herself a fish out of water, then she was the fish with the artificial lung. By the time the new year got under way, she had effectively buried her main competitor, Nell Nelson, who was to be read only once more during this period in the pages of *The World,* on March 3, 1889, when she visited an opium den. *The Journalist* noted that Nelson, "who came to notice through her admirable work upon the *New York World,*" had left the newspapers and was contributing to the Bacheller and Burr Syndicates.

For her part, Bly bobbed and weaved between investigations aimed at helping the downtrodden, exposing frauds, reporting the odd society ball, and a series of high-profile interviews. She visited the prison matrons to learn (and repeat for the third time) how difficult it was to get women criminals to reform. For that story, she went as herself. "I used to wonder what disguise you would come in," the matron at police headquarters said to her. "But I never thought I would see you as Nellie Bly." Then there was the mysterious veiled prophetess who told Bly what she already knew: that she was bright and had never known failure. "But you have an enemy," she warned.

Bly brought to light a scheme to defraud working girls who wanted to learn scarf making. She made fun of the French Ball, where the only place to get a drink after 1:00 A.M., when wine was banned, was policemen selling alcohol on the side. *Town Topics* groaned that the prohibitionary edict "took away the last vestige of its [the ball's] pristine glory . . . Five years ago, half the club men in town, both married and single, were present; last week not a baker's dozen could be found, which may or may not be an argument for the growing morality of the city."

In mid-February, Bly traveled to Boston to see for herself "the *bête-noire* of my childhood days," Laura Dewey Bridgman, the girl who had always been held up as an example when young Pink said, "I can't." Bridgman, deaf, dumb, and blind, had learned to read, to speak with her fingers, to sew and knit, and to do many more useful things. When Bly read Charles Dickens's account of Bridgman's life in his *American Notes,* her annoyance at the childhood example turned to spellbound admiration. She met her at the Perkins Institute for the Blind. While there, the director encouraged her to meet another pupil, a nine-year-old who he said "excels Laura in cleverness" and was bound to be "the marvel of the age." "Her name," wrote Bly, "is Helen Adams Keller."

✧

Bly's assignments, and those of like women reporters who were turning up at other newspapers around the country in the late 1880s, resulted from larger trends in the newspaper industry rather than a sudden openness from editors to having women on staff. Although magazines had already shown a willingness to have women even in top managerial posts, the daily press lagged far behind in this element of progressive thinking. The size and complexity of their operations, however, soon overtook the penchant to exclude. With the papers getting larger, the level of competition getting fiercer, and relays of editors and reporters and rewrite men working furiously to get out the papers, it became necessary to organize into departments. Larger staffs with specific duties required specialization. Specialization made way for different kinds of hiring. The voluminous Sunday supplements required designated editors and writers to oversee their weekly production. It was old news that women were ideal for home and society coverage. In addition, as Walt McDougall pointed out, they brought something novel to sensation writing. They also showed particular skill with "the interview." Although question-and-answer items had been appearing in American newspapers since the 1840s, it was in this period that the technique emerged as a popular, if objectionable, story form—criticized as an invasive and sensationalist tool aimed only at making "fools of great men." These disparate elements, taken together, created the first real and undisputed place for women reporters in daily journalism. Suddenly they were good for business.

Of course, there had long been the notable exceptions. In the mid–nineteenth century, there were standouts in daily journalism's more cerebral areas, such as the essayist Margaret Fuller and the political reporter Jane Grey Swisshelm. Other pioneers such as the columnist Fanny Fern or Jane Cunningham Croly, known in print as the fashion and food scribe Jennie June, started writing in the 1850s, when women were first identified as a newspaper-reading public. But none of these forerunners had succeeded in creating a mind-set among editors that made the women who followed them a sought-after commodity.

By the 1880s, a handful of women columnists, such as Bessie Bramble in Pittsburgh, had managed to eke out a respected place for themselves, and there were aberrations such as Middy Morgan of *The New York Times,* who led her all-male competitors in livestock coverage. But it was the advent of both the stunt girls and the large separate women's sections that created the first real place for women as regular members of the newspaper staff and an important part of the editorial mix.

Both those areas were ghettos, to be sure, but the stunt girls embodied one important distinction: Unlike the traditional women's interest writers, Bly and her female imitators in the intrepid detective field were able to bring women, as a class, out of the journalistic sideshow and into the main arena. Unlike the duties women had generally been asked to perform on newspapers, stunts did not appear on the women's pages. They also required daring, resourcefulness, a strong news sense, quick turnaround, and cunning—all the qualities of any good reporter. The work was often strong enough, as Bly had proved, to be lifted out of the feature sections and onto the front pages, providing women with their first collective opportunity to show editors they could perform with the brains, dedication, and selfless abandon of the most able men. Stunt girls, with Bly as the genre's leader, formed the human chute down which the next generation of women reporters plunged into journalism's mainstream. There would be issues and discrimination for years to come, but at least the way in had finally been opened.

At the end of February 1889, Bly came up with one of her more intricate escapades. She contrived her own arrest on a charge of grand larceny. At the station, police had a homeless woman strip-search Bly, while, she felt sure, a prying eye peeked through a crevice in the changing room wall. She spent the night in a coed jail. At court, a lawyer with access to the holding pen tried to bulldoze her into hiring him, and the detective assigned to her case made a pass at her. She was complimentary to the kindly male turnkeys but urged the authorities to put prison matrons on staff, which, in time, they did. Bly's exploit was the talk of the Nineteenth Precinct station house and the Jefferson Market Court the next day (she said Judge Duffy did not recognize her from the madhouse adventure; he said he did). And *The World* happily reported the stir in a follow-up column. Bly was roundly praised. Soon after, she was on the road again, this time to Washington, where she interviewed all the wives of members of President Benjamin Harrison's cabinet. Her versatility was impressive, as was her ability to latch onto subjects of high readability.

By March 25, 1889, *The World* proclaimed its Sunday circulation had reached the unprecedented high of 285,860 copies, no little thanks to Bly's relentless enterprise.

The young reporter's production onslaught continued through the spring and summer: an exposé of worthless washing machine swindlers; a report on women medical students; and a look, posing as the wife of a man who wanted her watched, at how good private detectives were at concealing their purpose and trailing their subjects. Bly's report on a wealthy woman diamond broker who was lending money without a license caused a "great stir among the fashionable up-town usurers," which *The Journalist* duly noted in a gossip column. It did not, however, credit Bly by name.

She wrote of a Harlem hotel, The Hamilton, where proprietor John Allen had the practical charitable sense to provide free dinners to the poor out the back door. She traveled to Belfast, New York, to visit the training camp of champion pugilist John L. Sullivan and pummel him with dozens of personal questions ("Do you take cold bath-showers?" "How are you rubbed down?" "Do you like prize fighting?" "How much money have you made?" "Do you hit a man in the face and neck and anywhere you can?"). He even gave her permission to pinch his muscles. Bly was enthralled and Sullivan, charmed. "You are the first woman who ever interviewed me," he told her, and, of course, she reported the quote verbatim. "And I have given you more than I ever gave any reporter in my life."

Although Bly is best remembered for her stunt work, her skill as an interviewer commanded just as much attention in its time. Her particular method was to establish a sense of intimacy with both her subject and the reader, letting both in on her thoughts and actions in a way that put the subject at ease, thus loosening his or her tongue. She cast the reader as eager voyeur. Even when the subjects would not tell her what she wanted to know, Bly's flirtatious prodding, and the way her subjects responded to it, revealed other interesting aspects of their personalities. As in everything else, she was always as much a part of the story as its ostensible point.

Bly's detailed article on the fifty-year-old Oneida Community, one of the early American experiments in structured communal living, was comprehensive enough for the colony to reissue it in pamphlet form as an explanation of their collective.

She loved the graduation ceremony for cadets at West Point, and *The World* loved its steadily increasing circulation, reporting an average per day during May of 345,808 copies. She tried out the latest in personal conveyances, the bicycle, and learned how to swim. At the end of the summer of 1889, she reported on the best resort playgrounds, fashionable Newport and Narragansett, where her subject was, in her contemptuous depiction, the "gay 'goings on' of people whose money is the sole thing that makes them known in the world." Then she was off to Bar Harbor and Saratoga Springs, along with a number of other women reporters. The gossipy *Town Topics* found it fascinating to watch these

> persistent and indefatigable working women . . . preserve their mental balance while being fawned on by one class of people and snubbed by another . . .
>
> Even more interesting, however, than to watch the women fawn and the women snub, is to notice the attitude of

the men towards the fair summer day writers, which is peculiarly cool and conservative when the world is looking on and
peculiarly friendly, gossipy and confidential at the far end of
the piazzas, in the retired corners of the parlors or during the
short walks that occur after supper and before night drops
her mantle.

A scandal broke on August 26 at the fashionable Noll Cottage
on Tennessee Avenue in Atlantic City, New Jersey. As the guests
seated themselves at the dining tables for luncheon they heard a
woman's screams and the crash of breaking furniture. A waiter ran
upstairs to find the distinguished former New York state legislator
Robert Roy Hamilton, grandson of Alexander Hamilton, trying to
subdue his wild-eyed, blond wife, Eva, who was "striking out in all
directions with a blood-stained dagger." A six-month-old child cried
helplessly on the bed, and her nurse lay bloodied on the floor.

The story unraveled over the coming weeks. According to *The
World,* Eva Hamilton was a woman with a past, several previous "husbands" and a good deal of time spent in brothels in New York and
Pennsylvania. She had met the illustrious Hamilton, who kept her,
while she continued her liaison with an unsavory character called
Joshua Mann and his "mother," a Mrs. T. Anna Swinton. Eva claimed
to be pregnant by Hamilton, who took the honorable course and married her. Forced at this point to produce a child, Mann and Mrs. Swinton bought one on Eva's behalf. Hamilton acknowledged the baby as
his daughter. But after a few days, unbeknownst to Hamilton, the
baby died. Mrs. Swinton bought a second baby, who also died, then a
third one, who didn't look enough like the first so she gave it away. A
fourth infant then was bought to serve as the Hamilton child.

Hamilton, unable to endure the social discomfort his marriage
was bound to cause, moved with his new wife and child to California.
They were unhappy in the West and soon moved back East, stopping
in Atlantic City to end the summer. Mann and Mrs. Swinton came
along, too. It didn't take long for the baby's nurse, Mary Donnelly, to
fill in the unseemly blanks. In a fight with her mistress, the nurse
shouted out Eva's secrets in Hamilton's presence. Eva, enraged, produced the knife.

Mrs. Donnelly survived the attack. Mann and Mrs. Swinton were charged with fraudulent production of an infant under false pretenses. By the time Eva Hamilton's case came to court September 19, *The World* was calling it "one of the most astounding stories of conspiracy, of turpitude, of plot and counter-plot, ever revealed outside the realms of improbable fiction."

Evangeline Hamilton alias Steele alias Parsons alias Mann was sentenced that day to two years in Trenton Penitentiary on a charge of atrocious assault and battery. Hamilton was by now thought to have renounced the adventuress who had duped him so mercilessly and dragged his good name into tawdry scandal. In an appearance before a New York grand jury, he sorrowfully revealed the intimate details of his life and his foolish ignorance of Eva's motives to the end. Yet, at the trial in Mays Landing, New Jersey, he was called to testify for the defense about the day of the knifing. Never once did he refer to the defendant as "my wife" as he dispassionately recounted the events of that fateful day.

Bly, in the meantime, was back from her summer of playful reporting and ready to claim her piece of the juiciest scandal yet. On Sunday, October 6, as *The World* reported on page one the incarceration of the now broken-spirited "syren" at Trenton Penitentiary, Bly claimed four columns of feature space with a harrowing report on the baby-buying trade in New York, including the statement of a woman who claimed to have sold one of the babies bought by Mrs. Hamilton and Mrs. Swinton. For her story, Bly posed as a would-be mother wanting to buy a child and found in at least four locations that she could buy a newborn from a broker for anywhere from ten to twenty-five dollars with no questions asked.

Three days later, Bly was in print with an exclusive jailhouse interview with Eva Hamilton herself. "Everybody has heard Robert Roy Hamilton's side of the story," Bly began. "It seemed only fair that the woman be given a show. I have seen her. I have talked with her and I write her story as she gave it. She has been judged in more ways than one. I smooth over nothing in the telling of what she told me."

Eva Hamilton spared no detail. Mr. Hamilton was fully aware of her relationship with Mann and Mrs. Swinton, whom she could not shake off because they were blackmailing her for Hamilton's money. It was true Hamilton kept her before they were married, but he actually owed her more money than he had given her. Her flashy diamonds were worth little, just over a thousand dollars, and besides she had most of them before she met Hamilton. Mamie was her own daughter. It was Mrs. Swinton who had bought the four babies on behalf of a client—not Mrs. Hamilton, though it was true she had accompanied Mrs. Swinton on two other baby-buying occasions. While she was his mistress, Hamilton had forced her to terminate two pregnancies and married her after she threatened to leave him. To escape censure, he promised to take her to California and tell his friends and family that the two had met and married there.

It was no coincidence that Bly's interview with Eva Hamilton appeared in *The World* on Wednesday, October 9, 1889, the day the cornerstone of Pulitzer's new gold-domed *World* headquarters was laid to much fanfare on one side of Park Row at Frankfort Street, just across from City Hall. The twenty-six-story skyscraper was ready for dedication fourteen months later, to the derision of Pulitzer's competitors, who still liked to think of *The World* as an outrageous upstart they would soon be able to shoo away. Charles Dana was said to have watched out the window of *The Sun* city room across the street as *The World* headquarters neared completion. "It looks serious," Dana was quoted as telling his new publisher, Charles A. Laffan. "Not at all, not at all," Laffan replied. "Still a mere episode, a mere episode."

When the building was completed, *The Sun* compared it to a brass-head tack. *The Times* said that looking out from its highest-story windows made "men below lose stature and become crawling bugs." The sour grapes must have given Pulitzer some measure of satisfaction, for by that point, *The World* had left the others, both literally and figuratively, in its shadow.

Inside the building's cornerstone, a metal time capsule had been lodged, containing numerous commemorative items, including, of course, the edition of *The World* for the day the cornerstone was laid. Bly's piece led the newspaper, front page, right-hand column, the only lead piece in which the writer was identified by name. The headline read:

MRS. EVA HAMILTON'S STORY

She Talks Fully to Nellie Bly in Trenton State Prison

༺༻

By the fall of 1889, Bly's first work of fiction had made it into print in the newest addition to Pulitzer's New York empire, *The Evening World.* The effort was out in book form by October 12. She busily promoted it herself, sending off copies to newspaper editors around the country accompanied by a note in her most careful and elegant

Park Row, showing The World, The Tribune, *and* The Times,
mid- or late 1890s

(Courtesy of The New-York Historical Society)

hand: "My dear sir:—I take the liberty of sending you personally a copy of 'The Mystery of Central Park'—my first attempt at novel writing. Any notice you may please to give it will be gratefully appreciated by Yours sincerely Nellie Bly." She was starting to hope that *The Epoch*'s prophecy would come true, that the personal sacrifices of her exhausting but highly visible life as a *World* "detective" would lead to a calmer career writing fiction.

The Mystery of Central Park is the story of a girl who commands her ne'er-do-well suitor to prove his worthiness by discovering the killer of a beautiful young woman the couple found slain in Central Park. The heroine, Penelope Howard, is fiercely independent, "in no hurry to marry," "slender to boniness," "willowy and graceful," with "bright, expressive eyes," "a murky complexion," and a "winsome smile." Her suitor, Richard Treadwell, is, of course, hopelessly in love with Penelope, doubly charmed by her "very obstinacy, her independence . . . even if it was provoking." Treadwell is financially comfortable, thanks to a modest legacy, but he lacks, in Penelope's estimation, "the spur of necessity which urged men on to greater deeds." She turns down his sixth proposal of marriage, saying he must accomplish "just one worthy thing, even" to earn the right to her hand. It is a dreadful book, loaded with nuggets of Bly's snide gibes at love and men—men seeking wealth, men seeking power, men as cads, men as weaklings—though not worse than much of the Victorian pulp fiction that passed for popular entertainment.

This fiction debut for Bly was mostly ignored, but *Town Topics,* in reporting on the recent release of Pearl Eytinge's new novel, *Velvet Vice,* gave some sense of how it was received around town: "The value of *Velvet Vice* dies in the worst series of spasms that has been revealed in public since Nellie Bly published her autobiography, *The Mystery of Central Park*, in the New York *Evening World*."

One of the novel's very minor characters is a former editor, John Stetson Maxwell, with Buffalo connections. The reference is too obvious not to be a play on the real-life name of James Stetson Metcalfe, the newly appointed drama critic of *Life* magazine. Metcalfe, at thirty-one, had arrived in New York a year before Bly, first directing *The People's Pictorial Express,* then managing for three years the American Newspaper Publisher's Association. Before that, in 1883 and

1884, he had edited and published his own failed magazine, *Modern Age,* based in his native Buffalo. Bly's name had been linked repeatedly with that of the handsome bachelor.

In the novel, the heroine recounts a tragic story told to her by Maxwell, which made her resolve "never to speak or act unkindly if I can help it." The story was of Maxwell's cold and brusque dismissal of a young visitor, a poet whose work he had once published and who was down on his luck. The young man then sent a packet of new work to Maxwell, who rejected it on sight with an impersonal, preprinted note. A few days later, the young poet killed himself.

Richard thought Maxwell bore no reproach for the death. Penelope felt otherwise:

> "I do and so does he," she replied stoutly. "It wouldn't have taken any more time to be kind to that man than it took to be unkind to him, and when he rejected the poetry, instead of sending back that brutal printed notice he could have had his stenographer write a line, saying the poetry, though meritorious, was not suitable for his journal. That would, at least, have eased the disappointment."
>
> "But editors haven't time for such things, Penelope."
>
> "Then let them take time. I tell you it takes less time to be kind than to be unkind," she maintained, nodding her head positively.
>
> "If they were not short, bores would occupy all their time," he persisted.
>
> "Richard, we will not argue the case," she said loftily, as a woman always does when she feels she is being worsted. "You can't make me think anything will excuse a man for being brutal and unkind."

There is no way to know, but the dialogue sounds as if it had come straight out of a discussion Bly had, or wished she had had, with Metcalfe in real life.

Notwithstanding her novel's cool reception, Bly's fame as a reporter had grown to such an extent that—as her mail revealed and she duly shared with *The World*'s quarter of a million Sunday readers—numerous impostors claimed to be Nellie Bly in sundry, often successful, efforts to win the hearts of young, eligible men, get dressmakers to sew for them on credit, and give celebrity interviews to newspapers. Bly detailed these amusing episodes and then wrote,

> I have no way to protect myself or the public against such people. I would only say to too confiding business people that I never run up bills, that I never under any circumstances use the name of "Nellie Bly" outside of print. I live quietly and am only known to the few I have come in contact with in business as "Nellie Bly." I exert every effort to prevent my being known as "Nellie Bly" and if people remember that, they cannot be imposed upon by those who try to impersonate.

That self-aggrandizement handled, Bly was on to her next ploy. Suffering from migraines, she visited seven reputable New York physicians, claiming at each examination the same ailment. Each made a different diagnosis—dyspepsia, malaria, defective eyes, neuralgia, shattered nerves. And each wrote out a different prescription. Two weeks later, Bly wrote of the enormous response from all over the country that her story had triggered. "I am still ill. Two weeks ago, I had seven physicians who charged large fees. Today I have 700 physicians who diagnose my case and prescribe without charge." What seemed like a fine idea, given the huge response, was terrific for Bly and the newspaper but certainly mortifying to the seven respected New York physicians, whom she had identified by name.

By *The World*'s own reckoning, circulation—still higher than that of any other newspaper—had started to ebb slightly, down 17,000 copies from the published May figures. It was time to crank up a phenomenon, a contest, something as compelling as *The World*'s 1885 campaign to finance the pedestal for the Statue of Liberty with the nickels and pennies of its readers. The editors huddled at their famed round table. They agreed on the need for an idea sensational enough to reestablish popular momentum. *The World* needed something with which it could stop the world.

❦ ❧

NUMEROUS AND HUMOROUS
RECIPES
ARE RECEIVED DAILY BY
THE EVENING WORLD
TO KEEP
A Husband
AT HOME IN THE EVENING.

The World

CIRCULATION GUARANTEED
GREATER THAN THAT OF ANY TWO OTHER
AMERICAN NEWSPAPERS COMBINED.

CIRCULATION BOOKS OPEN TO ALL.

CIRCULATION PER DAY
DURING LAST 7 MONTHS, 340,1

VOL. XXX., NO. 10,313.   12 PAGES.   NEW YORK, THURSDAY, NOVEMBER 14, 1889.   12

AROUND THE WORLD.

A Continuous Trip Which Will Girdle the Spinning Globe.

Nellie Bly to Make an Unequalled Rapid-Transit Record.

NOW, 30,000 MILES IN A RUSH!

Can Jules Verne's Great Dream Be Reduced to Actual Fact?

A VERITABLE FEMININE PHINEAS FOGG.

On a Four-Day Notice Miss Bly Starts Out with a Gripsack for the Longest Journey Known to Mankind—She Knows No Such Word as Fail, and Will Add Another to Her List of Triumphs—Circumnavigators of Other Days—Speed of Existing Lines of Travel to Be Tested—How the Idea Was Inaugurated—Judge Daly on "The World's" New Enterprise—Will the Imaginary Record of Eighty Days Be Beaten?

THE WORLD to-day undertakes the task of turning a dream into a reality. Thousands upon thousands have read with interest the imaginary journey which Jules Verne, that prince of dreamers, sent his hero, Phineas Fogg, on, when he undertook to win a wager circumnavigating this globe within the limit of Eighty Days.

THE LINES OF TRAVEL TO BE FOLLOWED BY "THE WORLD'S" FLYING REPRESEN

NELLIE BLY.

THE TWENTY-FOUR-HOUR WATCH.

5

⁓꩜ ꩜⁓

Globe Trotting

A S WITH ALL GREAT IDEAS, THE SHORTAGE IS NEVER OF PEOPLE
to take credit for thinking them up.

Bly's version, of course, was that the idea to girdle the globe
faster than the fictional Phileas Fogg was hers, that it came to her on
a Sunday in the fall of 1888 while she tossed and turned and wished
herself at the other end of the earth. Why not get *The World* to send
her? In the fifteen years since Jules Verne's *Around the World in Eighty
Days* had been published in English to immense popularity, no one
had succeeded—had anyone even tried?—in breaking the record for
global travel that was Verne's inspiration for his novel and Bly's
inspiration for the assignment of her life.

When Bly got to the office that Monday morning, she presented the proposal to her editor—Cockerill, presumably, though by
this point Julius Chambers had been on board serving alongside him
for a year. The thought of a timed world tour already had come up in
an editorial round table meeting, but it was the predisposition of
business manager George W. Turner to send a man. A man, Turner
argued, could be sent without a chaperon—for a lady of the late
1880s this was understood to be essential. Almost as important, he

would be able to travel without the encumbrance of, in Turner's words, a "round dozen trunks."

"Very well," Bly snapped back. "Start the man and I'll start the same day for some other newspaper and beat him."

By now, Cockerill knew her well enough to have no doubt she would do just that, an outcome he was not prepared to risk. Bly insisted she would travel light—and alone—and Cockerill in turn gave his promise that if and when the newspaper decided to go ahead with the assignment, it would be Bly's.

In the meantime the idea came independently from a half-dozen other sources: a reader of *The World* in Toledo, Ohio; a well-known Washington correspondent (probably the peripatetic Frank G. Carpenter); a writer from Bangor, Maine; another member of *The World*'s staff. All this took place over the course of a year. Then, Henry C. Jarrett, of the Jarrett and Palmer's theatrical enterprise, accepted a wager from his mates at the Player's Club on the time it would take to dash around the world. Several years earlier he had made a lightning trip across the Continent. He came to *The World*'s office to announce his planned departure. Told of the newspaper's intention to send Bly, Jarrett deferred with admirable grace and offered to help her with the planning.

The Jarrett offer pushed the newspaper into action. At 6:00 P.M. on a dank and rainy Monday, November 11, 1889, the orders came down. Could Bly be ready to travel by Thursday? What could she say except, why not?

Overseas correspondents were notified. Chambers set in motion a plan to arrange a visit between Bly and Verne himself. The editorial writer Edward S. Van Zile was dispatched to Washington to get Bly a temporary passport. Van Zile and his wife arrived late at night and went immediately to see Secretary of State James G. Blaine, who promised to have the document ready the following afternoon. At 4:30 the next morning, the Van Ziles returned to New York, Bly's Special Passport No. 247 in hand.

Bly, in the meantime, had gone home to spend Monday evening with her mother. At 10:00 A.M. Tuesday, she arrived at Ghormley, *robes et manteaux,* the fashionable dressmaker with studios on the rue Richelieu in Paris and just east of Fifth Avenue on Nineteenth Street.

There she ordered a traveling gown sturdy enough to withstand three months of constant wear. She wanted it in twelve hours. Bly was accustomed to getting things her way and on her time line. She explained the crux of her motivational methodology. Taking some perverse pleasure in asking for things to be done on dreadfully short notice, she also refused to accept the inadequate time frame as a reason for refusal. "Nonsense!" she would counter. "If you want to do it, you can do it. The question is, do you want to do it?" Almost invariably, she said, this psychology, though she did not call it that, would catapult the person into action.

William Ghormley needed no such spur. By noon, the blue plaid broadcloth travel gown was boned and shaped, and five hours later Bly was back in the studio for her final fitting. Ghormley delivered the gown Wednesday morning. Her own dressmaker, Florence Wheelwright, fashioned for Bly a lighter dress of brown camel hair for warmer climates, also ready in a day. She bought a heavy Scotch plaid ulster for warmth, a gossamer waterproof for the rain, no umbrella, and a "very English" double peaked cap. She wore some seventy-year-old heirloom earrings, a silver chain bracelet, a twisted gold ring, and a leather-banded wristwatch. On her left hand, she sported the lucky thumb ring she had worn the day *The World* employed her. Without specifying the nature of her misfortune, Bly said she had taken the ring off for only "three unlucky days" since her hiring.

The office gave her 200 pounds in English gold and banknotes. The gold went into her pocket and the notes into a chamois-skin bag, which she tied around her neck. She took some American money to find out where it could be used as currency abroad. She bought one piece of hand luggage no bigger than a gripsack, sixteen inches wide and only seven inches tall, and "the determination to confine my baggage to its limit." This she did, but only by sacrificing Miss Wheelwright's hot weather change of clothes. Instead, she crushed last summer's silk bodice into the satchel, along with two traveling caps, three veils, a pair of slippers, a complete outfit of toilet articles, inkstand, pens, pencils, and copy paper, pins, needles, and thread, a dressing gown, a tennis blazer, a small flask and a drinking cup, several complete changes of underwear, a liberal supply of handkerchiefs and fresh ruchings, and a "bulky and compromising" jar of cold

Nellie Bly, 1890
(The Bettmann Archive)

cream. She didn't consider taking any medicine ("I never was very sick in my life and I don't expect to be now") and decided against a revolver, which several people suggested she should carry. She also packed a twenty-four-hour watch that would be telling the right time when she started and again on her return to New York. "It will be seen," Bly later wrote, "that if one is traveling simply for the sake of traveling and not for the purpose of impressing one's fellow passengers, the problem of baggage becomes a very simple one."

Despite the newspaper's attempt to organize her travel, she left with no clear itinerary, a confused set of schedules, a ticket no farther than London, and a constant headache:

> For almost a year, I had been a daily sufferer from headache, and only the week previous I had consulted a number of eminent physicians fearing that my health was becoming impaired by too constant application to work. I had been doing newspaper work for almost three years, during which time I had not enjoyed one day's vacation. It is not surprising then that I looked on this trip as a most delightful and much needed rest.

The Hamburg-American Company liner *Augusta Victoria,* a White Star steamer, sailed from Hoboken Pier on the morning of November 14, 1889, at exactly 9:40:30. *The World* said Bly waved her good-byes "without a wince of fear or trepidation" although her own recollection was of ominous thoughts of the intense heat and bitter cold ahead, of killer storms and shipwrecks, of fevers and pain. But the day was beautiful, she said, and the ship glided into the sea.

"Do you get seasick?" someone asked, making friendly chitchat. It was enough to bring on the first attack. Bly bolted for the railing and, in her attempt at delicacy of expression, said she "gave vent to my feelings."

One man scoffed, "And she's going round the world!"

Later at dinner, while she was seated at the captain's left, the nausea recurred. On her third return to the table, the other passengers applauded, greeting her warmly with "Bravo!"

She went to bed and slept in the next day, until four in the afternoon.

The rest of the trip to England passed uneventfully for Bly in a "very creditable" total time of six days and twenty-one hours, despite head winds and choppy seas. Bly engaged happily in the mental pursuits of confined boredom: watching the man who took his pulse all day and the one who counted all his steps. *The World*'s London correspondent, Tracey Greaves, met her at Southampton with news that Verne had agreed to receive her at his home in Amiens. She could detour to see him without missing a connection, if she were willing to forgo sleep for two nights. She was. She had missed the last train to London, but thanks to Greaves's intervention, the London and Southwestern Railway had an extra engine fired up to deliver to London the mail carried on the *Augusta Victoria*. The railway made room for the two *World* reporters.

There was a quick trip to the *World* office to pick up her cables and then to see the secretary of the American Legation office for a real passport before heading for the Peninsular and Oriental Steamship Company, where she bought tickets to cover half her journey.

An amusing, and revealing, exchange took place between Legation Secretary Robert S. McCormick and Bly, the details of which vary with the teller. In Bly's version, reported in her book about the trip, McCormick asked Greaves to kindly move out of earshot while the secretary was obliged to put to Bly the "one question all women dread to answer"—her actual age. Bly said she laughed at his delicacy and then, in full voice, told him that she had not the least bit of hesitancy about disclosing her real age and would gladly swear to it in front of Greaves or anyone else. She invited her colleague to come out of the corner and listen, if he pleased.

Greaves's version of the encounter appeared in his dispatch from London dated November 28 and published by *The World* ten days later. In his account, he and Bly arrive at McCormick's West End residence, Bly swallows a cup of coffee as McCormick begins filling in the application, and then, at the point at which the diplomat is required to specify Bly's age, she "lures Mr. McCormick into a corner so that I [Greaves] shan't hear what she has to say." McCormick then regaled the two reporters with a series of anecdotes about "the peculiarities of women who come to the Legation for passports" in their efforts to keep their ages secret.

Both Bly's and Greaves's retellings neatly omit the age to which she swore. The actual passport application does not. Next to "birth date," it states: May 5, 1867. Age: 22. Without compunction, Bly shaved three years off reality for the rest of her days.

That the very youthful-looking Bly elected to declare for herself a new birth date, in or out of Greaves's presence, is of little consequence. As amply attested by McCormick's response in either version of the story, Victorian women were forever lying about their ages. The practice was a widely accepted nod to vanity, not entirely out of vogue even yet. Bly, for her part, looked even younger than twenty-two and had a great deal invested in being "that plucky *girl* reporter." What possible difference could it make to her government if she were born in 1864 or 1867? Her birth was never registered, and anyway, who would check? One could forcefully argue that a journalist, for whom facts were lifeblood, should never in any context interfere with their truthful dissemination. But whom could this minor infraction have hurt?

What is revealing in this episode is not only the brazen capacity Bly displayed to tell a white lie but the fuss she remembered herself creating, in a quick and instinctive burst, to buttress the credibility of her reply. True or not, it was a wily deception, in this Victorian context, to invite her colleague to bear witness to her oath, allowing the little deceit to dissolve into her favorite image of herself—young, charming, outspoken; modern and adorably bold.

Bly had enormous confidence in her ability to determine right from right and wrong from wrong and, once her judgment was formed, would always act out of her own vision of reality, her own set of rules, later even in willful contravention of business ethics, court procedure, and the sanctity of law. Bly genuinely believed the truths at which she would arrive; her recounting of the London legation incident for publication is but a small case in point. The anecdote made for amusing reading, but from Bly's standpoint, its more important feature was that it cast her in the light in which she wished to be seen. It was also indicative of a very subtle craftiness.

From the steamship office, Bly dashed off to Charing Cross Station, where, after a quick cup of coffee and a few bites of ham and eggs at the station hotel, she caught her connecting train by an eye-lash to the channel crossing at Folkestone for the Paris Express. She wasn't feeling well. As she wrote, "I know that cup of coffee saved me from a headache that day. I had been shaking with the cold as we made our hurried drive through London, and my head was so dizzy at times that I hardly knew whether the earth had a chill or my brains were attending a ball."

Bly and Greaves debarked at Boulogne and quickly boarded another train for Amiens. En route, she had her first cross-cultural insight of the journey as she pondered why the English, in their otherwise intense quest for privacy, insist on having strangers on trains sit face-to-face, knee-to-knee in locked compartments. Her reflections had the unmistakable Bly stamp:

> It would make any American woman shudder with all her boasted self-reliance, to think of sending her daughter alone on a trip, even of a few hours' duration, where there was every possibility that during those hours she would be locked in a compartment with a stranger. Small wonder the American girl is fearless. She had not been used to so-called private compartments in English railway carriages, but to large crowds, and every individual that helps to swell that crowd is her protector.

At Amiens, Monsieur and Madame Verne awaited Bly at the platform, accompanied by the Paris journalist R. H. Sherard. They greeted her warmly and escorted her to their home.

Verne told her that he got the idea for the novel *Around the World in Eighty Days* from an article in the French newspaper *Le Siè-cle,* which had a detailed calculation showing how such a trip could be made. He asked Bly her travel route. By now she had it memorized: New York to London, then Calais, Brindisi, Port Said, Ismailia, Suez, Aden, Colombo, Penang, Singapore, Hong Kong, Yokohama, San Francisco, and back to New York.

"Why do you not go to Bombay as my hero Phileas Fogg did?" Verne asked.

"Because I am more anxious to save time than a young widow," she replied, in a reference to the beautiful Aouda, who Phileas Fogg had saved on his fictional journey.

"You may save a young widower before you return," Verne said with a smile. Bly smiled wryly back in what she considered a calculated display of "superior knowledge, as women, fancy free, always will at such insinuations."

It was time to cut the visit short. If Bly missed her connection to Calais, she would lose a week, not to mention her passport to history. She asked before parting if she could see Verne's study, a surprisingly modest room when compared with the rest of the sumptuously furnished home, considered the most beautiful in Amiens. The visit with the Vernes was over, and Bly had enchanted them. Madame Verne even asked permission to kiss the young reporter good-bye, a rare gesture toward a stranger. Bly inclined her head to her diminutive hostess, and Madame Verne bestowed warm kisses onto each of her cheeks. When she put up her face for Bly's return buss, the traveler had to stifle a strong inclination to kiss Madame Verne on the lips in what Bly described as the American way. "My mischievousness often plays havoc with my dignity," Bly wrote afterwards, "but for once I was able to restrain myself, and kissed her softly after her own fashion."

Later, Verne would recall Bly as "the prettiest young girl imaginable . . . and what took the hearts of myself and Madame Verne was the complete modesty of the young person. Nobody, to look at the quiet, ladylike little thing, would have thought for a moment that she was what she is and that she was going to do what she is doing. Yet I must say she looks built for hard work." He said it was risky for her to have stopped to see him, "but it was a pretty and a graceful thing for her to do, and I am sure I was delighted to see her; and so, too, was Madame Verne, who has never ceased speaking of her since."

Before Bly's journey was completed, interest in her travels was so intense in France that Verne's book was being reissued in "no less than 10 new editions." And the Chatelet Théâtre in Paris made plans to mount a new production of the stage play, shelved years before because it was "quite played out."

No sooner had *The World* announced the departure of Nellie Bly, headed east in a mad-dash attempt to "add one more to the many feathers of triumph which adorn the journalistic cap of a plucky, nervy young woman," than John Brisben Walker, proprietor of *Cosmopolitan Magazine,* announced he would send Elizabeth Bisland in a westward attempt to outdo Bly. Although Bisland's itinerary was somewhat indefinite, *The World* estimated there was a good chance the two "Misses B," former colleagues at *The World*, might end up chumming for three days in Hong Kong, have Christmas dinner together, "and then Miss Bly will start away bound home with Miss Bisland left behind to spend a half-dozen or more days to idly wait." After that, *The World* virtually ignored the challenge, and Bly herself, already at sea, had no idea that at least some people thought her race was against more than time.

The Journalist reported Walker of *Cosmopolitan* had bet *The World* $1,000 to $500 that Bisland would triumph. "The practical value of the trip beyond the advertisement that it will secure has not yet been developed," Forman wrote in his magazine. "But I have no doubt that some great humanitarian project lies concealed in this race around the earth."

The World, on the day Bly sailed, conceded it did not really expect its intrepid reporter to come back with a new theory of the universe simply "because she will have traversed the visitable and accessible portion of it." But it did say the trip had "a valuable commercial aspect." Since Bly would be traveling without special assistance, in the manner of any first-class passenger, the trip would allow history to record the state of the art in facilities for travel and communication in the last quarter of the nineteenth century.

For Bly and *The World*, the accolades poured in from the city's most prominent citizens and newspapers around the country. A box full of marriage proposals arrived along with heaps of advice. At about the time Bly was leaving Verne's residence in Amiens, the collegial backbiting began. Forman of *The Journalist*, as could easily have been anticipated, led the teeth sharpening. He leaped quickly to the front of the Bisland/*Cosmopolitan* cheering squad in an item on

November 23, quashing what he termed the "absurd and idiotic rumors" that *The World* actually was sponsoring both travelers.

Joseph Howard, Jr., the columnist, fueled that speculation in a piece for *The Press,* which Forman's magazine reprinted in part. Howard was convinced—and "a million denials" wouldn't change the fact—that there was collusion between *The World* and *Cosmopolitan* in sending off the two women reporters. "Miss Nellie Bly and Miss Elizabeth Bisland are the best-known women reporters on the New York *World* staff," he wrote. "They have both started around the world and it makes no difference to anybody outside of the *World* office which of the two comes out ahead."

The Journalist stridently countered:

Miss Elizabeth Bisland is *not* on the *World* staff in any capacity. She has been employed in an editorial position on the *Cosmopolitan* magazine for about a year, as a reference to the files of that magazine would conclusively prove. She has a contract with Mr. Walker for her *exclusive* services on the *Cosmopolitan* at a good round salary which has yet a year to run.

Had Mr. Howard seen the feeling displayed in *The World* office when Mr. Walker announced that he had started Miss Bisland to beat Miss Bly, he never would have fallen into the error of supposing that both ladies were sent by the *World.* Further, doesn't it strike Mr. Howard as a little out of the *World's* ordinary custom to start two people and give somebody else the credit for one of them?

Bly, meanwhile, was too busy barreling from place to place to send more than the odd cable back to headquarters. As her London colleague assessed her possibilities for describing England on the basis of her visit: "It will be much the same as a man describing Broadway if he were shot through a pneumatic tube from the Western Union Building to the 23rd Street Uptown office."

At Calais, she boarded the fabled mail train bound for Brindisi, Italy, with its mere twenty-one passenger berths. Departure was at 1:30 A.M. The route skipped Paris by twenty miles, passing through Dijon and Mâcon in Burgundy, skirting Aix-les-Bains and arriving the next day at lunchtime in Turin, Italy. It passed through the plains of Lombardy to Bologna, hitting the coast of the Adriatic at Rimini and then heading south to reach Brindisi, in the heel of Italy's boot, at about 11:00 on Sunday night, November 24. Bly immediately reported back to *The World* in a brief cable that the rail journey was "tedious and tiresome," that she was "quite well though somewhat fatigued" and expected within hours to be "on the bosom of the Mediterranean."

The cabled news of her arrival in Brindisi appeared in *The World* on November 26, but it was not until twelve days later that the newspaper had in hand Bly's November 20 report of her transatlantic crossing on the *Augusta Victoria*—and that was days after the paper's London correspondent had regaled readers in minute detail with Bly's adventures in England and France. In the meantime, Bly had boarded the steamer *Victoria*, one of the best and fastest of the P. and O. line, and sailed for the Egyptian port of Ismailia on November 25.

It quickly became evident to the editors of *The World* that sustaining the eruption of interest in Bly's journey for another two and a half months with no more than the odd and very delayed letter was not going to be easy. In between reports, *The World* vamped. Hardly a day went by when the editors couldn't figure out something to print about the trip, if only the laudatory comments of the various out-of-town newspapers about Bly's astounding undertaking. Then, the saving stroke: A contest was announced for readers of *The World* to guess Bly's travel time. Grand prize? A free trip to Europe. Demands for ballots poured in, and the newspaper found a whole new way to generate copy in the absence of news. By December 2, some 100,000 readers had sent back the guessing ballots, and the stories of contest entrants droned on for days. Pity the rewrite desk.

The Journalist, meanwhile, led its next edition with a lavish and praise-filled profile of Elizabeth Bisland, in which Bly was never referred to by name. It said Bisland aimed to beat the announced seventy-five-day time allotment of "the *World* correspondent" by three days, if all went well, and would write a series of six articles for the monthly *Cosmopolitan*. "Miss Bisland," Forman wrote, in a not very oblique swipe at Bly, "is in no sense a sensational writer, but a lady of the most charming manners, of the greatest refinement."

*The Nellie Bly Guessing Match blank
which appeared daily in* The World *in
December 1889 and January 1890.*
(General Research Division,
The New York Public Library)

No passengers boarded the Brindisi mail train after Calais. The windows were too dirty for Bly to see much of France through them, so she confined her observations to what was going on inside. She was taken with the young English zealot, otherwise the sweetest and most gracious of girls, "of the uncompromising kind, that condemns everything, forgives nothing, and swears the heathen is forever damned because he was not born to know the religion of her belief." Bly was miserably cold. The train had been held up by bandits the week before, and Bly, shivering under the single blanket allotted her, pondered "with regretful envy, [that] if the passengers then felt the scarcity of blankets, they at least had some excitement to make their blood circulate."

By the time the train pulled into Brindisi, and Bly prepared to board a British ship, she already was working up an attack of her life-long antipathy for the English "and their much-talked about preju-dices." She took potshots at the food and the rude and insulting English captain and crew for the rest of the journey. Most of the women she met "frequently expressed their admiration for the free American woman, many going so far as to envy me, while admiring my unfettered happiness."

What she enjoyed most, she said, was "to sit in a dark corner on deck, above where the sailors had their food, and listen to the sounds of a tom-tom and a weird musical chanting that always accompanied their evening meal." Her description of them typified the level of most of her travel notes:

> The sailors were Lascars. They were not interesting to look at, and doubtless, if I could have seen as well as heard them at their evening meal, it would have lost its charm for me. They were the most untidy looking lot of sailors I ever saw. Over a pair of white muslin drawers they wore a long muslin slip very like in shape to the old-time nightshirt. This was tied about the waist with a colored handkerchief and on their heads they wore gayly [sic] colored turbans, which are really nothing but a crown of straw with a scarf-shaped piece of bright cloth, often six feet in length, wound about the head. Their brown feet are always bare. They chant, as all sailors do, when hoisting sails, but otherwise are a grim, surly-look-ing set, climbing about over the ship like a pack of monkeys.

She had not been aboard the *Victoria* many days when the rumor circulated that Bly was "an eccentric American heiress, traveling about with a hairbrush and a bank book." This produced two proposals of marriage, much to Bly's amusement, one from a man who traveled with nineteen trunks and was smitten not by Bly but by the notion of a woman who could travel light.

When the ship anchored for recoaling at Port Said, the men left the vessel with canes "to keep off the beggars" and the women took their parasols and the same intent. Bly refused all offers to supply her with makeshift weaponry, "having an idea, probably a wrong one, that a stick beats more ugliness into a person than it ever beats out." A small fleet of *falukas* sailed up to the ship to take the passengers ashore, its sailors competing noisily in a melee of "fighting, grabbing, pulling and yelling" for the few pence they would earn for being first to fill their boats with passengers. Out came the canes and parasols. In support, the captain ordered some of the sailors to beat the unruly Arabs into decorum with long poles. Bly was quick to judgment: "I thought the conduct of the Arabs justified this harsh course of treatment, still I felt sorry to see it administered so freely and lavishly to those black, half-clad wretches, and marveled at their stubborn persistence even while cringing under the blows."

Midway to shore, the Arab boatman demanded in plain and forceful English to be paid before landing. Bly thought this strange, but one of the Arabs explained to her that after many years of dealing with "the English and their sticks," the boatmen had learned that if "they landed an Englishman before he paid, they would receive a stinging blow for their labor."

At Ismailia, the passengers watched a juggler do a magic trick with a handkerchief. Bly knew the trick well and, after the magician had completed his performance, explained to her fellow passengers how it was done. This infuriated one man, who demanded to know why she hadn't revealed the trick while the fellow was performing it. "I merely explained that I wanted to see the juggler get his money," Bly reported she replied, "much to the disgust of the Englishman."

The passage to Aden [now the southern part of Yemen in the south Arabian peninsula] was leisurely and hot, and the *Victoria* arrived on schedule December 2. Officers on board warned the women not to go ashore for the seven-hour layover because of the intense heat. Bly, in the company of "a few of the more reckless ones," was not dissuaded. And although she described in detail everything she saw, she never described or mentioned any adverse effect of the heat.

She thought the Adenites had the world's most beautiful teeth—a result of their cleaning method, which employed a sort of toothpick made of soft, fibrous tree branches—and she found the black men with lime-bleached yellow hair particularly curious. She commended the Adenites for posting the prices to be paid to drivers and boatmen. This, she thought, compared favorably with the practice of New York's night hackmen to "demand exorbitant prices, and if they are not forthcoming, to pull off their coats and fight for it." She found the jewelry-laden women mysteriously beautiful—except for their ear adornments, which split the earlobe and weighted it down as far as the shoulder. And she found the performance of a group of "Somali-boy" divers with their "bullfrog" chorus of "Oh! Yo! Ho!" an amusing diversion.

The *Victoria* reboarded and set sail for Colombo. The days passed in quiet leisure. Despite her mounting distaste for all things British, Bly did allow how profound and impressive she found the loyalty of these subjects to their monarch. Every shipboard entertainment concluded with a moving chorus of "God Save the Queen," and when Queen Victoria's portrait was flashed on a white sheet during a lantern slide show, the applause was vigorous, spontaneous, and warm. This caused her to reflect in shame on her own lack of feeling for her country's national leaders, for reasons she did not give. "I could not in honesty speak proudly of the rulers of my land, unless I went back to those two kings of manhood, George Washington and Abraham Lincoln."

On the morning of Sunday, December 8, two days ahead of schedule, the *Victoria* anchored in the bay of Colombo, and Bly was the first ashore, cabling *The World* immediately of her well-being and whereabouts. The stopover was to have been brief but stretched into an unexpected five-day delay as the *Oriental* awaited the arrival of the old clunker *The Nepaul* before it could depart. But she cabled news of the delay to *The World* without explanation, leaving the newspaper's rewrite men to fill in the blanks.

"Nellie Bly Delayed," the headline read on Thursday, December 12. The story went on to explain that she would thus be leaving Ceylon on Friday, December 13, altering "that part of her itinerary which applies to the 3,500 miles between Colombo and Hong Kong." The delay would cut to seven days the time available to reach Hong Kong from Singapore but would probably still leave her enough slack to make the Occidental and Oriental steamship *Oceanic* for its scheduled departure for San Francisco on December 28. Then the real implications of the Ceylon delay were laid bare. To lose a day anywhere between Colombo and Hong Kong could set her behind schedule up to ten days. That would mean a New York arrival date of February 3 or 4, or two days late. "It is only fair to everybody to state that the elements are against her in that part of the journey where it is most essential that they should be propitious," the newspaper confessed.

Bly's descriptions of Ceylon were the most evocative of the journey thus far, probably because she had the most time to collect them. The Grand Oriental Hotel entranced her with its tiled arcades and easy chairs in comfortable corridors, where guests could sit and sip "cooling lime squashes or the exquisite native tea, or eat of the delicious fruit while resting in an attitude of ease and laziness."

She saw all the major tourist sites and gave in to the temptation presented by the local gems. After all, they added no discernible weight to her luggage. No woman who lands at Colombo, she declared, could possibly leave without a few new rings selected from the mountains of "deeply-dark emeralds, fire-lit diamonds, exquisite pearls, rubies like pure drops of blood, the lucky cat's eye with its moving line, and all set in such beautiful shapes" that even the men were drawn into temptation. "These rings are so well known," wrote Bly, "that the moment a traveler sees one, no difference in what part of the globe, he says to the wearer, inquiringly: 'Been to Colombo, eh?' "

Watching a couple under a veranda outlined against a gate lamp, Bly spoke sweetly of romance, as she had in her novel, and as if she long before had apprehended its mysteries: "I felt a little sympathy for them as wrapped in that delusion that makes life heaven or hell, that forms the foundation for every novel, play or story, they stood, until a noisy new arrival wakened her from blissful oblivion, and she rushed, scarcely waiting for him to kiss the hand he held, away into the darkness."

Of her first experience on a jinricksha, the seasoned equestrian told of the extreme discomfort she initially felt at having a man become the beast of burden to draw her around town. Then, after going only a short way, she changed her mind. "It was so comforting," she said, "to have a horse that was able to take care of itself . . . whose tongue can protest."

She could not decide whether to attribute the excellent condition of roads at all the Eastern ports she visited to the "entire and blessed absence of beer wagons or to the absence of New York street commissioners."

The five days passed and with them, Bly's patience. She recalled her behavior once on board *The Oriental*.

"When will we sail," she snapped at the polite and handsome elderly gentleman who had offered to help her with her deck chair. He was accompanied by a young, attractive blond woman in a starched white linen suit.

"As soon as the *Nepaul* comes in," he replied. "She was to have been here at daybreak, but she hasn't been sighted yet."

Bly offered a curse in reply: "May she go to the bottom of the bay when she does get in. The old tub! I think it an outrage to be kept waiting five days for a tub like that."

"Colombo is a pleasant place to stay," the elderly man offered in consolation, his eyes twinkling.

"It may be, if staying there does not mean more than life to one. Really, it would afford me the most intense delight to see the *Nepaul* go to the bottom of the sea."

They were surprised by her show of temper, and this amused her. They had no idea what the delay could mean to her as she conjured a mental image of "a forlorn little self creeping back to New York 10 days behind time, with a shamed look on her face and afraid to hear her name spoken." The thought of this made her laugh out loud "at my own unenviable position"; then she regained composure and quietly resigned herself to whatever fate held.

With that, the *Nepaul* came into view.

It was six days of sailing to Penang off the coast of Malaya, another two to Singapore, and a week more to Hong Kong. Bly's best shipboard tale was the story of the seemingly beautiful woman who, when accidentally burst in upon in her stateroom, turned out to be minus both hair and teeth. Bly awakened every morning to the sounds of that woman's husband and toddler in an unnerving morning ritual.

Bly made no secret of liking to stay up late and sleep in. "For heavens sake," she growled on the sixth straight dream-busted morning, "tell papa what the moo-moo cow says and let me go to sleep." The couple ignored her for the rest of the trip.

By the second day out from Penang, Bly "so longed for some new experience," she started wishing that some old-time pirates might show up for an attack.

Although the arrival at Singapore had been expected that night, the captain had slowed the ship down to let off a group of coolies at Penang near nightfall, forcing him to anchor out until morning for safety. Since the ship's mail contract made it compulsory to spend twenty-four hours in port at Singapore, Bly was livid. She considered the delay unnecessary and was very quick to fix blame. Gone was the relaxed forbearance and sensitivity she had shown toward the locals she had encountered at other stops en route. This time, they were in her way:

> While we might have been consuming our [mandatory twenty-four-hour] stay, and so helping me on in my race against time, I was wasting precious hours lying outside the gates of hope, as it were, merely because some black men had been too slow. These few hours might mean the loss of my ship at Hong Kong; they might mean days added to my record. What agony of suspense and impatience I suffered that night!

Once ashore, Bly and her fellow passengers made the usual touristic visits. The holy man at a Hindu temple barred her from entry because she was a woman.

"Why?" I demanded, curious to know why my sex in heathen lands should exclude me from a temple, as in America it confines me to the side entrances of hotels and other strange and incommodious things.

"No, señora, no mudder," the priest said with a positive shake of the head.

"I'm not a mother!" I cried so indignantly that my companions burst into laughter, which I joined after a while, but my denials had no effect on the priest.

On the way to the ship, Bly and her party stopped at the home of the group's driver to meet his pretty Malay wife, dressed in one wrapping of linen, with a large gold ring in her nose, rings on her toes and around her ankles, and several around the rims of her ears. She had several babies and, at the door of the house, a monkey. Bly moved into action: "I did resist the temptation to buy a boy at Port Said and also smothered the desire to buy a Singhalese girl at Colombo, but when I saw the monkey my will-power melted and I began straightway to bargain for it. I got it."

The ship left Singapore, sailing into a monsoon that Bly, with characteristic abandon, described only as "the most beautiful thing I ever saw." She was far less impressed with the fellow passenger who clearly fancied her but showed the poor form to become seasick at her feet.

"Do you think life worth living?" he asked her. The two were alone on deck.

"Yes," she replied. "Life is very sweet. The thought of death is the only thing that causes me unhappiness."

"You cannot understand it or you would feel different," he responded. "I could take you in my arms and jump overboard, and before they would know it we would be at rest. Death by drowning is a peaceful slumber, a quiet drifting away."

Alarmed by her proximity to what was "for the time a mad man," Bly kept the conversation going while she tried to figure out how to get away. Any false move, she feared, might mean her "burial beneath the angry sea." Fortunately, the ship's chief officer happened to stroll by and, sensing something was wrong, hurried Bly off to safety. The captain wanted the man put in irons, but Bly pleaded for his freedom. So much for her longing for robbers and pirates and loving the danger of monsoons. With the threat to her safety real and present, she decided "not to spend one moment alone and unprotected on deck."

Bly confessed to enjoying "the queerness of people," and delighted in the foibles and eccentricities of her fellow passengers. Particularly amusing were the newlyweds who, presuming this was a shipboard requisite, slept in their life preservers.

Despite the raging monsoon, arrival in Hong Kong was two days early, causing one passenger to sue the ship line for the cost of the additional days in a hotel. No such complaint from Bly, who rushed, in her elation, to the offices of the Oriental and Occidental Steamship Company to find out how quickly she could leave for Japan. She had just marked off her thirty-ninth travel day since leaving New York. The *Oriental,* on her maiden voyage to China from Colombo to Hong Kong, had broken all previous records.

At the O. and O. office, the young traveler was asked her name.

"Nellie Bly," she replied.

"Come in, come in," a man in the office said. "You are going to be beaten."

"What?" she shot back. "I think not. I have made up my delay."

"You are going to lose it," he said.

"Lose it?" she asked. "I don't understand. What do you mean?"

He then told her that time wasn't her only competitor. It was the first Bly had heard about the challenge of Elizabeth Bisland. Bisland's editor had offered a thousand dollars or more to the O. and O. steamship line if it could have the *Oceanic* leave San Francisco two days ahead of schedule in order to get Bisland to Hong Kong in time to catch the English mail for Ceylon. The O. and O. had declined the offer, but the ship had managed to reach Hong Kong long before it was due. And Bisland had made the connection.

"She left here three days ago," the man told Bly, "and you will be delayed here five days."

Bly tried to grasp what had happened. No cables or letters from *The World* awaited her. Perhaps the newspaper was unaware of the challenge? No chance, said the man from O. and O. Bisland had indicated that *The World* had arranged the race, although Bly was certain that could not have been the case. Bisland had brought along letters to the officials of the steamship lines at every port requesting them to help her. Bly only had one letter to the agent of the P. and O., requesting captains on their ships to look out for her because she was traveling alone.

Too proud to show her ignorance "on a subject of vital importance to my well-doing," Bly said only, "I do not understand it."

Thinking quickly, she stiffly told the O. and O. official that she had promised her editor to go around the world in seventy-five days, "and if I accomplish that I shall be satisfied. I am not racing with anyone. I would not race. If someone else wants to do the trip in less time, that is their concern."

Once in Hong Kong, she refused all invitations for social engagements, partly because she had nothing appropriate to wear and partly because she felt she should restrict her time to work-related pursuits. She played tourist, managing to see "everything of interest."

She decided she should see a real "Simon-pure Chinese city," so on Christmas Eve, she set out for Canton on the ship called the *Powan.* Chinese torture fascinated her, especially the lime-filled jars containing the heads of executed criminals and the brutal bamboo punishment whereby an offender was pinioned in standing position with his legs astride, fastened to stakes. Directly underneath the man, a sturdy bamboo sprout would be growing, starting its thirty-day climb to a height of sometimes seventy-five feet, targeted to penetrate straight through him.

What a Christmas. The morning was spent at a leper colony, followed by lunch in the Temple of the Dead. On came the pangs of loneliness, and Bly returned to the *Powan,* ending the day with one of her familiar sick headaches.

Shortly after her return to Hong Kong, on December 28, the *Oceanic* sailed for Yokohama, Japan, taking five days for the journey. Bly and her fellow passengers spent New Year's Eve on board. The five-day wait for the *Oceanic* to begin traversing the Pacific Ocean on January 7 must have seemed longer than the distance she had yet to cover.

Finally on board, the crew and its passengers joined Bly in trying to will her success, since few other means were at their disposal.
A couplet, composed by the chief engineer, was emblazoned on the
ship's engines:

For Nellie Bly
We'll win or die.
January 20, 1890

The runs were excellent, and Bly was greatly encouraged until
the third day, when a brutal storm hit and continued for more than
twenty-four hours. Hope sank. Her monkey must have been equally
distraught for, according to one report, he "showed his usefulness by
jumping on the back of the stewardess and attempting to bite off her
head."

"If I fail," Bly vowed, "I will never return to New York. I would
rather go in dead and successful than alive and behind time."

The chief engineer did what he could to console her, confidently
predicting she would make New York with three days to spare. Bly
couldn't see how. Day and night, she prayed in the classical mode for
God to show mercy on her sin-filled self. "As the mercy has not been
forthcoming," she said, looking for some fragment of a bright ray to
focus on, "the natural conclusion is that I'm not a sinner."

✦

Back in New York, Nellie Bly's race was having the desired effect on
The World's circulation. By Sunday, December 1, the number of
papers sold was back up to 268,230. A week later, it climbed to
270,660, and by December 16, a month after Bly's departure, it had
hit a whopping 273,090. Pulitzer had the figures splashed on the
right ear of the front page. On days when there was nothing first- or
even secondhand to report about Bly's travels—which were most of
the time—the newspaper did whatever it could to keep interest
primed. It carried snippets of reports about Bly from newspapers in
other cities, or columns of informed speculation calculating her
chances for success. When really desperate, the newspaper would

carry minitravelogues about the places on her itinerary and what she might or might not encounter. *The World* went so far as to claim Bly's race had given new meaning to the study of geography, which had turned into a veritable craze among schoolchildren and adults alike. "Everybody," the newspaper asserted, "will be, to some extent, improved by the Nellie Bly tour."

Every day, the newspaper reran "The Nellie Bly Guessing Match" logo and coupon accompanied by instructions for entering the contest. The coupons were returned by the thousands, and a "European Trip Editor" was appointed to catalog them. One the newspaper reprinted arrived in verse:

> *Nellie Bly is flying high*
> *On the China Sea;*
> *With her goes the hope of one*
> *Who wants to see Paree;*
> *She'll get here in 74,*
> *Sure as she's alive,*
> *Hours 12, minutes 10 and seconds 25.*

When circulation hit 270,653 for Sunday, December 22, even though it was down slightly from the week before, *The World* declared the figure a "total eclipse of all other Sunday newspapers."

By January 4, with Bly in Yokohama waiting to board the *Oceanic* for San Francisco, Allan Forman at *The Journalist* could no longer contain himself over the absence of interest in Elizabeth Bisland's challenge. He took it out on *The World:*

Now that *The World* is in a position to see how small a paper looks, which refuses to note matters of news for fear of advertising a rival, would it not look well to say a few words about Miss Bisland, who is going around the world for the *Cosmopolitan* magazine? I see a lot in *The World* about Nellie Bly but nothing about Miss Bisland. If one is news, is not the other? The New York papers which purposely neglected to mention *The World*'s Christmas Trees and Newsboy's dinner, were certainly below contempt, but *The World* preserves a singular silence in regard to Miss Bisland. It is too great a paper to allow itself to be guilty of an action which can savor of unfairness in the eyes of the most critical.

It is doubtful *The World* felt any sting from Forman, but three days later it did reprint a brief item from *The Albany Journal,* one of the papers following Bisland's progress. "Appearances today," the upstate newspaper said, "are quite as much in favor of Miss Bisland as Miss Bly."

For Bly, however, whose journey was nearing completion and success by her own measure—seventy-five days or less no matter who might be trying to beat her—*The World's* hyperbole knew no bounds. Elongating what would otherwise have been a scant five paragraphs on January 8, the rewrite men rhapsodized, prophesying for Bly a woman's homecoming unmatched in jubilation:

> Her grit has been more than masculine. Her perseverance has been more than rare Ben Jonson ever counselled or Philosopher Ben Franklin ever practiced. She is coming home to dear old America with the scalps of the carpers and critics strung on her slender girdle, and about her head a monster wreath of laurel and forget-me-nots, as a tribute to American pluck, American womanhood and American perseverance.

The World upped the prize package to include $250 in spending money and a private cipher code to keep down the cost of sending cables. The proprietor of Low's Exchange, the travel bureau, offered the facilities of the firm's London office to the winner. The popular comedians Hallen and Hart composed a song in three verses called "Globe-Trotting Nellie Bly." And all along Bly's route back to New York from San Francisco, local press clubs and citizens' committees prepared joyous receptions.

Town Topics, the stinging society gossip magazine, acknowledged that even when *The World* wasn't dignified, it was dazzling.

> As recently as a year ago it [*The World*] had the habit of celebrating Sunday with an extra quantity of good reading. All

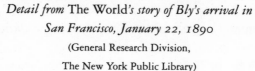

Detail from The World*'s story of Bly's arrival in
San Francisco, January 22, 1890*
(General Research Division,
The New York Public Library)

the bright boys, from A. C. Wheeler to Bill Nye, trooped gaily forward and seemed to be proud of their stations. Now they are spluttering under the voluminous whirlwind of Nellie Bly's skirts, and peeping timidly around the corner of the new prize package department, uncertain whether they are a newspaper or a policy shop.

The enterprise of *The Sunday World* is so overwhelming, *Town Topics* wrote, "that it loses an editor every month from brain disease," and both the "Nellie Bly Department" and the "Prize Package Department" had proved very profitable novelties.

A week later, *Town Topics* wondered out loud why *The Sun* didn't borrow a page from Verne's *Around the World in Eighty Days* and have someone like Mr. Fix, the detective Verne created to harass Phileas Fogg, try repeatedly to put obstacles in the way of Bly's success. It apparently had forgotten about Bisland. "The *Sun* might have commissioned a lively correspondent to do the same thing. Perhaps a man would not be ungallant enough to block the young lady's little game, but plenty of women could be found for the task."

Meanwhile, *The World* began deploying staff to the U.S. cities where Bly would be stopping. Fear of a snow blockade in the Sierra Nevada range had the editors concerned she would lose the time she needed to make New York before deadline. John J. Jennings was sent to San Francisco via St. Louis, where he stopped briefly. Other reporters awaited her arrival in Philadelphia. A "Nellie Bly Escort Corps" weathered a severe snowstorm on its arrival January 14 in Ogden, Utah. There was almost a stampede to the Walker House when rumor zipped through the town that Bly was staying at the hotel. Actually, it was the actress Helen Blythe.

"On the line out to this point," the crew in Ogden reported back to New York, "the name of *The World*'s globe-girdler is as familiar as President Harrison's and more familiar than the names of many of his Cabinet."

From Ogden, the escort corps took the fast mail train to San Francisco just after midnight, but got only as far as the Sierra Nevada town of Emigrant Gap, California, when the train stopped dead in a wicked storm dumping snowflakes reported to be the size of soda crackers. They had been stuck more than fifty hours by the time reporters were able to get word back to New York.

By January 20, with Bly expected to dock at San Francisco any hour, *The World* began speculating that it might become necessary to alter her overland route away from the Central Pacific, paralyzed under the worst snowstorm in more than a decade. The snowdrifts had become so solidly packed, and the snowfall so unprecedentedly heavy, it was expected to take a week for the tracks to be cleared.

Bly had traveled more than 21,000 miles in sixty-eight days without a mishap or a missed connection. Now, what should have been the most effortless 3,000 miles to cover lay perilously ahead.

༺༒༻

By January 20, at 7:42 A.M., the *Oceanic* was in sight of San Francisco, and Bly, by her own description, swelled "with a hopefulness that had not known me for many days." The ship's purser rushed by, blanching. "My God," he cried. "The bill of health was left behind in Yokohama." No bill of health, no landing in San Francisco. The vessel would have to await the arrival of the document on the next ship from Japan—not expected for another two weeks. Bly, bereft, got action in her own way. She simply threatened, quietly, to slit her throat. A second, more thorough search produced the bill of health, found neatly tucked in the ship doctor's desk.

A smallpox scare on board proved only a rumor, but more ominous than the threat of quarantine was the news in the morning papers, which revenue officers had brought on board, of the impassable snow blockade in the Sierra Nevada.

A tug, called the *Millen Griffiths,* sped out to the *Oceanic* to take Bly to shore, meeting her just across from Alcatraz Island. The monkey, by now called McGinty, was in tow. She skipped the farewells; there was no time. Her baggage was flung into the tug behind her, increased substantially by her many gifts. As the tug steamed off, the quarantine doctor called after her that she could not land until he had examined her tongue. She stuck it out. "All right," he yelled.

The San Francisco Chronicle gave only grudging notice to Bly's arrival, on page 8. Remember that Elizabeth Bisland of *Cosmopolitan* had started her journey westward with San Francisco her first stop after boarding the train in New York. Bisland spent five days in the city waiting for her ship, and, according to *The Chronicle,* "the general hope seemed to be that she [Bisland] would distance her rival and reach her goal first, for Nellie Bly was unknown as yet except by reputation."

The tug brought Bly in twenty minutes to Oakland Pier, where only a few people greeted her. In two minutes, she stepped into the special train laid on by *The World* to get her as far as Chicago by a more southern route. So much for the pledge to have her travel by regular passenger means, but given the snow blockade, who would quibble?

Bly's recollection of the transcontinental dash in only four and a half days was a blur, a "maze of happy greetings, happy wishes, congratulating telegrams, fruit, flowers, loud cheers, wild hurrahs, rapid hand-shaking and a beautiful car filled with fragrant flowers attached to a swift engine that was tearing like mad through flower-dotted valleys and over snow-tipped mountains." It was a queen's ride, she said, replete with ovations a royal could envy.

Bly's own explanation for the avalanche of emotion was that Americans could not help but do honor to an American girl who had broken the record for speed in world travel, "and I rejoiced with them that it was an American girl who had done it." When *The San Francisco Chronicle* reporter made a similar observation, saying what an extraordinary feat she had performed, Bly replied, "Oh, I don't know. It's not so very much for a woman to do who has the pluck, energy and independence which characterize many women in this day of push and get-there."

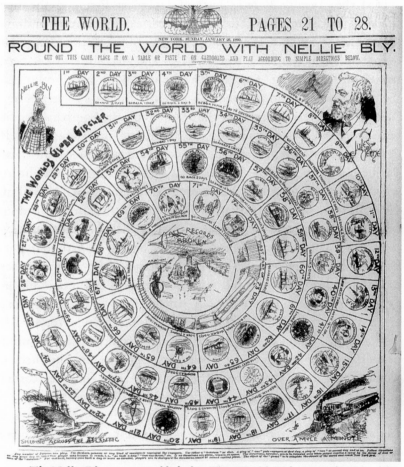

The Nellie Bly game as published in The World, *February 26, 1890*
(General Research Division, The New York Public Library)

She pinpointed her greatest success as "the personal interest of every one who greeted me." Interestingly, this would always be the form both her successes and her failings would take, an intense personal interest in whatever she was up to on the part of people who had no particular reason to be concerned. She had the fundamental characteristic of stardom.

No sooner had Bly set foot on American soil again than she began to rewrite history in a dispatch cabled back to *The World* from Fresno, California, typically altered just enough to suit her perception of herself. She conveniently forgot her first two nauseating days aboard the *Augusta Victoria* just off Hoboken Pier and the sick headache Christmas Day. She wrote of her experience that nothing pleased her so much as the "violent rocking of the ship, so long as it didn't endanger the success of my trip" and that she had not been seasick once, enjoying "good health ever since I left New York."

Her luxury train car, the San Lorenzo, drawn by The Queen, "one of the fastest engines on the road," took the Southern Pacific train route speedily down to Mojave, California, in a snow blockade detour. From Mojave, it took the regular route over the Atlantic and Pacific road—the "Nellie Bly Escort Corps" had finally caught up with her—continuing to Albuquerque. Three miles outside Gallup, New Mexico, Bly's train flew at fifty miles an hour over a deep canyon on a bridge under repair, its nails held in place only by jackscrews. The workmen heard the train coming too late to flag it, and only by a miracle did it traverse the ravine safely. Then, it was over the Atchison, Topeka and Santa Fe system to La Junta in southeastern Colorado, and on to Topeka, where a thousand people waited at the station, in spirited anticipation. Bly told the reporter for *The Topeka Daily Capital* that an ordinary person could make a trip like hers in seventy-five days for about $1,500, that an unprotected woman could travel the globe without fear, and that the worst cost of all was the incessant tipping required by just about everyone.

"There is really not much for Americans to see in the foreign lands," she told the reporter. "We've got the best of everything here; we lack in nothing; then when you go over there you must be robbed, you get nothing fit to eat and you see nothing that America cannot improve upon wonderfully. There is a great deal more to see at home than abroad. They are so very, very slow in Europe and to my mind are behind America in almost everything."

For its Albuquerque to Kansas City run, the train had broken the record for speed on a long-distance haul, reaching an average of forty-six miles per hour for the 918 miles, including stopovers and the crossing of both the Glorietta and the Raton mountain range.

Excitement overflowed in Chicago, where she transferred to a regular Pennsylvania Railroad carrier and the Pullman car Ilion to New York. Her stop in the Windy City was more than momentary, and the Press Club honored her with an 8:30 A.M. reception at Kinsley's, the second city's answer to Delmonico's. Stanley Waterloo, president of the club and editor of *The Sunday Times,* announced she had been voted "one of the boys." She was escorted to the wheat pit, where pandemonium on the trading room floor of the commodities exchange shifted instantly to respectful silence. Spontaneous applause erupted, "followed by three thundering cheers and a tiger for plucky Nellie Bly."

At Logansport, Indiana, where the train stopped briefly at 1:50 P.M., reporters tried to nail down rumors of Bly's engagement to one of their own, Dr. Frank Ingram. Ingram had been assistant superintendent of the women's lunatic asylum on Blackwell's Island when Bly did her exposé, and the two had become good friends. Told that he hailed from Logansport, Bly simply expressed surprise and explained that she knew the good doctor "intimately." She declined, however, to confirm the rumors, which had caused enough stir locally that *The Peru* (Ind.) *Journal* was moved to remark of Ingram's alleged ardor: "Since Indiana furnished the United States with a President, the average Hoosier seems to have multiplied his estimation of himself and is not satisfied with anything short of the earth and those who encircle it."

Even in staid Washington, D.C., through which she did not pass, there was a guessing contest frenzy involving senators and judges and even the visiting former governor of Louisiana, William Pitt Kellogg, found by a *World* correspondent in his rooms at the Shoreham Hotel, busily filling in the printed blanks. *The World* estimated the total number of guesses at somewhere between half a million and a million.

The Pittsburg Press sent a correspondent to travel with Bly on the six-hour train ride from Columbus, Ohio, to Pittsburgh, enabling the evening paper to carry an exclusive interview as part of its chronicle of her brief "hometown" welcome. Never in his memory, the Columbus stationmaster said, not for former President Cleveland in 1887 and 1888 or for President Harrison, had there been such pandemonium to greet an arriver—and fully half the crowd was women. The Pennsylvania Company presented her with exquisite flowers and a sandalwood box filled with bottles of rare perfume to sweeten and flavor the last hours of her journey.

"She was to all intents and appearances, Pittsburgh's own and only Nelly [*sic*], just the same attractive and pleasing lady she was in the old time Pittsburg hustling days," the *Press* reporter gushed.

She reboarded the Ilion, in drawing room 13—Bly claimed to be not at all superstitious, lucky thumb ring notwithstanding—a visual feast of peacock blue decor accented by fawn gray curtains and lambrequins. McGinty the monkey, now described as "a present from the rajah at Singapore" sat quietly in his cage, chained and suffering from an American bout with *la grippe* contracted at Mojave. As the flu had reached epidemic proportions around the country, Bly thought her monkey was taking the fashionable course. A Japanese mandolin hanging on the wall was described as a gift from a prince of the royal line at Yokohama.

Bly, when asked, said she had never encountered Bisland during her travels, nor had she for a moment considered the challenger a rival. "We are both on an errand which I look upon as infinitely higher in its import than some persons imagine," she ventured. "I am not the only person in America who will circle the globe inside of 75 days. It may be necessary some time in the future for one of our countrymen or women to make it in less time than my own. I have established, however, a standard schedule."

Bly then retired for a brief rest, during which time a prominent Pittsburgh manufacturer, not named by the reporter, agreed with Bly's assessment of her journey's value. True, he said, the primary purpose was aggrandizement of the two women and advertisement of their respective publications. But suppose Andrew Carnegie, on his more leisurely world tour over the same route some years earlier, got word at Hong Kong that the Edgar Thomson steel plant at Bessemer had burned down and his presence in Pittsburgh was urgently required? He would have had Bly's model of rapid transit to guide him home instead of the untried fictional notions advanced by Jules Verne. No doubt this new record "actually established a standard schedule which may be of inestimable value to many globe trotters or around the world loiterers in the future," the manufacturer said.

Bly reemerged after her nap and invited her escort corps to join her for a postmidnight snack of delicious fruit which had been presented at Fresno. The train pulled into Pittsburgh precisely on time at 3:10 A.M. Relatives and friends were on hand to greet her, along with a fair sampling of Pittsburgh's press corps. The Ilion then barreled on to Philadelphia, where Bly arrived nearly ten hours later, lavishly greeted by an estimated 5,000 well-wishers at the Broad Street station, led by her mother, quiet, small, bespectacled, and unrecognized, dressed plainly in black with a black velvet wrap and modest bonnet. Cora Linn Daniels also was on hand with the welcoming poem she had written in Bly's honor. She predicted her good friend would not have all that much to say about the journey. "She isn't much of a girl to talk," she told a *World* reporter. "I very seldom know what she is about until I read it in the papers."

Julius Chambers, *The World*'s managing editor, led the welcoming delegation, accompanied by Judge Leicester Holme as Mayor Hugh J. Grant's representative and a host of reporters, including James S. Metcalfe—the same Metcalfe who had rated a veiled reference in Bly's novel. Metcalfe would write a snotty parody of Bly's trip for his humor magazine, *Life*, which followed the journey of a certain Miss Sadie McGinty on her lightning tour around Manhattan Island.

Jules Verne proffered no such insult. He had cabled enthusiastic praise. French interest in her journey was intense, he said; he had been receiving piles of letters weekly. *World* correspondents also reported enthusiasm over Bly's achievement in both England and Germany, although there was criticism from some in France who thought she had done a grave disservice to the ideal of dignified leisure that a grand tour should represent. Verne disagreed. He found the accomplishment fantastic, and all the more noteworthy because it had been undertaken in the more treacherous winter months.

The Philadelphia crowd was in such tumult, Mrs. Cochrane had to be taken all the way through every train car to reach The Beatrice, the special car set aside for her reunion with her daughter, whom she apparently no longer addressed as Pink. *The World* described their tender meeting:

> Only when a goodly rate of speed was attained was Miss Bly summoned to enter the special car in which her journey was to be completed. There was cheering and applause. Everybody cheered. Old friends and newspaper co-laborers shook her hand, and she smiled glad, jolly smiles. Her sunburned face took on a new glow of delight. The mother awaited her in the state room, and through the throng of admiring friends she went to get the mother's welcoming kiss and rest in the maternal arms.
>
> The door opened and all the men stepped back from it. That meeting was a sacred thing.
>
> "Oh, Nellie!"
>
> "Mother! I'm so glad!" Then the door closed. The rest of it was their secret and none would molest them.

Bly alighted at Jersey City, and three timekeepers stopped their watches with a unison snap. Time? 3:51 P.M. The roar came up from "a thousand throats," and a battery of mortars boomed. The journey was done. Bly completed her mission on Saturday, January 25, 1890, seventy-two days, six hours, eleven minutes, and fourteen seconds after she began it, clocking an average speed, excluding stops, of 22.47 miles per hour. *The World* crowed that she had broken every record for circumnavigation.

She was ferried from Jersey to Manhattan, where she struggled through the surging crowd to a landau, carriage top flipped back so the crowds could cheer her, which carried the heroine to Newspaper Row. Once there, more crowds surged into the space between the main Post Office and Astor House, with the overflow filling the hotel rotunda. She reached the *World* office by 4:30 P.M. The cheering was wild. A private dinner was arranged at Astor House, and then a carriage took the triumphant "little traveler" and her mother to their home uptown.

As her train sped from Chicago to Philadelphia, Bly began dictating her travelogue to a stenographer so *The World* could publish it on Sunday to coincide with the four-plus pages of reports the paper carried about her arrival. By introduction, *The World* apologized for her story's lack of polish, prepared as it was under the impossible circumstances of hasty dictation interrupted by thousands of questioning well-wishers. "But there can be no doubt," the newspaper said, "about the brightness of the comment and the fresh spirit of the narrative." Across the top half of the Sunday feature section was printed a black-and-white facsimile of what would become the colorful and richly illustrated Nellie Bly board game, tracing square by square every day of her journey. *The Journalist* predicted it would become a sensation, as popular as Parcheesi, on which it was modeled, or the Fifteen Puzzle. *The World's* circulation on the day of her return was reported to hit 280,340, an increase of more than 10,000 over the previous Sunday record and only 5,520 below the previous high figure, published on March 25, 1889.

In its lead editorial that day, *The World* declared Bly's tumultuous reception across the United States utterly warranted, totally appropriate, devoid of excess. It was a fitting tribute to Nellie Bly, personification of pluck, that "combination of superb qualities which all sound-hearted men and women admire."

⋘❀⋙

On Bly's return to Park Row, among her many other tributes, a basket of rare roses awaited her, bearing the compliments and congratulations of John Brisben Walker. It was Walker, the editor of *Cosmopolitan,* who had sent Elizabeth Bisland westward in what turned out to be the vain hope of blighting Bly's achievement.

The World, with its victorious correspondent safely in port and Walker playing the gallant good sport, took the high road and wrote magnanimously of *Cosmopolitan's* ill-fated challenge. As *The World* recounted, Walker woke up on the morning of November 14 and,

Nellie Bly in her traveling clothes, 1890
(The Bettmann Archive)

reading about Bly's departure, got the idea to send a competitor westward. His staff member Elizabeth Bisland, late of *The World,* agreed to undertake the journey and left for San Francisco within six hours. Walker went to the *World* office and offered to make it a race. *The World* declined, but Walker sent Bisland nonetheless, convinced that, given the season, the westward journey would prove the faster.

For Bisland, there were disappointments and delays between Hong Kong, where she was well ahead of Bly, and Aden. According to *The World*'s account, by the time Bisland reached Brindisi for the mail train north, she was two days behind schedule. She had tried to meet the French steamer *Champagne* when it sailed from Le Havre on January 18 but missed the connection through what *The World* described as "some misunderstanding . . . although the vessel was obligingly held three hours for her."

The San Francisco Chronicle reported a slightly different version of Bisland's misfortune. First, she was delayed in San Francisco, having to wait two extra days for the *Oceanic* to leave for China. After that

> the energetic and plucky little woman pushed on and lost no opportunity to lessen the distance between herself and her goal. While she was on American or British ground she found the road was easy. She had all but won her trip when the red tape of the French Government defeated her. Had her train into Paris been on time, she would have been due at New York on Sunday next. She counted on catching the last steamer at Le Havre, but her train was delayed and she arrived two hours too late. She telegraphed to the agents of the steamer at Havre offering to reimburse them for the cost of any delay if they would detain the vessel until her arrival, but after a consultation, it was decided to send the fast steamer *La Champagne* out on time, and so the young lady was left.

So Bisland crossed the straits to Dover and hurried off to Queenstown, hoping to catch the Cunard Line's *Etruria,* a fast ship. Instead, the slow old *Bothnia* had been substituted and wasn't expected in port until January 28 or 29. *The World* made a point of saying that even if Bisland had managed to connect with the *Champagne,* which was not due in until Sunday, "she would not have been able to beat Miss Bly, as the returns show." Nevertheless, *The World* added, as Bly basked in celebration and Bisland wallowed "in the trough of the yeasty Atlantic," everyone, of course, wished the challenger well.

The objectivity of Allan Forman of *The Journalist* could never be trusted on matters concerning Bly, and he had long ago declared himself a great admirer of Bisland. Even as Bly's train pulled up at the station in Jersey City, *The Journalist* was in print with yet another tribute to Bisland, that writer of "daintiness and distinction," with the news gleaner's "observant and receptive faculties." There was no mention of Bly's impending victory, only a brief item stating that "Nelly [*sic*] Bly's real name is Pink Cochran [*sic*]. She came from Pittsburg, Pennsylvania, and began her career on the *Despatch* [*sic*] of that city."

A week later, Forman was in full vicious swagger. He began his "Bye the Bye" column with the snide statement and question raised in the magazine *The Metropolis*: "Nellie Bly has returned from her trip around the world. What of it?" *The Metropolis* did not bother to answer the question, but Forman could not resist a vitriolic rejoinder. In his view, the trip had shown that "a young woman sent around the world for no practical purpose will work to greater advantage in booming a newspaper than a dozen men sent out after facts." And more, "It has proved the immense resources of the *New York World,* and the vigor and intelligence with which they are utilized; and it has proved that the great majority of the American people dearly love a sensation—no matter how flimsy—so long as it gives them something to gabble about. It has been a great advertisement for the *New York World* and Miss Nellie Bly." Forman sniped that a trip so hurried could not possibly provide any facts of value to *The World's* readership, and for practical results, the paper would have done as well to send a "canvas-covered sugar-cured ham with a tag tied to it" instead of a woman.

"And yet," Forman lamented, "it paid."

More far-reaching in negative implication, he said, was that Bly's sensation signaled the end of the great tradition of American journalism, fathered by the likes of Horace Greeley and Henry J. Raymond. "Today we have the lightning press, the paragraphic editorial, the special railroad train, the Atlantic cable, the telephone, the phonograph and the Nelly [*sic*] Bly—'What of it?' forsooth. This much. If you don't like it, the people demand it, and—*Vox populi, vox Dei*, you know. If you can't keep up with the procession, there is no use in trying to stop it, for you can't."

Yet more than two years later, in a pandering tribute to the success of *Cosmopolitan*, Forman seemed to have forgotten how idiotic he once found it all and again took up the case of the "brilliant young writer" Bisland, charging that he could prove *The World* had pulled a trick in order to defeat the challenger, "a trick which would have disqualified the *World* among sporting men but which, under the very loose code of ethics which governs the conduct of a 'great' newspaper, is perhaps allowable to save the paper from ignominious defeat." Without elucidating on his charges, he claimed Bisland should have beaten Bly by three days. Nevertheless, Forman wrote, the race did manage to allow Bisland to showcase her "breeziness, originality and literary charm" in a series of seven monthly articles she produced for *Cosmopolitan* chronicling her trip, later compiled into a book.

The Bly adventure got a more amusing assessment on the editorial page of *The Pittsburg Commercial Gazette,* provided by her mentor, Erasmus Wilson, still writing his column under "The Quiet Observer" headline though no longer for *The Dispatch* or *The Bulletin.* This one carried the subhead "What Doth It Profit a Girl to Girdle the Earth?" and thoughtfully recounted, through the supposed conversation of two young women, the pros and cons, importance and insignificance of Bly's world race. Wilson speculated on what Bly might do next. No chance she would sit down and weep, Alexander-style, he said. "She isn't built that way. She will just wait until a new idea strikes her, and go straightaway and carry it out." So sure was his faith in her.

Bly, for her part, claimed no exhaustion or need for recuperation. She expressed regret that the journey had ended. The same went for the monkey, who, when let out of his cage in the Cochrane flat, managed to break every dish. Bly said she was considering donating him to the menagerie in Central Park. But she did not.

Asked what she planned to do next, she said without hesitation, "I expect to go back to work again. You know I must do something for a living. And I expect to work until I fall in love and get married."

On January 29, four days after her return, *The Philadelphia Inquirer* carried a report reprinted from *The Logansport* (Ind.) *Dispatch* via *The Cincinnati Enquirer* that Bly was engaged to marry thirty-year-old Dr. Frank Ingram. The report was attributed to Logansport friends, quoting "reliable sources."

Throughout that week, *The World* milked Bly's success for all it could, printing every cable of admiration, every iota of progress of the fourteen experts who were busily trying to determine the guessing match winner. There was, however, no report of a betrothal.

The World vowed scrupulous fairness in determining the victor of its Nellie Bly contest. No guess proffered after Bly reached Chicago would be considered, and if more than one entrant guessed correctly, the one whose coupon was dated earliest would win.

The Sunday World of February 2 carried a souvenir photo likeness of Nellie Bly, which she abhorred, and the first four detailed chapters of her travelogue, the last installment of which was published February 23. The name of the contest winner was released—

SHE'S BROKEN EVERY RECORD!

A Little Pardonable Consternation Among the Globe-Circlers at the Remarkable Achievement "The World's" Traveller

From The World's *front page, January 26, 1890*

(General Research Division, The New York Public Library)

F. W. Stevens of New York City, who guessed Bly's total travel time within two-fifths of a second. The newspaper prominently ran a listing of the 116 others who guessed within fifteen seconds of the actual time.

Before the trip, *The World* had done what it could to keep Bly's identity under wraps, considering the undercover nature of her most significant assignments. Now the time had come to release her "authentic biography," in which the story of her rise to sensational acclaim would be told in full. The newspaper described her as an unmarried woman, born in 1867, the same birth date she swore to in her passport application at the American Legation in London. She was living quietly in an uptown flat with her mother, endeavoring because of her work to know as few people as possible. Those who had gotten to know her, the newspaper said, liked her most for being

One of a series of Nellie Bly trade cards issued by various manufacturers, 1890

(Author's collection)

Latest Novelty

IN CAPS FOR YOUNG LADIES.

The "Nellie Bly."

In Plaids and Plain Colors, to retail from
50 Cents to $1.00.

. . SEND FOR SAMPLES . .

Walker, Stetson, Sawyer Co.,

83 LINCOLN ST., BOSTON.

*Postcard advertisement for the Nellie
Bly cap for young ladies, 1890*
(Author's collection)

so frank and so gentle. "Free from affectation or loudness, she is popular with all who have known her, except the people she has made uncomfortable through the columns of the *World*."

The newspaper went on to describe its reporter as a good-looking brunette with a slight, graceful figure and girlish appearance despite a serious cast to her thoughts and manners, no doubt caused by how earnestly she takes her work. "Still," *The World* said, "a jolly light-heartedness at times manifests itself."

Bly presumably provided much of the information for the profile and if so, took pains to mislead *The World*'s readers on several counts other than her age. Her inadequate education was an evident source of embarrassment, hence the false claim of two years at normal school, and the "threatening heart disease" that forced her withdrawal. On setting out around the world, Bly stated that

The cover of Nellie Bly's Book: Around
the World in Seventy-Two Days
(Library of Congress)

she had no need to cart along any medicine since she had never been
sick in her life.

This "authentic biography" also mentioned how her father's
sudden death without a will had left the family estate tied up and in
the hands of administrators. It went on to detail her entry into Pittsburgh and New York journalism, her insane asylum exposé resulting
in her permanent place on *The World* staff, and her "many and brilliant" achievements in the short two and a half years since, culmi-
nating in the trip which had made her "the best known and most
widely talked-of young woman on earth today. She has worked hard
and she deserves all her success."

Within days, the commercial advantages of Bly's new position
revealed themselves. To help fund the Washington Memorial Arch at

the foot of Fifth Avenue, Bly offered sale of one hundred collector's quality photographs of herself at five dollars each, all proceeds to be donated to the fund. The game was selling. Advertisers clambered to put her name and image on their products. Trade cards carried clever poems and full-color caricatures of Bly in her checked traveling coat.

On Sunday, February 9, she made the first of many lectures in a ninety-minute presentation at New York's Union Square Theatre, surprising everyone with her "modestly self-possessed" delivery and amusing anecdotes. She filled the theater again one week later, having sold out in advance for a highly acclaimed performance in Rochester during the week. *The World* could not understand how the other newspapers in town could be so small-minded as to ignore her success as a lecturer. After all, the newspaper said, she was no longer working for *The World* per se but was taking a well-deserved vacation.

In fact, that "well-deserved vacation" turned into an abrupt and unpleasant departure. Bly, full of herself and furious, left *The World* altogether, vowing she would never be back.

i, the able Washington correspon-
mmercial Gazette, of Cincinnatti, is
few weeks at Bar Harbor. She is
beautiful and wealthy Mrs. Alfred

er has some graceful summer letters
Inquirer.

that the correspondents continue to
books for their descriptive summer
it enough that the railroad should
tation?

hat Mrs. Frederick Rhinelander Jones
g article" from Bar Harbor in a
he World.

Emery is one of the br
men. Her work in th
won her much worthy far

Abbot, the wife of the famous
es an interesting editorial in the
ournal about elopments. She handles
knowingly that one is lead to conjec-
e has ever had any experience in that

ard's mother died a few days ago, and
h insane with grief. Being an un-
n, she had only her mother and her
her.

Harrison is having her portrait
Alfred Barney, of Washington.
le Willis is doing some excellent
he American Press Syndicate.
y fine article on Texan horses by
n, in a recent issue of the Herald, so
e is recreating in the wild's of the
te."

lkins, of the Toledo Bee, is one of the
n in the West. Toledo boasts of over
er women.
woman is Miss Anna A. Gallaner, of
She is about to start a daily paper

n newspaper woman, in a late clever
s just what she likes for breakfast.
ances any tales about newspaper
ing.
Libbey is to be congratulated upon a
the public also to be congratulated?
Sturges has an interview in the paper
a staff writer on newspaper women.
at, and worth digesting.
lie Bly? I don't mean the song, but

uilding is Stonier than ever, now that
n no more is seen. How soon one
fe and is forgotten?
there are any horses in heaven. I
, because so many nice reporters I
y could not live without "tracks."
aven be without the Adonis of News-
e "Victor" of all hearts?
an, of the Tribune, has begun to illus-
hecy of him in an early issue. He
n to the reading public a short story,
e merit of stamping itself upon the

nks, of the Boston Herald is one of
us of American writers. She writes
us" column, and has a hand in editing
zette besides.

MARGHERITA ARLINA HAMM.

NG AGENTS AS I HAVE FOUND
THEM.

N, BUSINESS MANAGER MANSFIELD (O.
EVENING NEWS.

een much said and written about the
e advertising agencies to the country
discussion still goes on.
why the publishers find so much fault
ng agents. They certainly don't have
ous offers for space and the agents

Like the buyer of any other commodity, the agent
buys space at as low a figure as he can. The publisher should control his own space and have business nerve enough to set a fair price on it. If one
advertiser doesn't buy it at that price, sell it to another. If the publisher doesn't possess the selling
ability, let him buy some by employing a man who
has it.

This idea of a man selling space in his paper, and
then forever and ever kicking about the low and
ruinous prices he gets is very tiresome and also
babyish.

It is not the agent's fault if he is successful in beat-
ing down the publisher when the publisher places the

The country publisher is too apt to look at a cheap
offer in the light that if he don't take it the "other
fellow will," so accepts the loss to keep his competitor
from getting it. Another thing he is also known to
do is to count the columns of advertisements and not
the price. Many of them would prefer to have ten
columns of advertisements at a dollar a column
than five columns at three dollars a column.

The advertising agents know this and other points
which work to their advantage and the publisher's
ruin.

During six years as business manager of a successful daily paper I have as yet to receive a "threatening" letter from an advertising agent, and have had
correspondence and dealings with all the leading
houses, and have doubts about the so-called "threatening" letters some publishers have seen fit to write
about.

To be sure the agents tell us if we don't accept
certain offers they will go to the other paper. Nothing wrong about that.

This whole disaffection between th
reputable advertising agent is a di
weak-kneed business policy pursued
themselves when brought in con
shrewd business agent, and all the 1
tions, card writings, annual conferen
tion cannot remedy it. The remedy 1
of the publisher, and any reputabl
what it is and how to apply it.

The Philadelphia Ledger says:
H. Welch, the widow of the lame
Philip H. Welch, is winning laurels |
profession of journalism, which she
hree years ago. For her
ully conducted the Sarat
New York Times, and fo
he department in the Su
that journal known as 'Her Point
department is unique among the 'Wo
which nearly all newspapers carry n
widely quoted from by the press alt
try. Mrs. Welch also writes New Yo
her own signature, which are among
their kind. She also contributes no
the columns of Life, Puck and H
Mrs. Welch is a graduate of the
Gardner School, in New York, and I
one of the most promising and brill
younger generation of newspaper wri

Owing to the disgraceful conduct of
Hinkle, of Ohio, it is probable that Gov
remove him from office and appoint
lowing gentlemen: W. W. Bond, who
tion under Governor Foster; Leo Hir
under Governor Foraker; J. H. M:
Ex—Congressman Enochs back of hin

IN THE GRAND SALOON.

THE STEAMERS

YMOUTH and PROV
— OF THE —
VER LINE

The Famous Business and Pleasure Route between

NEW YORK AND BOSTON,

are conceded to be the largest, handsomest and most perfectly equipped vessels of their class in the
by steam, are lighted throughout by electricity, and in every detail of equipment more than meet all
of the demands of first-class travel.
The Long Island Sound route of the Fall River Line is one of the most attractive highways of t

6

※ ※

Hiatus

B LY LEFT THE NEWSPAPER THAT HAD MADE HER THE MOST talked-about woman in America because what passed for a welcome back from her editors was, in her view, an unjust and galling insult. On August 12, Bly answered a letter from her colleague Frank G. Carpenter, the respected Washington travel writer and columnist, who had asked her to explain why she had left *The World.* She agreed to tell him on condition she not be quoted. Her editors never even said so much as thank you, she confided, let alone offered her any bonus, salary increase, or other reasonable compensation. This was all the more upsetting when the impact her feat had had on the newspaper's revenues was taken into account.

"Pulitzer cabled his congratulations," she wrote, "and begged me to accept a gift he was sending from India. I accepted the congratulations but have never seen the present." A movement was afoot in the office to have a medal struck in her honor, "but," she said, "I have it on good authority that the medal was given as a prize in a telegrapher's contest."

No thanks to *The World,* however, Bly took in $9,500 from her lecture tour, and two real estate men, enamored with her feat, presented her with property lots which she reckoned to be worth at least

$1,500. From *The World*, she said, "I did not receive one cent and my salary had been a very low one." Given how quick Pulitzer was with a bonus check for her insane asylum exposé, it is a fair assumption that something provoked his tightfisted response to her stunning feat.

Bly went on to say she had signed a three-year contract with her publisher, N. L. Munro, to write dime novel fiction in serial install-ments for his weekly *New York Family Story Paper*, at the impressive salary of $10,000 the first year and $15,000 for each of the next two years. This was as much as Cockerill was earning from Pulitzer as one of the nation's highest paid editors. It was a fabulous contract, one Munro, who had not bothered to determine if Bly had the makings of a fiction writer, doubtless lived to regret. It left Bly free to do any noncompeting outside work. She told Carpenter *The World* had given her a standing invitation to return, "but it is needless to add that in face of their shabby treatment of me I shall never do so."

In her private life and business dealings, Bly often relied on the reputation for valiance and credibility she had earned as a young reporter. This perception, coupled with her odd combination of charm and defiant self-righteousness, engendered trust among peo-ple in a position to advance her cause. Even when there was reason to suspect otherwise, Bly's version of events would stand as true, despite whatever slant, coloration, or omissions it might entail.

"Now, my dear Mr. Carpenter," she wrote after describing *The World*'s unforgivable behavior, "This is the story straight but you are at liberty to fix it to suit yourself. I shall back anything you say."

Bly's lecture tour and the preparation for publication of *Nellie Bly's Book: Around the World in Seventy-Two Days* had kept her out of public view for more than six months. During that time, she lost her beloved brother Charles to inflammation of the bowel at the age of twenty-eight. Surviving him were his widow, Sarah, and two small children, young Charles and Gertrude, for whom Bly would assume special responsibility.

By August of 1890, the book's first edition of 10,000 copies had sold out, and Bly busily prepared for the second printing. What actu-ally caused her break with *The World* was never fully spelled out, except in the version she presented to Carpenter, but it is clear the sympathies of the industry, especially its women, for once were with her.

There was one report, for which no documentation could be found, that *The World* behaved so dismissively toward Bly on her return because of a libel suit threatened by the seven doctors whose conflicting diagnoses and prescriptions she had published. Bly's doctor story had appeared in *The World* October 27, 1889, just three weeks before she boarded the *Augusta Victoria.* Pulitzer, who was maniacal about accuracy, had a deathly allergy to libel suits. Placards proclaiming "Accuracy! Terseness! Accuracy!" adorned the city room walls when the new *World* headquarters opened on December 10, 1890. Reporters who committed such offenses as inflating head counts at rallies could expect censure or even a fine. At the same time, they were under enormous pressure to produce colorful and compelling copy. It was a tricky balance to strike. Since Pulitzer's deteriorating health kept him out of the office so much, the publisher had to demand "impeccable reliability" from his editors and reporters, especially on the potentially costly score of legal action. It would stand to reason that if Bly's doctor story had precipitated a libel suit, hurled at the newspaper in the midst of her triumphant world journey, Pulitzer might have been put off the idea of offering her the kind of bonus that would have been within reason for her to expect. Although Bly's own version of why she broke with *The World* makes no mention of a legal wrangle, she wasn't in the habit of disclosing embarrassing details about herself.

By August, with her lecture tour and book behind her, she seemed quite ready to re-create herself in a less frenetic mold. *The World* kept parading through its Sunday columns the exploits of a new group of stunt girls—and sometimes boys. Leading the pack was Bly's old rival, Nell Nelson, who, after her syndicate stint and some writing for the second-tier *Evening World,* was rating personalized headline type in the Sunday paper as prominent as Bly's had been. *The World* kept reaching to fill the chasm Bly had left.

No copies of Munro's *New York Family Story Paper* for the period Bly was under contract are known to have survived, nor does any reference to the magazine during that time. It is therefore not known how many, if any, stories of hers were published or with what success. Two things are sure, however: First, that during the three-year period of her contract, Bly dropped so totally out of public view that colleagues were asking aloud and in print what had happened to her, apparently without reply—"Where is Nellie Bly? I don't mean the song, but the girl," "What is Nellie Bly doing now?"—and second, that her hopes were immense at the outset of her arrangement with Munro but as measured by the events that followed, they were never met.

On August 22, 1890, she wrote to Q.O. in Pittsburgh, having sent him a newspaper notice of the lucrative new contract. She said she already was at work on a story entitled "New York by Night." "Since I'm in luck again, I'm hunting up old friends who seem to have forgotten me," she wrote. She vowed never again to work for a newspaper and told him of her plan to use her position as a writer of serial stories to launch a new career as a novelist without leaving her house. "You know all the great English novelists began in this way, so I hope."

She reminded Q.O. of the stunning success of Henrietta Eliza Vaughan Stannard, whose pen name was John Strange Winter and who got her start writing for the story papers. Mrs. Stannard, who had written forty-two novels by the time she was twenty-seven, sold a half million copies of her 1885 novel, *Bootles' Baby*, which had been turned into a successful stage play in the United States and Europe. "And then Mrs. [Frances Hodgson] Burnett wrote for *The Ledger* until she made a hit as a novelist," Bly said. "So I feel encouraged."

Half a year into the contract, Bly was confined to bed under doctor's orders, only able to hobble around on crutches, due to an injury or ailment she did not name. Her condition was aggravated by an advancing case of depression. She wrote again to Q.O. on January 26, 1891, exactly one year after her record-breaking feat:

> You did neglect me frightfully but I forgive you because you wrote me such a nice letter at last.
>
> I am sitting up and I am writing my first letter in ink to you. It is lovely today and I am feeling so well that if the Pittsburg Press Club had not seen fit to ignore me and had sent me an invitation to the banquet I should be hauled down to the station and start at once for the smoky city. I think it was awfully shabby of them to leave me out but then—I suppose I can live with it.

I would have answered your letter at once but I was trying to catch up with my work and it's so tiresome writing in
bed that I soon played out.

Her letter was written three days before the Pittsburgh Press
Club honored Wilson at its annual dinner. Wilson's pal James Whitcomb Riley wrote a poem for the occasion and recited it. It well con-
veys a sense of the man whose friendship Bly cherished to the end of
her life:

> *'Ras Wilson, I respect you 'cause*
> *You're common like you allus was*
> *Afore you went to town and s'prised*
> *The world by gittin' "recko'nized,"*
> *And yit p'servin', as I say,*
> *Your common hoss-sense ever'way!*

Bly told Wilson how glad she was that he was one who always
hoped for the best. "Life cannot be entirely cheerless while hope
remains," she wrote. "It is a year since I have entertained such a feeling and, strange to say, I have not the least conception why I am, or
should be, blue." The benefit of psychology would have helped Bly
understand the letdown that would follow a switch from the white-
hot center of a bustling journalistic universe that had brought her
global renown unequaled by any reporter into a quiet, probably
lonely isolation, attempting work for which she had enormous
expectations and no demonstrated acumen. Despite the overwhelming national reception for her global feat, she was forced to endure an
equally affecting avalanche of jealous rebuke from her colleagues,
who, like Forman, enjoyed sneering at her every accomplishment.
And she had lost her favorite brother at a terribly young age.

There is also the matter of her love life. Nothing verifiable
about her romantic relations in this period has survived, although
there are repeated references to her in newspapers and gossip
columns as a popular object of male attention. Recall that her former
Pittsburgh colleagues remembered her as "coquettish" and "quite a
favorite with the gentlemen." There was talk, but no concrete evi-

dence, of a liaison with the drama critic James Metcalfe. And there were the published rumors of an engagement to Dr. Frank H. Ingram.

Although earlier she had scoffed at the idea of marriage, her position on the subject seemed to be softening, possibly in part because of her much improved position for landing what she would consider a suitable mate. She even told reporters on her return from the world trip that she needed to continue earning a living "until I fall in love and get married." Yet if there was an amorous side to her relationships with Metcalfe and/or Ingram, nothing came of either of them, and by early 1891 she was nearly twenty-seven, no longer so marriageable.

There were enough possible reasons for Bly's blues for them to spiral into what she described in March of 1891 as "the most frightful depression that can beset [a] mortal." She wrote Q.O. again. "You can imagine how severe it is when I tell you that I have not done a stroke of work for four weeks," she said. "The doctor says it is my blood that is responsible for this languor and weariness, still I am growing fat."

She urged him to come east to visit, see her mementos from the round-the-world trip, and meet her companions—parrot, monkey, and dog—before the inharmonious trio let their hostilities get the better of them and they obliterated one another.

⟨❀⟩

The New York Family Story Paper touted itself as a "lively, interesting and instructive weekly" with "the largest circulation of any family paper published in the world." Munro had begun the paper with a partner, Frank Tousey, inauspiciously on the first day of the Panic of 1873 with the business of publishing inexpensive books already very crowded and competitive. The magazine survived, even though the partnership did not, and stayed in print until 1921, despite several near brushes with financial disaster. Munro's wife, Henrietta, managed the company after his death in 1894.

In his 1926 memoir, Walt McDougall gave a detailed description of Bly's difficulties, recalling how amazed he was that she could accept with "intense complacency" such a splendid offer to write serial fiction when she had "no plot, characters or ability to write dialogue." Friend and colleague that he was, McDougall helped her, suggesting she have the hero or heroine start by falling into a rattlesnake pit and then just go on, week after week, getting him, or her, in and out of similarly terrifying scrapes "until they get married or take out accident insurance, when, of course, the story must stop." Bly was deeply grateful, McDougall recalled. "She went off and that was the last I ever heard about it," he said. "But she started the story off as outlined, and it ran I know not how many weeks."

In the meantime Bly's mother took a five-year lease on a farm in White Plains, perhaps thinking that the rural setting would bring up Bly's mood and creative spirit. Soon after, they left on a pleasure trip to Europe with the same intent. *The Journalist* mentioned Bly's return in an item by Margherita Arlina Hamm that was surprisingly conciliatory, considering the dismissive treatment Bly had thus far received from Allan Forman's weekly. Besides, she seemed to have well and truly left journalism behind and was therefore no longer a competitive threat. Hamm's defense was compelling. Without mentioning names, she condemned those, presumably like Forman and apparently many others among Bly's colleagues, who had maligned both her sensation writing and her unparalleled success. Hamm said these detractors had caused Bly "much unnecessary suffering."

"Miss Bly was always faithful, authentic and clever in her work," Hamm acknowledged, "and she certainly accomplished what

Masthead of The Family Story Paper

(Library of Congress)

no other woman has been able to." Hamm also said Bly deserved "a great deal of credit" for her "detective work," adding, with information that could only have come from Bly herself, that "a failure of health and strength" had forced her to give it up.

Bly, in her published statements, had generally liked to portray herself as a paragon of robust vitality, that plucky girl investigator whom nothing could stop. She had referred in print to the headaches she frequently suffered—once, for the sake of tripping up the New York physicians she investigated for *The World*, again on her arrival in London, and again in retelling the story of lunch in the Temple of the Dead. By this point, a year into the ill-fated Munro contract, those Victorian afflictions of mysterious origin had become part of even her public self-story.

Hamm went on to recall the miserable way *The World* had treated Bly, adding that such slights to women had become all too commonplace.

In the few short years since Bly's arrival on Newspaper Row, more and more women had made space for themselves in newspaper columns all over the country and soon began to clamor for equal opportunity. They bristled under the rigid prejudice that kept them, with the notable exception of the stunt girls, peg-posted to the women's pages. One real problem was the unprofessional behavior that some of their number actually displayed—enough in such a standout minority to saddle the rest with a stereotype that would take nearly a century to live down. Another was the prevailing vision of enlightenment: The newsroom was a crude, tobacco-stained, white male environment, and any outsider seeking entry would simply have to adjust. There was plenty for the women to complain about—even each other.

So, in the late 1880s and early 1890s, although the reality in newspaper life hadn't changed much for women, the climate for discussion certainly had. Bly led only by example. Her unfettered success, held up repeatedly, emboldened her colleagues in their own demands for greater professional leeway.

Not long after Bly's return from her world trip, there were enough women reporters in place across the country for *The Journalist* to drop its annual "Women in Journalism" issue in favor of a near-weekly column. The issues changed, too. No longer was the focus on getting the industry to open its doors enough to give women a chance. They had their chance, such as it was. The discussion now centered on what was happening to women once they got inside.

Mary Twombly, writing in August 1889, confessed that the easiest, indeed nearly the only way to break into the field was writing for the women's page. Although Bly's success with more general themes had its imitators, the growing majority of women reporters kept their subject matter "soft." Twombly urged the newcomers not to fight it but to make the best of it, to dress handsomely if they were covering fashion and to learn as much about varieties of flora and lace as they would a bill wending through the legislature: "Lapses in trifles like these not only tell against yourself, but lower the prestige of your calling and co-workers generally."

Twombly also felt it necessary to warn her colleagues not to let society women, reformers, or social workers manipulate them into promoting their various events or causes. Smile blandly and say nothing, Twombly advised. To enter journalism as what she called "a missionary" would only result in "a speedy ticket to leave." Bly, a congenital feminist, instinctively understood this valuable tenet. Her contribution to suffrage, which she certainly supported, was by example alone. As passionate as she was about issues of female concern, and as often as she wrote about them, she kept her journalistic bearings.

Thomas F. Anderson, writing for *The Journalist*, confessed that the male members of the profession greeted the arrival of women in the newsroom with outrage and disdain. "Now," he said, as if bestowing some generous compliment, "she is an indispensable reality, joyfully hailed as the deliverer of mankind from the horrors of high weddings, dry goods openings, woman suffrage conventions and fashionable balls." Anderson went on, "In the main, she is aggressively ambitious, a hard and conscientious worker, a paragon of persistency and—a woman." As a class, he said in another backhanded accolade, his woman colleagues were always ladies first, and newspaper workers second.

The writer W. T. Stead was much more farsighted. He wrote in the magazine *Young Woman* that any young woman who thought she might find a place in the field better do it as a journalist first, without reference to gender. "A woman who comes into journalism and expects to be excused anything because of her sex lowers, by the extent of that excuse, the reputation and worth of women in journalism," he said, adding that she better quickly get accustomed to the idea of foul language, scathing editorial scoldings, disgusting assignments, and late, unchaperoned nights. "You have a right to ask that your sex should not be regarded as a disqualification," he said, "but it is monstrous to erect that accident of your personality into a right to have opportunities denied to your brother."

It was not the opportunities denied her brothers that Margherita Arlina Hamm appealed for in *The Journalist* of May 28, 1892, but the same ones. Editors were still highly reluctant to entrust crime or disaster reporting to women. "It [is] a fact based on experience and supported by ample illustration," Hamm asserted, "that in the portrayal of crime or disaster, a clever, versatile and persistent newspaperwoman can more than hold her own with the opposite sex." As examples of those who had demonstrated this ability, Hamm named Julia Hayes Percy, Nell Nelson, and, of course, Bly.

The Atlanta Constitution, in tribute to Maria "Middy" Morgan, the respected livestock reporter of *The New York Times* who died in the spring of 1892, extolled the position on newspapers that women had managed to attain:

> It is admitted by everybody that the newspaper woman does better work than her male competitors on the society and fashion pages of the great dailies. Nelly [*sic*] Bly has shown that a woman can make her mark as a traveling correspondent and as a special writer. Margaret Sullivan stands in the front rank of editorial writers.
>
> Still, there is the general impression that the newspaper woman is confined to a narrow field. Perhaps this is a mistake.

The piece went on to say that even though some people might find a woman "unsexed" by the act of writing "political editorials, graphic letters of travel on a flying trip around the world, descriptions of slum life and first-class reports of horse races and cattle-markets, . . . in these days a woman must live, and it is much better for her to live by honest industry—brain-work or hand-work—than to give up in despair."

Salary levels for women in journalism varied but in nearly all cases were well under those of men. An article in *The Minneapolis Tribune* in the fall of 1892 reported that a few women journalists in New York had reached a salary of eighty dollars a week while "there are hundreds whose pay is $10 and even less. A fair average would be $12, but women who write and are paid by the column not infrequently earn $30 per week." Bly's salary at *The World* was never disclosed, but N. L. Munro, the story paper publisher, was paying her nearly $200 a week to start, an extraordinary sum. Albert Payson Terhune, for example, joined *The Evening World* in 1894 at $15 a week. By 1899, his weekly wage was $35.

Women in the newsroom were under scrutiny for "unfraternal" behavior toward each other—the catfighting Twombly described as "their willingness to undermine and supersede each other, and the uncharitableness towards beginners of those who are securely placed." On this score, there is little doubt that Bly, in her brief career, weighed in as both victimizer and victimized, given the friction with Bessie Bramble, Ella Wheeler Wilcox, Nell Nelson, Elizabeth Bisland, and others over the years.

Twombly said the best excuse for "the little meannesses is the pitifully narrow groove to which women are generally confined," shunted to the side as if they were some "necessary but illy defined adjunct of the press." This channel made it difficult to figure out the female hierarchy. For male reporters, it was a neatly laid out scheme of title and position. Men could vie for stature within an established and accepted framework. Not so for women, who were still a puny, amorphous minority.

"Consequently," Twombly said, "she who least understands her own value and place is often the most prone by word and action to make the most impossible claim for herself." And just to make things worse, the "lower" rather than the "higher" feminine contribution to the field always seemed to get the most attention. She did not elucidate on which was which.

Eliza D. Keith, a San Francisco writer known in print as Di Vernon, found it necessary to define for her colleagues just who could legitimately claim the appositive "newspaper woman" and who had no place in the breed. She assailed the dilettantes who fancied themselves reporters because newspapers, desperate for filler, would sometimes print without payment their flowery party notes. "Bah!" Keith ranted, indicating the just pride bona fide initiates took in their demanding craft. "Scribblers, writers, authors, anything but members of the press."

Friction also chafed relations between the more senior women in the field and their younger, more progressive counterparts. By the spring of 1892, the latter group had gone so far as to call for a second women's press club, since the now staid original group, controlled by the venerable Jennie June, was unresponsive to their needs.

Jennie June, pen name for Mrs. David (Jane Cunningham) Croly, was newspaperdom's dowager queen. She started Sorosis, America's first all-women's club, and later the Women's Press Club. As Jennie June, she effectively invented women's interest news for the daily newspapers in the 1850s and was credited with being the first woman ever actually to work in the newsroom. Over a forty-year career, she established herself as the grande dame of news about fashion and home, an achievement, to be sure.

But forty years had passed. There was no denying a very perceptible movement toward change. If nothing else, by the time the Gay Nineties got under way, the image of a woman on the job was altogether new. The name now synonymous with woman reporter was no longer Jennie June. It was Nellie Bly.

❧

During the years after Bly's abrupt departure from *The World*, Pulitzer kept his managers off balance in a dizzying game of editorial musical chairs. Acting on sometimes unreliable reports from informants inside the newspaper, Pulitzer, from his yacht or exclusive vacation spots, never allowed anyone to forget who was really in charge. By May of 1891, the men on *The World* to whom Bly—and Pulitzer, for that matter—owed the most, editor Colonel John A. Cockerill and business manager George W. Turner, were gone. Pulitzer, feeling his two lieutenants had gotten too lax, too full of themselves and their authority, fired Turner outright and ordered Cockerill back to *The St. Louis Post-Dispatch*, from which he had come. Cockerill, one of the most respected figures in New York journalism, quit in protest. Within two weeks, he had taken over *The Daily Continent*, the morning edition of *The Commercial Advertiser.*

In the months and years that followed, it would have taken a scorecard to keep track of who was running which department at the paper on any given day. Ballard Smith stayed on as acting editor-in-chief until August of the following year. E. A. Grozier, who had been managing editor of *The Evening World*, and editor of *The Sunday World*, was sent downstairs as business manager. The youthful Julius Chambers was sent over to head up the Sunday staff. Morrill Goddard became *The World's* city editor but soon shifted into other posts. And that was just to start.

The gossipy *Town Topics* seized on rumors that, by November of 1891, Pulitzer was vainly trying to win Cockerill and Turner back: "The loss of their service becomes daily more painfully apparent in the paper, until it would seem that they could not refuse to return out of very pity." The magazine was particularly critical of Smith, who, it said, "wobbles about in the editorial chair in a truly ridiculous manner, and keeps everybody wondering what *The World* will do next to stultify itself." His ouster came less than a year later. The positions kept changing; other names were added to the power roster, among them John Norris, S. S. Carvalho, and F. F. Burgin.

In the meantime, young Arthur Brisbane had been making his mark as editor of the evening edition of *The New York Sun* after his return from a highly successful stint in London as the newspaper's correspondent. By December of 1891, Pulitzer had lured him to *The World*, where he started out doing special work—interviews, squibs in the Saturday editions about what would be in the Sunday paper, and reports to Pulitzer about his co-workers, as they would, in turn, send notes about him. It was a common practice among *World* reporters and editors, one Pulitzer did nothing to discourage. Brisbane rose steadily in estimation and rank.

The newspaper, however, was still in editorial chaos. Circulation on the daily paper stood below its previous highs, and there had been a series of mortifying blunders. A published interview with John Roff, a boat pilot who had been dead for a year before the interview ran, was not the worst of them.

By August of 1892, Pulitzer dethroned acting editor Ballard Smith because of his inappropriate editorial handling of the violent worker lockout at Andrew Carnegie's huge Homestead steel mill. The newspaper, in editorials and reporting, came out heavily on the side of the workers who had charged the plant and taken possession. Smith was roundly criticized for propounding anarchy. When the company sent 300 Pinkerton guards to try to recapture the plant, the workers routed them with dynamite, missiles, and bullets, leaving ten dead and sixty wounded. When word got to Pulitzer of what Smith had done, he ordered a complete about-face in *The World's* position—and Smith's as well. The editor was out.

With the departure of Smith, all the men who had molded the newspaper into greatness were gone. George B. M. Harvey, the fair-haired boy whom Pulitzer had appointed managing editor two years before at age twenty-seven, assumed Smith's duties. By October 22, *The World* had fired twenty-five reporters, most of them men loyal to Ballard Smith. By December, *The Journalist* gossiped that "everybody in the *World* office feels like a jelly-fish, with the possible exception of [finance czar S. S.] Carvalho" and that things were worse for *World* reporters than for those on any other paper in the city. "The men are today on salary, tomorrow on space, now doing night work then assigned to day work and, of all press men, they are really the most miserable."

Nonetheless, when the tenth anniversary of Pulitzer's purchase of *The World* came around on May 10, 1893, the publisher and his staff had plenty to celebrate. To honor the date, a hundred-page colossus was published in which *The World* bragged about its every technological, architectural, and editorial advance. *Town Topics* immediately slammed it as "an exhibition of incomparable cheek," the way it "flopped on to our breakfast tables last Sunday like a big halibut, and was just a little less interesting than that creature before it is cooked."

Still, what was significant about the issue in this connection was its year-by-year synopsis, carried on ten consecutive pages, one for each year, in which the newspaper's most outstanding editorial achievements were summarized for the period of Pulitzer proprietorship. In the recounting of dozens of the newspaper's most remarkable exploits in the name of public service, only one reporter is credited by name for work performed on the paper's behalf. That same reporter's name appears on three different pages, once for each year she served on Pulitzer's staff. It was, of course, Bly, cited for her madhouse exposé, her unmasking of the Albany lobbyist Edward Phelps, and her trip around the world.

Considering the inconsequential position of most women on newspapers in general, considering that almost all Bly's colleagues on *The World* had moved on, considering that she herself had been off the staff and virtually out of public view for three full years when the issue was published, the tribute was sound testimony to the name she had made for herself against daunting odds both within and outside the industry.

Perhaps it was this retelling of her successes that got the new *World* elite excited about the possibility of inviting her back. Perhaps it was Bly seeing how warmly she was remembered who encouraged them to do so. Either way, for Bly the timing could not have been more opportune.

Since April, *The World* had been reported to be on a new hiring spree, "reaching out for good men to strengthen its staff." The campaign had resulted in the hiring of, among others, the respected *New York Sun* reporter David Graham Phillips.

At this time, Mary Jane Cochrane's lease on the farm in White Plains still had two years to run. Bly was enjoying her country weekends immensely but probably was ready for something to occupy her time more completely. The European tour and her restful new surroundings seem to have helped snap her out of despondency. Nothing else seems to have been going very well for her at the time: There was no money coming in, except Mary Jane's modest dower; abject inability had crushed her dreams of becoming a novelist; and at almost thirty, Bly's prospects for finding a husband had narrowed considerably. (If the rumors of her engagement to Dr. Frank Ingram back in 1890 had any basis, that relationship was fatefully doomed. In March of 1893, at the age of thirty-three, Ingram died of a heart attack, described in his obituary as angina pectoris.)

On August 1, 1893, Pulitzer made the decision to hand over the editorship of *The World* to a forty-five-year-old outsider, Colonel Charles H. Jones, an act he would soon regret. Jones showed appallingly poor judgment in two significant editorial episodes. Everyone resented him. Pulitzer understood his error and curtailed Jones's authority almost immediately. Carvalho was furious. Harvey ultimately resigned. A year later, Pulitzer was forced to suspend Jones outright and then, after complicated, costly negotiations, induced him to return to St. Louis.

With so much consternation at the highest editorial echelon, authority inevitably spiraled downward. By September of 1893, Morrill Goddard, the respected city editor who had already done his share of moving around the organization, took charge of the profitable Sunday edition. Richard A. Farrelly moved into the city editor slot. A new typeface was introduced. Goddard, a Dartmouth graduate not yet thirty, was a master of sensations mysterious or gritty, sexual or criminal. For coming up with feature ideas, he had no equal, often developing assignments from his own reading of an unnoticed paragraph in some obscure column. A great believer in the power of illustration, Goddard was able to use pictures to startling advantage. If the Sunday supplements hadn't already existed, they would have been invented for him.

Almost his first order of business was to offer a job to Nellie Bly. She accepted. Realist that she was, it was not an opportunity she could afford to ignore. Times were bad, and her ill-fated contract with Munro had ended. She no doubt missed the limelight. This time, she took pains in her negotiations to make sure she would be going back on her own terms—as a columnist. Although a long-standing offer from a Chicago newspaper still stood, New York was home. She had no desire to leave, even for a good job. If she were going to return to reporting in the biggest city, *The World* was the best place for her to work.

Part Three

1893–1914

The W...

"Circulation Books Open to All."

VOL. XXXIV. NO. 11,716.   PRICE FIVE CENTS.   NEW YORK, SUNDAY, SEPTEMBER 17, 1893.

NELLIE BLY AGAIN.

Interviews Emma Goldman and Other Anarchists.

WHAT JUSTUS H. SCHWAB AND JOHN MOST SAY OF CAPITAL.

Their Ideas of Marriage Do Away with All Ceremony.

SCHWAB'S WEDDING SERVICE READS, "HERE'S TO YOU."

Favor Freedom In Everything In Their Sucts—Emma Goldman's Opinion of the Woman Who Is Married and the Mother—What She Cares About the Wealthy and the Poor—Why There Are Criminals—If Everything Were Free, She Says, There Would Be No Criminals—Emma Goldman Speaks Russian, German, French and English, and Reads and Writes Spanish and Italian—Schwab Talks About His Wife and Smart Children.

JUSTUS H. SCHWAB.

EMMA GOLDMAN.

JOHN MOST.

PRESENT AND FUTURE RAILR...

THE TICKET AGENT   THE GATEMAN   THE CONDUCTOR

ARMOR-CLAD CASH CAR

McDOUGALL

THE HOPE OF THE FUTURE.

THE CANDY BOY   THE PORTER   THE...

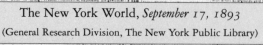

7

Comeback

ON SEPTEMBER 17, 1893, AS IF SHE HADN'T SKIPPED A BEAT, Bly scorched *The World's* front page with an illustrated jail-house interview with the anarchist Emma Goldman. The placement and display were the best a reporter could hope for; the headline, even better:

NELLIE BLY AGAIN.

She Interviews Emma Goldman

and Other Anarchists

No other American newspaperwoman could command such name recognition among readers or such glorification from her editors—and after three years out of newsprint. More than half a century later, leading women reporters would still be complaining about the edi-torial barrier that kept them from "making the front page." Bly managed repeatedly to violate this unwritten restriction. Unfortu-nately for her female successors, she had not unbolted the shackles of gender; she only slipped through them.

Although her years away from reporting had not diminished Bly's celebrity, they had played havoc with her signature technique. The most sophisticated members of the craft had very little patience for the souped-up snooping so closely associated with sensationalism which Bly had pioneered. Whatever glamour and novelty it once had long since had worn off from overexposure. Women reporters who had vied for the opportunity to emulate Nellie Bly began to see the kinds of assignments that evoked her name as degrading and déclassé. Without much choice if they wanted to stay off the women's pages, many continued to perform the feats of daring their editors would order up, and for much of the new decade, but they did so with greater and greater reluctance. In the fall of 1892, a year before Bly came out of repose, Margherita Arlina Hamm had already decried the "low grade of sensationalism" to which women in journalism had dropped, writing as they were with "the tinge of extravagance" that "lacks the essence of truth."

Shortly after Bly's return, the magazine *Town Topics* condemned *The World*'s practice of "employing women to degrade and humiliate themselves in order that they might write their experiences for its diseased pages." The gossip sheet cited in particular a recent article in *The World* in which a girl reporter, Dolores Marbourg, had posed as a street flower vendor to see what the life was like. At one point, she positioned herself outside the Union Club, where at least one distinguished and married gentleman, whom she did not name, propositioned her. *Town Topics* was outraged: "There is only one more step for Joe Pulitzer's crew of editors to take, and that is to employ a virtuous girl to go into a house of bad repute and write the story for the Sunday issue. Everything else has been done."

It is entirely plausible that this particular stunt stung the writers at *Town Topics* because it put the male members of its highborn readership at embarrassing risk. All the same, their response was further evidence of a deepening intolerance of stunt writing. This was not lost on Bly, who had always sought the respect of her colleagues, if not their admiration for her work. Indeed, her stunts usually avoided the demeaning quality of this one.

The distinctions are more than hairsplitting. Bly did not set up fishing expeditions for scandal; nor did her early work project the undesirable quality of stunt-for-stunt's-sake. Instead, she targeted specific situations or individuals in an effort to right wrongs, to explain the unexplored, to satisfy curiosity about the intriguing, to expose unfairness, or to catch a thief.

Her stunts were rarely frivolous or spurious in concept. Even when she donned tutu and tights to pose as a chorus girl, it was to examine what life was like for the young women who chose one of the few paths open to them for making a living. Although her technique of using disguises or false representation has long been discredited on ethical grounds as an inappropriate journalistic tool, this was by no means the case in her time. Bly distinguished her work with a style of ersatz investigation that her imitators could never quite match. Of all the "stunt girls" spawned by the New Journalism, it is little surprise that she built the legacy that has endured. She was not just one of the first, she was the best.

Bly had taken pains to win her new editors' agreement to give her a column of her own as well as wide latitude for special assignments. It was yet to be seen if she could hold them to their word.

Initially, her reappearance as a journalist provoked what might pass for enthusiasm among her New York colleagues. *The Journalist* announced her return to *The World* in a blind item:

Nelly [*sic*] Bly, of round-the-world fame, lunatic asylum experiences and other sensational doings, is back on *The New York World*. She has not been in a convent during the last three years, but only in a strange garret. When through her indomitable pluck with the assistance of *The World,* she awoke to find herself famous, she forgot that her successes were only in the line of doing odd things and that literary merit had little to do with them. Perhaps her bonnet did not fit; at any rate, she accepted an offer to write for the *Family Story Paper,* and *The World* dropped her. She made a good bargain financially, getting, I believe, $8,000 a year, but she can't write fiction and her work for Munro has been an expensive luxury for them. Now she comes back to *The World* to make her name over again. She has learned much during the interval that should be of service to her. Her command of language is improved; she is more of a woman of the world; and she has a better idea of what the public will read.

ᴄᴿᴀᴷᴺ

The Panic of 1893, set off by the failures of four major railroad companies and the National Cordage Company, spun the nation into its worst economic crisis in more than fifty years. By fall, hundreds of thousands of laboring people had lost their jobs. New York teemed with the hungry and idle. *The World* responded by starting its own bread fund, a promotional campaign that provided the newspaper with weeks of reportable pathos and opportunities for self-congratulation. The labor movement wrestled with how much of the socialist agenda being pushed by Samuel Gompers's rivals should be incorporated into the principles of craft unionism. And New York police, anxious to quell the rising unrest, turned attention to the city's anarchists, whose inflammatory oratory in meetings day after day exacerbated tension in an already fraught atmosphere.

The World could not have contrived a better vehicle than Emma Goldman's troubles with the law to bring back its own girl wonder. "Nellie Bly Among the Anarchists," Arthur Brisbane wrote in the Saturday promotional blurb advertising his pick of seven Sunday features to be printed the next day: "Who they are and how they live, what their hopes and plans are and what they say and do in their secret conferences. The mere announcement that this clever writer [Bly] is again in active service for *The World* is guarantee of original and venturesome undertakings."

Bly filled seven columns of type with her consideration of the three major "sympathizers, promoters and agitators" for open struggle between "capital and labor, the masses and the classes, between the rich men and the poor." She profiled the twenty-five-year-old Goldman as well as Johann Most, with whom Goldman was at odds, and Justus Schwab, the saloon keeper whose tavern served as social headquarters for the city's radical leaders.

"Do you need an introduction to Emma Goldman?" Bly asked. She took her readers into The Tombs, where she found her subject awaiting release on bail after pleading not guilty to three counts of incitement to riot. The charges stemmed from newspaper reports and detectives' notes on three incendiary speeches Goldman had delivered, including one particularly impassioned address to a protest rally in Union Square on August 21. *The World,* as it happened, had reported on the rally at length. Four days later, a warrant was issued for Goldman's arrest. New York detectives traced her to Philadelphia, seized her outside a mass meeting, and arranged for her extradition back to the city several days later.

"You have seen supposed pictures of her," Bly wrote of her youthful subject. "You have read of her as a property-destroying, capitalist-killing, riot-promoting agitator. You see her in your mind a great raw-boned creature with short hair and bloomers, a red flag in one hand, a burning torch in the other; both feet constantly off the ground and murder continually upon her lips."

Instead, Bly, clearly taken with Goldman's passion and sincerity, provided an unusual and highly sympathetic portrait. She punctured the notion that anarchists had some perverse fascination with filth—reporters favored referring to them as an "unwashed mass"—describing Goldman as neat, immaculate, and well-dressed in a "modest blue serge Eton suit." While *The New York Times* referred to Goldman as "the fire-eating anarchist," Bly sweetly dubbed her "the little anarchist, the modern Joan of Arc." Bly described Goldman as a "little bit of a girl, just 5 feet high, . . . not showing her 120 pounds; with a saucy, turned-up nose and very expressive blue-gray eyes that gazed inquiringly at me through shell-rimmed glasses." She gave Goldman and her colleagues full forum to expound on their most controversial ideas. The subjects ranged from marriage to murder.

Under Bly's questioning, the anarchist sketched out her early history: her birth in Russia [Lithuania], her upbringing in Germany, her siblings, her ill-fated marriage before the age of seventeen. She broadly outlined the evils of capitalism: how it made the poor seem lazy; how it promoted crime.

Bly asked Goldman what she thought should replace the institution of marriage. "The marriage of affection," Goldman replied. "That is the only true marriage. If two people care for each other, they have a right to live together so long as that love exists. When it is dead, what base immorality for them still to keep together."

Bly raised concern that unbinding marriage might lead to men deserting their children. Goldman disagreed. "And if a couple decided to separate," she offered, "there would be public homes and schools for the children. Mothers who would rather do something else than care for their children could put them in the schools, where they would be cared for by women who preferred taking care of children to, say, other work." The schools would be free, she said, and would promote development of the talents of every child, regardless of ability to pay.

Outright, Bly asked, "Do you think murder is going to help your cause?" The question was an obvious reference to the attempted murder of millionaire Henry Frick by Goldman's close compatriot Alexander Berkman after the deadly Homestead Steel Company lockout the preceding summer. Frick, as plant manager, had called out the rifle-toting Pinkerton guards, escalating the violence and earning the enmity of his employees. For Berkman, the situation presented what he perceived to be an opportunity for the first American *attentat,* that is, political assassination as an instrument of workers' revolution.

Goldman pondered the question, looked grave, Bly said, and then shook her head slowly: "That is a long subject to discuss. I don't believe that through murder we shall gain, but by war, labor against capital, masses against classes, which will not come in 20 or 25 years. But some day, I firmly believe we shall gain and until then I am satisfied to agitate, to teach, and I only ask justice and freedom of speech."

Goldman's trial lasted four days. At 5:05 P.M. on October 10, 1893, she was convicted on one count of incitement to riot and sentenced to a year in the women's prison on Blackwell's Island. Many years later, she still maintained her innocence, claiming that it had never been her intention to incite the unemployed to violence; that the conviction had resulted from a newspaper reporter's account of her speech that had been badly muddled by his editors at *The World*, and that she had done no more than urge the hungry to public demonstration in order to obtain what was rightfully theirs.

On the matter of the *World* report, Goldman, in her autobiography, recalled that the jury had been "loath to convict" and that it had seemed especially impressed with the testimony of one of her witnesses, an unnamed reporter for *The World* who had covered the Union Square rally. "When he saw his story in the paper the following morning, it was so garbled that he had at once offered to testify to the actual facts," Goldman wrote. While the reporter was on the witness stand, she said, a court attendant was sent out and soon returned with a copy of *The World* for the day in question. She went on: "The reporter could not charge some desk editor in open court with having tampered with his account. He became embarrassed, confused and obviously very miserable. His report as printed in the *World*, and not as testified to by him on the witness stand, decided my fate. I was found guilty."

On the day of Goldman's sentencing, her comrade Edward Brady informed her that *The World* had offered to carry in full—in a special edition distributed immediately after sentencing—the text of the speech she had prepared to read in court. Because of the many readers the newspaper was bound to reach, Goldman agreed. Still, she said, "I wondered that *The World*, which had carried a falsified report of my Union Square speech, should now offer to publish my statement. Ed [Brady] said that there was no accounting for the inconsistencies of the capitalist press."

As interesting as the anecdote is, Goldman apparently remembered the wrong newspaper. The embarrassed reporter was from the *Staats-Zeitung*.

Bly did not involve herself with the ins and outs of her newspaper's coverage of Emma Goldman over on the city desk. Her job had been to meet the woman, interview her, evaluate her impressions, and report them. Nothing more. Her sympathetic portrait implied no personal politics.

❦

Bly followed the interview with Emma Goldman with her first "very own" personal column for *The World*. The pen-sketched logo depicted her in a girlish pose under a fetching straw bowler, her portrait in an oval frame festooned with flowers and bows. In large outline letters, Bly's name unfurled from a banner above the drawing and beneath, set in type, were the words "Nellie Bly's Column." To have such a space allotment in which to parcel out opinions on whatever she felt like discussing squared perfectly with Bly's considerable sense of self. If she wasn't cut out for literature, the life of a columnist would do just fine. And so she informed her readers in her opening remarks:

> This is all my own.
>
> Herein every Sunday I may say all I please and what I please.
>
> Is it not a joy?
>
> It is one of the very sweet rights that come to an editor and owner of a newspaper, and although I am not an editor and only own the newspaper I buy from a boy still that joy is mine.
>
> Of course, my regular articles on various topics will appear from time to time, but in them I cannot write the little things that interest me and will, I hope, interest those who care to read my contributions. Of course, if you don't like me, the caption at the head of my column will warn you to leave this and go on to something else.

Most of the items were tedious. She wrote of why people have intense likes or dislikes for strangers, about pepper pots, about the new bells on the cable cars, about walking her dog, a little Maltese named Duke, along Twenty-fifth Street. One of the better items was about her namesake, the race horse Nellie Bly, and how a man who went to place a bet on the horse at the track at Sheepshead Bay was stopped by his wife, who warned him against it. "I hate her," the wife said of the human Bly, whom she did not know personally and who overheard the outburst. "I hated her when she was going around the world, and I've always hated her."

"Poor horse!" was Bly's rejoinder. "I felt so sorry for the poor, innocent beast, a beauty she is, too, that I doubled my bet on her out of sheer pity, and she won!"

Sadly, the seven years since her failed attempt at being a columnist at *The Pittsburg Dispatch* had done nothing to enhance Bly's ability to structure her ho-hum personal reflections into compelling paragraphs. Her editors realized this at once. Perhaps she did, too. The effort was buried on a deep inside page of the second Sunday feature section. Despite the trumpeting of its elaborate display and the promise in her introduction, "Nellie Bly's Column" never appeared again.

Morrill Goddard, who was running the Sunday feature section at the time, immediately directed Bly back to what she did best. It was just as well. *The Journalist* was quick to comment on the state of play at the city's largest circulation daily:

> Morrill Goddard of the *World* has been transferred from the city desk to the Sunday paper and [Richard] Farrelly is now city editor. [Arthur] Brisbane is doing interviewing and so is Nellie Bly. Col. [George B. M.] Harvey is in charge of the Washington bureau. Col. [Charles H.] Jones is editor-in-chief and the paper has a new dress of type. The new dress is very neat and trim and up-to-date.

Brisbane, himself destined for greatness in the field, watched Bly work with admiration. It was no mean distinction that colleagues both in and outside the newspaper would see fit to summon her name in company with highly regarded male members of the profession. Brisbane admired her pluck, her ingenuity, her doggedness, and the originality of her approach. A warm friendship based on mutual respect developed between the two.

On October 1, while Dolores Marbourg was telling *The World's* readers how flower vendors were forced to fend off the advances of prominent men, Bly led the feature report with a detailed account and comment on her inquiry into the workings of the Salvation Army. It began:

> I have been devoting myself to the Salvation Army for the last 10 days.

Arthur Brisbane, 1906
(The Bettmann Archive)

I began with an idea that it was some sort of a nonsen-
sical hullabaloo, run by a lot of fanatics incidentally for the
amusement of the curious, primarily for the financial benefit
of the chosen few.

I end—how?

I don't know. I can only tell, without an[y] frills, precisely what I saw.

I am without prejudice. Others may judge. I do not
care to.

Her visit to Salvation Army headquarters left her with several
questions she shared with her readers: If the purpose of this army was
helping the poor, why were there two quality grades of uniforms for
members to buy? Why did the army members have to buy the uniforms in the first place? Why did the organization charge its members
sometimes twice the going market price for items, such as watches,
available through its own distribution network? What were the lead-

ers doing with all the money they earned from trade and in-house publications? She didn't answer the questions, nor did she come to any conclusions about the organization. But there was authority to her work, even though, as usual, her reporting stopped short of seeking documentation to support her innuendos or even giving the courtesy of forum for rebuttal to officials of the organization.

She was at her best in describing her night at the army's food and shelter mission. As always, she injected herself fully into every scene, making the fact of her presence essential to the telling. She wound up buying one unemployed old man a week's worth of lodging for forty-nine cents to keep him from sleeping in the cold. She scolded the drunk who had let his friend buy him a beer instead of a bed, but then broke down and staked him two cents when she realized the street was his only alternative lodging. In gratitude, he offered to stay sober for a year, but Bly, long familiar with the ways of drinking men, was not fooled. In parting, she put up two dollars to cover breakfast the next morning for the more than sixty men in the shelter that night. Shenanigans at headquarters notwithstanding, Bly was clearly moved by what she had witnessed. Still, she warned her readers:

> Don't let my story move your heart to send it a lot of money. A few pennies, rightly given, does more good than dollars donated foolishly.
>
> I don't want you to send money to the Salvation Army Headquarters. Put on your old clothes, and when a cold night comes, go down to Front Street and watch those unhappy wretches come in. If they have no seven cents, give it for them. Don't give more. If you have work for them, blessed thing: clothes, good; but money given only pauperizes.

Five days later, by an act of what she described as editor persuasion, Bly traveled to Saratoga for the New York State Democratic Convention. Her assignment: to meet and report how she was treated by The Tiger, the nickname for the political chieftains of Democratic Party headquarters at Tammany Hall. Walt McDougall, the cartoonist, provided a wonderful illustration, portraying Bly

Detail from Bly's report on State Democratic Convention at Saratoga,
The World, *October 8, 1893*

(General Research Division, The New York Public Library)

with her tiny waist tightly cinched under a handsome ruffle-collared jacket. She was leading away a huge tiger, docile and cowering, by its broken chain.

The story is pure Bly, confident, unintimidated, acting her role as celebrity reporter in the company of powerful men: in short, her idea of a very good time. At the convention she met some of the most important sprockets in the Tammany machine: New York State Assembly Speaker William Sulzer, Charles Marrin of Harlem, Judge Daniel F. McMahon, Wiskinkie Donegan, and Tim Campbell.

Central to her story is what each of them thought of meeting her. (From Donegan: "What! Are you Nellie Bly? The real Nellie Bly? Why, bless me. I thought you were as big as Tom Brennan because I never thought a little thing could do what you've done. Come in, won't you, and see headquarters.") It was a practice her colleagues found infuriatingly indulgent. Her introductions at the Saratoga convention led her to follow up the next week by meeting her new political acquaintances again, this time back in the city, in Tammany Hall itself, for more conversations.

Enough of politics. An accused triple murderess awaited trial in the Sullivan County jail at Monticello, New York.

Authorities in the hamlet of Burlingham, in Walker Valley near the lonely Shawangunk Mountains, had arrested Eliza "Lizzie" Brown Halliday in September for the grisly slaying of her husband, Paul, along with Mrs. Margaret McQuillan and her daughter, Sarah Jane. It was a case for which *World* reporter Edwin Atwell contrived this exhalation: "From its circumstances, origin, conception and execution; its unique characteristics, the abnormal personalities and peculiar localities it involves, and, above all, in the strangeness and mystery of its great central figure, [it] is unprecedented and almost without parallel in the annals of crime."

Neighbors, suspicious about Paul Halliday's whereabouts, maneuvered Lizzie out of the house and conducted a search for their longtime neighbor. In the barn, under a pile of hay, they found the bullet-riddled bodies of both McQuillan women, the older already decomposing. Halliday's body, buried under the kitchen floorboards, was not unearthed for another two days.

Paul Halliday was in his sixties, twice widowed and once divorced when, through an employment service, he found Lizzie Brown and brought her home to keep his house. Soon he married the strange woman, forty years his junior—the neighbors said to avoid paying her wages. She wasn't well received in the peculiar little community. Neighbors thought she was a gypsy. They gossiped she had started the fire that burned down the Halliday home some years before and, in the process, killed Halliday's half-witted son from one of his previous marriages.

She had once been arrested for stealing a team of horses and taking them to another county to sell. At her trial on those charges, Lizzie Halliday put on such a bizarre and convincing performance that the judge had her committed to an asylum. She was soon pronounced cured, released, and sent back to her husband. Neighbors said she often bragged that her ability to appear crazy put her above the law. As soon as the bodies were discovered on the Halliday property, it is not surprising that suspicion fell on Paul Halliday's bizarre young wife. It is also not surprising that as soon as charges were brought, Lizzie again seemed to have lost her mind.

The third week in October, Bly journeyed to Monticello and landed the first interview Lizzie Halliday granted to a member of the press. The story ran seven columns, at the end of which Bly pressed hard to extract a confession. She reported this exchange:

"Did you or did you not kill those people?"

She looked up. There was real alarm in her face.

"I have been crazy; I was drugged," she ejaculated, defiantly.

. . . "Tell me," I urged, "you did it yourself?"

"What shall I say, dear?" she said, turning to the sheriff.

. . . "Are you guilty or innocent? Tell me now. I may be able to help you. Anyway, I am going away and you will never see me again," I said to her at last when it was drawing close to the hour of midnight.

"Some other time. My head feels bad now. Some other time," was her answer.

Within two weeks, Lizzie Halliday sent word through the sheriff that she wanted to see Bly again and tell her everything. Bly's interview appeared in *The World* on November 5 in a full-page story. To Bly, Lizzie revealed that she had been married six times—and she was only twenty-eight years old—and claimed she had been drugged by a "gang" of people she knew but could not identify in fear for her life and that they had forced her to witness the killings of her husband and the McQuillan women. She also gave details of the killing of a peddler some months before, twelve miles from her home, but said she hadn't committed that crime either. *The World* sent out three more reporters to verify Lizzie's story, and their report followed Bly's in the chapter format of a mystery in the same Sunday feature. The reporters were able to confirm all six of Lizzie's marriages—she was a bigamist for two of them, and several of the husbands had died under suspicious circumstances. Most, like Paul Halliday, were much older men with some sort of pension. The reporters also verified the peddler's slaying, which at the time had been blamed on wandering gypsies.

The local papers were slightly cynical about all the interest the Lizzie Halliday case had caused among the competitive New York sensation-mongers. "The reporters of the New York papers are still endeavoring to earn a dollar or two on the Burlingham tragedy," *The Middletown Daily Press* commented on October 23. "Nellie Bly of *The World* paid a visit to Monticello last week and wrote a three-column story, containing, however, nothing new." The Middletown newspaper suggested that the unnamed reporter from *The Herald* had fared better: "*The Herald* man has again taken up the story and writes, under date of Saturday, that there seems to be no doubt that Mrs. Lizzie Halliday is either rapidly regaining her sanity or has decided to cease feigning the actions and speech of a maniac. After her recovery from a severe attack of illness several weeks ago, Sheriff Beecher noticed a radical change in her demeanor."

Lizzie Halliday was tried and convicted of first-degree murder, but her sentence to death by electrocution appears never to have been carried out.

Week after week, Bly continued her investigations and news-related interviews, with an occasional break into something lighter, such as her cheerful visit to the Midway at the Chicago World's Fair. Whatever the topic, *The World* gave her top display, on the front page of the first or second feature section. The subject matter wasn't always earth-shattering, but it generally made for good reading—if one happened to be a fan of Bly's approach to reportage.

After four days of posing as a gambler, she produced an informative look at the city's illegal "pool rooms," establishments open to women who liked to bet on the horses. Bly learned of many of their locations, how the proprietors paid police protection to stay in business, what passwords were needed to gain admittance, how much money the owners took in each day. She drew word portraits of the women gamblers, many of them married and losing their husbands' money with approval, clearly finding it an appropriate and amusing pastime. Some lost continually, blaming their failures on cheating clerks, and the women gossiped about one another all the time. Bly reported this encounter with "Mrs. K—":

> "Will you go and play policy with me?" Mrs. K— asks,
> and I consent quite eagerly. Oh, I am learning so much—
> pool-rooms, policy shops—what next?

"I dreamed last night that I was going West. I looked out of a car window and saw a lot of white tents," she continued. "I asked some one what they were, and they said they were the tents of the Mohawks. 'No,' I said, 'They are the Last of the Mohicans.' You know, the novel? So I came here today and I see that Mohican is in the first race; but I had no money, and, of course, he wins. Now I'm going to play policy."

In December, Bly was the first to interview both Mary Hooker, a remarkably brave woman who had fallen down a dumbwaiter shaft and shattered three vertebrae, and Hooker's physician, Dr. Robert H. M. Dawbarn, who had performed the extraordinary surgery that saved Hooker's life.

Bly's reporting was clear and exact as the physician explained in detail how he had removed his patient's splintered tenth, eleventh, and twelfth dorsals, leaving the outside half of each intact to ensure the support of her back. It was surgery that had never been attempted before. The pain Hooker experienced in her legs after surgery, Dr. Dawbarn said, left him optimistic about her prospects for walking again. As for Mary Hooker, Bly told the story of her terrible fall and extolled the young woman for two qualities Bly found particularly exemplary: good spirits in the face of difficulty and pluck.

There were more high-profile interviews. For five hours, she closely questioned New York's leading moral reformer, the Reverend Dr. Charles Parkhurst, president of the Society for Prevention of Crime. Parkhurst had shot to prominence nearly two years earlier, on Valentine's Day 1892, with a sermon decrying corruption among police and politicians delivered from the pulpit of the Madison Park Presbyterian Church. To substantiate his charges, the clergyman launched a crusade involving undercover investigations of the city's brothels and other dens of iniquity, not unlike Bly's earlier efforts. Parkhurst always maintained his campaign was not against the "unfortunate inmates" of these corrupting locales, only against the collusion between their proprietors and police that allowed such decadent commerce to flourish.

He told Bly in depth about his effort to "fight the police as the guardian angels of crime." Along the way, she elicited his opinions on woman suffrage (against), woman's sphere (home and children), horse racing (a sin), foreordination (believed in it), free will (also believed in it and saw no contradiction with foreordination), immigration (restrict it), his prejudices (for the Caucasian but not against any race), and even his own idea of fun (mountain climbing).

Bly pushed the Reverend Dr. Parkhurst to concede that many women were winding up in prostitution because they had so few other remunerative employment opportunities. He said he was open to reforming any fallen soul who expressed interest but did not elucidate on what the alternatives might be. Bly found him "thoroughly honest in his views," if "a trifle self-conscious." The interview filled an entire page.

Bly was never succinct; likely she was paid on a space rate, by the column. For her utterly inconsequential exposé in mid-December of Britain's celebrated mind reader, Maud Lancaster, she filled one whole page and spilled over into a second—ten columns in all. She provided endless details of how Miss Lancaster—when her blindfold was tightened and her compatriots compelled to leave the room—failed to guess correctly where Bly and her guests had hidden objects for her to locate. The report was devastating for Lancaster's New York debut, and she was still reeling from its effects many months later, as *The Journalist* duly reported: "The English woman says she was bullied and misrepresented outrageously. That she was invited to Bly's house with the understanding that the fair Nelly [*sic*] was to interview her for the *World* and that she was treated most inhospitably."

Coincidentally, the multicolumn illustration that accompanied Bly's story about the mind reader provides the only surviving glimpse of Bly's duplex apartment at 120 West Thirty-fifth Street. This was where she had been living with her mother, Kate, and Beatrice for the past several years when not at the farm in White Plains. The decor was utterly Victorian—overfurnished, cozy, and elegant, gracious if not grand, but by all means an impressive residence for a "girl" with no material legacy out on her own and supporting several dependents.

To round out the year, Bly gave ten days to learning about "The Midnight Band of Mercy," what *The World* described in a headline as

"An Odd Gathering of Curious Women Who Are Devoting Their Lives to Alleviating the Suffering of Itinerant Cats." After a strong start, her assignments got more ridiculous every week. Only four months into her comeback, Bly was beginning to wonder if she had done the right thing.

✥

Unfortunately, in the new division of labour, it is not the lighter and more pleasant toil that has fallen to a woman's lot. As a rule, she sues for employment in forma pauperis; *not in the strength of her superior capacity for the task, but because she must have some task, and because she is willing to take anything that is given to her, however burdensome and ill-paid. In fact, she is willing to undersell her male competitor,—and, under the circumstances, who shall blame her? But the natural result is that she thereby undertakes the most disagreeable and thankless of the labours which are entailed by a journalist's life.*

—The Spectator, *June* 17, 1893

By the spring of 1893, there were a reported 250 bona fide newspaperwomen working in the United States, an estimate that pointedly ignored the several thousand women who did "a little space work" in between their social or business obligations. The arduous nature of the journalist's calling, and the particular toll this took on female practitioners, had begun to be seen and felt. Expressions of empathy with the burdensome lot of the woman reporter appeared in numerous publications, like this one in *The New Orleans Picayune*:

She will be tired and disappointed and heart-sick much oftener than even her intimate friends imagine; the good work of one day will be overshadowed by failure on the next, and her record begins anew each morning that she reports for duty, and on the day's work she must stand or fall back. It is the old story of the cat climbing out of the well. Her sex will hinder one hundred times to once that it helps her; the air-castles she has spent months in erecting may be demolished by a word; her best work will be taken as a matter of course, and anything less than her best as a deliberately planned and personal injury. If at last a combination of these conditions leads the unfortunate woman to lie down, fold her hands over her tired heart and conduct a funeral over her own remains, 10 to one she will be called upon to write a page story; and of course it must be done at once.

As the months passed, Bly found her expectations on the job were not being met. Although when she first returned to full-time newspaper work, she was commanding the best assignments a woman could expect, that changed very quickly.

In early January 1894, for example, Bly was sent to seek out five truly destitute families for the apparent purpose of promoting *The World*'s free bread fund. The next week she spent the night in a desolate, haunted house in Woodport, New Jersey ("Afraid of ghosts? Oh, no! Not I!"). She exposed a furniture swindler and arranged to have herself ensnared by Mrs. Allie Clemisphere, "The Siren of The Coleman House," a schemer who lured wealthy women into secret gambling dens in the old hotel for a fleecing. In the process, Bly ran into Pat Sheedy, probably the best-known gambler in the country, who cleverly blew her cover and gave her yet another opportunity to compliment herself in print. "My God!" he said to Bly while shooting a warning glance at Mrs. Clemisphere and her companions, "You're smart enough to be Nellie Bly!" With that, everyone scattered. The stories were amusing to cover but of too little consequence to satisfy Bly's sense of what she ought to be accomplishing.

As if her own assignments weren't demeaning enough, *The World* had other woman reporters competing with her in the same sorts of embarrassing tasks. It had gotten to the point that the Sunday female stunt slot had taken on the aspects of an assembly line. The Sunday editors had gone so far as to designate "Meg Merrilies" the byline to be used by any number of woman reporters doing lead feature stunts alongside Bly. The composite competitor had written at length about walking around New York for seven days in the divided skirt known as trouserettes to see if she could endorse the style being pushed by the Boston dress reformers. Then, she went underground to learn what the "mud miners" experienced as they burrowed deep under Blackwell's Island to complete the East River Tunnel. No one said so, but it makes sense that the "fits-all" byline would have been devised to head off creation of another prima donna with Bly's ego, stature, and attendant demands.

The World's editorial gambits, as well as Joseph Pulitzer's social climbing and miserly management, not to mention his Semitic heritage—Pulitzer's father was Jewish, which he himself didn't really acknowledge—were a constant target in the scathing columns of Town Topics. The society magazine was quick with its satirical take on the Meg Merrilies ruse. In this lampoon, Pulitzer himself was said to have come up with the byline, then bestowed it on a fledgling reporter. She was said to have made such a hit with admiring fans that they began sending her mail to The World's office, addressed to the Merrilies nom de plume. Pulitzer, fearing that his creation was about to be usurped, took the name away from the young sensationalist and gave it to someone else. He then got the idea of having the Meg Merrilies articles written by different employees each week, garbed in "an article of feminine attire" emblazoned with the initials "M.M." The lampooning went on:

> As custodian of this article, it is now Mr. Goddard's duty to take it from the safe every Monday morning, and, while the World's female staff is lined up on the portion of the roof at the base of the dome, select someone that is to wear it until the following Saturday night. Before handing over the garment, however, he takes a written pledge from the fortunate woman, in which she promises to wear it for only a week, return it in as good condition as received, and relinquish the right to be called Meg Merrilies when the article is, on the following Saturday night, locked in the safe again. During the interval, the woman is addressed by no other name than Miss Meg, and it is understood that her future career on the World depends on the daring of her week's adventure, and the condition in which the article of apparel is returned. I should, perhaps, state that the garment is laundried in the

stereotyping room, and that it was only slightly damaged by the mud in the East River Tunnel last week.

Despite the attempts at sophisticated derision, there is no question that *The World* saw the work of its stunt girls as an essential element of its winning Sunday mix. Although Goddard's leadership and New York's expanding immigrant population deserve credit for the growth of the newspaper's Sunday circulation in this period, Bly, as Miss Derring-do Nonpareil, could fairly claim a share of that success. It may have been no more than coincidence, but Sunday readership at *The World* dropped the year after Bly left the newspaper, hovered around the 260,000 level for the three years she was gone, then jumped to 323,471 in 1894, which was Goddard's first full year in charge of the Sunday paper and Bly's first full year back on staff. The daily paper experienced a similar growth pattern. On the eleventh anniversary of Pulitzer's stewardship of *The World*, the newspaper proudly announced its average daily circulation had reached 433,167, a climb of 67,858 papers per day over the previous year and of 125,629 over 1891.

Nevertheless, *The World*'s sensation-mongering was the object of much industry ridicule, with its exploitative use of women reporters especially singled out. "Nell Nelson has made a number of bad breaks," *The Journalist* said in March of 1894, speaking of a reporter it had practically deified six years earlier. "But perhaps [she] is not to be censured, for it is well-known in the office that she is expected to furnish and keep a grade of patronage for which *The World* caters." Of Bly, the trade magazine said, she "has been put at work unworthy of her enterprising pen." At the same time, the magazine conceded, she still stood "easily at the head of the press women of today."

Bly bore up in the months from March to July, although neither her assignments nor apparently her attitude toward her work improved much. She visited the mysterious "Hindoo Idol," and the jugglers and contortionists from India who had entertained on the Midway Plaisance during the Chicago World's Fair. They had stayed in the United States in order to perform "private entertainments" in New York. She spent a day at the Bloomingdale Insane Asylum before the facility was moved to White Plains and its historic build-ing became part of Columbia College. She described the history and condition of some of the asylum's most famous inmates, past and present, including her old acquaintance Billy Scanlon, the actor, who was suffering from what the doctors called "the actors' disease," pare-sis, a slight or partial paralysis.

Bly made no secret of her dissatisfaction, and industry wags picked up on it:

> *The World* understands how to manipulate women. I am told that when Miss Nellie Bly made her first great hit, she was put off with a compensation which would make an ordinary cow laugh. Little by little she advanced until, receiving a bet-ter offer from some publishing house, left. Now she's back again, her copy mutilated, her feelings hurt, herself put in the background, or assigned to do work repulsive or revolting.

She must have gotten her message across, because after that item appeared in a widely read column of *The Journalist*, the quality of her assignments seemed to improve, at least in the short term. On May Day, she was sent to Washington to provide her version of the biggest national story of the day, the march of "Coxey's Army," a protest demonstration started in Massillon, Ohio, by Jacob Coxey, who had assembled thousands of out-of-work supporters from across the country to march on Washington and demand relief for the unemployed and destitute. For the most part, Eastern newspapers ridiculed this ragtag effort, which resulted in only about a thousand of the weary, hungry marchers actually making it to the Capitol, a haunting spectacle nonetheless. Bly, like her colleagues at other papers, expressed only contempt for Coxey and his lieutenants: "My whole heart has always been with the working man and woman, but I believe in justice and right as well. I do not think workmen should make a circus of themselves or their wrongs, and I do believe they are strong and powerful enough to right their wrongs in a dignified way and without the aid of selfish and greedy schemers."

On her return, Bly interviewed John Jacob Astor on publication of his first book, *Journey to Other Worlds*. She learned that the young millionaire was a supporter of woman suffrage, Canadian annexation, and asphalt pavement. In her story, she admitted to a practice widely scorned in later journalistic procedure. She mentioned that she had allowed Astor to read the interview in manuscript form before it was published and then remarked on how pleased she was that he had liked it. She did not say if he had asked her to change or omit anything, or if she had done so.

By this point, Bly had reestablished herself as enough of a presence in New York journalism for *The Journalist*, which had been so uncharacteristically friendly of late, to start nudging her off her pedestal.

> Newspaper women are here to hunt the almighty dollar same's other folks. Of course, the dear things have souls and exalted ideals and all that, but it's rubbish to talk of any one of them never writing anything trivial or light. They all do—unless, perhaps, it's Nelly [*sic*] Bly.
>
> Speaking of Miss Bly, now I, for one, was glad *The World* had to bring her back. I am always glad when a woman has the least little bit of triumph, and this is a big one for Miss Cochran [*sic*]. However, it would be more grateful all around if Nelly would not take herself quite so seriously and would let up on these periodic descriptions of her glorious eyes and her career. Of course we all know that she is the smartest woman who ever lived, and has accomplished more than all the men journalists of this century put together and still her continuous special ownest own little boomlet is a trifle wearisome at times.

The columnist feigned astonishment that Bly had gotten through her entire interview with young Astor without his once commenting on her beautiful eyes, her figure, or her past success.

She also was careful to avoid self-flattery in the best assignment she snared in early summer—an exclusive interview with State Senator Clarence Lexow, chairman of the senate committee then deep into an investigation that was about to produce overwhelming evidence of corruption against the New York police. In the weeks before the Lexow interview, she had produced a steady flow of fairly typical Bly probes: witnessing the whipping and pillorying of eight men accused of crimes in New Castle, Delaware, where the law still allowed such barbaric punishment; critiquing the usefulness of a new charity-driven, low-interest pawn shop; submitting to the "gold cure" for alcoholism with other women at the Keeley "Institute" in White Plains; then stopping off to see William Muldoon, the champion wrestler, who was running an all-male health spa nearby on his picturesque farm.

On Friday, June 29, Lexow's committee recessed until fall after hearing six weeks of highly incriminating testimony. Witnesses had leveled accusations of blackmail and other crimes against a police commissioner, two inspectors, and sixteen captains out of thirty-seven in the department. Bly interviewed Lexow the next day, traveling by train and carriage to South Nyack, where he awaited her arrival in his large and beautifully appointed home. Her interview appeared in *The World* the day after.

Lexow suggested his den for the interview's venue. That suited Bly. "I always try to have a man at perfect ease before I begin to talk to him," she told her readers. "And if possible I always try to talk with him where he feels the most at home. A drawing-room interview is always frosty and unsatisfactory."

She described Lexow, his house and grounds, and then pelted him with questions, direct and to the point: What did he think was the best way to regulate gambling and the social evil? Did he expect that the revelations of his committee would spur legislation providing for a chief of police completely independent of political commissioners? Was the system so rotten that merely changing officials would not lead to reform? Had Governor Roswell P. Flower's veto of an appropriation to cover the committee's expenses hampered its work? Would the investigation put a stop to police blackmail? Would there be new legislation in Albany as a result of his committee's work? Would any police officials be going to jail? Would a jury convict on the basis of the testimony of people as disreputable as most of the committee's witnesses? Were any of them paid a bonus to testify? Had they been offered any protection? If

Lexow himself were superintendent of police, could he stop the blackmailing? Lexow answered whatever questions he could without jeopardizing the progress of his investigation, expected to resume September 10.

Having established that she had done her homework, Bly applied her own branding iron to the inquiry. She wanted to know if Lexow was superstitious. ("I have an aching desire to find a man who will acknowledge he is superstitious or whom I can prove to be honest in saying he isn't.") Lexow said no, but that he did believe in dreams. He told her that he read mostly law books and Charles Dickens, that he spoke five languages but his Italian and Spanish were rusty, that he didn't care much for horses but enjoyed shooting and fishing, and that he had no particular fondness for children other than his own.

She asked if he thought life was worth living, if he ever became despondent, if he thought it paid to try to reform the world. Yes, no, and yes were his replies. Did he think giving women the vote would help purify politics?

> If all women voted, yes, but I fear the proportion of good women that would stay at home would be larger than among men, which condition is responsible for the misgovernment under which we suffer. I fear women voting would aggravate instead of ameliorate. I think that with few exceptions the class of women who would vote would not help the Commonweal—would, rather, hurt it. But I can see no harm in giving women the right to vote on all questions non-political—on such matters as affect education, taxation and etc.

The following Sunday, *The World's* lead feature section carried Bly's report on the women who spent the Fourth of July betting on horses at the track at Sheepshead Bay. But Bly herself, by then, was en route to Chicago, where railroad workers were eight weeks into a strike against the Pullman Palace Car Company. A national emergency was looming, and Bly was about to produce what would later be remembered as some of the best reporting of her career.

By the time Bly arrived in Chicago, the city was in turmoil. Federal troops had been called in to restore order. The nation's railway system was on the verge of paralysis, and the federal government was moving swiftly to ensure this did not happen.

With the country in deep recession, George M. Pullman, like so many other large employers, had laid off half his workforce and cut wages by 25 percent for those who remained. Although he had accepted unprofitable contracts to keep his plants open, he did not lower rents at his model worker town in Pullman, Illinois, to reflect the decrease in wages. A workers' committee met with management representatives to protest the situation. A day later, three of the committee members, all members of the American Railway Union, led by Eugene V. Debs, were fired.

To protest the firings, the union called a strike on May 11, 1894. Pullman countered by laying off the rest of the workers and closing the plant. A month later, the union proposed arbitration, but the company refused. The union then declared that until the company accepted the principle of arbitration, no union member would work on a Pullman car on any railroad line.

President Cleveland, focused on ensuring the movement of the mails and interstate commerce, swore in 3,600 special deputies—selected and paid for by the General Managers' Association. The GMA represented the owners of twenty-four rail lines affected by the strike, extending over some 41,000 miles of midwestern track. Reaction from the strikers was swift and vehement. Riots broke out in the Chicago area and sporadically elsewhere. Legions of the disaffected and unemployed joined the strikers.

A federal injunction was issued against Debs and the strikers on July 2 to stop interference with the movement of trains after 2,000 protesters had refused to disperse when ordered by a federal marshal. The information was cabled to Washington, where officials cabled back to the U.S. attorney's office in Chicago to convene a grand jury, which slapped Debs with a federal indictment.

By July 5, the streets had erupted in looting and destruction. Flames consumed buildings, stores, and hundreds of trains. On July

6, President Cleveland sent 2,000 more federal troops into the city. Illinois's progressive governor, John P. Altgeld, who had opposed federal intervention, called up 5,000 militiamen to assist the regulars in the restoration of order. The skirmishes raged on for several days, exaggerated or minimized by newspapers, depending on their persuasion for or against labor. And then, on July 14, the strike was over, the workers utterly defeated. Six days later, the government withdrew the troops. Debs was convicted on contempt of court charges and jailed.

The World, for the year preceding the Pullman strike, had been under the disastrous leadership of Colonel Charles H. Jones. Don Seitz, a longtime Pulitzer business manager, remembered Jones as bewhiskered in an era when newsmen preferred a clean-shaven look. He was considered a total misfit among *The World*'s increasingly conservative "hardened old hands."

> Colonel Jones' ideas reflected much of the Populism that was soon to capture the Democracy, remote from those ideals which had solidified in *The World*, and they involved the dawning Free Silver heresy. His beginnings were full of mistakes. He was fortunately under guard of the established forces and could not, luckily for the paper, enforce obedience.

In the summer of 1893, Seitz recalled, *The World*'s Washington correspondent, John H. Tennant, had been forecasting repeal of the Sherman Silver Act in his dispatches. As soon as President Cleveland placed the matter of repeal before Congress, Jones sped down to Washington, "big-footed" Tennant, and started writing dispatches himself—against the repeal. Editors back in New York held a war council and simply canned all the copy that their chief editor produced. *The World* remained staunch and consistent in its support for the gold standard, which passed. Jones slunk back to New York, whatever remained of his aura greatly diminished.

Nevertheless, he still had charge of the editorial page a year later when the U.S. government issued its injunction against Debs and the Pullman strikers. Aroused again, Jones dashed off a much-discussed editorial headlined "Government by Injunction," in which he assailed President Cleveland's decision and endorsed Debs. Pulitzer interpreted the editorial as a direct challenge to his long-held position against outlaw violence and summoned Jones to his vacation home in Bar Harbor for censure. But Jones refused to back down. Pulitzer, in a reliving of the Ballard Smith episode during the Homestead crisis, suspended Jones from editorial page responsibilities. Five days later, the newspaper was back to its traditional position, appealing in an editorial to the calm reason of working men.

Town Topics, always looking for an opportunity to skewer Pulitzer, gave its own eviscerating spin to *The World*'s bizarre flip-flop, which must have been hard to fathom outside *The World*'s inner sanctum. *Town Topics* saw it simply as "insane ignorance" reflecting *The World*'s consistent ineptitude in discussing questions of law or government.

> Mr. Pulitzer's position was substantially that of the pulp-headed anarchist jack pudding who is Governor of Illinois. While ostensibly opposing Debs and violence, *The World*'s . . . protests against federal interference were virtually invitations and incitements to arson and murder . . . When he found out that public opinion was practically solid against the rioters, and when some office boy had explained the Constitution to him, he reversed himself, and took a position exactly the oppose of the one he had been maintaining with so much heat. The trouble with Mr. Pulitzer seems to be [that] . . . his point of view is essentially foreign and alien. He does not comprehend the American spirit. He seems to think the American people are about on a level with his friends in the Elmira Reformatory.

In the midst of this embarrassing episode, Bly boarded the train for Chicago to cover what turned out to be the last week of the strike. Her feelings on the way out to the Midwest were of vehement opposition to the workers. That soon changed. Bly headed straight for the town of Pullman, from which, in a series of three lengthy features, she decided to tell the story of the strike from the vantage point of the strikers and their families.

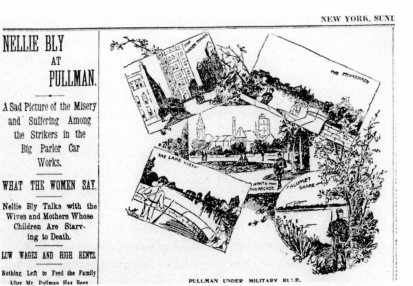

NELLIE BLY
AT
PULLMAN.

A Sad Picture of the Misery
and Suffering Among
the Strikers in the
Big Parlor Car
Works.

WHAT THE WOMEN SAY.

Nellie Bly Talks with the
Wives and Mothers Whose
Children Are Starv-
ing to Death.

LOW WAGES AND HIGH RENTS.

Nothing Left to Feed the Family
After Mr. Pullman Has Been

PULLMAN UNDER MILITARY RULE.

Detail from Bly's first report on the Pullman strike, The World, *July 11, 1894*
(General Research Division, The New York Public Library)

Her suddenly sympathetic presence worked like an open flood-gate. Families brought her into their clean but modest homes. They told their hard-luck stories. They showed her their leases. They provided the pathetic arithmetic of their distress. They explained how Pullman had effectively coerced them into living in the company town if they wanted to work for him. They complained about how much more he charged in rent and gas and water than at comparable locations; how everything was priced to Pullman's advantage. Bly's conversation with a tidy, black-haired woman in a flowered challis dress and freshly laundered apron was indicative of the kind of material she had elicited:

"Can you tell me, please, where I shall find the poorest strikers?" I asked, and she replied with a smile.

"Across the street is the letters. They are mostly foreigners and I guess you won't find any that speak English. Not many of them belong to the unions and they are suffering most."

"What do you mean by letters?" I asked.

"The row is known by letters instead of numbers. They begin at A and end at R, I think. These houses are called the 200."

"And you are all in the [Mrs. Astor's] 400, now," I told her, and she smiled without knowing why and asked me what I meant.

"At present you are a leisure class; so is the 400," I explained.

"It is not our fault," she answered promptly, as I had reproached them.

"It was only a few that wanted to strike. They shut up the shops and the others did not dare go back for fear of their lives. My husband doesn't belong to the union and we have to be careful what we say—only sometimes I have to break out and tell them what I think when they talk too much."

"What did your husband work at in the shops?"

"He is a wood-carver, but work has been very slack and he did anything he could. He hadn't any carving to do in a long time until two weeks before the strike. You know, business was dull everywhere and Mr. Pullman claimed he didn't get any orders, and I suppose that was true. He couldn't give the men work if he didn't have it to give."

"Was that the sole cause of the dissatisfaction?"

"That was not all. There were many charges against the bosses. Of course, Mr. Pullman got the blame, and, as he is the head of the whole thing, it was his duty to inquire into things. He can't expect his bosses always to be right and just, for they have their likes and dislikes, just like everybody else, and when they have the sole power they will do things that are wrong. But strikes do no good. The poor man is the only one to suffer. I told them when they first talked about it that they couldn't starve out a millionaire. You can't make him hungry or back in his rent. Why Mr. Pullman only had one order in the shop. That was for a hundred elevated cars for New York. They were to be finished by the first of August but they can't be now even if the men went back. So what does Mr. Pullman care how long they stay out? As I told them, it doesn't hurt Mr. Pullman's vacation; he doesn't go hungry; it is only the workman who hurts himself."

"I suppose you are the cause, then, of your husband not joining a trade union?" The little woman smiled at me.

"I talked against it, but he wouldn't have joined anyway. He belonged to the Knights of Labor and was in their strike, and it taught him a lesson. He is an American, but I am from Holland. I came to Pullman when I was twelve years old and I never left it. I know all about workmen and strikes, and I know there are wrongs on both sides, but striking and destroying property and killing rich men isn't going to help the working man."

The workers seemed to adore having the celebrity reporter in their midst and, on the day the strike was called off, invited her to address a rally of the American Railway Union at Turner Hall in Kensington. "I told them I came to Chicago very bitterly set against the strikers," Bly reported herself saying in a story about the meeting, "that so far as I understood the question, I thought the inhabitants of the model town of Pullman hadn't a reason on earth to complain. With this belief I visited the town, intending in my articles to denounce the rioters and bloodthirsty strikers.

"Before I had been half a day in Pullman," she concluded, "I was the most bitter striker in the town." One of her pieces began:

I don't know which amuses me the more—the sight of the army in Chicago or the stories in the newspapers. The whole affair impresses me as being a huge joke—a sort of Coxey burlesque on an immense scale. Everywhere I go, everywhere I look, I am confronted by the soldiers. Officers, chock full of importance and trying to look as if the safety of the land rested upon their well-padded shoulders, strut around and dine in the hotels and enjoy themselves immensely. Soldiers in squads, with a man in command, march hither and thither, and wheel about and shoulder arms and stack arms to the intense appreciation of curious spectators.

Bly said the newspapers thumped with stories of bloodshed and riots "until I reach the last line, by turning a page, which tells me that it is so rumored. I see blood-curdling pictures—men falling dead and others with flaming torches, clubs and revolvers in their hands. Then I go out to see the strikers in Pullman. The town has a Sabbath-day look. Very few people are on the streets and they are mainly women on some errand. I go into the quiet homes and I find the strikers nursing the babies." The picture she drew was of earnest, hardworking, well-meaning people, caught in mean realities created by management bosses and the unions. In Bly's view, Pullman himself bore most of the blame: "They [the strikers] are not firebrands; they are not murderers and rioters; they are not Anarchists. They are quiet, peaceful men who have suffered beneath the heel of the most heartless coward it has ever been my misfortune to hear of."

None of the other major New York newspapers carried stories of a similar type.

Bly left Chicago for the Illinois state capital of Springfield and headed straight for the executive mansion to interview the controversial governor in the center of the Pullman controversy, John P. Altgeld. Earlier in his administration, Altgeld, to rounds of abuse from conservatives, had pardoned the three anarchists still serving murder sentences on charges stemming from the Haymarket Riots of 1886.

"I went in fear and trembling," Bly recalled, "for I had heard hair-raising tales of the governor's hatred of all things and persons journalistic; that the sight of a newspaper man was to him what the toreador and his mantle are to a bull. Still, I wanted to see him. I rather enjoy an encounter with fierce people."

Bly thought she could jump-start the interview by catching her subject off guard.

"Tell me," she blurted out. "Are you an anarchist?"

"Nonsense," Altgeld replied, but gave her leave to keep on asking questions. She started way off the main subject, "hoping by talking of different things to pave a way for introducing more important topics." She wanted to know if he read newspapers or novels, what he thought about woman suffrage—he was the first governor to appoint a number of women to important government boards—and then she began in earnest: What hope did he think there was for the working man? Did he know how difficult conditions were at Pullman? Did he believe in arbitration? What about the deployment of federal troops to Chicago? Did he think the strike taught anything to capital and labor?

> "No strike in this country has ever yet settled a principle or benefitted the employer where he won the strike." [Altgeld said.]
>
> "Then you think Pullman has hurt himself in this affair?"
>
> "I think in the long run Pullman will be hurt by the strike. The public's attention has been drawn to Mr. Pullman in rather an unfavorable way, and in the end I think he will be very seriously affected."

She reeled off her strike-related questions, ending with whether the governor thought the federal government ought to own and control the railroads. "I don't want to answer that," he said, and then wanted to know why she was asking him so many questions. Bly replied, "I'm asking you these questions because I want to know if you are an Anarchist." "Pshaw," he exclaimed in disgust.

She went on to other subjects. Soon, Altgeld started to interview her. She asked him if he didn't think the country had enough of the Democrats.

> "You are a little Republican," he interrupted, shaking his hand at me.
>
> "Well, if I am, my father was a Democrat, and so is my newspaper. Now then, what party do you think will elect the next President?"
>
> "Democratic party, of course," [he said] emphatically.
>
> "That's your opinion . . ." [she replied.]

Altgeld wanted to know about what Bly had witnessed in Pullman. As she told him, Bly wrote, "the Governor listened in breathless silence, his blue eyes growing moist when I told him about a number of pathetic cases."

"Did you write about all you heard and saw?" he asked in surprise.

"Certainly; that is what I went there for," I answered.

"And were your articles published?" wonderingly.

"Certainly."

"Then the *World* is very unlike the Chicago newspapers. I did not believe any paper would publish anything against capital."

"The proprietor of the *World* hires people to find out and publish the truth about everything, regardless of all other considerations, and if the truth is not given it is solely the fault of the writer, not the paper."

Through their conversation, Bly had charmed Altgeld, utterly. He wanted to know if he had been "the softest subject" she ever interviewed. She confessed how afraid of him she had been because of stories that he hated reporters. "So I do," he replied, "but it was your smile that did it. You come in and smile and sweep everything before you. It's the smile, young lady; it's worth a million dollars to you." She recounted the rest of the flattering episode, which, she was deliberate in pointing out, took place in the presence of the governor's wife. Mrs. Altgeld expressed her delight in the opportunity to meet the famous globe girdler she had heard so much about. Bly, the ever shameless self-promoter, committed three more paragraphs to the impact of her winsome beam:

"Oh," I gasped. "How I wish I could sell it." He laughed with me.

"That's all right. You keep it. It's your success. You can get anything you ask for when you smile."

"I'm smiling now," I reminded him. "So do tell me, are you an anarchist?"

This time Altgeld responded with a long and reasoned reply, tracing his vocational history as a farmer, a soldier, a schoolteacher, a lawyer, a county attorney, a judge and governor, drawing the conclusion for her that this was not exactly the profile of an anarchist.

"But," he did say, answering her real question, "I believe that the toiling masses are entitled to justice and I have lifted my hand to secure it for them whenever I could. I have never asked anything of them, but have dealt honestly with them, and they seem to have confidence in me."

For Bly, whose encounters with the Economites and the Oneida Community had left her very hopeful about what she might find in Pullman, the conditions under which striking families were living were a terrible shock. She was quick to follow up on the suggestion that she visit a real model worker town, one supposedly functioning with great success since its establishment four years earlier on 150-plus acres of Madison County, Illinois, about an hour east of St. Louis. The town was called Leclaire, Illinois, in honor of the French originator of profit sharing in his housepainting and decorating business, Edmonde Jean Leclaire.

This town was the creation of a businessman by the name of Nelson Olsen Nelson, owner of the N. O. Nelson Manufacturing Company, a plumbing supply concern he started with "a pocketful of quarters." He was also the author of an 1887 book titled *Profit-Sharing*. As soon as Bly's Chicago duties were over, she headed for Leclaire to see if Nelson had succeeded where Pullman had failed in finding a solution to "the dissatisfaction of the employed, the misery of strikes and the cruelty of corporations . . . What I had seen and learned in Pullman had not only converted me into a striker, but had left me very despondent as to the ultimate fate of the employed, men and women. Even Governor Altgeld, who has the subject very much at heart, could only suggest one hope when I interviewed him, 'Let them all stand together; it is their only hope.' "

Like the stand-up painted wooden scenery of a vaudeville set, Pullman's settlement had impressed her immediately with its pretty park and lake, its fine station and hotel, its impressive arcade of shops. "But when I walked to the rear of the town and saw the miserable 'letter' blocks and the 'brickyard' frame tenements, I felt like tearing down the sham front and showing the filth and poverty behind it."

Leclaire had the opposite effect. The more she explored the pretty town, the more she liked it. Every worker had his own house on a minimum of a third of an acre, set back at least twenty feet from the pavement. There was no hotel or train station. Rent was low, and everyone had the option of buying his own house, at the same monthly payment as the rent. The factories were arranged in a one-story campus-style setting, and there was a clubhouse, a library, a strong educational program, and the town motto, "Individual Independence." There was a Provident Fund to help workers with home payments when they were too sick to work. Men got an increase in wages when they married, and a trade school system had been instituted for boys from the age of twelve so that by the time their education was complete at eighteen, they would have mastered a trade. Every person Bly stopped to interview seemed to be basking in a workers' idyll.

Nelson she described as a plain, unassuming man, with bushy whiskers and a tan, about five feet five inches tall.

> There is something about this N. O. Nelson that prevents one knowing whether his eyes are dark or light. It is by the greatest effort I recall his appearance, and yet I remember vividly every word he said to me and I spent the good part of a day conversing with him. There are men I have talked with whom I could afterwards describe to the very lines in the palms of their hands and still not be able to recall one word they said to me.
>
> There is that difference in men, and my reader can solve it to suit his pleasure.

Nelson eschewed meat because of the brutality of butchery and actually encouraged his workers to join unions and associations, "a protection for laborers who would singly be helpless in the face of combined capital."

Bly said she wanted to bring two people in particular to see Leclaire: one was George Pullman, who needed an encounter with another capitalist's approach to labor, and the other was Herr Johann Most, "the anarchist of man-destroying beliefs," who, she said, needed a lesson in what it really takes to benefit the world.

Bly returned to New York to find a very welcome letter waiting for her from Erasmus Wilson, who invited her to attend a reception in Pittsburgh. By the time she opened the letter, however, the entertainment had taken place. Although Bly had intended to stop in Pittsburgh on the way back from Illinois, the unplanned interview with Altgeld and her tour of Leclaire had forced a change in her schedule.

Bly's sense of accomplishment and satisfaction should have been boosted by the splashy share she claimed in her newspaper's coverage of the Pullman strike, a national story of enduring significance. Yet the letter she wrote back to her old friend and mentor betrays depression, a sense of burdensome resignation and numbing disappointment.

"How I would like to see you!" she wrote. "What a long time it is and how little I am doing. And I used to have such hopes!"

Although her stories appeared regularly in *The World* on Sundays, she told Wilson she worked only "off and on—and have a worse temper than ever." Her only source of pleasure, it seemed, was the farm in White Plains, now her permanent address, although she still maintained the apartment on West Thirty-fifth Street. She invited Q.O. to visit: "Can you picture me as a farmer? I helped plant a barrel of potatoes this spring and I thought I was having loads of fun. But I soon got over it. The most I can do now is to walk through the garden and see how things are coming on." Bly described her orchard, the lawn with its handsome shade trees, her horse named Chaperone, her cow named Lady Anna Lee II "with a pedigree as long as her tail," her five dogs and sixty-four chickens.

During this period at *The World*, "Meg Merrilies" survived "the most thrilling experience" of her life by deflecting a silver bullet off a newfangled contraption called a bullet-proof vest—while she was wearing it. *Town Topics* was quick to complain that the invention of such effective protective equipment would end any hope of silencing those "long-winded Sunday creatures," from whom Bly had been trying vainly to disassociate herself.

The World carried Bly stories all through August. Her interview with "the world's greatest detective," Police Superintendent Thomas F. Byrnes, appeared on a Wednesday in the news section of the paper with Byrnes's views on women kicked back to the "Women and Home" section of the same day. On another day, Bly repeated the advice of world champion wrestler William Muldoon, urging young boys not to start smoking cigarettes.

For her Sunday feature, she spent two days in a flat *The World* had rented for her in the city's largest double-decker tenement, at 222 Second Street, between Avenues A and B. It was one of the hottest days of the year. Bly counted 117 people living in the building's sixteen three-room flats. There was a funeral for a man who had left a widow and eleven children with no means of support. His upstairs neighbors had eight boarders. The constant din kept her up most of the night, and the odors from the street caused her head to ache. "But poor people have got to put up with such things," a visitor told her. Bly's story lacked the eloquence and documentation of Jacob Riis's *How the Other Half Lives*, published four years earlier while she was busy ascending to the status of peripatetic national heroine. But squalor and overcrowding remained a fact of tenement life, and the story of the struggle to live under such conditions could not be told too many times.

There were, however, stories that could be told too many times, and Bly wrote those, too. Recalling her interview with John L. Sullivan, she filled nine columns with ten illustrations and her report on meeting with the new champion prizefighter James J. Corbett. This time, she slipped into the clumsy padded leather gloves and had him teach her how to box. She brought William Muldoon, the wrestler, as her second, but Corbett insisted Muldoon serve as referee. Corbett acknowledged he thought the sport too violent for women, but Bly found it exciting and recommended it. She even managed to knock Corbett down at one point and caused his mouth to bleed.

> "See what I did," I said proudly to the spectators.
> "Oh, that's nothing," Mr. Corbett said. "You hit me in the mouth with your elbow."

"You won't confess that I drew blood with my fist," I replied, as my pride vanished.

"Well, I bear you no ill-feeling. I'm glad the championship stays in America," he said.

The 1890s were a time of heightened consternation over the need for moral reform, and Bly played her part. She charged into Saratoga to expose the legions of gambling men and lowlife painted women, many accompanied into sin by children who were heard asking such questions as "What's a scratch?"

"Crime is holding a convention there," she wrote of the place she called the most wicked in the country, "and vice is enjoying a festival such as it never dared approach before." She visited the gambling dens. Of the women's pool room for horse betting, she wrote haughtily, "If one enjoys a democratic crowd, then one would love this woman's pool-room. If woman's suffrage would produce such a scene, then God prevent suffrage. I claim to be liberal in my views; I believe in liberty and the right to do as one pleases, but I don't think I should like to see such an assemblage again, even at the day of judgment."

She met the man most responsible for the descent of Saratoga, village president Cales W. Mitchell, who was also proprietor of the community's most notorious gaming rooms. It upset her to find him pleasant, bright, gentlemanly, earnest, attractive, even forthright.

"I am sorry I've met you," I say again, "but I must be true to my convictions and say your gambling resort is a wicked place."

"All right; give it to it," he said heartily.

"But you will not like it when you see it in print?" I insisted.

He smiled and laid his hand on my shoulder.

A follow-up story the next Sunday, which ran without a byline, said Bly's exposure of the evils of Saratoga had fortified its decent citizens with a hope for reform. What Bly had described in detailed word pictures, the follow-up writer summarized:

The element of unrestricted gambling and of wild plunging on the races by men and women, and in many instances by young boys and girls, is the poison that has diseased the social body of Saratoga, and by its opportunities for wanton pleasures has drawn hither the low and the depraved from all the big cities, East and West. Here State laws and man's laws come to a full stop, and every statute that threatens to interfere with vice is killed before it can become operative.

The women here who are really bad make the fact so plain that nobody can mistake them.

Back in New York City, the fine impression Bly had made on Governor Altgeld of Illinois in July paid off. He arrived in New York unexpectedly in mid-September, resulting in another front page story for her: "Governor Altgeld a Sick Man," the headline read. "He Informs Nellie Bly that He Is Threatened with Nervous Collapse." Because Bly was out of the office when Altgeld appeared unexpectedly in *The World* city room, another reporter was quickly assigned to interview him on the spot. Altgeld told this reporter that his sole purpose in coming to the city was to see Bly. The unnamed reporter explained that the governor and Bly had not seen each other since she "gave him a new introduction to the American people in her famous interview with him." The reporter did not manage to extract from Altgeld the real purpose of his visit but said that his "charming" explanation "was one of those little white lies that Governors and other great folks are privileged to tell."

Bly had no such problem. She called on the governor that evening at the Holland House hotel and learned immediately that he was in New York to consult a specialist about locomotor ataxia, a condition that had plagued him for some time. He described it as "the outcome of a general undermining of the nervous system" that had left him despondent. Of this she wrote:

I have said that John Peter Altgeld will be President if he lives a few years longer.

But will he live?

That is what he has come to New York to find out.

The only other major New York paper to carry a story on Altgeld's visit was *The Herald*, but without any of Bly's explicit details. Later, after her story had sent alarm bells clanging all the way to Chicago, Altgeld's doctors said he would likely recover, with rest and care. He also gave Bly his heartbreaking impressions of the miseries of life for the strikers in Pullman and how he had failed to convince George Pullman to improve conditions.

She must have loved this. Not only had the notorious news-making governor of Illinois sought her out first on his trip to New York but her story took front page lead position and the main headline in Saturday's paper, ahead of that of her male colleague whose flat, no-news interview with Altgeld was relegated to a long sidebar appended to the end of her piece.

Altgeld delayed his return to Chicago by a day, reportedly because of train scheduling. Bly's sensationalized story clearly had not angered him; he filled his extra time in New York accompanying her to the ill-kept Central Park menagerie. From the story she wrote about the visit, it was evident she knew the place well. She liked to talk to the monkey "inmates," as she called them, and translated their gibberish for Altgeld, who did not share her facility with primate-ese. *The World* had been campaigning against the zoo's inhumane conditions. Bly got Altgeld to add his voice: "I don't want to see any more," she reported him declaring. "It is the worst managed and most filthy place I've ever seen."

The next day, after Altgeld's departure, Bly headed over to see Superintendent John P. Haines, president of the Society for the Prevention of Cruelty to Animals, who confirmed that conditions at the menagerie were deplorable but that the society did not have the jurisdiction to intercede.

There is no reason to suspect there was more to Bly's relationship with Altgeld than zoo walks and interviews; in any event, the Altgeld holdings at the Illinois State Archives in Springfield contain not even the most innocuous note of thanks between them. But even in cases where there might have been reason to suspect more, evidence is scant or nonexistent. Fierce discretion ruled Bly's approach to romance. Through her stories, she flirted and teased. The peculiar habit of glorifying her smile, her body, her sway over powerful men in print may have been her way of coding messages to her beaux to enhance her aura, to swell their ardor by giving cause to jealousy. As much as she liked to rehearse her desirable attributes for the public, she held firm to her independence and choosiness. "Nell" was much more than the second syllable in the name of Penelope, the heroine of Bly's novel back in 1889. Penelope had been modeled after Bly herself—adamant in her obstinacy and independence, two qualities that charmed her suitors as much as they provoked them. Penelope was slender, willowy, and graceful, with bright, expressive eyes and an alluring smile. Just like Bly. The fictional character's resemblance to Bly's newspaper depictions of her own eye-batting encounters with men of all stations was striking. From prizefighters to governors, Bly seemed to be able to wile anyone into telling her a good deal of what she most wanted to know.

In the late summer of 1894, *Town Topics* dropped a nasty buzz of odd gossip into two of its columns that seemed to herald her imminent betrothal. In August it was

MISS DASHAWAY: How many proposals have you had this summer, Jessie dear?

MISS HIGHFLY: Sixteen, dear.

MISS DASHAWAY: What a terribly persistent fellow that Tommy Noodles must be!

The gossip sheet sounded the same theme a month later:

DARLING DELIA: Nellie Highfly is the most original and outrée girl I ever saw!

SWEETEST SUSAN: Why so?

DARLING DELIA: She is actually going to marry one of the fellows she was engaged to during the summer.

All the same, no announcement of any engagement for Bly was forthcoming.

In October, Bly busied herself with the $900 purchase of a farm in White Plains from a man named Lawrence McCarthy. No story of hers appeared in *The World* until November 11, when she exposed the medium Patrick Jules Wallace as a "spiritualist fakir," a "wonderful" piece rating that gratifying adjective in the personals column of *The Journalist* for November 17. Bly's report began:

> Fakirs! Fakirs! Fakirs!
> It is humiliating to one's love for one's country to see how easy it is for fakirs not only [to] gain a foothold but a deluge of idiotic followers. I speak strongly, but I feel so. I have lost my patience with the people who could and should see but will not.

Her indictment of spiritualism was blanket: "I wish for all time to make myself clear to my readers on the point of spiritualism. I declare it fraud from beginning to end, and all mediums impostors. I have studied the business. I can do any trick any medium can perform, and it is needless to add that spirits are not my aids."

In addition to duping Wallace into giving her information about brothers of hers who did not exist and prognoses of ill health for her long-dead father, Bly provided a long list of Wallace's run-ins with the law in cities from Honolulu and Denver to St. Louis and Indianapolis. It was one of the only times a report of hers included lengthy corroboration from sources other than her own impressions.

During this period, the rival Meg Merrilies byline appeared on stories of the usual sort with increasing frequency: Merrilies spent the night among the "tortured inmates" of the Chambers Street Hospital; she "faced death" in front of a trolley car to show why public conveyances needed to be equipped with lifesaving devices; she witnessed cataracts being removed from the eyes of a six-month-old baby at Manhattan Eye and Ear Hospital; she got a job as an extra with a traveling theatrical troupe; she rescued a child from a burning tenement as a volunteer fireman; she served as an official poll watcher in the city's worst election district; and then joined the crew of Pilot Boat No. 15 and steered the vessel through a fierce gale.

Bly was spared the stunt work. She finished out the year with a series of interviews, starting with the "Astor Tramp," a man by the name of John Garvey, who somehow got into the Astor mansion and went to sleep in a servant's bedroom, roused only by the police who came to make his arrest. She gave a brief three columns, carried in the news section of *The World* on page 3 of Monday's paper, to the moral reformer Elizabeth Grannis. Mrs. Grannis led the National Christian League for the Promotion of Social Purity; she was superintendent of the New York County Women's Christian Temperance Union and of the Social Purity Central Union, and she owned and edited *The Church Union*. In Bly's story, Mrs. Grannis was railing against the indecency of low-cut dresses, which, Bly got her to confess, she herself had worn as a young girl.

Bly pursued Thomas C. Platt, the Republican boss so much in the news, to produce a pandering profile. One of her favorite questions to male subjects, one she had asked of Lexow, of Altgeld, even of Mitchell in Saratoga, she also put to Platt: "Are you superstitious?" Platt, like the others, said no but added he would rather see a new moon over his right shoulder than his left.

For the requisite holiday pathos piece, she visited the miserable tenement homes owned by the Trinity Corporation, the real estate arm of Trinity Church, which, she said, was busy spending thousands of dollars to celebrate Christmas, ordering masses of green foliage and holly and mistletoe while its tenants were subsisting in barren, cold, and leaky quarters.

For New Year's Eve, a Monday, she told the real-life fairy tale of the rise of socialite Edith Kingdon Gould, wife of the financier George Gould, son of Jay. Bly both admired and identified with the subject of her piece, a very poor girl and the sole support of a widowed, wise, and Napoleonic mother who had instilled in her daughter the value of being well-groomed, well-dressed, sweet, and pleasant. Edith's mother decided that her daughter should become an actress—the most expedient way for a poor girl to meet better-born eligible men. She probably did not expect the likes of George Gould to come along, but he did. Although his parents objected to his marrying an actress, they ultimately accepted Edith, whose reputation was, as the expression goes, beyond reproach.

Mrs. Gould produced what Bly considered a "generous" number of children for the wife of a millionaire, then lived a life of quiet deference until her father-in-law's death. At that point she felt free to pursue her social ambitions. Bly took credit for enabling her launch.

Bly wrote the story as a tale, starting with her own decision to help out a young woman acquaintance who needed a job. Bly suggested the young acquaintance's name to the editor of *The Mail and Express,* who was looking for someone to start up the newspaper's children's department. The young woman was hired and did her work ably. In the course of her duties, she came up with the idea for two charitable drives to benefit children's causes. Bly then gave her protégée the idea of inviting Edith Gould to chair the events. Mrs. Gould agreed. The younger newspaper writer repaid Mrs. Gould's efforts by writing flattering items about her in the newspaper, thereby establishing her importance with her would-be peers.

It was a start, but true arrival in New York society would require more. Bly's tale continued. The Goulds set out for England, where social success in those rarefied aristocratic circles greased the way for newly monied Americans to quench their social yearnings back home. The Goulds bought a yacht, *The Vigilant,* and soon George Gould was able to count the Prince of Wales among his racing companions.

By the time the Goulds returned to New York, mothers of society's marriageable sons and daughters were busy cultivating the former actress. Bly was delighted with the ascension.

> The Goulds are in "society," and though those on the inside know that New York "society" has "pantatas" as well as the New York police, and that a female pantata and a male pantata both supposed to be "society" leaders, cost the Goulds almost as much as *The Vigilant*, yet it is entirely due to the fact that George Gould married a poor girl who had brains and ambition that they are where they are today.

Edith Gould, Bly said, would always reflect credit on George Gould and his home. "That," she said, "is the moral in the story for rich men. The moral for mothers is all through the story. At any rate, who can help feeling an admiration for Edith Kingdon Gould."

The reason for Bly's fascination with Edith Gould was obvious. Both were poor girls whose mothers had groomed them to know no limits. Bly, now thirty, bored, even somewhat embarrassed by the only work by which she could earn a good living, may have started to find some decided appeal in the prospect of a life of security and honor as the wife of a wealthy man. Mrs. Gould, in Bly's estimation, had distinguished herself from the snobbish vacationers of Newport and Narragansett, whom Bly had once described as "people whose money is the sole thing that makes them known in the world." Having money and position did not, by definition, deny one the possibility of other, more noteworthy achievements. Bly, in any event, could already claim those. To her mind, Mrs. Gould symbolized not only the legitimacy but the many advantages of wealthy scions deciding to marry outside their class.

Readers, not privy to what may have been Bly's interior dialogue, could only evaluate her strange fable about Mrs. Gould at face value. Why had she written such a peculiar story? *Town Topics* thought her "charming condescension" outrageous and quickly slipped out the machete: "If Mrs. Gould ever does any literary slumming and reads *The World*, she must have been delighted to find in last Monday's issue a long article from which it appears that she owes all her success in society to Nellie Bly. This will be a revelation to many of my readers, who know of Mrs. G's tact, beauty and *savoir vivre*, but it must be true—for Nellie Bly says so."

The gossip magazine mocked Bly's self-promoting account of Mrs. Gould's rise, sneering that not only had Bly given herself credit for getting Mrs. Gould to chair the charity benefits that launched her social climb, which was true, but that it was also Bly's idea to buy *The Vigilant* and get to know the Prince of Wales, which was not. It didn't stop there: "And now Nellie Bly is going to fix it with St. Peter so that Mrs. Gould will have entrée into heavenly society. Really, it is the most charming example of unassuming but powerful protection that I ever remember to have read of. And how Mrs. George Gould must enjoy the story! I do not wonder that the infant Goulds are taught to pray each night, "And p'ease, Dod, b'ess Nellie Bly.""

In the world of modern wild-cat journalism, the woman reporter lasts about four years. She brings her education, her personal attractions, her youth, her illusions, her energy, her ambition and her enthusiasm to the encounter, and the first year she rises rapidly. The second and third years she enjoys the zenith of her popularity; with the fourth year she begins the descent, lingers about the horizon for a time and then she disappears from view.

—Haryot Holt Cahoon, 1897

Through her sympathetic reporting at Pullman, Bly had established enough credibility with the labor movement to feel perfectly comfortable showing up unannounced in a small Illinois town for a jailhouse interview with Eugene V. Debs, leader of the American Railway Union, in January of 1895. Debs and other labor leaders were serving time on contempt of court convictions stemming from the Pullman strike. Because the vermin-infested Cook County Jail was jammed to capacity, Debs and his compatriots were being held in rather pleasant, if locked, quarters behind the sheriff's house in Woodstock, Illinois.

Although the two were not personally acquainted, Debs knew who Bly was as soon as she introduced herself. He expressed his pleasure at the opportunity to submit to her interview, and she obliged with a very flattering portrayal. With what she herself acknowledged was considerable impertinence, she did not hesitate to ask him how much money he made or if he had money of his own: Debs was known to have agreed to a decrease in salary from the union on more than one occasion. The newspapers had charged that Debs was insane, a dipsomaniac who had impaired his memory with excessive drinking, but Bly presented a picture of a modest, intelligent, rational man, whom she described as "temperate" without further comment.

It appears Bly's contract with *The World* had changed by this time. When the Debs interview appeared in the newspaper, it bore the tag line "Special to the *World*," usually the designation for a story bought from a writer not on a newspaper's permanent staff. None of

Bly's previous work from Chicago or other out-of-town venues had ever been so marked. From Chicago, she traveled west for more than a week to report on the hunger, suffering, and hardship resulting from a spell of severe drought throughout the Midwest. Those stories—datelined Valentine, Nebraska; Fairfax, South Dakota; and Butte, Montana—were tagged "Special Correspondence of the *World*." Neither the Debs piece nor any of the reporting from the drought-stricken region appeared in a Sunday newspaper, which may indicate that Bly, after months of dissatisfaction, had finally fallen out completely with Sunday editor Morrill Goddard. Actually, her last "long-winded" Sunday piece was the Thomas Platt interview, which had run in early December. So her break with the Sunday editors may have come well before the trip west. The daily editors adorned her work with the same marqueelike display she had long been accustomed to in the Sunday feature pages of *The World*, but her stories ran three columns instead of the usual seven or eight. If she was being paid on a space rate, which she probably was, this would have meant a severe slash in earnings.

On arrival in Nebraska, Bly engaged as her guide U.S. Special Agent George Crager, an interpreter of Native Americans who had captured Big Turkey during the Indian Uprising of 1891. They drove through the hardest hit areas of Nebraska, stopping at every home they found, so Bly could report a series of tragic personal stories. From Valentine, she wrote of the vista:

> Imagine one broad and level stretch of land, with a sky closing over it like a dome, and sky and land apparently meeting and forming a perfect circle. The sky is of Italian blueness, not a cloud in sight, and the air as soft and balmy as on a perfect October day. But all the land lies desolate, covered with the yellow stubble of corn stalks that never matured and grain that never came to a head. The dust in the roads is many inches deep, and one finds it difficult to realize that it is winter.
>
> Cheered by the blueness of the sky and the balminess of the air, I thought Nebraska not a bad place to live in until I

remembered to look for signs of life. I could see for miles, but not a single sign of li[f]e, man, beast or plant, met my gaze. Trees there were none.

From there, she went straight to Lincoln and Omaha to meet with state relief officials and visit the warehouses to see what kinds of stores they had. She came up against the traditional problem in relief efforts: abundant supplies and no effective means of distribution to those in most dire need. Said Bly: "Charity is a difficult matter to deal with. The sufferer usually receives the smallest share. But in this case there are thousands of families . . . in Nebraska who will have to be fed until next September. That is a big work and caution is necessary or the sympathy and the money will be exhausted before the people are really helped. Indiscriminate money-giving is bad."

By the time she reached Fairfax, South Dakota, Bly's advice was that unless a person felt inclined to do penance for his sins, "Stay East! Life in the West is one dreadful routine of hardships and privation without any compensations, unless it be the blue sky and endless stretch of level land."

Back in Nebraska, she expressed her disdain for the State Relief Commission, which she decided was too incompetent for the magnitude of the task. However, she singled out the local relief commission in Boyd County for praise. The leaders in Boyd had taken pains to form eight subcommittees, one for each of the county's precincts. After freight charges had been paid on any food coming into the county, the supplies were divided for equitable distribution to the districts. This plan, she said, actually worked.

By the end of her weeklong stay, Bly was convinced that the seed cause of misery in Nebraska was the overwhelming desire of the settlers to own their homes.

I never realized before what a strong feeling is the love of home and what a universal one. It is the desire to own a home to which is due the untold misery of the settlers in Nebraska. They were poor people who saw no chance of owning a home, and they read the flowery tales that emanate from the western land-boomer, the railroad employee, that tell how men can take up a claim and live thereon at no cost and in perfect ease and comfort.

"It is a horrible and ghastly delusion," she concluded about lives lived out in houses of sod far from the nearest railroad, of settlers buying fuel at exorbitant prices and hauling it great distances, contending with scarce water, no churches, no schools, no industries, and "children who must grow up in ignorance and of necessity become farmers, there being no other work." The series represented some of her most compelling work.

At some point back in New York, Bly had read an advertisement about "Abdullah the Mind Reader," and, sensing the opportunity to expose another fakir, she had paid the seer a visit. She found Abdullah rather engaging and used the occasion of their meeting to tell her readers a little more about herself:

> "Why do you wear a veil," he asked . . .
>
> "Because I am better-looking seen through one," I answered laughingly.
>
> "You would get along better in life if you were vainer," he observed.
>
> "Possibly," I replied. "At least I would be happier could I be vainer."
>
> "You are a remarkable young lady," he said, watching me closely.
>
> "Only for my frankness," I answered, lightly.
>
> "You are indifferent to everything," he asserted.
>
> "Not to dogs," I declared.

Abdullah then admitted to Bly that there was no art or gift to his seemingly mystical powers, that he was able to perform his startling feats through the knowledge of a neat trick which had been taught to him by a fellow passenger named W. Irving Bishop during an ocean crossing.

Bly's Abdullah story appeared in *The World* on Monday, February 18, after the final piece in her drought series was already in print.

She may have written the piece and handed it in before she left for the Midwest because, while there, she landed a new job.

At the end of February 1895, James W. Scott assumed control of both *The Chicago Herald* and *The Chicago Evening Post*. He quickly merged *The Herald* with the city's only other Democratic newspaper, *The Chicago Times*. As *The Times-Herald*, one of the paper's first acts was to lure to Chicago the best-known reporter in America; the best-known woman, at any rate.

Scott, who had been business manager of *The Herald*, had as partners in the merger Willis J. Abbot and his brother-in-law, Harry W. Hawley, who had recently acquired *The Times*. Abbot recalled Scott as a man "of ability and great personal popularity," somewhat tainted by his relationship with the banker John R. Walsh, who was *The Herald*'s previous proprietor and Scott's partner. Abbot cryptically noted that Walsh "had been useful to him [Scott] in many ways not commonly looked upon with favor by ethical journalists."

Chicago, like the other great American newspaper towns in this period, was part of the movement to consolidate the number of morning papers in each city, a result of the growing importance advertisers saw in evening papers as a means to reach women readers. In 1892, Chicago had six morning newspapers. By 1902, there were only four, and by 1918, the number of morning papers had been reduced to two.

The new *Times-Herald* was part of that consolidation trend in a situation of increasingly intense competition, every bit as vicious as that in New York. The onus on Bly was to dazzle Chicago readers, and that is what she set out to do. Long after her death, Walt McDougall would describe her as the lady reporter with "fire and flame" unmatched. Now Chicago got its chance to supply the kindling.

"Nellie Bly in the County Jail," the first blaze of headline read on Sunday, March 10. "Misery Among Crowded Prisoners." Acting on her tip from Debs, Bly spent nearly two days investigating conditions at the Cook County Jail, which she described as not fit for "a lot of mad dogs." She visited the men in their cells, the unfortunate women, and boys as young as ten years old—one even held in a dungeon on some minor prison infraction. Her eye for quirky and telling detail was, as always, what distinguished her work. She questioned the inmates about how often the sheets were changed, how frequently they could bathe or if they were required to do so. Learning that singing was a favorite pastime, she asked which songs they favored. The answers could not have been more apt: "The Widow's Plea for Her Son" and "Home Sweet Home."

Back in New York City, the thought of Bly reenacting for Chicago readers what she had been doing in New York over the past seven years had her detractors seized in paroxysms of hilarity. *Town Topics*, of course, led the nasty assault with its usual satirical sting:

When Nellie Bly entered Chicago last Saturday, joy bells were rung in all the churches. Cannon boomed from the lake front. Mayor Hopkins turned handsprings in the City Hall. Washington Hesing rushed over to the Grand Pacific and had his whiskers trimmed. Flags were flung to the breeze from the roofs of all the tall buildings and Papa Gillett sprinkled the downtown streets with perfume through his own garden hose. Every newspaper, save *The Times-Herald*, suspended publication and their editors rushed pell mell to the bogs of Bridgeport, where they spent the day in swallowing revivifiers of river water. As the young woman stepped from the train the entire *Times-Herald* staff lined up in military order on the platform and broke into the following beautiful hymn composed expressly for the occasion by Janitor [*Times-Herald* editor] Ole Jansen:

> *Hail to Nellie! Hail the holy*
> *Day that we secure such game*
> *Scotty may be roly-poly*
> *But he gets there just the same!*

At which stage in the proceedings Mr. James Scott, superbly attired as Falstaff, tore his cloak from his shoulders and following the example of the gallant Sir Walter of old, cast it manfully into the first puddle through which the lady was compelled to paddle. After this there was a procession through the streets and a reception at *The Times-Herald* office.

The magazine, indicating how highly Bly had been paid to make the switch, made prominent mention of Scott's supposed dismissal of twelve reporters to make room for her, imagining them as sacrificial offerings at this fantasized reception, feasting on fried giblets and milk. Then, "having expressed a preference of death to starvation," the twelve reporters were treated to fatal belts on the head from Jansen's baseball bat. The lampoon concluded: "Miss Bly made her debut in the columns of the *Times-Herald* in triumph the following morning. She was assigned to 'do' the Cook County Jail, and none of Mr. Scott's rival publishers, apparently, could raise sufficient money to bribe a turnkey to lock her in."

The *Times-Herald* contrived a follow-up piece on Bly's prison exposé a couple of days later. A knowledgeable reader's unsolicited response to Bly's article corroborated her charges, as did a second reporter's follow-up visit. If ever there was a "reach" for copy, this was it: "Nellie Bly's story of the frightful conditions in the county jail, printed in *The Times-Herald* Sunday, has had no apparent effect upon jail or other county officials."

Eleven days later, however, the sought-after results did emerge: "In the county jail they are blessing Nellie Bly," the story began. "Her exposure of the methods prevailing there, her criticisms of sanitary conditions which stung because true, her plea for better treatment, better food, unvitiated air, and better opportunities for cleanliness for the poor unfortunates there contained, many of them only awaiting the opportunity to show their innocence, is bearing fruit." Although prison officials were not about to give credit to Bly, it was no coincidence that in the three weeks since her story had appeared, a rash of improvements in everything from sanitary procedures and conditions to ventilation had been carried out.

In the meantime, Bly interviewed Frank Wenter, the not-yet-unsuccessful Democratic mayoral candidate, finding out what kind of mayor he thought he would make, what kind of friend he considered himself to be, what he put in his coffee.

Bly's success at the Cook County Jail led her straight to Bridewell Prison for her second act. The superintendent, Mark L. Crawford, had given her unrestricted access to the facility and its prisoners, saying, "I suppose when Nellie Bly comes I might as well throw up my hands." To this she replied slyly, "That depends." Crawford had nothing to fear. Bly described The Bridewell as "the best managed institution I ever visited."

Her story, which appeared in *The Times-Herald* on Sunday, April 7, was the last Bly ever wrote for the newspaper. Her Chicago career began and ended in five short weeks, punctuated by Scott's unrelated though eerily timed death from apoplexy while vacationing in New York the following Sunday.

Bly's situation was unenviable. She was one month shy of her thirty-first birthday, maligned again by her New York colleagues, unwilling to resubmit to the editorial dictates of *The Sunday World*, on unsteady ground in Chicago, and lacking acceptable alternative financial prospects.

The next thing anyone knew—and it was a closely held secret for some weeks—Nellie Bly had eloped. On April 5, 1895, with the Reverend Theodore N. Morrison officiating, Elizabeth Jane Cochrane plighted her troth in the rectory of Chicago's Church of the Epiphany on Ashland Avenue. The groom was Robert Livingston Seaman, a bachelor industrialist originally from Catskill, New York, as well-known in New York business circles as Bly was in newspapering. He was rich. And he was just turning seventy.

THE WORLD. PAGES

WANT DIRECTORY

NEW YORK, SUNDAY, APRIL 21, 1895

MR. AND MRS. NELLIE BLY.

The World's Famous Reporter Marries an Aged New York Millionaire.

THIS IS NOT AN EXPOSE; THIS TIME

Mr. Robert Seaman the Happy Husband, Is Seventy-Two Years Old and Never Married Before.

LAST WEEK AT THE THEATRES.

A Critical Study of "Trilby," "Pudd'nhead Wilson" and "Fortune."

SOCI

MR. AND MRS. NELLIE BLY

the World's Famous Reporter Marries an Aged New York Millionaire.

THIS IS NOT AN EXPOSE, THIS TIME.

Mr. Robert Seaman, the Happy Husband, Is Seventy-two Years Old and Never Married Before.

The New York World, *April 21, 1895*
(General Research Division, The New York Public Library)

8

❧ ❧

Marriage

NELLIE BLY TOOK A HUSBAND IN A QUICK, INSTINCTIVE, hastily calculated burst, the way she did everything else. Despite an ample selection of appropriate suitors, she had demurred for years on the question of marriage. Now, there was talk of devious motivation in her surprising choice.

The newlyweds did not announce their marriage immediately. This was, according to Bly, "owing to my business affairs and to his." More likely, it was because of opposition to the marriage from Seaman's prospective heirs, who, smelling a young adventuress after an old man's millions, had tried to talk him out of it. Seaman's hometown paper, *The Catskill Examiner*, said that the family had tried to dissuade him from marrying Bly and that their odd and sudden union had caused "no end of talk."

Finally, more than two weeks after the marriage, the New York newspapers began carrying confirmation that the rumors were true. *The Advertiser* said Bly had met Robert Seaman at a dinner in Chicago's Auditorium Hotel, that the attraction had been instantaneous, that they had married two weeks later, and that Seaman then had returned to New York the following day while she settled her affairs in Chicago.

What awaited Bly in New York was a new life as wife of a reputed multimillionaire; mistress of a "metropolitan residence" in the prestigious Murray Hill district, at 15 West Thirty-seventh Street, between Fifth and Sixth avenues, and of a magnificent Victorian "cottage" set on well-manicured, terraced gardens overlooking the Hudson River for weekend and holiday retreats. In addition, Seaman owned a farm on 300 of Catskill's rolling acres.

Those who knew them both were incredulous. Seaman's Catskill neighbors found news of the confirmed bachelor's impulsive marriage so preposterous they dismissed it as a newspaper joke. The ever-merciless columnists of *Town Topics* mused that Bly might be perpetrating yet another of her notorious "fakements," having plunged the embattled genre to a new low: "Such is the degradation of the press that nobody would be surprised to see in the Chicago paper upon which Nelly [*sic*] Bly has been engaged a sensational article headed: 'Is Marriage a Failure? Nelly Bly Tries It with a Good Old Man!! Her Experiences and His!!! A Divorce Applied for to Set Our Contributor Free!!!! Full Details by Seaman's Journalistic Wife!!!!!' "

From bits and scraps, it is possible to construct at least a reasonable version of how this marriage came so suddenly to pass. To start with, Bly's good friend Walt McDougall wrote in his memoirs that fractured romance more than her fractious relation with *The Sunday World* had precipitated Bly's original decision to quit New York in February of 1895. "Nellie was deeply attached to a friend of mine," McDougall wrote, "and when he suddenly married another, she abandoned New York." McDougall did not name the man in question, and from the many men he cataloged in his book as close friends, none sticks out as the obvious heartbreaker.

McDougall did, however, mention James Stetson Metcalfe, the drama critic of *Life*, as one with whom he was well-acquainted. Metcalfe had figured in Bly's life for some time. He was a fictionalized character in her 1888 novel and two years later met her in Philadelphia on her return from her round-the-world trip and wrote about it for *Life*. Bly had been heard in the offices of *The World* to speak wistfully of a loan "to *Life*" of $8,000, the sum total of her bank account at the time, which had not been repaid even years later.

Nellie Bly, 1896, 1890, 1895, left to right
(The Theater Collection, Museum of the City of New York)

On top of that, *The World*, in announcing her marriage to Seaman under the headline "Mr. and Mrs. Nellie Bly," made note:

> Miss Bly has been greatly admired by many, and has had more than one opportunity to become a bride before this. Mr. James Metcalfe, one of the editors of *Life*, has been very persistent and devoted in his attentions for several years. It has, in fact, more than once been reported that they were engaged. Cranks, too, wrought up to a state of frenzied adoration by her brilliant work, have thrown themselves at her feet with offers of marriage. But it remained for the aged millionaire to be made happy in his declining years.

One discrepancy: Metcalfe did not marry at the time of Bly's abrupt departure for Chicago. Rather, Metcalfe's marriage to the widow Edith Williams Dowling took place in August of 1896. However, McDougall could have meant that word of Metcalfe's new romance sent Bly packing. The memoirs were, after all, composed a good thirty years after the events described.

In any case, it seems clear that Bly was on the rebound, unhappy to have left her friends and family behind in New York, uncertain of her future with the wobbling *Chicago Times-Herald*, fed up with her line of work, and facing her thirty-first birthday. Said McDougall, "I never knew, nor does anybody, I suspect, what her intentions were" when, "to everybody's amazement," she married the elderly man.

Seaman was distinguished if not a society dandy—good looking, with military bearing, serious countenance, combed back if thinning white hair—a man of the same honorable country background as her own. He was *someone*, respected but not effete or snobbish, wealthy enough to insulate her from difficulties, secure, a onetime go-getter with a formidable history of financial success, and instantly smitten with the notion of being wed to the plucky Nellie Bly. She had happened upon a haven from chaos, disappointment, and exhausting employment, a replacement for the father she hardly knew, a man who was likely to demand little while providing the first opportunity of her adult life to rely on someone other than herself. It was a chance to put Lonely Orphan Girl permanently behind her. It was time to think more like Edith Gould.

The World announcement had the richest details. Its version was that the couple had met on the train to Chicago only days before the wedding. As a habitual reader of *The World*, Seaman had long been familiar with the famous Nellie Bly as a newspaper writer, but the two had never been introduced. Intimates estimated Seaman's fortune at $3 million, "and, if so, Bly has accomplished one of the ambitions of her life," the newspaper said. It went on, "At any rate, Miss Bly becomes the mistress of a metropolitan residence, a magnificent country seat, a whole stable of horses and nearly everything the good fairy of the story books always pictures. Few young women have had more worldly experience at the age of 30 than Miss Bly, and few are more capable of enjoying the pleasures of a 'millionaire existence.' "

Seaman's people were prominent residents of Catskill, the seat of Greene County on the banks of the Hudson River, 125 miles north of New York City. His paternal ancestors were English Quakers who originally settled in Jericho, Long Island, in the seventeenth century. Robert's father, Williams [*sic*] Seaman, moved from Jericho to Catskill in the early 1800s, hoisting a wooden sign shaped like a rocking horse above a shop on Main Street to start his business of sad-

Robert Livingston Seaman, circa 1896
(*Moses King's Notable New Yorkers of 1896–99*)

dle, trunk, and harness making. He was a beloved member of the small community, an "ardent and active" Democrat who was town supervisor from 1823 to 1828 and a member of the State Assembly in 1823 and 1826.

Robert, as near as can be determined, was born in 1825, the penultimate of the eight Seaman children—one girl and seven boys—who survived childhood. Three others died in youth. He got his education in the Catskill public schools, not at "Yale or Harvard, I do not know which," as one of his friends quoted in *The World* recalled. At eighteen, four years after his father's death, he left for New York City. The elder Seaman left no direct bequests to his children, entrusting all his real and personal property to his wife, Ellen, who lived another twenty-one years, until 1860.

At first, Robert Seaman clerked at a wholesale grocery concern known as Park, Smith, and Bruce. When Smith and Bruce retired soon after, a new company was formed by young Seaman and the partner who had originally hired him, Charles F. Park. Their business thrived—so much so that by 1862, the Seamans bought the West Thirty-seventh Street town house. Title was in the name of Robert's older sister, Ellen. The neighborhood was the best. The house was within baby steps of Tiffany's, of Brick Presbyterian Church, of the exclusive St. Nicholas Club with its membership roster of Remsens, DePeysters, Rhinelanders, and Roosevelts. The Union League's gabled clubhouse stood two blocks away, and two doors east of the Seaman brownstone lived the Valentine G. Halls, maternal grandparents of Eleanor Roosevelt.

After Charles Park died in 1866, Robert Seaman carried on alone in the business for four years before making partners of several of his clerks and ceding day-to-day management of the firm to them. He had moved on to other interests.

In 1869, he had formed a partnership with H. W. Sheppard for the manufacture of milk containers for rail transport. The business, known as the Iron Clad Manufacturing Company, was named for the historic Civil War naval battle, "the fight of the iron clads," the *Monitor* and the *Merrimac.* The company expanded over the years to encompass the manufacture of all sorts of hardware. Showrooms were on Cliff Street in Manhattan, and the factory site encompassed one square block of the Bushwick section of Brooklyn. At some points the firm employed as many as 1,500 workers. Sheppard's health was delicate, so Seaman, as treasurer and later as president, undertook major responsibility for running the company. He became a respected enough member of the New York business community that both Merchants' Exchange Bank and the Irving Savings Bank invited him onto their boards of directors.

In 1885, he closed out the grocery business, then known as Robert Seaman & Company, but kept Iron Clad going, more and more in the hands of hired managers. In the meantime, he accumulated valuable real estate in New York City and Kings, Queens, Westchester, and Greene counties.

In his younger days, friends recalled, Seaman was "what was then called a beau and now called a man-about-town. He never married. He was precise and modish in his dress. The habit never forsook him."

When Seaman met Bly, he was apparently just turning seventy, although the newspapers said he was seventy-two. A friend describ-

ing him to a *World* reporter said he had "a clean-shaven face, bald
head with kindly eyes, a rather strong nose and a well-set jaw, which
controls the muscles about the corners of the mouth until deep lines
are formed. There is something very reminiscent of Clay or Calhoun
or some of the famous early American statesmen, whose physiog-
nomies are today described as Roman." The friend continued:

> The old gentleman has dropped the assumption of jauntiness
> that was characteristic of him in his earlier years. He still
> scorns a cane, but has compromised on a tightly rolled
> umbrella with a firm steel rod. The swallow-tail, knicker-
> bockers, high collar and stock and ruffled shirt of the first
> half of the century would become him naturally. Should he
> conclude to entertain at his palatial home on the Hudson or
> his mansion on Murray Hill, New York City will meet a rare
> old gentleman of the Sir Roger [de] Coverly stamp.

Census records show that although Catskill remained the permanent residence of Seaman's unmarried siblings—Ellen, Henry,
and Edward—all three spent long periods with Robert at the town
house until Ellen's death in 1888 and Henry's three years later.
Edward, *The World* recorded, who was only a year or two younger
than Robert, was his brother's constant companion and had been for
forty years. Edward suffered from alcoholism, and all three of his
older siblings took a custodial relationship to him, as evidenced by
their wills. For years, Robert and Edward had taken their "daily air-
ing" together in a "cumbersome and expensive carriage drawn
sedately by a well-appointed team of large black horses." Robert was
said to have an avid amateur interest in science.

"He is today one of the most carefully dressed men in New
York," *The World* said. "In his style he is rich and quiet, never obtru-
sive. He does not look his 72 years. In fact, walking with his brother
Edward, he would be taken for the younger of the two. Notwithstanding his advanced age, he always was, and is today, a keen man of
business. His marriage is a surprise to all who know him, but then he
was always a man of strong convictions and an inflexible will. His
associates have always known this."

If anyone could be counted on to refuse to tally her good fortune on the abacus of press reports, it was Bly. Still, it is hard to imagine she could have been fully prepared for what awaited her on her return to New York as the new Mrs. Robert L. Seaman. It is safe to say that the situation was not at all what she had been led to expect.

True, she was probably braced for the family trouble. This was likely why the wedding took place in Chicago and not Catskill or New York City. What she may not have anticipated was how directly this situation would affect her daily life. The unexpected horror was that grand "metropolitan residence," with its impressive estimated value of $150,000. She took in the dusty, outdated furniture that Robert's sister had installed when the house was purchased more than thirty years earlier and its wall coverings and appointments, exhausted by years of transience and bachelor neglect. Bly dubbed it "Bleak House." In the understated assessment of another newspaper reporter who happened to see it at the time, "Mr. Seaman is said to be worth some millions but the interior of his home does not indicate that the owner is possessed of great wealth."

The living situation would prove as dismal as the interior. Edward Seaman did whatever he could to make Bly miserable. He undermined her position as lady of the house. He spied on her and her friends. He fomented conflict over money between Bly and his brother, and worst of all, he showed not the slightest inclination to move out.

There were other problems. Bly couldn't tolerate Seaman's longtime housekeeper and had her fired. Seaman declined to honor an antenuptial agreement to support Bly's mother and sister. Bly refused to have dinner at home—she couldn't bring herself to stomach her husband's "fare," she said at the time, not to mention the company at table. They agreed that she could dine out at any of a number of restaurants at which he kept accounts, but he positively refused to give her money for meals. On top of this, Bly found her new husband "unaccountably jealous." All summer she felt sure he was having her watched.

The very public collision of two headstrong souls locked in matrimony for seven short months was about to take place.

Saturday evening, November 9, 1895. Bly left the house at 6:30 P.M., got into her hansom cab, and instructed her driver, Barney, to head for the Imperial Hotel at Thirty-first Street and Broadway. She felt sure she was followed, and indeed, the man she suspected of tailing her entered its café. Bly, being Bly, wanted proof. She asked a porter to walk to the corner of Thirty-fourth Street to find a policeman and have him await the arrival of her cab. She left the café, again entered her hansom, and ordered Barney to proceed slowly and by a circuitous route toward Thirty-fourth Street. The second cab, as expected, followed closely behind.

Bly's cab stopped suddenly at the southwest corner of Thirty-fourth and Broadway, where a policeman stood waiting. At the northwest corner, the second cab stopped.

"Officer," she called as she got out of her cab. "There is a man in that cab who has been following my every movement. I want him arrested."

The policeman approached the second cab and ordered the man to get out. He resisted at first, then flashed a deputy sheriff's badge. The policeman told him he would have to explain his actions at the station, then ordered the man's driver to take him there. Bly followed in her own cab.

A *New York Tribune* reporter witnessed events at the West Thirtieth Street station house:

> The prisoner, who was a short, stout, well-dressed man, appeared ill at ease while Mrs. Seaman glared at him, and confided to a bystander that she had frequently seen him in her husband's library. To Sergeant Marron, Mrs. Seaman said that every place her cab stopped the prisoner's cab would stop also, and that she had seen the man make notes of the places she entered. For three weeks, she said, she had been followed and had made up her mind to put a stop to it.
>
> "Why," said the man, "her husband has employed me to follow her."
>
> "Oh, that is what I wanted to know," said Mrs. Seaman.

A charge of disorderly conduct was lodged against the prisoner, who turned out to be Seaman's Catskill caretaker of seventeen years,

Henry Hansen. The fact that Bly did not seem to know him indicates she had not spent much time, if any, at the country house since her marriage.

Hansen asked Sergeant Marron to send for Robert Seaman, who would put up his bail. Bly did not wait for her husband to arrive. "Barney," she commanded. "The Imperial Hotel."

Half an hour later, Robert Seaman walked into the station house to post bond for his caretaker. "Hansen should not have been arrested," Seaman told a reporter for *The World*. "He has only been in New York two days from Catskill. Somehow or other my wife got it in to her head that he was a private detective whom I employed to follow her, but that is ridiculous. She is mistaken." The bonds were signed. Seaman smiled when Hansen came out of the lockup, and the two left the station house together.

Hansen's loyalty reflected his long years of valued service. With a staff of four, he created and maintained the most admired gardens in Catskill behind the ornate iron gates of the Seaman property, accented with wandering peacocks strutting their feathers for passersby. Only a month before the arrest in New York, Hansen had come to the old man's aid in his shocking fistfight with Catskill neighbor F. A. Titus over their long-disputed property line. Hansen, as a special deputy sheriff of Greene County and accompanied by police and constables, led the arrest of Titus and a group of men he had hired to tear down an old boundary fence that separated the two properties. They were later released pending trial.

Events do not corroborate *The New York Sun*'s gratuitous one-word description of Seaman in this period as "feeble."

The day after Hansen's arrest for spying in New York, both he and Bly appeared before Magistrate John O. Mott at the Jefferson Market Police Court. Seaman stayed home. Hansen confirmed under oath that he was caretaker of the Seaman estate in Catskill, that his employer had called him to New York a week ago Friday but hadn't asked him to do anything until Saturday evening. At that time, he called him into his study and said, "You will find a cab on the corner; enter it and follow my wife, who is about to drive away in another cab. See exactly where she goes and what she does and report to me."

"I obeyed," Hansen said, "and my arrest followed."

The judge asked Bly if Hansen had molested her. "Of course, he didn't touch me," she said. "He simply followed me, just as I have stated."

"Then he has done nothing legally wrong," the judge said. "What do you expect of me?" The exchange continued:

> "I expect protection, your honor," replied she. "I have been annoyed by men following me for three weeks, and two or three nights ago someone tried to force the door of my sleeping apartment. I want protection."
>
> "Was it this man who attempted to enter your room?"
>
> "Well, I can't look through a door and so, of course, I am unable to say exactly who the intruder was, but I can say that I have seen this man sneaking about the halls."
>
> "What you can prove and what you can't prove," exclaimed the Court, peevishly, "are two entirely different things; for all I know the old man is trying to get a divorce from you. Now tell me exactly what you want."
>
> "I want this man put under bonds."
>
> "Bonds for what?" snapped the Court and yet with a laugh.
>
> "To make him keep away."
>
> "No," replied the magistrate, still in a cross tone. "I can't do it. The prisoner is discharged."
>
> "Very well," exclaimed Mrs. Seaman as she left the bridge. "I see I can't get justice here, so I'll go where I can get it."

Hansen tried to apologize, but Bly ignored him and got into her cab and left.

Later, reporters for *The Sun* and *The Recorder* came calling at the Seaman house. To *The Sun*, Seaman made the following statement:

> Really there is nothing in it, nothing in it at all. On Saturday evening, Mrs. Seaman's carriage was at the door to take her out to dinner. As she left the house, I told my butler to

step down into the basement and ask Hansen to see where she got her dinner. Hansen did so and did it so bunglingly that he got caught and was arrested. I have a right to know where my wife takes her dinner, I believe. She refuses to dine at my table, and I wished to know where she did dine. Now that's all there is to it.

Hansen is not a detective. The man has been in my employ 17 years as caretaker of my country place in the Catskills. He is no more a private detective than you are. He is, I believe, a special deputy sheriff of Greene County. He came to New York on Tuesday to make his annual accounting to me. I think the manner in which he followed Mrs. Seaman clearly shows that he is no professional detective. He did his work like a countryman, rattled around in a cab and got caught like a mutton-head.

Flat out, the reporter asked Seaman if he had engaged Hansen or anyone else to follow his wife. "It is not true, emphatically not true," Seaman replied. "I have never had detectives or anyone else in my employ to track Mrs. Seaman, and I am frank to admit that it was foolish of me to send Hansen out on Saturday night. It was a hasty act on my part, and I'm sorry I did it. I have no intention of trying to obtain a divorce from my wife, and so far as I know, she has no desire to obtain a divorce."

The reporter for *The Recorder* also took the initiative to go to the Seaman house. There, he witnessed what he described as a strange seriocomedy, one he titled "The Mating of May and December," or "When Love Has Flown Away."

Bly took the reporter to the back drawing room to meet her husband. She introduced him and then said, "He wants to know why you had a detective following me." The reporter found Seaman pacing rapidly up and down while "puffing vigorously at a cigar" and described the gentleman as still handsome at somewhere between sixty-five and seventy years of age.

As Seaman started to answer the question, Bly decided she needed to interject. *The Recorder* reporter repeated the exchange:

"I have no statement to make," he said, "I don't know that I had any one following her."

"But," broke in Mrs. Seaman, "he swore he was obeying your orders, and that you had asked him to follow me."

"I don't ask my servants," Mr. Seaman replied. "I direct them what to do."

"But that man isn't a servant," Mrs. Seaman explained. "Now, didn't you tell him to follow me?"

"Well," said Mr. Seaman, turning to the reporter. "I guess he went of his own accord as much as anything else; but perhaps I did say that she was going out that evening"—

"Don't put me in a wrong light," broke in Mrs. Seaman, with a queer smile. "Remember I go out to dinner every night; I'm going out now."

"And that he had better look after her," Mr. Seaman went on, just as though his wife had not spoken. "I may have been wrong, and perhaps I made just as much of a fool of myself then as she did when she had him arrested. But it can't be helped now and I don't know that I have anything more to say on the subject."

With that, Bly left the house with her brother, not giving her husband as much as a backward glance. She had smiled continually during the exchange, and Seaman "seemed very much excited and never for a moment ceased walking up and down and puffing clouds of smoke from his cigar." Edward Seaman was in the house as was a woman Bly said she did not know by name. She turned out to be Seaman's niece. Bly passed the reporter as she left. "They are trying to make all the trouble possible for me," she said in an apparent reference to her husband's family.

Later that night, she again appealed to the authorities for help. Seaman had invited two guests that she didn't like. She walked two blocks down Thirty-seventh Street to Park Avenue and found a policeman walking his beat. She told him about the men. "My husband is in the house," she said, "and I want you to see them and get them out. I am afraid to stay in the house with them." The officer accompanied her to the house, where Seaman confirmed that the men were his guests and that he wanted them to stay. Bly would have to go to the station house and see the captain if she wanted further action, the officer told her.

To a *Sun* reporter, the policeman repeated what Bly had told him about her marital difficulties. Her problems with Seaman were not "of the divorce sort," she said; rather, they were brought on by Seaman's brother Edward, who "had control of him" and made trouble about financial matters between her and her husband. Bly then got into her cab and drove to the West Thirtieth Street station house, where she saw Sergeant Henry Halpin in private. Soon after, she left, apparently satisfied. No details of the discussion were disclosed.

Despite Seaman's emphatic denials, Bly was not imagining things when she suspected she was being followed before the Hansen incident. Three years later, it would be learned that Seaman had hired a better-trained private detective to follow his wife around during this period. The man was John Hanley, an advance agent for William H. West's minstrels who had once worked at a detective agency. In court papers, Hanley charged that Seaman had paid him $1,000 for his services prior to February 1896 but still owed him another $1,265 for work in February, July, and August of that year investigating the "actions and conduct" of "one James Metcalfe of 17 West 27th Street," "a certain person known as and by the name of Nellie Bly," and an attorney identified only as "Mr. Webb."

❧

Within three days of the Hansen episode, a far more embarrassing scandal rocked the Seaman household, this time having nothing directly to do with Bly. *The Chicago Evening Post* reported the story on November 23, and by the next day it had made *The New York Times*:

> Chicago, Nov. 23—The litigation between L. H. Bisbee, a Chicago attorney, and Robert Seaman, the New York millionaire and husband of "Nelly [*sic*] Bly," involving the recovery of $50,000 from the lawyer, assumed a sensational

phase yesterday in the Court of Master in Chancery [Jeremiah] Leaming, before whom evidence is being taken.

In a long cross-examination conducted for the millionaire, Mr. Bisbee stated that he visited New York in 1887 and effected a settlement between Mr. Seaman and Ernestine Sanderson, who claimed to be Mr. Seaman's common-law wife, whereby the woman was to go away and cease to be a burden upon his mind. The defendant said he had a verbal agreement with the millionaire that his services in effecting a release of the woman's claims were to liquidate any amount for which Mr. Seaman might hold Mr. Bisbee's notes.

John C. Patterson, counsel for Mr. Seaman, was surprised at the revelation of the "woman in the case." Mr. Bisbee said Mr. Seaman deeded property to the woman and a lot of jewels and that Mr. Seaman agreed to relinquish all claims against the defendant on the further payment of $5,000.

Bisbee, a Chicago attorney and former Illinois state legislator, was a sometime business partner of Seaman. Although Seaman's case against Bisbee had been in litigation for some time, the lawyer said he had never before brought up the matter of the Sanderson woman because of "its extremely confidential character." He only brought it up at this point, he said, in retaliation for the way Seaman's attorneys had "viciously and maliciously and outrageously and wickedly and designedly and corruptly" used legal instruments to prevent Bisbee's wife from securing a loan to cover the mortgage on their home. Seaman's counsel, John C. Patterson, shot back that Bisbee's real motivation in falsely raising the matter of Ernestine Sanderson at this time was to fuel the "unfortunate gossip" about Seaman's marriage to Bly that had been circulating for the past several weeks and to further embarrass the old man.

According to Patterson, Bisbee obtained information in 1882 that the claims of the defunct Cook County National Bank and the bankrupt B. P. Allen estate of Des Moines, Iowa, would be worth far more than the purchase price. Seaman loaned Bisbee $39,000 to buy the two claims. Bisbee, in turn, gave Seaman promissory notes for about $12,000 and agreed to repay the notes along with the balance of the loan still owed and half the profits accruing from realization of the claims.

The claims yielded handsomely as expected, but Seaman never saw a cent. "We sued for the recovery and an accounting," Patterson said, "and in the various phases of the hearings Bisbee's side was closed, only to be opened again. And now he comes out with his false tale of a common-law wife of Mr. Seaman and his alleged services in effecting a settlement between her and Mr. Seaman solely to delay the suit and worry the old gentleman. Why did he wait ten years to tell such a story?"

Patterson said further that Bisbee would not be able to produce even a scrap of evidence to substantiate his contention and that anyway, he had written Seaman "scores of letters acknowledging his indebtedness and [had] made all sorts of promises to pay." Seaman's side charged that Bisbee had only invested $7,000 of Seaman's money in the gilt-edged claims and put the rest in Chicago real estate with Bisbee's wife's name on the deeds. Bisbee countered that he could account for all of Seaman's money, that he had paid back what he owed, and that the claims purchased with Seaman's money had not been profitable. The court ultimately found in Seaman's favor, awarding him an $80,000 settlement. Since Bisbee was virtually insolvent at that point, it is unlikely Seaman ever actually collected. Interestingly, one of Seaman's lawyers in the case was the New York attorney Ernest C. Webb, one of the men Seaman hired detective Hanley to investigate early in 1896.

As for Ernestine Sanderson, Bisbee was vague and confused on details of events that allegedly had occurred as much as ten years earlier. He also was unable to produce any evidence to support his impugning statements. Nevertheless, he told the court that she had cohabited with Seaman; that Seaman often brought her along to dinner and theater with the two men when Bisbee was in New York; that Seaman felt a nagging responsibility toward her because his sister, Ellen, before her death, had acted to prevent a marriage; that Seaman was insistent that the matter stay confidential to protect his reputation and hers, and this was the reason he used a Chicago attorney to arrange a settlement. Bisbee also said the woman had continued to harass Seaman for money until as recently as 1892. Bisbee also mentioned that he and Seaman had once met Ernestine Sanderson on the street when she was accompanied by a young girl whom Seaman identified as the lady's niece. The innuendo of his testimony was that the child might have been Seaman's, although there is no evidence of this.

Seaman responded to Bisbee in testimony, categorically denying every element of his accuser's story. He did acknowledge an acquaintanceship with Ernestine Sanderson and her family, all of whom he said he held in the greatest esteem. Ernestine was born in France in 1850 and immigrated to the United States with her parents at the age of six. She would have been in her mid-thirties during the period Bisbee described. Seaman, at the time, was about sixty.

Back in New York on Christmas Eve 1895, Robert Seaman drew up a will which left a measly $300 to Bly in addition to her widow's dower right in the estate. He also gave 250 shares of stock each to a number of his trusted employees at the Iron Clad, $10,000 each to two of his nieces, Arlisle and Nellie Young, and a like amount to a woman, not identified further, named Sarah Fawcett.

The action surely jolted Bly into the realization that this marriage might not ever provide the financial security she may well have imagined. Her mother's experience doubtless supplied a haunting specter. To the Cochranes, the widow's dower of a wealthy man meant only virtual poverty. Bly had no interest in repeating a sordid history. She had long ago determined that no man was going to undermine her independence or her ability to provide for her own security, which were inextricably linked. She would show Seaman what he may not have bargained for in marrying Nellie Bly. No more would she play the role of wealthy matron without sure, undisputed access to the attendant means to do so in perpetuity.

Bly moved at once to secure her own future the way she knew best: by earning her own way. By reporting and writing for *The New York World*.

~❧~

Since Bly had left *The World* a year earlier for Chicago and then marriage, affairs at the newspaper had churned in the chaos the staff had long accepted as routine. In this period, however, there was a new

dimension to the struggle in the form of some highly focused competition from William Randolph Hearst. The owner of *The San
Francisco Examiner*, Hearst had purchased the moribund *New York
Journal* in September of 1895 and set himself up as Pulitzer's main
rival. From *The Examiner*'s office inside the Pulitzer building, Hearst
quietly negotiated with *The World*'s valuable Sunday crew, inducing
them all to move to his new paper. Pulitzer was outraged, threw *The
Examiner* out of the *World* building, upped the cash offer, and won
his staff's return—but only for twenty-four hours. Hearst quickly
outbid the ailing Pulitzer again, and Goddard and his crew left for
good. To Pulitzer, Hearst's behavior was tantamount to a declaration
of war.

Triage was performed on the talent hemorrhage. Pulitzer
moved fast. Arthur Brisbane assumed Goddard's position as Sunday
editor and immediately assembled a competitive new team. He hired
newspaper novices such as Harriet Hubbard Ayer, a reputed beauty
expert, and added the star-reporter byline of Nellie Bly. Brisbane was
a great admirer of Bly, and the feeling was mutual. The timing suited
her perfectly. She could help out an old friend in a way that would
earn her good money, and, at the same time, she would have the
chance to irritate her uncooperative husband in a reasonably
respectable way. Maybe she thought she could even cause her former
editor, Morrill Goddard, some grief, too.

Pulitzer was likely referring to Bly in his cable to business manager John Norris of February 2, 1896: "Please don't write in Delphic
phrases/ Name person reemployed and out of office twice/ I know
nothing about it."

Without fanfare, the byline of Nellie Bly had been appearing in
the daily pages of *The World* for several weeks before the great Goddard defection. On Monday, January 13, *The World* published Bly's
four-column interview with Patrick Jerome Gleason, the charming
seventy-five-year-old mayor of Long Island City, Queens, just a ferry
ride away from Manhattan across the East River.

At this point, Bly's purpose in writing for *The World* again was
as much to secure an independent income as to slip a few prickly
metaphoric burrs beneath her husband's undershirts. He was the
obvious target of many of the questions she posed to her subjects in

this period, this subject in particular. Gleason was Seaman's contemporary in age, and Bly was quick to make much of the parallel.

Bly charmed the old widower into telling her his whole life story. With loving warmth, he described his twelve-year-old daughter, who was being raised since his wife's death in a house other than his own, and, in response to her prying questions, he reeled off his philosophies and some of his more intimate thoughts:

"What is your greatest ambition now?" I asked this very original man.

He leaned back and laughed so heartily that although I was feeling as blue and bitter as the great briny deep, I had to smile in sympathy.

"There's another point, young lady, you and I will have to argue," he said teasingly. "Supposin' I said my greatest ambition was to get married? What would happen?"

"I would write it and you would be besieged by thousands of maidens all forlorn," I answered guilelessly.

"And what would I do? You wouldn't help me out of it by taking me yourself," he questioned jokingly.

"There are matrimonial reasons why I couldn't," I sighed. (A woman only has to sigh when she talks about such topics. It always flatters the men and they think, "Well, by jove! If I haven't made an . . ."—But this is a different story.)

Almost before Gleason realized it, Bly had him describing a handsome girl he had once loved and was asking if she were his first affair:

He laughed again; all the sentiment gone.

"Supposin' I interviewed you on your first love affair," he suggested.

"I'd tell you: women like to recall such things," I responded, "But"—I changed the subject instantly.

She wanted to know what Gleason thought of "The New Woman," the independent late-nineteenth-century feminist ideal whom Bly certainly thought she personified. "I don't know exactly," he replied, doubting. "I think a woman's greatest ambition should be to take care of a good home."

Here was something her new husband was not giving her much chance to realize, if indeed Bly considered homemaking a primary value. If not, she seemed too enchanted with Gleason to challenge him on attitudes toward women she had never endorsed. In this instance, it didn't matter, since the real target of her word-loaded BB gun was Robert Seaman, the very reason for her feeling "blue and bitter as the briny deep." The question most on her own mind she put to Gleason:

> "Do you think marriage a failure?"
>
> "By jove, no. Why should it be?" he asked in surprise.
>
> "I don't know," I confessed.
>
> "What is a woman's best attribute?" I asked this very original man.
>
> "To love her husband and to think that everything he does is just right," was the instant reply.
>
> "Her best accomplishment," he added, "is to know how to have a good table, know what to order and how it should be prepared."

By Gleason's yardstick, Bly was not even getting an opportunity to prove her wifely worth at 15 West Thirty-seventh Street.

"What's a man's greatest attribute?" she asked the mayor. "Honesty," he replied.

Bly discussed with Gleason his prospects for remarriage but seemed strangely intent on learning the color of his lost sweetheart's eyes:

> "And you won't say whether her eyes are blue or brown?" I urged imploringly.
>
> "I don't care. If a young girl like you was to marry an old man like me, I'd be grateful. I'd love the ground she'd walk on."

"You can find one," I said.

And I believe it. Good men are too scarce for Patrick
Jerome Gleason, with his true blue heart, to pine.

For the following Monday she interviewed John Daly, "The
Gambler King." The story was, by her description, the first interview he had ever given to the press. Bly had read in the newspapers
that Daly was planning to sell his gambling establishment—since
gaming had been outlawed three years before—and move on to
Europe. Daly told her he had no such intention, that he would continue to run the place as a men's club, "to keep people off the streets,"
for another few years and then, if gambling was not reintroduced,
would simply close down.

As with Mayor Gleason, Bly found her subject utterly charming. She couldn't resist the opportunity to quiz another attractive
man on the subjects of matrimony and bliss:

"What gives the greatest happiness in the world?" I
asked. "You have known everything—hard work, money and
ease, excitement and quietness."

"Married life gives the greatest happiness in the
world," he said, firmly.

"For you, possibly, because you are a good husband," I
argued.

"I have said it depends entirely upon the man," he
answered, smiling, "and being right, it is the only real happiness in the world. I look at men who come here, rich bach-
elors, who don't know how to spend their time or their
money, and I think their lives must be wretchedly cold and
lonely. It gives me a shiver. I don't see how they stand it. I
can almost think that any sort of a wife and home is much
better than none at all."

When Bly announced to Seaman the next week that she would
be going to Washington to cover the National Woman Suffrage Convention, he quietly called John Hanley, the private detective, to

shadow her. Hanley's suit against Seaman for nonpayment of fees two years later listed his trip to Washington to observe and report on Bly's "actions and conduct."

Her reporting from the convention was Bly at her very best. The story from the Church of Our Father, where the convention was held, had everything: details, descriptions, atmospherics, boredom, excitement, highlights of the proceedings, humor, ironies, the struggles with parliamentary procedure, comparisons and criticisms—all delivered with high readability. No wonder Brisbane was glad to have Bly on staff. She was able to create the sense that the reader was really a delegate, sitting all day and following the proceedings, stopping to whisper to a neighbor from time to time, making comments on various aspects of the discussion, observations and plain old gossip about people and platforms. The length alone gave a sense of how the day must have been experienced by those who attended. The story took up almost a full page.

World editors played the convention report on page 4 of the news section—impressive prominence for a movement that would not reach its stated goal for another quarter of a century. Or maybe the significance was that Bly had covered it. Here is her initial observation: "The first thing I learned was that woman's suffragists do not differ from women of lesser ambitions. The hour of the meeting was announced for 10 o'clock, and it was exactly 10:20 when the President, Susan B. Anthony, appeared upon the platform."

In the course of the day, Bly seemed especially irked by the tendency of many of the suffragists to pay so little attention to how they dressed. Alice Stone Blackwell's double-breasted broadcloth coat with two rows of enormous pearl buttons was at least six years old and hideous, Bly said. And her black cashmere skirt was a horror— never had Bly seen one hang worse. Charlotte Perkins Stetson, she said, must be "daft on dress reform or some other abomination. She was decidedly wider at the waist than she was below it. We did not need to be told that she was corsetless and, I fear, petticoatless! . . . I never could see any reason for a woman to neglect her appearance merely because she is intellectually inclined. It certainly does not show any strength of mind. I take it rather as a weakness. And in working for a cause I think it is wise to show the men that its influence does not make women any the less attractive."

Personal appearance was a fixation. She pounded the keyboard again later in the story: "Dress is a great weapon in the hands of a woman if rightly applied. It is a weapon men lack, so women should make the most of it. As their motto seems to be 'the means to gain the end,' why not use the powerful means of pretty clothes?"

Bly advised the suffragists to take a cue from men at political conventions and remove their hats when they appeared onstage. She said the one man who addressed the gathering was simply no match as an orator for the movement's impressive women speakers. The struggle of the movement to fund itself disturbed her. "When one hears the women talk about it being difficult to collect the dues and one realizes that it is less than a cent a week, one feels that woman cannot be given suffrage too soon, or anything that will make her less the slave of poverty," she wrote.

She followed carefully the debate over fund-raising methods. By far the most lucrative of the moneymaking schemes was the minstrel show staged by the North Dakota suffragists, which netted $300, according to that state's delegate, Dr. Cora Smith Eaton. "We blackened our faces and gave a minstrel show and oh! it was so popular! . . . The ladies hesitated to advertise themselves so we called it the Daughters of Ham. The first part was a minstrel show; the second part was a plantation scene. It was very, very comical. In part III we had the Highland fling and part IV was a cake walk. Oh! It was very funny!"

At least one woman was not amused. "Madame President," she called out to Susan B. Anthony. "Do you think a minstrel show stamps us with dignity? The Woman Suffragists should not do anything that will cause reflection to be made upon them. A minstrel show is rowdyism and lowers us."

Bly made note of the fact that there was only one "colored" delegate to the assembly and almost no one between the ages of eighteen and twenty-five. No one opposed the minstrel show idea on racial grounds. Suffrage was still largely a movement of and for the white middle class.

The next day, under the headline "Woman in the Pulpit," Bly provided endless detail on Mrs. Charlotte Perkins Stetson's sermon preached at the People's Church Typographical Hall at Number 423 G Street. Mrs. Stetson's sermon was full of humor—"This is exactly what is needed in churches," Bly remarked—and she repeated the story of Mrs. Stetson's that had provoked the greatest laughter:

> "Industry is part of the maternal function," she continued. "Women produced children, and man ate them if he could catch 'em. The subjection of women was necessary for the elevation of man. The savage could eat and hunt. He could not work. His wife did that. Now, when he began to want to keep his wife shut up so she could not be seen by others, he had to find food for her, for his children and his maiden aunts and things, and thus, through his jealousy and selfishness, he learned to labor."

Bly saved for the following Sunday her interview with the movement's leader, the venerable Susan B. Anthony, to which *The World* again gave huge display. Although Anthony had been interviewed scores of times during a half-century in the suffrage movement, never had she revealed more information about herself than she did in her exchange with Bly.

Anthony spoke for many of the suffragists at the convention in voicing concern about the subjugation of Cuba by Spain and the talk of U.S. intervention to win Cuba's independence. Both *The Journal* and *The World* were at the forefront of newspapers revving up concern about alleged atrocities against the Cuban nationalists. The era of Yellow Journalism counts some of its most notorious moments from this episode, taking its name from the Yellow Kid, a comic strip character in both newspapers.

"Tell me about Cuba!" Miss Anthony implored Bly after the two exchanged greetings. "I am so interested in it. I would postpone my own enfranchisement to see Cuba free."

Bly fulfilled the suffragist's request to be brought up to date on Cuba and then asked a slew of very personal questions, to which she got answers:

"Were you ever in love?"

"In love?" she laughed merrily. "Bless you, Nellie, I've been in love a thousand times!"

"Really?" I gasped, taken aback by this startling confession.

"Yes, really!" nodding her snowy head. "But I never loved any one as much that I thought it would last. In fact, I never felt I could give up my life of freedom to become a man's housekeeper. When I was young, if a girl married poor, she became a housekeeper and drudge. If she married wealth, she became a pet and a doll. Just think, had I married at 20, I would have been either a drudge or a doll for 55 years. Think of it!

"I want to add one thing," she said. "Once men were afraid of women with ideas and a desire to vote. Today, our best suffragists are sought in marriage by the best class of men."

Bly seemed relieved to be able to report that "unlike most suffragists or 'brainy' women, for that matter, Miss Anthony is very particular about her dress. She is always gowned richly, in style and with most exquisite taste."

"Do you pray?"

"I pray every single second of my life. I never get on my knees or anything like that, but I pray with my work. My prayer is to lift women to equality with men. Work and worship are one with me. I know there is no God of the universe made happy by my getting down on my knees and calling him 'great.'

"True marriage, the real marriage of soul, when two people take each other on terms of perfect equality, without the desire of one to . . . make the other subservient. It is a beautiful thing. It is the highest state of life. But for a woman to marry a man for support is a demoralizing condition. And for a man to marry a woman merely because she has a beautiful figure or face is degradation."

Had Bly asked "Are you religious?" she would have been unlikely to have elicited a comparable response. It was indicative of her exemplary skill as an interviewer.

Back in New York, Police Commissioner Theodore Roosevelt announced plans to abolish on Valentine's Day the homeless women's shelters inside various police station houses around the city. For her story on the Sunday before the projected closures, Bly spent the night with the women at the Oak Street Stationhouse, observing them in all their wretchedness, most brought low by "misfortune and whiskey," as they slept on bare boards and told their tales of misery. Her full page of sympathy-engendering pathos led the feature section, which Brisbane had taken to entitling *"The World*'s Sunday Magazine."

One woman captured the general mood: " 'There's no use lying about it,' said a sad-faced woman and the most intellectual one in the lot. 'Whiskey is our curse. It robs us of everything and we get down to this, and then we drink to forget our misery.' " Bly asked another if she had any interest in reforming, a favorite theme of hers from years past. This woman confirmed Bly's long-established view. "No," she replied. "What's the use? I only want enough drink to forget."

Of the fifteen women listed on the station house blotter, thirteen gave their place of birth as Ireland. Bly closed her piece, appearing to suggest that the sorry plight of these women could at least be understood in the context of their recent arrival in the country and their inability to adjust. "Only two Americans in the unhappy lot," she wrote. "Only that thought was a grain of comfort at least."

For the following week, someone got the idea to pair Bly's interview with eighty-year-old suffragist leader Elizabeth Cady Stanton with another woman in the news: Mary Alice Fleming, who was tending her two-month-old son, Robert, as she awaited trial in The Tombs prison for the slaying of her own mother. The two stories ran under one headline: "Nellie Bly and Two Women Contrasts." Stanton was touting publication of her new Woman's Bible. The suffragist had immersed herself in the project to help women break free from what she called the shackles of religious "degradation" by providing context and explanation for every biblical text about women. As an example of a biblical passage that women might find problematic, she cited the Old Testament on the slaying of the Midians in which women were classified just behind the jackasses.

Mrs. Fleming, from her makeshift jailhouse nursery, provided an intriguing counterpoint. The fact that male editors would think to set up in tandem the stories of two such different women was in itself a reflection of the times. Women's lives were undergoing jolt-

Nellie Bly as an elephant trainer, The World, *February 23, 1896*

(General Research Division, The New York Public Library)

ing transformations, and every aspect was news: changing mores, political action, the expansion of job opportunity, dress reform, bicycle riding. If Elizabeth Cady Stanton and Mary Alice Fleming had been men, their stories never would have appeared in such purposeful juxtaposition. There would have been no point. As for Bly, she was never one to miss a good news angle.

A ridiculous assignment followed. Bly's love of animals helped her transcend her disgust with stunt work, and she seemed delighted to accept the challenge of spending a day helping train the eight new elephants who had joined "The Greatest Show on Earth." When the trainer told her she had performed feats that even the professionals feared to attempt, she shared a confidence with her readers: "I did not tell him I had no nerve through it all. I merely did it because I hadn't courage to say I was afraid."

⌇⌇⌇

The World's circulation bounded forward, but so did *The Journal's*, at an even faster rate. The competition swerved into dangerous excess. Editors on both papers too often fell into the practice of inflating the significance of events or exaggerating in headlines to keep readers primed. This was sensationalism at its most reckless. The crisis in Cuba, and the passions it inflamed among Americans after Cuban nationalists rose against Spain in 1895, was a case in point. On March 8, 1896, a lavish illustration covered three quarters of a page of *The World* over the caption "Nellie Bly Fin de Siecle Joan of Arc." Accompanying it was the headline:

NELLIE BLY PROPOSES TO FIGHT FOR CUBA

Women Have More Courage than Men and Would Make Braver Officers.

READY TO RECRUIT VOLUNTEERS FOR HER FIRST REGIMENT.

Perhaps the featured report was only Brisbane's idea of a way to feed interest in Cuba as the story waned. Perhaps Bly, aroused by her feminist immersion of recent weeks and embittered by her marital disappointments of recent months, actually heard the call to arms. Either way, the story could not have more perfectly suited *The World*'s immediate purpose:

Nellie Bly is the busiest person in New York, man or woman. In fact, there are few persons of the billion and a half that toil and groan on this round earth that are so occupied as she. And, as always, she is doing something entertaining and novel and interesting.

Nellie Bly is arranging to add a new terror of war!

Could anything be more delightful? Now, adding a new terror to war in this day of all manner of dreadful inventions is no easy matter. And at first thought you would say that it would be impossible for a slender, comparatively frail young woman to do such a fearsome thing. But that is because you are not thoroughly acquainted with Nellie Bly.

It is very difficult to get her to talk about her plan. She is so busy arranging details that she has "no time for chat" as the gentleman said to his friends on the corner who called to him when he was being towed down the street by a wild steer. This interview was got only by accompanying her in a cab as she was riding from one place to another. She was looking very charming, but decidedly weary.

She had already designed a handsome uniform, so well styled and comfortable she thought it would encourage recruitment. She had been to all the most prestigious men's clubs, seeking formation of a committee of men "whose names will carry conviction to the community." Her plan was for these men to raise the necessary funds for the regiment, secure subscriptions, send money and supplies to the regiment at the front, look after the wounded when they returned home, and arrange funerals for those "who have died gloriously on the field of honor." *The World* reporter offered: "Miss Bly has a plain, matter-of-fact way of speaking and such a record of daring and unique achievement that it was impossible to suspect her of indulging in illusions. Miss Bly is not a dreamer."

Bly's contention was that war was "no longer a matter of muscular force" but of putting together forces of brave men who will obey orders. The key, she said, is the right kind of officers—"brave, capable of endurance, faithful, sober, intelligent, full of personal magnetism that will inspire the soldiers to do and dare." Women, she declared, embodied all these qualities far better than men.

As to a woman's ability to inspire male troops, she argued:

Do you think a company or a regiment of men soldiers, led by a woman would ever dare run away? Do you think that if a woman were watching them any man of them would flinch? Do you think that if a woman drew her sword and said, "Come on!" there would be a single soldier in the whole army who would not "come on" until his wounds made it impossible for him to crawl any further? No, indeed. With calm, intelligent, noble women leading the way there would be no such things as drawn battles. Every battle would be fought out to the bitter end, and wars would be brief and decisive and less destructive. You see you have no ground left to stand on. The wars of the future must and will be planned and officered by women. There is no mistaking the way the hands on the signboards point.

Bly was not disturbed by the reporter's incredulity. New ideas have that effect on people, she said. "Century after century you men have been jeering, imprisoning, burning, scoffing [at] every person who came forward with a new idea. You do not welcome it, ask it to sit down and get warmer, and interrogate it with the hope of learning something. Oh no: you just bar the door and bawl out to it as it stands pleading in the storm." She went on: "I shall simply go ahead and raise my regiment. It will be led and officered by women. And if the United States goes to war with Spain, why this woman regiment will go to the front, and you will see war such as there never was before." Bly acknowledged that the undertaking was great but vowed to persevere. "And I shall raise up such friends for poor, harassed Cuba as no nation fighting for liberty ever had before."

No more was heard of the plan, nor of Bly for quite some time.

༺ৡৣ৵

The marriage survived its roily first year. Rapprochement must have been effected sometime after the anniversary. Perhaps the vision of his wife marching off into battle snapped Seaman into the realization that he really did care for her. Bly gave up newspapering once again, which probably meant that Seaman had reevaluated his financial attitudes toward his spouse, as well as his refusal to honor his agreement to support Bly's several dependents. By August, the Seamans had left for Europe, with some of Bly's family members in tow. There was her mother, Mary Jane; her sister Kate; and Kate's daughter, Beatrice, now almost thirteen.

While in Paris, Seaman drew up yet another will on November 17, 1896, indicating the dramatic extent of their reconciliation. This one named Bly his sole executrix, awarding her new and powerful leverage with his family. To Edward, his brother, he gave Newton Farm, the 300-acre Catskill property, not to be confused with the mansion, and an annuity of $4,000 to be paid by Bly in equal quarterly installments for the rest of Edward's life. A handwritten insertion in the typed document instructs the executrix to pay off the outstanding mortgage on the farm from Seaman's estate. Seaman further instructed her to make one-time gifts of $1,000 apiece to his one living sister-in-law, each of his four nieces, and his two grandnieces. The rest, an amount not specified, was to be Bly's.

Given the financial panics of the preceding few years, it is hard to evaluate the worth of his holdings. They included bad debts, such as Bisbee's; devalued real estate; and the sludge of once-promising speculation. Still, the estate potentially represented more money than Bly could ever have dreamed of amassing on her own. The Iron Clad Manufacturing Company was still a going concern. Its factories occupied a full square block of Brooklyn property, bordered by Flushing and Bushwick avenues and Varet and Evergreen streets. There was the Catskill mansion on ten beautiful acres on Prospect

Avenue, some smaller pieces of property in the New York and Catskill areas, the Thirty-seventh Street town house in Manhattan, plus stock in two banks, bonds of the New York Central Railroad, shares of the New York, Haven and Hartford Railroad, 2,000 acres of land in Nebraska, and another 640 acres in Iowa.

A Christmas to celebrate at last. Presents were sent back over the Atlantic to Mary Jane's widowed daughter-in-law Sarah and her children, Gertrude and Charles Cochrane, now living in the Pittsburgh suburb of Oakmont. The cards were saved as keepsakes, and several have survived: "To Charlie. Merry Christmas from Paris. Love, Beatrice," "To Sarah, Wishing you Merry Christmas, from Mary Jane." And again from Mary Jane, "To grandson Charles."

To perfect his wife's contentment, Seaman, acting from Paris, transferred title of the house at 15 West Thirty-seventh Street to her

West 37th Street, New York, April 1907, north side from Fifth Avenue. Seaman's brownstone is the eighth staircase, moving right to left

(Courtesy of The New-York Historical Society)

name on Christmas Eve 1896, "in consideration of natural love and affection." In a pointed eviction notice to brother Edward, he granted Bly the right to "quietly enjoy the said premises" and to receive it as his outright gift, free from debt. Bly took the further precaution of having Seaman commit in writing, as part of the transfer, to "forever warrant the title to said premises." The execution of a "warranty deed" bound Seaman to uphold Bly's right to ownership of the property against any future challenge. Her main concern, of course, was Edward and the Seaman nieces, who were quick to make their fury known. At about the same time, Seaman took steps to put the Iron Clad in Bly's name as well. In this family warfare, he had placed himself firmly in the camp of his feisty young wife.

The Seamans remained in Europe for nearly three years, having originally departed in an effort to improve Seaman's health, which had started to deteriorate. They may have spent the summer before they left at the Catskill house, but there is no documentary indication that Bly took wifely charge of the two homes until a couple of years later, when she owned them outright.

Europe clearly suited them. Paris, Vienna, Rome, Wiesbaden, and even hated London were known venues. Seaman's failing eyesight was a source of great concern, and like Joseph Pulitzer, who shared the affliction, he spent much time consulting specialists and seeking cures, apparently with some success.

The Seamans were in London in the early fall of 1897. After they began traveling, Seaman's attorney Treadwell Cleveland began acting as his business proxy. Cleveland secured Seaman's power of attorney, then requested that that power be widened, with which Seaman complied. On July 13, with the Seamans still away, the Iron Clad Manufacturing Company's only four stockholders—Cleveland as proxy for Seaman; David D. Otis, the Iron Clad secretary; Henry B. Haigh, the president; and Frank E. Young—had voted to increase the company's board of directors from three persons to five without specifying the names of the new appointees.

On September 16, from the U.S. Consulate in London, Seaman gave Otis his power of attorney, acting through attorney Cleveland. Less than a month later, Seaman revoked Otis's power of attorney and the next day gave it to William R. Montgomery, a clerk in the Wall

Street law firm of Evarts, Choate and Beaman, with which Cleveland had been associated.

Two months later, the Iron Clad had filed a new certificate of election with the New York Superior Court. A new board had been named, including Robert L. Seaman; Bly, identified as Elizabeth C. Seaman; Thomas Diehl; Willis B. Richards; and David Barnes King.

Three weeks later, while the Seamans were billeted at the Rhein Hotel in Wiesbaden, Germany, Bly got her husband to draft yet another will. This one, rendered without punctuation in Seaman's sprawling, oversized hand, was only two sentences long:

> Wiesbaden Nov 29/97
> I give and bequeath all my property personal and real of any
> kind and in any place whatsoever to my wife Elizabeth C Sea-
> man and hereby appoint her sole executrix
> This is my last will and testament
> Robt L Seaman

In the hotel's smoking room, a German notary, Dr. Hermann Romeiss, made the will official. At Seaman's request, Carl Ebbighausen, the hotel's headwaiter, and Alfred Raab, a porter, witnessed the document in writing. Ebbighausen and Raab both later recalled that Bly was present at the signing, along with Seaman and the notary, Dr. Romeiss. Ebbighausen remembered that Seaman's "eyesight was greatly affected," and it had rendered him "quite helpless." Ebbighausen said he remembered that Seaman was expecting to undergo surgery shortly.

Attached to the new will was a long and revealing letter, typed and similarly notarized. Although it bears Seaman's signature, its contents strongly suggest the influence of another, more facile, scribe:

> Wiesbaden, Germany
> November 29, 1897
>
> TO WHOM IT MAY CONCERN:
> I have given and willed to my wife Elizabeth C. Seaman
> all my property entire and absolute to be hers alone and to do
> with as she wishes. In view of the repeated threats of certain

persons that they will break my will and take my property from my wife, I desire to make this statement, which I shall swear to and sign in the presence of witnesses and which I intend to be used in Court as my affidavit, if any attempt is made to carry out the threats to take my property from my wife and divide it among those who have no rights to it and to whom I am taking every precaution it should not go. During my life I did all I ever intended to do for my relations and more than by their treatment of me they deserved and should have had. I gave my brother a farm at his own request and at his own assertion that it was all he wanted or needed, though I included a condition as to the farm being his only on his remaining sober for a certain period, which condition he failed to keep, and recorded the deed without my knowledge and before the time limit had elapsed and when he had not remained sober. However, he has the farm and this is as much as I intended or do intend to do for him.

I have also during my life given all I ever intended to my nephew and nieces and grandnieces and everybody else, who may fancy they had some claim on me. It has been my great desire to make amends to my wife for all these same persons and others who wanted my property [and] made her suffer. They persecuted her and endeavored to poison my mind against her in order to get my property which I have now given to my wife. As they have asserted they will claim undue influence in order to break my will, I will provide against any such claims by giving my wife during my life the greater part of my property, further directing by my will that she shall receive the remainder at my death and so become the sole possessor of all I own.

I only regret that I have not more to give her. She gave me all the money she had saved to buy her mother a home when I was pressed for debt and everybody else, even my oldest friends and men I had helped to fortune turned against me. So I in turn give her my all.

I repeat I have given during my life all I ever intended to give to relatives and others and claim the right of every

American citizen to dispose of my property as I wish and my
wish is to give it all absolutely and entire to my wife.

Robt. Seaman

So, Bly had won her husband's trust by offering her tender care
in his debilitated state and by giving him all her savings to help bail
him out of unspecified financial difficulties. She came away with his
devotion and the not inconsequential rights to whatever he owned.
In her view, Seaman's family had mistreated and harassed her and
now would pay dearly for what she saw as their suspicion, hostility,
and greed. Bly was back where she best liked to be: in control.

⌇⌇⌇

Rome and Vienna were the Seamans' primary stopping places of
1899. The couple had been married four years by this time, and the
tumult of their first twelve months together had become as remote as
Seaman's meddlesome family. Bly finally had everything she wanted,
and Seaman, her latest dependent, appears to have settled into their
companionate arrangement with contentment. At the very least, he
was in no position to protest.

In January, the Seamans were in Rome, evidenced by a slender
volume of Wilfrid Scawen Blunt's *Love Sonnets of Proteus*, which came
into Bly's possession and which she inscribed, "Nellie Bly, Roma,
Italy, January II, 1899." A month later, New York newspapers
reported that they were thought to be in Vienna.

In late February, word had come from New York that the U.S.
consul in Vienna, Carl Bailey Hurst, had been instructed to put a
series of questions to Seaman in connection with a case before Justice
Lewis J. Conlan in New York's City Court. The questions had been
framed by Maurice Meyer, the attorney for sometime detective John
M. Hanley, whose clear intent was to shame Seaman into paying a
long-outstanding bill for his services as a snoop.

Hanley had filed suit the preceding November, claiming Sea-
man owed him $1,265 for spying on both Bly and James Metcalfe in
February of 1896. This would have been during the brief period of
Bly's reemployment by *The World*. If Seaman ever responded to the

questions, the record has not survived, nor has any indication of the final disposition of the case. Given the nature of the questions, it is likely Seaman would have agreed to a settlement before submitting his wife's reputation to so scandal-suggestive an inquiry:

> Did the plaintiff [Hanley] about February 14th, 1896, submit to you any information relating to the actions and conduct of James Metcalfe and as a consequence of the communication of much evidence to you, did you accompany plaintiff to 17 West 27th Street [Metcalfe's address], New York City, or the vicinity thereof, late on the evening of February 14th, 1896 or early on the morning of February 15th, 1896 and there did you meet or see James Metcalfe?
>
> If so, who accompanied you and who accompanied James Metcalfe at the time you met or saw him? From where did they come? What happened when you met? What became of the person who accompanied James Metcalfe? Where did she go?
>
> What was the name of such person and what did you say to her? And where did you ascertain James Metcalfe and the person who accompanied him had been just previous to the time you met them?

Originally, the Seamans had planned to spend four years abroad, but trouble with the management of the Iron Clad forced them to cut their stay short. There was concern about the reach of the company's creditors. Bly, who by then had been named company president, must have feared some personal liability. While in New York on April 22, 1899, she had the deed on the town house transferred into her mother's name.

From the Continent, though, she had begun to take an active interest in the management of her two homes. She returned to the United States in February and fired Henry Hansen, Seaman's longtime caretaker and friend in Catskill, who promptly opened a nursery and floral business that became highly successful. She also initiated the renovation and redecoration of the West Thirty-seventh Street town house in anticipation of a more permanent return.

The difficulties at the Iron Clad stemmed from the way the company was being run by Seaman's attorney Treadwell Cleveland and Willis B. Richards, who was then vice president and secretary of the company and its general manager. From Rome, on May 14, Bly wrote to "Jennie," who was performing the duties of personal assistant. Jennie possibly was a nickname for Bly's sister-in-law Jane. Bly signed the letter "Affectionately, Pink" and concerned herself only with questions involving her personal affairs and those of her immediate family.

Bly reported that she "had just written Mr. Richards a blast, though I rather feared to do so on account of what he may do in other matters." Richards, as manager of the Iron Clad, was apparently taking care of the Seamans' bills in their absence. She had Jennie instruct him "not to pay Mr. Miller unless the glass shelves fit." Miller was apparently a hired man in Catskill, since she also asked him by separate letter, she said, to pay a visit to the farm. "Tell me all about the new man in Catskill," she went on, "and how Hansen took his dismissal. When did the new man go there? And when is Kate going? Did you get the furs put away in storage? And did you send that trunk to the Manhattan Storage Co.? You will have to send the silver in a second trunk. Make a list of the silver."

She asked about Beatrice, her niece; about how Jane's husband, Al, was getting along, "better or worse?" Bly's new financial stature had drawn both of her brothers to New York with the apparent hopes of feasting off the imagined bounty. By 1899, Albert and Harry and their wives were listed in the city directory as living in the Seaman house at 15 West Thirty-seventh Street along with Mary Jane. Albert no longer had his job in Pittsburgh, perhaps the reason for his not getting along so well, and Harry had come from Wisconsin, where he had met and married the former Adele Graeber. Like Bly, neither of her brothers had children. Kate had remarried since her divorce to a man named Arthur Sanchez, about whom nothing is known. But they were soon divorced as well.

As a postscript to the letter, Bly asked Jennie to "have everyone make a list of what they want and send size of gloves for *all*. Do it at once," she urged, "I can't tell how long I may stay."

The Seamans knew they would have to do something about the management of the Iron Clad. Throughout their time abroad, Treadwell Cleveland had written periodically to assure the couple the firm was doing well. As soon as they announced their plans to return to the United States, his story changed. Cleveland urged them to stay away. He told them that the company had fallen into substantial debt and that he had secured notes worth $150,000 with the company's stock. He had managed to forestall creditors pleading the Seamans' absence from the country, but if they returned, he warned, the notes would surely be called—at the Iron Clad's certain peril.

If Bly equivocated about leaving Europe, a death in the family quickly superseded her indecisiveness. Kate, her thirty-two-year-old sister, contracted tuberculosis and died on July 27, 1899, while summering at the Catskill home. Bly sailed back to New York, bereft. Seaman did not return until November. They fired Richards and Cleveland and installed a new general manager at the Iron Clad.

Once in Catskill to spend the remaining summer months, Bly rudely refused to see neighbors who hoped to pay their respects. A local oral tradition holds that Bly was so dismissive of the women of the town, fulfilling their time-honored obligation to call on one another, that she took out a newspaper advertisement asking them in so many words to stop pestering her. She was inconsolable in her grief. On September 25, *The Coxsackie Union* carried a report on the funeral pyre she heaped with Kate's belongings. The Coxsackie paper quoted *The Catskill Examiner*:

> "Nellie Bly" who made herself famous as a reporter at home and abroad for the New York newspapers, married Robert Seaman of Catskill and is spending the summer there. Recently her sister Mrs. Sanchez died and *The Enterprise* reports that a few days ago Nellie had a funeral bonfire upon which she sacrificed all the personal effects and belongings of the deceased sister. Thousands of dollars worth of property were destroyed, beautiful silk dresses, jewelry and cases, white hair mattresses, tapestries, bedding, a $50 harness, a $175 wagon, and many other valuable articles. Besides these a valu-

able dog and horse were chloroformed. However bright Nellie might be in some respects, she has shown her fool points very conspicuously by this silly performance. How much better it would have been to sell these articles if she did not want them, and donate the proceeds to the deserving poor. But some people seem to lose all the sense they ever had when they get the benefit of a little money.

Bly went straight to the editor of *The Enterprise* to demand a retraction for the insulting description, threatening a libel suit if it were not forthcoming. Editor F. A. Gallt said it was the only time in the history of the small weekly that he had entertained such a threat. Gallt issued the retraction at once.

The following year, Catskill would be the site of further misery. Shortly after 11:00 P.M. on Friday, May 25, Mrs. Spencer Van Loan, who lived on the Seaman property, smelled smoke and sent her son Bert out to discover its source. Bert ran up the hill from the river to find the mansion engulfed in flames. He ran to the firebox at the corner of Liberty and King streets to call for help.

Citizens Hose Company No. 5 responded quickly, training their hoses on the burning structure for more than five hours to keep the fire from spreading to neighboring properties. The Seaman mansion was a near-total loss before the firemen even got to the site. *The Examiner* raised the suspicion of arson: "There is hardly a doubt that the fire was of incendiary origin. The house had not been occupied for some time, Mr. and Mrs. Seaman being in New York. The house was insured for $3,500 and its contents for $700, Bennett and Heath carrying the insurance." Once the fire was extinguished, only the foundation of the house remained. Firemen, at the time, were quoted as saying they found the living room carpet soaked when they arrived and watched it burst into flames. They also discovered several new kerosene cans on one of the porches, all empty.

No criminal charges were ever filed. The house was never rebuilt. Its destruction ended Bly's very tenuous connection to the Greene County community. It was no doubt dreadful for Seaman but for Bly, probably little more than a case of good riddance.

In New York, the Seaman brownstone was loaded with Cochranes. There was Mary Jane, of course. Bly's two brothers and their wives were in and out, deciding whether to remain in New York. Kate's daughter, Beatrice, was in Bly's charge until she married at the age of nineteen in 1903. Even Charles's two children, Charles and Gertrude, by this time teenagers, were making extended visits, and Bly is known to have sent Charles for business training while he was in the city. Bly clearly liked having her family around, and with a four-story brownstone, there was no problem with accommodation.

Many years later, Gertrude would recall how beautiful the living room was once Bly had redecorated it. She had chosen a color scheme of red and white with a border relief of decorative rope in bright gold leaf on the walls. The room was elegantly furnished. Dueling white marble fireplaces stood at either end, setting off a magnificent all-marble floor.

It was probably at this time that the Seaman home became a gathering place for Bly's friends, whom she would invite regularly for Sunday evening receptions and dinner parties. The actress Beverly Sitgreaves, a great friend and impersonator of Sarah Bernhardt, once recalled often being at these parties, attended by men and women well known in the literary and artistic worlds.

There was plenty of household help and all the problems that invariably accompany a large service staff. Gertrude remembered a young butler from India whom Bly had hired. When Bly discovered he had used his cousin's references to get the job, she fired him. "She didn't like underhanded things," Gertrude said, "and didn't think his acts were moral."

Another household upset made the newspapers. On February 26, 1904, Bly grew suspicious about her new maid, Jane Murray, when she noticed the woman's velvet coat missing from the hall in the middle of the day. Bly went up to her own third-floor bedroom and found it strewn with bits of jewelry and hat pins. Brother Harry happened to be in the house, and Bly sent him straight to the nearest pawn shop, at Thirty-fifth Street and Sixth Avenue. There he found the maid, attempting to pawn $800 worth of Bly's jewels. Bly had Murray arrested for theft.

The Seamans were in the newspaper again a few weeks later, but this time with another death notice. On February 6, Robert Seaman had been struck by a horse and wagon rig while crossing the street. The impact knocked him down and left him with a fractured rib, but he soon recovered. On the morning of Thursday, March 10, however, while reading his newspaper, Seaman suddenly collapsed. Bly called in three physicians to attend him, but to no avail. He died two hours after midnight in his own bed. Doctors attributed his death to heart disease, brought on by the accident. He was nearly eighty years old.

Bly held visitation at the house on West Thirty-seventh Street on Saturday, March 12, then had the casket transported by special train to Catskill that night. Funeral services were held the next day at St. Luke's Church, with the Reverend E. P. Miller officiating. The church's vested choir attended, singing amidst dozens of handsome floral tributes. Among them was a miniature gunboat sent by his employees at the Iron Clad, sixty of whom accompanied the casket to Catskill. Seaman was buried in the fenced-in family plot in the village cemetery with his parents and the rest of his siblings. He was the last of the line. Younger brother Edward had died in Catskill two years before.

Even prominent members of the Catskill community agreed that however much the Seaman family may have complained about Bly, and however dismissive she may have been to Seaman's neighbors, she had cared for her husband lovingly through the nine years they were married, and for that, she had earned their respect.

Some months later, Bly filed for probate in New York County Surrogate's Court the will Seaman had drafted in Wiesbaden back in 1897. Not surprisingly, his disinherited family members contested. They presented for probate the earlier version of his will, under which each of them was to receive a substantial bequest. They further charged that Seaman had been physically incapacitated when he signed the new will; that he had not been of sound mind, memory, or understanding; and that Bly had exercised her influence over him to prevent him from disposing of his property as he wished.

Since Seaman's most significant holdings had all been placed in Bly's name long before his death, the argument over what remained of his estate was effectively moot. Nevertheless, the relatives persevered. Time-eating elements, such as arrangements to take the depositions of the Wiesbaden hotel witnesses, caused the case to drag on for five years. Ultimately, the court ruled in Bly's favor.

As a widow, Bly might have decided to pursue a renewal of her relationship with her old beau James Metcalfe, whose wife, Edith, had died unexpectedly two years before Seaman. This, however, was not to be. Shortly after Seaman's death, Metcalfe became engaged to the actress Elizabeth Tyree. For Bly at this time, Metcalfe was old news. Her attention was elsewhere, trained on the man her husband had hired back in 1899 to replace Willis Richards as the Iron Clad's general manager. His name was Major Edward R. Gilman.

NELLIE BLY THE HEAD OF A BIG LOCAL INDUSTRY

Former Newspaper Writer Worked as Factory Hand to Learn the Business.

RECREATION FOR EMPLOYES.

Clubroom and Library Maintained and Entertainments and Weekly Lectures Provided.

CLUBROOM OF THE IRONCLAD LIBRARY ASSOCIATION.

"Nelly Bly."
Mrs. Elizabeth Cochrane Seaman.

Mrs. Roosevelt's

Library of the Ironclad Library Association.

Business Printing

Every merchant needs printing. It's impossible to conduct business without it. The point is to

had in the use of time and labor-saving appliances.

Brooklyn Eagle Job Printing Office

CHINA FROM W SOUGHT BY

Specimens of Se ous Presi Fancy

MANY ARE MEN

Not a Piece of C Roosevelt Has the M

INNOVATIONS AT THE IMPERIAL.

Manager William T. Grover's New Ideas of Conducting a "Somewhat Different" Theater.

CRESCENT SOCIETY'S PLAY.

"The Tale of a Coat" Successfully Given at Prospect Hall.

A BIRTHDAY PARTY

9

❧ ❧

Business

FROM THE TIME OF KATE'S DEATH, "PURELY AS A MENTAL DIS-
traction" from her intense bereavement, Bly immersed herself in
the duties of president of the Iron Clad Manufacturing Company. She
brought the full force of her abundant prestige and personality to the
post as well as the insights she had gleaned over the years as a
reporter—at Leclaire and Pullman in Illinois; at Oneida, New York,
and in Economy, Pennsylvania. From the time she took over in
November of 1899, Bly put in eleven- and twelve-hour days at the
factory in Brooklyn and brought her correspondence home for attention each night.

   She introduced more modern, more efficient processes, of which
she said, "many I devised myself." She had new buildings erected on
the factory site in Bushwick and reorganized the operational system.
Bly drafted and secured passage in the state legislature of the law
under which the Brooklyn Rapid Transit Company changed the way
it did business, enabling the railroad to come into the factory yard for
loading and unloading. She learned how to operate every machine in
the plant and even claimed to have designed several new ones. By
1905, she held twenty-five patents in her own name. She instituted

a social welfare system for her employees. Gilman, the general manager, once told a reporter about Bly's amazing adaptation to industry:

> She discarded steam engines and oil lamps and substituted electricity for power and lighting, and now we have a plant for generating 1,400-horse power—one of the finest in the country. She sent men to Europe as well as to other parts of this country to study the most modern machinery, and whenever they reported a new machine the old one in the factory was discarded and a new machine bought. Now we manufacture our own machinery, except such parts as have to be cast, and the entire plant has been practically reorganized.

By the time of Robert Seaman's death, Bly claimed to have quadrupled the company's business, to have brought it out of a debt she calculated at $300,000, and to have increased its sales to $1 million a year at an annual profit of $200,000.

Bly concentrated on the manufacture, promotion, and sale of Iron Clad's startling array of products: milk cans, dairy supplies, cold weld range boilers, gas and gasoline hot water heaters, riveted range boilers, expansion tanks, brazing tanks, air tanks, galvanized ware, enamelware—even kitchen sinks. The details of the company's finances did not interest her in the slightest, and she happily left their conduct to Gilman and his team of accountants. Bly once said she felt comfortable doing this, "having no personal use for money beyond that which supplied the very moderate living expenses of my mother and myself" after her husband's death. Although she was on the books of the Iron Clad for a salary of $25,000 a year, she claimed never to have drawn the entire amount in any year.

The well-being of her 1,500 employees, however, did concern her greatly. The lessons of Pullman and Leclaire stayed with her. Gilman once explained Bly's philosophy on labor to a reporter:

> Mrs. Seaman's theory of life is that it is the duty of the head of every family to take care of his own children and of the people in his household. Likewise, she maintains that it is

the duty of every employer of labor, whether he employs one or 10,000, to do what he can to make their lives happier and brighter, and that they ought not to give money away in waste (as so many do), but to take care of his own, who have produced his wealth.

In this pursuit, Bly eliminated piecework and instituted weekly wages for every Iron Clad employee. She had a six-story structure built to house new offices and a recreation center for her workers. Showers were installed in the basement for their use, with soap and towels furnished free of charge. There was a gymnasium and bowling alley in the building and on the fifth floor, a 5,000-volume library with two librarians. The club room had Ping-Pong and billiard tables, a piano, parlor croquet, and other games, and there was a host of employee committees involved in running these facilities.

Entertainment was provided every Saturday night, and there were frequent lectures. A mutual aid committee visited the sick and those in distress. The company maintained a mini-hospital on site and arranged for a doctor to make house calls at fifty cents a visit, with the company paying the balance of the bill. There was a base-ball team and a hunting and fishing club. The company dining room, with its Japanese chef and waiters, was open to the company's clerks, department managers, foremen, and heads of the factory at the end of 1905. "Later," Gilman said, "we hope to extend it for the use of all employees."

Like Bly, Gilman, as general manager, brought considerable prestige to the operation. Born in Thomaston, Maine, he was the son of General Jeremiah Gilman, who commanded Fort Pickens in South Carolina at the start of the Civil War. Young Edward attended the public school in Fort Leavenworth, Kansas, while his father was stationed there and at the age of fourteen went to work on a ranch in Colorado. A year later, he was with a surveying party in New Mexico and by the age of seventeen had entered West Point. As a graduate of the academy and an army second lieutenant, Gilman was sent to Fort Kehoe, Montana, and later served at the Cheyenne Indian Agency on the Tongue River. He rose to the rank of major.

While still in the army, Gilman studied law and entered the bar. Later, he took up electrical engineering and became one of the better known electrical contractors in the Northwest, before heading for New York and yet another career in finance. An avid and accomplished yachtsman, he belonged to numerous clubs around the city.

When Robert Seaman hired Gilman on his return from Europe in 1899, he told Bly he considered him one of the ablest financial men in the country, awarding him a salary of $10,000 a year as general manager. According to Seaman, the year before Gilman joined the Iron Clad, he had amassed the impressive sum of $150,000 in Wall Street trading. Both Gilman and Bly were thirty-five years old at the time. Seaman was by then seventy-four.

Bly and Gilman had rejuvenated the Iron Clad, doubling the amount of business under her control by starting the first plant in the United States to manufacture steel barrels. Bly called the operation the American Steel Barrel Company, though its actual operation was somewhat difficult to distinguish from that of the Iron Clad. "They [steel barrels] are my own invention," Bly once said. "I hold the patents on them." On a trip to Europe after her husband's death, Bly saw steel containers made to hold glycerin.

> When I got back, I determined to make steel containers for the American trade. My first experiment leaked and the second was defective because the solder gave way, and then I brazed them with the result that the liquid inside was ruined by the brazing metal.
>
> I finally worked out the steel package to perfection, patented the design, put it on the market and taught the American public to use the steel barrel.

Bly was quick to apply the strength of her still considerable name recognition to the company's promotion. She had her photograph emblazoned on the company's advertising cards. For the National Bottler's Convention in October of 1901 in Cleveland, for example, Bly's face appeared on the card, elegantly posed in hat and feather boa next to the words

*The Iron Clad factories are the Largest of their
kind and are owned exclusively by
NELLIE BLY
The only woman in the world personally managing
industries of such a magnitude*

She may not have been "the only woman in the world" so engaged, but there were very few. Most, like Bly, were conducting and expanding businesses they had inherited or become involved with through family connections. Henrietta Chamberlain King, for example, was running the enormous King Ranch in Texas, and Kate Gleason of Gleason Works proved a phenomenal international marketer of the bevel gear, which her father had invented with the help of a machinist. Of those women who ventured out on their own, Florence Nightingale Graham, the Canadian better known as Elizabeth Arden, founded what became an international cosmetics empire—but not until 1910—and the European, Helena Rubinstein, followed Arden to New York soon after in the same field.

For Bly's large enterprise, Christmas 1905 was clearly a high point. *The Brooklyn Daily Eagle* ran a five-column feature on her and the Iron Clad. The company's Library Association was hosting a ball in the new premises of the steel barrel factory and apparently had put the word out. Bly, at the employees' request, held up the installation of eighteen carloads of new machinery and material so the building would be empty for the celebration. She then volunteered to pay all the expenses of heating and lighting for the occasion. Three thousand people attended. Both *The Eagle* and *The New York Times* carried stories about Bly's gift to each of her employees of a basket filled with Christmas dinner for six with all the trimmings, a custom each year since she had started running the firm. The baskets contained dressed chicken, English plum pudding, oranges, apples, cans of soup, baked beans, biscuits, and something called the "Iron Clad" cigar.

Her alma mater *The Pittsburgh Dispatch* had also featured her in a story, and by the spring of 1906, her old friend Erasmus Wilson had written about her in his "Quiet Observations" column for what was at that time called *The Pittsburgh Gazette-Times*. Wilson and Bly had stayed in touch, and he had recently visited her on his return from being honored at a banquet in Boston. Back in January, she had invited him to stop in New York. Although two years had passed since Seaman's death, the letter was written on the engraved mourning stationery with the thick black border she had used for condolence responses. To Q.O., she signed herself in the warm and deferential way she often had, "Your friend and kid, Nellie Bly."

Wilson's item about Bly appeared on May 16 in response to the question of a former schoolmate of Bly, who asked, "What has become of our old friend Nellie Bly?" Wilson replied:

> Oh, she's all right. She's worth about $5 million and has been busying herself with the expert management of her husband's Iron Clad works in Brooklyn. Now that things are going along smoothly and successfully, one might find her ready to retire from the business world. But that is not her way. One of her pet schemes, and one she has long nursed, is to start a model town, and remove her extensive works to it. Those who know her best think she will yet build it. For there is no such word as fail in her lexicon. She has, moreover, begun the manufacture of steel barrels, of which her new plant turns out 500 or more daily. She has installed a gymnasium for her people and an up-to-date kitchen. Entertainments are given every Saturday night by the literary and social clubs and she is always the honor guest.
>
> And what is her part in all this wonderfully complex world? She is the whole thing. She watches every detail in office and shop, and cares for the physical and social welfare of all her people, sick or well. Such is a brief answer to the question: "What has become of Nellie Bly?"

The notice thrilled Bly, and she wrote Wilson immediately to tell him so. "It is just like your dear, good self to write so nicely about me," she said. "Aren't you afraid I will finally get a big head?"

The company issued an "Approximate Financial Statement" on July 1, 1906, presenting a picture of vigorous financial health. The statement showed a net worth of $2 million and excellent liquidity.

Promotion was not the only business art Bly had mastered. Litigation was another.

Two major legal wrangles occupied her in this period. One was the case of the Iron Clad's ousted manager, Willis Richards, who had not gone quietly. After his dismissal in 1899, Richards filed suit against the Seamans for back compensation. Outraged, Bly countersued, charging that Richards had conspired with Seaman's former attorney, Treadwell Cleveland, and another company director, Frank Cazenove Jones, to loot the Iron Clad as well as Seaman's major personal assets for their own profit. The complaint further charged that the three men had formed an executive committee for the sole purpose of paying themselves high fees and large salaries.

Cleveland called the suit "malicious prosecution" and declared that he could account for every cent of the Iron Clad's money. The case, which first came to court in 1901, dragged on for four and a half years, until well after Robert Seaman's death. It was settled in the defendants' favor. Bly agreed to pay $5,000 in back compensation to Richards and to give general releases to the other two defendants.

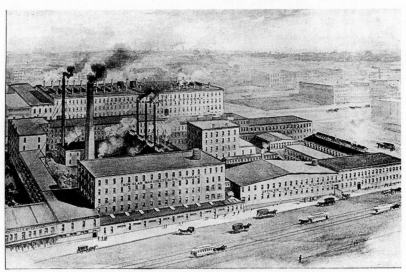

The Iron Clad Manufacturing Company, Brooklyn
(*King's Handbook of New York City, 1893*)

The next major case threatened to cause a milk famine in the New York area. It was initiated by Bly in late May of 1905 against the Dairyman's Manufacturing Company of Jersey City, New Jersey, a large milk dealers' cooperative. Bly charged that Dairyman's was manufacturing and using a double-necked unbreakable milk can on which she held the patent. She asked the court for an injunction to prevent the firm from using the cans and for patent infringement penalties of up to $1 million. Dairyman's, she charged, had been using the cans illegally since 1900. A temporary restraining order was issued but was soon vacated when Dairyman's argued that to restrain them from distribution—a huge number of cans in use could be classified as infringements on the Iron Clad patent—would severely affect milk supplies and cause too great a hardship on the community.

There was one case in this period for which Bly had no stomach for prosecution. Not long after Seaman's death, she discovered that Gilman had defrauded her of $50,000 in a business transaction involving his brother in St. Louis. "As he seemed overcome with remorse and told me that he had had heavy losses in Wall Street," she later explained, "I forgave him."

Even for someone with the tender good-heartedness so long ascribed to Bly, such merciful absolution to a well-paid, confessed embezzler who had been entrusted with the combination to the safe strains credulity. Most amazing is that she allowed Gilman to stay on as general manager. Other factors must have been in play: an attachment and involvement, for example, that extended well beyond the offices of the Iron Clad.

༺༒༻

While Bly busily established herself as "the only woman in the world personally managing industries of such a magnitude," Arthur Brisbane had become one of the most significant figures in American journalism and its highest paid. In 1897, he left his $200-a-week job with Joseph Pulitzer at *The New York World* to become number two to William Randolph Hearst at *The New York Journal*. From Hearst, he accepted a contract for fifty dollars less per week plus a bonus on circulation. He would not regret it. The Spanish-American War broke out, and in Hearst's words, Brisbane was the big man for the big occasion. His bonus "assumed war-time proportions," and Hearst, the ultimate beneficiary, was only too glad to pay. Brisbane was soon put back on salary, and before too long Hearst was paying him more than $250,000 a year—a staggering amount at the time.

Bly and Brisbane were the same age, both Civil War babies of 1864. As colleagues on *The World*, they had become good friends. The blond, good-looking Brisbane remained a bachelor until his marriage at the age of forty-eight. Although he was rumored in the meantime to have pursued romantic relationships with numerous newspaperwomen, including Bly, he was not one to kiss and tell. It is sure that he was a great admirer of Bly's work and her loyal friend, that she consulted him on business matters, that they saw each other socially, and that she was close to his sister, Alice. Why he was so soft on her is anybody's guess. Perhaps it was the residue of the intense platonic bond that a newsroom's neurotic frenzy so often fosters among male and female colleagues. Perhaps it was his affectionate bow to a long past entanglement of a romantic sort. There is no way to know.

Shortly before his death in 1936, a would-be biographer of Bly asked Brisbane for personal details of his relationship to Bly. He replied,

> I knew Nellie Bly, concerning whom you write, quite well for a number of years. She worked for me as a reporter and I believe she was the best reporter, man or woman, with the possible exception of Dorothy Dix. I cannot give you any personal details concerning Nellie Bly, as I knew her only as a working newspaper woman. Her hair as I recollected was brown; later, when I saw her . . . just before she died, it had turned gray.

But a perusal of Brisbane's correspondence in the early 1900s suggests a much closer relationship. Bly's courtroom battles of this period had gotten Brisbane's attention, and he showed concern, interest, and not a little amusement with her new persona. In 1907, she started to think about selling the house at 15 West Thirty-seventh Street. The town house may have become too large for Bly and her mother. Beatrice was no longer living there. By then, she had divorced her adulterous first husband, William R. C. Latson of Brooklyn, a physician and editor of medical literature who was twice her age, and had married Richard E. Brown, also of Brooklyn, who was twenty-five to her twenty-two and a department manager with the Edison Company. Albert and Jane had moved to Bridgeport, Connecticut, where Al became a salesman for the Canfield Rubber Company, and Harry and Adele appear to have gone back to Wisconsin. The most likely possibility is that Bly wanted to sell the house because she needed cash, for reasons she herself did not yet understand.

In May of 1907, Bly asked Brisbane's advice about the prices of residential property she had seen in Flushing. Two months later, she invited her former colleague to go for a Saturday drive in her racy new red automobile. She even wrested Gilman from the handsome yacht he had anchored in Sheepshead Bay to accompany them on the ride.

Brisbane was so taken with Bly's daredevil motoring, he published a cartoon about it for *The Journal*. Titled "The Gentle Sex," it depicted, in five squares, the tale of a woman first seen standing on a chair, frightened by a mouse, then in her chauffeured convertible ordering her driver to speed up beyond the seventy miles per hour he had already reached. "Over take that machine," she shouts. "Hurry up!" "My but this is great sport." "We missed that tree by an inch!" In the last square, a judge slaps on a ten-dollar fine for reckless driving. "Tee hee," she laughs, "I don't care."

The cartoon was something of a prophecy. Two years later, police arrested Bly's chauffeur for speeding while he was rushing her to a stockholders' meeting. The arresting officer charged him with driving at over forty miles an hour, to which Bly remarked, "Dear me, this thing can't go five miles an hour. I am sure you are mistaken." By the time they got to the station, Officer Edward Van Clefe apologized and changed his story, reporting that Bly's car was traveling at only twenty-one miles per hour. Bly bailed her chauffeur out, giving her West Thirty-seventh Street home as what must have been considered ample surety, since she reported its valuation at a generous $200,000. "She is extremely comely," *The Brooklyn Daily Eagle* gushed in its report of the incident, "and was the center of considerable attention in court today."

Brisbane sent Bly a copy of his cartoon with a page-long typed letter of thanks on June 26. Allaire was the New Jersey estate he had just purchased, in which he was building a palatial estate. Hampton was probably a pet. Under a salutation of teasing endearment, "My dear Law-suit Lucy," this is how it read:

Thanks for your letter. I shall have a better picture made today. I won't delay it at all—that will be the difference between you and me, for you always delay except when you are in the automobile, and then you explode.

I hope you observed my feeble effort to put in the paper my impressions of you as a motorist. I enclose clipping.

I trust we shall have another automobile ride together before long. I enjoyed the last one very much. I enjoyed it so much, that I think it will last me until I get a new set of nerves. My carburetor isn't working.

Our next ride will be in MY machine, a calm, cautious Cadillac that goes 14 miles an hour and groans all the way. In this Cadillac a man may live to reach middle age.

Young people, like you and General [*sic*] Gilman, may dash around at 60 miles an hour, taking the bark off of trees. But no more for this old gentleman. I have had trouble enough keeping alive 42 years, and I don't want to be mixed up in my death with a bright, red automobile duster, a West Point general and a crazy chauffeur, or found with an iron axle driven through my liver.

I appreciate none the less your kind, courteous and persistent effort to kill me last Saturday.

Yours sincerely,
A. Brisbane

P.S. Things are much better at Allaire, I am glad to say. Remember me to the General. I wonder if you and he would take it as a demonstration of unfriendliness if I took out accident insurance on both your lives in favor of myself and

Hampton. You two mean a good deal to me and Hampton, and you ought to be willing to have us protected.

᷍

Bob Kerr was a barefoot teenager spending the summer of 1906 on Sheepshead Bay when Gilman's big yacht—one of the finest Kerr had ever seen—was at anchor in the harbor with its stern too far up. "With a kid's curiosity," Kerr recalled in a newspaper interview many years later, "I made for it."

Immediately, young Kerr realized that when the tide ran out, the yacht was bound to tilt to the breaking point. Kerr towed alongside it and yelled up to a crew member, "Hey mister, you're going to break your boat!" The sailor ignored him, and so did the captain. Gilman heard the commotion and appeared on deck. Kerr tried again.

"Mister," he yelled out, "they're going to break your boat in two because they're too lazy to put down kedge anchors." Gilman asked what a kedge anchor was, and Kerr supplied an explanation. Gilman ordered the crew to put the anchors down and promptly invited Kerr on board. He offered the young man a job as his private secretary at twenty-five dollars a week.

"I thought I could bear to quit my $16-a-week job for that," Kerr said in the same newspaper story. So Gilman had Kerr outfitted at the fashionable Fifth Avenue tailor Jim Bell's, in pressed white flannels and a navy blazer with brass buttons, and the younger man traveled up and down the coast with Gilman for the next three years. He went on to make his own fortune and settled on Long Island in the chic town of Great Neck, where, in the early 1920s, he got to know F. Scott Fitzgerald.

Kerr and Fitzgerald were "buzzing" one night, and Kerr regaled the young author with stories of how he got his start, of his days in Gilman's fascinating company. The tales made enough of an impression on Fitzgerald that he folded parts of what he had heard into the descriptions of some of the characters in the novel he was then writing. Of this, he informed Kerr in a letter, written but not dated, from the Villa Marie in St. Raphael, France. The letter thanked Kerr for selling off his membership at a Great Neck country club at a good price:

> The part of what you told me which I am including in my novel is the ship, yatch [*sic*] I mean, & the mysterious yatchsman [*sic*] whose mistress was Nellie Bly. I have my hero occupy the same position you did & obtain it in the same way. I am calling him Robert B. Kerr instead of Robert C. Kerr to conceal his identity (this is a joke—I wanted to give you a scare. His name is Gatsby.)

Kerr, then, was a partial inspiration for Gatsby; Gilman for Dan Cody, the wealthy yachtsman Gatsby met in Little Girl Bay, Minnesota; and Bly for Ella Kaye, "the newspaper woman, [who] played Madame de Maintenon to his [Cody's] weakness and sent him to sea in a yacht."

⁘

On October 31, 1907, Gilman rented what was known as the Scherman Cottage on Emmons Avenue, opposite Coyle Street in Sheepshead Bay, the Brooklyn harbor where he kept his yacht. Gilman had an option to buy the cottage at any time during the yearlong lease at a preset price of $25,000. By the following July, however, he had chosen to buy a more desirable property closer to the bay in Hog Pen Sprout and backing up onto Emmons Avenue, the main thoroughfare. Gilman's chief cashier at the Iron Clad, Charles W. Caccia, notarized the document.

The same week that Gilman was investing in waterfront property, Bly was taking out a first mortgage on her Manhattan town house in the amount of $62,500, loaned by the Greenwich Savings Bank, to raise needed funds for the Iron Clad. Despite the company's impressive sales volume and profits, Bly recalled, "there never seemed to be any money on hand."

By the start of 1909, she had begun to suspect wrongdoing. "I spoke about the matter to Major Gilman again and again," Bly said. "He would tell me that the growth of the business required the employment of more money; and, as we were carrying from $350,000 to $400,000 worth of stock, I believed him at first."

In July of that year, Gilman was experiencing another personal financial crisis and, in the process, lost his yacht and the house at Sheepshead Bay, which was put up for auction. Bly sent word back to Apollo, Pennsylvania, for her half niece Grace McLaughlin, the daughter of Bly's half sister Mildred, to come to New York and bid on it. Although the house became Bly's, it was bought in Grace's name, presumably to avoid any appearance of impropriety given Bly's close association with Gilman. For a number of years, the Cochrane clan made Sheepshead Bay their playground. At some point, Grace quietly transferred title on the house, 3164 Emmons Avenue, to Bly's mother.

Major Edward R. Gilman
(*Brooklyn Daily Eagle,* February 10, 1911,
Library of Congress)

Gilman's financial troubles did nothing to cool Bly's evident ardor, nor was she willing to take any action against him personally once she started to suspect that he may have been a source of the Iron Clad's troubles.

By the fall of 1909, Gilman told Bly that he had arranged to borrow $60,000 for the Iron Clad from the Western National Bank of Philadelphia "in order to clean up a few small debts and have something in the bank." He convinced Bly that it was good business for the Iron Clad to carry some debt, that all big companies in the process of expanding employed this practice.

Ten days after the loan was made, Bly made one of her infrequent visits to the finance department. There she found Gilman deep in conversation with Chief Cashier Caccia. As Bly entered, Gilman angrily threw his pen across the desk. "Mrs. Seaman, I give up," she recalled him saying. "That $60,000 we got from Philadelphia is gone and we are not a bit better off."

At this point, Bly declared in Caccia's presence that she was sure she was being robbed. Despite Gilman's protests, she immediately sought an independent auditor to go over the Iron Clad's books. She chose the Safeguard Accounting Company, which had been suggested by William A. Nutt, one of the Iron Clad's own auditors. Nutt previously had served as Gilman's private secretary.

Safeguard sent an accountant named Arthur Coons to head up the audit. He and his assistants spent several weeks going over the Iron Clad's financial records. He instituted the Safeguard system of bookkeeping and, Bly said, by December, reported that the Iron Clad was "in a flourishing condition." Coons gave the financial department a clean bill of health. Gilman was clearly relieved. "Mrs. Seaman," Bly recalled him telling her, "you owe an apology to every man on this floor."

Still, the Iron Clad's financial difficulties deepened. Starting in 1907, as a result of conditions in the Brooklyn real estate market, the Iron Clad's property underwent a 40 percent depreciation, bringing down by $280,000 the valuation of its real estate and thus severely cutting into the company's net worth. Gilman had been securing loans using the real estate as collateral. With so little money on hand all the time, the real estate depreciation in itself had the potential to put the company into insolvency.

As 1910 got under way, Bly had other problems to distract her. First, Gilman became seriously ill. By spring, his physician diagnosed an advancing case of stomach cancer, and Gilman soon took to his bed. Bly gave herself over to his care. She later recalled,

> I felt myself to a certain extent responsible for his condition in that the doctors told me that his worrying over the affairs of the Iron Clad might have superinduced the malady, and it was for that reason that I devoted my spare hours to him . . . I had him moved to Sheepshead Bay, where I took a house for him and provided him with nurses, physicians and servants, all at my own expense. I spent so much time with him that I got little sleep.

Still, Bly managed to be at the factory every day. On March 31, at 6:30 P.M., she was at her desk when fire broke out in one of the seven wooden buildings on the Iron Clad site. According to *The New York Tribune*, watchman John Kenney discovered the blaze while

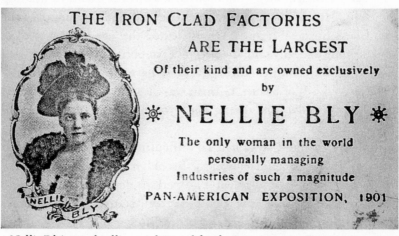

Nellie Bly's metal calling card created for the Pan-American Exposition, 1901
(Author's collection)

making his rounds and immediately informed Bly. Bly got the company telephone operator to summon the 200 employees who had been trained to respond to fire. They assembled but were unable to put out the blaze. An alarm was sounded to the fire department. One unit responded, then another, then another until all the apparatus in the lower end of Brooklyn had been brought out. The firemen kept their hoses pointed at the company's japanning, or varnishing, factory, which adjoined the burning building, and kept the flames from igniting it. Reserves from six station houses were called out to keep in check the 15,000 spectators who gathered to watch. As for Bly, according to *The New York Tribune*, "Mrs. Seaman said that she regretted more the loss of 75 valuable pigeons that were caged on the roof of the factory than she did the loss of the building."

The New York Times reported that Bly led the firefighters through alleyways and wagon paths to where the blaze could be fought to best advantage. Hearst's morning paper, *The American*, said Bly

also ventured into the building in the dense smoke and encouraged the men there. The atmosphere was so suffocating that the firemen worked in relays, each man remaining inside but a few minutes at a time.

The courage of Mrs. Seaman and the determined work of the firemen conquered the fire after $30,000 worth of property was destroyed. The origin of the fire is unknown.

Two months later, *The American* carried more news of Bly in a happier connection, this time a brief item reporting her gift of two very rare Antarctic gray geese and a dozen ducks of varying species to Central Park. There was no explanation of how these fowl had come into her possession, but her passion for fauna, and for the park, was well known.

There also was activity of a more questionable sort at this time, involving the desperate monetary juggling act that had become necessary to the Iron Clad's survival. The following story is the recollection of W. H. Hands, the late retired secretary to a partner in the Wall Street investment house known in this period as Brown Brothers and Company.

Brown Brothers, an already venerable Wall Street firm, counted the Iron Clad among its clients. In that capacity, the company issued commercial letters of credit to the Far Eastern suppliers of the large quantities of tin which the Iron Clad used to produce many of its products. Hands explained that the shippers would draw on Brown Brothers for the value of their shipments, attach the usual shipping documents, and when the shipments arrived, Brown Brothers would deliver the documents to the Iron Clad to enable it to obtain the tin. Brown Brothers delivered the documents on its usual form of trust receipt. This allowed the Iron Clad to take over and manufacture its usual products while retaining, in Brown Brothers' name, the ownership of the imports, crude or manufactured, until the banker's acceptances were paid off. Hands continued,

> Nellie, not being of a nature to darn her husband's socks or sew buttons on his shirts, became very active in her husband's company, so active that she was shortly practically running it. However, her management didn't prove quite as successful as her husband's had been, and the company was soon in a rather bad cash position and had trouble in meeting its regular bills.
>
> About that time, a large shipment of tin arrived under one of our credits and, without knowledge of the position of the company, we delivered the documents as usual which only permitted the manufacture of the tin in the usual way and its sale to the company's customers.
>
> However, Nellie saw a way to obtain some quick cash and, instead of taking the tin into their factory to be manufactured and sold as usual, in which case the proceeds would enable the company to pay our drafts, and notwithstanding the terms of the trust receipt, Nellie simply sold the documents and the entire shipment to some competitor and used the cash to bolster the position of the company.

Hands said the action was clearly a criminal offense, but it did not come to light for some time. "Evidently," he said, "it was hoped to help the company out of its troubles." In fact, it only made them worse.

God proves men in the furnace of humiliation, but for Bly was reserved the all-boys club represented by the American banks and courts of law. The way Bly experienced the years 1910 to 1914 would have reduced any lesser soul, man or woman, to cinders.

At the end of 1910 and into the New Year, Gilman's health further deteriorated. His relatives ignored him, and no one else visited, so Bly got in the habit of spending her late afternoons and evenings at his bedside. She later recalled,

> His physician told me that mental trouble was hastening his death, and that if I could induce him to unburden his mind, his life might be lengthened. I made every effort in this direction. I told him that I was his best friend, and assured him that no matter what he might have done to injure me, I would freely forgive him. Although I brought the matter up many times . . . for the doctor told me that the only relief from his mental suffering would come with his making a clean breast of whatever secret he was concealing, he never gave any other answer than tears. He would turn his head to the wall and weep silently for a quarter of an hour at a time, but . . . he never uttered a word as to the cause of his grief.

She must have had some expectation of trouble, because on November 23, 1910, she took the precaution of finally recording the 1899 deed granting title of the house at 15 West Thirty-seventh Street to her mother, presumably to make certain the property was out of the reach of creditors.

In December, the freight agent of the Brooklyn Rapid Transit Company, Captain Alexander Piper, reported to Bly that he had come upon cash discrepancies in the settlement of the Iron Clad's bills of lading. Bly delayed starting an investigation of her accounting department because she said, "I feared for the effect of such a move on Major Gilman, who was almost at death's door. I saw many other indications that there were sinister happenings in the finance department of the Iron Clad about that time, but I could not bring myself to take steps that might add to the unhappiness of a dying man."

The same month, the Western National Bank of Philadelphia notified Bly of a $26,000 overdraft. In January, it reported an even larger one, of $40,000. Bly couldn't believe it. In January, the bank's president, George E. Shaw, and Edward Dunn, president of the Philadelphia Warehouse Company, which the bank controlled, visited her at home to discuss the matter. Bly asked Charles Caccia, chief cashier of the Iron Clad, to join them for the meeting, but personal obligations kept him away. Caccia assured her, however, that he could account for the missing funds and would be able to cover the overdraft in a day or two.

The bank was not prepared to wait. To save the Iron Clad's credit, Bly gave her personal guarantee for the amount of the overdrafts and signed documents to that effect. Shaw agreed to honor any checks Bly might sign for necessary expenses, providing she let him know the total sum of her checks each day. Over the next four days,

Nellie Bly, circa 1910
(The Bettmann Archive)

she wrote checks totaling $1,100 or less each day and notified Shaw of the total spent by telephone each evening.

On the fourth day, Shaw informed her that her checks totaled $15,000 more than she had told him and that he had protested them. She recounted, "I went to Philadelphia the following morning and spent the day in the office of the Western National Bank, the entire board of directors being present. I did not believe the story about the $15,000 worth of checks, being aware that I had not signed them, and thought that Shaw was lying in an attempt to trick me in some manner. He did not produce the checks in question, and I never thought of asking for them."

Before she left for Philadelphia, Bly went to the office of former New York City Controller Herman A. Metz, who advised her on business matters. Metz had agreed to cover the Iron Clad's $5,000 payroll for a week if needed. He advised her not to sign anything at the bank, but, under threat of legal action, she did—a new $40,000 note, with which she took up the mysterious $15,000 worth of checks as well as fees Shaw said were due the bank. She called Metz at 2:00 P.M. from Philadelphia and asked him to dispatch the $5,000 to the Iron Clad's offices, which he did.

In the meantime, on January 15, again in an obvious effort to secure her ownership of the West Thirty-seventh Street brownstone, Bly had her mother transfer title on the house to Gustave Meyer, an apparent family friend, who, five weeks later, put the deed in the name of the Dundonald Estates. By September, Dundonald transferred title to Bly's brother Harry, who, in turn, put it in the name of a Milwaukee friend named Martin Linden.

Gilman died on Thursday, February 9. On Friday, while Bly was in Sheepshead Bay attending to his funeral arrangements, an agent of the Bank of Commerce of St. Louis appeared at the Iron Clad's offices, presenting notes bearing Bly's signature in the amount of $40,000. Bly had no knowledge of them. "I remembered that the major had got me to sign several notes some time before, which he had told me were for the Iron Clad's business purposes," she then recalled. "Somehow I was not surprised by the Bank of Commerce incident. I had been subconsciously expecting unpleasant developments after Gilman's death."

Gilman's funeral was Sunday, and Lincoln's Birthday holiday was celebrated on Monday. William A. Nutt, the Iron Clad auditor who also had been Gilman's personal assistant for many years, came to see Bly at the West Thirty-seventh Street house that day. "Mrs. Seaman," she recalled him saying, "you have been surrounded by a lot of rogues and scoundrels, and the biggest one of them was E. R. Gilman. You have been robbed right and left and he has been paying his St. Louis brother's debts with your money." Nutt confessed that he had been corresponding for many months with the Bank of Commerce in St. Louis on Gilman's behalf and that drafts amounting to $65,000 had been paid out of the Iron Clad's funds into the St. Louis account of Gilman's brother.

Bly met with the St. Louis banker the next day in Herman Metz's office. The banker presented $40,000 worth of notes issued over several years and all past due. He acknowledged that the bank had never made a demand on the Iron Clad for payment. On Metz's suggestion, Bly allowed the St. Louis man to see the Iron Clad's books. He found no record of any transactions with the Bank of Commerce. "Mrs. Seaman," the banker said. "I am sorry for you." He left for St. Louis that night, and Bly heard nothing more about it.

Even many months after the theft was disclosed, Bly could not bring herself to believe that Gilman had intended to betray her and rob her into ruin. "The amounts out of which I was defrauded by Major Gilman reach the comparatively small total of $100,000," she rationalized, "and I still believe that when he began to steal he thought that he would be able to make restitution before his thefts were discovered."

Bly immediately ordered another investigation of the Iron Clad's books. This time she assigned the work to the Audit Company of New York. Two weeks into the probe, on a Saturday, the chief investigator, a Mr. Cadwalader, notified Bly that he wanted to see her privately at home.

He came over that evening, and told me that he had "struck something queer" in an account that showed an indebtedness of $30,000 to L. F. Lawrence, an employee of the Iron Clad . . . Cadwalader said that he had spoken to [Chief

Cashier] Caccia about the matter several days before, and he had put off explaining it from day to day on the ground that he was particularly busy that week.

Bly immediately put Cadwalader in charge of the Iron Clad's finance department. Within a day or two, he had compiled enough evidence to warrant the arrest of Charles W. Caccia on charges of forgery and conspiring with other members of the department to defraud the Iron Clad Manufacturing Company.

As for Gilman, Bly later said,

> While I do not believe that he was a member of the conspiracy to loot the Iron Clad, his dishonesty made that conspiracy possible, for if the others in the finance department had not been aware that their chief was using the credit and cash of the company for his own purposes, they would never have ventured on the audacious campaign that ruined it. Of course it is possible that Gilman shared the proceeds of the forgeries, but I do not think that he did. My belief is that he merely yielded weakly to temptation when he was in stress for money.

She had already known for many months that while decoding mysterious entries in the Iron Clad's books, the auditors had discovered such surprising expenditures as a $5,000 political campaign contribution and a $25,000 yacht.

News That's to Print."

THE W
Fair Sunday an
moderately w
yinds. mostl

W. F. BAKER IN MILLINERY.

Former Police Head Now Concerned in the Finance of Feathers and Ribbons.

William F. Baker, ex-Police Commissioner, has gone into the millinery business. He has joined the firm of Warren M. Lincoln & Co. of 12 East Thirty-third Street, and is devoting his time to the trials of office. Not that Mr. Baker poses as an expert in feathers and finery, for he leaves that to his partners. He is concerned with the financial end, and as these days of close competition and large investments that is enough to keep one man busy.

Though for ten years Mr. Baker had served the city as Civil Service Commissioner, Deputy Police Commissioner, and Police Commissioner, he has had plenty of experience in business, and he is, in reality, only returning to the kind of life that seemed his fate till he decided to enter the public service. In his younger days he was a clerk in business circles and is an intimate friend of many of the men prominent in the commercial life of the city.

"I'm quite satisfied with the change," said Mr. Baker yesterday. "My friends may laugh a little at the contrast between millinery and the police, but I've found enough to be in private life again. I can see my home now from time to time, and I couldn't do that as long as I was in politics. Of course, I shall still take an interest in public affairs, and I don't regret having been for a time behind the scenes, but I'm going to be content to stay in the ranks and leave the excitement of the front places to some one else now."

SILENCERS ON FIELD GUNS.

Tests Made by the Army Show That Improvements Are Needed.

Special to The New York Times.

WASHINGTON, July 1.—The ordnance experts of the army have of late been making a the interesting tests of the silencer invented by Hiram Percy Maxim, son of the noted English inventor, Sir Hiram Maxim.

TRAIN KILLS THREE IN A STALLED AUTO

Mr. and Mrs. Newell and Son of Trenton Caught by Fast Express Near Albany.

DAUGHTER ALSO IS INJURED

MRS. SHONTS TO SUE?

Report from Paris That She Will Seek a Separation Unconfirmed Here.

ROBBING NELLIE BLY
AN AMAZING GAME

Checks Clumsily Forged or Raised —Bills of Lading Altered in Scramble for Loot.

BANKS EASILY DECEIVED

State Superintendent's Men Wonder How Any Teller Passed Bogus Paper and Even Certified It.

When nine forged and raised checks of the two Brooklyn manufacturing plants owned and managed by Mrs. Elizabeth Cochrane Seaman, who gained her first fame as "Nellie Bly," were shown to the present officials of one of the Brooklyn banks which, it is alleged, hurried her Ironclad Manufacturing Company into

BRITISH WARRANTS FOR BOMB SUSPECTS

Scotland Yard After Kaplan and Schmidt for Complicity in Los Angeles Times Explosion.

BELIEVED TO BE IN ENGLAND

Detective Burns There—Bow Street Magistrates Issue Warrants at State Department's Request.

10

❧ ❧

Bankruptcy

"I CANNOT BLAME MYSELF ENOUGH FOR NOT HAVING LEARNED banking methods and commercial accounting when I first went into the Iron Clad," Bly confessed. "However I never in my life had taken any interest in money for itself, and financial details bored me terribly." It was this predisposition compounded by Bly's apparent romantic involvement with Gilman and her yearlong preoccupation with his illness that provided the perfect circumstances for the Iron Clad conspirators to "make their harvest."

As the criminal case unfolded, Bly needed to raise more cash. Again she pursued the idea of selling or renting the brownstone on West Thirty-seventh Street. In early March, she wrote Arthur Brisbane to see if he might know someone who would be interested in her house, desirable enough to fetch a good price. Brisbane was in Chicago, where, he explained, union problems at Hearst's *Chicago American* might keep him at least half the time. "Sorry to hear you are working so hard," he wrote in response to her note. "The other day I went to the old *Herald* office and thought of you, and the days you came out here to work for our old fat friend [James Scott]—I forget the old fellow's name now." Brisbane said if he heard of anyone "who wants a building in 37th Street, you may be sure that I will send him to you." Bly had spared Brisbane the details of what she meant by "working so hard."

On Monday, March 6, Bly arranged for the auditor, Cadwalader, to be in her office along with Captain Piper from Brooklyn Rapid Transit; Detective David Wilbur of the Brooklyn Detective Bureau; and her attorney in the case at the time, H. Ludlow Christie. She telephoned Caccia, asking him to meet her. He made excuses, delayed, but finally appeared. Bly went on,

> We had asked him a few questions when he begged me to see him alone. I took him into my private office, where he fell on his knees, confessed he had robbed me, and implored me to forgive him.
>
> "You have forgiven others who have defrauded you," he pleaded. "Only forgive me, and I will make complete restitution if I am compelled to be your slave for life. I was not alone in this. I will tell you about all the others. I can bring you back $30,000 right away, and I can get all that has been stolen from you if you will only save me from going to prison."

Bly told Caccia she would forgive him if he would go into the other room and repeat his confession in the presence of the four men she had assembled. Detective Wilbur had already heard the confession through the partly opened door and had called for reinforcements in case there would be need for more arrests. Caccia first implicated Stanley Gielnik, assistant cashier. Gielnik initially denied complicity, then broke down and confessed. The detectives took him to his house—a house Bly charged he had bought for his mother with the Iron Clad's money—and returned with vouchers for $30,000 worth of forged checks.

Next came William Traphofner, the keeper of a nearby saloon, who had cashed a number of the checks. Bly continued:

> Until four o'clock the next morning the three pallid thieves in craven fear told tearfully of their crimes, alternating pleas for mercy with promises to make restitution. Stenographers,

one after another, came in to take down the confessions for an hour or two at a time. Late at night I sent out for coffee and sandwiches, which was the only refreshment any of us took during the long inquisition.

According to Bly, Caccia had agreed to bring back the $30,000 the day after he confessed, then stalled for nearly a week until he engaged a lawyer. At that point, Bly rescinded her forgiveness and had Caccia, age thirty-seven, and Gielnik, age twenty-two, arrested on March 16. Traphofner, in the meantime, unloaded his Brooklyn property and fled for his native Germany.

The following day, the two cashiers were arraigned in Manhattan Avenue Court in Brooklyn on the specific charge of Bly's forged signature on one $650 check drawn on the People's National Bank of Brooklyn. A witness told the court that investigators had uncovered evidence of a "systematic peculation" that would bring the total amount of the forgeries to at least $100,000. Other reports put the figure even higher. Caccia entered the courtroom from his cell, took one look at his beautiful blond wife, and burst into tears. Bail for each man was set at $10,000. Bly, her face layered in three veils to avoid being photographed, declined to make a statement. "I am better at getting interviews than giving them," she told reporters, then flashed her trademark smile, visible even through the netted shield.

When Caccia confessed to Bly, she said he told her that he began practicing how to forge her name the day he was promoted to chief cashier; that while he was forging checks, he was always the first man in his department on duty in the morning and the last to leave each night; that he never took vacation, lest his crimes be accidentally exposed in his absence. At the arraignment, Caccia entered a plea of not guilty. Gielnik pleaded guilty to aiding and abetting the forgery, which the magistrate refused to accept. Caccia and Gielnik claimed that they forged Mrs. Seaman's signature only in the course of paying the Iron Clad's bills when she was not available to sign checks, and that the money had been put to no other purpose.

On May 4, when the cashiers were to appear in the Adams Street Police Court, Kings County Assistant District Attorney LeRoy Ross had the indictments there dismissed for reasons not explained at the time. He proceeded immediately to have the two men rearrested and brought directly before a grand jury in Kings County Court, where they pleaded not guilty to six counts of forgery and larceny. Bail for each was set at $30,000. The larceny charges were new, stemming from evidence that they had cashed checks coming into the company as payment from Iron Clad customers, another element of the alleged scheme. At this point, the extent of Iron Clad funds lost to theft was thought to have reached as high as $400,000.

At the same time, Bly, in her position as president and treasurer of the Iron Clad Manufacturing Company, was starting to experience difficulties of an even more disastrous sort.

⸙

By May of 1911, the Iron Clad's numerous creditors had started to grow anxious about recovering what the company owed them. With Bly's consent, a creditors' committee was formed to examine the Iron Clad's books and accounts; it consisted of George Shaw, president of the Western National Bank of Philadelphia; Franklin Potts, president of the Philadelphia Warehouse Company; and E. R. Crawford, president of the McKeesport Tin Plate Company. The three were thought to represent a total of $310,000 of the Iron Clad's estimated $450,000 debt. There was talk of a company reorganization based on the committee's findings.

Bly said she signed two different agreements with these creditors, then repudiated both. On the first, they inserted too many interlineations, which she refused to initial. For the second, the creditors offered to install a new, distinguished board of directors to restore confidence in the company and stay the pressure of immediate demands. She agreed to this, but when the creditors supplied only the names of inconsequential men she described as "dummies," she reneged again. "I decided it was no use and I would make them wait a little while and let me run along as I was doing or make them close me out," she said. "They did the latter," despite the fact that she had never missed a payroll and was doing a business of $135,000 a month.

On May 4, Bly was at the Adams Street Court House for the first arraignment of her accused employees, Caccia and Gielnik.

Anticipating her presence, eight process servers converged in an effort to serve Bly with summonses from her various creditors. With a human barricade of lawyers and friends, Bly managed to elude confrontation with all but one of them. He had slipped into the building next door to the courthouse, climbed on the roof, then stealthily walked along that building's window ledge until he was opposite the window of the stenographer's room, where Bly had taken refuge. He flung the papers into the room and managed to land them right at her feet.

Assistant District Attorney Ross later explained that this was the reason he had made the unusual decision to move the case directly to the grand jury at Kings County Court. Bly, he said, "had been treated outrageously by some people, among them several creditors." When Ross found Caccia and Gielnik's lawyers demanding that Bly bring the company books to court, and that process servers queued up to harass her, he stepped in. "Now there was absolutely no cause for the production of Mrs. Seaman's books in this criminal case against alleged forgers," he said. "It would have been vastly to the advantage of the group of creditors, however, to have Mrs. Seaman's books in the courtroom."

By May 23, another group of creditors led by Brown Brothers and Company filed a petition of involuntary bankruptcy against the Iron Clad in U.S. District Court, charging that Bly "committed acts of bankruptcy by settling bills amounting to $24,118.76 in the last four months while practically insolvent." For its part, Brown Brothers was reported to have a claim against the Iron Clad for $33,000 for the purchase of tin, the Seaboard Coal Company was trying to collect $4,000, and a stationer named Oscar Uns said the company owed him $130.

U.S. Bankruptcy Commissioner Richard P. Morle appointed Appleton Clark as receiver for the company. Clark got down to work immediately, taking possession of the plant the next day. He met with Bly, who told him she was an officer and director of both the Iron Clad and the American Steel Barrel Company. Bly, now barred from the Iron Clad, concentrated on American Steel Barrel, which was still profitable and which, she maintained, was entirely separate from the embattled company that had spawned it.

But Receiver Clark had his attorney, Adolph Kiendl, file a motion before Judge Thomas I. Chatfield in U.S. District Court on June 20 to extend the Iron Clad's receivership to the steel barrel company. In the meantime, Bly sued Clark personally for loss of income and damages for having the gates to her freight shipping yard locked to prevent the steel barrel company from using them without the goods first being subjected to time-consuming inspections by the receiver's staff. Bly found this particularly outrageous because the freight shipping yard stood on her personal property. Clark responded that he had indeed asked the South Brooklyn Railway company to lock the gates to the yard when he realized Bly was removing valuable assets from the Iron Clad and storing them in the steel barrel plant. That suit dragged on for three years in the New York Supreme Court, ultimately ending in a discontinuance.

At the same time, in May of 1911, Judge Chatfield had started to hear arguments as to whether the Iron Clad and American Steel Barrel Company were one and the same. Bly made her case in a feature story on a special women's page of *The Brooklyn Daily Eagle* carried June 21. What upset her most, she told the reporter, was that for the first time in her life people had started to perceive her as a failure:

> Some of the creditors are pointing to me as a business failure and saying, "That's what comes from letting a woman run things." But the biggest banks and business houses in the country have been robbed by dishonest employees. That is what happened to the Iron Clad. Why don't they look at the sales that have been made during the past 12 years, at the steady progress of the company, at the inventions, instead of pointing to me as a failure in business? That's what hurts.

The reporter described Bly, by then forty-seven years old, as "thoroughly womanly and charming in manner, simply but modishly garbed, she looked the capable woman that her direction of the mechanical side of the Iron Clad and the Steel Barrel companies has proved her to be." She spoke with a remarkable calm, even able to smile occasionally—"a charming smile, incidentally"—about the terrible betrayal of trust that had brought on her misfortune. All she wanted now, she said, was to be able to run the Steel Barrel company "unmolested."

> I am the only manufacturer in the country who can produce a certain type of steel barrel for which there is an immense demand at present, for the transportation of oil, gasoline and other liquids. I invented and developed it. The machines were all made after my designs which I had patented, and the process is a secret one. I worked night and day on that steel barrel . . . but I persevered and now have a barrel that defies comment.
>
> I began with an output of five barrels a day. Now I can turn out a thousand a day—if I am let. But, owing to interferences and restrictions, I can ship but 500 a day just at present and customers are complaining. I have canceled many orders because of my inability to get the barrels shipped within the required time.

The reporter asked her what one company had to do with the other. "Nothing really," she replied, "but I am threatened with an injunction so that the Steel Barrel company may be turned in as an asset of the Iron Clad. Why, I can show by the books that I turned over hundreds of thousands of the profits of the Steel Barrel to help out the Iron Clad."

Once everything was straightened out, was she planning to get out of business? "Never," she said. "I want to see that everything is made right for the creditors of the Iron Clad. And I'll keep on making steel barrels till I die."

The same day's paper carried a report of Bly's "obdurate" performance before Judge Chatfield and the jury in U.S. District Court, where she had been asked to produce the steel barrel company's books. She arrived in court without them, stating they were nowhere to be found, then declined to answer numerous questions put to her during fifteen minutes on the witness stand.

As Bly's knowledge of the scheme broadened, it became evident not only that forged checks had been written to total a staggering $1.6 million but that reputable banks where neither Bly nor the Iron Clad kept accounts had apparently cashed the forged checks repeatedly over the years and without question. Bly began to press for an investigation by the state banking authorities, determining that the banks were a clear potential source of recourse and restitution. Her first stop was Albany, where she made her appeal directly to Governor John A. Dix.

Dressed in black satin trimmed in green, set off by a small but stylish black bonnet, she was ushered into Dix's office. She told the governor she had come to him because she felt she had no place left to go. Caccia and Gielnik, despite two indictments, still were not being brought to trial; their bail had been reduced to $5,000 each, and they both had been released from jail. Bly said Assistant District Attorney LeRoy Ross was handling the case at first, but he soon turned it over to Assistant District Attorney Robert H. Elder. Elder, when questioned, claimed to have nothing to do with the matter.

Ross then confirmed that the district attorney's office wanted to drop the criminal prosecution and leave it to Bly's personal counsel to pursue a civil suit. She protested this, saying that her personal finances had been so reduced by the forgeries, she could no longer afford lawyers to look after her affairs. Besides, her present counsel, James A. Allen, was so deluged with work resulting from the bankruptcy proceedings that he couldn't possibly take on the forgery case, too.

On top of all that, while Receiver Clark had barred Bly from the Iron Clad premises, she had seen Caccia coming and going from the offices, giving him access to the company's books and the possibility of altering evidence, since his release from jail. All this had led her to Governor Dix's office.

"I came here," she explained to the governor, "to ascertain if the State of New York will permit a woman engaged in a legitimate business to be robbed as I have been—robbed in a way which would not have been possible were it not for loose banking methods which seem to call for rigid inquiry by the proper state authorities."

Bly named specifically the Broadway Bank of Brooklyn, which was only two blocks from the Iron Clad and had cashed a total of $1.4

million in forged checks despite the fact that Bly had no account with the bank. She also named the Guardian Trust Company of New York, which had cashed $200,000 worth of checks, and the First National Bank of Jamaica [Queens], which had cashed $32,000 worth.

Dix listened attentively and promised to make further inquiry into her case, then referred her to Banking Superintendent George C. Van Tuyl, who saw her the next day.

Broadway Bank of Brooklyn, through its attorney and board member Henry Weismann, was quick to issue a statement in response to Bly's assault:

> The checks of the Iron Clad Company—claimed to amount to $1.4 million—if this is the amount—were paid by the Broadway Bank during a time approximating three years, in the regular course of business and pursuant to the regular banking methods. A great part of them were paid by the bank upon which they were drawn and the other proportion over the bank's counter upon proper identification of the parties presenting them and upon endorsement which the bank had no reason to question.
>
> The trusted employees of the Iron Clad Company now charged with larceny appear to have had full charge of the financial matters of the concern, which seems to have been conducted in a most extraordinarily loose manner, which latter appears to be responsible for whatever losses the company may have sustained through this source.

Three days later, the First National Bank of Jamaica stated that there was no impropriety in the method in which the Iron Clad's checks had gone through that institution, either.

Banking Superintendent Van Tuyl advised Bly to secure as many of the forged checks as she could and not to attempt to prosecute her own case but to hire the best possible counsel. He asked her to meet with him the following week in New York and present her evidence.

The end run to Albany and the extensive publicity it occasioned in the New York City newspapers stirred the district attorney's office into action. As soon as Bly got home, Assistant District Attorney Elder sent word that he wanted to meet with her to discuss developments in the forgery case.

The New York Times published a major feature on Bly and her complicated case, in which she described herself as "a fighting woman who has a fight to make and is determined that nothing shall stand in the way of carrying it to a last extremity." With three cases involving her then before the various courts, Bly told *The Times* she planned to start yet another effort in federal court, this time to have Clark ousted as receiver in favor of "a practical businessman put in this lawyer's place, so that the lawyers will not get it all."

When the reporter suggested that many people had the impression she was no more than a figurehead for the Iron Clad, Bly bristled:

> They said I married [Robert] Seaman for his money. They are wrong. I had an idea and I loved business. There was in Europe Bertha Krupp, a woman who was doing great things in a business left her by her people. But she was nothing more than a figurehead in it. And there was also Mrs. Cadbury, who makes the famous Cadbury Chocolates in London. But she only interested herself in the social welfare end of her business.
>
> These two women were my only rivals. I could prove what an American woman could do in actual practical, cold and hard business, and seven years after the burdens of one great plant came upon my shoulders, I added to that plant another almost as large.
>
> That was my success and I was going to see if an American woman could not lead the world. And did men help me? As wolves might help rabbits.

She described how a "well-known" New York bank, which she approached for a $25,000 loan, advised her to hire a team of lawyers to draw up the papers. That firm demanded an outrageous retaining fee, which she refused to pay. A member of the law firm told her he was also a director of the bank and would see that her loan was called if she didn't pay the retainer.

"I went right to the bank, exhibited his letter to the president and dismissed [?] him. The loan was not called. The lawyer was dismissed from the directorate. That was my first fight," she said.

I learned that the woman who would go into business when there is no such weapon as the ballot to help her along has an orphan-like struggle all the time. She is not treated according to that code by which men deal with one another. Her finances are free-picking for every law firm that can get its clutches on her and to stir any group of men to resentment against it is very, very hard.

I have not heretofore been a suffragette. Now I am one and the first legislation I want to see enacted is a law changing radically the bankruptcy methods.

The tragedy was that despite efforts that resulted in the building of a great company, "a man in my closed-down Iron Clad plant is answering telephones at $10 a day and they want the Steel Barrel plant, too. It is not a great victory for an American woman who has had her fling at business and done her best," she said.

"But the end is not quite yet."

❧

Bly pressed her effort to have Appleton Clark removed as the Iron Clad's receiver and in the meantime found every way she could to aggravate him. In May, she sued him over locking up the freight shipment yard. In June, she sent a raiding party to tear down the outdoor staircase leading up to the office he was occupying at the Iron Clad plant. The raiders overpowered Clark's watchmen, who were forced to call in federal deputy marshals. The marshals had to draw their revolvers to chase the interlopers away. They were back the next day, intent on their task. Bly insisted that the staircase stood on her personal property and was therefore not part of the bankruptcy proceedings. Clark gave in and let her have the staircase torn down, which meant the only way to his office was by a circuitous route through the factory. Bly's reaction was spiteful, petulant, and small, even childish. It indicated the level of her sense of exclusion from the all-male world of New York big business. She reacted to the bankruptcy proceedings as if they represented a personal vendetta against her. Her behavior in such episodes only made matters worse.

What enraged Bly most was something in bankruptcy proceedings that causes just as much consternation to latter day operators of companies in trouble: that Receiver Clark's only duty in carrying on the Iron Clad's affairs seemed to be to sell the stock on hand—not to figure out how to get the company running again at a profit. In Bly's view, Clark was needlessly putting 1,300 men out of work. A factory expert Clark had called in declared the Iron Clad "too large and too expensive to be operated under prevailing conditions." Clark would

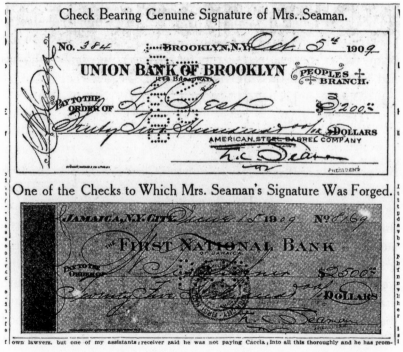

Facsimiles of checks bearing Bly's actual and forged signatures published by
The New York Times, *June 29, 1911*

(UMI)

not disclose the expert's name. Bly was convinced this decision had been reached only because the creditors were bankers, the receiver was a lawyer, and neither could think like a businessman. If they would run the company instead of selling off its assets, the jobs could be saved, Bly said, the debts could be paid, and everyone would be better off.

By June 28, Bly had served notice on Receiver Clark that he should proceed at once to bring suit against the four banks—she added the Union Bank of Brooklyn to her list—that had cashed forged Iron Clad checks. Clark replied that this was outside his jurisdiction and should be taken up with the bankruptcy trustee, once one was appointed in the case.

At the same time, Bly's case against Caccia and Gielnik gained momentum. Assistant Kings County District Attorney LeRoy Ross produced for reporters a packet of checks cashed by Caccia and Gielnik, some paid in favor of the saloon keeper Traphofner and often in amounts well into the thousands of dollars. "There may be some question about a few of these checks," Ross said. "We cannot tell if all the funds represented were stolen until we examine the company's books very thoroughly." Nevertheless, he said, on the basis of his preliminary investigation, it was already "absolutely certain" that a systematic plan to loot the company had been in place.

In the federal motion to have Clark removed from the Iron Clad, Bly's attorney, James A. Allen, questioned why Caccia, under criminal indictment, was being allowed repeated access to the Iron Clad offices while Bly was barred. Clark responded by saying that Caccia was helping him get a grasp of the company's affairs and added that he was not being paid anything for the service. Clark said he had informed Caccia that he could not see the books of the company and that Caccia had not expressed any interest in seeing them.

Bly's attorney also charged that Clark was obstructing the supply of heat and power from the Iron Clad to the American Steel Barrel Company, which was dependent on the Iron Clad for energy, and that when a coil on an electric generator snapped, stopping the barrel company from filling orders, Clark repeatedly refused to have it fixed. Judge Thomas I. Chatfield, who, among others, was hearing the case, declined to issue a written order forcing Clark to repair the coil—his existing orders already covered such an eventuality, he said—but he told the receiver that he had better go ahead and do it. When Clark said he didn't know how to fix the generator, Bly volunteered that she could do it in ten minutes and always kept a special replacement coil on hand for just such an emergency. The judge agreed she should get immediate access to the machine. When Clark finally admitted her to the premises—a week later—Bly made the repair just as quickly as she said she would.

Another part of Chatfield's order was favorable to Bly. Clark was told to hire however many men he needed to inspect the steel barrel company's freight in a way that would not impede the movement of its shipments to customers.

In arguing for his side, Clark's attorney, Adolph Kiendl, would bow low with a flourish of his hand every time he invoked Bly's name, to which he would add in operatic sarcasm, "Her Royal Highness."

"These vexatious problems," Bly told a reporter,

are of course merely incidents of a warfare every woman must make who tries to brave the upper financial circles. They tolerate us women now down in the clerical classes, but when we try for anything more, why we get ahead only so far as we can fight our way against obstacles from which a businessman, with the prestige that surrounds his success, is entirely, or almost entirely free.

The supposition in the case of those who deal with a successful man manufacturer is that he knows just what's fair and just what isn't and that they must play the game within certain fixed limits. But with the woman manufacturer— well, the supposition is entirely different. I wish I might make public some of the offers—very tempting offers—of supposedly reputable law firms of the basis upon which they would like to undertake the prosecution of my case.

And I would like to tell also what an audit company asked and demanded in fact, as a consideration for installing a new set of books.

Judge Chatfield had gotten fed up with all the quibbling between the two attorneys in the case, acting as messenger boys for Bly and Clark, who were too hostile to communicate directly. "Authority to buy a paper of tacks doesn't need a court order," the judge said. "Ever since these bankruptcy proceedings began attorneys have been coming before me seeking orders and injunctions in matters already covered in my instructions to the receiver."

Chatfield delayed decision on ousting Clark until Judge Van Vechten Veeder returned to take over for Chatfield, who was going on vacation. Chatfield similarly postponed deciding whether the barrel company was an Iron Clad asset. His delays effectively bought Bly time to keep the barrel company running and out of the receiver's hands.

Bly was convinced that getting her story to the public through the newspapers was her only hope of success. "Under this system of lawyer-receiverships," she told a reporter for *The New York Times,* "everything they touch is done for. I don't want to close down my barrel plant. There is no need to. I understand its needs and its capacity and the extent of its business. I sold 500,000 barrels last year. And yet, if they beat me, as my own trusted men employees beat me, they will close it down and turn its employees out just as they have the Iron Clad."

Bly's attorney produced two of the Iron Clad's salesmen, who showed orders for more than $100,000 worth of goods, which they'd had to reject when Clark arrived. Factory manager L. F. Lawrence testified that he canceled 500 orders a day for three weeks after the forced closing of the plant, and the sales manager of the dairy supply department, T. J. McHale, said his department alone turned back $75,000 worth of orders.

Bly for her part said that she was conducting the affairs of the barrel company on a cash-only basis and that on the night of June 30 had the largest balance on hand that the firm had seen for many years.

Several days later, she told *The New York Times* she would have absolutely no objection to her creditors putting their own men on the steel barrel company's books and on handling its cash if, in return, they would refrain from interfering with her business in a way aimed at shutting her down. She declared that if the courts would only leave her alone, she would have enough money within two years to pay off the last of her debts. "I hope this all comes out," she said. "It has got to come out. Publicity is the only weapon left and I want the guilty punished even if it should turn out that I am guilty. I'm going to stay right on the job and fight."

⚜

A reporter for *The Times* tried to ferret out the details of how the forgery scheme against the Iron Clad had worked. Bly handed over to him a packet of more than a hundred checks, from which he chose nine to examine more closely.

One check drawn originally for $101 and paid to the order of a cement contractor was altered to have a face value of $801 by the time a teller named Trimble certified it at the People's Bank of Brooklyn. "The 'eight' obviously had been written over the word 'one,' the printed number had been scratched out, and a number in ink substituted, and an awkwardly written figure 'eight' had been superimposed upon the figure 'one' beneath it. Clumsier forgeries have rarely been exhibited," the reporter wrote.

> The history of this check as traced by a *Times* reporter through the records of Denton and Company, payees, shows that it had been cashed through the forgery of their endorsement. They had received, as their ledger showed, only the amount due them, $101, whether in cash or by check they could not tell.
>
> When the check, with a statement from Denton and Co. that they had received only $101 and that their [e]ndorsement was a forgery, was taken to the People's Bank it would find that its doors were closed and that the State Banking Department was in charge, the bank having gone into liquidation a year ago as a branch of the Union Bank of Brooklyn.

Bank examiners looked closely at the nine checks. The reporter said they found acid stains clearly showing where dates and numbers had been erased and in some cases even where the name of the payee had been erased and another substituted. Faint letters and figures showed beneath the acid stains.

Assistant Banking Superintendent W. C. Penton said it was "past belief" that a teller at the People's Bank could ever have received these checks in good faith. He proposed another explanation: "There is one thing I can think of that may save the banks," he said. "As I have studied the system of these two forgers, they made a constant practice of stealing the Iron Clad Manufacturing Company's checks as they came in through the mails from customers. Then they would forge Mrs. Seaman's name and would cash these stolen checks at a saloon, and receive in return the saloon keeper's check on the Broadway Bank of Brooklyn." Penton thought it was possible that Caccia and Gielnik were increasing the face value of Iron Clad checks paid out to suppliers only *after* these checks were received back in the Iron Clad's offices for filing away. The sloppy "raisings," then, would have been done solely to give the books some semblance of balance, to show—on paper at least—that money was going out of the company to pay bills instead of to enrich its crooked employees and a barkeep who took a percentage for his laundering services. If that wasn't the scheme, Penton said, "I cannot conceive how such shabby work would otherwise escape detection."

Under Penton's theory, the banks would not have liability to the Iron Clad at all, except insofar as they might have raised question about the arrangement between Traphofner and Bly—E. C. Seaman by her signature—who seemed to be endorsing an extraordinary number of Iron Clad checks over to a saloon.

The investigation became so cumbersome that Assistant District Attorney Elder offered to postpone his vacation in order to keep collecting evidence against the accused forgers. Among the papers collected was a note for $15,000 made out by the Iron Clad to Traphofner. On the back of it was an endorsement showing that $2,000 of the amount had been paid. Across its face in large and nervously written letters was the word "Canceled," written by

Traphofner in the presence of detectives when they found the note and questioned him about it before he fled the country.

The Times said it also appeared that not all the money obtained in the scheme was stolen. For example, one check written on December 23, 1910, for $3,000 was made out to Traphofner against the Iron Clad's account in the Western National Bank of Philadelphia. Of the money received for it, the company's books showed that $2,500 had been put to the company's credit in the People's National Bank, and other sums had been scattered through various small accounts. Caccia and Gielnik tore up the vouchers of one account, called "the Lawrence account," as soon as they were received from the bank. It was thought that the account was one operated by the two men to give the books a "semblance of regularity," the reporter explained.

The Times also disclosed that Caccia had been indicted on July 21, 1893, on charges of stealing from a previous employer, Hyman Sonn, of the Sonn Brothers wholesale liquor dealers. After Caccia spent a month in The Tombs, Sonn dropped the prosecution. The indictment was dismissed five years later.

The question that remained was where had all the money gone? Investigators had yet to turn up any trail of large financial transactions by Caccia, although he was said to have a penchant for gambling at the racetrack.

༄

Bly's old friend Arthur Brisbane could help through his editorial page column in *The New York Evening Journal*, and he did. The Hearst papers liked to support the causes of beleaguered women. "Women Are Robbed About Nine Times Out of Ten—Sometimes Oftener," the headline on Brisbane's column read. "Men That Wouldn't Cheat Each Other, for Some Mysterious Reason, Seem to Take Delight in Cheating Women. Have You Noticed That? The Case of Nellie Bly."

He went over the details of Bly's case, inserting his trademark all-capital-letter attention-getters as appropriate, and then admonished: "Women, before you get into any kind of business, or before you trust any man, no matter how ingenuous his expression, how curly his hair or how deep his interest in you, REMEMBER THAT MEN USUALLY CHEAT WOMEN WHEN THEY GET THE CHANCE. If you don't know that, read about the case of Nellie Bly."

The New York Times also produced an editorial supportive of Bly's cause and very damning to the powerful banks and Receiver Clark. *The Times* questioned how banks had cashed such crudely forged and "raised" checks and how none of the people concerned in "these most curious transactions" had manifested any uneasiness as to the possible consequences, nor had they provided any convincing explanation of their long-continued carelessness.

As to Clark, *The Times* said, he had continued to make it hard for Bly to conduct the affairs of the barrel company. "The difficulty of suspending judgment, as regards the receiver, is made cruelly difficult when he gets himself savagely scolded by the court that appointed him, for mysteriously delaying the shipment of goods, and professes inability to repair a machine which Mrs. Seaman, as soon as she can force her way to it, promptly starts running as well as ever." The editorial concluded:

> These things are producing an extremely painful impression that "the woman in the case" is not getting fair treatment, to say nothing of consideration, and that she had excuse, if not reason, for declaring herself the victim of a large, elaborate and continuing conspiracy. It would be judicious for the court and the receiver to remove this impression from the public mind at once.

As if Bly's life wasn't legally complicated enough, a tangent of a much older case involving the infringement on the Iron Clad's patent for double-necked milk cans surfaced again in early July of 1911 in upstate New York's Herkimer County.

Bly expected to be called to Utica to testify as the state's principal witness in the trial of a prominent and politically powerful Utica attorney, Edwin H. Risley, who was accused of inserting the words "the same" into an affidavit of Bly's that already was a matter of public record—a criminal offense. The insertion of the words had entirely changed Bly's intended meaning.

The case grew out of Bly's failed injunction against the Dairyman's Manufacturing Company back in 1905 for patent infringement. When she could not get Dairyman's to stop using the milk cans on which the Iron Clad held rights to the patent, she informed the inventor that unless he could protect the Iron Clad from patent infringement, the company would cease to pay him royalties, as provided for in their contract. The inventor was from Herkimer County, and Risley was his attorney.

"The other companies kept on making cans. We ceased paying the patent holder and he sued," Bly said. "In the meantime I devised alterations in our cans which avoided conflicts with the patent and in seven or eight years the patent [holder's] suit found its way to the Herkimer County court calendar." In the course of that case the preceding spring, the alleged affidavit alteration occurred. When Bly discovered it, she informed the judge, who immediately stopped that trial and commenced criminal proceedings against Risley.

Bly claimed to have received a telephoned warning that she would "keenly regret her action" if she went to Herkimer to testify against Risley. She wrote immediately to Herkimer County District Attorney Frank A. Schmidt, explaining what had transpired. Bly said if Schmidt still required her testimony, the threat had made her all the more anxious to appear in court. She said a lawyer with whom she was acquainted had called and asked her if she knew an attorney from Utica by the name of William Grant Brown. She said she did not, then was informed that Brown had suggested

> that it would be a fine thing for me and my fortunes in the financial entanglements connected with the receivership of my Iron Clad Manufacturing Company if I should fail to appear at Herkimer, and should give no testimony damaging to the defendants there.
>
> There was added to the suggestion another to the effect that many of my present difficulties had their origin in my activities against the Utica law firm charged with altering a

public document, and that if I ceased these activities my fortunes here would begin to look up.

Bly said she told the caller she would testify when called. He called back again, this time saying that "Mr. Brown had offered his most sincere assurances that I would be arrested the moment I set foot in Herkimer if I should go there, and would be harassed and followed by powerful people."

To *The New York Times*, Bly said, "For more reasons than those involving my own welfare, I cannot afford to lie down under any such threats as those conveyed to me. Until businessmen learn that the woman in business is entitled to the same fairness that exists between men, there will be no place in business for women and at present we have only to fight the infinitely numerous crooked games tried upon us." Schmidt was quoted as saying if Bly had been so threatened, he was certain the court would investigate the matter. *The Utica Observer* reported that no attorney named William Grant Brown was known in the area.

The case was continued until the fall. Bly testified on the second day of the weeklong trial. On October 11, Risley, who was seventy years old, was convicted on charges of fraudulently altering evidence. The maximum sentence was a $1,000 fine and seven years in prison. Risley was spared the prison term but was fined the $1,000 and later disbarred.

～～

On July 11, 1911, U.S. District Court Judge Van Vechten Veeder issued his first major ruling in Bly's favor. He said there was not sufficient evidence for him to consider the American Steel Barrel Company part of the Iron Clad in spite of the obvious intertwining of their books and operations, as well as Bly's previous statements, presented by her opposition, which gave credence to the contention that the two companies were one and the same. In effect, Judge Veeder ruled that Receiver Clark had no jurisdiction over the steel barrel company.

In both September and November of 1910, in filling out her returns for what she referred to as "federal incorporation tax," Bly had prepared an affidavit in which she stated that the steel barrel company had "never been separated from the main company. It is simply a department. The same presses do the work for both companies. The same payrolls are used for both companies and no separate books were kept, so that it is impossible for us to divide or separate them. The one report covers both." Bly's opposition thought record of this affidavit should have proved to the satisfaction of the court that the companies were one. Judge Veeder ruled otherwise, in effect saying that Bly's affidavit didn't necessarily represent a statement of absolute fact.

Bly told the court that she had explained the problem of the tangled books to the government before filling out the affidavit but had made the statement anyway because the filing date was fast approaching, Caccia had the books as confused as possible, and the authorities had assured Bly, she said, that they would "deal liberally with such questions [as whether the companies were separate] until the matter of corporation tax was better understood."

To buttress her claim that the companies were separate, Bly used the example of the account with Brown Brothers. Although Brown Brothers, according to Bly, repeatedly requested that she pledge both the Iron Clad and the American Steel Barrel Company as collateral for obtaining credit for tin being furnished to only one of them, Bly said she consistently refused. Her "constant aim," she said, was to build up both companies as separate entities.

Although Bly had succeeded in the short run in holding on to American Steel Barrel, Veeder did allow the creditors to reintroduce their motion if they gathered more evidence. The judge also suggested it might be necessary to appoint a bankruptcy referee to sort out the differences of Bly and the Iron Clad's receiver, but he reserved decision for the moment.

By July 12, *The Brooklyn Daily Eagle* reported that Bly had hired the firm of Moos, Prince and Nathan to plan a new defense strategy. Moos met with counsel for the Iron Clad's unsecured creditors and said they were planning to apply in federal court for an order to have officials of banks that had cashed the forged checks of the

Iron Clad examined before U.S. Bankruptcy Commissioner Richard Morle. The hope was to gather enough information to file civil suits that would force the banks involved to repay the Iron Clad for the forged checks they had cashed, a requirement under banking law. But no more was heard of the plan.

Things had started to look up by July 17, when prosecutors withdrew a motion to hold Bly in contempt of court for refusing to answer questions about the books of the American Steel Barrel Company. But on July 24, Judge Veeder came down hard on Bly's motion to have Receiver Clark ousted:

> The petition might well have been disposed of summarily since it consists almost entirely of simple assertions by the petitioner unsupported by any statement of facts, as to all of which the receiver's express denial is sufficient. The various terms in which the petition has attributed malicious and wrongful motives to the receiver are without any support whatever in the facts. There is absolutely nothing in the conduct of the receiver tending to show that he has not performed the duty to which he was assigned by the court with entire good faith and solely in the interests of the estate of the alleged bankrupt.

Veeder further accused Bly of an "attitude of hostility" in all her dealings with Clark, going so far as to refuse to receive his letter from the postman. Veeder dismissed her every argument and called her decision to tear down the staircase to Clark's office a "gratuitous and petty display of spite." He supported Clark on every point, even his failure to bring suit against the banks, affirming Clark's view that this was well beyond a receiver's mandate.

The judge's ruling prompted *The New York Times* to produce a second editorial on Bly's predicament, adjusting its sympathies substantially to reflect the new developments. It said in part:

> Judge Veeder's ruling on Mrs. Seaman's petition that a part of her property might be kept out of the receiver's hands brought the hope [that women could get fair treatment in

business] to realization. It vindicated the honesty as well as the wisdom of the receiver's course, declared that all his acts had been of the strictest legality, and with impatience dismissed the charges against him as without weight or substance. This decision, of course, must be accepted as conclusive as between Mrs. Seaman and Mr. Clark, the receiver. The losses that brought about her bankruptcy properly excite indignation and commiseration, but they in no wise affect the validity of her creditors' claims or the propriety of protecting and enforcing those claims.

Her belief that every man's hand is against her simply because she is a woman in business can be understood and excused, but fortunately it is not true. Further proclamation of it, now that the court has spoken, might lead to the suspicion that what the woman in business wants is not justice, or such justice as would be accorded a man, but consideration of her femininity—which would be both unreasonable and impractical.

The next week, Judge Veeder issued a restraining order to stop Bly from taking electrical power from the Iron Clad to run the steel barrel company. The court had previously ordered her to pay $150 a month to the Iron Clad for the service, but Bly had declined to do so, Veeder's order said.

Judge Chatfield was back on the case at the beginning of August and issued several rulings against Bly's interests. He directed Bly to show cause by August 11 why she should not return to Clark property she was said to have removed from the Iron Clad and why she should not be held in contempt of court for violating various court orders over the course of the proceedings. The rulings gave Clark an opening wedge into the affairs of the steel barrel company, about which Bly steadfastly refused to answer questions.

On August 11, Bly sent word that she was too ill to appear at trial. The day before, she had successfully avoided Clark's attorney Kiendl when he came to her house to serve her with a summons. Chatfield issued a continuance.

The case resumed August 30 with Judge Veeder on the bench. Bly did appear that day, informing the court that she had resigned as president of the American Steel Barrel Company as of April 29, then saying there was a new board of directors on which she served as vice president. Veeder still insisted she answer the questions being put to her by attorney Kiendl and Bankruptcy Commissioner Morle. Bly maintained that Judge Chatfield had previously ruled that she did not have to answer the questions, so she didn't see why she had to now. Veeder told her the alternative was to be held in contempt of court. Bly retorted that the questions had to do with "private matters."

"Characterize them as you see fit," the judge said, "but you must answer them. I should be extremely loath to commit you for failure to comply with the court's order. I should sincerely regret, in the first exercise of my authority in this respect, to commit a woman. It is impossible for the court to accomplish anything if it submitted to the violations you have displayed."

"I have had no intention to violate," Bly said.

"Your intentions will be judged by your actions," the judge said.

"I understood from Judge Chatfield that I need not answer these questions," said Bly. "My lay mind won't take in Judge Chatfield's reversing himself."

"That's neither here nor there," Veeder said. "He's done it and I want the directions obeyed."

Bly then testified, keeping her responses as vague as possible. She said she was a stockholder in the Iron Clad, the barrel company, the Iron Clad of Baltimore, and Mary Milling and Mining Company. Sometimes she purchased goods for the barrel company, and sometimes the Iron Clad's purchasing agent did it. Both companies had one telephone number. Both had offices on the same floor in the same building. The barrel company bought most of its material from the Iron Clad—$1.5 million worth in five years. She said she didn't know where the steel barrel company kept its bank accounts, nor if she was president of the company in January of 1910 nor if the company's minutes would show this or any of a number of other things Kiendl was trying to find out from her.

The judge tired of the proceedings, which he characterized as a "mere quibble," and left the room, instructing Commissioner Morle to report to him. Morle then asked the court stenographer to take down every question Bly declined to answer or replied that her memory had failed her on so they could be presented to Judge Veeder, who would decide whether to hold Bly in contempt of court.

The next day Bly was at the Iron Clad with Receiver Clark and Kiendl, his attorney, looking at documents in order to prepare to answer the questions being put by the court. Bly's contention had been that since the steel barrel company was independent of the Iron Clad, the court had no jurisdiction over its affairs, nor the right to ask her to submit to Kiendl's twenty-one questions about it.

In the afternoon, she did consent to answer the questions, asserting, among other things, that the books of the steel barrel company were in the possession of company treasurer George A. Wilnik. She said further that the directors of the company included George A. Wheelock, whom the court later described as a bookmaker for the horse races and who Bly said now had bought controlling interest in the firm. The other directors were Bly's cousin Robert Lee Cochrane, who was a secretary at the company; Bly herself; C. A. Guibert; and Charles Gehring.

The case dragged on through September and into October, after Bly's return from testifying in the Herkimer County patent case. There was a skirmish over machinery and barrelheads which, Clark asserted, Bly had removed from the Iron Clad premises just before he took on his duties at the plant. Bly agreed to return them, then said she would sue immediately to get them back. But she didn't pursue the matter further.

Judge Chatfield was back on the bench. Clark complained about paying a bill of $2,900 which arrived at the Iron Clad for two welding machines Bly was using at the steel barrel plant. Chatfield advised Clark to seize the machines and let the court decide who owned them later. Clark complained that Bly would laugh at him if he did that and would refuse to give them up. Chatfield reiterated his decision.

On October 25, Bly was back on the stand giving every possible excuse, none very plausible, for why she couldn't produce the steel barrel company's books. Maybe they were with the district attorney's office, she suggested. Maybe they'd been left with a handwriting expert she had hired. Chatfield ordered the marshal of the court to take Bly into technical custody.

One week later, Bly's friend Herman A. Metz, the former New York City controller, appeared with a surprising offer: to take over the Iron Clad and the American Steel Barrel Company, reorganize and run them both, pay off the creditors, and make everyone happy. The creditors at first seemed interested in the idea, then rejected it for reasons not explained. The bankruptcy proceedings continued.

Bly was not in court the day Metz presented his offer. She was attending the funeral of the man to whom she owed a great deal, Joseph Pulitzer. Of the more than thirty people listed by his newspaper, *The New York World*, as among the prominent mourners, Bly was the only woman.

Three weeks later, before U.S. District Court Judge Thomas I. Chatfield in Brooklyn, the jury sided with Bly's creditors and declared the Iron Clad Manufacturing Company to have been bankrupt since May 23, 1911. Bly's attorneys moved at once to have the verdict set aside. The creditors moved to get a reversal of Chatfield's refusal to determine whether the Iron Clad and the steel barrel company were separate. And Bly, never say die, commenced action against the banks she held responsible for hastening the Iron Clad's downfall.

⌘

December 11th, 1911.

My dear N.B.:—I am back from my vacation. I had a very good vacation riding, then came back, did something queer and then went to bed. Now I am out again for a day or two at least I hope.

I will be glad to see you at any time—although I suppose when I do see you, that as usual you will listen solemnly to my feeble advice and forget all about it.

I hope that your business affairs are going well and that you will start this year cheerfully.

Please remember me to your mother.

Yours sincerely,
A. Brisbane

Bly decided she needed new counsel and had sought Brisbane's advice in the selection of new attorneys. He suggested two— Clarence J. Shearn and Samuel Untermyer, both of whom were highly successful in the service of William Randolph Hearst. Bly thought maybe she should employ both.

One hundred of the Iron Clad's creditors met on January 10, 1912, to try to agree on a trustee in bankruptcy for the firm, presumably under the court's direction. Bly supported the election of Don Seitz, business manager at *The New York World* and a trusted deputy of Pulitzer, but the position went to Adolph Kiendl, who had been Receiver Clark's attorney in the federal court proceedings and no friend to Bly.

For the second issue of *Fair Play*, a new weekly magazine being published by her friend Marcus Braun, Bly wrote a detailed description of her travails under the headline "How I Was Robbed of Two Million Dollars"; it led the publication. Within hours of its availability on newsstands, the magazine distributing firm of Ward and Gow ordered it removed from all subway and elevated stations, which they controlled, because of material in Bly's piece considered potentially libelous. Artemus Ward, head of the distribution company, declined to say who had called his attention to the article.

By the end of the month, with the property of the Iron Clad factory about to go on the auction block, Bly frantically contacted everyone she knew in a position to do so to buy it on her behalf. Since both the presses and the $100,000 power plant were to be sold as part of the land, she considered it a great bargain. But everyone, including Brisbane, who claimed too many financial encumbrances of his own, turned her down.

With Brisbane's influence, Bly tried to get Untermyer to take her case, but he had refused. "Mrs. Seaman or some of her numerous friends have gotten this thing in such an inextricable mess that I can do nothing with it," he confided to Brisbane. Shearn begged off with a similar assessment. On February 8, Brisbane warned Bly that he had heard from someone in a position to know that "there is a great prejudice against you 'in the atmosphere' of the federal court in Brooklyn." He quoted another attorney, David Gerber, echoing

Untermyer's sense that Bly had been "very badly advised and your case very badly mixed up." Indeed, Bly, without the benefit of legal knowledge, wanted to direct the strategy for her legal cases, largely basing her approach on an overly emotional, overly personalized response to events. She tied herself up with lawyers willing to do her bidding and in the process compounded her difficulties.

On February 8, the creditors renewed their fight to gain control of the steel barrel company in federal court in Brooklyn.

Bly pelted Brisbane with an endless barrage of requests, all of which he responded to with grace and patience, a winning air of responsive compassion and loyalty, and a virtually imperceptible unwillingness to act on her behalf in matters that might compromise his financial or editorial stature. Bly was shameless in her requests for advice and help from her influential former colleague. She even asked him to help her mother sell the house at 15 West Thirty-seventh Street. Brisbane, in typically polite refusal, volunteered that he thought it wise to sell the house but said he could not get involved with the actual sale.

In the meantime, the court had appointed a bankruptcy referee, Robert J. Tilney, who presented on February 15 his determination that Bly was guilty of contempt for removing Iron Clad company assets from the premises after the company had been deemed bankrupt. Bly had done nothing to curry Tilney's favor, treating him much the way she did Clark.

In the meantime she continued her pursuit of a friendly buyer for the Iron Clad real estate, onto which she hoped to be able to expand the steel barrel company's operations. Twice more she asked Brisbane to reconsider, and twice more he charmingly declined.

On the scheduled day of the sale, Bly wrote to Brisbane in Chicago: "I shall still fight, but I hardly know any more what I am fighting for, except to fight," she wrote. "They have taken every-thing—they have wrecked everything. They lie about me and per-secute me. I shall be glad to talk to you about things when you come back."

Brisbane forwarded a letter to Bly which he knew she would find interesting. The letter itself has not survived, but Bly's response has. "I know that the attorneys [for the creditors] had gone to the *Times* to induce them to print nothing favorable about me, but that is one of the things I have met frequently," she told Brisbane.

By the end of the month, Judge Chatfield had ordered Bly to vacate a large parcel of property in use by the steel barrel company, since, the court had determined, the land belonged to the Iron Clad. At the same time, Chatfield allowed her to take steel barrel company belongings off the property before she surrendered it, provided she gave the court a list of what she had removed. The same order denied the receiver's application to search the barrel company premises, but it did require Bly to surrender to the control of the court—until ownership could be determined—some $15,000 worth of furniture and paintings she had put in storage.

Bly had made it clear she felt unable to get justice in Brooklyn. Responding to this sentiment, Judges Chatfield and Veeder invited Judge Charles M. Hough to come over from Manhattan and rule on whether Bly should be held in contempt of court for her repeated refusal to answer questions and produce the steel barrel company's books. Bly pulled another disappearing act when attempts were made to serve her with a summons. Her attorney, James Allen, announced in court the next day that she was too ill to appear. Judge Hough maintained that Bly's behavior might be the result of "ignorance unenlightened by advice" and suggested that her good behavior as a witness over the two weeks until March 26, when the order was to take effect, would determine whether she could expect clemency.

On March 15, 1912, Bly won an immense victory. Judge Chatfield ruled against the creditors' petition to have the steel barrel company declared a subsidiary department of the Iron Clad. The creditors responded by moving immediately to have Judge Chatfield charged with bias under a new judicial code. On the basis of the charge, which Chatfield categorically denied, he still readily consented to an order from Senior Circuit Judge E. Henry Lacombe to have him taken off the case.

In the meantime, the creditors renewed their petition to take control of the steel barrel company, hoping for a favorable ruling from a new judge appointed to hear the rest of the case. For his part,

Chatfield said he regretted that the creditors thought so little of him but that if they had merely expressed this sentiment to him, without filing an affidavit, he would have removed himself from the case at once. Insofar as the affidavit had been submitted, however, he readily had himself withdrawn from the case in accordance with the new procedures.

On March 16, Bly finally appeared in court before Judge Hough to respond to the contempt citation pending against her. She stated,

> I am told that my conduct in court has not been all that is expected of a litigant and I regret that fact. While I do not ask any consideration on the ground of sex, however, I may say that I have been under a physical and mental strain for something like two years that would have broken down many a strong man. To be forced to look helplessly on at the destruction of the property one has spent the best years of one's life in building up, that experience following months of wearing anxiety due to the events that precipitated the catastrophe, is not conducive to suavity of deportment.

She told the court that when she refused to answer questions it was because she knew they were being put for the purpose of obtaining information to be used against her in depriving her of her rights. Or, she said, she had "cried out against the admission of false testimony on the part of the associates of the indicted forgers and thieves," or it had been because "I honestly could not believe that the court really comprehended the situation."

The performance did not sway the judge. He declared Bly in contempt of court and fined her $600, of which $100 was due the court and the rest payable to the Iron Clad's creditors within four days. Hough then asked Bly to address the court. She said in part,

> Perhaps I have done wrong, but it was only through a desire to fight the men who have slandered me in court and out. The representatives of the secured creditors have plotted to cheat me, wreck me, crush me . . . This case means 12 years of my life work wasted.

I am not fighting the court but these men. They are powerful and I am weak. They have money and I have none. I have given my time, money, health and, I fear, my mind to these proceedings . . .

I will fight these wreckers until the breath leaves my body and until my unsecured creditors' claims are secured. It is a fight to the finish against these men who are striving to ruin me.

Still, she did not pay the fine. Kiendl, now the Iron Clad trustee, said he was willing to be patient if she would just show a willingness to abide by the court's ruling, even if she lacked the funds to do so. "Nobody wants to be mean," he said, "especially since she is a woman."

On the same day, April Fool's Day, 1912, Caccia and Gielnik were arrested for the third time on the forgery charges, this time on a bench warrant, although it is not clear what happened to the earlier attempts to prosecute them. The two were arraigned in the Court of General Sessions.

Bly, meantime, was furious about the unfair assault on Judge Chatfield. She cabled Brisbane in Chicago, suggesting he devote an editorial to this unwarranted charge of bias against such a fine man. Brisbane replied by return cable on April 2: "Glad to write it," he said. "Mail me his decision and full explanation." Bly cabled back that she already had posted a copy of the decision and a full explanation would follow.

At the same time, Judge Hough signed an order committing Bly to jail for contempt of court and failing to pay her $600 fine. While marshals combed Manhattan in an effort to arrest her on April 3, Bly showed up in Brooklyn, at the offices of the district court, and paid the fine. With her was Marcus Braun, the publisher of *Fair Play*.

Brisbane, meanwhile, had further thoughts on writing an editorial about the Chatfield matter. He couldn't figure out what there was to base it on. "The man in charge undoubtedly was honest, in deciding in your favor," Brisbane concluded; at the same time he advanced that he had "no right, however, and cannot under the law take it for granted that the man who now will sit in the case

[Mayer] will judge unfairly. That can only depend upon what he actually does."

Since Bly was "as good a newspaper worker as myself," Brisbane suggested that she "sit down and write out exactly what you would like to have said in our paper, as though I were writing it. If the facts are as stated, and if the article, or something like it can be published under the libel law I shall lose no time in printing it. Write exactly what you would like to say in a thousand words. Send it to me and if I can use it in that shape or in another shape of my own, I'll do it." No such editorial was ever produced.

Brisbane renewed his concern that Bly needed to get herself an "energetic, progressive, capable lawyer IN GOOD STANDING WITH THE COURTS." He again suggested Shearn, who handled so much of the Hearst company business, even offering to sign a personal note to guarantee the price of a retainer for him on Bly's behalf. Shearn, however, declined to take on a case that had been mucked up by so many incompetent hands. Brisbane was out of ideas.

There was no end to the legal avalanche unleashed on Nellie Bly. The creditors initiated new contempt of court proceedings against her for failing to produce documentation they said would prove the connection between the Iron Clad and the steel barrel company. The Caccia-Gielnik case seesawed between the Court of General Sessions and the New York State Supreme Court, with no evident progress, and Bly's troubles with the Iron Clad creditors intensified exponentially, no matter what she did. Her desperation had driven her to barking at even her most tolerant friends.

The accusation of indifference rolled off Brisbane, who, in response to her whine of frustration, enumerated the extent to which he had supported and would support her:

> June 13th, 1912
>
> My dear N.B.
>
> I am on the train going to Buffalo—to speak at the Banker's Convention tonight. I wish you were going to speak in my place—you could tell them some pretty interesting truths, I guess.
>
> But honestly I do not see what I can do.

If you will give me any definite statements of facts to be published, if you will make any statements over your own signature that can be published with due regard to the libel laws, which as the agent of another I must respect, I shall be very glad to give full publicity to your side.

I talked to a number of lawyers as you know, Untermyer, Gerber, Osborne. I believe that any one of these men could have taken care of your case, and won it for you. Unfortunately, however, it seemed impossible to make any arrangement between you and them.

I do not think that you feel that I really showed lack of interest in that matter. In the case of Mr. Shearn, as in the case of the others, I offered to guarantee the expense of litigation up to $5,000 or more in case an advance payment were made which you could not meet at the time.

I have no doubt whatever that men have robbed you— as they usually rob women in business and out of business— whenever they get the chance.

I myself am very much pressed, trying to carry on four times as much work as I am able to do, and I cannot give the time that I should give to the affairs of my friends.

But if you will show me something definite that I can do, or supply me with ammunition that I can actually USE in your defence [sic], I'll be glad to use it.

I know that Mr. Hearst will be more than willing to have his newspapers take up the cause of a woman unjustly treated.

We cannot of course attack judges without definite statements of facts, nor can we attack others unless we can get facts upon which to base statements.

Brisbane then planted an idea that no doubt he thought would be as helpful to Bly as it could potentially be to his newspapers. For Bly, it was the unguent of opportunity, perhaps not exactly what she thought she needed, but relief grounded in reality and within the Brisbane sphere of influence and control.

He reminded Bly of what she may have forgotten: that even if she lost everything, she could still easily earn more money than she and her mother would ever need "and doing much more useful work than making tin cans. . . . Being tied to a factory and a lot of scoundrels cannot have been such very great happiness," he said and then pledged, "Be sure, when the time comes, if this business of yours goes wrong, which I don't think it will, I'll be glad to help you in some other direction. And if you can tell me anything definite that I can do now, tell me, and I will do it."

Bly pondered Brisbane's advice. She was about to face another contempt citation that could easily land her in jail. The only judge she trusted had been taken off her case. Her finances were in shambles. Maybe a reporting assignment—an out-of-town assignment—was, as Brisbane would have put it in his column, EXACTLY WHAT THIS BELEAGUERED DAMSEL REQUIRED.

⌘

One week later, Bly was in Chicago, adding her typewriter to the clatter being produced by legions of reporters covering the Republican National Convention of 1912. Bly was there as representative of *The New York Evening Journal*. Only one story of hers appeared, on June 22. Brisbane had teamed Nellie Bly with his paper's gifted illustrator Nell Brinkley, whose work usually accompanied theatrical stories. Bly wrote in classic vein about the clever and dogged schemes these two Nells employed in order to steal a glimpse of "Teddy" Roosevelt. The two women hid behind a broad-backed policeman stationed outside Roosevelt's hotel room, No. 1102, winning the officer's cooperation. Bly flirted him into offering his chest as a writing board so that she could dash off a note to the former president.

Roosevelt was locked in what was to be an unsuccessful battle to take the Republican nomination away from incumbent President William Howard Taft. Roosevelt formed the independent Progressive or Bull Moose Party, splitting the GOP vote with Taft so that they both lost the election.

When Bly finally saw Roosevelt, she wrote:

It was Teddy, the great and only, the glorious and independent and original Teddy! One glance and he went down the hall in a flying wedge, past that great mass of people, before any of them realized what had occurred.

One glance at his face and I felt my heart sink. He was pale. He was tired. He looked worried or unhappy, and as he was rushed down the hall, surrounded by policemen, followed by a bodyguard and led up in the rear by friends, all in a running trot, it was exactly as if he had been put under arrest and was being rushed off a prisoner.

Brinkley's delightful drawing consumed the top third of the newspaper's third page. Most amusing to anyone who had recently seen Bly, by then a matronly forty-eight, was the depiction of both women as svelte and gamine coquettes, as befitted the text. It was vanity rather than modesty, then, that had kept Bly so heavily veiled and impossible to photograph during her recent court trials. She could tell Brinkley how she'd like to be portrayed.

On June 26, U.S. District Court Judge Julius M. Mayer, the new judge appointed to hear the rest of the case, issued the second contempt of court order against Bly. This one was much more severe,

Nell Brinkley sketch of Nellie Bly at the Republican Party Convention, Chicago,
The New York Evening Journal, *June 22, 1912*
(Ransom Humanities Resource Center, University of Texas)

including a $3,000 fine and a sentence of twenty days in jail. But by the time Mayer issued it, Bly was on the train to Baltimore, where *The Journal* had sent her to write more features. The Democratic National Convention was about to start. Mayer issued a stay on the order until July 1. When Bly still did not appear, because she was out of town on assignment, he extended the stay until September, when the bankruptcy case was set to resume. Bly had her first reprieve in eighteen months.

From Baltimore, *The Journal* gave Bly star billing and great display. Her first piece occupied the left two columns of the front page under the headline "Nellie Bly Tells What She Saw at Baltimore." It was the only signed piece on the page.

The convention got under way with William Jennings Bryan and Senator James A. O'Gorman imposing their populist notions on the framing of the party platform, the main news lead of the day. Bly led her piece with a survey of the powerful New Yorkers the convention had brought to Baltimore. She began with a verbatim account of her chance encounter with New York Governor John A. Dix:

> "How are you getting on with your troubles, Miss Bly," the governor asked, as we shook hands. I had forgotten for a moment that I had any troubles and that a prison sentence is sitting behind a judge's bench waiting for my return to New York because some men stole most of my money.
>
> "They're worse every day," I told him.
>
> "Didn't Mr. Van Tuyl [the state banking superintendent] help you?" he asked.
>
> "Mr. Van Tuyl is perfectly lovely, but I didn't see that he did much for me," I said.
>
> "I told you to come back to me if he didn't handle your case successfully," he reminded me.
>
> "Well, I may come later. Mr. Frank Moss is handling the criminal side of it now and afterward I may come back to you to have the banking institutions investigated."
>
> "I am glad you have Mr. Moss," said the governor. "You couldn't have a better man."

A few paragraphs down she greeted big Tim Sullivan and her good friend, the former Controller Herman Metz, "who says he is making money and Herman likes money. And I like Herman so what's the difference?"

> But we all like money. Some of us say we don't. It's the style at the present time to cry out against money and I never remember seeing the world work harder to get money than it does now.
> Everybody's doing it. Somebody got most of mine. That's one of the reasons I'm here. I do mind losing the money, but still, I'm awfully glad to be here.

When Bly's old friend "from racing days" Jack McDonald saw her, he said the convention might as well be "Nellie Bly's reception." The compliment so honored her, she said, she had to run upstairs and change her hat. Bly's story had little to say about the convention proceedings, but, as always, much about her experience of the moment and the impact of her own presence on it. For example, "Then Mr. Tom Powers [illustrator] came over to show me a sketch he had made while I was shaking hands in the lobby. I told him if he dared to make me fat and showed my double chin I'd have a real photograph taken to show how extremely thin I am (if you really want to know something about the Democratic Convention this must interest you dreadfully)."

For the next day's story, Bly was loping, covering the convention in much the enthusiastic, gossipy way she had the woman suffrage convention sixteen years earlier—with hour-by-hour, blow-by-blow descriptions of proceedings and comings and goings that went from four o'clock in the afternoon until seven o'clock the next morning. The newspaper carried her report on two columns of the front page, all of the third page, and a half column on the fourth page.

Bly made only two brief personal, or at least semipersonal references, both about money. The first was a response to Bryan's resolution to exclude from the convention the delegates Thomas F. Ryan and August Belmont and those representing them and their heavily monied interests:

It was a bully move of Mr. Bryan's. It appeals to those who haven't got any money.

Have you ever noticed how those who have no claim to fame struggle to belittle the famous? Do you notice how those who have not the ability to make money hold up as if in shame those who can?

Oh, that master stroke! Who conceived the idea, no one tells, but it was a speech that appealed to the envy and hate of the people.

I had to like the man because he dared to say what we all know.

It takes courage to do that. But he had the courage because he was face to face with defeat. It was dare or die.

Bly seemed perplexed by the honor accorded "our captains of industry," the way the success of a Rockefeller, a Ryan, or a Morgan gives a sense of family pride to every American—except at a political convention.

And I say of all this, who has the best right to cry out against the power of money? I have seen its evil when least it should be felt and when it is most dangerous. I have fought its influence single-handed. For in one year I have lost a million dollars through its use and abuse, and though this day I stand a victim to its power, yet I am fair enough and I trust broad enough to recognize the power, of goodness in money as well as its power of evil.

There is to me no evil in the making of money. The evil is in its use.

On June 28, with the convention meeting for its thirteenth ballot and no sign of a presidential nominee, the hall was awash in rumors that Bryan would try to take the nomination for himself. Bly decided she should find out. Other reporters dismissed her. Don't bother, they advised, Bryan was too shrewd to tell. But, as she said,

My vanity was piqued. "I can know and prove in ten minutes whether Mr. Bryan wants and expects to steal the nomination," I declared.

The reporters laughed at me. In a second I jumped upon the reporters' table and stepped from one to the other. It was the only possible way to get through the crowd.

"Come with me," I said to the others. "I will make Mr. Bryan declare his intentions." I reached the stand above Mr. Bryan. The crowd was standing and yelling so loud that one could not distinguish what they yelled.

I yelled for Bryan. He heard me. He jumped to his feet and came over to the gallery where I stood. He took my hand.

"Don't," he said earnestly. "Don't start a stampede for me."

He held my hand and I looked into his eyes.

"Yes," I argued. "You want it," and I gave the loudest Bryan yell I could.

"I don't," he begged earnestly. "I would not accept the nomination."

"You don't mean it," I argued, and I yelled again.

"I will leave the hall if you don't stop," he called desperately to me.

He started rapidly for the door, pushing his way through the mass of people.

I was satisfied; I laughed too. It amused me to know I could make Mr. Bryan run away. I went back to my chair.

"He means," I said to the newspaper men, "that Mr. Bryan may have some bombs to explode, but not one to make himself the nominee."

In fact, both the nomination and the election went to Woodrow Wilson.

Bly's convention coverage continued two more days. One paragraph of the story which ran July 1, however, would echo back to federal court in Brooklyn the following year. It was in reference to a description she wanted to make of Tammany Hall boss Charles Francis Murphy, but she restrained herself to avoid having to apologize to him the next day.

> And I never apologize. It's tiresome. Apologies are the food of the humble in mind. I never was humble. That's why I was fined.
>
> If you ever get in court remember you must be a liar. Truth is tabooed. If you tell the truth you'll lose your case, sure, and your reputation. The lawyers on the other side will swamp you in a sea of lies. They will trim every act you have done since your big toe ceased to be the most fascinating object in the world, until your own mirror looks cracked and you gaze at yourself as the biggest stranger on earth. I've gone home from court after listening to a representative of the money trust tell all about me—and almost fallen over when my mother recognized me.
>
> Such is eloquence.

~❦~

The case of accused forgers Caccia and Gielnik was postponed three times during August and September of 1912. By October, the two had made bail of $1,000 each after five months in jail and were again set free. Brisbane encouraged Bly to write more features for him, even sending a letter to Abe Erlanger, one of *The Journal*'s main editors, introducing Bly as a new special correspondent just as soon as she got back from Baltimore. "She writes a better story than anybody else in town," Brisbane said, "and I know it will interest the readers."

But Bly's old headaches were back, for reasons not very difficult to fathom, and she had to put him off. There were her continuing financial difficulties to distract her as well. For a wedding gift for Brisbane, who had married his young cousin Phoebe on July 30, Bly and her mother had sent a painting from her own collection which Brisbane clearly appreciated—so much so that his sister Alice Thursby, Bly's friend, was moved to write her own letter of appreciation for it.

Soon after, Bly asked Brisbane if he would buy her home in Sheepshead Bay. He declined, as he always did such requests from her, claiming he was out of money and just getting payments together for his own holdings as they came due.

Five days later, a firm called City Real Estate Co. took out a $10,000 mortgage on Bly's house at 15 West Thirty-seventh Street, and two weeks later, the property was transferred into the name of Bly's brother Harry C. Cochrane. Harry, in turn, put the house in the name of his Wisconsin friend Martin Linden about a month later.

On October 28, 1912, a new steel barrel company was incorporated in Newark, New Jersey, with the name Steel Barrel Company of America. Bly now had plans to reincorporate and find a new factory site, keep the business accounts of her original company but effectively start over. In the meantime, as the various court cases continued, she managed to stay out of jail and avoid the punishing fine. It seems Brisbane figured quietly in this reprieve.

Bly wrote him a long letter just before Christmas:

> I do not know what they asked you to do, but I know it was something to help me, and I know as usual you did it. It must be that it bore fruit in this case. Of course I am glad that I am not going to jail, and that I do not have to pay a fine of $5,500 and now that this is settled I am ready to go to work. As long as this sentence hung over me which you know has been since we were in Baltimore, I did not want to undertake anything which might possibly be interrupted.

She told him the last court battles were before her in the new year—the trial of Caccia and Gielnik and the renewed effort of her creditors to have the American Steel Barrel Company declared part of the bankrupt Iron Clad's assets. "I do not know how it will end," she said, "although three times before it was tried, and in every case the American Steel Barrel won."

All three times, however, the judge was Chatfield—"a man I believe to be the most honest and fearless on the bench, for in many cases he lambasted me showing me he was not favoring me in any particular, and in one case he gave me the verdict and two weeks after it was given, these men . . . filed a certificate of bias against Chatfield. It was the most outrageous thing, especially since they waited for the verdict to be handed down before they did a thing."

Bly suggested some story ideas. What if she went to Albany to cover the inauguration of Governor-elect William Sulzer? "I don't know how it will appeal to you, but it seems to me that it will make a first-class story giving in detail every single step of the proceeding, who was there, what they did and all the ceremonies and have it well illustrated."

Brisbane said no, he didn't want inauguration coverage from Albany or from Washington, either. "That isn't the kind of thing I care about especially for the *Evening Journal*," he said, although he offered her services to Bradford Merrill on *The American*, the Hearst morning paper, and to Hearst himself.

That letter, of December 14, included a handwritten note in which Brisbane offered Bly some holiday advice:

> *Be a good girl—*
> *Have white servants—*
> *Save your money.*
> *Trust no one—*
> *Merry Xmas*
> *Happy New Year*
> *That's enough   A.B.*

Judge Chatfield suddenly came under investigation by the grievance committee of the Brooklyn Bar Association on complaints against him in fifteen cases involving "discourtesy to counsel, delay and neglect and of giving consideration to matters without both sides being heard." The complainants were led by the attorneys for Bly's creditors. Chatfield, when asked to comment, said that he had been questioned for "doing certain things and treating certain persons in a way that did not meet with a certain man's approval. He thought I had a little hard feelings against him. But before the meeting of the grievance committee was over, I think he was satisfied he had made a mistake."

Bly at this time was finding new ways to complicate her legal life. Attorney James A. Allen had presented her with a bill for

$45,755, which she found excessive. She further charged, through her new attorney, Louis C. Van Doren, that Allen had prepared her brother Harry so poorly for testifying that his appearance in federal court resulted in an indictment for perjury.

Allen was appalled. "Unless by 'adequate preparation' counsel infer that I should have told him [Harry Cochrane] what to say and what not to say, which I confess is not my custom with witnesses, I am at a loss to understand how lack of adequate preparation can be said to be responsible for the indictment of this witness for alleged perjury." He went on,

> I charge that aside from the general indisposition of Mrs. Seaman to pay lawyers in particular, she is led to seek the substitution of another attorney herein because I have, in the course of the litigation, refused to do things which would have been unprofessional and because I have discouraged the doing of things which would not only have been unprofessional and calculated to obstruct the administration of justice, but which would also have been unlawful.

Bly told Brisbane she was looking forward to her return to newspaper life—"I believe it is only that that keeps my courage going"—as soon as her legal tangles unraveled themselves. She presented him with a proposal for a beat she hadn't attempted since Pittsburgh: as a first-night theater critic. Shades of her old friend James Metcalfe. "Are you the editor brave enough to publish the truth about plays and theatres?" she asked. "It was my idea to write of first nights just as one sees them, and if you had liked the idea I would have been glad to do it for you."

Brisbane replied:

> Thanks for your letter. About drama criticism, I can only say that I shall be very glad to see what it is you have in mind. I don't believe much in CRITICISM. Anybody can criticize, few can work. My notion is that the real critic should be a man pointing out that which is good, and ignoring that which is bad. The good needs encouragement. The bad dies of itself.

On February 27, Bly's attorneys filed suit in the U.S. Supreme Court to bring Judge Chatfield back onto the bench for the continuation of her bankruptcy proceedings. Her contention was that he had been wrongfully removed from the case. The high court determined that even if Judge E. Henry Lacombe had been in error when he removed Chatfield, he had been within his authority to do so, and the high court could not compel him to undo what had been done more than a year ago. Judge Mayer, then, much to Bly's chagrin, remained on the case.

Bly had other business in Washington, too, about which she was greatly excited. She had been invited to ride as a herald in the "greatest demonstration for women's suffrage the world has ever been called upon to view," featuring a *tableau vivant* of 250 young suffragists costumed and barefoot (some finally donned silk hose and sandals because of the cold) on the steps of the Treasury depicting Hope, Peace, Columbia, Charity, Justice, and Liberty, among other virtues. Bly covered the parade for *The Journal* but missed the protest demonstrations of thousands of men who had to be restrained by police from disrupting the spectacle, which Hearst's morning *American* made front-page news. She also covered President-elect Woodrow Wilson's inaugural festivities.

She had "stunning" riding togs tailored for her first time back on a horse in sixteen years. The long coat was of a new gray tweed, as were the trousers, dotted in her favorite emerald green, and a small green hat with a turned-up brim to complement. She wore her beautiful jade beads that matched her eyes and for once didn't mind being photographed. "Some persons with a mistaken idea that I might not like to confess to having green eyes have called them black and gray and blue," she wrote. "Or they may have been colorblind. But I always know the truth."

She had tea with the father of the suffragist and chief herald for the parade, Inez Milholland:

> "Why all the green?" asked Mr. Milholland.
> "Can you look at my nose and ask that?" I laughed.
> "When did you arrive?" he retorted.
> "I haven't arrived," I said. "I'm on the way."

Nellie Bly in riding togs, The New York Evening Journal, *March 3, 1913*
(Ransom Humanities Resource Center, University of Texas)

"If I could copyright your smile, I could make a million dollars on it," he said.

"And if I use it in court I get fined and sentenced to jail."

The next day she described the parade in enthusiastic detail:

Can you imagine it? Ten thousand women in line? They say that was the number by actual count. I believe there were more.

Picture if you can an endless chain of butterflies, divided into sections according to color. Imagine ten thousand of these beautiful dreams of color fluttering along and it will give a little impression of the exquisite parade which made history.

Add to this the knowledge that women of ability and fame in all lines of art, literature, medicine, schools—why waste space in repeating all the fields occupied by women today?—was represented and still add to this the knowledge that women in that parade came from every state in the Union with a few from foreign countries, and some slight conception of the appearance and quality of the paraders may be conceived.

She concluded with the trumpet blast of a woman reborn: "I never was so proud of women; I never was so impressed with their ability; I never so realized their determination and sincerity. I am glad I am one."

Of the inauguration ceremony itself on March 5, Bly wrote her experience for *The Journal* before heading back to New York for the start of the Caccia-Gielnik forgery trial. The crowd had gathered to witness the ceremony. Bly got a guard to look the other way and mounted the podium. She wanted to take in the scene from the president-elect's perspective:

I stood alone on the platform where in 15 minutes the President of the United States would take his oath of office.

Before and beneath me in a hollow square was Brigadier-
General [Leonard] Wood and his aides on beautiful, impatient horses. On my left were the cadets from Annapolis in
straight rigid lines and in their long black—or perhaps blue-
black—overcoats and white leggings, they looked as immovable as statues and as handsome as gods.

On the left, the West Point Cadets were just as
straight, immovable and handsome in their splendid uniforms. Lined up at their side, but facing the inaugural stand,
was the mounted Culver Cadets, who came as a guard of
honor to Vice President [Thomas] Marshall.

On an elevated fortification back of all this was a line of
camera men.

I stood, a woman on this stand sacred to men. I looked
at the vast assemblage surrounding me and I wondered!

Will you and I ever see a woman stand there and take
the oath of office?

⌒⌒⌒

The state's case against Charles W. Caccia and Stanley Gielnik finally
came to trial in the criminal division of the New York State Supreme
Court in Manhattan on Thursday, March 6, 1913. Much to Bly's irri-
tation, the trial date came two years after the initial arrest of the two
confessed forgers, probably to the detriment of her case. There had
been a total of ten postponements in either the Supreme Court or the
Court of General Sessions, each of which had the case on its calendar
at various points. Assistant District Attorney Frank Moss led the
prosecution. Caccia and Gielnik were represented by the prominent
criminal lawyer George Gordon Battle.

The prosecution brought this final round of indictments for the
specific forgeries of two checks, one in the amount of $2,800 and the
other for $4,000, which had been made out to an office boy of the Iron
Clad. Moss said the prosecution intended to prove that some $2 mil-
lion of the company's money had been stolen in this fashion, and that
most of it had gone to benefit people other than the two accused forg-

ers. Battle contended that the defendants had signed the checks but had done so in perfect propriety in their positions as cashier and assistant cashier. He said the money had all been paid out for the benefit of the company. The liability of the banks which cashed the checks also was raised, a prospect *The New York Tribune* called "the most interesting contention involved" in the case.

Bly was in court daily and dictating correspondence to her secretary during recesses. Brisbane got one of her missives. She told him that while defense attorneys were interviewing prospective jurors, they kept impressing upon them that Bly worked for *The Journal*. "I don't know what point they seemed to want to make of that," she said, then added, "This is the most vital part of my life. Your support now will save me. The conviction of these confessed forgers means the end of my trouble. Do all you can for me in every way."

She was on the witness stand on both the first and second day of the trial. The proceedings were getting scant coverage in the New York press. The newspapers did note when attorney Battle asked Bly about the story she had written from Baltimore in which she said that it is impossible to tell the truth in court without risking one's case and one's reputation. Bly looked over the article and replied, "At the time that article was written, I was in the federal court in connection with this case and was in a state of mind—I had seen the triumph of lies. I was simply relieving my mind when I wrote the article published."

The case recessed for the weekend. As it resumed on Monday, March 10, Brisbane wrote a very pointed letter of instruction to his managing editor:

> Dear Mr. Speed:
> Please let us make the Nellie Bly story REALLY CON-
> SPICUOUS. I want to help her regardless of the news value.
> Mr. Hearst feels that she has been very badly treated, and has
> asked me more than once to see that she gets a hearing.
>
> Print her picture, print the picture of [David M.] Car-
> valho, the hand writing expert. Print his opinion.

Send reporters to the banks, and ask them whether or not they are paying the lawyers of these forgers.

And ask them why they hire lawyers to defend forgers—what their interest is?

Ask Mr. Battle who is paying him his retainer.

Find out who is on the bond, the bail bond, which puts these men at liberty.

Give the matter two or three columns or more if necessary. Let us do something about this, to show that we are really interested, and have it on the front page for a column or more every day for the present.

Yours very sincerely,
A. BRISBANE

The same day, Brisbane wrote Bly to tell her what he had told Speed and even sent her a copy of his letter to the editor. Brisbane reiterated that he would do whatever he could to help Bly but warned, "If I should prejudge your case, or lecture the court in advance of a decision, I should render you a very bad service—besides laying the paper open for contempt of court."

Speed followed orders. The photograph of a sad-eyed, somber, matronly Bly appeared on the front page of *The Journal* for Tuesday, March 11, over the headline "Say Nellie Bly was $1,680,000 Fraud Victim."

This was the lead:

The trial of Charles W. Caccia and Stanley Grienik [*sic*], formerly cashier and assistant cashier of the American Steel Barrel Company of which Mrs. E. O. [*sic*] Seaman (Nellie Bly) was the head, affords today a striking example of the obstacles which are placed in the way of the woman in business by the men.

There clearly was not much happening in the trial that day, for the article was only six paragraphs long and didn't say very much. It did point out, however—without backup or attribution—that "it was hinted that the banking interests, which are closely watching developments in the case, because they face the possibility of having to refund the money they paid out on forged checks, had secret influences at work to delay the case as long as possible."

The case continued until Thursday, March 13, a total of six days plus three night sessions, representing 1,181 pages of stenographers' minutes and the testimony of forty-eight witnesses, thirty-six for the defense. As Brisbane said it would, his *New York Journal* did what it could for Bly's side.

The newspaper reported that Battle, the defense attorney, had been hired by the firm of Jonas, Lazansky and Neuberger; and that Jonas was employing Caccia to collect checks and other evidence to be used in the trial. Caccia claimed he never removed any checks from the Iron Clad offices to be presented at trial. The newspaper reported how Caccia and Gielnik worked to lay blame for the theft on the late E. R. Gilman, who, they claimed, had been the major beneficiary of ill-gotten company funds. The newspaper said, "The story of her fight for her property is replete with charges of espionage, petty tricks on the part of attorneys and alleged bribery, all of which would form a fitting plot for a true portrayal of how a kind-hearted and sympathetic woman can be 'trimmed' by dishonest employees when she enters the financial field."

Again, aspersions were cast on the banks without benefit of evidence:

> To all intents and purposes, it appears that certain well-true banking interests are vitally interested in the outcome of the present proceeding. Added credence is given to this report because of the belief that should the state win in its fight that victory will pave the way for suits to recover from the banks the two million dollars which Mrs. Seaman declared was paid out by them on bogus checks.

The story further noted that the accused men, despite the serious charges against them, were free on bail. The reporter asked— without answering—who the wealthy backers were who had provided the funds to secure Caccia and Gielnik's release. Attorney Battle, the newspaper said, would not disclose who was paying his fee of $1,000 a day against a $10,000 retainer.

Brisbane gave his editorial column over to the subject as well. This time the headline was "In Business Men Usually ROB Women." He was hard on the banks:

> It will interest the public, and perhaps the district attorney and it will certainly interest the honorable judge in the case, to find out the source of the bail and the lawyers' fees provided for these forgers.
>
> Have the banks who cashed the forgeries—and who should be made to refund where they did cash the forgeries—by any chance interested themselves in the welfare of the criminals?
>
> Has any bank supplied money to protect a forger from the result of his crime? IF SO, WHY? AND HOW OFTEN DO BANKS DO THAT?
>
> Did any bank supply money to bail out men who had confessed forgery? Has any bank supplied the cash to hire able lawyers to defend criminals and if possible secure for them acquittal—thus depriving Nellie Bly permanently of the money stolen from her?

The jury retired at 10:07 P.M. on Thursday night, returned to court at 11:40 P.M., and, after retiring, returned at 1:25 A.M. Friday morning to announce they could not reach a verdict. The judge discharged them. Interviews with various jurors established that they had stalemated at eleven for acquittal and only one for conviction.

Caccia and Gielnik were again released on bail. Bly considered the result a victory and felt conviction of the two men would be swift and sure in the second round.

That hope died fast, as did the whole case. Nothing happened until January of 1914, when repeated motions failed to produce a second trial. A year after that, on January 15, 1915, Caccia and Gielnik, through their attorneys, asked that the court dismiss the indictments against them since two years had passed with no action taken. On April 28, 1915, the court acceded to the request.

Without a conviction in the criminal forgery case, Bly's prospects for winning the civil suits she had filed against the banks dimmed to darkness. With her financial resources almost exhausted, she let the cases fold. Even she had recognized that the prospects for victory were too slim to warrant the expense and aggravation of further pursuit, especially against what had proved so formidable a group of foes.

Brisbane's question as to what interest the banks had in the outcome of the forgery case never was answered. It seems evident, however, that it would have been in the best interest of the banks to see that Caccia and Gielnik got top-notch legal representation in order to facilitate their exoneration and thereby blunt the potential impact of the pending civil suits against the banks. There was nothing illegal about the banks' interceding. In fact, it would have made good business sense.

For Bly, the possibility of recovering any part of the money she had lost evaporated. The only hope that remained was to hold on to what was left.

❧

Just after the forgery trial ended, in April of 1913, yet another fire broke out at the factory site, causing about $5,000 damage to the facilities of the American Steel Barrel Company. Bly seemed unaffected by the relatively minor disaster. The bulk of the barrel operations were being conducted by this point in the name of the Steel Barrel Company of America, with Mary Jane Cochrane as head. By mid-May, Bly was aboard the *George Washington*, headed for Cherbourg. She had told the court she needed rest and gained permission to leave the country. She sent a note to Brisbane the day before to give him her departure details. Her address in Paris, she said, would be care of Crédit Lyonnaise on the Boulevard des Italiens. That day, *The Brooklyn Daily Eagle* seemed somewhat startled to report that the late Major Edward R. Gilman, illustrious member of so many prominent clubs and boards, had left an estate of only a few hundred dollars.

Brisbane asked Bly if she would write a couple of stories for *The Journal* from Paris—"the kind you can write if you feel like it. I'll be glad to pay for them and make them conspicuous. And it would do you good to be remembered by your friends and especially by your enemies."

As Brisbane's wife, Phoebe, had given birth to a baby girl, Bly recalled that the preceding June, when she and Brisbane were both in Chicago for the Republican convention, he had found a fifty-dollar bill in his pocket and handed it to Bly for safekeeping. Bly wrote him in that connection: "I have put it to better purpose. I have instructed Mother to put it in the bank in the name of your baby, and Mr. Guibert will bring the book back to you." As a postscript, she added, "The original fifty dollars I am still carrying, because it was yours, hoping the Gods will send me good luck."

By late July, Bly was back in New York. She finally paid the $2,666 due on a fine for contempt of court that had been standing since the preceding December, when the Circuit Court of Appeals had affirmed the original citation.

On August 4, she wrote to Brisbane about how she had practically given up on finding an honest lawyer in New York. She had soured on Van Doren, too. "I get away from one crook only to get tied up to another; each one getting a lot of money and no one doing any particular good." The prospect of returning to newspaper work was increasingly appealing.

In late November, Brisbane had his editor return to Bly a manuscript she had written from the ship while en route to Paris. The newspaper hadn't published it because, Brisbane said, "your lawyer said he didn't want you to be well and strong enough to write when you were in Europe for reasons known to you." Brisbane went on to explain that he had his own reasons for withholding publication: "It was not a real Nellie Bly article . . . only an imitation. It wouldn't do you any good to print something that didn't show you at your best."

By mid-December, Bly's mother had become seriously ill, and her youngest brother, Harry, had been indicted for perjury for testimony he gave during the Iron Clad bankruptcy proceedings. There seemed to be no prospect for relief for Bly in 1914.

A vicious labor strike broke out at the copper mines in Calumet, Michigan. Brisbane, entertaining reveries of Bly's splendid performance at Pullman twenty years earlier, had a bright idea. On January 9, he sent her a two-sentence note: "Will you do the Calumet strike NOW? How much and expenses?" With an unconvincing list of excuses, she replied that she could not. Brisbane did not take her refusal well:

> About Calumet, after I made the suggestion to you to go there and report the strike, it occurred to me that the job would not suit you. Your viewpoint and sympathies have changed since the days when you reported the strike at Pullman.
>
> I did not want, needless to say, to have somebody go out there to find out how badly rich people are treated by their employees. The rich are well able to take care of themselves.
>
> But I want an impartial investigation of the conditions and the plain truth written about the miners and their lives if they are as miserable as alleged. You did this admirably in regard to Pullman and conditions there. I am afraid, however, that your mind would take a different turn now.
>
> And besides, as you say, it is frightfully cold and the trip would hardly be worth the trouble. It would be worth it, if you went out there as the enthusiastic Nellie Bly of other days, with a natural tendency to help the under dog.

Brisbane's letter did not embarrass Bly into action. She never went to Calumet. She couldn't have left town anyway. On January 23, 1914, a settlement at last had been worked out to end the bankruptcy proceedings. Bly was reinstated as president of American Steel Barrel, she and her mother withdrew their $500,000 worth of claims against the Iron Clad estate, and Bly paid out $50,000 to the Iron Clad's creditors as settlement against all their claims. By March 28, Judge Mayer discontinued all proceedings evolving from the case, to everyone's great relief. By January 29, the house in Sheepshead Bay had been foreclosed upon and put in the hands of a referee.

As for Harry Cochrane's perjury case, it stemmed from his statement under oath that the late E. R. Gilman had never owned shares in the American Steel Barrel Company. Another former Iron Clad employee, H. C. Roberts, testified to the contrary, that shortly after Gilman died in early 1911, Roberts had gone to Bly's home at her request and altered a stock certificate for 100 shares of the American Steel Barrel Company made out to Gilman, changing the number of shares to 50 and the owner's name to Bly's. The date of the certificate was changed from December 11, 1905, to February 3, 1911 — shortly before Gilman's death. The certificate bore the signature "Harry C. Cochrane, President."

Ultimately, the court ruled that even though Cochrane's name appeared on the certificate, indicating he had known of Gilman's ownership of the shares, there was no way to be certain that the signature actually was Cochrane's. The judge dismissed the case on April 7. It never even went to the jury.

Within two weeks, attorney Louis O. Van Doren had his chance to sue Bly in the Supreme Court of Bronx County for nonpayment of a $25,143 legal bill. It was Van Doren who had obtained a settlement for Bly in her previous financial skirmish with lawyer James A. Allen.

A new indictment was returned against Bly on July 24 on charges of obstructing justice for refusing a week earlier to obey Judge Mayer's order to produce the books, ledgers, and papers of the American Steel Barrel Company and thereby concealing its actual relationship to the Iron Clad.

Fleeing prosecution, at least for a few weeks, until she could figure out what to do, was now the only way out. Bly arranged for a wealthy Viennese friend, Oscar Bondy, to pay off the $10,000 second mortgage on 15 West Thirty-seventh Street, plus interest on that loan. Still, the Greenwich Savings Bank held the first mortgage on the house in the amount of $62,500 plus mounting unpaid interest.

Although Bly had entrusted everything she still owned to her octogenarian mother, Mary Jane, both Albert, who had grown obese, and Harry returned to New York full-time to oversee the company in their sister's absence. Within a week of the indictment, Bly quietly set out for Europe aboard the RMS *Oceanic*. The ship left August 1, bound for Southampton, England. Bly's intention was to make her way to Vienna to discuss further financing for her steel barrel company with Bondy and to return in a few weeks. What she had not counted on was the outbreak of World War I. Four days before her departure, Austria declared war on Serbia and Germany invaded Luxembourg. Bly boarded ship without a second thought.

Part Four

1914–1922

BOMBARDMENT OF CRAC

Famous Writer in Austria for the Journal
NELLIE BLY ON THE FIRING LINE.

Nellie Bly

The following is the first of the articles to come from Miss Nellie Bly, special correspondent for the Evening Journal, who is now at the front in the beleaguered fortress of Przemysl in Austria.

Przemysl, Friday, Oct. 30, 1914.

—I went on the firing line yesterday. It was Thursday, October 29, 1914. I was called at 5 o'clock. I made my unsatisfactory toilet in the dark. My electric light had gone to sleep and the daylight was not yet on duty.

At six I walked down four long flights of stairs dirty stairs pushing through a crowd of soldiers who were raising a frightful and unmilitary dust for brushing and polishing officers uniforms and boots.

I walked one back to the interior house cafe Mother. Three miniature waiters how all for like dwarfs in this country in the same dirty clothes they have been since we arrived stood talking to the girl behind the counter. All tables were smeared with ashes of cigarettes so I resignedly sat down. There was no chance.

But I think they would be clean if they were taught and knew the importance of cleanliness. It is something, perhaps the fact that we will teach them—the importance of cleanliness.

BREAKFAST FOR 15 CENTS

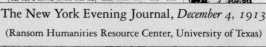

I I

❦ ❧

War

BLY WIRED AHEAD TO OSCAR BONDY IN VIENNA, BUT THERE had been no word from him before she boarded the RMS *Oceanic* on August 1, looking happy and carefree as she waved to her trusted assistant at the Iron Clad, Margaret Collins. "Good bye, Miss Collins," she called out. "I'll be back in three weeks. Take care of everything."

By midvoyage, the outbreak of further fighting left the ship's destination in question. "There is no telling where we shall land, or if I shall ever get to Vienna," Bly wrote her mother during the crossing. With everything in such unsettling flux, Bly displayed her usual fearless abandon: "So I have as plans—I shall simply do what the moment calls for." She repeated rumors that the Germans were expected to try to seize the ship, given its cargo of $4 million in gold. "I hope they do," she wrote. "It will be a fine experience." The trip had been dreadfully monotonous. Every nationality clustered to itself. "They all seem afraid of each other," she said.

Since it was not known where the *Oceanic* would be allowed to land, Bly could give no address. Fraught as was the situation that lay ahead, she kept thinking about the troubles she had left behind. She felt cursed. "My luck is too bad for anyone to be near me," she wrote. Bly's primary concern was that attorney Van Doren would try to

Oscar Bondy
(Courtesy of Ivo Rie)

attach whatever assets he could trace to her in efforts to settle his large bill. She warned Mary Jane not to "let anyone bluff you out of the house."

Once in Paris, on August 11, Bly headed for the U.S. Embassy, where she requested and received an emergency passport, giving Switzerland as her destination. From there, she made her way to Vienna, registering at the U.S. Embassy on August 22. She gave the city's most fashionable transient address, the Hotel Imperial, as her own. The supremely elegant hotel—with its statuary, mosaic floors, Corinthian columns, and wide marble staircases—was only a short walk along The Ring, Vienna's grand, encircling boulevard, from the sumptuous apartment of her wealthy friend Oscar Bondy, with his phenomenal private collections of art, antiques, and musical scores.

By September 18, Bly was desperate to know what was happening at home. Her half niece Grace McLaughlin had written vaguely to confirm that Van Doren had gotten the court to grant him an attachment, but Bly wanted to know the details. She wrote to C. A. Guibert, manager of her ailing steel barrel company. The letter was on the stationery of Prague's Hotel Blauer Stern, but she gave Vienna's Hotel Imperial as her return cable address. In the meantime, Bondy had put Bly in touch with Harold Nathan, his attorney in New York, who had offered to lend Bly some assistance with her legal entanglements.

The letter to Guibert was loaded with directives, many of them blatantly crooked. Bly's attention had clearly turned from the ways she could use the legal system to protect herself to the ways she could get around it to protect the assets she had left. Keeping the house at 15 West Thirty-seventh Street from being attached or repossessed had become paramount. She was especially worried about Van Doren in this regard.

"Will Nathan do nothing for you?" she asked Guibert. "If not, apply to William McCombs, 96 Broadway." McCombs was the powerful chairman of the Democratic National Committee, whom Bly had gotten to know when she covered the Democratic National Convention in Baltimore for *The New York Evening Journal*. "Tell him I told you to go to him for salvation," she wrote, "I am tied up here. No one except those having tickets can get to Holland. Everything is sold to the last of October. I am forced to stay here as I could not afford to live in Holland until I could get passage. My trunks were lost in France and I am without clothing."

These were her instructions for the disbursement of the steel barrel company's money:

> Pay all your bills daily. Pay mother's house bills and give her $100 per week if possible, also my salary. Don't have any chairs in the office except yours and Florence and Miss [indecipherable]. If you can't get the others [chairs] out, pile things high on them so they can [not] be used. If [G. Murray] Hulbert [Van Doren's attorney] walks in don't show him anything. No attachment allows him to look at books or papers or letters. Ask Nathan or McCombs if the bill of sale to mother which you registered in Brooklyn is good. If so, remove all machinery and store it in some warehouse in Hoboken or Jersey City. Then, when the factory is empty, have it boarded up and nailed up. Board up windows every-

where, even on roof and in the back. Don't pay interest on the mortgage and don't pay taxes. Take your money to pay my salary and mother's debt. If the Grievance Committee of the Bar Association should ask you about Van Doren and Hulbert, tell them everything and spare nothing.

Write me immediately and fully—all about our troubles—what Van Doren did, what money you have, what to collect, whether you get orders, what you did about the house.

Nathan, with a power of attorney from Bondy, she said, was trying to obtain a $66,000 loan to pay off the mortgage on 15 West Thirty-seventh Street which Bly had taken out back in 1908 from the Greenwich Savings Bank. "If this is done," she said, "please see that the house is rented at once to its best advantage either entire or by room. Get as much as you can but whatever you get, will help pay off the interest. Or if Nathan can sell the house at a few thousand more than its mortgage, let it go." She went on,

Buy nothing for the business. Contract no debts. Give up your office. Take one little room somewhere and have the post office deliver all the mail to 15 W. 37th St. Remember you can sign papers as secretary and as cashier and as I wrote you, by proper appeal to the courts, anything can be stayed because I am unable to get back until later. I can't possibly get passage . . . Only those who had secured passage before can get away. If nothing else, apply to the Bar Association and ask them to help you hold off litigation until I can get back.

She was "crazy for news, even if I can't help" and urged Guibert to send a letter "by Holland boat" at once. "I hope and pray luck will change for us," she wrote, "and that you can successfully hold out. Lock up the office if you want. Hulbert will scarcely dare break in."

As an afterthought, she suggested that if McCombs was unable to help, Guibert should "appeal to Arthur Brisbane, *Journal* in my name."

Bly knew very well that the best way to stall the engine of justice was to prolong her stay abroad, remaining barricaded in Europe by the exigencies of war. This was the call to return to journalism again. The fact that circumstances enabled her to do it as a war correspondent had its own seductive appeal. Much later, when asked, Bly would say that her reason for heading straight for Austria when the war broke out was to cover the fighting between the Austrians and the Serbs. Back in 1897, she recalled, her marriage to Robert Seaman had kept her from covering the Spanish-American War in Cuba. She saw the start of the World War as her last chance for battlefield initiation, a life experience she didn't want to miss.

Clearly, journalism was not the impetus for Bly's arrival in Austria, but it was only a matter of weeks before it might as well have been. She managed very quickly to put her worries over the steel barrel company aside. Her primary preoccupation became "getting to the front."

⌇⬧⌇

Anyone who was anyone passing through Vienna billeted at the luxurious Hotel Imperial, and Bly used the hotel as her permanent address, although she also spent a good deal of her stay at the Hotel Bristol nearby. She got to know everyone of importance that she came in contact with and used this to her advantage in her efforts to win permission to be the first woman, and one of the first foreigners, to visit the war zone. Her first inroad came when a U.S. aid committee arrived in Vienna, headed by a man Bly identified only as the U.S. assistant secretary of war. He asked for Bly's help with arrangements during the visit. Georg de Pottere, an Austro-Hungarian foreign ministry official, expedited every impossible appeal Bly made, from passport validations to requests for special trains. Through de Pottere, Bly obtained an introduction to Count Leopold Berchtold, the foreign minister. Berchtold treated her "as if he had all the time in the world to see to my needs. His calm demeanor, his quick grasp and appreciation of my task encouraged me to tell him everything. He offered his help and he also delivered."

During her few weeks in Vienna, Bly had also gotten to know Princess Alexandrine von Windischgrätz, who offered support for Bly's plan to see military action. So did Camille MacCollum, another American guest at the Imperial who had come to Vienna to study for

six months but liked it so much she stayed two years. MacCollum
introduced Bly to Baron Franz von Schönaich, a philanthropist Bly
described as a man of great and genuine generosity and compassion.
The baron had recently founded a fund for military widows and
orphans, and Bly had heard much about his efforts. Of him she said,

> There are so many motivations for benevolence: To see one's
> name in print, to arouse envy, to be honored with a medal, to
> buy a reward from heaven, or a profound love for humanity. I
> needed not more than the warm handshake of Baron Schö-
> naich, his tenderness for his charming wife, his concern for
> everybody around him to perceive his untiring support given
> to his friends and how each of his deeds was spontaneous and
> dictated by his heart.

The baron put in yet another good word for Bly with the foreign
minister, Berchtold, whom Bly described as a model of "exceptional
graciousness and consideration."

Bly's prospects were further enhanced by the fact that she had
been acquainted for fifteen years with the U.S. ambassador to Austria, Frederic C. Penfield, and that he thought well of her. Penfield
did not hesitate to write a letter of introduction for Bly to Ritter
Oskar von Montlong, head of the press department of the Austro-
Hungarian Foreign Ministry.

When Bly arrived in Penfield's office to pick up the letter, he
interrupted the signing of a foot-high stack of documents and offered
her a chair next to his desk, speaking in an easygoing manner made
possible by their long acquaintanceship. Bly recalled him saying:
"You have filed a request with these gracious people and our petition
will be granted. But you must promise me personally that you will
remain what you have been all along: an advocate of truth, an apos-
tle of justice and, last but not least, you must never forget that you
are an American." Bly interpreted the last remark as an "appeal to my
freedom of speech and thought."

In the ambassador's letter to von Montlong, he described Bly as
a "journalist of standing, who desires, if it can be arranged, to go to
the front to personally view certain phases of the war." He continued,

I can vouch for her in every way and have her promise to submit to the censor all that she writes on the subject of the war.

It is Mrs. Bly's promise to write of the war in a manner at once truthful and creditably to the Dual Monarchy in which she is a visitor.

In the meantime, Countess Nandine Berchtold, wife of the foreign minister, invited Bly for a visit, of which Bly later wrote,

If I tell you now that the American press is full of inspired stories written by mysterious authors who sign their articles "ex-diplomat" or "ex-attaché," and make brazen allegations that the Imperial Court of Austria is the only unapproachable court in the whole world, and that the Austrian nobility is unequalled in terms of arrogance, you may understand the degree of interest with which I followed an invitation to visit the Countess Berchtold. However, when she greeted me with an outstretched hand, with openness, spirit and confidence in her eyes and an appealing smile, and when she addressed me in my very own "American" mother tongue, I realized that yet another prejudice against Austria had to be abandoned.

The two women made small talk, of magazines and personalities and visits to the United States. The countess mentioned briefly that she understood Bly was interested in visiting the war zone. Bly acknowledged that was the case but made no further comment about it, and the conversation moved on to other topics. "When I left, she admired my coat," Bly recalled. "Wasn't that charming, tender, truly feminine and quite natural?"

Bly did not deliver Penfield's letter to von Montlong right away. There was no need. Her authorization strategy had been quite effective without it, and she quickly obtained all the necessary permissions. Arrangements were made for her to go to the Kriegspressequartier, the military press office for the Austro-Hungarian army at Alt Sandez, in Galicia, and to visit the firing line that separated the Austrian forces from the Russians to the northeast. From there she would travel to the Austro-Hungarian front with Serbia to the south.

On October 22, two months after her arrival in Austria, Baron Vladimir Giesl von Gieslingen, the foreign ministry's representative to the Army High Command, presented to the foreign ministry the names of four foreign correspondents who had been granted credentials to cover the war: Aldo Borelli of the Italian newspaper *Il Mattino*; Royal Italian Navy Lieutenant Cesare Santorre, technical correspondent of the Italian military magazine *Aero Marittima*, and two Americans representing publications which he did not identify, William G. Shepherd and "Mrs. Bly." Shepherd worked for the American news agency United Press.

The first morning before setting out, Bly's small group had an opportunity to meet Field Marshal Baron Franz Conrad von Hötzendorf, whom she carefully observed:

> The expression of his eyes was frank and forthright with a nuance of sadness. The contour of cheeks and chin, the line of his head and his slim figure gave him a youthful appearance. He told us about the dangers of the front. Then he turned to me and asked with concern whether my clothes were warm enough for the strain ahead of me. As we shook hands at our departure, he said, "It may not be very diplomatic. But do take a close look at everything, go everywhere and write nothing but the truth."

Bly sent her first cable back to Brisbane at *The Evening Journal* on October 26. She was en route to the battlefront near the beleaguered fortress town of Przemyśl, on the present Polish-Czech border, which would be under siege on and off for a total of six months, "visiting on the penned-in garrison of 150,000 Austrians deprivation and misery indescribable." Bly couldn't wait for the encounter. She wired back to New York:

> I will send three articles. Now on way to Przemyśl. I go to the fighting line. Will write all I can and will cable important things when possible. Cables will go by telegraph to Wilkie Vertreter, Heilbronnerstrasse 19, Berlin. Get up a movement among your readers to send packages of cotton, as

I cabled, by parcel post to the Red Cross, War Department, Wien. All out here. Poor wounded soldiers suffering. Have the privilege of taking camera to the front. Return to Wien in two weeks. Will get camera and come back. Cable Imperial, Wien, Bly, care of Bondy, Kolowatring 3, Wien, if you wish to communicate. Everything going well with Austria—winning. Everybody—soldiers, officers and officials—splendid. Yours, Nellie Bly.

As it happened, Bly's stories reached New York only after her return to Vienna on November 25, and they did not start appearing in *The Journal* until December 3. Instead of the battlefront trip lasting the two weeks she had anticipated, it continued for a full month, with a rest stop in Budapest between visits to the Russian and Serbian battle zones. From Przemyśl, Bly and the rest of her party went to Budapest, then south to the Serbian line and then back to Budapest. The original party included Santorro, the photographer Alexander Exax, the painter Baron Laszlo Mednyanszky, and the man she described as "the amiable artist" Carl Leopold Hollitzer. Others—Austrian, Hungarian, and foreign—joined the group along the way.

Field Marshal Conrad's strategy was to strike down the Serbians while taking the offensive against Russia in Galicia, where he focused the greater part of his forces. The plan was rash and presumptuous for a junior partner in the Central Alliance in the view of later historians, as defeat would prove.

The Journal carried Bly's reports under the logo "Nellie Bly on the Firing Line," parceling out her reports on a month in the war zone in relatively brief installments of two or three half columns each. There was nothing else like it in the newspaper. Bly had transmitted enough copy to fill twenty-one of these reports, which were published in three- and four-day spurts over two and a half months. So rare were descriptive, human interest accounts of what was happening on the war's Eastern Front that *The Journal* seemed delighted to be printing almost every word she wrote, even when the dates of her reports lagged far behind the events described. Bly's final report, dated November 25, 1914, as she left Budapest for Vienna, ran in *The Journal* more than two and a half months later, on February 19, 1915.

In this new guise as war correspondent was the same old Bly: fearless, by no means impervious to discomfort or pain, but willing to endure anything for the sake of the adventure and the chance to tell about it. She was sensitive, self-confident, reflective, compassionate, often banal, and almost oblivious to the significant overview.

As always, Bly was exacting in her descriptions, and conscious of her own consciousness. Her writing centered not on the wider situation at hand but on descriptions of her personal experience. She gave equal space and gravity to the nausea she felt when ordering coffee in a grimy café and the description of a soldier whose shrapnel-shattered jaw fell slack and shapeless against his chest. Her work read like the animated chatter of a practiced raconteur at a table of intimate friends. The stories were frank and personal, sometimes inane, sometimes beside the point in the midst of such dire events, sometimes parabolic and, as often, deeply moving. Her approach was brave, brazen, a little whiny, and a lot narcissistic.

She told *Journal* readers of how she responded to Field Marshal Conrad's admonition to "Write the truth."

"I am," she wrote. "I write it for the sake of humanity. The first and most important thing for Austria is an able, efficient sanitary commander and corps with power."

Bly was undone by the filth. From Przemyśl, after having been wakened at 5:00 A.M. to board wagons for the front and having dressed in the dark, she wrote:

> I walked one block to the coffee house—Café Steiber. Three miniature waiters—they all look like dwarfs in this country—in the same dirty clothes they have worn since my arrival, stood talking to the girl behind the counter. All tables were smeared with ashes of the night's smokers, so I resignedly sat down. There was no choice.
>
> But I think they would be clean if they were taught and knew the importance of cleanliness. It is one thing, perhaps the first, this war will teach them—the importance of sanitary cleanliness.

A smiling, pleasant woman with a bucket of cold, dirty water, a dirtier rag and no soap, came rushing to wipe my table and the floor underneath with the same rag.

Six wagons conveyed their party. In a "dream of blue color," the cavalry rode by in haste in all directions, yet the only sound was "of constant and steady cannonading. It was like a moving picture with the cannon effect behind the curtain."

The wagons passed the village of Hermanowicz, coming to a river spanned by two new fortified bridges. The embankments were only two miles from the Russian line. Alongside the banks were deep dugouts covered with thatch and lined with straw holding scores of saddled horses.

Bly's fur coat weighed fifty pounds—far too heavy for her to manage on the long treks required for the journey. This she described at length. She was ready to forsake the coat without a second thought, she said, ready to brave the cold without a wrap. Herr Hollitzer then said she could wear his cape. She accepted gratefully, even though Hollitzer was six feet tall and weighed 250 pounds. Bly folded the leaden length of woolen fabric into a shawl. "The burden was martyrdom," she said. The group set out, led by their army guide, whom Bly referred to only as "Col. John."

So we started up the muddy road, Col. John striding along the muddy channel cut by the flat rims of the wagon wheels. I followed after, breathless and perspiring under Mr. Hollitzer's cape. The rims of the wheels are narrow. To step on the side was to get five inches deep in slush. To keep both feet in the narrow wheel rut was to walk like a pigeon-toed Indian. It was painful, walking a tightrope could be more dangerous but not more difficult.

They walked on and on, passing streams of sick and wounded soldiers. "Sometimes they saluted, more often they staggered unconsciously and forlornly on, their sunken eyes fixed pathetically on the west. Blind to their surroundings, their ears deaf to the near and ceaseless thundering of cannons, their nerves dead."

A woman, wounded by shrapnel in her right arm, walked along in the single line headed westward. Bly described the woman's boots, her short, full, balloon-shaped purple skirt, and her flower-bordered white handkerchief. "Her right arm was bound with a ragged shawl tight to her breast," she wrote. "In a fortnight she will be a mother."

Nothing that Bly encountered escaped her need to describe it. On the cholera:

> On the ground was strewn straw. In that straw was a mixture of senseless human beings, knapsacks, flasks, discarded bloody bandages, a shoe, a gun and matter unspeakable.
>
> One motionless creature had his cap on his head. He had a short, stubby brown beard. Great black circles were around his sunken eyes. Black hollows were around his nose and his ears were black. Still he lived. Dying, I believe.
>
> Near him, completely covered by his coat was a form. Occasionally it shivered convulsively. That was all.
>
> Nearest us was another on his face. He never moved. Perhaps he was dead.
>
> Beside him sat a soldier, his chin on his breast. Some one shoved him and yelled at him. He heard. He tried to lift his head. Useless. It sank again, his chin against his chest. Cholera, the posts were marked, dear friends. Human creatures they were, lying there in a manner our health authorities would prohibit for hogs or the meanest beasts.
>
> I staggered out into the muddy road. I would rather look on guns and hear the cutting of the air by a shot that brought kinder death.

She got her "baptism by fire." As the group walked along, they climbed into a trench to see what it was like, then moved on. A shell exploded behind them. Black smoke rose from their just-vacated trench. Three weeks before, under Austro-Hungarian fire, the Russians had retreated from the same trenches.

Another shell exploded 200 feet beyond them, throwing off another shower of black mud. It missed the camp by 50 feet. The

scene changed from repose to frantic action. Cattle were driven westward; campfires were deserted. Horses were hitched to wagons and
whipped to highest speed. From the stables, horses were led running
in groups. Bly described it:

> Colonel John yelled for us to fly to the trenches. But like the
> famous lady who turned to salt, I turned to look!
>
> Another frightful explosion in the east; another cloud
> of black smoke and one after the other six shells fell and
> buried themselves in the same soft earth.
>
> Then I got into the trench. Two hundred feet was near
> enough for me. I was not afraid. I would not run. Yet my
> mind was busy. I thought another shot would follow. It will
> doubtless be better aimed. If it does, we shall die.
>
> And if so, what then?

She wrote of the makeshift battlefield hospitals set up by the
Red Cross, of makeshift altars where priests said mass for the sol-
diers, of the black pockmarks that scarred the hills and valleys where
Russian grenades had burned into the ground, of ceremonial presen-
tations, of medals of honor, of the long, circuitous train ride through
Galicia and on to Budapest.

During the train trip, there was a dreamlike sequence with the
dimensions of a parable:

> Many of the men carry alcohol lamps. They [the Hungarians]
> are always cooking tea, as they express it. Some of them seem
> to be eternally eating. At one place we stopped, a ragged
> bare-footed woman, with an old shawl wrapped around her
> head, stood watching our waiting train. Some of our party
> talked to her and finally persuaded her to go to the cluster of
> houses in the valley way below and get them some chickens.
> She returned after the long trip with four young broilers—
> pullets. She said they cost five kronen—one dollar. A man
> laid four kronen on the ground and grabbed the chickens.
> The woman protested. Either give back her chickens or give

her five kronen. The man left her crying, took the chickens to the other side of the train and killed them.

What Bly described as her "own sense of justice" compelled her to step in. The woman had covered her face and was crying. Bly confronted the man: "Either give the woman what she asks," she demanded, "or give back her chickens."

"She's had enough," the man shot back and went on with his butchering.

"It is not right or fair," Bly scolded. "If you don't give her the right amount, now you have killed her chickens, I shall pay her."

The man's friends tried to convince him to give the woman the balance, but he still refused. Finally, one of them offered the woman another krone. She turned to Bly and kissed her hand.

Bly drew no parallel for her readers between the monetary plight of the poor peasant woman and her own financial troubles, also instigated by men, which had driven her to Austria. Moved by her sense of justice, and through the power of her own intercession, Bly had been able to accomplish for the peasant woman what she had so recently been unable to achieve for herself. If her faith had been shaken in her long-held belief in the force of energy rightly applied, in this moment, perhaps, she saw it restored.

Still, there was a price. After the woman got her money, several of the men pelted the peasant with pebbles to shoo her back down the valley side, forlorn, barefooted, so raggedy in her faded old shawl.

The incident was forgotten. The men turned their attention to preparing a great feast of chicken and rice. They ate with gusto. Bly quelled her own hunger with five small biscuits. Chicken only agreed with her under some conditions, she explained, and this was not one of them. "At any rate," she added without further comment, "I was not invited to eat."

On November 6, in the Hungarian village of Sátoralya-Ujhély, where the train had stopped en route to Budapest, Bly walked away from the station toward the churchyard. An officer approached her

Nellie Bly at the war front with unidentified Austrian officer, 1914
(UPI/Bettmann)

and asked to see her papers. Bly had left everything on the train. A crowd gathered. Two gendarmes appeared and held back the growing mob.

"Everybody was excited except myself," Bly said. "I was enjoying the new experience. I studied the faces of the mob as the officers and gendarmes endeavored to obtain information from me. They spoke Hungarian. I spoke Americanish. We did not make rapid progress."

The officers, "fierce, grave and determined," ordered Bly to follow them. A woman stepped out of the crowd and laid a sympathetic hand on Bly's shoulder.

"You are American, not English?" the woman asked in broken English.

"I am," Bly replied.

"I knew," she answered back.

The woman, who had lived briefly in Cleveland, intervened with the gendarmes. She then explained, "They think you are a British spy."

Bly told her to tell the gendarmes that she was from New York and traveling with representatives of the Kriegspressequartier and that their train was stopped at the village station.

The gendarmes led Bly to a low-ceilinged room inside a courtyard, where uniformed men at desks rose unsmiling to greet her. The woman tried to accompany her but was roughly pushed outside. Bly recounted:

> The room was filled with men in uniforms and civilians' dress. A very tall man in a brown suit got up and gazed at me. I held out my hand. He hesitated. I still held my hand outstretched. He gave me a gingerly touch with the stiff tips of his fingers.
>
> I began to speak.
>
> "How do you do," I began. "It is nice of these gentlemen to bring me to visit you, but I must hurry."
>
> He did not thaw. He even frowned. He asked me in German where I came from. I replied:
>
> "Przemyśl." He looked his unbelief. He asked where I was going.

"Kriegspressequartier," I replied.

He was angry. He said in German this was not the route from Przemyśl to the press headquarters. I knew it, but I did not know enough German to tell him that blown-up and destroyed bridges were the cause of our wide detour.

Another military figure arrived, apparently of higher rank. Bly tried to explain the situation again, but he ignored her. She tried to leave but was shoved back into the room, alone. "I heard the key turn," she said. "I sat down resignedly. I wondered what they would say when the train pulled out and I was not there. I imagined several days more would elapse before they would search for me. I dreaded the anxiety of those in power and wondered if my escape would cause them to send me back to Vienna."

Soon the door unlocked and Bly's captors returned with an English-speaking gentleman in a black frock coat. "He was pale and thin," Bly said, "and the news they gave him seemed to worry him. He looked at me as they talked. He approached me. A sudden silence fell on the crowd."

What happened next could only have happened to this suspected British spy:

"I am Dr. Friedman," he announced. "You are English, they say."

"I am Nellie Bly of New York," I answered.

Both hands flew up above his head.

"My God! Nellie Bly," he cried excitedly.

The next instant his arms were half around me and he was repeating, like a father to his child, "Nellie Bly! Nellie Bly! Nellie Bly!"

The men had cleared a space around us. Their mouths were not open but their eyes were.

They were speechless, dumbfounded. My new friend began to talk rapidly to them. They listened aghast.

"I have told them every child seven years old in America knows Nellie Bly," he said aside to me.

Other correspondents had joined the group when they got to military press headquarters at Alt Sandez in Galicia. On November 7, the famous Austrian reporter Alexander Roda-Roda did a story for the *Neue Freie Presse* about the visit to press headquarters of U.S. Ambassador Penfield's secretary, Thomas Hinckley. Hinckley had come to meet with correspondents for American publications. Bly never mentioned Hinckley's visit in her reports, but she did note with great delight that the illustrious Roda-Roda, as the writer was known, had mentioned her by name in one of his stories. He had shown her in the midst of his German text where her name appeared in the Austrian paper. Roda-Roda's story contained no description of Bly other than that she represented "the Hearst concern" and had met with Hinckley along with William G. Shepherd of United Press, George M. Schreiner of Associated Press, and Robert Dunn of *The New York Evening Post*.

Once in Budapest, Bly visited the hospitals and described the heroism of doctors and nurses; the unimaginable suffering of the victims of war. She wrote poignantly of the Russian who was shot and lay unattended for eight days in a trench while his feet froze. On the way to the American Red Cross Hospital at Budapest by freight train, his feet dropped off. When he arrived at the hospital, his last blood poured from his open veins. Bly came to his side. She described the scene:

> —I shuddered. The clay-pallor of death. The ribs cutting the skin. Bones, bones, no flesh anywhere.
>
> The head turned. Great, hollow black eyes looked into mine. Transfixed I stood heartsick, soul-sad. Those great hollow eyes searched mine. They tried to question me. They spoke soul language to soul. The lips parted, a moan, a groan of more than physical agony. He spoke. I could not understand. His words were a sound my ears shall never forget. The appeal, the longing, the knowledge!
>
> "What does he say?" I cried, unable to stand it. "Can no one understand? Can't you find some one to speak to him?"

A nurse smoothed his forehead. An attendant held fast the pale, pale hands.

"The attendant understands," the doctor said; and to him, "What does he say?"

"He is asking for his children," was the low reply.

The hollow, black eyes turned again to search mine. I could not endure their question. I had no answer to give.

"Let me go," I said to the doctor.

The low moan seemed to call me back, but I walked steadfastly toward the door and down the corridor.

"Could Emperors and Czars and Kings look on this torturing slaughter and ever sleep again?" I asked the doctor.

"They do not look," he said gently.

In Budapest, Bly was thrilled to see her old friend Mihály Gellér, owner of the Budapest Astoria Hotel and nephew of the owner of Haan's restaurant at the St. Regis Hotel in New York, who had invented "Eggs à la Nellie Bly." The Astoria, she said, was equal to any in New York, and the bar produced "real American cocktails." She praised the establishment repeatedly in her series and evidently could share openly with her readers that the hotelier did not charge her for the exquisite room and bath. By the highest present-day American journalistic standard, Bly could not have accepted the gesture.

Just before she left Budapest for the Serbian war front on November 14, Dr. Charles MacDonald of the American Red Cross showed Bly what was thought to have been a poisoned Serbian bullet. Fastened around and between the cap and lead was a bit of cloth and a smear of a soft, pinkish white substance.

"Dr. MacDonald warned me to be careful," Bly said. "I thought I was. But the agony I have endured for three nights and two days convinces me I was less careful than I might have been. The most agonizing pains from instep to waist, a fever and a mass of inflamed spots from ankle to knee is not comforting."

She told her group nothing of her misery. "I would not be pronounced ill and left behind," she said.

In Budapest, they boarded the *Zsofia Herczegno* for the 185-mile trip down the Danube to Újvidék, opposite the picturesque fortress village of Peterwardein. Ludwig, king of Bavaria, had made the maiden voyage on the elegant vessel named, Bly said, for an assassinated crown princess. This was its second trip. Bly was ushered into King Ludwig's suite, splendid quarters with a reception room adorned in pearl-inlaid mahogany and a bedroom of white enameled walls. "I might have called this article 'The Story of the King's Bath Tub,' " she wrote. "I am bathing in the King's tub."

Once in Újvidék, the group awaited their departure by wagon on the thirty-mile trip to the Serbian frontier town of Mitrovica, from where they hoped to get to the firing line. Bly reflected on the impressive performance of the women of Austria-Hungary of all classes. "Grand duchesses scrub floors and perform the most menial services for the injured soldiers," she wrote. "And peasant women, unsolicited, bring their last pillow as well as their only pillow." She went on, "And all men know and appreciate. Women are standing shoulder to shoulder with them, dry-eyed and brave. There can never again in this land be any question as to the equality of women."

From Mitrovica, on November 19, the group set out for battle. The trip was expected to take two days. Bly took a sleeping bag, biscuits, chocolate, tea, and Hungarian candy, unable to tolerate the salamis and other dried and preserved meats favored by her colleagues. She had soured on trekking. "I hope I don't have to walk," she said. "If I do, someone else will have to write my story. My mysterious ailment still makes my nights wretched and my days helpless."

She was uninspired by the town's Croatian inhabitants. "They are badly mixed," she said. "Five languages are spoken in the town by the regular inhabitants." The group then planned to see the destroyed Serbian side of the town, also called Mitrovica. Bly described it thus: "It was raining, muddy, cold. Same old story, I only repeat lest you forget and think it lets up here sometimes. We were to walk. Not I. Couldn't if I wanted to. Wouldn't if I could. I remembered the advice of my best friend, that there is no glory in the death of a non-combatant on a battlefield."

Bly asked for and got permission to hire a carriage at her own expense. Fifty small houses had been totally wrecked. She saw a few smashed pieces of furniture and an empty birdcage. Nothing else remained.

Two days later, in heavy snowfall, the journalists and their Austrian guard set out in wagons for the battle zone. At one stopping point, Bly spied a haystack. "I do not believe in looting to please one's greed," she said, "but I could not resist asking the gendarme to let the men take enough hay to feed their horses. He readily consented and procured permissions from the soldiers on guard."

The horses ate heartily. And soon after, Bly made another war-induced readjustment in her long-standing principles:

> Never again, I hope, shall I preach anything as admitting of no deviation. I am not one who cares to drink or could ever see any excuse for it. I have been one of those who argued that in no instance was drink ever a necessity. I have changed my mind. I consider it a necessity at the cholera barracks in Przemyśl, or elsewhere. I considered it a boon to our drivers. They had had nothing to eat since the day before. They had neither coffee, tea nor water. They could obtain none. They were stiff and cold. One had a large bottle with water-like fluid.
>
> He offered it to me first. He said:
> "Schnapps! Goot [*sic*]! Warm!"

Bly drank, then gave the drivers the cigarettes she had brought along for wounded soldiers. Their consideration of one another and thoughtfulness for everyone touched her deeply. "I have not traveled with royalty," she mused, "so I can express no opinion in that regard. But of the middle class and the lower or peasants, give me the lower. Selfishness and the lack of consideration is the predominant characteristic of the middle classes. It is also true of America."

Bly then recounted how one of her colleagues in a fur-lined coat had ordered his driver to take off the sheepskin coat he was wearing and drape it over the correspondent's legs for warmth while he slept. She told the story: "The driver did. He had a little thin black vest and that was all. He shivered with the cold. But when I asked him if he were not freezing, he shook his head and said the 'head master' was cold and needed it! 'Even as ye do unto the least of these.'"

They saw no fighting at the Serbian line but did see the spoils of it. Bly told of the magnificent loot that had been seized from the Serbian homes—hand-loomed materials, embroideries, and knitted and worked woolens "such as I never saw in my life," antique silver bracelets, chains, and brooches.

She was taken to see 400 Serbian soldiers. "I gasped with amazement," she said. "There was not a man in the entire lot with the look or appearance of a soldier. They looked like poor farmers." Many were barefooted, bareheaded, "and almost bare-legged since they had what seemed to be trousers made out of coffee sacks," she said. "They looked frozen and hungry, but not severely malicious or savage. They were undersized, thin men."

There was an overnight in Serbian territory, in the village of Zrnabara, then the return to Mitrovica. There was to be no trip to the firing line after all and no explanation. Bly's group returned to Budapest in two shifts. She picked the earlier, an all-night train ride from Mitrovica with arrival in Budapest on the morning of November 23. There, the group remained for several more days, billeted again in the plush Astoria Hotel. Bly spent her days at the hospitals, seeking out and finding a poignant conclusion to her report:

> I enter a ward where some 40 men with horrible wounds hover between life and death.
>
> In the two end beds are two gypsies. There is only one face between them. Each has half a face blown off by shrapnel. They cannot speak. They can only grunt and make signs. Out of the bandages peer their black bulging eyes, half of a disfigured nose and an upper distorted lip. By signs each conveys the information to the nurses that the looks of the other disgusts him. When they grunt too energetically, great chunks of blood gush from their mouths.
>
> And yet when some one brought a fiddle into the ward, the one grabbed it as if it were heaven. He played wild sweet refrains until the one beside him snatched it away to play a wilder, sweeter one. And all faces not hidden by bandages beamed and glowed. For the moment, the voice of the violin had stolen their pain away.

Bly never concerned herself with assessment of the Dual Monarchy's strength on the battlefield or the progress of the war. She made no more trips to the front. As S. L. A. Marshall observed in his history of the war, Austria-Hungary remained throughout the conflict "a chronic invalid, without vitality or inspiration, though its ability to resist final dissolution passed understanding."

⟊

While braving the hardships on the Serbian frontier, Bly at least was in blissful ignorance of the renewed assault on her barrel company back in New York. On November 16, 1914, three creditors filed a bankruptcy petition against Bly's original American Steel Barrel Company in U.S. District Court. The creditors, representing relatively modest claims, totaling less than $4,700, charged that the machinery and tools of the firm had been transferred to the name of Mary Jane Cochrane on July 30—two days before Bly sailed for Austria—and that the company had stopped doing business altogether, surreptitiously passing its remaining accounts to the Steel Barrel Company of America. This was the company Bly had formed in a defensive action against the creditors of the Iron Clad back in October of 1912. The newer company, incorporated in New Jersey, was also held protectively in the name of Bly's octogenarian mother.

Oscar Bondy's New York attorney, Harold Nathan, rescued the situation, staving off the bankruptcy action by negotiating a settlement with the petitioners under which Bly's new company agreed to pay off the old firm's debts.

Nathan was not so successful, however, in his attempt to save the house at 15 West Thirty-seventh Street. The Greenwich Savings Bank repossessed the property on December 16 and auctioned it off a month later for $65,000—about the value of the mortgage. Mary Jane moved in with Albert and Jane and Harry and Adele in the pretty new South Prospect Park area of Brooklyn, where they had rented a neat frame house at 332 East Sixteenth Street. In Bly's absence, Mary Jane had shifted her dependency to Albert and put him in charge of the barrel company's affairs.

The war played havoc with transatlantic communications, slow even under the best of circumstances, and Bly's ability to keep track of what was happening back home was haphazard at best. She did, at Nathan's suggestion, instruct Mary Jane to have Nathan reregister the Steel Barrel Company in the name of Oscar Bondy. This was a way for Bly both to protect the company from further assault and to relieve her debt to Bondy for his help and kindness, which by this point extended well beyond paying off the $10,000 second mortgage on the West Thirty-seventh Street brownstone.

With distance and the inability to exercise control, Bly's interest in her personal matters across the Atlantic flagged. She turned her attention to cultivating the good graces of the Austrian establishment, starting with the foreign ministry's press chief, Oskar von Montlong. Her first effort was directed at grasping the new and peculiar nuances of military censorship. The Vienna newspaper *Die Zeit* invited Bly to write for it after the battlefront trip, and she was surprised when the story, published in German, didn't run until December 27 and then after huge excisions that seemed arbitrary and unrelated to the need for military secrecy.

Other colleagues from the trip had experienced even worse problems. George Schreiner, the Associated Press correspondent, left immediately after the group got back to Vienna for his home bureau in The Hague. He sent Bly two postcards instead of a letter in a closed envelope, which, he acknowledged, would have been in better taste, "it being all the same to the censor." He complained bitterly that a story of his sent November 6, 1914, from Vienna to his office in The Hague for retransmission, arrived the day after Christmas. "Can you beat it?" he asked.

> So I said: "Welcome little stranger. Thou has tarried long but thou wilt serve well as an exhibit." Hardly had I said this to myself when the porter enters with a letter from M. E. Stone, [president of the AP] sayeth he in effect, "We have received just two letters from you since you joined" the merry gang thou speakest of as the "Kriegspressequartier." For some seconds, much mental business on my part and then exclama-

tion! No wonder! I hope that I am the only one who has fared thus and so.

Schreiner said he was glad to have gotten out of Austria and had been credited with sound judgment for doing so. "What's the use?" he asked. "If those people haven't sense enough to get our stuff through[,] what can be done for them. They want to have the situation cleared up and then most efficiently fail our efforts to do so. Far be it from me to attempt it again. I wrote a most beautiful bit of *timely* copy on Nov. 5 and it gets as far as The Hague on Dec 26. Wonderful, indeed!"

Bly had asked for Schreiner's help in locating her still-missing trunks, thought to be somewhere in Holland. He told her there was really nothing he could do, least of all through the American consulate, which she apparently had suggested. "The gentlemen are so very busy," he told her, "and trunks, kindly believe me, are their very pet aversion." He said he had no plans to return to Vienna until "the pups of war are leashed again, which is not one of the things likely to make copy in a hurry."

Schreiner asked Bly to tell von Montlong the story of the unreasonably tardy transmission of his copy from Vienna and to assure the press chief that it wasn't a question of what Schreiner had written: The "assanine [*sic*] retarders" hadn't even cut a word of it before it was sent, he said. "Meanwhile, I would like to know where my other stories are. I wrote 13 in all. Do the gentlemen of the 'K[riegspressequartier]' keep adding to a museum on 'manuscripts?' "

As Bly's series ran in *The Journal*, Konstantin Dumba, the Austro-Hungarian ambassador to the United States, cabled back to Vienna via the Austrian embassy in Rome his complaint that the stories had been "critical of the military's sanitary conditions in Galicia." He similarly slammed William Shepherd, the United Press reporter, for his coverage of the Serbian retreat, characterizing Shepherd's work as "highly unfavorable."

Bly happened to run into von Montlong, who made a passing remark about her "unfriendly cables." He was certainly referring to her newspaper series in *The Journal*, even though it had been sent by mail and not by wire. Bly, confused by his reference, assumed he was referring to two brief telegrams she had sent, one from Vienna on October 17 and one from Przemyśl, both urging Americans to send cotton and medical supplies by parcel post for the aid of wounded Austrian soldiers.

Von Montlong was not an enemy she could afford to make, and Bly wrote at once to placate him on February 6: "I want to thank you again for your very generous offer the other day. I have not written anything since I returned from the pressequartier, but if I should it will be a pleasure to submit all articles to you for your approval and valuable suggestions as to what may be of greatest aid to the country we both love." She used the occasion to forward the letter of introduction which Ambassador Penfield had written back in October but which she had never delivered. She reinforced its flattering contents by telling von Montlong she had known the American envoy for "fully 15 years." Then she raised the matter of the press chief's remark about her "cables," immediately jumping to paranoiac conclusions inspired by her recent troubles: "If unfriendly cables were sent bearing my name they were forgeries. I sent no cables except these two I have mentioned. Can you ascertain more about them? It would be a great favor to me."

She went on to explain that she had written "a great number of articles which I gave to the censor to mail. I believe he mailed them to America or otherwise I would doubtless have been informed of their detention. The very fact that the censor passed and mailed them shows they must have been fair and honest and *not unfriendly*."

The story she wrote for *Die Zeit*, however, she said, had been severely cut. She sent him an unedited copy of the piece, which was about how she had engineered her opportunity to get to the battle-front. She drew diagonal lines through the parts that had been eliminated when it was published—nearly half the story. The excised parts did include some brief references that identified locations she had visited too exactly for military comfort. But most of the eliminated paragraphs were her fawning references to the Austrian nobility and government officials she had gotten to know during her quest to gain permission to go to the battle zone. She told von Montlong:

I am curious to know why what I wrote the censor thought must not be published. And I believe my story was retained by the censor almost three weeks. A story like this, published in America, would arouse the *love* of the public for the persons mentioned. It is by such things our officials become popular and the beloved of the citizens. I should value your frank opinion on the matter. *Die Zeit* wanted more articles but I refused to write them.

For his perusal, Bly enclosed the two postcards from Schreiner as well as one from D. Thomas Curtin of *The Boston Globe*, another reporter Bly had gotten to know. Curtin simply noted that he would soon be in Vienna and hoped to see her.

Von Montlong answered Bly's letter within a couple of days, on February 10, but she did not receive his reply for more than a week. She had been out of the city. Von Montlong explained that in the *Die Zeit* article, it had not been the censors who had made the cuts but the newspaper itself, since those parts of her work did not reflect its liberal, progressive viewpoint. Bly responded on February 21:

> What you tell me of the "*Zeit*" is indeed a surprise and I apologize for my unjust suspicions of the censors. I have heard such things have happened occasionally in America but never to me. Fortunately, my articles are always printed as I write them, whether they coincide with the editorial opinion or not. Is it not a pity the Austrian readers would not know how kind and thoughtful those in position are of others? I shall send that same story to the *Zeitung* in New York. I am sure Herman Ridder, the owner, will see that not a word is cut out.

Her focus had shifted from being a foreign correspondent in Austria to being as helpful to the Austrian war effort as a foreigner could. A fine new life was opening up for her. Bondy's connections and her own status as a famous American correspondent gave her wide and immediate access to a fascinating array of people in an immersing situation. The issues were, quite literally, of world-shaking importance. Bly's own horrendous five years of thrashing in the enervating swamp of litigation, aggravation, victimization, ridicule, and near-destitution could safely recede by contrast into stunning insignificance. In Austria, she had important friends, influence, and the potential for serious purpose. Even her lifelong hatred of the British could be put to positive use. The blackout on news from the other side skewed her perspective, made her oblivious to the growing public sentiment among her own countrymen against the Central Powers' cause, and at the same time cemented a new and earnest loyalty to her gracious hosts. Doing her part to save Austria in this terrible crisis swiftly became her personal battle cry.

❧

Oscar Bondy, thanks to the legacy of his grandmother Hellman, owned the Central Bohemian Sugar Enterprises, one of the monarchy's largest sugar producers. Vienna, where Bondy was born, worked, and lived, was the company's headquarters, although the factories were in the Bohemian towns of Meziřič and Zditz, bearing his name in huge letters above the entrance.

Bondy was an inveterate collector and creditable musician, blondish, balding, polyglot, fun-loving, and as adept in business as he was with women, favoring those with theatrical flair. Born October 19, 1870, he remained a bachelor into old age, marrying his faithful bookkeeper during World War II. He was six years younger than Bly, who was by this time a full-figured fifty years old.

Bondy's factories in Bohemia were in the capable hands of his nephew Norbert Rie, the grown son of his sister Melanie. Bondy's practice was to visit the production facilities only once or twice a year, always accompanied by a different "auntie." Rie would use the occasions of his uncle's visits to organize chamber concerts, bringing together a string quartet in his Biedermeier-styled music room with himself on the violin and Bondy on the viola. Bondy's interest in music extended to collecting precious manuscripts of scores by great composers. At various times he owned both Stradivari and Guarneri violins.

As a family, the Bondys were thoroughly assimilated Viennese Jews—educated, cultured, and private. Oscar was the second of four children and the only boy, sandwiched between Ida, the oldest daughter, and the twins, Melanie and Marie.

Bondy's particular passion for music had put him on the very short list of benefactors of Vienna's prestigious Musikverein, a society of friends of music and patrons of the Vienna Philharmonic whose select circle included mostly royalty and high-ranking aristocrats. He was one of the few commoners among the organization's patrons, a testament to his wealth and standing. Another was Paul Wittgenstein, son of the rich Jewish industrialist, brother of the philosopher Ludwig Wittgenstein, and himself a concert pianist who continued to perform after losing his arm in the war.

The war and its inflationary consequences had a disastrous effect on Bondy's business, and he began to entertain notions of immigrating to the United States during Bly's Vienna sojourn, although he would not do so until many years after her death. As a foreign national and an American, she may have seemed a useful friend to have at this time, and Bondy's willingness to help her extended far beyond the bounds of warm acquaintanceship or friendly business dealings. Between them there was genuine affection. They may even have been lovers.

By mid-March of 1915, through Bondy's influence or on her own, Bly had thrown herself into the local war relief effort. She became involved with the Imperial and Royal Austrian Military Widows and Orphans Fund, founded in August of 1914 by Austrian Archduke Leopold Salvator and his wife, Archduchess Blanka. It was a formidable committee. The board of directors included two former ministers, high-ranking federal legislators and bureaucrats, representatives of Vienna's religious communities, and leading industrialists, bankers, and editors of the major daily newspapers.

Unlike the imperial government, the organization worked only with the Austrian half of the monarchy and spent its time raising money for charitable work, activities that included arranging for the adoption of war orphans; providing medical, material, and financial help to the pregnant wives and infants of soldiers; arranging low-premium life insurance; and distributing gifts at Christmas. Bly had determined that she could serve Austria best by using her influence to encourage Americans to send money and relief supplies for these innocent bystanders by letter or parcel post. She had completely abandoned any pretext of journalistic objectivity. The United States was still officially neutral in the conflict, with President Wilson pursuing a course of peaceful nonintervention. Although public sentiment tended toward the Allies from the start, the Teutonic countries had their very vocal supporters. Germans still represented the largest immigrant group in the United States, and the Irish population was anything but pro-British. Bly's personal declaration for Austria, then, was not untoward, except insofar as the position of war correspondent would preclude the taking of sides. Furthermore, her attitudes squared perfectly with the Hearst-Brisbane position. According to Brisbane's biographer, Oliver Carlson, Hearst's newspapers advocated peace at all costs but with a highly anti-British slant and the use of "one type of appeal for its German-reading audiences and another for its English-reading section." News and interviews in this period were often faked to support the editorial bias.

Bly wrote to von Montlong on March 22:

> Here are three articles for the widows and orphans—and three personal letters on which I have placed postage. I think they will go quicker through you.
>
> The cable for flour I have written at the bottom of a page. The addresses to whom it should be sent are at the top of the page.
>
> Following your advice, I went to the German Embassy Saturday and gave them a cable for flour. I told them I had given *you one*, first. They telephoned me yesterday it had been sent. I gave them nine addresses to send separately. So if you still think well of it, I think we ought to send these additional ones for Austria.
>
> Is there anything *special* you want me to send for Austria in the way of news?

Bly addressed her collective cable to every major newspaper editor or personality with whom she had any friendship or influence.

"Appeal American citizens send by parcel post only packages of wheatflour for orphans and widows to Nellie Bly—Vienna Austria," it read. Brisbane topped the list of intended recipients, followed by his counterparts at *The Pittsburgh Dispatch*, *The Chicago Post*, *The Washington Star*, *The San Francisco Chronicle*, Herman Ridder of the German-language *Staats-Zeitung*, Erasmus Wilson of *The Pittsburgh Commercial-Gazette*, *The New York Sun*, *The Saturday Evening Post*, *The Chicago Daily News*, and *The Chicago Tribune*.

Von Montlong forwarded the cable to Ambassador Dumba in Washington, accompanied by a letter of explanation and caution, which said in part:

> There are two major objections against this certainly well-intended request:
>
> The first is that such an appeal in its telegraphic brevity could feed new fuel to the unfortunately prevalent erroneous supposition abroad about the resources of the Monarchy.
>
> Second, according to news reports, the government of Great Britain has not refrained from confiscating American postal packages, if those contain foodstuffs for enemy countries.

Von Montlong aired his concerns with Bly, who responded she was sure there was no reason to worry. Widows and orphans anywhere were a worthy cause even in peacetime, she said, and if Americans learned that the British were seizing foodstuffs intended for the benefit of needy mothers and children, there would be a public outcry. Bly thought even this would be a situation Austria could turn to its advantage.

Von Montlong's own advice to Ambassador Dumba was to hold on to the cables. However, he left the matter to Dumba's judgment, adding,

> For your personal information, I am mentioning confidentially that I left Miss Bly in the belief that her telegrams had been sent, in order not to turn her against us. She can blame their failure to arrive later on our enemies. Following our example, the same procedure has been used

by the German embassy whom she had approached in an analogous matter.

It took Ambassador Dumba nearly two months to respond to von Montlong, informing him on May 12 that he had not forwarded Bly's cables to the newspapers for the reasons von Montlong expressed and for another reason of his own. Five days before Dumba wrote to von Montlong, the German submarine *U-20* unleashed two torpedoes aimed at the British Cunard liner *Lusitania*, sinking the great ship within eighteen minutes of the first hit. The attack killed 1,198 of the liner's passengers, among them 128 American citizens, mostly women and children. Although Brisbane brushed the incident off in an editorial as "no cause for a declaration of war," American public sentiment turned swiftly against Germany and its allies. It was in this atmosphere that Dumba explained to von Montlong why he had not delivered Bly's cables:

> I was motivated primarily by the concern that the antagonistic press would immediately interpret the undeniable fact that this telegram was conveyed by the Embassy as evidence that the aforementioned war correspondent was only used by us as a cover for the project. I would like to add that the German Embassy, too, has turned down a series of similar offers received so far.

Oddly, the very next day, Bly rewrote her telegrams and presented them for transmission in Vienna again. This time, they were sent to Washington through the Austro-Hungarian Embassy in Berlin and were almost immediately forwarded to the newspaper editors and publishers to whom she had addressed them. *The Evening Journal* of May 18, 1915, carried a two-column boxed item at the top of page 3 under the headline "Nellie Bly Pleads for Food to Feed Austrian War Victims":

> The *Evening Journal* is in receipt of the following telegram from the Austro-Hungarian Embassador [*sic*] at Washington:

Washington, D.C., May 17

Editor Evening Journal:

I beg to inform you that the following message from Nellie Bly addressed to you has been forwarded to the Austro-Hungarian Embassy by the Foreign Office in Vienna. "Please appeal to the citizens of America to send packages of wheat and flour by parcel post for distribution by me among orphans and widows. Nellie Bly, Vienna."

Austro-Hungarian Ambassador

Five days later, on May 23, Dumba cabled back to Vienna to confirm that he had forwarded Bly's cables. No explanation for the about-face was offered.

In the meantime, *The Journal* ran the first story Bly had sent since her trip to the firing lines. She made no attempt at impartiality. It was essentially a solicitation for silver quarters to be sent to Austria "to someone you know" so that they could contribute them to the widows' and orphans' fund. In gratitude, the names of contributors were to be inscribed in the country's "Gold Book and placed among the imperishable records of Austria." Bly explained that this was one way to "perpetuate your name. There are records in Vienna now 600 years old, and for the next 600 your descendants can come and see your name among the sacred treasures of Austria."

She also explained the *"Wehrmann in Eisen,"* the Iron Man for Austria's Defense, a carved wooden statue, later to be cast in iron, into which people were driving nails as a reward for their contributions to the widows' and orphans' fund. The *Wehrmann* statues had become a popular fund-raising device throughout the Teutonic countries. One in Berlin, dedicated to Field Marshal Paul von Hindenburg, had raised thousands of dollars.

Bly said Archduke Leopold Salvator had driven the first nail into Vienna's *Wehrmann,* then inscribed his name in the Gold Book. "He is a splendid man," she said, "amiable, modest and not one bit snobbish. He is very good-looking, also." She went on in an anti-British tirade:

He is just the opposite to an English personage—just as the English chill one's blood with repulsion, the Archduke Leopold Salvater [*sic*] warms one's blood with friendliness. There is not the faintest hint of the "loftier than thou" about him. He makes one believe that he feels it a great pleasure to make one's acquaintance.

But that is true of all Austrians—they are the most cultured, refined and modest people of the world, from Emperor Francis Joseph down to the simple folks.

In closing, she repeated the assertion heard often in Vienna in recent months that American-made guns and ammunition "enable the English to continue this war." She suggested that under such circumstances, American citizens would do well to show "they mean to help the orphans and widows and send over thousands of quarters."

Completely oblivious to the turn of American sentiment against the Central Powers, Bly was busy envisioning "nail driving clubs" sprouting up all over America and producing enough in contributions to her beloved Austrian widows and orphans to warrant an "American nail-driving day" in Vienna. In what she thought would encourage generosity, Bly explained that if such an event were to take place, moving pictures would be made of it and sent back to the United States to be shown.

༺༒༻

On April 1, 1915, after seven months in Austria, Bly informed her mother by letter that her trunks had finally arrived. She complained she was missing several things she had asked for specifically: her blue wrapper, the white feathers from a hat, her furs, her steamer coat, and, worst of all, her notebooks and sketchbook. These last two she requested be sent at once by registered mail. "All the ideas I ever had are in that one book," she explained.

She had other, more pressing issues to air as well: "I am most anxious to hear from you and to know if you transferred the Steel Barrel Stock to Mr. Bondy *as Mr. Nathan wished you to.* I need money but I cant [*sic*] accept any from Mr. Bondy until he has the stock. And it must be hurried as I am not overly anxious to starve to death."

Actually, Mary Jane had effected the stock transfer four months earlier, but the difficult communications with Europe apparently had delayed the news getting to Bly. Bly also asked about her protégée, Margaret Collins, from whom she had not heard for many months. Margaret was Bly's most valued employee at the steel barrel company. Bly was curious to know if "in spite of all the opposition made to her, she stuck to the business." Without her, Bly felt sure, the company would "go to ruin."

Margaret had worked for Bly since 1908, when the barrel company got started. She was hired as a twenty-five-year-old business school graduate with some experience in real estate. Bly immediately made her a protégée, promoting her ahead of others, giving her opportunities, and depending on her. It was Margaret's job to solicit orders from various companies. Sometimes she accompanied Bly on speaking engagements, such as to the Independent Petroleum Marketer's Convention in St. Louis after the Iron Clad's troubles started. Bly gave a talk on how she lost her millions and "made many new friends, as usual." Margaret recalled what a good time they had together, how Bly was known as the woman with "the million dollar smile." She recalled how Bly had once gone to visit an elderly cousin of her mother, referred to as Aunt Mary. Bly then brought the woman and her canary back to live with her in New York, where both died and were buried together a few years later.

After Bly's departure for Europe, much of the thankless burden of fending off the barrel company's creditors fell on Margaret, and as she confided to her children years later, the job became extremely stressful. On a sales call to the Tidewater Oil Company, she met the company vice president, Dennis Carey, and the couple married soon after. Margaret was no doubt relieved to be getting out of the barrel company mess. She remained with the company until shortly before her wedding, on January 16, 1916, at the age of thirty-five, and quickly got busy making a family. The Careys had six sons in all, the third of whom, Hugh, became a governor of New York State.

Bly was in fine humor through the spring and summer of 1915. She may have been doing some traveling, since the U.S. Embassy in

Vienna had record of her reporting a lost passport on June 4. At summer's end, she sent a postcard to Erasmus Wilson in Pittsburgh on which was printed a black-and-white photo of the Serbian prisoners she had seen in Mitrovica. She was still working hard for the widows and orphans with evident enthusiasm:

> Dear Q.O.
>
> Thanks for the precious letter and all. Write often. Letters reach me because everybody knows me here and trusts me. Ask your readers to send 25 cts and their names to me "c/o *Hotel Imperial*" my permanent address here. Names will go in Gold Book with Emperor and money will drive nails into Iron Man for benefit of orphans. *Send your own name* and 25 cts silver comes all night. See other side. I was there when photo was made. The "movie men" had me walk along with prisoners and films were exhibited everywhere. Write soon. Your kid, Nellie Bly.

To her mother, she wrote again on October 21. From the letter's contents, it appears that Mary Jane had moved into the newly rented house in South Prospect Park with Albert and Jane and that Harry had gotten into a terrible squabble with his mother, which Bly was trying to mediate through the mails. Albert had effectively taken control of the barrel company, much to Bly's regret. "Are you still friends with that Cochrane who gets so much out of the barrel company while we get nothing?" she asked angrily. She was solicitous of Mary Jane's needs ("Have you got heavy winter clothes? And did you get nice new underwear? Thank you for sending me that check but I think you needed the money."). The problems with Albert and Harry rekindled the embitterment she had successfully put aside since her arrival in Austria. She told her mother, "Don't deny yourself comforts to support others. You now have seen by this time that no one denies themselves anything to give to you. Learn to think only of yourself. Selfishness is the only thing which gains in this world.

"And keep your own secrets," she continued. "What you trust to Guibert [the barrel company manager] is discussed by others.

Don't tell him anything." In closing, she wrote, "Write me a long letter all about yourself. And have no discussions with anyone and live for happiness alone."

More than six months later, on May 24, 1916, Bly surfaced again in *The New York Evening Journal* with a lengthy report on the results of her nail-hammering drive. This was her lead: "For every American who has sent me money for the widows and orphans to whom the war has brought suffering, there is a nail driven into Vienna's great soldier statue, the *Wehrmann*. Of this I am certain, because I drove the nails."

At the ceremony, Countess Nandine Berchtold welcomed Bly in English. She thanked her "with all my heart for the warm interest which you take in our country, dear Miss Bly, and especially for having come here today, showing your sympathy with our patriotism, as expressed in the *Wehrmann in Eisen*, by driving nails into the statue in the names of some of your friends and compatriots. Will you have the kindness to transmit to them our very best and warmest thanks."

A raw wind blew as Bly drove the nails into the statue one by one. Someone suggested a substitute be permitted to finish Bly's task, but Countess Berchtold objected. "No," she said. "It is a duty Miss Bly owes to those who sent the money to her. She must drive each nail herself." Bly continued her account: "And so, while the Countess patiently passed the nails to me as reverently as one in an act of devotion, I hammered away until the last one had been sunk into the big *Wehrmann in Eisen*—one for each name on my list."

Bly did not give the full list of names she had gathered for her cause. Perhaps there were not so many. But she did name a few from *The Journal*'s circulation area, among them both her mother and her sister-in-law Jane; George Horace Lorimer, editor of *The Saturday Evening Post*; Mrs. Helen Hampton of Brooklyn; Charles F. Koster and Katherine Koster Winslow of Sheepshead Bay; Theodore Olmstead and William Dawes of Newark, New Jersey; Mr. and Mrs. J. J. McCable of Bridgeport, Connecticut; Florian L. Treumann and Margaret G. Relihan of New York City; and J. N. Brandenberg of New Dorp, Staten Island.

President Woodrow Wilson kept the United States out of the war for nearly two and a half years, despite such incidents as the sinking of the *Lusitania*, which could have been considered provocation enough to trigger American entry. Wilson campaigned on the slogan "He Kept Us Out of War" and won reelection in 1916. On January 31, 1917, Germany notified the United States of its intention to begin unrestricted submarine warfare the following day. By February 3, Wilson had broken off diplomatic relations with Germany but still held off making an all-out declaration of war, awaiting an overt act of hostility to which he could point for his change of mind. That would come soon enough.

British naval intelligence intercepted a coded message to the German ambassador in Mexico signed by German Foreign Minister Arthur Zimmermann. In it, Zimmermann offered Germany's assistance to Mexico in efforts to recover Texas, New Mexico, and Arizona in return for Mexican support for Germany should it go to war with the United States. That message, passed by the British to the Americans on February 25, coupled with the German sinking of four unarmed American merchant ships in mid-March, spurred Wilson to approach Congress on April 2. Within four days, both Senate and House had approved his request, and Wilson declared war against Germany at noon on April 6, 1917. Brisbane and *The Journal* kept up the anti-British attacks, unmindful of the shift in public opinion against the Germans. Efforts to recoup came too late and dearly cost Brisbane in prestige and the Hearst papers in circulation.

Where relations between Washington and Vienna would stand in this new turn of events became a source of immediate concern in Vienna. In fact, the very day of the U.S. declaration of war against Germany, the Austrian foreign ministry put forward to the United States its proposal for how the two countries should treat each other's visiting or resident citizens in the event of a rupture in their diplomatic ties.

The actual break in diplomatic relations came on May 17. Spain's embassies in Vienna and Washington handled communications between the two nations. Four days later, the United States agreed to an amended version of the Austrian proposal, the gist of which was that so long as the visitors did not behave in an untoward manner, they would be able to go about their business "unmolested," and that they would be able to leave and enter the other country on a case-by-case basis after having met certain requirements.

The United States tightened this agreement in a presidential proclamation issued on December 11, 1917, which said that Austro-Hungarian citizens who remained in the United States and refrained from actual hostility or from aiding or giving comfort to the enemies of the United States or did not disturb the peace were free to go about their business. In fact, numerous Austro-Hungarian citizens were interned in the United States during this period, specifically at Fort Douglas, Utah; Fort Oglethorpe, Georgia; Ellis Island; Fort McPherson, Georgia; and Fort Bliss, Texas. The Austrians similarly maintained internment camps for American nationals they deemed troublemakers.

When the U.S. government asked about the status of American internees in the monarchy, the foreign ministry responded that only those whose behavior was belligerent were subjected to house arrest or internment, and that other than being required to register with the police, Americans were free to move about the empire. On the question of leaving or transiting the country, the Austrians said they would allow Americans to enter Austria-Hungary or cross the Swiss border after the usual quarantine and with special authorization on a case-by-case basis, and that Americans who had already obtained permission to cross the Swiss border could do so unless the border were otherwise closed to travel generally.

Bly, as the American darling of the Austrian regime, never endured any of the potential hardships of enemy alien status. She traveled throughout the monarchy without difficulty and made no requests to exit. On March 31, 1918, the Imperial and Royal Police Headquarters in Vienna requested permission from the War Ministry on Bly's behalf to enable her to visit Budapest for a museum tour and antiques auction to which she had been invited. The letter read:

> The American citizen Nelly [*sic*] Bly, born May 4, 1877 [*sic*], where a resident, Protestant, widowed, living in Vienna at

the Hotel Bristol for several years, requests permission to travel to Budapest and return to Vienna. The above-mentioned was, until the interruption of relations with America, active as a correspondent for local newspapers in connection with the best circles and known as an Austria-phile. There are no objections against the request.

The Hungarian Ministry of Interior echoed the Viennese police in its easy affirmation of the request, and Bly's permission to travel was granted on June 3, 1918.

Thus, there is no indication she ever was subjected to any sort of house arrest or internment. In any case, her recognized status as an "Austria-phile," as well as her impeccable connections to Austria's "best circles," ensured against that happening. As an enemy alien, however, she probably was barred from further reporting. No stories of hers from Austria-Hungary appeared again in the American press. She proudly wore her American flag lapel pin and remained "unmolested" in her temporarily adopted country until the winter of 1918–19.

*

Once war was declared, Austria and the United States had to contend with more than the question of how to deal with each other's citizens on enemy ground. There also was the matter of each other's citizens' property. The Steel Barrel Company of America, of which Oscar Bondy now held virtually all the shares, was a clear case in point.

Bondy, as a citizen of the monarchy, had become, by definition if not in spirit, an enemy alien of the United States. For this reason, the U.S. government's Alien Property Custodian took steps to seize the 490 shares of Bly's barrel company which Mary Jane Cochrane had put in Bondy's name back in January of 1915. Bly, it will be recalled, had transferred those same shares to her mother's name shortly before leaving for Europe in 1914. Mary Jane, in turn, assigned them to Bondy at her daughter's behest in the office of Harold Nathan, Bondy's New York attorney. Mary Jane reserved for herself all the dividend income from the shares to be paid for the rest of her life.

Nathan was the attorney who had saved the new barrel company from creditors of the old barrel company in December of 1914, a month before the shares of the new firm were transferred to Bondy. By the time the Alien Property Custodian got into the picture, the new company was on solid footing and worth an estimated $200,000.

Nathan had occasion in March of 1918 to write Mary Jane concerning the stock transfer, and in her reply a few days later, she suddenly announced that she had no recollection of ever signing such a document. This was odd, since, according to Nathan, she had been in his office reviewing it only four or five months before.

When it became clear that the Alien Property Custodian had the power to sell off the barrel company shares, Mary Jane, heavily prompted by Albert, filed a bill of complaint against the government office on August 23, 1918. In it, she claimed that Nathan had defrauded her into signing the shares over to Bondy. She asked for an injunction to stop the Alien Property Custodian from selling off the shares until the fraud question could be resolved. To this, the agency agreed, even though it saw the case as a "flimsy" attempt to tie its hands and prevent sale of a firm it considered fully enemy-owned. The fraud case proceeded in U.S. District Court.

On October 7, Mary Jane was deposed in the case. She claimed her only reason for transferring the barrel company shares into Bondy's name was to protect the new company from the old company's creditors—something the judge found highly questionable but decided to overlook. She also contended that it was her understanding that she had not been divested of the title and that the stock would eventually come back to her.

Nathan, enraged at the accusation against him, disputed Mary Jane's version of events. He said that she had fully grasped the nature of the stock transfer, that she had wanted Bondy to be reimbursed in this way for the money he had advanced her daughter, and that she had trusted that Bondy would see that the shares ultimately were returned to Bly, to whom they rightfully belonged.

Clearly in the intervening three years, Mary Jane had changed her mind about all that—probably under Albert's tutelage. Albert's only chance for getting title to the company was as an inheritance from his mother. At this point, he saw himself responsible for the company's success in Bly's absence and probably felt the shares were his just reward. Bly, he knew, would never give them to him. As Bondy's, they would either revert to Bly or be sold off. Over Mary Jane, now at least eighty-eight years old and totally dependent upon him, he could prevail.

Bly could no longer delay her return to New York. A brand-new fight had to be waged. This time it was not a stampede of powerful bankers, high-priced lawyers, and conniving employees against a solitary woman in business. This time it was a devoted daughter against her mother.

⌘

Mary Jane Cochrane's lawsuit against Oscar Bondy's control of the barrel company shares forced Bly to take immediate steps to gain permission to leave for New York. As she did, the empire was near collapse. A new republic of German Austria was about to be declared.

On November 3, 1918, Austria surrendered. The Armistice followed eight days later, the same day that Emperor Karl signed his after-the-fact note of abdication. One day later, the newly formed National Assembly resolved unanimously that German Austria was a democratic republic and a component part of the German republic. The Social Democratic leader Karl Renner became head of the new coalition government.

Austria's only spoils of four years of war were chaos and economic misery. Communists convulsed the fledgling republic with threats of a revolution. Bly, amidst the chaos and uncertainty in Vienna, heard a new calling. As the archetypal American Austrophile, she saw a unique role for herself in the pursuit of salvation for her adopted country. Someone had to make President Wilson understand the dire nature of the dual threat to Western civilization posed by starvation and the Bolsheviks. She decided she was uniquely equipped for the task.

Immediately, on November 26, Bly cabled her closest contact to the president, William J. McCombs, chairman of the Democratic National Committee:

I beseech you tell the President what you have told and written me that through my psychic influence on you he became candidate and beg him to grant the prayer of my cable and reward faith and belief of these new-freed people—whose God he is—and save them from approaching starvation by the immediate shipment of food. Starvation will produce the horrors of the Russian Bolschewismus which lies here on the frontier with no army to keep it out and hunger to incite it. Hunger breeds Bolschewismus. Food kills Bolschewismus. These long suffering newly liberated people must be saved from perishing.

Nellie Bly.
Imperial Hotel.

A second, more detailed cable on the same theme went out the same day to someone else with the ability to circulate a message widely: Arthur Brisbane, of course, at *The New York Evening Journal*.

Have wired President Wilson an urgent appeal to save the Austrian people from starvation by immediately shipping meals land [*sic*] flour potatoes and clothes. Everything here quiet and orderly but deaths from starvation rapidly increasing. People astoundingly patient. Believe the land who has freed them from slavery will not allow them to perish. President Wilson worshipped by all as the saviour of mankind. Faith and belief in him unbo[u]nded. I am perfectly familiar with conditions not only among the rich but among the masses. Bolschewismus lies on the frontiers (We realize daily more and more its horrors). Austria now has no army and no frontier's protection. Bolschewismus finds fertile soil in the minds of the starving. The Pangs of hunger and pain, of cold, strip mankind of every vestige of civilization and transforms them into a beast of prey. Hunger breeds Bolschewismus. Food kills Bolschewismus. Austria is the barrier between Russian Bolschewismus and France, Italy, England and America. Once it gains footing here it will also spread to the Entente lands. Even nobility here rejoiced for a Republic but all stand in deadly fear before the starvation which confronts us. America must not allow the people it has freed to perish. Bohemia and Hungaria [*sic*] being agricultural lands are well provided but will not share with us. Austria not an agricultural land, only mountainous produces no food and has our 10,000,000 souls to feed. The people America has freed must not be allowed to perish.

Nellie Bly

As ever, Brisbane obliged. Editors cleaned up the syntax, inserted the missing articles and pronouns, and published Bly's cable in full under a huge picture of her on page 2 of *The Journal* of December 7.

By the middle of the month, Bly received a cable from her mother, who had been ailing, reporting herself in good health and again demanding that Oscar Bondy surrender the stock certificate of the barrel company before everything was lost. Bly could delay no longer. On December 27, she applied for U.S. permission to leave Austria on a special train to carry American expatriates to Berne, Switzerland, on January 25, 1919, a week after the scheduled start of the Paris Peace Conference. Bly routed herself on to Paris as Austria's anointed if ad hoc emissary.

She arranged with no difficulty an exclusive interview with Renner, the republic's new chancellor, on January 18. She submitted her questions in writing in English. Renner answered in German, which his office translated into English for her benefit. The questions were clearly framed to present Austria in the best possible light to President Wilson and the American public. At the same time, Bly asked for and received letters from both Renner and Foreign Minister Otto Bauer establishing her impeccable credentials with the new Austrian government. The letters were meant to be presented at the meeting she hoped to arrange with President Wilson. Renner's letter of authorization said in part:

> It gives me great pleasure to confirm to you, that you, as an eyewitness to our prevailing conditions and having been briefed personally by key members of the Government, have been authorized by the State Chancellery of German Austria

as well as by other Government Departments to give all desired information to the President of the United States, Mr. Woodrow Wilson, who is held in high regard in all of Austria, and to impart to him in person the trust of the Republic of German Austria in the justice, fervor, humanity and statesmanly wisdom of the great President.

In the interview, Renner laid out what the new republic needed from the United States. First on the list were German Bohemia and the Sudetenland, which housed the empire's most important industries and "the most intelligent segments of our population." Second was German West Hungary, just outside Vienna's city limits and the capital's main supplier of meat, flour, and vegetables. Although the Magyars had ruled the area for many years, Renner explained, it had remained German in character.

From the United States, he said, the Austrians were seeking economic aid in the form of shipments of desperately needed grains and fats, loans to restore the nation's currency, and financial aid to improve water works and electrical power systems. The need for coal was dire. "The Czechs have taken our German-Bohemian coal mines; moreover, those mines of Bohemia are succumbing in increasing numbers to socialist anarchy . . .

"By disarming ourselves and entrusting ourselves totally to the Peace Congress," Renner said, "our country and its people have committed themselves tacitly to the protection of the United States." The army, actually, had fallen into confusion and disarray with the breakup of the monarchy and the moves toward independence of several of its numerous parts.

Renner said that there was no doubt Austria would remain a republic, that the question of future revolutions depended "as much on the powers of the Entente as on ourselves," and that the Socialists would not break up the big corporations or large estates but instead would try to bring those operated by cartels under government control. There would be ample room for free enterprise, he said, and for American investment.

Bly asked what had become of Emperor Karl and the rest of the imperial family. Renner said they had moved quietly to a castle in

Eckartsau, outside Vienna, and were expected to leave the country once the borders reopened.

"Our most fervent desire," Renner said, "is for the blockade to be lifted and for free communication between us and America to be restored. Many thousands of German Austrians with whom we would like to have contact again are living over there. In our country many good working people are waiting for the opportunity to go to America and be gainfully employed there. Therefore, the best remedy for us is something all the world needs, that is the restoration of peace and friendship between the nations."

Bly's response was immediate. She would take on the difficult task herself.

STORMS REPORTED RAGING IN BERLIN A

ROADS' RETURN DEMANDED BY CONVENTION

Reconstruction Congress Asks Government to Remove Restrictions.

ATLANTIC CITY, N. J., Dec. 7.— The great Reconstruction Congress of American industry in its closing session gained little shedding opinions and apparent unanimity of sentiment reconstruction and agriculture, not of those concluding a meeting to-day urgently by the hands of food...

WRITER WHO ASKS AID FOR AUSTRIANS

NELLIE BLY.

EXTENSION OF ARMISTICE EXPECTED

Germans Are Unable to Surrender All Materials in Period Agreed Upon.

By Universal Service.

Washington, Dec. 7.—The statement has appeared here that there is little in the belief...

CASUALTY LIST WORK BEING SPEEDED

16,000 of Major Character to Complete Pershing's Report Next Week.

By Universal Service.

WASHINGTON, Dec. 7.—There are 16,000 major casualties yet to be tabulated in General Pershing in Washington...

Measles the Pes
American Arm
Camps

By Universal Service.
WASHINGTON, Dec. 7.—

8 WORDS T
TREVES OF U
BOYS' COMI

Newspapers Reduce Bre Style to the Minimum— tility Is Concealed

By DAMON RUNYO
Staff Correspondent of U
Service.

HULBERT'S PLAN FOR DOCKS INDORSED

18 HURT AS
CRASH ON "
ONE HEL

GIRL'S DEATH RIDDLE SOLVED BY MOTHER

222 Harvard Men Killed.

MISSISSIPPI TRAFFIC

New Zealand Referendum.

CONGRESS PASSPORTS

12

Peace

S O PLEASED WAS THE NEW REPUBLIC OF GERMAN AUSTRIA BY
Bly's offer of intercession with her own government that Chancellor Renner's office paid for her train ticket and provided her with a private compartment for the trip to Paris. There was a warm expression of gratitude and concern she be sent off "in the best possible way."

The special train for Berne, Switzerland, left as planned on January 25, 1919, carrying Bly and nineteen other American citizens, a few of them children. From Berne, they proceeded immediately to Paris, where Bly registered at the Hotel Montana on the Avenue de l'Opéra.

On February 4, she applied at the Passport Bureau in Paris for a visa to return to the United States. Because of her well-publicized activities on behalf of an enemy nation, the U.S. War Department's Military Intelligence Division investigated her request with arched scrutiny. In talking with the U.S. official, a "G-2 representative," Bly got her first opportunity to tell her story. She explained that she had set out for Austria at first word of the outbreak of war in 1914, sailing by way of England since that was the only passage she could secure. The British detained all passengers for questioning, but Bly

said she managed to elude the authorities and made her way straight
to Austria as she had planned. She told the passport official how
much she hated the English and how she would do anything against
them. She said she felt the same way about the French. All this, of
course, only served to call her loyalty as an American into question.
Her sentiments also reflected the fact that during the four years in
Austria, Bly had had no exposure to Allied propaganda or point of
view. All her opinions were formed on the basis of what she had
learned from and in the nations of the Central Powers, where information from enemy sources was blacked out.

When she raised the issue of creeping Bolshevism and how
much she knew about it, the official offered to put her in touch with
"his friend" Second Lieutenant John A. Chamberlain, who, accompanied by another officer, interviewed Bly at Rumplemayer's. She
refused to have the conversation in any official location.

According to Lieutenant Chamberlain, who sent his report to
U.S. Military Intelligence in Paris:

> Miss Bly stated upon investigation that the only remedy for
> the Bolshevik evil was the upholding of the Governments of
> Austria and Germany. She also said that she believed in
> democracy, that she thought the only monarchy which was
> satisfactory in the world was the German monarchy and the
> Kaiser was the only great monarch; this due to the fact that he
> had given his people a government which had made them
> healthy and happy. She stated that if large debts were put
> upon the Austrian and German people by the Allies, they
> would become Bolsheviks and that she had worked in con-
> nection with the Prefect of Police in Vienna, who she states is
> a fine man, giving him information with reference to the Bol-
> shevik movement in Austria, she claiming to be a confidential
> and intimate friend of the Bolshevik movement there.

Chamberlain went on to say that Bly was willing to provide
such information as the names of Bolsheviks serving as Red Cross
workers in Russia, what part the Bolsheviks played in the recent riots
in Austria, and how the Bolsheviks forward their propaganda to Eng-

land and the United States. The massacres of Jews in Galicia, she said, had resulted from the religious prejudice of Roman Catholics who believed all Jews were Bolsheviks. Of the repatriates who left Austria with her, two she identified as Bolsheviks had disappeared upon arrival in Paris. She had information that one had already arrived in England.

Bly offered these tantalizing bits and then stopped. She was willing to give more complete information on these matters only if an interview could be arranged with Colonel Edward M. House, Robert Lansing, or President Wilson himself.

Chamberlain concluded, "Miss Bly is a woman about 45 years, stout, fairly tall and of a rather masculine type. She is staying at the Hotel Montana with a little Austrian dancer and an Austrian violinist, who are both naturalized Americans, who have been in Austria for the entire war."

On February 6, Bly sat down in her room at the Hotel Montana to draft in her own hand another letter to President Wilson on stationery bearing a simple "NB" monogram. She explained how she had come from Vienna to describe to him personally the prevailing conditions in Austria, Hungary, Bohemia, and Germany. "I know all the different party leaders from the Monarchs down to the Bolschevicks [*sic*]," she said, "understand their aims and are acquainted with their intentions." She told Wilson that only he had the power—after hearing the information she planned to give him—to "save from destruction the peace and the cultivation of the world . . . After the revolution in Austria, I cabled you and later succeeded in sending you a letter. Every moment increases the danger in these lands. I pray you may soon find a few minutes for me. *You can save the world from the horrors of Bolschewickism.*"

The next day she was off to the General Headquarters of the American Expeditionary Forces at Chaumont for interviews with General John J. Pershing, commander of the force, and Brigadier General D. E. Nolan, the assistant chief of staff. Lieutenant Chamberlain had arranged the meetings at headquarters since Military Intelligence was having a hard time deciding what to do about her.

Bly was back in Paris the next day and, while walking down the rue de Rivoli at about three o'clock in the afternoon, saw the 700th

Motor Transport Company at work. She stopped one of the soldiers, John N. Moffitt, and asked him what they were doing. Moffitt replied that they were hauling coal for the Hotel du Louvre, where officers on leave in Paris were billeted. She told him she had just come from Vienna where conditions were terrible and where the Bolsheviks were holding full sway.

Private Moffitt found the encounter interesting enough to file a report on it with Military Intelligence. He reported Bly's view that Italy, France, and England were overrun with Bolsheviks and the United States was in peril.

> I asked her if she had ever been in Germany and she replied she had. I asked her how the German people as a whole felt towards the people of the United States and she replied that they had shed tears when our men first fell on the field of battle, or something to that effect. Then I said that I did not think that it was as much the German people as a whole that were to blame as it was the Kaiser. She replied that he was the finest man she had ever seen, that she knew him personally.
>
> She said that all France was not worth one American life. Said the Germans were more like our people in regard to their attitude towards women.

Moffitt said Bly was exercised over the fact that Canadian soldiers were not allowed in American canteens while the English were, and said this was because the English were afraid the Canadians would become too friendly with the United States and would wish to be annexed. "She seemed to talk more for the Bolsheviks than against them," Moffitt said. "[She said] some people had a lot of money and some were starving and you could not help wanting to keep on revolting."

In the meantime, Bly received a reply to her letter to President Wilson. It was from his confidential secretary, politely refusing her request for a personal interview with the president because of the deluge of work produced for him by the peace conference. "If you would care to send him a statement in writing of the information which you have secured, I am sure he will be glad to receive it," the letter said.

Bly responded by letter at once. "Mr. President," she began. "Believe me, if my communications were not more important than the Peace Conference for the safety of the world, I should not ask for a personal interview at this time. But of what use will be the Peace Conference or the League of Nations if meanwhile Central Europe becomes a second Russia? For once the middle countries are in the clutches of the Bolschewicks, *nothing* can save the rest of the world from the same dreadful fate. *The salvation of the world depends upon what you do now. Every hour is precious.*"

Bly impressed upon the president the urgency of her request to see him, summoning every persuasive wile:

> The truth regarding the Bolschewicks is not published any-where. No one dares print the real facts. Excepting Bolschewicks, the citizens of these countries, from the nobil-ity to the street-venders [*sic*], want to make a republic but they dare not make a real one. They are like a banker who opens his safe at the command of masked robbers. All the people believe in you and are depending on you for succor. The nobility, the college proffessors [*sic*], the business-people—even the beggars upon the street who see the Amer-ican flag upon my arm, say to me, "Ask President Wilson to save us!" The Bolschewicks fear you. They know you can destroy their power and prevent their increase. I cannot trust to paper what I can tell you in five minutes. I am convinced the fate of the world depends upon you or I would not urge.

In case her reputation had escaped the president's notice, Bly encouraged him to ask William McCombs of the Democratic National Committee for a personal reference. "He will tell you as he has told and written me—that only my influence upon him pre-vented him in Baltimore from withdrawing your name as candidate as you wired him to do." Or, she said, he might want to ask Generals Pershing and Nolan, whom she had met two days before. They would give him assurances, she said, "that I plead for five minutes only from the conviction that you can save the world from Bolschewick horrors. And that is the greatest of all deeds."

Bly's letter was sent on Sunday, February 9. That afternoon, as she told Wilson in the letter, she traveled back to General Headquarters in a car Nolan had sent for her. She told the president of her plan to return to the United States during the week. Since that was also his intention, she asked, "Perhaps you would give orders that I should be included in the passengers allowed to travel on the same vessel with you. This would allow you at your leisure on the way over to learn the details of all conditions in Central Europe. I am convinced this information will be most useful and valuable to you."

No such arrangements were made, nor was record of an answer to her letter found.

Bly did undergo a long debriefing at Chaumont with Nolan, the assistant chief of staff, and his assistant, Colonel A. B. Coxe. At that time the State Department was asked to investigate her citizenship status and sent inquiries back to Vienna. Bly remained at headquarters for three days, at the end of which Military Intelligence requested from headquarters a full report on what had been learned from Bly there "in order that our information in this case may be as complete as possible." Nolan clearly harbored no more doubts about Bly's American loyalties or the reasons for her pro-German views. He told the inquiring officer from intelligence, Lieutenant Colonel Cabot Ward, on February 15:

> She went to Austria in 1914 when war was declared by that country against Serbia. She was with the Austrian Army as a correspondent until our entry into the war, when she returned to Vienna and did not again go to the front. She had met and is on friendly terms with many of the government officials and men in public life. She has not corresponded with her friends or relatives in the United States and has received no news directly from the United States since our entry into the war. Her only information regarding our participation in the war has been received from German and Austrian sources. She is convinced that England brought on the war for commercial reasons and believes that we entered the war to recover the money we had advanced to the Allies. She is apparently a perfectly loyal American woman, who has

heard only the arguments of the Central Powers regarding the war for four years and who knows nothing of the Allied point of view.

Nolan went on to mention Bly's interest in having the United States provide food, clothing, and coal for the Austrians and the fact that she wanted to return to New York for business reasons, having recently learned by telegram that her company was in financial difficulties.

Ward of Military Intelligence responded again, confirming to Nolan that the Passport Bureau had been instructed to facilitate Bly's return to the United States "at the earliest possible date." He also explained why his office had investigated her so thoroughly:

> The question of this lady was also taken up with Col. [Ralph H.] Van Deman before your letter was received and he advised us that in agreement with G.H.Q. [General Headquarters] Miss BLY was to be allowed to go to the United States. At the same time this office showed to Colonel Van Deman reports which it had made on this subject and copies of which are enclosed with this letter [Lieutenant Chamberlain's and Private Moffitt's]. We feel that we were not in possession of all the facts which would show that Miss BLY is a loyal American woman, for up to the present our investigations had shown that she had strong pro-German leanings. In any case we are signalling her departure for the United States.

Immediately on her return from Chaumont, Bly wrote urgently to Bondy back in Vienna, asking him to pass her letter on to every major government official. "Bohemians, Poles, Roumanians, Jugoslavs and Italians have presented to the Peace Commission large colored maps showing the territories they claim," she wrote. "They assert the right of old boundary-lines and there is no one here to contradict them or make any claim for Austria. The commission would like to see what Austria claims and also copies of old maps showing boundaries." Bly said that she could recall seeing such maps and that a new one of what Austria claims should also be prepared. "You must furnish proofs of these old claims for the commission desires to be just and restore only boundery [*sic*] lines. To rob anyone or to be unjust is not the intention," she assured.

Bly urged that the maps and documents be sent under seal to the Austrian Legation at Berne, which should see that they were taken personally to the military attaché of the American Legation there. Bly said he would have instructions to forward them to the proper authorities in Paris. She asked Bondy to greet all her official friends and thank them again for "the continued kindness and courtesies I received during my four years in Austria." Although the letter's salutation was a formal "My dear Mr. Bondy:" in light of whom she intended to be reading his mail, she closed by saying,

> With renewed thanks to you who never failed in kindness and thoughtfulness to me and with best wishes for your success and welfare, believe me,
>
> very sincerely yours
> NELLIE BLY.

Bondy forwarded Bly's letter to State Chancellor Renner, who passed it on to the appropriate parties. At the same time, Renner asked Foreign Secretary Otto Bauer to explain why Austria's maps were not at the Peace Conference. Bauer gave a detailed description of all the relevant documentation that was in Paris and to whom it had gone. "Moreover," Bauer said, "it is a well-known fact that a special American study commission under the directorship of a Professor [Archibald S.] Coolidge is in charge of procuring all material needed for the peace negotiations in Paris. All maps and other material have been made available to this Commission as well. This has been done to an extent that even caused repeated requests to reduce the material to the absolutely necessary."

Bauer concluded that Bly's "complaints" were based on incorrect information. "We have to leave it for you to decide," he wrote Renner, "if and to what extent an illumination would be in order, conceivably in combination with expression of appreciation for the good intentions of the complaining person."

With that, on Renner's behalf, the section chief of the State Chancellery sent Bondy a note of thanks for passing Bly's letter along and informed him that the maps and documents she mentioned had been sent to the American Mission. Graciously, he added, "Should it be possible for you to get in touch with Miss Bly in some way, I would very much appreciate it if you could convey to her our warmest gratitude for this recent manifestation of her friendly attitude towards German Austria."

With American clearance to travel, Bly boarded the SS *Lorraine* at Bordeaux for New York on February 22, 1919. Two days later, despite the unequivocal opinions advanced by Brigadier General D. E. Nolan at General Headquarters, Military Intelligence in Paris cabled its Washington headquarters to signal that Bly would be arriving in New York on that ship. By letter the same day, the intelligence officer following her case, Lieutenant Colonel Cabot Ward, sent his Washington office a copy of the earlier, more suspicious reports on Bly submitted by Lieutenant Chamberlain of the Passport Bureau and by Private Moffitt. Ward told his counterparts in Washington that the reports demonstrated Bly's "pro-Germanism and her attitude toward Bolshevism," on top of which she was "outspoken in her opinions going to the extent of being aggressive and defiant."

Unsure if she should be granted permission to return to the United States, Ward explained that his office had referred the question to Brigadier General Nolan at General Headquarters and to Colonel Van Deman. Both, he said, "were of the opinion that she would do less harm in America than in France where at this time tendencies such as she has manifested may be serious in their consequences." This, of course, had not been the view of Bly from headquarters at all.

❧

Word of Bly's departure was cabled immediately from Military Intelligence at the port to General Headquarters in Washington. From Washington, Colonel J. M. Dunn forwarded the information to Captain J. B. Trevor in New York, adding, "Although residents of New York, Mayflower descendants and original members of the Pilgrim

Society will remember Nellie's activities, our files however are not sufficiently antiquated to furnish any information." Two days later, the Bordeaux office sent another wire reminding Washington that Bly was "believed to be pro-German." Dunn passed that information on to New York as well.

Trevor met Bly at Military Control House in New York following her arrival in New York February 28, and on March 6, he dutifully filed a report to Washington headquarters on what he had learned. The report largely repeated information already passed along to Washington from Paris, although Trevor had her arriving aboard the SS *Rochambeau* instead of the *Lorraine*. He added several new details:

> Nellie is a bit hazy as to her exact reason for visiting the Central Empire, and still more hazy with regard to prolonging her stay there even after the entrance of her native land into the world war, and there is no doubt as to Nellie being a bit pro-German. Nellie is an avowed hater of England and all that is English, and out of this hatred of the land of the Lion and the Unicorn grew her hope for the success of German arms. She avows and declares, however, that the United States of America is nearest and dearest to her heart, and that her reason for returning to this country was to save us from the perils of Bolshevism.

He went on to explain how Bly's unrequited desire to see soldiers under fire drove her to Austria at the end of July 1914, that she had visited the front, "and that she did not mind at all whether or not she was killed because of her discouragement over her financial affairs in this country previous to her departure." She had told Trevor of her travels around Austria-Hungary and Germany between 1914 and the latter part of January 1919, when she left for Paris.

> She maintains steadfastly that even after the entrance of the United States into the war she was treated with the utmost courtesy both by the Austrians and the Germans, and pointing to an American flag which she wears conspicuously on

her fulsome left arm emphatically declared that she had worn
it throughout Germany and Austria, even though her native
land was then embattled against the Heinies.

She told of her efforts to give President Wilson the benefit of
her advice and how the Austrians had encouraged and enabled her to
do so, how she had laid this information before General Pershing,
who, in turn, had put her in touch with Generals Nolan and Coxe.
Her report so impressed Coxe, she told Trevor, that he assigned a
stenographer to make a verbatim transcript of her remarks while
promising never to reveal their source. "We are hereby violating that
agreement" was Trevor's facetious aside.

As to specifics, Bly told Trevor that while in Austria she
"enjoyed the rare and distinct privilege of being in the inner councils
of the Bolshevik leaders," that the leader of the movement was the
scion of a wealthy family and "somewhat of a writer." Trevor reported
the man's name as "Kiss," possibly a misspelled reference to the journalist Egon Erwin Kisch. Trevor said Bly "avow[ed] and declare[d]
that one Bauer, Secretary of the Austrian Foreign Office, is one of the
ring leaders of the Bolshevist group in Austria" and claimed that both
men had entrusted her with valuable secrets. Trevor's report went on:

> What these secrets were Nellie did not dilate upon. How-
> ever, she states that the Bolshevist headquarters in Austria is
> sending forth forty agents amply provided with funds and
> with a diversified supply of passports, their objective being
> the United States; that the Bolsheviki feel that if they can
> win the United States to their cause they have conquered the
> world. Nellie could not be specific as to the routes to be
> taken by these agents but was certain that they would obtain
> entrance into the United States. She praised the cleverness of
> the leaders of the Bolshevist cause, and declared that they
> were not a lot of long-haired, dirty peasants, but were astute
> and clever diplomats.

Trevor decided not to "bore" headquarters with Bly's detailed
plan for defeating Bolshevism, but he summarized:

Suffice to say that her main weapon is the throwing of a line of troops along the Russian frontier to cut off the passage of agents to and fro, and so having prevented the Bolshevik agents from entering or departing from Russia that the cause would burn itself out of the late Czar's land without spreading into the other countries of Europe. She warns us that France is soon to succumb to Bolshevism and that our day is not far distant. Nellie is eager to devote her remaining days, and give her life if necessary to putting a stop to Bolshevism and is eager to get in touch with such Government officials as may wish to make use of her efficient self, to send her back to the Dual Empire and from there into Russia where she can get into the confidence of the leaders.

Trevor said Bly could be found at the McAlpin Hotel for the time being but that "her funds have been so dissipated that she will have to seek cheaper quarters." In this connection, he added,

Miss Bly, whose real name is Mrs. Elizabeth Y. [*sic*] Seaman, was arrested yesterday on the charge of perjury and interfering with justice and held in $1,000 bail in the Federal Court in Brooklyn. It will be recalled that back in 1914, previous to her departure abroad, Mrs. Seaman was president of the Ironclad [*sic*] Manufacturing Co., of Brooklyn which went into bankruptcy and brought Nellie into considerable prominence in the courts. It was charged that she was secreting books and documents so that the Commissioner in Bankruptcy could not get possession of them.

Back at Chaumont, a brief item in *The New York Times* about Bly's federal court troubles renewed General Nolan's interest in her. On April 29, he wrote to his director in Washington, Brigadier General M. Churchill, seeking "all of the information readily obtainable in New York regarding the history, antecedents and reputation of Miss Bly." Churchill replied, sending along a copy of Trevor's glib report from New York accompanied by a single comment: "It is our opinion that Miss Bly's aspirations should not be taken seriously."

༼ༀ༽

The Brooklyn Daily Eagle said Bly, garbed in silks and fur, was "just like her old self" to spring a sensation after debarking from the *Lorraine*. She submitted to the interview with Captain Trevor of Military Intelligence at the Customshouse, then surrendered to U.S. Marshal James M. Power on the five-year-old indictment stemming from the Iron Clad's demise. Bly found herself before U.S. District Court Judge Thomas Chatfield once again, pleading not guilty to charges of willfully obstructing justice and failing to obey an order of Judge Julius Mayer, who had replaced Chatfield in the bankruptcy case. After a short discussion, Bly was released on $1,000 bail, and an April court date was set. She was still wearing her American flag pin. Asked about her mission in enemy Austria, Bly said it was a secret, "locked here in my heart." The reporter said she could "still overpower one with her striking personality."

When it became clear that she was unwelcome at the home of her mother and Albert at 332 East Sixteenth Street in Brooklyn— Jane had died while Bly was abroad—Bly went to stay with her brother Harry at 156 Clarkson Avenue, also in Brooklyn. Soon after, she moved to the Hotel McAlpin, only a short walk from her old Manhattan brownstone. The brownstone, forfeited in a mortgage default, had been targeted for demolition and new industrial development on the formerly elegant residential street.

The McAlpin was a commercial hotel but with plenty of its own panache. The reception rooms were gilded and mirrored, and twenty-six tapestries depicting the history of New York City adorned its walls. There were exercise rooms and even a "silent" floor for guests who needed to sleep in the daytime. Bly took a small two-room suite, Number 1805, but later moved to different rooms.

It was clear from her return that Albert now felt he had full entitlement to the barrel company and would bar any attempt by his sister to regain control. Mary Jane's suit in federal court against the Alien Property Custodian moved ahead. Bly was in another enervating legal mire, this time with a cast of characters sure to create real heartbreak. What followed was the inevitable despair, and Bly's attendant surge of will to fight once more.

819 Woolworth Building
March 29, 1919

New York c/o Harry C Cochrane

Dear Q.O.

Thank you for your very kind letter and forgive me for the sad one I must write you. I returned after all these years to find my mother whom I cared for so tenderly since my early youth is under the evil influence of my brother Albert P. Cochrane and a band of conspirators—(lawyers). Before leaving, I put my last property in my mother's name under an agreement whereby she was to return it to me on my demand. [T]his agreement I left with other valuable papers in a safe deposit box to which my mother had access. This box was discontinued, all my papers stolen, and my mother claims the property was paid for by her money and that I own nothing. A man running my company mother has put in at a salary of $7,800 and a 4% commission which in the poorest year was $20,000. My mother has been drawing dividends of $1,500 weekly. *I am penniless.* She not only refuses to give back my property but has deeded it to Albert Cochrane, my drunken brother whom I supported for 25 years. I have exactly $3.65 and a trunk full of Paris evening dresses! These I shall sell to replenish the $3.65—that is, if I can. Can't you ask Charlie Rook [a Pittsburgh editor]—who wrote me a nice letter to Austria, if he can't give me some sort of a position or accept letters from New York for the Sunday addition [*sic*]?

And dear Q.O., can't you write me what you know of my supporting my family since I began on the *Dispatch* [.] You have talked to mother and me enough to know that mother had nothing and that I was the sole support—You visited us in New York and we all talked to you then. Have you seen them since I left? And you talked to Jeff Cochrane [Bly's half brother in Pittsburgh, Thomas Jefferson Cochrane] and knew from him doubtless family conditions. Please try to recall everything and help me by writing me all you remember and know.

I am so glad you are well and cheerful. You see the sad, sad ending of your kid! I have been betrayed by my employees and now by my mother! I mean to die—I would have kill [*sic*] myself at once but I have a duty to my dear brother Harry to perform and until that is completed, I must live. And then you may write of the kid who wrote an orphan girl letter and got work which enabled that orphan girl to care for her family and how at last betrayed by her mother, she died. I struggled all my life to gain comfort and independence for my mother and that mother deserts and crushes me. Forgive me, I can't help but pour my news out to you. You can reach me through Harry, address at the top of letter. Live happy and long and well and never forget the affection of your kid

Nellie Bly

Within nine days, Bly had filed a complaint against Albert in Flatbush Police Court, charging that in July 1914, shortly before her departure for Europe, she stored $5,000 worth of machinery for manufacturing dental supplies in the plant of the American Steel Barrel Company, which Albert sold without permission, pocketing the proceeds. At the same time, Harry complained that while he was still living at the East Sixteenth Street house, he had stored $1,900 worth of silk bought in Japan on a world trip the family took in 1907, which Albert had disposed of or sold.

A week later, Albert was arrested, formally charged, and held for the grand jury in Flatbush Court on $1,000 bail. In retaliation, Albert charged Bly with malicious mischief, for which she too was arraigned before Magistrate Mortimer S. Brown. Albert claimed that Bly had deliberately destroyed a crayon drawing of him by cutting away the bottom half of the face. Bly pleaded not guilty. On the stand, she explained that she had gone to live with Harry because she was hungry and penniless and "I wanted food and could not get it at my mother's home." Bly was asked if she could identify her mother's handwriting, and she said she could sometimes but not always because it had so frequently been forged. She did not say by whom.

The next day Magistrate Brown dropped the charges against Bly, despite her own mother's testimony against her. The case against

Albert was heard May 22, but the grand jury declined to indict him, accepting his version that he had acquired both the silk and the dental machinery in legitimate business transactions.

At the same time, Bly was busy trying to obtain from the State Department a copy of the cable Mary Jane had sent her in December 1918, in Vienna about the barrel company's troubles. She was gearing up for her part as an additional defendant in the case Mary Jane had brought against the Alien Property Custodian. This concerned Oscar Bondy's ownership of the voting trust certificate for the barrel company's shares of stock, which gave him effective control of the firm. Bly had won a court order allowing her to participate in the suit before her she got back to New York, probably through attorney Nathan's good offices. On May 21, the old perjury indictment was dismissed in federal court in Brooklyn. Even the district attorney's office could see it didn't matter anymore.

All that settled, Bly needed money until the barrel company dispute was resolved and maybe even after that. She needed work. The obvious place to turn was back to Arthur Brisbane, who gave her a job as an editorial page columnist on *The New York Evening Journal* at a salary of $100 a week. It was half of what she had commanded as a writer thirty years earlier.

Her first column ran May 24, 1919, the day after Albert was cleared of those internecine charges in the dental machinery and silk disputes. It was she, not her brother, who inspired the lead sentence: "A man may be down but he's never out."

❧❧

, 7 Hurt in Jersey Arsenal

☆ ☆ ☆ ☆ ☆ ☆ ☆ ☆ ☆ ☆

BLY SETTLES OURT OF BABY'S

☆ ☆ ☆ ☆ ☆ ☆ ☆ ☆ ☆

Coldest De____ 0 Years

The Real Baby" an____
Three Pri____
Tangle ____
from Des____

MRS. LISA RECOGNIZED AS REAL MOTHER

Mrs. Wentz Relinquishes Child to Authorities Pending Legal Disposition of Case

"Love O' Mike," the baby claimed by Mrs. August Wentz as her kidnaped son, was taken

MRS. LI____

MRS. AU____

HARRY LISA.

Photos by International.

---

cial Refuses Raise; ys $400 a Year Is Enough

ed Anderson, secretary of the ey., N. J. Board of Health, refused an increase in sal. The Board voted to raise his which is now $400 a year. e job isn't worth any more y," Anderson said. "The holds only twelve meet a year, and it would be an tice to the townspeople to t an increase in pay." erson was appointed secre f the health body four years Previously he had served as ber of the Kearney Town

RAL DECKER GIVEN VORCE FOR DESERTION

PORT, R. C. Dec. 18.—Real the Key West Naval Station, ated an absolute divorce from , Mary, Ida. by Judge Doran Superior Court, on the grounds ful desertion.

ral Decker stated his wife fe come to Newport after the in 1912. He went to Wash where his wife was living, and again asked her to come port. She refused, and since ay had lived apart.

E JACK" AND STILL AIDED IN NEW JERSEY

BRUNSWICK, Dec. 18.—A several jugs of New Jersey Jack" cider was found in the t of a dwelling at No. 10 street last night, according to ice. The discovery was made g a fire which broke out in rtition around the still. The e soon under control, and the und in the supposed coal bin the fire broke out, was con the police say.

00,000 CANADA'S HARE FROM CANTEENS

WA, Ontario. Dec. 18.—Lieu Colonel Cherry, of the pay and ranch of the Canadian army, here to-day from England ,000,000, Canada's share of the of the canteen system of the expeditionary force. A dis expected dividing the money the Canadian soldiers at as time.

SCHANEL'S ELECTION MAKE HIM PRESIDENT

, Dec. 18.—Paul Deschanel elected President of the er of Deputies to-day. It is be e possible that this victory the way for his election to idency of France if Premier eau declines to be a candi Deschanel was opposed to one other candidate.

DALMENY WINS IVORCE IN SCOTLAND

URGH, Dec. 18.—Lord Dal ho fought with distinction in ld War, got a divorce in the to-day. Lady Dal s accused of desertion and defend the suit. Lord Dal es the heir of the late Earl

OAD TRAFFIC IN EAST AGAIN NORMAL

INGTON, Dec. 18.—All rail affic east of Chicago is now the Railroad Administration et to-day. All trains taken g the coal strike have been

NDED BRITISH SHIP IS SAVED BY TUGS

L LOOKOUT, L. I., Dec. 18.— itish freighter, Grange Park,

MAN KILLED, 20 FIREMEN FROZEN

Hundreds Driven to Streets, Thinly Clad—"L" and Surface Lines Blocked.

One man was killed, a score of firemen sustained frozen hands, families from fifty dwellings were driven out into the zero weather and two elevated and a surface car lines were tied up for more than an hour as the result of a fire to-day in Deutsch Brothers' furniture store at No. 1481 Broadway, Brooklyn.

Although the blaze finally was confined to the three-story brick building in which the store is located, it was necessary to sound three alarms in order to get sufficient fire apparatus to combat the flames because of frozen water mains.

When news of the three alarms reached Mayor Hylan, who lives several blocks away, he hurried to the scene and watched the firemen in their battle against the fire and cold.

USED KEROSENE IN FURNACE

James Swsling, sixty, of No. 116 Penn street, Brooklyn, but his life in the fire. He was employed as a watchman at the store. He was at tempting to start a fire in the fur nace in the cellar of the building. He threw kerosene on the fire to make it burn more quickly Swsling caused an explosion which set fire to his clothes and the building. His body was found in the waterfilled cellar after the flames had been extinguished.

The blaze in the furniture store was first seen by one of three porters em ployed there. He dashed to the street and notified Patrolman Garvin of the Ralph avenue station. Garvin turned in two alarms and called for addi tional police aid. Reserves from the Gates avenue and Ralph avenue sta tions were sent.

Fire Chief James O'Hara arrived soon after the first fire apparatus and upon seeing that the water mains were frozen turned in a third alarm.

Fifteen or twenty firemen had their hands frozen and ambulances from St. Mary's and the Bushwick Hos pitals came thuzinted from. Several firemen had their hands frozen to the street or quickly aid the falling water freeze in its zero temperature.

A photographer had a remarkable escape from death. He was asleep in the Administration building which was close to the experimental labor atory, but escaped with a bad shaking.

100 Families Flee Fire in Dancing School with Mercury 1 Above Zero

With the mercury 1 above zero more than one hundred families were driven into the street shortly after 1 a. m. to-day, when fire broke out in Remy's Dancing of the upper part of the Nos. 913-91 ents corner clad and belongings.

(column center, bottom photo)

rream of water upon the fire.

The explosion occurred shortly after midnight and was very heavy. It broke windows in Dover and many people hurried into the street, some of them recalling the wild prediction that the world was coming to an end.

The explosion occurred on the ex perimental laboratory from an un known cause. In this laboratory ex periments were made with shells and explosives. The structure was badly damaged. Fire quickly spread to the carpenter shop, machine shop and several smaller structures.

LOSS MAY BE MILLION.

No official estimate of the damage could be obtained. Unofficial esti mates put it variously from $500,000 to $1,000,000.

Private McCormick's abdomen and upper part of his legs were badly torn by a heavy shell fragment while he stood fifty feet from the burning ad ministration building, where shells were frequently exploding. (He was carried on a door into the hastily rigged up emergency hospital and was later removed to the Deer Gen eral Hospital, where he died. His home was in Akron, O. He was re cently married.

Pending the compilation of an ac curate list, the army officers declined to make known the names of the in jured. Two of them are Private Paul Green, of Boston, Mass, and Private Luce, address not obtainable. Three other men besides McCormick were taken to the General Hospital. One had a badly cut head and the other was wounded in the leg.

MARINES BRAVE DEATH.

Immediately after the explosion, Colonel F. H. Miles, Jr., commander of the arsenal, took charge of the fight against the flames. He first di rected the efforts of the soldiers and civilian guard. These were quickly reinforced by marines from barracks at the naval powder depot which is within a comparatively short distance of the arsenal.

The marines upheld the traditions

NEW CLUE AIDS PRISONERS IN DANSEY CASE

ATLANTIC CITY, Dec. 18.—Prosecu tor Edmund C. Gaskill and County Detective Charles Wilson have given out portions of new evidence in the "Billy" Dansey death mystery which may clear Charles S. White and Mrs. Esther L. Jones, held in jail at Mays Landing.

Mr. Gaskill has admitted that this evidence apparently establishes the innocence of the prisoners and Mrs. Susan White, for whom a warrant

Baby Campaigners in Paris War on Birth Control Leaders

PARIS, Dec. 18.—War was de clared on advocates of birth con trol today by leaders of the "more and better babies" movement. Followers of the birth control campaign had placarded billboards with advertisements calling for a baby strike. Their opponents made a tour of the billboards, tearing down all the posters and destroy ing them.

M. Michel, who is the father of six children, declared that the birth controllers aim to depopu late France.

TRAIL NOW L WA

By Internatio WASHINGTO General Palmer the investigation preme Court de sued them for hi The Attorney-G with all develop immediately in from the West.

The scope of tigation and the into will easily several cases of the called on to ernment agenc These agen in advance of down, are of hands and co and the state lands used to whose discover at the Departm There are six law to

RAVE COLD GET N. J. DEER

N. J., Dec. 19.—The of hunters in the Blue Pahuaquarry township and Blairstown townsh ships, in spite of the cold weather. Only buck deer may be shot, accord ing to the law.

There are fifteen or twenty game wardens of the State on guard in Pahuaquarry township. Mayor Harry Searles brought home a two-year-old buck on Tuesday night.

PREMIER BORDEN MAY BE AMBASSADOR HERE

OTTAWA, Dec. 18.—The report that Premier Sir Robert Borden is to

---

(bottom center)

---

bill to the east of the arsenal. The two reservations join. There are some sixty large buildings on the Naval Reservation, most of them be ing used to store large quantities of powder. None of them was affected by the explosion.

The fire was a brilliant sight to one approaching it from Dover. The ex perimental laboratory, which was a one-story brick building, was flaming from every window, and fire was rising through the hole where the roof used to be. On each side were

sel. G. Arthur Boltz, will apply to Supreme Court Justice Swayze at Newark to-morrow for a writ of ha beas corpus. The prosecutor does not expect to be present, but his office will be represented.

NEW ARRESTS EXPECTED.

Detectives representing the Prose cutor and the White family are placing together links in the new chain of facts which are expected to result in new arrests.

Two mysterious men figure in the

13

✢ ✢

The Journal

BLY'S COMEBACK WARRANTED A FOUR-COLUMN HEADLINE emblazoned across the top of the editorial page of *The New York Evening Journal*, with her byline in type as large as the title. In bold-face italics spread across the same four columns, the newspaper with one of the largest circulations in the country and still the great bastion of sensationalist reporting, proudly reintroduced its latest recruit:

> *Nellie Bly, the famous woman writer, noted the world over for her feats of journalism, has engaged to give the readers of The Evening Journal the benefit of her keen observation and her experience, gained in every country in the world.*
>
> *Miss Bly has recently returned from Europe. During the great war she was literally in the thick of it — sharing with the soldiers of many armies their fortunes in the trenches of the first line.*
>
> *This is the first of a series which Miss Bly will write. Her subjects will be various, and to each she will bring the human sympathy and keen insight for which she is so well known.*

The subject that first grabbed Bly's attention was a doughnut drive the Salvation Army was sponsoring for the dual purpose of saving mankind and raising money. "The whole idea one gets in this drive is man and doughnuts, doughnuts and man; to aid man, to save man!" she wrote. No one at the Salvation Army, she pointed out, had mentioned the salvation of woman. "Of her no one has written those hope-inspiring words: A woman may be down but she's never out. No, and if one dare acknowledge it, a half-formed, unexpressed idea exists that a woman down is a woman out—forever! Or, if she is not 'out' she will be 'out' finally, just because she is down."

The inspiration for Bly's choice of theme was obvious, but its tone was a far cry from the despondent outpouring to Erasmus Wilson just two months before. Her resolve had returned. A renewed determination prevailed over her otherwise debilitating personal circumstances. She went on, "Among our millions of women hundreds of thousands get down. Working women lose their jobs, wives lose their husbands, widows lose their money. Fate finds innumerable ways to strike. The more reputable the woman the bitterer the blow. Her decency is her greatest handicap. No one is helping a pure woman stay pure. Not until she is 'out,' and only then will she find aid."

A week later, Bly was urging men whose hair had gone gray to take their cue from the Europeans and dye it dark. Appearances count, she said; dyeing one's hair would be no different than replacing a missing tooth. She also became a great promoter of the new field of plastic surgery.

For June, she wrote only two editorial page columns, one at the beginning of the month on the vital need for everyone over the age of eighteen to have a home and a little ground, and the other at the end of the month on the importance of constant fresh air for babies' health. In the middle of the month, Brisbane had her deployed the way he best liked to see her work. She was sent to Toledo, Ohio, to cover the training and upcoming heavyweight boxing championship match between titleholder Jess Willard and his challenger, young Jack Dempsey, "giving her own impressions from the viewpoint of her sex," according to *The Journal*'s front page introduction of Bly's reports.

Her first piece put her back on the front page. It was an interview with Dempsey, a man with "the brown questioning eyes of a very big, good-natured boy." She learned about his Colorado upbringing in a family of eleven children and how he felt about boxing and the world. She hadn't lost her penchant for injecting her own views into the story. Waiting for him to arrive for the interview, she thought to herself:

> Would I hesitate and feel dumb and at a disadvantage in the presence of a great big fighting machine? I had been with soldiers in the trenches and had seen them fight and die; I had been lost in pity and in the horror of the thing; I had felt the helplessness of humanity, thousands and thousands butchered and dying, without will or volition, at the command of a few. I have sat through bull fights and watched the poor, helpless animals having their entrails gouged out and being forced to fight by man until they dropped dead; I have seen roosters thrown into a pit and forced into a death fight. I have seen dogs set one upon the other in a death struggle. All instituted by man, planned by man, and carried out by man—for sport!

She was fascinated by Dempsey and was sure she wanted him to win until she met Willard, who caused a similar reaction. Her interviews with the two fighters were as much about her experiences getting in to see them—and how she felt once she had—as they were about the men. It was her favorite technique, but without the full force of its old appeal. The pace of the age had quickened, and a far less ponderous journalistic style had come into fashion. Women finally had won the right to vote, and along with suffrage had come increased opportunities in many fields, newspapering among them. The feisty-woman-braves-man's-world aspect of Bly's reporting had lost its novelty. Still, *The Journal* trusted in what it hoped was the enduring ability of her byline to draw and hold a segment of the newspaper-reading public. The editors approached her copy as if she were the star she had always been, bouncing her to the front page with notable frequency, as they had done for Dorothy Dix and her legendary "sob sister" coverage of the major court trials while she was on the Hearst payroll. Front page play was as significant for a woman reporter in 1919 as it had been thirty years earlier.

In Toledo with the male sports reporters, Bly did all the usual stories associated with a major upcoming sports event but brought her own perspective to the task. She watched the fighters spar and observed that football was more brutal than boxing. She watched them train, and didn't faint when blood was drawn. She told the readers what it was about Willard's training quarters that kept everyone laughing. Sick with bronchitis or stomach or heart trouble—depending on which diagnosis she was prepared to accept—Bly arranged for Willard's personal physician to attend her. He put her on a diet of cantaloupe, stewed rhubarb, and orange juice, cutting out everything else.

The fight itself, on the Fourth of July, 1919, became another in Bly's long string of firsts. It also put her on page 1 again, with a long jump onto page 3.

TOLEDO, July 5—The king is dead. Long live the king!

Success is dragging all the world at its chariot wheels.

Defeat, forgotten and abandoned, is hauled away in an ambulance.

This fallen champion, who lies within, perhaps does not hear the groans of disapproval which the sight of the ambulance brings from the crowd.

Willard's day is done.

Dempsey's day has begun.

The new moon which hung in a cloudless blue sky, on the left of the fighting ring, boded good fortune for Dempsey, who faced it, and ill-luck for Willard, whose back was to it.

I, the first newspaperwoman in the world to sit with the press and telegraphers at the end of the boxing ring, felt what?

I expected to be frowned upon and to feel like a stranger thrust upon a family Christmas party. But everybody was so nice; the telegraph operators became messenger boys for me; the ushers brought pails of water that I might drink from the edge and not be thirsty; the newspapermen

did their loyal best to show me they were glad I was there
and were at my service.

She had the obligatory victory interview with Dempsey, conducted the day after the fight. It ran on the sports page three days
later with fine display.

While Bly was gone, letters from readers responding to her first
stories arrived at *The Journal* offices. They gave birth to an advice column of sorts that would run on the editorial page whenever Bly ran
short of opinions or exclusive interviews worthy of placement up
front. Bly's column was modeled in part on the prototypical advice-
to-the-lovelorn column which Dorothy Dix had developed and
written for *The Journal* from 1901 to 1917. Dix left the Hearst organization to join the Wheeler Newspaper Syndicate, commanding
even higher recompense. She got her start in journalism in 1896, as
Bly was on her way out. Her real name was Elizabeth Meriwether
Gilmer.

Bly had long ago made a specialty of the jailhouse confessions of
accused avengers and murderesses, from Eva Hamilton to the
Shawangunk Mountain slayer, Lizzie Halliday. Such reporting had
been a staple for many years for the "sob sisters" who followed Bly's
early success. These included Dix, "Annie Laurie" (Winifred Black),
and Ada Patterson. Although Bly was making steel barrels during
the heyday of sob-sisterhood, she could still jerk tears with the best.
In fact, other than Bly, only Dix had managed to achieve the stature
of front page *maestra* of the huge sensation story.

As an early assignment for *The Journal*, Bly interviewed seventeen-year-old Edward O'Brien, a clerk in a Wall Street trading firm
who took a hammer and bludgeoned to death his aged, miserly boss,
Gardiner C. Hull. Not only did young O'Brien graphically describe
for Bly the slaying and his reactions to it but she extracted from him
the sorry tale of his life to date. His father had left home when he was
small, and his mother farmed him out to a state children's home, as
she did all his siblings who were too young to be put to work.

"Do you know," he began impressively. "I never can get
a vision of Hull's face. I don't know why. Lots of times I lie in

my bed and try to get Hull's face, but I can't get a vision of him, before or after. Queer, isn't it?"

"But you remember how the blood looked as it gushed over his face," I reminded him.

"Yes, and how glassy his eyes were and how they stared knowing at me, but his face—I can't see it. I turned back as I left the office to look at him. He was still sitting in his chair. I wondered why he did not fall, and then I thought what a cruel guy I had been not to think of my mother or Mrs. Hull."

Bly was convinced, and O'Brien confirmed for her, that all his troubles started because he didn't have a father or a real home. "I tell you we guys hate everything," he said. "We hate what ruins us. We could kill with joy. We rob and feel we are not getting revenge enough. We help each other rob. We want some kind of satisfaction. Our own bitterness and hatred burns us up. It makes us hate and thirst for revenge. We kill. We don't kill enough. The boys of New York are killed—their souls, their lives—you don't understand."

If he had had a father, he said, the father would have paid attention to him; he would never have degenerated as he did. "But who'll save the homeless boy?" he asked.

Bly said his emotional outburst left her trembling. Then she told him,

"You must die . . . You can before you die tell your life's struggles to the world. It will help the lives of other boys. The good world will hear and reply. Then you will not have died in vain and the good your revelations will bring about will help atone in heaven for your sin. Spare no one. Tell the evils which beset the homeless boy."

He looked earnestly and questioningly into my eyes.

"I shall do it," he said. "They will kill me if I tell, but I shall tell."

A new idea was taking shape in Bly's mind. When a woman who had fallen on desperate financial circumstances wrote asking Bly if she should give up her two-year-old son, "Jack O'Hearts," Bly did not hesitate to advise against it. "Don't do it!" she wrote. "If you could have sat with me in a cell last Sunday listening to the life story of the seventeen-year-old murderer, Edward O'Brien, you would fold Jack O'Hearts in your arms and keep him there through thick and thin. Don't—as you value his soul—let him get away from you. You brought him into the world. On you rests the responsibility of his future, of his weal or woe." Bly didn't stop there. She offered to help the mother find work near where the child could get daytime care.

To the woman who filed divorce papers after catching her husband in an affair with another woman, Bly advised, "Can't you make up? Don't you think perhaps you failed somewhere and that led to your husband's falseness? Were you not jealous and 'nagging'? You were suspicious or you would never have thought of following."

In the meantime, the stories of poor little Jack O'Hearts and the unfaithful husband brought in scores of letters, from some wanting to give the child a home, from others seeking jobs like the one Bly offered to find for little Jack's mother, from those affirming her advice that a wife had to stay a coquette and keep her husband guessing to stop his interest in her from flagging. She found herself an instant clearinghouse for fractured families in distress. She invited more:

Dear Troubled Mother: There must be some one who will provide a place for you and baby. I am so glad you love it and will stick to it. Tell me what work you can do besides clerical work—something you know, or have an aptitude for or wish to learn. Write me confidentially. Tell me everything, I shall not publish your letter. I only publish this one to open some heart to you—which I am confident it will. Write me and let me help you and be your friend.

Whatever her motivation—and her need to feel vital and important was certainly part of it—the question Bly always seemed to ask of God and life was how she could do her part to save the world from wherever she happened to be standing. This was true as a young reporter, as an industrialist, as a war correspondent, as an expatriate in Vienna, as an American in Paris in the aftermath of war. Now, with the power of empathy in a column for a major daily newspaper, armed with her experience with helping widows and orphans of war in Austria and her need for a place in history, Bly found herself pointed in a brand-new direction. She embraced it.

　　　　　　　　　　　　　　　　✧

The letters poured in, from those with plans to improve the subways, from those needing jobs, from those needing homes, from those wanting wives or husbands, from those offering advice to others who had already written in, and from those just wanting a chance to tell their own life stories, sad or heroic. There was even one from a woman who wanted to know how to get a song she had written published.

By the end of the summer of 1919, Bly had turned the column into an occasional pulpit. At what point, and on what basis, she had summoned the moral authority of the ages is not clear, but "Am I my brother's keeper?" was the question she posed in her piece on August 25. Her answer, decidedly yes. And who was brother? "The whole wide world of mankind: good, bad and indifferent." And women who were down on their luck, she said, were most in need of this universal guardianship.

In addition to the human misery she was encountering in her work day after day, Bly may have been alluding to her own sense of abandonment by old friends when she wrote:

> It is a story as old as the hills that a man in hard luck loses all his friends. He is avoided and shunned. Everybody wishes to forget him. No one holds out a helping hand.
>
> With women it is even worse. Misfortune of any character sends all friends scattering like chickens pursued by a hawk! The one who needs aid is treated as if she had a deadly plague.

The giving and passing along of advice became the staple of Bly's work for *The Journal*. The clearinghouse sideline kept her busy enough to warrant the hiring of secretaries; Beatrice Alexander was one of them. They, assisted by legions of well-meaning volunteers, crowded the little suite at the McAlpin at all times of day, helping to sort Bly's mail. The column had spawned a makeshift nursery for abandoned babies Bly was attempting to place with stable families, and she was trying to get a "Mother's Club" off the ground, a support group for women with children and limited resources. *The Journal* provided a private office for Bly in its city room at 238 William Street, but she rarely appeared there. Ishbel Ross, writing in 1936, said *Journal* colleagues remembered seeing Bly brush through the city room, mysterious and anachronistic in her large hat with the chenille-dotted veil, but no longer the object of very much speculation. Bly never socialized with the sassy new generation of young women reporters in their increasingly short skirts, nor did they show much interest in her. Women in the newsroom by this point had become commonplace. To them, Bly was not so much icon as relic. The reporter Mildred Gilman, who went to work for *The Journal* in 1927, said she had no recollection of anyone at the paper ever even mentioning that Bly had been a member of the staff.

This was of no consequence to Bly. She had learned long ago that success did not depend on the adulation of her peers, although, like everyone, she wanted their respect. But Bly had defined a specific and highly receptive audience for her work. She tapped into the social issues and concerns that affected *The Journal*'s vast working-class readership. She had Brisbane's imprimatur, which was all that really mattered.

On September 20, 1919, a large boxed, boldface announcement ran at the head of the column:

IMPORTANT:

Dear Friends—I receive hundreds of letters and shall answer each one, but only in rotation. Consequently it is necessary that friends needing immediate assistance must send name and address, which I shall never publish or divulge, but preserve forever in sacred secrecy. I need immediately address of "L.M.," "A Failure" (a disowned boy consumptive in hospital), "Herbert's Mother," "L.M.G.," "M.R.A.," "P.Z.," "M.L.D.," "V.D.H.," "Lonesome," "F.S.," all those who wish to adopt babies, and those who have written about work.

On October 2, Bly reported in another boxed announcement over the column that the backlog of letters awaiting replies was up to eight weeks.

By this point Mary Jane had purchased a spacious, turreted three-story frame house at 1028 Beverly Road in South Prospect Park. Likely the house was actually Albert's, put in Mary Jane's name for business reasons and certainly purchased with money taken out of the barrel company. Mary Jane, who now admitted to ninety years of age, was still sprightly and in full command of her wits. Albert's wife had been dead more than a year, and given Mary Jane's still-strained relations with Bly and Harry, their mother was more directly dependent than ever on Albert.

If Bly was as infuriated as could have been expected by her mother's beautiful new home, her published writings bear no hint of it. There is no sign of any response, in fact, except a new ability to transcend anger, a new serenity which had grown out of repeated opportunities to perform acts of unbounded benevolence toward unfortunate strangers. In the column, she testified to the rewards of her new humanitarianism.

"Nellie Bly Gives Day Out of Her Life," the headline over her column of October 14 read. "Grievously Wronged, She Finds Satisfaction in Life Through Making Other Unfortunate People Happy." The column did not go into what was meant by "grievously wronged," although Albert and Mary Jane, if they were reading, probably got the idea. The column dwelt instead on the happiness she had found in her good works. Perhaps she had chosen this way to let her errant family know that their avarice had not defeated her. In any event, it enhanced the image of "angel of mercy" she had been so busy cultivating with reports of her many good deeds.

A long deferred goal had been achieved. Bly was finally a columnist with a following. The first acknowledgment came early: After less than five months on the job, Brisbane increased her salary by a stunning 50 percent to $150 a week. The figure was not extraordinary by the going standard, but it wasn't insulting, either. It wouldn't make her rich again, but she could get by on that amount.

Bly doled out advice to her readers throughout the fall. Success was a theme she still felt comfortable expounding upon. She evinced no sense of defeat despite her years of setbacks. The school of failure had taught her as much about success as her long list of victories in so many of the things she had set out to do. As she told her readers on November 6:

> Know yourself.
> That is the first essential for success.
> If one would become great, two things are absolutely necessary. The first is to know yourself, the second is not to let the world know you.
> If you do not know yourself, you are a slave. Your hands and feet are tied; your mouth is gagged; your eyes are blindfolded.
> If the world knows you, you are a prey. Your heart and soul are exposed and unprotected; your abilities are undefended, your progress is defeated.
> . . . Smiles, expressions and words should be the shield or mask to protect you. By these means, one can avoid being the victim of the unscrupulous.
> If you are an open book to the world, you are doomed.
> . . . If you have been flattered and praised, don't gulp it down wholesale. Chew it carefully before swallowing it. Exaggerated praise is prompted by a desire to be agreeable. Accept praise for its worth—politeness. Be brutally frank with yourself. It's safer.

Bly's story of November 29—"a fairy tale come true"—made page 3 with a banner headline: "Nellie Bly Finds A Home and Father for Little Waif." A photograph of a cherubic four-year-old accompanied the article. He was adorably dressed in a dark knee-high suit with a white frilly collar and identified only as "Richard ———." The birth mother, unmarried, had abandoned the child, and a poor young crippled woman had found and raised him as her own. Lacking the means to educate him properly, the woman had turned to Bly for help. She decided that her only recourse was to put the boy up for adoption, to which Bly reluctantly agreed. At the same time, a wealthy widower, a grandfather whose own children had grown up and left home, met Bly at the McAlpin and expressed interest in adopting a child. Bly checked his credentials and set to work playing the happy matchmaker.

Thanks to Bly, little Richard was united with "Mr. O." The story had two more installments over the next couple of days. Not only did the grandfather and little Richard take off for the West but Bly had also engineered the rescue of the poor foster mother, who had been desolate at the thought of giving up the child. Bly wrote,

> My heart stood still with pain. Could I inflict upon this sweet, devoted girl an agony worse than that of death? Was it not better to let her keep the boy, for whom she had slaved and whom she worshipped?
>
> "I cannot!" I answered hurriedly. "She loves the boy so devotedly. Her love for him was too noble and too holy to deserve this blow. I will not!"

But the wealthy man pleaded with Bly to let him have the boy. And, seeing how shaken the foster mother was by the prospect of separation, he instantly offered her a home as well. Her only task, he said, would be to look after the flower arrangements in the house and buy new ones as necessary.

> The crippled girl sank upon a bench, I beside her. She was white and speechless. I was laughing and crying.
>
> "Run! Pack your trunk! You are leaving at once for your new home," I said. But she would not. It would not be fair for the matron [her employer]; she must give her a few weeks' notice.
>
> I did not intend to let Fate have a chance to dim the glorious sunshine which had burst upon her. It was her one great wonderful chance. I saw the matron. I rattled off all sorts of explanations. I held her hands close and pleaded.
>
> She smiled and yielded and the crippled girl asked us to go on to my hotel, taking Richard and leaving her to pack her trunk and join us.

As Christmas approached, Bly wrote on the theme of disappointment, which, in this new state of inner peace and enlightenment, she had come to understand as a form of selfishness. "Disappointment is the state of being balked, defeated, hindered of result, tantalized. In plain words, deprived of something one wanted," she wrote. "To grieve over something one wanted and did not get is a species of selfishness."

She confessed, "I have had several keen disappointments which have left my heart bleeding." But the examples she enumerated concerned only her disappointments in relation to helping her readers. There were the four families awaiting adoptive children who would not have them in time for the holiday. There was the lonely chorus girl who had signed herself "Nameless" and had confided that her only dream was to have a woman friend whom she could truly trust. She wrote Bly three times without signature but missed Bly's effort to contact her through a notice in the paper. "So," Bly reported, "she drifted again into the wide, wide world alone and embittered by the fact that her one appeal had been denied." Bly expressed remorse at her own powerlessness to help. This, she said, was one of those disappointments "which do not heal."

It must have helped Bly to have the troubles of the destitute, lonely, and sorrowful to focus on as the source of her pain instead of the more gnawing and emotionally destructive issues of familial betrayal and monetary loss. Consciously, at least, she was not going to submit to that or any other kind of defeat.

The staff at the McAlpin adjusted to having the famous Nellie Bly in its midst and the streams of sometimes ill-clad, unwashed visitors who often waited in the lobby for their chance to tell her their problems. She published her address in *The Journal* all the time, not the least bit concerned about who might come calling. One employee remembered the retort she flashed at friends who feared she was being exploited by many of the unfortunates who sought her help. "Relieve immediately," she would say. "Investigate afterwards."

In the meantime, there was more satisfaction and more happy results from her sanctioned trafficking in the placement of foundlings. She had started to discern a divine pattern in the circumstances:

One woman buoyed up with spiritual exaltation is eager to welcome the new little angel from another world.

One woman listens in fear and dread for the first feeble cry of the unwanted.

One woman, denied motherhood, ever unsatisfied and lonely, dreams of clinging curling fingers and a warm bundle, nestling confidingly against her heart.

Might it not be that some merciful, All-wise Power so arranges that there shall be childless homes for homeless children? That the sin of one shall be blotted out because of the blessing of the other?

Who knows?

The Journal boldly displayed Bly's story of little "Ann Randolph," a name given to a beautiful month-old foundling by the nurses at Bellevue Hospital; a man going to work after midnight had stumbled over the bundle in which the baby had been left at Grand Central Station. The last foundling at Bellevue Hospital had been baptized a Catholic, so little Ann, by the rotation system then very strictly in force, was declared a Protestant. "So the city shapes the destiny of foundlings," Bly wrote. "This is one of the unbreakable rules." It happened that a wealthy Protestant couple owning "three ranches in the West" had arrived in New York in search of an infant to adopt. Their youngest daughter was fifteen, and they very much wanted a third child. Bly arranged for them to meet little Ann and, as the headline said, worked her magic to "shuffle" another baby girl waif into a life of luxury.

The most momentous of the foundling stories was published on December 10. *The Journal* reported on page 5 that Bly was making every effort to adopt a seven-month-old baby boy who had been abandoned in Grand Central Station with the following note pinned to his clothing:

To Somebody—For the love of Mike, take this kid. He is too much for the family. Give him to Nellie Bly of the New York *Journal. He is seven months old and as healthy as they make them.*

*Can't afford him at the price they are charging for milk today.
There are others I am trying to support.*

A man had handed the baby to Harry J. Loise, a special officer
on the New York Central Lines, ostensibly for only a moment while
he went to another part of the station. The man never returned, and
Loise, seeing the note, took the baby to Bellevue. *The Journal* said,

> Miss Bly was notified of the finding of the baby and of the
> request of the note. She went to Bellevue to claim the baby
> forthwith, but was told there were many yards of red tape that
> should have to be slowly unwound before she could carry the
> infant off. Miss Bly went to the ward where the baby was and
> spent several hours getting acquainted with him.
>
> After leaving the ward Miss Bly said it would be the
> twenty-eighth baby she has found a home for. She said she
> and the baby understood each other perfectly, and that the
> foundling had patted her on the cheeks.

The story then took a strange and sensational twist. Mrs.
August Wentz declared that the abandoned infant was actually her
own little Arthur, who had been kidnapped in July from a department store in the Bronx. Her husband, the newspaper reported, was
not fully convinced the child was theirs but expressed his willingness
to adopt the baby boy to appease his wife. Wentz had already rejected
another child his wife had claimed since the kidnapping. This time
she said she was able to identify the baby by a birthmark on his neck,
and the child was given to the Wentzes. Bly, meanwhile, had initiated legal proceedings to adopt the child herself.

The next day, the newest development in the case put the story
on the front page again. The Society for the Prevention of Cruelty to
Children reclaimed the child on the complaint of Lena Lisa, a
twenty-four-year-old widow who confessed that the child was her
own son, Harry. When Mrs. Lisa read that the baby had been claimed
by the Wentzes, a family not much better off than hers, she came forward to reclaim him. This was not the future she had envisioned for

her son. She went to Bly, who brought her to the Society for the Prevention of Cruelty to Children, where she told her story. Bly had offered to help Mrs. Lisa in any way she could. *The Journal* reported the end of the touching saga:

> Mrs. Wentz wept when the baby was taken from her. Miss Bly and Mrs. Lisa sought to comfort her. Mrs. Wentz threw both arms about Miss Bly.
>
> "My dear woman," said Miss Bly, "you simply made an honest mistake out of pure mother-love. We will do all we can to help find your own boy."

Mrs. Lisa explained she had been left a widow with two young children and no way to support them both and got the idea to give the baby to Nellie Bly, who, she thought, could arrange to place him in a better home. Unable to take off from her job making artificial flower arrangements, she gave the baby to a neighbor to take to Bly. The neighbor became confused, too intimidated to enter the McAlpin Hotel, and, by then distraught, he left the child with Loise at the train station with the note pinned to his clothing. With Bly's intervention, the children's society made the decision to give "Love of Mike," as *The Journal* had dubbed him, back to his mother.

Bly wrote her own page 3 follow-up five days before Christmas. Love of Mike was back at Bellevue—not abandoned this time but suffering from several illnesses. Who was there helping Mrs. Lisa with arrangements for the child's admission? Bly, of course, as well as Mrs. Wentz, who not only had resigned herself to the fact that Love of Mike was not her kidnapped son but was experiencing the satisfaction of being of service to the needy and overburdened young mother. Bly pronounced herself utterly satisfied with the turn of events.

When the news services reported from San Francisco that a Mr. and Mrs. Hubert Barnett were offering to sell their third child as soon as it was born because they were not going to be able to keep it, Bly went into a rage that *The Journal* found worthy of front page treatment the following day:

Nellie Bly with "Love o' Mike" baby, his brother and Mrs. Lena Lisa,
December 1919

(UPI/Bettmann Newsphotos)

A man who offers his child for sale ought to be put to death.

Slavery is supposed to have been abolished some years ago. Selling a baby, whether it be white or black, is slavery. Even offering it for sale, I imagine, would come under this law. The very thing to be done is to punish Mr. Hubert Barnett as severely as the law permits.

Bly emphasized she was not making a case against adoption, which she felt should be made easier to give unwanted children a better chance in life, but that she was railing against the idea of *selling* an unwanted child. That she found anathema.

Her experience in the children's wards and orphanages had made her a strong advocate of birth control, still a controversial theme. She wrote,

The greatest crime that has ever been taught the world and particularly the American portion of this sphere, is the theory of large families. Almost without exception large families occur only among the very poor. Generally those who have the most children are, for the benefit of humanity, those who should have the fewest.

When we are once truthful with ourselves and really love our fellow creatures and hope to better them, then we shall stop all this talk about encouraging large families. We shall without doubt not only teach birth control, but enact new laws which will prevent children being born in the world to those who shouldn't have them.

One needs only be familiar with the children's wards in hospitals and with public institutions and children's asylums, to be appalled and horrified at the sight of born misery.

Bly's Christmas Eve appeal was for the rights of adoptive parents. She urged that those who "open their hearts and homes to little abandoned children see that all legality possible is employed to secure [their] rights." She called for enactment of a law whereby a mother who abandoned or gave away her child forfeited all right or claim to it forever. It was something of a contradiction to the stance she had taken in the Love of Mike episode only a few days before, but consistency was never Bly's strong suit. She acted only on whatever passion she felt at the moment: "It is terribly unjust to those noble beings who take abandoned children to drag those little ones away later on when it suits the caprices of the heartless women who deserted them. Affection developed after a child is beyond the helpless age and is approaching the time when it can be a wage earner is unworthy of consideration."

The column included the stories of readers to whom this had happened, one a woman who had raised from age three to thirteen a child whose birth mother had just come back to claim her. "Write me more," Bly urged. "Give me the mother's name, your own, the history of your taking the child and everything else. And I shall see if there is any way to help you. I presume you did not secure the necessary legal papers of adoption. It is totally wrong and I hope we shall find some way to restore the child to you."

The open, caring tone was the same in her responses to every reader who sought her help.

⚬⚭⚬

Before leaving Vienna, Bly had given Oscar Bondy her power of attorney, and he, in turn, had entrusted to her 150 shares of stock he held in U.S. sugar companies on which dividends had been accumulating in her name since 1916. As she left for Paris, Bondy had given her a large sum of Austrian currency to exchange into dollars or francs in Switzerland and a magnificent brooch and earrings that had once belonged to Queen Victoria. The Austrian currency could not be sold, however, and there were at first technical complications in getting the sugar stock funds released to Bly, even though they had been held in her name in Switzerland for some time. She wasn't exaggerating, then, when she told Erasmus Wilson of her $3.65 in liquid assets.

Bondy, in the aftermath of war and the breakup of the Habsburg monarchy, was experiencing business troubles of his own. "I have just returned from Bohemia where the workmen and employed situation has come to almost untenable conditions," he wrote Bly on July 8, 1919, shortly after she started work at *The Evening Journal*. As his difficulties increased, Bly urged him to immigrate to the United States. She even offered to adopt him to expedite the process. "Don't worry," she wrote in January of 1920, "You know I have all that sugar dividends—it is at least $2,500—safe and secure. I am saving it for *Thee* every penny."

She had written Bondy of all the hardship she had endured since returning to the United States, to which he had replied:

> It's *terrible* that you underwent hardships and fell ill of them. But pray, if that unfortunate Austrian money was really unsalable (at your departure its market value was [instead of $8,000 before the war] indeed about $3,000. *Now* only it has fallen down to $1,000) why did you not pawn the "Victoria" and earrings, for instance, since you *knew* the s. stock with all its dividends since 1916 on it was your property and was bound to be placed in your hands in a few weeks? I could cry, I have not better provided for you, but of course assumed you could better sell our crowns in Switzerland than buy francs or dollars in Vienna! Darling, you must not doubt you will regain your health and strength but, if you possibly can, abstain from new excitements and *pray*, feed well and regularly and nurse yourself. Don't have any crazy ideas about owing anything to me (!!) which is too silly, or not touching what is your undisputed property, and has only a sense of existing as long as you use it. Though I am glad to hear you have a newspaper position again, *you must no more overexert yourself, I beseech you.*

Bly refused to spend a cent of the sugar stock income he had entrusted to her, and overexertion had for too long been her way of life for her to change. She suffered recurrent bouts of bronchitis, which forced her hospitalization more than once. Still, she produced an average of two or more stories a week for *The Journal*. Her self-styled charitable enterprise grew.

Over the coming months, Bondy continued to implore Bly to cash in the sugar stock to add to her comfort. "Pray don't be foolish about that sugar stock and *use* it for *your* personal daily require-ments!" he wrote on February 7, 1920.

> I am *not* poor yet, the factories and art collection still belong
> to me, only our money has lost its buying force and tremen-
> dous property taxes are imminent. All foreign (including
> German) stock seized by the government. Unfortunately, I
> had no other deposits in N.Y. to give you at the time than
> that stock, all my other American papers lying in London
> (and some copper stock in Paris) having been seized after the
> outbreak of the war by the Entente.

At the end of February 1920, Mary Jane's suit against the Alien Property Custodian resulted in a judgment in Bly's favor. U.S. District Court Judge Edwin L. Garvin ruled that Bly—not her mother—was entitled to the 490 shares of Steel Barrel Company of America stock and that attorney Harold Nathan had done nothing improper in getting Mary Jane to sign the stock certificate over to Oscar Bondy. Mary Jane retained her life interest in the income from the shares, which was to revert to Bly upon her mother's death.

Judge Garvin did mention, however, "the irresistible conclu-sion" that although it was Bly's energy and activity that had made the new company possible, "its later prosperity does not seem to have been due to her connection with its affairs." This, of course, was the source of Mary Jane's—actually Albert's—claim to the company, not to mention the difficulties they had all lived with during the Iron Clad's wearying collapse. Nevertheless, the judge's opinion thor-oughly discredited Mary Jane while remarking on the "extraordinary keenness of mind" she had displayed throughout the trial, despite her advanced age. The judge also took special exception to Mary Jane's repeated assertion that she had signed the stock over to Bondy "to save the company from the creditors." Garvin wrote,

> It may be noted that if her contention is correct she was lend-
> ing herself to a scheme to put property out of the reach of
> those entitled to it, an act which does not make her a more

believable witness, and which of itself abundantly justifies refusing to set aside the transfer. The plaintiff has not come into court with clean hands if she asserts that the transfer which she now seeks to avoid was made by her in order that creditors might not be able to find property to be applied in payment of their claim.

Judge Garvin said so much bitterness between the parties surrounded the case that the court had made every effort to reconcile their conflicting interests "and to restore the natural relation of mother and daughter between plaintiff and defendant Seaman which had ceased to exist." In the end, he said, that proved impossible. The history of Nellie Bly and the steel barrel company ended in dissipation by litigation. Albert responded to Bly's victory in district court by attempting to have the number of shares in the company increased to 1,250, thus diluting his sister's stake and creating a much larger one for himself through Mary Jane. Bly refused to agree to such an arrangement. She instituted another round of legal proceedings to block the plan. Still, the defeat was evident.

On March 15, she explained the sorry state of her finances to an officer at Bankers Trust Co.:

Salary from *NY Journal* began June 1919
$100—per week
Oct 15-1919 increased to $150 per week.
No other source of income. Have spent for babies (charity) over
$500 since August 1919.
Losses—furniture $20,000
      books $5,000
      paintings $20,000
      American Steel Barrel—$25,000

There the story of Robert Seaman's fortune in the hands of the Cochranes effectively ended. It had brought Bly's own life story from the age of six full circle, from orphan back to orphan, from impoverishment back to impoverishment. It also represented the third pivotal instance in Bly's life when her mother's actions and inactions had left her life in turmoil. Perhaps the exemplary care Bly had shown for Mary Jane throughout the years had been a mask for seething anger, the most acceptable response to feelings so inappropriate they had to be submerged. Could a woman of such take-charge independence so fully forgive and excuse her mother for never having insisted that Judge Cochran provide for his young family in writing before he died? Did Bly absolve her mother without recrimination for subjecting her to the five-year horror of life in a house with the drunken Jack Ford? Maybe all Bly's legal battles and crusades against wrongdoing emanated from a displaced need to confront Mary Jane for the weaknesses that had failed her in such a fundamental way.

Throughout the years, Bly, in a seeming need to overcompensate, drenched her family—even Albert—in concrete acts of lovingkindness. She made Robert Seaman agree to support her mother and sister before she married him. She got Seaman to improve her position in his will three times, which was for their sake as well as her own. She educated her nieces and nephew. She gave her brothers jobs. She housed her family members whenever needed and even when not. She lavished them all with concern, attention, and gifts. It was as if she had to show her mother, by inverse example, how a responsible person manages a family, how loved ones really care for loved ones.

In this final instance, Mary Jane's weakness pitted child against child and left Bly at the short end of her mother's loyalty and affection. This time the mistreatment could not be ignored. Bly did not let her anger at Mary Jane go.

❧

Bly's tales of abandoned, abused, and missing children made for startling, often front page headlines throughout 1920. In January, she reported the story of a fifteen-year-old girl unable to read and write who was living in the middle of the city. Her mother had kept her locked in a room of her apartment for fear something would happen to her if she were let out. There was a sensational follow-up in the Love of Mike case. It turned out that the baby's mother, in an effort to make her story of giving up her child more palatable, had

lied to authorities about being a widow. Her husband, Albert Lise—
Bly gave a different spelling for the family name at this point—had
joined his wife in deciding to give the baby to Bly in the hope that
she would be able to place him in a wealthier family. The hapless carrier who had abandoned the child at Grand Central Station before
finding Bly was Lise's brother, Joseph.

When Love of Mike ended up with a family not much better off
than the Lises, Albert Lise encouraged his wife to reclaim the child
but couldn't come forward himself because of the bad light the lie
about her widowhood would cast on the couple in their efforts to
retrieve their son. When Willard Parker Hospital sent the Lises a
cable saying that their child was gravely ill, Albert Lise became
remorseful over the lie and desperate to visit the baby. That was
when he decided to reveal the truth to Bly. "The fault I committed
was done not through a desire to do wrong," Bly quoted him as saying, "but through a desire to secure the happiness of my baby boy. If
it were wrong it was a wrong committed through ignorance and
prompted by love of my child."

Bly readily overlooked whatever embarrassment the case might
have caused her and saw it as an opportunity for yet another headline.
In her story, she appealed for forgiveness in Lise's behalf. "Who has
been hurt by this little tragedy?" she asked. "If punishment they
should have, they certainly have had it in the fullest measure. Let us
put ourselves in their places. IF we love our children, what will we
not do for their good and benefit?"

In another follow-up column, a month and a half later, Bly
reported that little Love of Mike never lived to leave the hospital. She
blamed his death on all the red tape involved in settling his case and
the inordinate number of strangers to whom the infant had been
exposed in the process. The child, who had been robust and healthy
at the outset, was by the time of his return to his parents, suffering
from bronchitis, whooping cough, measles, chicken pox, and double
pneumonia. He bit off his tongue in a convulsion and died. Bly exon-
erated the Lises, who, she said, were only trying to find a way to give
their child a better life.

Although Bly was getting very involved in publicizing the
names and descriptions of adorable infants she had available for

adoption, a good hard news story still could attract her attention. On January 29, she accepted Brisbane's challenge to be "the first woman to witness an execution in 21 years" at the electrocution for murder of Gordon Fawcett Hamby at Sing Sing. Bly traveled to Ossining for the solemn event, describing every detail of the day and her every reaction. According to a colleague, Brisbane, witnessing the first electrocution at Sing Sing in 1891, had turned green from the spectacle and decided to miss the official autopsy. Bly stayed for everything, then fashioned her story as an indictment of capital punishment:

> Horrible! Horrible! Horrible!
> Hamby is dead. The law has been carried out—presumably the law is satisfied.
> "THOU SHALT NOT KILL."
> Was that Commandment meant alone for Hamby? Or did it mean all of us?

Bly watched the execution and described the gruesome scene: "I looked. I shall never forget. None of us who looked on what was there can ever forget. It must haunt us to our graves, that face, that open mouth, those sunken cheeks and deep sunken eyes. It was horrible."

She also reported that shortly before the electrocution, Hamby, who had been corresponding with Bly, sent her his Ouija board with a carefully written note, signing with one of his aliases.

> *January 29, 1920. A slight remembrance (all I have at this time) for your infinite kindness and friendship.*
>
> J. B. ALLAN

The following week, Bly continued the anti–capital punishment theme, vowing to work unceasingly until the practice was abolished. "I shall never forget," she wrote. "I shall never cease to work to abolish this premeditated killing. I shall never cease to pray for forgiveness for having been an accessory to a killing."

For three days before the scheduled legislative hearings in Albany on the Boylan-Pellet bill to abolish capital punishment, Bly urged support for the measure from common New Yorkers and clergy alike. Hamby, she reported in one column, had told her he confessed to murders in Brooklyn that he did not commit for the sake of warranting the death penalty in New York instead of a life in solitary confinement for the crime he had committed in Washington State. Bly wrote,

> If the death penalty is abolished and the Boylan-Pellet bill of solitary confinement (life imprisonment) is passed, I am positive this crime of murder will decrease in New York State. But with this bill must go the positive declaration that pardons are not possible. That solitary confinement means what it says. That the man who commits murder, or the woman who commits murder, shall at the moment of conviction enter a living tomb, and unheard of, uncommunicated with, shall remain within that tomb until death.

She took up other crusades: against the evils of gambling and the degradation of society through low moral standards. Among these, she mentioned how accepting society had become of men being seen with much younger women. She did not refer to her own experience in this regard. She made a strong case for offering real jobs to the blind in occupations they could handle instead of giving them licenses to peddle pencils, which she considered tantamount to enforced charity. She suggested special communities be established where the blind could safely live and work.

To the homeless boys who so often wrote her, she replied in a long group letter, giving them advice about their futures, explaining how much worse it was to be from a bad home than from no home, and professing her sincerest devotion:

> And as so many of you have written to me, so pathetically that you have no one in the world and never had, and that you just love me, remember that I love you, too—every single one of you. I think of you daily. I am your true friend. I want you to live to be happy, to accomplish great things in the world, to be the builders of your own homes and your

own families. To make your families what you want them to be, not as fate has given them to others.

Don't despair for one minute. Remember, if the world sees you are determined to make something of yourself it will help you.

And don't forget. I love you.

Bly reported that a column she had written about loneliness had provoked charges from scores of women that she lacked understanding. Bly responded with apology, "I have never written a word that did not come from my heart. I never shall. I have never had but one desire, and that was to benefit humanity, to encourage, to uplift, to point out the way called straight."

In the same column, she told how she cured a lonely wife of the mistaken feeling that she had found her true soul mate in someone other than her husband. Bly had applied reverse psychology to the case, although she didn't call it that. She repeatedly encouraged the woman to go to her lover and let Bly arrange to introduce the husband to a beautiful, wealthy friend of hers. In time, Bly said, the wife began to realize that it was her husband she really loved after all.

Amidst more tales of the pathos of unwed mothers were appeals to give first offenders a second chance before carting them off to prisons full of hardened criminals and for society to help men released from prison in their efforts to readjust to life in the world.

In this connection Bly was instrumental in the reintroduction to society of a young man who had served a jail term for theft. Convinced of his sincere reform, Bly did whatever she could to help him land a job. However, when he came to the McAlpin to thank her, a secretary happened to mention that she was going downstairs and was leaving her bag. "I'd take it along," the secretary recalled Bly as saying in the presence of the beneficiary of what had seemed her unending kindness. "This young man here has light fingers."

Bly speculated on what she would do with a spare million dollars—"I would become the greatest benefactor in the world. I would become to suffering humanity what no human creature has ever been. I would immortalize my name with undying fame. The great names of history would pale beside the renown of mine." First on her list of projects would be a cure for cancer, the establishment of excellent day-care centers geared to the needs of mothers who had no choice but to work at outside jobs for a living, and the creation of a city for the blind and a school for maimed soldiers.

"For money," she said, "does everything."

Her personal indictment of Charles Newton Harvey, the confessed Los Angeles "arch Bluebeard and slayer" of five of his twenty-five or twenty-eight wives, was presented on the front page. "A selfish, unfeeling monster," Bly called him, scoffing at the plea of insanity of this "evil freak of humanity" with the "abnormally developed case of ego." She added, "Now let some one tell us what is wrong with these silly but good women who become the hypnotized slaves of such merciless, soulless, selfish monsters?"

After the vanishing of a fifteen-year-old Harlem schoolgirl, Henrietta Bulte, Bly offered a $1,000 reward for information leading to the arrest and conviction of her abductors, if she had been kidnapped. Clues flooded in from all over the country. Bly's stories ran on the front page of *The Journal* for eleven of the thirty-six days Henrietta was missing. From the information she collected, Bly finally surmised that the girl had not been kidnapped, but had left home bound for Hollywood. She wrote the girl an open letter, urging her to return to her loving parents. Police acknowledged their debt to Bly and her relentless attention to the case. Henrietta finally made her presence known in Los Angeles and agreed to come back home. The girl had discovered how difficult becoming an actress really was. On her return, her parents decided to move to another neighborhood to spare their daughter the embarrassment of having to answer the questions of curious neighbors.

On June 1, Bly hosted an all-expense-paid picnic trip to the Coney Island Luna Park for 750 orphans from the city's various asylums. The Twentieth Century Brown and White Taxicab Association lent 100 cabs, and the Manhattan Tourist Company gave its biggest sightseeing bus to transport the children. Mayor John Francis Hylan greeted the orphans representing "half a dozen nationalities" at City Hall before they took off for Brooklyn to feast on food donated by The Nedick Company and play with balloons from the House of Balloons. Bly said the day was perfect.

Hearst's International News Service put Bly under contract to cover the Republican National Convention in Chicago the second week in June. *The Journal* carried her stories, all angled on the role of women in their first official political performance since gaining the right to vote.

Probably mindful of her horror at the way women at the suffrage convention of 1896 had dressed, Bly must have taken satisfaction in the fact that women at the Republican convention were very well turned out. She had extremely fixed ideas on the importance of appearance and the value of female attractiveness, and she had no problem reconciling these more sartorial concerns with her ardent feminism. Observing the women who had gathered in Chicago, she said,

> They have all arrived dressed in the latest style and accompanied by trunks filled with the prettiest gowns obtainable.
>
> Still these women are not frivolous, empty-headed specimens of humanity. They are the cleverest and brainiest of their kind. That is why they have not neglected their appearance. For while they have fought and won the battle for equal rights with men, they did not forget that man is a creature of his eyes.
>
> Nor do these same women intend to let the world believe that suffrage will make her anything else than she has been heretofore, a womanly woman, a mother, a wife and a sister and the uplifter and sustainer of all that is good.

Bly wrote of her certainty that by the time of the conventions of 1924, women would have taken over politics altogether—since they seemed to bear the strain so much better than their male counterparts—and would certainly put an end to the rowdy, rabble-rousing way that men, acting like lunatics, had gone about nominating Warren G. Harding as their candidate for president.

Once back in New York, Bly was put to work playing detective again in the mysterious slaying of Joseph B. Elwell, a womanizing turfman and whist expert shot to death in the reception room of his West Seventieth Street home. She offered no reward this time, nor anything much but days explaining her theories in the case.

In the middle of July, Bly wrote a long column asking people to think before they griped or grouched and cited the case of a loud and obnoxious group of restaurant customers who had cost a waiter his job by complaining of his suggestion about what they should order. Bly recalled other episodes of brutish behavior and couldn't resist an evident swipe at Albert:

> If it weren't an insult to brutes, I would say I know a brute of a man. But I apologize to the brutes. I don't think even the name monster can begin to describe this terrible monstrosity whose existence is a torment to every creature with whom he comes in contact.
>
> He is not a wage earner. He never was. He simply exists first upon the income of a sister and now upon that of another.
>
> But it is his kind and sort that has no consideration for the other person.
>
> If a child runs a hoop along the pavement, or dares to have a soapbox wagon, he calls the police and has the child driven from the street.

Bly viewed the late July yacht races from aboard the vessel of Sir Thomas Johnstone Lipton, the English tea merchant and yachtsman, in the company of ambassadors, commissioners, a baron, a du Pont, and her niece Beatrice, who had divorced her second husband in 1917, after ten years of marriage. Much as Bly still resented the English—her staff of assistants at the McAlpin said she steadfastly refused to give aid to any troubled young women who had a hint of a British accent—for Sir Thomas there was only her ever-ready smile and charm, perhaps because he had climbed to wealth and prominence from nothing, the American way.

Bly was frantic with activity during this period. She detested the telephone, preferring to do her work in person, and would rarely answer of her own accord. Her assistants at the time recalled that the only calls she would place herself were to the editors at *The Journal* when she didn't like the placement given her column. Then it was merciful angel turned wrathful diva. Bly's fingers would clench, a tight line would appear around her mouth, and a tirade would follow. Brisbane would get the next call and a full report from her on whatever dressing down she had given his editors. She neglected her health, refused to take prescribed medicines, raced around in the worst weather in taxicabs, skipped meals often, and was picky when she bothered to eat.

There was more illness in the fall of 1920, of which Bly complained in a letter to Bondy. She made a case in her column for the wonders of plastic surgery and the importance of women dressing well (again) and emphasized the importance of buying American goods and deporting foreigners who commit crimes. She even warned Americans against marrying foreigners. "Like belongs to like," she wrote. "Different nationalities cannot marry and find happiness and compatibility." As for the children of such unions—Bly declared they were "as wretched in their way as children born to parents of different race and color." And yet, when a young man wrote her of the love of his life, lost because he feared going against his parents to marry one of a different religious faith, even though she was pregnant by him, Bly's advice was unequivocal: "My dear young man. MARRY THE GIRL AND DO IT AT ONCE. You love her and she loves you and that is sufficient to justify your marriage even against the opposition of anybody of a different religious belief. You owe a duty to that girl, but you owe a still greater duty to the little one that is coming. That is holy and above everything else in life . . . Do your duty first. Your duty is to that unborn child. Then come to me and I shall try to help you."

As the holidays approached, Bly had many ideas for bringing happiness into her readers' lives by helping the less fortunate: the worthy but sickly electrician who needed medical care and a job and scores of needy families awaiting the kindness of strangers to cheer their Christmas. The philosophy she expounded was this:

I have never yet written of the misfortunes of anyone that I did not instantly get responses from every part of the United States containing offers of aid and sympathy. I hate charity as it is known. I love kindness and, above all, I reverence the great Biblical precept: "Do unto others as ye would that they should do unto you."

There are cases when one must necessarily give money, but the real charity, and the only constructive and true-hearted aid, is to help others help themselves. The greatest act of kindness is to help another to be independent and self-supporting.

Bly had established herself as cultural commentator, addressing the needs and concerns of *The Journal*'s vast readership.

✦

The volume of newspaper work Bly produced in 1921, in failing health at age fifty-seven, was as great as in any of her most stellar years as a young reporter. Most of her columns for *The Journal* grew out of her clearinghouse operation: The letters she received and the interviews she granted inspired almost every column and sparked all of her crusades as well as most of her comment on larger social and moral themes.

Bly's services for homeless babies continued through 1921, occasioning new friendships with prominent New Yorkers, such as the philanthropist Edwin Gould and the respected attorney John Warren Hill, later presiding judge of the Court of Domestic Relations. Her columns would often detail, sometimes in two or three installments, the woeful gothic accounts of fallen women trying to remake their lives, of desperate fathers trying to raise their children without wives, of reformed convicts trying to make new lives, of wives who nagged themselves into abandonment and husbands who did the same, and of the disturbing displays of ingratitude of some of the people she had helped.

She told the story of Zita, the empress of Karl of Austria, and how her interference in the affairs of state had hastened the monarchy's downfall. Her subjects, Bly said, found everything about her insufferable, from her decorating to her poor taste in clothes.

Her small treatise on happiness, a mind cure, really, gave advice almost in direct opposition to what she had told her mother by letter from Vienna only two years before. No longer did she advocate self-ishness. Now, her best wisdom was:

To be happy, to know how to find happiness under all circumstances and out of all conditions is the acme of wisdom and the triumph of genius.

Only those who have mastered the art of happiness can prosper and progress. The happy spirit sees no obstacles, is not blinded by gloom and invokes the strength and ambition that surmounts all difficulties and gains success.

The world would be a happier and better one if everybody cultivated happiness. Don't be a grouch and waste life; don't be disgruntled and dissatisfied; don't be a growler; don't be a crank.

During Bly's illness in the fall of 1920, she had been treated at St. Mark's Hospital for several weeks. "The Hospital with a Heart," as she dubbed it, was at the corner of Eleventh Street and Second Avenue, opposite St. Mark's Church. "Like a streetcar, it takes in without a question every patient so long as there is the possibility of crowding another in," she wrote in a column of appreciation. "There is no red tape. The need of assistance and aid is the only passport required." Housed in a gracious old private residence that once belonged to Peter Stuyvesant, the hospital was supported by private contributions with no government assistance. "I spent many weeks myself in St. Mark's Hospital in a big airy room filled with sunshine the whole day. The whole atmosphere was so remote from the usual with hospitals that my stay there seemed more like a pleasant visit than a struggle to regain health." It was the place she had sent many of her charitable patients, and she was close to the hospital's administrators.

Bly had developed some oddly set ideas on the sphere of women since the harangue in *The Pittsburg Dispatch* that had launched her career thirty-six years earlier. These ideas were not entirely out of step with the times and were largely molded by her work with children. The story of what had happened in one family in which the mother was working outside the home prompted her to decry women with outside jobs who worked for reasons other than absolute financial necessity. It was a theme she hit on more than once:

> No home can be a home where the wife and mother works outside. No marriage life can be ideal or true or worthwhile where the wife and mother "goes to business." No children can be cared for and brought up and developed as they should where "mother works downtown."
>
> That women should work is necessary. That they should be treated with equality for their labor is just and right. There should be no difference in the recompense for work, whether done by a man or a woman, so long as it is done equally well. There should be no barrier to woman's work in kind or place or time. Sex makes no difference in regard to labor either mental or physical; only habit, custom and prejudice control.

Bly suggested that the influx of immigrants over the preceding twenty years—with foreign women being much more accustomed to life as "drudges" than their American-born counterparts—had, in effect, poisoned the society to the point that women now continued working after marriage and often thought nothing of boarding out their offspring to avoid having to alter their style of life. Bly was appalled by this development:

> For the good of our country, laws ought to be passed prohibiting the employment of married women unless those women are deserted by their husbands. Then the laws should be so strict that deserting husbands would be kept under bond for the maintenance of their families. The law should prohibit the employment of married women and daughters of well-to-do men. Work should only be given to widows, girls who must support themselves and deserted wives. Thousands of women and girls are working today not from necessity but in order to avoid the irksomeness of household duties, to pro-

vide themselves with an easy method of making acquaintances and to obtain fine clothing. These women are parasites. Morally they are a detriment to the world. They are keeping out of employment girls who, of necessity, must be self-supporting and widows who have children to provide for.

But the issue that most inflamed her passions in 1921 was the plight of the nation's seamen. Recession in the shipping industry had left some 20,000 Americans jobless, a problem compounded by the propensity of U.S.-owned ships that did have business to hire the cheaper labor of foreign crewmen, a situation that Bly, in her new "America for the Americans" mode, found outrageous. In the process, she had found a new cause over which to tweak the British:

It is known and acknowledged that a big force has been retained to spread propaganda in America for the benefit of English ships and English seamen. This propaganda is working steadily and hourly with the greatest keenness and cleverness to undermine and disqualify American shipping and American lines and American seafaring men. England is not only determined to control the shipping of the seas, but includes the American lakes, Long Island Sound and even the East and North Rivers.

This is no exaggeration. The truth of these statements is easily verified. And it is up to the men who earn their living on the water, to the Americans who desire to enter the Merchant Marines and to the officials of the United States Government to make a housecleaning and to right what is today so palpably wrong.

Week after week from late February until the middle of October, she wrote on the subject, demanding that American shippers hire American. She urged travelers and shippers to use only American vessels and to be certain they were staffed with American crews. Letters from disaffected, jobless seamen and their families poured in, many naming specific ships and companies that were sailing with foreign crewmen.

By mid-May she had started formation of the American Seamen's Association, "in care of the McAlpin Hotel," the aim of which was "to establish American seamen exclusively upon American boats, to defend the rights of American seamen, to expose injustices and wrongs done them and to aid in every way toward their betterment and supremacy." By the end of the month, the organization's first meeting had been held to an overflow crowd in a reception room at the McAlpin provided free of charge by the hotel. Bly was elected president. The second meeting had to be held in much larger quarters. The response was enthusiastic as members agreed on the organization's guiding principles and its constitution. By August, she reported a membership roster of 20,000 mariners.

On February 26, Bly's mother died of bladder cancer at her home on Beverly Road in Brooklyn, at the reported age of ninety-four. Albert took control of all Mary Jane's possessions, leaving in her estate only $400 which remained in a bank account. Bly's newspaper columns in this period betrayed no trace of a reaction to the news, although months later, in September, the theme of familial pain surfaced in her choice of letters to respond to from her many anguished readers. She wrote about the "delusion" of "the ties of blood":

> Life is a mask of uncertainties and surprises. Families produce children totally unlike [each other] . . . Children have hated parents and parents have hated children. Brothers and sisters have despised each other and have been unable to live in peace in the same home. I have known mothers who abhorred the very presence of their daughters and I have known daughters who despised their mothers. I have known fathers to hate their children with a murderous hate and I have known children who could not endure the presence of their fathers.

In October, she devoted a lengthy column to reflections on the regrets that do not go away.

> Death, which leaves no opportunity for forgiveness, is the severest reproach one can harbor in heart and soul in the very

grave. Regret that comes from some word or act which ends a friendship or a love is like an incurable illness—it is always with one and cannot be driven away. Millions of people have borne to their deaths the regret of a hasty action which deprived them of that success in life that is the due of every living creature.

Before you are unkind and ill-tempered to anyone, try to think what you would do if that one was forever removed from your life. Would you not alter your action immediately? Would you not try by word, as well as by act, to retain that person—be it father, mother, sister, brother, lover or friend? If you are a child, are you laying up a life of regrets in your conduct toward your parents?

. . . You may evade and fool an acquaintance, or even those near and dear, but you cannot fool your own soul. It is your master and you cannot still its voice so long as you live. And the older you get the louder gets that voice of your soul.

You cannot evade, you cannot shake off, you cannot kill that voice which will make you say in deepest misery: "If I only had—"

As the article was being published, Bly's health was again imperiled, and doctors had her readmitted to St. Mark's Hospital for treatment. On October 15, she got word that Albert had spent the preceding two days auctioning off the furniture, tapestries, and curios in their mother's house at 1028 Beverly Road, which Mary Jane had turned over to him before she died. Bly claimed the furnishings as her own, saying they had been lent to her mother when Bly left for Europe in 1914. Accompanied by a St. Mark's nurse, Bly took a taxi to the Flatbush address to stop the auction. She had arranged to be met by detectives who arrested Albert and a "co-conspirator" on charges of grand larceny. Bly put the value of the items she claimed, including souvenirs from her round-the-world trip, at $75,000.

Albert, for his part, said that Mary Jane had left him her entire estate, including the furnishings of the house. Even if Albert were correct, Bly said, since Mary Jane's will had not yet been probated, he had no right to sell anything until the estate was settled. Albert and Paul W. Towner were arrested and held pending arraignment in the Parkville Police Station. Towner was general manager of the Steel Barrel Company of America. Ultimately, there was no case against them, and the matter was dropped.

⟡

Two other women journalists at *The Journal* commanded as much space and notice as Bly during this phase of her employment by Brisbane. One was Julia McCarthy, known in print as Margery Rex, considered an ace among the younger generation of women reporters. When in 1921 Bly moved exclusively to editorial page altruism, Rex took over the big-headline kidnappings and other women's-interest tragedies and scandals. She had not yet reached the rank of journeyman, but Rex, too, rated front page bylines, although she lacked the luster to get her name planted in the headline as well.

Dorothy Dix had left *The Journal* in 1917, before Bly signed on for daily work. Editorial page competition instead came from Winifred Black, whose column appeared regularly alongside Bly's. Black was another contemporary of Bly, a respected San Francisco reporter known in the West as Annie Laurie. She had been with the Hearst organization since her first assignment for *The San Francisco Examiner*: covering Elizabeth Bisland's departure from the Bay City on her race to outpace Bly in her round-the-world hustle. Black's columns covered many of the same themes as Bly's, though without the dimension of personal involvement with her correspondent-readers, of playing angel of mercy. This was Bly's peculiar contribution to advice work, one that subordinated her role of journalist to that of crusading activist. The column became a vehicle for publicizing Bly's charitable efforts, expanding her constituency, aggrandizing her reputation, eliciting ideas for new causes to support, and in Bly's own words, providing her with endless opportunities to savor her own "taste of the bliss of heaven." Bly, in her maturity, had turned the full force of her undiminished will to the task of saving souls, among them, her own.

Yet to New York's child welfare professionals and the well-established voluntary organizations, such as Catholic and Protestant Big Sisters, Bly's unorthodox, even rogue approach to helping unwed mothers and facilitating the adoption of their offspring was objectionable. By November of 1921, she felt the need to devote two long columns to defending her work in response to a letter from a man she identified only as J.T. The gentleman had expressed interest in helping Bly expand her operation but had to withdraw the offer when his wife found out about his plan.

Bly told her readers that since her return to the United States in 1919, she had placed thousands of children in happy homes, provided thousands of unwed mothers with a new chance, and "saved their names and spared their families the slurs of the world." J.T.'s wife had expressed "a strongly developed antagonism" to Bly's work, based on criticism from a volunteer group with which the wife was associated. He told Bly the leaders of that group, which Bly did not name in print, "have accumulated considerable data that are in their opinion, derogatory to your [Bly's] particular way of doing things." He had asked them to produce the documentation so he could form his own judgment.

Bly's response was to publish the accusations in J.T.'s letter and to explain herself. She said her method was to "shield the name and reputation of the girl, to allow her to return to her family and friends without the fear of being disgraced or hounded, and to give her a chance to live a pure and upright life." Furthermore, she said, she made sure every child was adopted by "reputable, substantial, comfortably fixed, childless families, so that the little one is spared the knowledge that would blight his life and is assured of an education and love and devotion." She stated that she had never failed a child or an adoptive family in all those thousands of instances, a figure that was likely exaggerated. What she did not mention was that it was also her practice not to reveal to authorities in New York the names of the adoptive families, whose privacy she guarded as fiercely.

I should like to see what "accumulated data" any one could have derogatory to this holiest of ways of treating the girl who has failed and the innocent child that has come into the world.

I have spent years studying this subject, in close contact with these unhappy girls, and I have come out of the darkened prejudiced ways of antediluvian ages into the light.

Bly then recounted the stories of three unwed pregnant girls with whom she had made agreements for the placement of their children but who, during the requisite twelve-day hospital stay after delivering their babies, had been pressured by representatives of charitable organizations such as the one with which J.T.'s wife was involved. The volunteers, Bly said, threatened these vulnerable girls with exposure, punishment, and disgrace if they gave their infants to Bly. Bly said each of them took her newborn and fled the hospital in terror upon release. In each case, she said, the babies soon died in the inadequate care of their teenaged mothers. She went on,

I have now given strict orders in hospitals where I send girls that they are not to be molested, bullied or nagged by any one. If they are, I mean to proceed as far as I can legally against those who seek to persecute them. I don't intend to allow any girl's life to be wrecked or children to be killed by this malicious interference and persecution.

Bly said arranging the adoption of these children had given her greater happiness than anything else in the world, "a joy unspeakable." Happily, she said, she had dedicated her life to this task. "There is no reason for any baby to be abandoned," she vowed, "so long as I live."

⌘

In this period, Bly probably spent as much time arranging foster parentage and adoption for the children of unwed and indigent mothers as she did writing columns for *The Journal*, which appeared two or three times each week. But Bly's behavior in the delicate proceedings of child placement was as unambivalent and unconventional as it had always been in everything else. Her life, to the end, was a study in resolute if shoot-from-the-hip action, of talking straight and doing what she thought was right, whether it was or not, and regardless of anyone else's opinion. Among child welfare professionals, she had as many detractors as friends.

At Christmastime in 1919, the case of six-year-old Dorothy Coulter had been brought to Bly's attention by the New York Society for the Prevention of Cruelty to Children. She had been admitted to Willard Parker Hospital with a case of presumed fatal diphtheria. Efforts to locate her mother had failed, and the agency hoped that an article by Bly about the child's dire condition would encourage the mother to come forward.

What is known about the case and Bly's involvement in it provides a most complete illustration of why Bly's participation in child placement proceedings was not always welcomed. It also is emblematic of the way Bly operated and the liberties she would take to achieve a desired end.

In the heartrending story Bly wrote about Dorothy's condition, she identified the little girl's missing parents. The mother, "somewhere," was Grace Coulter, once a member of the Glorianna Company, a vaudeville troupe. The father, Bly said, was a member of the vaudeville team called Lane and Coulter. Bly said Dorothy hadn't seen her mother since the preceding July, when the New York Society for the Prevention of Cruelty to Children had removed her from what were said to have been "unfit surroundings," but she did not elaborate. The child was placed for six months with a woman approved by the court, with whom the mother had arranged to board the child. But the woman turned the child back over to the court just before Christmas because the mother had never paid the agreed upon boarding fees, nor had she visited.

In her story, Bly portrayed the dying Dorothy clutching a teddy bear Judge Samuel D. Levy had sent her as a gift. The image sparked an outpouring of letters. Most contained offers to adopt the child if she survived. One came from a woman who claimed to have information about the child's missing parents. Bly took that letter to Judge Levy and presented it in court, along with the offers of adoption. It was in this way that she insinuated herself into the process of determining Dorothy's future.

Dorothy had come into the care of the Society on June 27, 1919, a day after police arrested her mother for stealing a doll from Riker and Hergemane, a drugstore in Times Square. Grace Coulter had heroin in her purse when police took her into custody, and she admitted to being an addict. She also told authorities of the six-year-old child she had left at home in the care of a maid. An officer of the Society was dispatched to the apartment, taking Dorothy into custody as soon as she learned the child had not been fed since her mother had left the house.

Dorothy's case came up three times in Children's Court before anyone appeared on her behalf. It was not until July 29 that the mother, identifying herself as Grace Coulter, came before Judge Levy. She was out on bail after pleading guilty to the charge of petty larceny for which she ultimately received a suspended sentence. She brought with her the woman who had agreed to board Dorothy until Grace's case could be decided. That was the arrangement that continued until just before Christmas. After her late July appearance, Grace Coulter never came before the court nor did she see her little girl again.

So Dorothy, without proper guardianship, was remanded into the custody of the Society for the Prevention of Cruelty to Children once again. The diphtheria was diagnosed almost immediately, and Dorothy was sent to the hospital. Investigators in the meantime tried to piece together the child's past. They kept up the search for the missing Grace Coulter, who, in two interviews, had given authorities conflicting information about Dorothy's religious faith—once saying that she was Catholic and another time that she was Protestant. This caused great confusion and delay in determining Dorothy's future. Because of Bly's story in *The Journal*, there were now several families interested in taking Dorothy in, but the court could not place a Catholic child in a Protestant home or vice versa. Her religion had to be determined first.

The Society spent months looking into the matter. Letters went out to the health department of Rhode Island, where Grace Coulter was said to have been born, to see if her identity could be traced. Investigators tracked down her former husband, Clarence Coulter, a vaudeville harmonica player who turned out not to be the child's father. In fact, he claimed that he had only met the little girl once, when she seemed to be about three years old, well after Grace had left him.

Bly's article about Dorothy's sad case brought in a letter from Helen Love-Beauregard, the woman in New Haven, Connecticut, who had boarded the child before Grace had brought her to New York in February of 1919 and tried to raise her on her own. Grace Coulter, it turned out, was the married name of the woman who also identified herself as Marie Frances Harris and, at other times, by the stage name Grace Clifford. Despite the investigation's wide net, it did not produce conclusive evidence of Dorothy's religion, nor did Grace surface.

Clarence Coulter said he believed his former wife had loved the little girl dearly, considering how she treated her during their one meeting. But Grace had made his life "living hell" when they were together, he said, and if Dorothy were his child, "I would never leave her in my former wife's hands to raise."

Mrs. Love-Beauregard was more explicit:

> She [Grace] was addicted to the use of drugs and during the last few months I cared for Dorothy, Mrs. Coulter was an inmate of a house of ill fame conducted by a Mrs. Alice Dreyfus of Boston whose husband maintained the notorious Cafe de Dreyfus.
>
> Mrs. Coulter in appearance is refined, is tall and graceful in carriage, very thin because of the use of drugs and slovenly in dress as all addicts are. She has light brown hair and eyes like Dorothy's. Her whole being indicates good birth but bad environment.

Mrs. Love-Beauregard said she recalled Grace telling her that Coulter was not the child's father, that Dorothy was the illegitimate daughter of a "prominent and wealthy Providence young man who at an early age and under rather pitiful circumstances, seduced her."

At about the same time, in February of 1920, Bly paid a call on the general manager of the Society for the Prevention of Cruelty to Children, Ernest Coulter, who was no relation to Dorothy's mother or her former husband. Coulter filed a memo about the meeting, at which Bly said she had a prospective home for Dorothy, but declined to disclose any details about said home. He wrote, "Mrs. Seaman said she was not willing to have any of the homes in which she placed children visited or on record in the courts or visited by probation officers or institutions or agents, this to save foster parents from any annoyance that might be caused by those visits and to prevent the history of the child being known."

Coulter explained to Bly that an investigation would have to be made before a child could be placed. Bly said Judge Levy had all the details necessary to reveal and that she would drop the matter before she would subject the prospective parents to such a procedure. Coulter said Bly did explain "in a general way" that the proposed family lived on Long Island and conducted a large business, but that she was not willing to say more.

In the meantime, the Society stepped up efforts to locate Grace Coulter. There were reports she was staying at a house on West Fifty-first Street kept by the wife of Max Alexander, a gambling impresario, but she was not located. Dorothy was released from Willard Parker on February 18, 1920, and sent to the Campbell Cottages for further convalescence. Catholic and Protestant Big Sisters played tug-of-war over her future, and Bly took it upon herself to hire an attorney, John Warren Hill, to represent the child's interests. Still, the child's religion remained in doubt. All the parties to Dorothy's case agreed to allow her to be placed in Catholic hands upon her release from the hospital until a determination of her faith could be made.

After her convalescence, on May 7, 1920, nearly a year after she had been turned over to the Society, Dorothy was sent to Peekskill to the St. Joseph's Home, overlooking the Hudson River, in the care of the Missionary Sisters of the Third Order of St. Francis.

By then, finding Dorothy's mother had been written off as hopeless. Ernest Coulter recommended in a memo that a general guardian be appointed for Dorothy until she turned twenty-one. When Mrs. Love-Beauregard wrote to Coulter again on August 12 to ask what had become of Nellie Bly's effort to find Dorothy a home, Coulter wrote back that the journalist's intervention "was not considered by the court to be in Dorothy Coulter's best interest" but that

Bly had certainly given the case enormous publicity. In Peekskill, he reported, "the little girl has excited the affection of all with whom she came in contact. She is receiving good, kind care and affection. She is very happy in her present surroundings."

Two months later, Marie Frances Harris, alias Grace Coulter, alias Grace Clifford, came out of hiding. Penniless, dying of pulmonary tuberculosis, and with nowhere to turn, she appealed for help to Nellie Bly, who arranged for her admittance to St. Mark's Hospital on October 6, 1920.

In a lengthy two-part story which ran in *The Journal* October 19 and 20, Bly explained everything she knew about Grace and Dorothy and how she had become involved in their lives.

She recalled how the Society for the Prevention of Cruelty to Children had asked her to write about Dorothy when she became ill in the hope of forcing Grace Coulter to surface and how "the great big heart of New York throbbed with pity" in response to her column.

Bly had searched everywhere for the mother, who, she learned, had left New York as a member of a theatrical troupe that disbanded on the road. Grace's decision to leave town for work while still under suspended sentence for the petty larceny conviction had caused the authorities to issue a warrant for her arrest. Her acquaintances in New York told Bly she would never return to the city so long as a jail term was hanging over her. Bly went on:

And so time passed, and, wonder of wonders, little Dorothy recovered. And I went to the courts and laid before them offers from families of wealth to adopt the child. I wanted to give her—the little one—the chance her mother had never had. I wanted to know that she would have love and comfort and the proper surroundings and a father and a mother to adore her and an education and a chance to live.

But there were others of a different mind who wanted the child to go to an institution and they fought to carry out their ideas and I fought to carry out mine, and all the while I searched and searched for the missing girl mother, who feared her sentence in jail.

Bly had pressed for Grace's sentence to be set aside so that she could return to New York unafraid. Others had wanted the woman captured and punished. In the early fall of 1920, Bly herself had been admitted to St. Mark's Hospital for treatment. A call came in from a friend of Grace Coulter, whom Bly identified as "Mrs. H." The woman said Grace was with her. Bly had her come to St. Mark's at once:

> Tall and slender, with thick auburn hair, and eyes as blue as the waters of the "Blue Grotto," and skin as white and soft as the petals of a lily, she stood before me.
>
> We had a long talk, and I understood the heart of the broken flower that was the mother of Dorothy. And while I had sympathized with her when I did not know her, my sympathy doubled and trebled after we had talked. For I saw the heart of a girl who had never had a chance, of a girl who was her own worst enemy; of a girl who was possessed of every fine instinct that is inbred in the most wonderful and finest of womankind. And this girl had been forced to live through the brutality of a brutal world.

Grace told Bly of her simple country upbringing in a small New England village, where she attended Sunday School in the Methodist Church. She said that she and her sister had been orphaned in childhood, that she became pregnant with Dorothy when she was only fifteen. She told Bly of her brief, unsuccessful marriage and how she had struggled to maintain herself and her child. She gave her version of the drugstore arrest, to which Bly gave her full, unquestioning support:

> She walked into a drug store and, looking around, saw a red-painted face of a plump doll. Even if she had to go without a meal or two, she thought the doll would bring joy to her baby. And she picked it up and held it in the corner of her arm as she looked leisurely about. The cashier's desk was by the door, but before the girl reached it a hand of steel clasped her arm and she was accused of shoplifting!

Shoplifting a little doll marked $2.79! In vain she protested her innocence, but she was dragged over to the police station, where she was searched. Twenty-two dollars and some cents was in her purse. But there was something else! A little package of cocaine!

She confessed that she had been ill and had been given cocaine. That finished her! Her story that she was not shoplifting, and did not mean to steal the doll, but was going to pay for it as she would pass the cashier's desk by the door was unbelieved. And when she was held for stealing, the lawyer advised her to plead "Guilty." He told her it would be easier, and that it would save the necessity of a long and expensive trial for which she had no money and it, so he said, would bring LESS PUNISHMENT.

And she yielded to his advice, with the result that she went out of the court under probation and with a suspended sentence hanging over her head. That was the beginning of the end. That painted face little doll, priced at $2.79, cost Grace her life and Dorothy her mother! For they never met again.

Bly tried to convince Grace to go with her to the courts and hope for leniency, but the younger woman feared jail. Bly called the judge herself to plead for leniency but was told that there could be no such promise, that Grace would have to take her chances with the system. "What could I do?" Bly asked her readers. "What would you do? What would any one do with a heart in his breast?"

Grace went back out on the road in a little company, earning thirty-five dollars per week, paying all her own expenses except train fare. She promised to write Bly, and Bly promised to try to get Dorothy back for her.

But there was no word from Grace until early October, when a note arrived in a hand so feeble it was hardly legible. "Dear Miss Bly," it read. "The doctor said it is T.B. and is trying to have me sent to Otisville." Bly sent friends to rescue Grace from a "cold, bare room in a house in Jersey," where she had lain chilled and hungry for a week. They brought her to St. Mark's Hospital, where Bly, herself a patient at the time, secured Grace's affidavit as to Dorothy's religion and her own guardianship of the child. Grace's two-paragraph will bequeathed to Dorothy all her property: a suitcase containing a ten-dollar dress. She died on October 16, 1920.

On December 7, Bly again appeared in Children's Court on Dorothy's behalf. Attorney Hill read the deathbed affidavit of Marie Frances Harris also known as Grace Coulter into the court record. On the basis of the testimony, Judge Levy adjudged Dorothy a Protestant and ordered her immediate transfer from the Catholic home in Peekskill to the Leake and Watts Orphan Asylum, a Protestant facility in Yonkers, New York. One month later, a Surrogate Court order appointed Bly the legal guardian of Dorothy Harris. Sorting out Dorothy's case had taken twenty-two hearings over eighteen months. Bly immediately made her interest in the child known to the superintendent of Leake and Watts, who wrote to her on January 3, 1921:

> My dear Mrs. Seaman:
>
> I understand that you are very much interested in Dorothy Coulter, one of the little girls committed to our care, and am writing to ask if you will not come out some day soon and take lunch with us and see Dorothy in her surroundings.
>
> Under separate cover, I am sending you one of our latest catalogues, which will tell you something of the nature of our work. However, nothing can give you as good an idea of the spirit of the place and the happiness of the boys and girls here as a personal visit to the home.
>
> Dorothy is well and seems to be very happy here. She has been transferred to our main building and entered school this morning.
>
> Hoping to have the pleasure of meeting you soon, and with the season's greetings I am,
>
> A. S. McCLAIN
> Superintendent

By April 6, 1921, Dorothy's case file at Leake and Watts indicated the interest of several families in adopting her "because of her attractive looks and ways." Protestant Big Sisters had put forward the name of one promising family. Ernest Coulter of the Society for the Prevention of Cruelty to Children was asked if he considered Dorothy eligible for adoption, and he agreed that she was. Coulter, however, may not have been aware of Bly's legal guardianship, a fact that was conclusively established two weeks later, when an attorney acting for Protestant Big Sisters reviewed the probate of Marie Frances Harris's will. The attorney's opinion was that Bly had legal claim to Dorothy and that her adoption would require Bly's consent.

Superintendent McClain was at a loss for how to deal with Bly, who was trying discreetly to find her own family to adopt the child. Bly's column in *The Journal* of May 6, 1921, gave descriptions of six pretty little girls she had available for adoption. The one she called "Gloria" and referred to as "the little princess" was obviously Dorothy:

> She isn't really a princess even of American dollars. But she ought to be one.
>
> She is seven, slender, graceful, blue-eyed and brown-haired, pretty and intelligent. She is a darling. The princess comes from old New England stock, and when her girl mother was buried a year ago, little princess Gloria was left alone in this big, big world.
>
> She is a sensitive child, delicate, refined, affectionate. She is not bold, yet she is not afraid. She is modest and unobtrusive. In every characteristic is Gloria a real little princess. Unselfish to a degree, considerate of others, truthful in the extreme, with a love for all the beautiful things in the world. She adores music and pictures, is fond of dancing, and is always and everywhere a dainty little lady.

Bly asked anyone interested in adopting one of the six little girls to write her, including details she promised to keep in the strictest confidence. She wanted full names and addresses, occupation, religion, whether homeowner or not, and references. She explained, "Under no circumstances can these children be given to persons who do not own their own home and they should have a country place. They must be people comfortably and permanently

situated in life. To them will be given full and absolute adoption."
Or, if the prospective parents preferred, the children could be taken
for a probationary period of several months.

Bly's article must have worried Superintendent McClain, for he
began seeking a strategy to keep her from deciding Dorothy's future.
He received a letter from Joseph H. Applegate on May 15, 1921, on
the letterhead of the Newspaper Feature Service. Applegate wrote on
the suggestion of a mutual friend "to tell you that I may be able to
do something with Nellie Bly, who is an old friend of mine. I will be
glad to talk to you about this matter whenever you can find it convenient to call at this office." The case file notes that an interview
with Applegate took place two days later, but there are no recorded
details of the conversation. That same day, McClain confirmed by
letter an arrangement for Bly to visit Dorothy at the orphanage on
May 20 and have lunch with him. "I shall be very glad indeed to have
you see our large family of 300 children and something of their life
here," he wrote her in confirming the appointment.

Bly visited Leake and Watts that Friday as planned. She found a
verdant country campus with more the look of a prestige boarding
school than of a home for unwanted children, true even seventy years
later. She renewed her acquaintance with Dorothy, whom she had gotten to know during their numerous joint appearances in Children's
Court. And she told Superintendent McClain she wanted to take
Dorothy away for a few days' visit, to which he reluctantly agreed.

On June 7, 1921, Leake and Watts closed its file on Dorothy
Coulter, noting that the child had been taken away by Mrs. E. C. Seaman on May 20 for a short visit. Three days later, Bly wrote McClain,
informing him that she had made other plans for the education of
Dorothy Coulter and that the child would not be returning to Leake
and Watts.

✦

For *The New York Evening Journal* of January 9, 1922, Bly produced
what would be her last newspaper column. She recounted the stories
of two lifelong women friends, to whom she eerily gave the fictitious
names Mary and Jane. The friends had started out in life on even

terms, born a few months apart in the same southern village, but ended up in vastly different circumstances. The choice of a play on her late mother's name to identify the two women probably had no more than subconscious significance, since the stories do not parallel, even in composite, those of any of Bly's close family members.

The essay was reflective and wry, a story about people Bly said she had known for a lifetime, if they indeed existed. There were no reader letters to round out her thoughts as usual. She used the opportunity to pose a hard life question: What governs destiny? She gave no pat, decisive answer or strident opinion, as was her customary practice. She did not ask her readers to offer up their own ideas on the subject, a device she often employed for generating new material. Perhaps she sensed she would have no need for more material. She simply shared the conundrum that stumped her as she looked back over her own remarkable life:

Are we not governed by destiny over which we have no control?

Is it possible for us to struggle and overcome fate or are we merely being swept along a course which all our efforts fail to alter or change?

Can it really be that the planets which control and influence plant life may also be the governing factors in our destiny?

Both women had fathers who deserted the family; both turned to the stage to make their way. Both married. They both had sons. But Jane, the less comely of the two, ended up wealthy and Mary, destitute. Mary's son had to enlist in the war and fell. Jane's son landed a comfortable wartime position in Washington. "What governed the destinies of these two?" Bly asked. "Was it fate or did each make her own life?"

The day the essay was published, Bly entered St. Mark's Hospital with a severe case of bronchopneumonia complicated by heart disease. The headline on that last piece of published work held its own comment on a life not so much lived as waged, a life turned by fate and fortune at defining moments. "Nellie Bly," the boldface type read, "On Pranks of Destiny."

Insofar as it was possible, Nellie Bly had governed Nellie Bly. As she had said so many years before, "Energy rightly applied and directed can accomplish anything." It could have been an epitaph.

Two days after Bly entered St. Mark's, she gave her brother Harry and niece Beatrice $800 to cover any expenses that might arise during her incapacitation. She signed her will on January 11. As executors of her estate, she named both Harry and Beatrice along with her attorney, John Warren Hill. To Oscar Bondy she bequeathed, as she had said she would, the sugar company stock; the Austrian currency he had given her when she left Vienna; and the balance in her bank account at the Union Dime Savings Bank, which represented the cumulative interest on the sugar stock since he had put it in her name five years earlier. She had never spent a dime of his money, just as she had told him. She even returned Queen Victoria's brooch.

To Beatrice, she gave her "Octagon Plate Diamond Ring in platinum setting," her pearl necklace, and all her furs. To Harry went her diamond earrings, and to her half niece Grace McLaughlin she bequeathed a ring or brooch which the executors were to select and send her back in Apollo. Nothing was left in the will to Gertrude and Charles, her other full niece and nephew, or to their mother, Sarah, although Gertrude had the jade beads Bly brought from Asia and a beautiful strand of turquoise beads, said in the Cochrane family to have been a gift of the artist and illustrator Frederic Remington.

To Hill, the attorney, she gave her pedigreed German shepherd and a scarf pin. Scarf pins also went to her physician at St. Mark's and to the hospital's superintendent, Ernst F. Lohr, a witness to her will and a great supporter of her work with children.

As to the still-disputed shares of stock of the American Steel Barrel Company, Bly instructed that they be given jointly to Harry and Beatrice at the point at which the shares came into her estate. The wording of the will makes clear that Bly held out hope her lawsuit against Albert would eventually be resolved to bring real and valuable assets into the hands of her heirs. In fact, from years of neglect, the company had been operating at a loss for some time, with an accumulated debt to the Internal Revenue Service alone of more than $50,000. There was nothing left to fight over. Within a year of Bly's death, her executors agreed to drop the suit.

The strange and surprising provision of the will was the one numbered "Thirteenth." It called for Harry and Beatrice, upon their own deaths, to leave all property still in their possession which had been inherited from Bly to one of the scores of children she had helped over the years, the one she described as "my ward, Dorothy Harris, known also as Dorothy Coulter, and also known as Elizabeth Cochrane Bly."

After payment of her debts, including $9,000 owed to attorney Harold Nathan for his work on the barrel company, the estate's net value amounted to only about $8,000, very little of which was cash. Bondy's share had claimed the bulk of what remained, leaving only jewelry, furs, and little more than the $800 for Harry and Beatrice to squabble over, which they did for years. As a *per stirpes* legatee, Dorothy Coulter or Dorothy Harris or Elizabeth Cochrane Bly would never benefit from her guardian's intended largesse. The hovering question was why this little girl, among the scores of children Bly had helped and harbored over the last three years of her life, should have been chosen for such recognition.

Death came eighteen days later, at 8:35 A.M. on January 27, 1922. Beatrice organized the funeral two days after, at the Church of the Ascension at Tenth Street and Fifth Avenue. According to *The Journal*, it was attended by newspaper workers, personal friends, and representatives of the American Seamen's Association. No mourners were mentioned by name. The Reverend Percy Stickney gave the eulogy, praising especially the charitable efforts of Bly's final years. Bly was buried at Woodlawn Cemetery in a grave that remained for half a century "unmarked by loving hands"—Bly's own sad description of a grave she saw in Mexico on her first foreign assignment back in 1886.

New York newspapers gave ample notice to her passing. Her obituary even ran over the wires of the Associated Press, which said her life was "more active than falls to the lot of more than one woman in ten thousand." Every story mentioned the feats that first brought her to the country's attention: the madhouse exposé and her trip around the world. *The New York Times* noted her marriage to Robert Seaman, a man forty years her senior, and her success in running his companies. "Luck turned against her, however," *The Times* said, "and a series of forgeries by her employees, disputes of various sorts, bankruptcy and a mass of vexatious and costly litigation swallowed up Nellie Bly's fortune. Her courage and liveliness remained, however, and she returned to journalism with all her old spirit." *The New York World* reported her death on its obituary page with a ten-paragraph story, noting her close friendship of so many years with Erasmus Wilson and the irony of his death having occurred only two weeks before hers, on January 14.

Nellie Bly, circa 1921

(UPI/Bettmann)

The most elaborate tribute came from Arthur Brisbane, who devoted his column to Bly's memory the day after her death:

Nellie Bly, whose work and character are known to millions, died yesterday. Newspapers will tell of her work as a newspaper woman, the trip around the world when she was a young girl, in which she traveled more rapidly than Jules Verne's imaginary hero, and her other exploits.

More important to Nellie Bly and to her friends is the work of which the world knew nothing.

She died leaving little money, and what she had was tied up, pledged to take care of children without homes, for whom she wished to provide.

She went to work again, living economically in a single room, always having with her at least one child that had no other home.

The children upon whom she spent money earned by hard work in spite of illness, were strangers to her, with no other claim upon her except the fact that they were poor and friendless. Her work for the children, and for the American seamen, in whose behalf she fought constantly the entire record of her life as a newspaper worker, proved that her "heart was ever with the weak and miserable poor."

Nellie Bly was THE BEST REPORTER IN AMERICA and that is saying a good deal. Reporting requires intelligence, precision, honesty of purpose, courage and accuracy.

Her courage was first proved when she, a young girl in her teens, deliberately had herself committed as insane, to an asylum against which serious charges of cruelty had been made.

Shamming insanity and keenly observing, she lived among the maniacs as one of them, often in danger. When she came out she wrote articles that improved the conditions of thousands of unfortunate inmates all over the country.

Nellie Bly died too young, cheated of the fortune that should have been her own, suffering for years from ill health that could not diminish her courage or her kindness of heart.

But her life was useful and she takes with her from this earth all that she cared for, an honorable name, the respect and affection of her fellow workers, the memory of good fights well fought and of many good deeds never to be forgotten by those that had no friend but Nellie Bly.

Happy the man or woman that can leave as good a record.

. AND JAPAN AT LAST REACH AGREEMENT ON SH

MISS NELLIE BLY, GREAT WOMAN JOURNALIST

This photo was taken in 1883, when Miss Bly won fame by circling globe in record time.

LUALDI AS POPE IN DEADLOCK COMPROMISE

Archbishop of Palermo Mentioned if Neither of Opposing Factions Can Elect.

By International News Service

ROME, Jan. 28.—Cardinal Alessandro Lualdi, Archbishop of Palermo, may be selected as a compromise candidate in the Papal election in the Vatican next month, in the event of a deadlock, it was learned to-day from an eminent prelate of the Roman Catholic Church.

It is reported that negotiations have been conducted between the factions headed by Merry Del Val and Cardinal Gasparri, but without any result. The adherents of Cardinal Merry Del Val are known as the "Irreconcilables," and are opposed to reconciliation between the Vatican and the Quirinal.

The followers of Cardinal Gasparri, the Papal Secretary of State, wish to continue the policy of the late Pope Benedict X.

The names most prominently mentioned follow in the order named: Cardinal Ratti, Archbishop of Pisa; Cardinal Ratti, Cardinal Laurenti

Dr. Catt to Entertain Club.

Mrs. Carrie Chapman Catt will entertain the New York Alumnae Club of Pi Beta Phi at her home, No. 404 Riverside drive, February 4, at 2:30 p. m. Mrs. Catt will address the club on "College Women as Citizens,"

the end of the week. A survey of the details yet to be gathered up, however, has led the conference officially to believe it will not be possible to adjourn until possibly the 15th of February.

The resolution providing for another conference to consider rules of warfare was adopted by the Armaments Committee this evening, and the Far Eastern Committee disposed of the Chinese wireless question.

The rules of warfare here, which is termed a commission, will consist of two delegates from each of the "Big Five" Powers. Changes in international law to cover new agencies of warfare will be recommended to the five Governments, which, it they adopt them, will ask other nations to accept them. The meeting will be called by the United States not earlier than three months after the present conference adjourns. The date and place of meeting will be agreed upon in consultation with the other Powers.

In the wireless matter, the resolution of December 7 was reaffirmed after French objection had blocked other proposals. This measure restricts wireless stations in legation quarters to Government messages, and other stations to the terms of concessions under which they were erected.

Unauthorized stations are required to be turned over to China upon fair reference, with due compensation.

U.S. SENAT
KERN-B
SCAND

Continued from

ington, one time Chie
Supreme Court of the
lumbia—by appointe
Wilson—who resigned to accept the
signments of profitable cases involving properties seized by the Custodian.

In the Bosch instance, it is said,
he got first $1,000 from the Govern-
ment, then $15,000 from Kern. He
collected $6,000 when representing
the Heyden Chemical Works and
$15,000 when appearing for the Bayer
Company. He was retained by the
new managements of the seized Berlin Aniline Works, Synthetic patents
Company, Hudson River Aniline &
Color Works and the Kalle Color &
Chemical Co., Inc.

More important than all this is the
fact that he appeared for the Chemical Foundation, Inc., the wealthy
dye manufacturing company of which
Garvan is the head and which, it is
reported, obtained from the Custodian's office 4,600 German dye for-
mulas for $250,000.

LAST RITES FOR NELLIE BLY TO-MORROW

Funeral services over Nellie Bly, in private life Mrs. Robert L. Seaman, a special writer on the staff of The Evening Journal and probably the best known woman newspaper worker of her time, will be held at the Church of the Ascension Fifth avenue and Tenth street, to-morrow afternoon at 2 o'clock. It was announced to-day. They will be conducted by the Rev. Percy Stickney

has given rise to the report that the
Government is determined to put an
end to the rum runners who are alleged to have been infesting the Jersey coast for the past year.

It is generally believed that Lieutenant Hutson will be extra vigilant
in maintaining a scrutiny over Two
Mile Beach, the only uninhabited
beach between Sandy Hook and Cape
May. Two Mile Beach is on the
harbor here, and there have been reports that rum runners have been
using this place as a cache for whiskey, said to have been brought from
the Bahamas in schooners and fast
motor boats.

Despite the fact that members of
the coast guard station at Two Mile
Beach deny the report that "booth"
has been landed there, a lone fisher-
man was held up recently and forced
to witness the loading of two trucks
with some from a cache in the sand
dunes, which are over forty feet high
in some places on the coast. The
Kickapoo will keep a sharp watch on
the Delaware Capes and see that no
liquor is smuggled through there under cover of dark-ness. There have
been reports that several craft have
succeeded in getting through the
Capes and unloaded their cargoes
along lonely stretches of the wooded
beach from Cape May to Maurice
River.

RITES FOR
LIE BLY
MORROW

ices over Nellie Bly,
Mrs. Robert L. Sea-
Journal and prob-
known woman news-
er her time, will be
ch of the Ascension
and Tenth street, to-
oon at 2 o'clock, it was
day. They will be con-
he Rev. Percy Stickney

of pneumonia in St.
erday after-
en ill about two

Born at Cochrane's Mills, Pa.,
town founded by her father, Judge
Cochrane, she was fifty-six years old.
Finding herself virtually penniless,
Miss Bly took up newspaper work
while still in her teens—at a salary
of $5 a week. Later she was able to
earn $25,000 a year with her pen.

AROUSED THE WORLD.

One of her best known journalistic exploits was her famous trip
around the world, started in November, 1889, to prove the
Jules Verne's imaginative romance
"Around the World in Eighty Days"
was possible. She made the trip in
seventy-two days, six hours, eleven
minutes and fourteen seconds, arriving back in New York on January
25, 1890. On her way around the
globe she found time to visit and interview Jules Verne at his home at
Amiens, France.

Another feat that attracted coun-
try-wide attention was her action in
having herself committed to the
Blackwell's Island insane asylum as
a patient in order of study and expose conditions in that institution
through the columns of a morning
New York newspaper on which she
was then employed. So well did she
feign insanity that her life was able
to get a mass of detailed inside information, show up startling defects
in the management and force important reforms.

Nothing was too daring for her to
undertake in order to get a "good
story." She went down into the sea
in a diving bell, up in the air in a
balloon and attempted and carried
out numerous other feats in order to
be able to give a vivid first-hand
story of her sensations and observations to her thousands of readers.
She has been called in later years
the country and numbered her

MRS. STILLMAN
TO SHOW LACK
OF FUNDS

John T. Brennan, commenting on
the decision of the Appellate Division of the Supreme Court reversing the order granting Mrs.
James A. Stillman $7,500 to defray
expenses in Canada, said to-day that
he would apply to Supreme Court
Justice Morschauser in Poughkeep-
sie for a new commission, and
would prove by affidavits that his
client has not the money necessary
to take the Canadian testimony.

The decision pointed out that Mrs.
Stillman has already received a
greater sum than most people are
able to accumulate in a lifetime of
toil. This includes monthly al-
mony of $7,500, $10,000 counted fees
and $12,500 expenses.

The history of the commission
began several months ago, when
Mrs. Stillman's counsel applied to
Justice Morschauser for a Canadian
lawyer to take testimony of North
Woods witnesses contradicting the
banker's witnesses.

this larger field of activity. At that
time Mr. Wilson was conducting a
column on the Pittsburgh paper under the caption "Quiet Observer."

Curiously enough, Miss Bly was
stricken with illness in her apartment in the Hotel McAlpin on the
same day that Mr. Wilson died—
January 14. He was seventy-nine
years of at the time of his death,
and had acquired a wide reputation
as a historian, in addition to being
a "columnist."

MISS BLY'S ROMANCE.

In 1895 Miss Bly went to Chicago,
to work on one of the dailies there,
and at a banquet met Robert L. Seaman, an aged and wealthy Brooklyn
manufacturer to whom she was later
married. They came to New York
and established their residence at
No. 15 West Thirty-seventh street.

Mr. Seaman, who was seventy-two
years old at the time of his wedding,
died fifteen years later, leaving his
fortune to his wife. His properties
included the Ironclad Manufacturing
Company, makers of enameled iron
ware, and the American Steel Barrel
Company.

Mrs. Seaman assumed the management of these properties herself upon
the death of her husband and proved
highly able and efficient in her new
field of endeavor. Later, however,
she got into difficulties through
questionable transactions by associates in the companies. The properties were finally forced into technical
bankruptcy, and Mrs. Seaman was
robbed of most of her fortune,
subjecting to hundreds of thousands
dollars. Her fight in the courts
where hostile associates lasted for
four years, but she finally won
victory in the litigation.

TO JOURNALISM.

returned to the field of
and her evening engag-
in the Evening Journal re-
to the time of her final
illness.

Nellie Bly's work among the poor
endeared her to many of the city's
population. She had found homes
for many homeless children, causing
friends to take care of waifs whose
mothers had been brought to her attention. Some of these children were
cared for in her own home.

EPILOGUE

IN THE EIGHT MONTHS BETWEEN LITTLE DOROTHY COULTER'S removal from the Leake and Watts Orphan Asylum and Bly's death, it is not clear how much time they actually spent together. In interviews with Dorothy in April of 1991, trace memories of her birth mother, of the orphanage on the river, and of how much she loved Nellie Bly fell from the deep freeze of a memory somewhat altered by age and early signs of dementia.

Yet she remembered with precision a story that sounded too much like an orphan's fantasy to have any basis in reality, until it was corroborated by documents some months after it was told. It was about the famous writer Nellie Bly, who came to the orphanage in a big black car and picked Dorothy out among all the other children to carry her away to a new and happier life. "Dorothy," she remembered Bly saying as they got into the backseat together, "I'm kidnapping you today."

From the woman of eighty came the singsong voice of a seven-year-old girl, reliving the amazing moment that changed the course of her life. "That's all right with me." She beamed. "I'll go anywhere with you."

Dorothy remembered how beautiful her mother was, how she once dropped a milk bottle on the way out of the store and cried so much that the clerk gave her a new one for free. She remembered her mother accidentally burning her head with curling irons while fixing her hair. She remembered being taken by her mother to Boston once to see a show and to meet a man. She remembered being alone in a room most of the time and how neighbors who found out about it complained.

Dorothy remembered liking the orphanage because it provided so many playmates and so many chances to sing and dance. She remembered the view of the Hudson River and the time she got so sick someone wrote about it in the newspaper.

She remembered life at the McAlpin Hotel after her "kidnapping," and that Nellie Bly had arranged for her to study piano and German. Bly taught her how to curtsy, a grace she performed every time she answered the door of the hotel suite. People were constantly in and out. The special attention she attracted made the other chil-

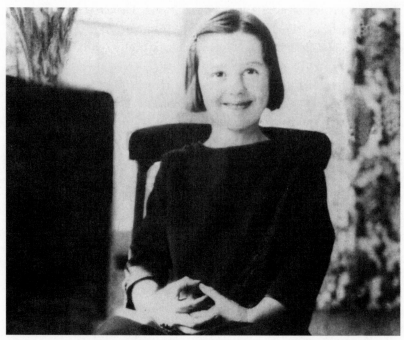

Dorothy Coulter, circa 1924
(courtesy of Roberta Liming)

dren in Bly's care jealous. There were always plenty of children around. She couldn't remember where she slept at the hotel, but she did recall eating in restaurants every night and getting the Bly course in how one behaved at table. She remembered Bly teaching her how to tell time by the hands of a huge clock visible from their hotel window. She remembered Central Park, where Harry often took her, even though she never liked him, and she thought perhaps she went to school somewhere nearby. She remembered that Bly almost changed her name to Elizabeth but suddenly decided against it over concern that people might take to calling her Lizzie, a nickname Bly told Dorothy she had always hated.

Dorothy remembered Bly's tales of her trip around the world and how fascinating and loving a woman she was. Her memory had inspired Dorothy to want to travel someday. Bly had let her try on a corset that she had worn at the age of twenty-five. It was already too small for the child, whom Bly had again described in a story published on July 2, 1921. That time she called her "Helen," "a dainty princess," "unusually brilliant, gifted in music, able to dance, refined to a degree, possessing a most admirable character. She is a little lady of exquisite manners and to see her is to love her." It went on: "Helen's mother is dead and her father was a millionaire Bostonian who went his way uncaring after breaking the heart and wrecking the life of a 15-year-old girl, the pretty girl that was Helen's mother."

By August 19, 1921, Superintendent McClain of Leake and Watts wrote to Bly at the McAlpin: "I am very anxious indeed to see you personally about Dorothy Coulter. I have a very fine home for her and I am wondering if it would be possible for me to call at your convenience sometime during the early part of next week."

Bly replied three days later: "I would be pleased to see you if I had a moment to spare but all my time is engaged as far ahead as two months. Won't you write me full particulars about the home you have? Name, address, nationality, religion, business and age of the persons. Then I will give it my serious consideration, believe me."

There was no further correspondence on the subject in the superintendent's file. Three days before Christmas 1921, just over a month before Bly's death, her column for *The Journal* told of plans to have a "great big fat" Christmas tree in her room at the McAlpin, even if it were just a hotel, for the sake of her "kiddies," all awaiting adoption. Among them was yet another evident description of Dorothy, disguised in chronology and details. This time Bly wrote of the girl

> who lived in poverty with her poor little mother, only a bit of a girl herself . . .
>
> The mother did her best, but that best was most pitiable. She kept her child and tried to support it. She went to work each day, locking the child in a room alone, where it remained until she came back at night. A cold room and poor food—she and her baby barely existed until finally Nature took its revenge.
>
> The mother became a victim of consumption. Then she appealed to me. There was nothing to be done except to give her care and comfort during her last few hours. She was beyond help. I comforted her as best I could and promised her to care for her little girl. I sent the child to the country, where she was fed and nursed into health and strength while the mother lay in a hospital receiving the tenderest care that could be given to her, but gradually fading away. She died with a smile on her lips as I said my last words to her, "I would care for her [*sic*] little girl."
>
> I buried her and the child does not know yet that her mother has gone away forever. This will be her first Christmas.

Sensing her new protector was not well, Dorothy remembered making a promise to Nellie Bly that she would take care of her for the rest of her life. She also remembered a red velvet coat and bonnet with white fur trim that Bly had bought for her to wear when she went to meet her new parents.

And then she remembered some confusion, being taken to stay with Bly's niece Beatrice for a few days and someone saying, "Aren't you sad that Nellie Bly died?" Soon after, her uncle-to-be, Morris Bosworth, picked her up in his car and drove her to Cleveland to live with his sister, Clara Belle Watson, and her husband, Harry, a cashier for H. Black and Company. The three-story, two-family frame house they had recently moved to was at 3202 Sycamore Road, a lovely tree-lined street in Cleveland Heights and a great place to raise a child. The couple, in their forties at the time, had been married and childless for fourteen years.

Dorothy arrived at the Watson home on February 3, 1922, a week after Bly's death. Three days later, the Watsons enrolled her in Lee Elementary School in Cleveland Heights, giving her last name as Watson even though her formal adoption would take nearly two years to complete. Dorothy entered Miss Kate Phillips's third grade class, although her age as of the nearest September 1 was noted on her school record with a question mark. The Watsons left Cleveland in 1926 for St. Petersburg, Florida, where Harry Watson opened a restaurant. Dorothy finished high school there, married Robert

Dorothy Coulter Watson Brauer, April 1991
(Brooke Kroeger)

Brauer, and had her own family, sharing in whispers with her daughters and closest friends, and later her granddaughter, the amazing stories from her past. While she was growing up, her adoptive mother had forbidden her to talk about her previous life.

Since no birth certificate could be found for Dorothy, her actual date and place of birth have never been determined. In an affidavit to police after her arrest, Dorothy's mother had given the child's birth date as September 23, 1912, although this was never verified. Grace—Marie—herself had given different names and birthplaces for her own parents every time she was asked.

The inability to establish a place of birth also meant that Dorothy was never able to fulfill her dream to travel as Bly had done. Dorothy's husband of fifty years, Robert Brauer, spent the better part of their marriage trying to track down his wife's early history so that she might obtain a U.S. passport. Scores of requests for documents from her past over the course of forty years yielded no answer to that question. Dorothy's daughters, Anita Scheublein and Roberta Liming, took up the search after their father died in 1988. Anita's daughter, Carolyn Craige, shares the fascination with Grandma's past. It was Carolyn who brought Dorothy from St. Petersburg to Black Mountain, North Carolina, in 1990, to live with her and her three children after it became apparent that Dorothy could no longer manage on her own.

In 1991, much of Bly's description of Dorothy seventy years earlier still held. There were the eyes "big and wide and blue as the water in Capri's famous grotto," "soft cheeks," "bewitching dimples," a mouth that "seemed formed for kisses," and a manner "gentle and winning," "filled with music." The genteel charm, the ability to please that had served her so well in much less settled times were all intact—there was no evident embitterment in the old woman whose first ten years on earth were a study in fear, loneliness, abandonment, deadly illness, and jarring change, softened by the goodwill of strangers. Dorothy had managed to transmute the memory of her birth mother into a passion for music, dance, and exotic costumes, evidence of which bulges from her many albums of photographs. In Dorothy's memory, Bly became the fairy godmother, a designation that would no doubt have delighted her had she lived to tell the story herself.

ACKNOWLEDGMENTS

I t is astounding how many minds are required for one person to write a book about another.

Elizabeth Blackmar provided insightful criticism, comment, and correction to early drafts of the manuscript, as did my husband, Alex Goren; Gail Gregg; Michael Ridder; Arthur O. Sulzberger, Jr.; and David and Helen Weinstein, my cheerleading parents.

Attorneys Mendel Small and Jay Russ helped me through the nuances of turn-of-the-century bankruptcy proceedings; James McClister elucidated on early Pennsylvania estate law; Dennis Mandell on early property deeds; and Leah Keith on prosecutorial procedure. The expertise of Professor Solomon Wank saved me from several embarrassments in the Austria chapters. Ingeborg von Sitzewitz ably translated dozens of German documents into English. John F. Englert's contributions to Bly's early family background were enormous.

Marilynn Abrams in Harrisburg; Russell B. Adams, Joseph L. Galloway, Marsha Pinson and David Vine in Washington; Alex Beam in Boston; Donna Elkins in Austin; Jane Field in San Francisco; Sylvana Foa in Los Angeles; Hans Fritz and Alison Smale in Vienna; Theodore Hogeman and Charles R. Kroeger in Utica; Trudy

Rubin in Philadelphia; Ricki Weiss in Cleveland, and Vickie Weiss in Albany, responded cheerfully to brazen requests to do bidding on short notice.

For the patient, informed, intelligent hearing given to long sections of this book during the years of its work-in-progress phase, I must single out Alex Goren and Gail Gregg, especially, along with John F. and Jane Englert, Paula Span, and my brothers, Arlen (Avi) and Randall Weinstein. Analyst Carmela Mindell helped me understand Bly's psychological profile. Geraldine Baum, Malka Margolies, Molly O'Neill, and Marsha Pinson also proved thoughtful listeners.

Collectors Patrice McFarland and Starr Ockenga guided my assembling of a personal collection of Bly memorabilia, an irresistible outgrowth of this undertaking. Starr also photographed it. April Bernard, who did not know me, generously gave me her copy of *Love Sonnets of Proteus* with Bly's signature on the flyleaf, which I treasure. Muriel Nussbaum was a wellspring of encouragement and lore, as was Peggy Cochrane Potts.

Philippa Brophy was much more than a literary agent to me throughout, and my editor, Steve Wasserman, was an unfailing source of enthusiasm and expertise. My gratitude to Times Books extends as fully to publisher Peter Osnos and the superb production team. Special thanks to Susan M. S. Brown, who elevates copy editing to an art form.

Gina Breuer ably assisted me in the last few months before deadline, finding arcane references and missing first names. Cathy Crane stepped in to help with bibliographic precision in the final weeks of preparation.

Gail Gregg willingly absorbed most of the angst of the project. Alex and our children, Andrea, Selina, and Brett, patiently endured my distraction and neglect. Alex, only sometimes complaining, performed a thousand tasks that enabled the completion of the manuscript on deadline. Without him, there simply would not be a book.

NOTES AND SOURCES

Bly's Letters

The Department of Special Collections, Syracuse University Library, houses the Brisbane Family Papers. All correspondence with Bly is in the Arthur Brisbane papers, which included, for reasons undetermined but welcomed, several letters from Bly to her family and one to her company's general manager. Particular thanks to Carolyn A. Davis and Karen D'Agostino for locating material no one else seemed to know existed.

Bly's letters to Erasmus Wilson are in the Manuscript Collection of the Carnegie Library's Pennsylvania Department. Marie Zini, now retired, was extremely helpful during my work there and later graciously responded to scores of calls for assistance.

The Frank G. Carpenter Papers, Sophia Smith Collection, Smith College, contain one letter from Bly to Carpenter.

The World (NY) Papers, involving documents from *The New York World* and correspondence of Joseph Pulitzer, are in the Rare Book and Manuscript Library, Columbia University. A second collection at the Library of Congress, Manuscript Division, has both overlapping and different material. At Columbia, the papers of W. A. Swanberg concerning his preparation of the biography *Pulitzer* were also consulted.

The Woodrow Wilson Papers (Paris Peace Conference, 1919) at the Library of Congress, Manuscript Division, include a brief correspondence with Bly.

Peggy Cochrane Potts, Bly's grandniece, provided family Christmas cards, letters, photographs, and encouragement from the outset.

One letter of Bly's to Bankers Trust was found buried in her estate file with the Clerk of the New York County Surrogate's Court. Others surfaced in the national archives in Vienna.

Doris Kerr Brown kindly provided the copy of F. Scott Fitzgerald's letter to her father, Robert Kerr, and the interview with Kerr in *The Great Neck News,* both first seen in a 1976 article by Joseph Corso in *The Fitzgerald-Hemingway Annual,* a monograph edited by Dr. Matthew Bruccoli of the University of South Carolina from 1969 to 1979.

Bly's Books

The Library of Congress has all four of Bly's books, *Ten Days in a Mad-House, Six Months in Mexico, The Mystery of Central Park,* and *Around the World in Seventy-two Days.* The New York Public Library has all but the Central Park mystery novel.

Real Estate, Vital Statistics, and Court Records

All Armstrong County records involving deeds and mortgages, marriages, divorces, and estates of the Cochran/Cochrane family are in the Armstrong County Courthouse in Kittanning, Pennsylvania, in the Prothonotary (marriages and divorces), the Register and Recorder's Office (estates, deeds, mortgages), and the Tax Assessment Office (tax rolls). The Armstrong County Historical Society has some valuable material. Similar searches were made in Somerset and Westmoreland counties in Pennsylvania. In this connection, the voluntary and sacrificial efforts of John Englert, president of the Armstrong County Historical Society, went on for a year after I had left the area and defy description or adequate expression of gratitude. He and his wife, Jane, have become wonderful friends. In this connection, I also want to thank Mildred Thomas.

Michael Cochran's estate, from which comes much documentation, including Bly's case against her guardian, Col. Samuel Jackson, is in the Armstrong County Orphans' Court records of the Register and Recorder's Office, Estate No. 2043.

New York City Vital Records (including Brooklyn) for the relevant period are housed at the New York City Municipal Archives, 31 Chambers Street, where Ken Cobb ably fielded scores of requests.

New York City wills and estates are lodged with the New York County Surrogate's Court Clerk, also at 31 Chambers Street. Other helpful archives at the same location were those of the New York County courts. Some useful district attorney and criminal court records were in the Municipal Archives, as were minutes of relevant civil proceedings and tax assessment rolls.

In Brooklyn, the Kings County Surrogate Court clerk provided relevant wills and estate documents. Brooklyn real estate records came from the Kings County City Register's Office.

New York City Real Estate Records (deeds, mortgages, titles) cited are housed in the City Register's Office.

The Westchester County Historical Society in Elmsford, New York, retrieved leases on the farms the Cochranes rented and owned in White Plains from the Westchester County Deed Book.

Property, tax, and church records as well as some details of Seaman family history are in the Greene County Historical Society in Coxsackie, New York. Thanks to Raymond Beecher. The Greene County Surrogate's Court clerk's office in Catskill had probate files on several members of the Seaman family. Additional genealogical research on ancillary members of the Seaman clan was provided by Marsha Saron Dennis.

Some material from Chicago—mainly Bly's articles for *The Times-Herald* and the Bisbee-Seaman case—was retrieved by Terry Fife's staff at History Works. The Illinois State Historical Library in Springfield also was helpful.

Records involving Bly are variously found under Nellie Bly, Pink Elizabeth J. Cochran, Elizabeth J. Cochrane, Elizabeth Cochrane Seaman, and Mrs. Robert L. Seaman, and under her mother's name, Mary Jane Cochrane.

National Government Archives

The U.S. National Archives State Department Files cited in Chapters 11 and 12 were from the Vienna Embassy, registration of American citizens, 1907–1920++; U.S. Ambassador to Vienna Frederic Penfield's correspondence, 1914; Spanish Embassy representation of the United States in Austria, 1917–1922.

Also from the U.S. National Archives, files on the Alien Property Custodian suit brought by Bly's mother against Oscar Bondy are from the Alien Property Custodian, Record Group 131, Entry 139, Exhibit D-19; Entry 199, Report 1709 Cochrane v. APC; Entry 289, Box 4, APC Records, Bureau of Law File No. 54. Russell B. Adams, Jr., a longtime Bly buff, had collected these some years before and graciously passed them along.

Military intelligence files on Bly came from the U.S. National Archives, Record Group 165, M.I.D. Files, M.I.D. 19297-331. John Taylor was especially helpful to me over and over again in this area of research.

Consular records of Bly's passport activity and the like are listed individually in the notes. Dane Hartgrove, Sue McDonough, and John Butler of the National Archives assisted repeatedly.

From Vienna, the Haus-, Hof-und Staatsarchiv files cited in Chapters 11 and 12 include the Foreign Ministry Archive on the treatment of Americans under the monarchy, Administrative Registratur, F-36, Boxes 607–608. All letters and documents concerning, from, or to Bly at the Haus-, Hof-und Staatsarchiv are in the Press Department (Presse Leitung) Files, P.L. 202/1915, Folios 109–146, and not as indexed. Without Dr. Leopold Auer, this part of the story simply would never have been told.

Kriegsarchiv files from Vienna are few and noted specifically in the text. Special thanks to Dr. Rainer Egger for handling my requests by mail while the archive was closed for renovation.

From the Archiv der Republik, files on Bly were from the Staatskanzlei No. 441-1919 and No. 1207/1-1919; the Allgemeines Verwaltungsarchiv, Ministerrats Praesidium, Presse Leitung Mixta, and the Deutschösterreichisches Staatsamt für Ausseres No. 2054/4-1919.

Files on Oscar Bondy were from the Vermögensverkehrsstelle L.G. No. 9165 VA 50842. At the Nottendorfergasse location of the Österreichisches Staatsarchiv, I was helped enormously in this work by Dr. Rudolf Jeřábek.

Peter Bograd, an American Fulbright scholar in Vienna in 1991, helped with research on Oscar Bondy's sugar refining enterprise, on Bondy's role as a music patron, and on the activities and membership roster of the Military Widows and Orphans Fund.

The bulk of information on Bondy, however, came from his grandnephew, Ivo Rie, who also provided family photographs. His contribution was supplemented by the recollections of Ruth Blumka, Mrs. Otto Kallir, and Hildegard Bachert, all of whom knew Bondy or his wife personally.

Frederika Zeitlhofer of the Austrian Cultural Institute in New York expertly mined the institute's library for obscure facts.

Other Archives

The Brown Brothers Collection in the Manuscript Room of the New-York Historical Society Library was useful in Chapter 10. The Historical Society also had a few letters concerning James Stetson Metcalfe and Arthur Brisbane, and some of Robert L. Seaman's business correspondence.

The New York Public Library's Manuscript Division was consulted for possible sources, yielding only Edward S. Van Zile's poem to Don Seitz. Richer use was made of the Billy Rose Theater Collection at the New York Public Library at Lincoln Center for information on James Stetson Metcalfe, on Eddie Cantor's failed Broadway production in 1946 of *Nellie Bly*, a musical very loosely based on Bly's trip around the world, on the staging of *Around the World in 80 Days*, and on the actress Beverly Sitgreaves.

The New York State Archives at Albany has state legislative records, which Vicki Weiss ably and efficiently combed on my behalf in response to specific requests.

David G. Badertscher, principal law librarian of the State of New York Unified Court System Supreme Court, First Judicial District, expedited my search for case summaries.

Special Collections and Archives, Stapleton Library, Indiana University of Pennsylvania, has Bly's registration and school records, as well as the early history of the normal school. Record Group 52, Boxes 25 (p. 101) and 31, Office of Registrar, Registration Ledger—Ladies, 1875–1896. Special thanks to Pamela Pletcher and Denise Visconti.

Buswell Memorial Library, Special Collections and Archives, Wheaton College, Wheaton, Illinois, has the Mignon Rittenhouse Collection, which contains excerpts from a letter to her from the late Margaret Collins Carey, Bly's secretary from 1906 to 1916, which includes some of Mrs. Carey's recollections of Bly. Mrs. Carey's son, Edward, shared his memories, too. Thanks to David Malone at Wheaton, who found the Rittenhouse collection by chance among the library's uncataloged papers months after I had asked if they existed on the advice of the author's daughter, Lois Kellerman.

Peter M. Kenny of the Metropolitan Museum of Art graciously allowed access to the museum's files on the family of James Stetson Metcalfe. Christopher Gray of Metropolitan History was especially helpful in efforts to picture New York neighborhoods in Bly's time. Walter Kidney performed the same service for early Pittsburgh.

Biographers Kathleen Barry and Alice Wexler shared their insights about Bly's interviews with Susan B. Anthony and Emma Goldman, respectively, and Allan Farnham took time to discuss his long-standing interest in the life of Arthur Brisbane.

Access to confidential files of the New York Society for the Prevention of Cruelty to Children and the Leake and Watts Children's Home in Yonkers, New York, concerning Bly's ward, Dorothy, was arranged with the kind permission of Dorothy Brauer and her granddaughter, Carolyn Craige, and the equally kind cooperation of both organizations. Carolyn and her mother, Anita Sheublein, provided copies of all the documentation Dorothy's husband had collected about her early life. Likewise, I am grateful to NYSPCC Director Ann Reiniger and to Director James Campbell of Leake and Watts and his assistant, Ruth Schoen, who allowed access to their respective records. I also must mention the phenomenal necrology files of the Western Reserve Historical Society in Cleveland Heights, Ohio, and a young man named Gary Silverstein, without whose help I would have failed to trace Dorothy to Florida. It was there that Jack Payton and Natalie Watson of the *St. Petersburg Times* provided the key information that led to finding Dorothy in Black Mountain, North Carolina. That is, of course, another story.

Newspapers

As many of Bly's articles as possible have been mentioned in the text or indexed in the notes in rough chronological order.

The relevant years for *The Pittsburg Dispatch* are on microfilm at the Pennsylvania State Library at Harrisburg and at the Library of Congress. The Pennsylvania State Library also has complete files for other Pittsburgh newspapers of the period. I had able assistance in reeling the microfilm from Muriel Nussbaum, another Bly buff, who accompanied me to Harrisburg to help put together the file of Bly's two years at *The Dispatch*—for the fun of it—and from David Vine, who went back over those same years at the Library of Congress to make sure we hadn't missed anything. We had missed a few. Marilynn Abrams, of Harrisburg, a thorough and proficient researcher and a wonderful friend, made dozens of trips back to the State Library to request and copy all kinds of related material.

The New York World is on microfilm at the New-York Historical Society, where I reviewed it for the most part, and at the New York Public Library and the Library of Congress. Most other major New York newspapers are on microfilm at one or more of these facilities.

The New York Evening Journal, however, is complete only at the Harry Ransom Humanities Research Center, University of Texas at Austin, which also houses the *New York Journal-American* morgue, a crumbling but wonderful index. Ken Craven of the HRC proved helpful repeatedly. Donna Elkins copied *Journal* and *Journal-American* stories from the microfilm and found many that otherwise would have been missed.

The Brooklyn Daily Eagle morgue is housed at the Brooklyn Public Library, where librarian Judith Walsh enabled the unearthing of many unanticipated surprises. The New York Public Library newspaper collection has the morgue of *The New York Sun*, which also proved invaluable.

The Albany newspapers are on microfilm at the New York State Archives in Albany, where Vicki Weiss searched them for articles on the Phelps case on my behalf.

The Library of Congress has a complete collection of *The Journalist* for the relevant years as well as most of the other magazines of the period. In between my numerous trips to Washington, David Vine spent many more hours at the Library of Congress, pulling articles I had requested from turn-of-the-century periodicals, rechecking some sources, and arranging for the photocopying of long-out-of-print books not available in New York.

The New-York Historical Society has bound volumes of *Town Topics* in pristine condition and a very civilized microfilm reading system. May Stone and other members of the library staff were courteous and helpful during the many months I spent in that treasure chest.

The Catskill (NY) *Daily Mail* ran a multipart series June 20–24, 1977, tracing the history of Robert Seaman's mansion property in Catskill, New York, and Bly's brief sojourns there. The series was written by then Greene County Historian Mabel Parker Smith and included excerpts from newspaper articles she had clipped and interviews she had conducted many years earlier with Catskill residents who had known Seaman or met Bly—even some who had worked on the Seaman property. Mrs. Smith, when interviewed May 7, 1991, was unable to retrieve the notes and source material she had used in the series but verified their authenticity.

The Greene County Historical Society also has a large collection of nineteenth-century weekly newspapers from the immediate area.

Public libraries and historical societies in Albany, Batavia, Buffalo, Great Neck, and Sullivan County, New York; Bridgeport, Connecticut; Topeka, Kansas; St. Louis, Missouri; Edwardsville, Illinois; Milwaukee; Logansport, Indiana; Cleveland Heights, Ohio; Pittsburgh; and New Orleans, among others, were prompt and courteous in response to written and telephoned requests for newspaper photocopies and other material.

Unpublished Essays

In light of the limited contemporaneous material for this project, three unpublished essays proved especially valuable:

"Memories of Apollo" by Dr. Thomas J. Henry was written but not published sometime before his death in 1945. It recounts boyhood memories of Bly's hometown at the time she was growing up. Dr. Henry, the town physician and self-styled historian, was close to Bly's family: He was a friend and contemporary of Bly's brother Albert and was married to Bly's half niece Cora Cochran Henry. Mrs. Leland Henry, Jr., provided me with a copy of the essay. Another Henry descendant, Linda Henry Champanier, shared her copy of *Chronicles of the Cochrans*.

Irene Ravitch's "Nellie Bly: A Biographical Sketch" was written in 1931 in fulfillment of Mrs. Ravitch's requirements for a master's degree from the Columbia University Graduate School of Journalism. Mrs. Ravitch interviewed several people who knew Bly well or had specific recollections of pivotal moments in her life and career. The essay is in the Arthur Hays Sulzberger Library, Graduate School of Journalism, Columbia University. As she no longer had possession of the source material, Mrs. Ravitch kindly gave permission to quote from her work.

Alfred Frantz Myers, "Nellie Bly: Fact or Fiction, The Life and Legend of Elizabeth Jane Cochrane," was written in 1970 while Myers was a student at Indiana University of Pennsylvania, formerly the Indiana State Normal School, which Bly attended. Myers, a distant relative of the Cochranes, interviewed James Agey, Bly's grandnephew, in Oakmont, Pennsylvania, in 1970. Agey showed him Bly's two letters to her brother Charles, from which Myers transcribed excerpts. After Agey died in 1981, the letters fell out of family hands. Fortunately, Myers included the excerpts in his college paper, the only extant record of their existence. Mr. Myers could not locate his notes but kindly gave permission to quote the excerpts from his paper.

I

✨ 🐮

Childhood

p. 3 **May 5, 1864** The commonly accepted birth year for Bly is 1867, which was deduced from the age she claimed to be at the height of her popularity, when she was in her twenties. Her baptismal record in a logbook of the United Methodist Church of Apollo, Pa., however, confirms 1864 as correct. Further, in court testimony on Oct. 14, 1878, she gave her age as fourteen, and at entrance to Indiana Normal School in Sept. 1879, she gave it as fifteen.

p. 3 **early-nineteenth-century Irish settlers** Haughton, *Chronicles of the Cochrans*, p. 87. Michael Cochran's parents, Robert and Catherine Risher Cochran, came from County Derry, Ireland, via Baltimore, to settle in Westmoreland County, Pa., around 1804. Michael was born in 1810.

p. 3 **prominence and financial success** Ibid., pp. 87–89.

p. 3 **bound out** Set to work as an apprentice, indentured.

p. 3 **own indentured apprentices** *Armstrong Democrat and Farmer's and Mechanic's Advertiser*, July 2, 1834. Michael Cochran offered a reward of six cents for the return of his runaway "indented apprentice" Andrew Shannon, age seventeen.

p. 3 **ten children** On Sept. 13, 1922, NB's brother Albert, in connection with the ongoing settlement of his father's estate, quoted the entry in the family Bible giving all the names and birth dates of the children of Catherine and Michael (Michael Cochran's Estate, Armstrong County Courthouse) as well as the five by his mother. Files of Apollo's United Methodist Church show a baptismal record for a Lester Wayne Cochran, as a son of Michael and Mary Jane, but there is no reference to him in any family history or on Albert's list, nor is there a tombstone for him to indicate an infant death.

p. 3 **bitter campaign** *Armstrong Democrat and Farmer's and Mechanic's Advertiser*, June 29, 1843, et seq.

p. 3 **buying up the property** Armstrong County Deed Book, Vol. 5, p. 286, Armstrong County Courthouse. The house built for the Cochrans stood until 1940, when what remained of the village was carted away as part of a state flood control project.

p. 4 **prospered quickly** County tax assessment rolls published in *The Armstrong Democrat* in the 1850s show Michael Cochran paying the highest amounts. Armstrong County Historical Society.

p. 4 **five-year term** Section 3, Act of 1851, P.L. 648; Pennsylvania Constitution of 1838, Art. 5, Sec. 2, "if of good behavior." An associate justice was an elective official under the Constitutional Amendment of 1850. The office was abolished by Schedule of Judiciary Art. 5, Sec. 8, effective Jan. 1, 1969. Also, Eastman, *Courts and Lawyers of Pennsylvania*, 1623–1923, Vol. 2, pp. 497–501; *Standard Pennsylvania Practice*, Vol. 1, 1960, pp. 183–185.

p. 4 **covered wooden bridge** Beers, *Armstrong County, Pa.: Her People, Past and Present*, Vol. 1, p. 188.

p. 4 **into a snake** Recollections of Jane Englert, of nearby Ford City, Pa., whose mother and grandmother grew up in Cochran's Mills. Descriptions include the written reminiscence of Mrs. Englert's grandmother Mildred Cartwright Jobson (1885–1959), set down sometime in the decade before her death.

p. 4 **best fishing** Oral history in undated article from *The Vandergrift News*, Summer 1947, containing old-timer recollections dating back to the 1870s. Armstrong County Historical Society.

p. 4 **Catherine died in 1857** Her tombstone in the Apollo cemetery records her death on Apr. 24, 1857, at the age of fifty years, five months, and fifteen days. The bodies of Catherine and Michael originally were buried in Cochran's Mills but were moved to Apollo by the family. Apollo Public Library. Also, Wiley, *Biographical and Historical Cyclopedia of Indiana and Armstrong Counties*, p. 391; U.S. Census for Armstrong County, Burrell Township, 1860.

p. 4 **born a Kennedy** Minutes of Court of Quarter Sessions of the Peace, Somerset, Pa., 1810–1825. Various applications of Thomas Kennedy for licenses to operate his tavern, Somerset County Courthouse.

p. 4 **first sheriff** Welfley, *History of Bedford and Somerset Counties, Pa.*, p. 161. Somerset County first assessment list, U.S. Direct Tax Lists, 1798, Roll 21, Stoney Creek No. 0398, Somerset County Courthouse. Also, Cassady, *The Somerset County Outline*.

p. 4 **rank of captain** Smith, *History of Armstrong County*, pp. 83–86. Capt. John Cochran was honorably discharged from the military after a court-martial resulting from a prank pulled with another officer in which the two introduced themselves to a group of women using the names of other officers in the regiment. They were ordered to apologize and resign, but Cochran refused to do so. All the same, the 103rd Regiment "had no braver officer than he, and he was, perhaps, as strict a disciplinarian as was in the Regiment." Dickey, *History of the 103d Regiment, Pennsylvania Veteran Volunteer Infantry, 1861–1865*, pp. 82–83. Upon dismissal, he married Rebecca Christy, Oct. 13, 1863, but deserted her eighteen months after the marriage, according to her divorce testimony (Register's Docket Vol. 6, p. 151, File no. 10078, Divorce No. 86, Armstrong County Courthouse). In 1891, he was committed to the State Hospital for the Insane at Wernersville, where he died in Nov. 1919.

p. 4 **run away to enlist** Haughton, *Chronicles*, pp. 87–89; Smith, *History*, pp. 83–86. William enlisted June 10, 1863, and died a few months later. Dickey, *History of the 103d Regiment*, pp. 83–86.

p. 4 **long since married and left home** Haughton, *Chronicles*, pp. 87–89; Smith, *History*, p. 85. Information in this paragraph amalgamated from Beers, Smith, and Wiley entries on the various Cochrans; Haughton, *Chronicles*; Henry, *1816–1916: The History of Apollo, Pennsylvania*, testimony in estate records of Michael Cochran, Armstrong County Courthouse, and the Shoemaker family genealogy. Armstrong County Historical Society.

p. 4 **The season brought** Descriptions of Cochran's Mills on May 5 courtesy of Marian S. Doyle, Vandergrift, Pa., and Jane Englert.

p. 5 **Full brothers** Baptismal records of Methodist Episcopal Church of Apollo, now the Apollo United Methodist Church. Courtesy of Dorothy Knepshield, church historian.

p. 5 **The Reverend J. S. Lemon** Ibid.

p. 5 **While the other mothers** NB's contemporary in Cochran's Mills, the late Lillie Elliott Myers, repeated this story to her grandson, Alfred Frantz Myers, who included it in "NB: Fact or Fiction," and to her granddaughter, Sue Myers, who recounted it in a telephone interview with the author Jan. 20, 1992. A similar version appears in Burke, "NB Started This Globe-Girdling."

p. 6 **same age as her stepmother** Mary Jane's death certificate gives her birth date as Dec. 29, 1826, which could mean she was thirty-three when she married Michael in 1860. Census records, however, show her three years younger.

p. 6 **wealth burgeoned** Deed book entries in the Armstrong County Courthouse show Michael Cochran's real estate speculations, purchases, and sales over the years of his adult life, e.g., Vol. 125, p. 365; Vol. 17, pp. 315–316; Vol. 27, p. 602; Vol. 28, p. 76; Vol. 30, p. 132; Vol. 33, p. 465; and numerous others painstakingly collected by John F. Englert.

p. 7 **evaluated his own holdings** U.S. census records, Armstrong County, Pa., Michael Cochran, 1850, 1860, 1870.

p. 7 **Burrell Township** "Origin of Armstrong County," *Western Pennsylvania Genealogical Society Quarterly*, Aug. 1980, p. 2.

p. 7 **By 1869, the hamlet** 1870 U.S. Census for Armstrong County, Burrell Township, Cochran's Mills, Pa.

p. 7 **"The seed which . . ."** *NY World*, May 27, 1888, 19:3.

p. 8 **purchased three acres** The house still stands at 505–507 Terrace Avenue in Apollo, verified by a title search back to Michael Cochran's original lot purchase in 1868, conducted by John F. Englert.

p. 8 **enough surrounding land** Apollo Borough Tax Assessment Records, 1869–1891, Armstrong County Courthouse.

p. 8 **William Worth died** Smith, *History*, p. 85. William died Jan. 6, 1864, of chronic diarrhea. Dickey, *History of the 103d Regiment*, pp. 79–80. His remains were buried on Roanoke Island but were moved to the National Cemetery at New Bern, N.C., Plot 7, Grave 108.

p. 8 **all Catherine's other children** John abandoned his wife in 1865, wandered for a few years, then returned to Cochran's Mills to work on his sister Juliana's farm in about 1868. Thomas Jefferson, called Jeff, moved to Pittsburgh and had a job in publishing, and George, who suffered from alcoholism, went to Iowa, then returned to Pennsylvania to live out his days. John, Jeff, and George had no children.

p. 8 **loving relationship** Of the obituaries of Catherine's children who remained in the area, only Mildred's (*Vandergrift Citizen*, Sept. 8, 1911, and *Apollo Sentinel*, Sept. 8, 1911) cite Mary Jane and her children as immediate family. Also, Mildred's youngest daughter, Grace McLaughlin, actively involved herself in NB's business affairs many years later.

p. 8 **"learned in the law"** *Standard Pennsylvania Practice*, pp. 183–184.

p. 8 **judge was described** *NY World*, Feb. 2, 1890, 5:1.

p. 9 **entrepreneurial risk** George went off to Iowa; John tried the "oil country" during the rush of the 1860s; Albert tried Iowa and several Pennsylvania towns and went on into entrepreneurial ventures later in life, describing himself as a "capitalist." Robert Scott Cochran, before settling down in Apollo, was a "49er and was at one time in the oil business," according to his obituary in *The Vandergrift Citizen*, Jan. 16, 1914.

p. 9 **medical book** Burke, "NB Started This Globe-Girdling."

p. 9 **Allegheny College** Armstrong County Deed Book, Vol. 19, p. 410. According to Allegheny's librarian, Margaret Moser, the college, in an attempt to avert a funding crisis, offered "endorsements" at perpetual free tuition in return for a twenty-five-dollar contribution. Soon, the program became so expensive it caused a financial crisis of its own. Ultimately, the college was forced to renege on the arrangement.

p. 9 **college has no record** Letter, Margaret Moser, librarian, Lawrence Lee Pelletier Library, Allegheny College, to author, Apr. 28, 1992.

p. 9 **paralysis** *NY World*, Feb. 2, 1890, 5:1.

p. 9 **never bothered to make out a will** Estate of Michael Cochran, Armstrong County Courthouse.

p. 10 **demanding an inquest** Ibid.

p. 10 **state intestate law** *Barnard's Estates*. Before the Intestate Act of 1917, neither husband nor wife was an heir to the other as to real property.

p. 10 **equitable distribution** Letter, Attorney James McClister, Kittanning, Pa., to author, Mar. 1992.

p. 10 **Apollo house and acreage; mill and surrounding fourteen acres; Two other parcels** Estate of Michael Cochran, No. 2043, Armstrong County Courthouse. Also, Deed Book entries: Vol. 40, p. 49, 51; Vol. 46, p. 188; Vol. 40, p. 52, representing allotments A, B, C, and D of the Cochran estate.

p. 10 **"the widow's third"** Under the Intestate Act of Apr. 1833, Sec. 1, a widow was entitled to "one third part of the real estate for the term of her life." Schall's Appeal, 40

Pa. 170, 1861. Under provision of the Orphans' Court Partition Act of Mar. 29, 1832, the widow's portion, whether there be one or more lineal descendants, or collateral heirs only, could be assigned to her by metes and bounds, if the estate could be divided without prejudice: Bishop's Appeal, 7 W. and S. 251; McCall's Appeal, 6, P. F. Smith 363. Kurtz's Appeal, 2 Casey 465, says that "whatever doubt there may be as to the nature of the widow's estate, it is certain that, so far as relates to the principal sum, it is simply a charge on the land in the nature of a lien, payable at the widow's death to the heirs of the intestate, to be recovered as personal only."

p. 11 **Mary Jane ended up** Apollo Borough Tax Assessment Records, 1869–1891, Armstrong County Courthouse.

p. 11 **Her dower** Testimony of Samuel Jackson in suit brought by NB, Armstrong County Orphans' Court, Sept. Term, 1886, charging he mismanaged her trust. Mortgage settlement documents in Estate of Michael Cochran, Armstrong County Courthouse.

p. 12 **wage of a well-paid factory worker** Abbott, *Women in Industry*, wage tables, p. 302; also chapter on wages, pp. 262–316.

p. 12 **764 inhabitants** Smith, *History*, p. 245.

p. 12 **contrast between the two dwellings** Armstrong County Deed Book, Vol. 34, p. 109; Vol. 33, pp. 421–422; Vol. 60, p. 503.

p. 12 **a name she would detest** Author interviews with Dorothy Brauer, Apr. 1991.

p. 12 **Pinkey or Pink** Myers, "NB: Fact or Fiction." In addition, various court testimonies involving NB in adolescent years refer to her as Pink or Pinkey, which she also put as the first name of her signature. As late as 1915, she signed a letter to a family member "Affectionately, Pink."

p. 12 **long white stockings** Author interview with Josephine Myers, daughter-in-law of the late Lillie Elliott Myers, Ford City, Pa., Jan. 21, 1992.

p. 12 **to play the piano and organ** NB, *Ten Days in a Mad-House*, p. 55. Also, Jackson's accounting for NB's trust in the estate of Michael Cochran shows payments for organ, music, etc.

p. 13 "... Jack and the Beanstalk ..." *NY Evening Journal*, Feb. 5, 1915, 3:4–5.

p. 13 **School was a two-story** Smith, *History*, p. 243.

p. 13 **By the time Pink entered school** Henry, "Memories of Apollo." Henry's first wife was NB's half niece, Cora Cochran, daughter of Robert Scott Cochran. Cora was the same age as NB. She and her two-year-old son were killed while crossing the Beaver Run Railroad Bridge, according to *The Kittanning Times* of July 2, 1895, when a freight train ran over them. The story handed down in the Henry family is that Cora's high-topped shoe got caught in a railroad tie, and when she could not loosen it quickly enough to free herself, she flung the child to safety. He fell into a puddle face-first and drowned.

p. 13 **voracious reader** *NY World*, Feb. 2, 1890, 5:1.

p. 13 "... **riotous conduct** ..." Haughton, *Chronicles*, p. 95. (Personality sketch of NB in this volume supplied by T. J. Henry, M.D.)

p. 13 **"rather wild"** Henry, "Memories of Apollo."

p. 14 **"When [she was] a very little girl ..."** *NY World*, Feb. 2, 1890, 5:1.

p. 14 **After school** Henry, "Memories of Apollo."

p. 14 **almost fully self-sufficient** Ibid.

p. 15 **By January of 1873** Marriage certificate, Mary Jane Cochran and John J. Ford, Jan. 19, 1873, Armstrong County Courthouse.

p. 15 **Ford was a Civil War veteran** Henry, *1816–1916*, p. 85. Also Ford's obituary, *Apollo News-Record*, June 9, 1906.

p. 15 **younger than Mary Jane, and childless** Headstones, Apollo Cemetery, for Jack, Henrietta, and infant Ford.

p. 15 **taxable assets** Apollo Tax Assessment Records, 1873.

p. 15 **forfeited to debts** Divorce proceedings of Mary Jane Ford v. John "Jack" Ford, No. 123, Mar. Term, 1879, Court of Common Pleas, Petition Oct. 14, 1878, Divorce granted June 3, 1879, Divorces Book I, p. 96, Armstrong County Courthouse.

p. 15 **She had given up** Apollo Tax Assessment Records, 1873.

p. 15 **"squire"** Obituary of Cora Cochran Henry, *Kittanning Times*, July 12, 1895.

p. 15 **Cousin Thomas A. Cochran** *Atlas of Armstrong County, Pa.* Also listings on T. A. Cochran indexed in Smith, Wiley, Beers, and Henry.

p. 16 **Mary Jane added some details** Divorce file, Mary Jane Cochrane v. John "Jack" Ford.

p. 16 **set Albert up** Testimony of Mary Jane Cochran in case of NB v. Samuel M. Jackson, Mar. Term, 1886, Armstrong County Orphans' Court, Armstrong County Courthouse; **and confectionery business with his stepfather** Tax Assessment Book, Apollo Borough, Armstrong County, 1874, Armstrong County Courthouse.

p. 16 **status of women** Brown, "The Woman's Rights Movement in Pennsylvania, 1848–1873," p. 153. The state woman suffrage association was formed in Philadelphia on Dec. 22, 1869. Developments in the movement in Pennsylvania basically paralleled the national scene. The Constitutional Convention of 1872–73 in Harrisburg included suffrage debates.

p. 17 **Jennie Stentz** Miss Stentz's name appears in two of the county histories and again in Henry's *1816–1916*. However, there are no supporting tax or census records in which her name is mentioned, and no copies of the newspaper are known to have survived. Although Henry probably copied his information from earlier sources, he would have had firsthand knowledge of her existence as a publisher because he was a young adult in the town at the time of publication. Furthermore, his brother-in-law, Michael Hermond Cochran (one of NB's many half nephews), was a subsequent owner. Beers, *Armstrong County*, p. 151, says Stentz started *The Kiskiminetas Review* in 1875 and transferred it after a short time to J. Melhorn. The name was later changed to *The Herald*, and in 1883 the plant was purchased by William Davis, who later (in 1886, according to Henry) sold it to Michael Hermond Cochran. Cochran died in 1883, and his widow assumed editorship and management.

p. 17 **fire of 1876** Smith, *History*, p. 246.

p. 17 **fondness for alcohol** Letter, NB to Charles M. Cochran, Sept. 23, 1879, citing Albert's intemperance, quoted in Myers, "NB: Fact or Fiction."

p. 17 **Michael Hermond Cochran** Henry, *1816–1916*, p. 91.

p. 17 **New Year's Eve, 1878** Unless otherwise cited, all information in this section comes from the divorce proceedings.

p. 19 **one of only fifteen divorce actions** Analysis of Armstrong County divorce filings, 1800–1900, by John F. Englert, based on U.S. census chart of Armstrong County growth from 1800 to 1910.

p. 20 **"My age is 14 years . . ."** NB's testimony from divorce proceedings.

p. 21 **"normal schools"** Brown, "The Woman's Rights Movement in Pennsylvania," p. 159.

p. 22 **"conceded to be the best . . ."** Caldwell, *History of Indiana County, Pennsylvania*, p. 332.

p. 22 **head of the . . . Apollo Savings Bank** Beers, *Armstrong County*, p. 150.

p. 22 **coincidentally had made him kin** The late Judge Cochran's nephew Thomas A. Cochran, son of the Judge's oldest brother, John, was married to Jackson's sister, Martha. Beers, *Armstrong County*, p. 150.

p. 22 **Jackson petitioned the court** Testimony in NB v. Samuel M. Jackson.

p. 22 **Expenses at the Indiana State Normal School** Merryman, *Indiana University at Pennsylvania: From Private Normal School to Public University*, extracted by Denise Visconti, archivist, Stapleton Library, Indiana University of Pennsylvania. Also, Caldwell, *History of Indiana County*, pp. 332–333.

p. 23 **enough money to graduate** NB's testimony in NB v. Samuel M. Jackson.

p. 23 **Jackson signed her registration** Registration ledger, 1879, Indiana University of Pennsylvania.

p. 23 **"In the intercourse . . ."** Caldwell, *History of Indiana County*, p. 333.

p. 24 **In a childish, penciled script** Letter, NB to Charles Metzgar Cochrane, Sept. 23, 1879, quoted in Myers, "NB: Fact or Fiction." NB's niece Peggy Cochrane Potts also recalled seeing the letter when it was in the possession of NB's grandnephew James Cochrane Agey, before it was lost.

p. 25 **"Elizabeth J. Cochrane"** Registration records, 1879, Indiana University of Pennsylvania.

p. 25 **Pink appears to have acted first** Pittsburg City Directory, 1880–81.

p. 25 **Miss Cochrane enrolled** Registration records, 1879, Indiana University of Pennsylvania.

p. 25 **Colonel Jackson paid** NB testimony, NB v. Samuel M. Jackson.

p. 26 **Pink sued the colonel** The suit was filed in the spring of 1886. Attorney James McClister feels certain that Jackson misadministered NB's money, evidenced by his confused testimony during the proceedings and apparent forgeries of signatures for withdrawal and disbursement of funds. By the time the auditor submitted his report and conclusions a year later, Pink was off to New York as a reporter for *The NY World*. At that point, the amounts involved must have seemed too insignificant to continue the suit. She let it drop.

p. 26 **check mark** Registration records, 1879, Indiana University of Pennsylvania.

2

✤ ✤

The Dispatch

p. 29 **visit to . . . "the oil country"** Testimony, NB v. Samuel M. Jackson, Mar. Term, 1886, Armstrong County Orphans' Court; Estate of Michael Cochran, Armstrong County Courthouse.

p. 29 **"When Miss Cochrane . . ."** *NY World*, Feb. 2, 1890, 5:1.

p. 30 **visiting a physician** NB v. Samuel M. Jackson.

p. 30 **Suffragists Parade** *NY Evening Journal*, Mar. 3, 1913, 3:1–4.

p. 30 **February 4, 1880** Burgoyne, *All Sorts of Pittsburgers*, p. 75.

p. 30 **third largest city** Cornell, *History of Pennsylvania*, p. 365. Population in 1889 was about 125,000. *History of Allegheny County*, p. 519.

p. 30 **a painter** Pittsburg City Directory, 1880. There is no *e* at the end of *Cochran* for the family members until the 1881 directory. NB used it as of 1878. NB's letter to Charles from boarding school, Sept. 23, 1879, asks him to send money to Mary Jane in Apollo, indicating he was already in Pittsburgh.

p. 30 **Cochrane and Co.** Pittsburg City Directory, 1881–82.

p. 31 **$300 at sheriff's auction** Armstrong County Deed Book, Vol. 79, p. 559, Armstrong County Courthouse.

p. 31 **50 Miller Street** Pittsburg City Directory, 1880–81.

p. 31 **Manchester** Ward map of Allegheny City, 1883. Descriptions courtesy of Walter Kidney, architectural historian of the Pittsburgh History and Landmarks Foundation (author interview, Jan. 21, 1992, and subsequent correspondence).

p. 32 "**I venture to hope . . .**" Letter, Charles M. Cochrane to Mr. and Mrs. John Hamilton Gillis, dated May 16, 1881, private collection, Peggy Cochrane Potts.

p. 32 **Arch Street** Descriptions of Walter Kidney, Pittsburgh History and Landmarks Foundation.

p. 32 **taken in . . . boarders** Interview with Thomas Smiley, Jan. 20, 1931, quoted in Ravitch, "NB: A Biographical Sketch," pp. 13–14. Smiley rented a room from Mary Jane circa 1885–86. City directories indicate that everyone in the family except Charles and Sarah lived in the house on Chartiers. The young couple moved to 97 Preble in a much less desirable, industrial area of Allegheny and then to 34 Market Street. Within a year of Mary Jane's move to Arch Street, however, Charles and his family moved back in with his mother, Harry, and, presumably, NB. Albert would by this time have married and moved out. The boarders, according to events Smiley described, would have been living with the Cochranes at this time. NB would have been working at the newspaper.

p. 32 **Catherine May . . . married** Birth certificate, Beatrice Cochrane Kountze, Allegheny County Vital Records, Vol. 1, p. 310, Allegheny County Courthouse.

p. 33 **Albert married** Wedding announcement, *Pittsburg Gazette*, Apr. 30, 1885, p. 5.

p. 33 **Dithridge and Fillmore** Author interview with Walter Kidney, Pittsburgh History and Landmarks Foundation, Jan. 21, 1992.

p. 33 **Beatrice Cochrane Kountze** Birth certificate.

p. 33 **Charles Grant . . . Gertrude** Information supplied by Charles Grant Cochrane's granddaughter, Peggy Cochrane Potts, in various telephone conversations with the author, 1991–1993.

p. 33 **adored her** Ibid. Also, recollections of Gertrude Cochrane Agey, who died in May 1979, in "Relatives Agey Proud of Aunt Pink," *Pittsburgh Post-Gazette*, Nov. 16, 1966.

p. 33 **nothing is known for certain** The Pittsburg City Directory for 1882 lists a teacher by the name of Miss Lizzie J. Cochran at 142 Pennsylvania Avenue. Given NB's already noted aversion to this diminutive, the listing may refer to some other person. The 1883 directory includes both a "Miss L. J." at 142 Pennsylvania and a "Miss Elizabeth" Cochran in a row house at 1 Grant Avenue in the industrial Manchester neighborhood of Allegheny City. The Lizzie J. and Elizabeth entries could indicate short-lived positions as a nanny, private tutor, or housekeeper with "Elizabeth" being her own or a different employer's correction of "Lizzie J." NB's family members variously appear in the directories as Cochran or Cochrane. Interestingly, in the directory for 1884, the year before NB went to work for *The Pittsburg Dispatch*, Lizzie J. and Elizabeth both disappear and are never listed again. This supports the notion that Pink returned to live with her mother and other members of the extended family at 246 Chartiers. It would have been odd, in this time, for a woman living at home with her family to list herself separately.

p. 33 **One can easily see** The scenario is supposition. All that can be said conclusively is that the dates and entries for the Cochran/Cochranes in the Pittsburgh directories during this period square with its supposed sequence.

p. 34 **"blackest, dirtiest . . ."** Cutler, "The Gilded Age in Pennsylvania," p. 11, quoting J. Ernest Wright, "Pittsburgh Seventies," *Western Pennsylvania Historical Magazine*, Vol. 26, 1943, p. 137.

p. 34 **"distraction from the all-absorbing . . ."** Cutler, "Gilded Age in Pennsylvania," p. 13.

p. 34 **phenomenal fortunes** Cutler, "Gilded Age in Pennsylvania," pp. 12–13. Also Baldwin, *Pittsburgh, The Story of a City*; Lorant, *Pittsburgh, The Story of an American City*; Marcosson, "The Millionaire Yield of Pittsburgh," pp. 783–789.

p. 34 **newspaper industry** Baldwin, *Pittsburgh*, p. 351.

p. 34 **"Quiet Observations"** Wilson, *Quiet Observations on the Ways of the World*, p. x.

p. 35 **"homely wisdom . . ."** Baldwin, *Pittsburgh*, p. 351.

p. 35 **"pose the same old topics . . ."** Wilson, *Quiet Observations*, p. x.

p. 35 **for more than three decades** Obituary, Erasmus Wilson, *Pittsburgh Chronicle Telegraph*, Jan. 14, 1922.

p. 35 **"terse, breezy . . ."** Nevin, *The Social Mirror*, pp. 36–37. Also, Zurosky, *The First One Hundred Years, 1891–1991*, pp. 12–13.

p. 35 **"gray-haired, sharp-nosed . . ."** *Pittsburg Commercial Gazette*, Jan. 25, 1890, 1:7.

p. 35 **"Woman's Sphere"** Wilson, *Quiet Observations*, pp. 138–140. The column and response it provoked reflect the passions in an ongoing nineteenth-century debate over the place of women in society.

p. 36 **"Anxious Father"** *Pittsburg Dispatch*, Jan. 14, 1885, 4:5.

p. 36 **"In China . . ."** Ibid.

p. 36 **". . . couldn't hold a candle . . ."** *Pittsburg Dispatch*, Jan. 18, 1885, 9:3.

p. 37 **father wrote to Q.O. again** *Pittsburg Dispatch*, Jan. 27, 1885, 4:6. Also, Wilson, *Quiet Observations*, p. 167.

p. 37 **Becky Briarly** *Pittsburg Dispatch*, Feb. 3, 1885, 4:4. Also, Wilson, *Quiet Observations*, pp. 170–174.

p. 37 **Fatima** *Pittsburg Dispatch*, Feb. 3, 1885, 4:4. Also, Wilson, *Quiet Observations*, p. 173.

p. 38 **"with no style . . ."** *Pittsburg Commercial Gazette*, Jan. 25, 1890, 1:1, 7:3.

p. 38 **George Madden** Burgoyne, *All Sorts*, pp. 158–159.

p. 39 **"If the writer . . ."** *Pittsburg Dispatch*, Jan. 17, 1885, 4:5.

p. 39 **Sunday edition** Boucher, *A Century and a Half of Pittsburgh and Her People*, Vol. 2, p. 427. Although the Sunday edition had been planned since 1880, under the management of Alexander W. Rook, it was his successor, Eugene O'Neill, who got it off the ground in 1885, when, according to Boucher, it "at once gained a great circulation and has continued to gain steadily over a vast field and with immense advertising patronage." A search of issues of *The Dispatch* on microfilm shows Sunday issues of the newspaper as far back as the spring of 1884.

p. 39 **"a shy little girl"** *Pittsburg Commercial Gazette*, Jan. 25, 1890, 1:1, 7:3.

p. 39 **"The girl's countenance brightened . . ."** Ibid.

p. 40 **Bly herself recalled** Ibid.

p. 41 **"The Girl Puzzle"** *Pittsburg Dispatch*, Jan. 25, 1885, 11:6–7.

p. 41 **"The schools are overrun . . ."** *Pittsburg Dispatch*, Jan. 25, 1885, 11:6–7.

p. 42 **"Let the young girl know . . ."** *Pittsburg Dispatch*, Feb. 1, 1885, 10:4–5.

p. 42 **Pattison's recent proposal** was passed June 1, 1891, as an act of amendment to the further supplement No. 629 to the act concerning divorces which was passed May 8, 1884. It allowed that any marriage procured by fraud, force, or coercion could end in divorce; that the husband or wife of a party convicted of a felony and sentenced by a court to the penitentiary could sue for divorce, and that a wife could sue when she was subjected to "cruel and barbarous treatment" which rendered the "condition of her husband intolerable or life burdensome." *Laws of Pennsylvania*, No. 629, p. 644.

p. 43 **"A young man drawing . . ."** *Pittsburg Dispatch*, Feb. 1, 1885, 10:4–5. Albert Cochrane married about three months after the article appeared.

p. 43 **The article** Both "The Girl Puzzle" and "Mad Marriages" refer to Q.O. (Wilson) and "Anxious Father," which may mean she conceived them at the same time. The second piece appeared a week after the first. Wilson, in the Jan. 25, 1890, piece in *The Commercial Gazette*, said that NB's first assignment from Madden was the working girl series. But that did not begin until a week after "Mad Marriages."

p. 43 **"contributed to causing the salutary change . . ."** *NY World*, Feb. 2, 1890, 5:1.

p. 44 **Foster's "Nelly Bly"** The original Nelly Bly remained with the Woods family for many years after slavery was abolished and died at an advanced age. "Echoes of Early Hazelwood and Glenwood, Pittsburgh," p. 217.

p. 44 **the song "Nelly Bly"** Howard, *Stephen Foster, America's Troubadour*, p. 265. The rest of the verses are

> *Nelly Bly hab a voice*
> *Like de turtle dove,*
> *I hears it in de meadow and*
> *I hears it in de grove*
>
> *Nelly Bly hab a heart*
> *As war as cop ob tea*
> *And bigger dan de sweet potato*
> *Down in Tennessee.*
>
> *Heigh! Nelly, Ho! etc.*

p. 44 **Pittsburgh's poor working girls** "Girl Puzzle" (*Pittsburg Dispatch*, Jan. 25, 1885, 11:6–7), "Mad Marriages" (Feb. 1, 1885, 10:4–5), and "Perilous Paths" (Feb. 8, 1885, 12:5–6) all dealt with this subject. "Our Workshop Girls" ran Feb. 15, 1885, 9:1–3; Feb. 22, 1885, 9:1–3; Mar. 1, 1885, 9:1–4; Mar. 8, 1885, 9:1–3; Mar. 22, 1885, 9:1–3; Mar. 29, 1885, 9:1–3; and Apr. 12, 1885, 10:1–2.

p. 45 " 'Risk my reputation!' . . ." *Pittsburg Dispatch*, Feb. 8, 1885, 12:5–6.

p. 46 **personality sketches and juvenile biographies** Rittenhouse, *The Amazing Nellie Bly*, pp. 28–30; Noble, *Nellie Bly, First Woman Reporter*, pp. 20–24. Study of *Dispatch* files for NB years reveals nothing to substantiate these accounts, repeated in Ross, *Charmers and Cranks*, pp. 203–204.

p. 46 **"I'm through school . . ."** *Pittsburg Dispatch*, Feb. 15, 1885, 9:1–3.

p. 47 **"The 'helpers' are the smallest . . ."** *Pittsburg Dispatch*, Mar. 1, 1885, 9:1–4.

p. 48 **investigation and exposé** The era of the muckrakers dates roughly from the 1890s. Jacob Riis's *How the Other Half Lives*, for example, was published in 1890.

p. 48 **hastened to imitate it** Livermore and Willard, *A Woman of the Century*, pp. 186–187. *NY World*, Feb. 2, 1890, 5:1.

p. 48 **standardized this type of reporting** With NB's Oct. 1887 asylum exposé, *The World* began running such features, by NB and others, regularly.

p. 48 **Madden moved Bly** There is no evidence Bly was moved to women's news because Madden succumbed to pressure from business interests to take her off the labor beat, as stated in Rittenhouse and repeated elsewhere. In her private correspondence, Rittenhouse acknowledged that she never located the *Dispatch* file for NB's years of employ and that she had fictionalized parts of her book. Letter, Mignon Rittenhouse to Legal Department, Metro-Goldwyn-Mayer Pictures, Feb. 14, 1959, Mignon Rittenhouse Collection, Wheaton College. Special thanks to David Malone.

p. 49 **start planting trees** *Pittsburg Dispatch*, Apr. 5, 1885, 8:1–2.

p. 49 **selections for spring planting** *Pittsburg Dispatch*, Apr. 12, 12:3–4.

p. 49 **annual flower show** *Pittsburg Dispatch*, Apr. 12, 1885, 12:3–4; Apr. 16, 1885, 5:1–2; and Apr. 19, 1885, 2:5.

p. 49 **fashion reporting** *Pittsburg Dispatch*, May 3, 1885, 7:6, 9:4, 11:6; May 6, 1885, 4:5; May 10, 1885, 9:4, 9:5, 10:6; May 11, 1885, 3:2; May 16, 1885, 4:5; May 17, 1885, 7:6, 9:6, 10:2, 12:2, 12:5; May 23, 1885, 4:5; May 24, 1885, 6:2, 9:4.

p. 49 **Economites** *Pittsburg Dispatch*, May 24, 1885, 8:1.

p. 49 **"A Plucky Woman"** *Pittsburg Dispatch*, May 31, 1885, 7:7.

p. 49 **chorus girl** *Pittsburg Dispatch*, June 7, 1885, 11:6.

p. 50 **musical prodigy** *Pittsburg Dispatch*, June 7, 1885, 12:6.

p. 50 **"In person 'Nellie Bly' . . ."** Nevin, *Social Mirror*, p. 29.

p. 50 **Tom Smiley and Tony Orr** Interview of Irene Ravitch with Thomas Smiley, Jan. 20, 1931, quoted in Ravitch, "NB: A Biographical Sketch."

p. 51 **the difficulty florists have** *Pittsburg Dispatch*, June 14, 1885, 9:4.

p. 51 **hay fever** *Pittsburg Dispatch*, July 5, 1885, 12:7.

p. 52 **"In this age of wonders . . ."** *Pittsburg Dispatch*, July 12, 1885, 11:6–7.

p. 52 **Schenley mansion** *Pittsburg Dispatch*, July 19, 1885, 3:1–2.

p. 52 **Colonel William Sirwell** *Pittsburg Dispatch*, Aug. 23, 1885, 5:3.

p. 52 **Colonel Samuel Jackson** NB v. Samuel M. Jackson.

p. 53 **For her debut** *Pittsburg Dispatch*, Sept. 6, 1885, 8:2–3.

p. 53 **By the next week** *Pittsburg Dispatch*, Sept. 13, 1885, 6:3.

p. 53 **By the third week** *Pittsburg Dispatch*, Sept. 20, 1885, 5:2.

p. 53 **Young Men's Christian Association** *Pittsburg Dispatch*, Sept. 27, 1885, 6:4.

p. 53 **it provoked response** *Pittsburg Dispatch*, Oct. 11, 1885, 6:5.

p. 53 **Bessie Bramble was quick** *Pittsburg Dispatch*, Oct. 4, 1885, 12:1.

p. 55 **Bly respectfully told Bramble** *Pittsburg Dispatch*, Oct. 11, 1885, 6:5.

p. 55 **". . . If we had more people . . ."** *Pittsburg Dispatch*, Oct. 17, 1885, 4:6.

p. 55 **rubber raincoats** *Pittsburg Dispatch*, Oct. 17, 1885, 4:5.

pp. 55–56 **tree grafts** *Pittsburg Dispatch*, Nov. 21, 1885, 6:2.

p. 56 **50,000 butterflies** *Pittsburg Dispatch*, Nov. 22, 1885, 10:1–2.

p. 56 **hair care** *Pittsburg Dispatch*, Nov. 29, 1885, 9:3.

p. 56 **she hated it** *Pittsburg Commercial Gazette*, Jan. 25, 1890, 1:1, 7:3.

p. 56 **"self-sacrificing Christian ladies"** *Pittsburg Dispatch*, Jan. 24, 1886, 9:1–2.

p. 56 **"IN MEXICO"** *Pittsburg Dispatch*, Feb. 21, 1886, 9:3–4.

3

✿ ✿

Travel

p. 59 **"too impatient . . ."** NB, *Six Months in Mexico*, p. 5.

p. 59 **"a lot of good stuff"** *Pittsburg Commercial Gazette*, Jan. 25, 1890, 1:7.

p. 59 **young railroad men** Interview of Irene Ravitch with Thomas F. Smiley, Jan. 20, 1931, quoted in Ravitch, "NB: A Biographical Sketch," pp. 14–16.

p. 59 **"something that no other girl . . ."** *Pittsburg Commercial Gazette*, Jan. 25, 1890, 1:7.

p. 60 **thousands of miles of track** Meyer and Sherman, *The Course of Mexican History*, p. 442.

p. 60 **she secured train passes** *Pittsburg Commercial Gazette*, Jan. 25, 1890, 1:7.

p. 60 **"beautiful in the extreme"** *Pittsburg Dispatch*, Feb. 21, 1886, 9:3–4.

p. 60 **"New buildings are rapidly going up . . ."** Ibid.

p. 62 **"So many have come here . . ."** Ibid.

p. 62 **a second Humboldt** Alexander von Humboldt (1769–1859), Berlin-born explorer and scientist who made a five-year expedition to the Spanish colonies in South and Central America, 1799–1804.

p. 62 **Theo Gestefeld** was a reporter for *The Chicago Tribune* in 1884–85 but had a longer prior association as reporter and editor with *Staats Zeitung* in Chicago. He left Chicago in 1886, returning to the city in 1890 to work for *Der Beobachter*. Chicago City Directories, 1884–1902.

pp. 62–63 **"Maybe I'll not be more fortunate . . ."** *Pittsburg Dispatch*, Feb. 21, 1886, 9:3–4.

p. 63 **with one four-year term off** After his first term, Díaz followed Mexican election law prohibiting reelection and retired in favor of Gen. Manuel González. Pletcher, *Rails, Mines and Progress*, p. 10. González's rule was beset with problems, and the nation returned Díaz to the presidency in 1884.

p. 63 **Porfiriato** See Pletcher, *Rails, Mines*, p. 10; also Rodman, *A Short History of Mexico*, pp. 89, 93.

p. 63 **Díaz was being widely extolled** Rodman, *Short History*, p. 93; Pletcher, *Rails, Mines*, pp. 10–14.

p. 63 **subjects that would cut against** *Pittsburg Dispatch*, Feb. 21, 1886, 9:3–4.

p. 64 **Bly made it a point to praise** *Pittsburg Dispatch*, Feb. 24, 1886, 4:4.

p. 64 **"great heaps of human bones"** *Pittsburg Dispatch*, Feb. 21, 1886, 9:3–4.

p. 64 **moved by the reverence** *Pittsburg Dispatch*, Feb. 28, 1886, 9:4–7.

p. 64 **"a curse to the poor"** Ibid.

p. 64 **Mexican bureaucracy at its most hardened** *Pittsburg Dispatch*, Feb. 27, 1886, 6:3–4.

p. 65 **intricacies of bullfighting** NB, *Six Months in Mexico*, pp. 37–47.

p. 65 **intermission at the theater** *Pittsburg Dispatch*, Apr. 2, 1886, 16:1–2.

p. 65 **cigarettes** *Pittsburg Dispatch*, Mar. 7, 1886, 9:3–5.

p. 65 "spit on their hands . . ." Ibid.

p. 65 tiny coffin of his dead child Ibid.

p. 65 laborers covered the body Ibid.

p. 65 "As a people . . ." Ibid.

p. 66 the Sabbath *Pittsburg Dispatch*, Mar. 14, 1886, 9:3–4.

p. 66 Lent *Pittsburg Dispatch*, May 23, 1886, 9:1–3.

p. 66 customs of love and courtship *Pittsburg Dispatch*, Apr. 18, 1886, 9:3–4.

p. 66 value of the sombrero *Pittsburg Dispatch*, May 18, 1886, 3:1.

p. 66 protested the incarceration *Pittsburg Dispatch*, Apr. 1, 1886, 4:5.

p. 66 "Men are seldom killed . . ." Ibid.

p. 67 "For the last year . . ." *Pittsburg Dispatch*, Apr. 17, 1886, 4:5.

pp. 67–68 "flaunting tales of their riches . . ." *Pittsburg Dispatch*, Apr. 17, 1886, 4:6.

p. 68 Bly bragged to brother Charles Letter, NB to Charles M. Cochrane, Apr. 3, 1886, quoted in Myers, "NB: Fact or Fiction."

p. 68 Joaquin Miller *Pittsburg Dispatch*, Apr. 17, 1886, 4:6.

p. 68 every doorway led to a coffin maker *Pittsburg Dispatch*, Apr. 25, 1886, 9:1–2.

p. 68 "floating gardens" at La Viga *Pittsburg Dispatch*, May 9, 1886, 9:3–5.

p. 68 detailed travelogues *Pittsburg Dispatch*, May 30, 1886, 9:1–2; June 6, 1886, 9:3–4; June 20, 1886, 9:1–2.

p. 68 "The Mexicans surveyed myself . . ." *Pittsburg Dispatch*, June 20, 1886, 9:1–2.

p. 69 "try once again . . ." *Pittsburg Dispatch*, May 23, 1886, 9:1–3.

p. 69 back in Pittsburgh *Pittsburg Dispatch*, June 23, 1886, 2:5.

p. 69 "a sort of horror . . ." Ibid.

p. 69 found themselves in jail *Pittsburg Dispatch*, Aug. 8, 1886, 12:3–4.

p. 69 "tools of the organized ring" Ibid.

p. 70 "The subsidized sheets . . ." Ibid.

p. 70 "I did a good deal of . . . 'bluffing' . . ." *Pittsburg Dispatch*, June 23, 1886, 2:5.

p. 70 "My residence in Mexico . . ." *Pittsburg Dispatch*, Aug. 1, 1886, 12:3–4.

p. 70 Díaz arranged for Manuel González Pletcher, *Rails, Mines*, p. 10, says Díaz "possibly" thought González would hand back the presidency after his term.

p. 71 "President Díaz has two years . . ." *Pittsburg Dispatch*, Aug. 1, 1886, 12:3–4.

p. 72 "half-breeds and Indians" *Pittsburg Dispatch*, Aug. 22, 1886, 9:3–4.

p. 72 **"There was little in Mexico . . ."** *Pittsburg Commercial Gazette*, Jan. 25, 1890, 1:7.

p. 72 **"Mexican Manners"** NB's *Pittsburg Dispatch* stories on return from Mexico: June 27, 1886, 9:1–2; July 4, 1886, 9:1–2; July 6, 1886, 8:1–2; July 11, 1886, 9:1–3; July 18, 1886, 12:1–2; July 25, 1886, 12:1–2; Aug. 1, 1886, 12:3–4; Aug. 8, 1886, 12:3–4; Aug. 15, 1886, 12:3–4; Aug. 29, 1886, 12; 3–4; Sept. 10, 1886, 8:1; Sept. 19, 1886, 8:1–2.

p. 73 **suit she had filed** NB v. Samuel M. Jackson. Jackson filed his exceptions to the auditor's report in 1888, but Bly never responded. The case was taken off the books nearly forty years after it was filed. Armstrong County Courthouse.

p. 74 **"In Stage Circles"** . . . **"Some Stage Secrets"** *Pittsburg Dispatch*, Oct. 24, 1886, 10:1–2; Oct. 31, 1886, 13:1.

p. 74 **features on other topics** *Pittsburg Dispatch*, Nov. 7, 1886, 12:3–4; Nov. 14, 1886, 12:3–4; Nov. 28, 1886, 10:3.

p. 74 **longer, timeless features** *Pittsburg Dispatch*, Jan. 9, 1887, 14:4–5; Jan. 16, 1887, 16:4–5; Jan. 30, 1887, 16:4; Feb. 6, 1887, 16:5–6; Feb. 13, 1887, 9:5–6; Feb. 20, 1887, 16:4–5; Feb. 27, 1887, 9:5.

p. 74 **"Footlight Gossip"** *Pittsburg Dispatch*, Jan. 23, 1887, 12:4; Feb. 13, 1887, 12:4; Feb. 20, 1887, 12:5; Feb. 27, 1887, 12:4; Mar. 13, 1887, 12:4; Mar. 20, 1887, 12:4.

p. 75 **"Among the Artists"** *Pittsburg Dispatch*, Jan. 2, 1887, 13:1; Jan. 9, 1887, 13:1; Jan. 16, 1887, 12:5–6; Jan. 23, 1887, 12:3 and 12:4; Jan. 30, 1887, 12:5; Mar. 6, 1887, 12:6; Mar. 13, 1887, 12:6.

p. 75 **"It is certainly time . . ."** *Pittsburg Dispatch*, Jan. 2, 1887, 13:1.

p. 75 **"The city editor couldn't find anything . . ."** *Pittsburg Commercial Gazette*, Jan. 25, 1890, 1:7.

p. 75 **"DEAR Q.O."** *Pittsburg Commercial Gazette*, Jan. 25, 1890, 1:7.

4

🎕 🎕

The World

p. 79 **arrived in May** *NY World*, Apr. 19, 1888, 1:1, 2:5.

p. 79 **Park Row** *How to Know and Find New York*, Boston: Rand Avery, May 15, 1887, p. 40.

p. 79 **15 West Ninety-sixth Street** Letter, NB to Erasmus Wilson, Nov. 13, 1887, Carnegie Library.

p. 79 **most successful, most imitated** See Mott, *A History of American Magazines*; Emery, *The Press and America*; Bleyer, *Main Currents in the History of American Journalism*.

p. 81 **The manned balloon** *NY World*, May 1, 1887, 11:1–7; May 8, 1887, 12:1; May 10, 1887, 13:3; May 15, 1887, 17:1–2; June 3, 1887, 3:4; June 5, 1887, 17:1–3; June 11, 1887, 5:2; June 14, 1887, 5:3–4; June 15, 1887, 2:1–2; June 17, 1887, 1:3; June 18, 1887, 1:5–2, 2:1–2; June 19, 1887, 1:1–4; June 20, 1887, 2:5. Similar for *St. Louis Post-Dispatch*.

p. 81 **note of introduction . . . The rejection** . . . *NY World*, Feb. 2, 1890, 5:1.

p. 81 **writing women's features** *Pittsburg Dispatch*, June–Oct. 1887; specifically, June 19, 1887, 16:5; July 10, 1887, 13:1; July 17, 1887, 9:7; July 24, 1887, 14:3–4; Aug. 7, 1887, 9:7; Sept. 18, 1887, 9:7; Oct. 9, 1887, 9:3.

p. 81 **"empty glory and poor pay"** *Pittsburg Dispatch*, Aug. 21, 1887, 9:3–4.

p. 83 **a job-demanding frenzy** Legends contained in Ross, *Ladies of the Press*, and Rittenhouse, *The Amazing Nellie Bly*, have NB fighting past guards until she wangles her way into Pulitzer's private office to present the story idea that lands a job. The story is first presented in Livermore and Willard, *A Woman of the Century* (1893), written during NB's lifetime but six years after the fact. Earlier (1890, *NY World*, *Pittsburg Commercial Gazette*) profiles make no such claim. Theodore Dreiser, in *Newspaper Days* (1931), told a similar story about his own hiring at *The World* a few years after NB. Both 1890 newspaper profiles of NB mention her last hundred dollars, a situation she herself described in "Among the Mad," *Godey's Lady's Book*, Vol. 118, Jan. 1889, p. 20.

p. 83 **"We have more women now . . ."** NB, "Among the Mad," p. 20.

p. 83 **coming to blows** Swanberg, *Pulitzer*, p. 132.

p. 84 **"Miss Nellie Bly [who] . . ."** *The Journalist*, Oct. 15, 1887, 4:1.

p. 84 **"The standard it raises is high"** Tarbell, "Women in Journalism," p. 395.

p. 84 **"bright and talented young woman"** *NY Mail and Express*, Aug. 27, 1887, 2:7.

p. 84 **"I was penniless . . ."** NB, "Among the Mad," p. 20.

pp. 84–85 **"I really think . . ."** Ibid.

p. 85 **"Energy rightly applied . . ."** Ibid.

p. 85 **travel to Europe and return steerage** *NY World*, Feb. 2, 1890, 5:1.

p. 86 **Blackwell's Island** *How to Know and Find New York*.

p. 86 **"You can try . . ."** NB, "Among the Mad," p. 20.

p. 86 **"preferred that she should try . . ."** *NY World*, Feb. 2, 1890, 5:1.

p. 86 **"asked by *The World*"** *NY World*, Oct. 9, 1887, 25:1.

p. 86 **"Conspicuous Feature"** World (NY) Papers, 1888, Columbia University.

p. 86 **"A good while ago . . ."** Ibid., 1887.

p. 87 "frequent reports of shocking abuses . . ." *NY World*, May 7, 1893, p. 56.

p. 87 "charges seriously affecting the character" *NY Times*, Aug. 14, 1887, 9:2; Aug. 16, 1887, 8:2.

p. 87 "very ugly and painful stories" *NY Times*, Aug. 18, 1887, 4:3.

p. 87 Pulitzer's "New Journalism" Mott, *American Journalism*, pp. 430–445.

p. 88 something altogether new Although sensationalism had been an element of newsgathering since its very beginnings, Pulitzer came under heavy criticism for reviving it and bringing it into the mainstream.

p. 88 Joseph Howard's column *The Journalist*, Oct. 15, 1887, 4:1.

p. 88 Bill Nye . . . in a letter Bill Nye to James Whitcomb Riley, Oct. 21, 1887, cited in Nye, *Bill Nye: His Own Life Story*.

p. 89 to book length NB, *Ten Days in a Mad-House*, includes her *World* reports "Trying to Be a Servant" and "Nellie Bly as a White Slave" at the end of an edited version of the madhouse story.

p. 89 East Coast Annie Oakley McDougall, *This Is the Life*, p. 186.

p. 89 The strategy for getting into Most details of Bly's escapade in this section, unless otherwise specified, come from her asylum reports in *The World*, Oct. 9, 1887, 25:1, 26:1, and Oct. 16, 1887, 25:1, 26:1; and from NB, *Ten Days*.

p. 89 "I looked at the little woman . . ." *NY World*, Nov. 17, 1889, 15:3–5.

p. 90 Charles Dickens Dickens, *American Notes and Picture from Italy*, pp. 109–110.

p. 90 Margaret Fuller Fuller, "Our City's Charities," *NY Tribune*, Mar. 18, 1845. Fuller worked for *The Tribune* in 1845–46.

p. 91 size two and a half shoe An 1897 Sears catalog gives the range of women's shoe sizes as 2 to 8. Costume Institute, Metropolitan Museum of Art.

p. 91 *The Sun* played the story *NY Sun*, Sept. 25, 1887, 1:7.

p. 91 "She never seems . . ." *NY Herald*, Sept. 25, 1887, reprinted *NY World*, Oct. 9, 1887, 26:5.

p. 91 "undoubtedly insane" *NY Evening Telegram*, Sept. 26, 1887, reprinted *NY World*, Oct. 9, 1887, 26:5.

p. 92 "mysterious waif" *NY Times*, Sept. 26, 1887, 8:3.

p. 93 Bly barely escaped exposure NB, *Ten Days*, pp. 76–77.

p. 93 "a raging crowd of female maniacs" McDougall, *This Is the Life*, p. 188.

p. 93 *The Sun* reported the mysterious waif's *NY Sun*, Oct. 7, 1887, 5:5.

p. 93 *The Times* provided a longer account *NY Times*, Oct. 7, 1887, 8:2.

p. 94 "PLAYING MAD WOMAN . . ." *NY Sun*, Oct. 14, 1887, 1:6–7, 2:1–4.

p. 95 "ALL THE DOCTORS FOOLED . . ." *NY World*, Oct. 15, 1887, 5:1.

p. 95 Bly refuted *NY World*, Oct. 17, 1887, 5:1.

p. 95 And the doctors *NY World*, Oct. 17, 1887, 5:4.

p. 95 "We all know that in times . . ." *NY World*, Oct. 16, 1887, 26:4.

p. 95 "She is well-educated . . ." *Pittsburg Dispatch*, Oct. 18, 1887, 2:2.

p. 96 "Even the most passionate pleaders . . ." *Pittsburg Dispatch*, Oct. 16, 1887, 10:5–6.

p. 96 "The World Their Savior" *NY World*, Oct. 28, 1887, 12:1.

p. 96 "I have one consolation . . ." NB, *Ten Days*, p. 98.

p. 97 "overcrowded and entirely inadequate" Minutes, Board of Estimate and Apportionment, City and County of New York, 1887, pp. 455–456, NY Municipal Archives.

p. 97 On October 25, Dr. Charles Simmons Ibid., pp. 354–355.

pp. 97–98 On December 18 . . . By December 29 . . . Ibid., pp. 328–939. Also, *NY World*, Oct. 28, 1887, 12:1; *NY Times*, Nov. 2, 1887, 3:7; Nov. 3, 1887, 4:6; Dec. 18, 1887, 2:4.

p. 99 "hit the ground running" The derivation is unclear, but it is probably paratrooper or airborne-assault unit terminology or Navy-Marine slang. See William Safire, *New York Times*, Jan. 11, 1981, 6:9:1.

p. 99 A letter arrived Letter, NB to Erasmus Wilson, Nov. 13, 1887, Carnegie Library.

p. 100 "That a streak of good luck . . ." *Pittsburg Dispatch*, Nov. 20, 1887, ?:4.

pp. 100–101 "They are very good to me . . ." Letter, NB to Erasmus Wilson, Nov. 13, 1887.

p. 101 pretended to be a maid *NY World*, Oct. 30, 1887, 9:1.

p. 101 clandestine trafficking in newborns *NY World*, Nov. 6, 1887, 10:1.

p. 101 in paper box factories *NY World*, Nov. 27, 1887, 10:1.

p. 101 Fannie B. Merrill *The Journalist*, Dec. 17, 1887.

p. 102 rolled tobacco for cigarettes *NY World*, Nov. 20, 1887, 25:1.

p. 102 matrimonial agencies *NY World*, Dec. 4, 1887, 2?:1.

p. 102 "I went begging . . ." *NY World*, Dec. 11, 1887, 11:1.

p. 103 "at once handsome and brainy . . ." *The Journalist*, Dec. 17, 1887, 20:3–4.

p. 103 "considerable literary ability . . ." *The Journalist*, Dec. 24, 1887, 13:2.

p. 103 "Learning Ballet Dancing" *NY World*, Dec. 18, 1887, 25:1.

p. 103 "Our Women Journalists" *The Journalist*, Dec. 31, 1887, p. 12.

p. 103 giving too much for the money *The Journalist*, Dec. 24, 1887, 3:2.

p. 104 by remote control Swanberg, *Pulitzer*, pp. 146–147. See also Barrett, *The World, the Flesh and Messrs. Pulitzer*; Seitz, *Joseph Pulitzer, His Life and Letters*.

p. 104 "Her appearance . . ." McDougall, *This Is the Life*, p. 186.

p. 105 pitting talent against talent Chambers, *Newshunting on Three Continents*, p. 312; Swanberg, *Pulitzer*, pp. 107–110.

p. 105 "enhance suggestiveness" Barrett, *Joseph Pulitzer and His World*, p. 98. Also Swanberg, *Pulitzer*, pp. 107–110.

p. 105 "at least two editors to drink . . ." McDougall, *This Is the Life*, p. 107.

p. 105 " 'Activity and accuracy' were . . ." Chambers, *Newshunting*, pp. 331–332.

pp. 105–106 Van Zile wrote to congratulate Poem, Van Zile to Don C. Seitz, undated, circa 1924, New York Public Library.

p. 106 steady income from the . . . newspaper McDougall, *This Is the Life*, p. 197. The paper was well-paying for its male correspondents, but, as NB explained in an 1890 letter, she considered her salary low. It was, however, steady income.

p. 106 202 West Seventy-fourth Street NY City Directory, 1888–89.

p. 106 Magdalen Home *NY World*, Feb. 12, 1888, 29:1.

pp. 106–107 She went onstage *NY World*, Mar. 4, 1888, 15:3.

p. 107 sham mesmerist *NY World*, Mar. 25, 1888, 19:1.

p. 107 learned how to fence *NY World*, Mar. 11, 1888, 12:4.

p. 107 "gray-blue eyes . . ." McDougall, *This Is the Life*, p. 187.

p. 107 "treader upon tender toes" Mott, *History of American Magazines*, pp. 564–565.

p. 108 several letters charging bribery *NY World*, Apr. 19, 1888, 2:5.

p. 108 "Conspicuous Features" World (NY) Papers, 1888, Columbia University.

p. 108 which ran April Fool's Day *NY World*, Apr. 1, 1888, 19:1–6.

p. 109 "The remarkable narrative . . ." *NY World*, Apr. 2, 1888, 1:7, 2:1.

p. 109 "I have read with some amusement . . ." Ibid.

p. 110 "a romance . . ." *NY Times*, Apr. 2, 1888, 5:3.

p. 110 *The World* stood by its stunt girl *NY World*, Apr. 2, 1888, 2:1.

p. 110 comments of legislators Ibid.

p. 111 "The place to expose the lobby . . ." *Albany Times*, Apr. 2, 1888, 2:2.

p. 111 six lawmakers named *Albany Times*, Apr. 6, 1888, 1:5.

p. 111 The Assembly Judiciary Committee agreed *Albany Times*, Apr. 6, 1888, 2:3.

p. 111 *The World* produced a second exposé *Albany Morning Express*, Apr. 5, 1888, 4:4.

p. 111 By Friday, April 6 *NY World*, Apr. 6, 1888, 1:5.

p. 111 "there will be a great deal . . ." *Albany Argus*, Apr. 7, 1888, 3:3.

p. 112 By April 11, a grand jury *Albany Argus*, Apr. 8, 1888, 6:1.

p. 112 "The assembly judiciary committee began . . ." *Albany Argus*, Apr. 13, 1888, 4:5.

p. 112 "In the opinion of the Grand Jury . . ." *Albany Argus*, Apr. 17, 1888, 6:3.

p. 112 Phelps testified as well *NY World*, Apr. 19, 1888, 2:5.

p. 113 "She proved to be a slender woman . . ." *Albany Argus*, Apr. 19, 1888, 4:5.

p. 113 "The 'crash' had come and gone . . ." *Albany Morning Express*, Apr. 19, 1888, 4:4.

p. 114 Phelps left Albany *NY World*, Tenth Anniversary Issue, May 7, 1893, highlights of 1887–88.

p. 114 "A: Yes sir" *NY World*, Apr. 19, 1888, 1:1.

p. 115 her "odd" fan mail *NY World*, May 27, 1888, 19:3.

p. 115 "the most beautiful reporter . . ." *The Journalist*, June 9, 1888, 8:3.

p. 115 Pulitzer's ever-shifting editorial staff *The Journalist*, June 9, 1888, 8:3.

p. 115 Bly to police court *NY World*, June 17, 1888, 13:1.

p. 115 "mind healer" *NY World*, July 1, 1888, 17:1.

p. 115 Colonel Bill Cody's Wild West Show *NY World*, July 8, 1888, 9:3.

p. 116 "I give his stories . . ." NB, *Six Months in Mexico*, "Munro's Library," John W. Lovell, New York, Jan. 16, 1888, p. 15.

p. 116 Bly's next big piece *NY World*, Aug. 5, 1888, 9:3.

p. 116 "A fair reader who confesses . . ." *Town Topics*, Aug. 16, 1888, 9:1.

p. 117 Belva Lockwood Bardes and Gossett, *Declarations of Independence*, p. 162.

p. 118 "What class of women support you . . ." *NY World*, Aug. 12, 1888, 13:3.

p. 118 New York's famous "VouDou Knave" *NY World*, Aug. 19, 1888, 11:1.

p. 118 "fun-loving hop-pickers" *NY World*, Sept. 16, 1888, 17:1.

p. 118 all the presidential candidates' wives *NY World*, Sept. 9, 1888, 9:1–4; Oct. 7, 1888, 12:1.

p. 118 all the former and present living first ladies *NY World*, Oct. 28, 1888, 17–19:1+++.

p. 118 **Frances Cleveland** Anthony, *First Ladies*, pp. 230–299.

p. 118 **Bly went calling at Oak View** *NY World*, Oct. 28, 1888, pp. 17–19.

p. 119 **nor the editorial support** Bleyer, *Main Currents*, p. 331.

p. 120 **Nell Nelson** *NY World*, Sept. 23, 1888, 17:1; Oct. 14, 1888, 17:1; Oct. 21, 1888, 20:1.

p. 120 *The Journalist . . .* **produced a two-column piece** *The Journalist*, Oct. 13, 1888, 13:1.

p. 120 **Roseboro as "a charming little lady . . ."** *The Journalist*, Sept. 15, 1888, 7:1.

p. 120 **"reporter's notebook"** *NY World*, Nov. 4, 1888, 9:3.

p. 120 **"Miss Falls [*sic*] . . ."** *NY World*, Nov. 4, 1888, 9:3.

p. 121 **"When a charming young lady . . ."** *The Journalist*, Nov. 10, 1888, 12:3.

p. 121 **Nell Nelson finished out** *NY World*, Nov. 11, 1888, 12:3; Nov. 18, 1888, 9:1; Nov. 25, 1888, 21:1; Dec. 2, 1888, 20:1; Dec. 16, 1888, 22:1.

p. 121 **"In this day of almost equal rights . . ."** *NY World*, Nov. 11, 1888, 12:1. Also, Nov. 18, 1888, 17:3; Nov. 25, 1888, 17:3.

p. 121 **"throngs of poor invalids"** *NY World*, Dec. 2, 1888, 9:1.

p. 121 **Elizabeth Bisland** *The Journalist*, Dec. 8, 1888, 3:1.

p. 122 **"cozy little flat" at 120 West Thirty-fifth Street** *Epoch*, Mar. 22, 1889, p. 113; Also, NY City Directory, 1889–90, Mary Jane Cochrane, widow Michael.

p. 122 **"If there is a brighter newspaper woman . . ."** *The Journalist*, Jan. 26, 1889, 14:3.

p. 122 **"The *New York World* has called . . ."** *The Journalist*, Jan. 26, 1889, 12:3.

p. 123 **"Her real name is Elizabeth Cochrane . . ."** *Epoch*, Mar. 22, 1889, p. 113.

p. 123 **"Nothing was too strenuous . . ."** McDougall, *This Is the Life*, p. 187.

p. 123 **Connecticut's most notorious haunted houses** Ibid., p. 188.

p. 124 **"I knew in a vague way . . ."** *The Journalist*, Jan. 26, 1889, 12:2.

p. 124 **"The privilege of being the receptacle . . ."** Flora McDonald, "The Newspaper Woman: One Side of the Question," *The Journalist*, Jan. 26, 1889, 13:1–3.

p. 125 **she visited an opium den** *NY World*, Mar. 3, 1889, 13:1.

p. 125 **Nelson, "who came to notice . . ."** *The Journalist*, Mar. 23, 1889, p. 13.

p. 125 **visited the prison matrons** *NY World*, Jan. 13, 1889, 11:1.

p. 125 **mysterious veiled prophetess** *NY World*, Jan. 20, 1888, 13:1.

p. 125 **scheme to defraud working girls** *NY World*, Feb. 3, 1889, 17:1.

p. 125 **French Ball** *NY World*, Feb. 10, 1889, 10:1.

p. 125 "took away the last vestige . . ." *Town Topics*, Feb. 7, 1889, 9:1.

p. 125 Laura Dewey Bridgman *NY World*, Feb. 17, 1889, 10:1.

p. 126 Charles Dickens's account of Bridgman's life Dickens, *American Notes*, pp. 37–52.

p. 126 Helen Adams Keller *NY World*, Feb. 24, 1889, 11:3.

p. 126 question-and-answer items Stephens, *A History of News*, p. 246.

p. 126 "fools of great men" Mott, *American Journalism*, pp. 444–445, quoting *The Nation*, July 17, 1873.

p. 126 good for business Emery, *The Press and America*, pp. 325–328.

p. 128 She contrived her own arrest *NY World*, Feb. 24, 1889, 10:1.

p. 128 Bly was roundly praised *NY World*, Feb. 25, 1889, 5:4.

p. 128 interviewed all the wives *NY World*, Mar. 10, 1889, 13:1++, 14:1–2.

p. 128 circulation had reached the unprecedented high *NY World*, Mar. 25, 1889 (front page box).

p. 128 washing machine swindlers *NY World*, Mar. 31, 1889, 13:1.

p. 128 women medical students *NY World*, Apr. 14, 1889, 23:1.

p. 128 private detectives *NY World*, Apr. 28, 1889, 13:1.

p. 128 woman diamond broker *NY World*, May 12, 1889, 21:3.

p. 128 "great stir among the fashionable . . ." *The Journalist*, June 1, 1889, 5:1.

p. 128 Harlem hotel, The Hamilton *NY World*, May 19, 1889, 13:1.

p. 128 John L. Sullivan *NY World*, May 26, 1889, 13:1.

p. 129 Oneida Community *NY World*, June 2, 1889, 13:1.

p. 129 in pamphlet form Oneida Community, Leaflet No. 30A, "Outline of Bible Theology," Syracuse University Library.

p. 129 West Point *NY World*, June 9, 1889, 13:4–5, 14:1.

p. 129 *The World* loved its steadily increasing circulation *NY World*, June 23, 1889, p. 1.

p. 129 the bicycle *NY World*, June 23, 1889, 13:1.

p. 129 learned how to swim *NY World*, Aug. 18, 1889, 9:5.

p. 129 Newport and Narragansett *NY World*, Sept. 1, 1889, 9:1.

p. 129 Bar Harbor and Saratoga Springs *NY World*, Sept. 8, 1889, 16:1–5.

p. 129 "persistent and indefatigable working women . . ." *Town Topics*, July 18, 1889, 3:2.

p. 130 **A scandal broke on August 26** *NY World*, Aug. 27, 1889, 1:3.

p. 130 **The story unraveled** *NY World*, Aug. 28, 1889, 1:1, 2:3; Aug. 29, 1889, 1:3; Aug. 30, 1889, 1:5; Sept. 1, 1889, 3:1; Sept. 4, 1889, 1:5; Sept. 5, 1889, 1:1; Sept. 7, 1889, 1:7; Sept. 8, 1889, 6:1; Sept. 18, 1889, 1:3.

p. 131 **"one of most astounding stories . . ."** *NY World*, Sept. 19, 1889, 1:5–7.

p. 131 **he sorrowfully revealed** *NY World*, Sept. 7, 1889, 1:7; Sept. 18, 1889, 1:3; Sept. 19, 1889, 1:5–7, 2:1.

p. 131 **baby-buying trade** *NY World*, Oct. 6, 1889, 21:1.

p. 131 **exclusive jailhouse interview** *NY World*, Oct. 9, 1889, 1:8, 2:1–2. According to *The World*, July 7, 1894, Eva Hamilton died circa Aug. 23, 1890. She served out her term of imprisonment, embarrassed the Hamilton family by going onstage, "married" two more times, and sued Hamilton's estate for her rightful share as widow. On July 6, 1894, a document was entered at the office of the registry clerk, confirming that for the sum of $10,000, Lydia Gaul (alias Evangeline L. Hamilton, Evangeline L. Steele, Eva L. Mann, Mrs. Fred Tilton) relinquished any future claim against Hamilton's estate.

p. 132 **new gold-domed *World* headquarters** *King's Handbook of New York City*, p. 622.

p. 132 **"It looks serious"** Churchill, *Park Row*, pp. 43–44. Also *Times* response.

p. 133 **"MRS. EVA HAMILTON'S STORY"** *NY World*, Oct. 9, 1889, 1:7.

p. 133 **out in book form** NB, *The Mystery of Central Park*.

p. 134 **"My dear sir:—I take the liberty . . ."** Letter, NB to editor, *The Herald*, Omaha, Nebr., dated "Tuesday morning" [Oct. 1889], author's collection.

p. 134 **Penelope Howard, is fiercely independent** NB, *Mystery of Central Park*, p. 10.

p. 134 **"the spur of necessity . . ."** Ibid., p. 12.

p. 134 **"the value of *Velvet Vice* . . ."** *Town Topics*, Oct. 17, 1889, 9:2.

p. 134 **James Stetson Metcalfe** went on to become one of New York's most respected theater critics, best known for his 1906 lawsuit against theater managers for barring him from shows because of unfavorable reviews. (See *NY Times*, Mar. 30, 1906, 9:3; Apr. 8, 1906, 9:2; July 13, 1906, 9:2. Also Metcalfe file at Billy Rose Theater Collection, Lincoln Center, New York Public Library. Obituary, *NY Times*, May 27, 1926, 23:1.)

p. 135 **" 'I do and so does he' . . ."** NB, *Mystery of Central Park*, pp. 54–56.

p. 136 **"I have no way to protect myself . . ."** *NY World*, Oct. 20, 1889, 18:1.

p. 136 **visited seven reputable New York physicians** *NY World*, Oct. 27, 1889, 13:1–5.

p. 136 **"I am still ill . . ."** *NY World*, Nov. 10, 1889, 27:1.

p. 136 **down 17,000 copies** *NY World*, Nov. 11, 1889, p. 1.

p. 136 **Statue of Liberty** *NY World*, Mar. 16, 1885, cited in Swanberg, *Pulitzer*.

5

Globe Trotting

p. 139 **Bly's version** NB, *Nellie Bly's Book: Around the World in Seventy-Two Days*, pp. 3–4. All descriptions and details of NB's trip in this chapter are from this book except where otherwise indicated. Direct quotations are cited.

p. 139 **Julius Chambers had been on board** *The Journalist*, Oct. 27, 1888, 9:2. Cockerill did not depart until early in 1891.

p. 139 **The thought . . . already had come up** *NY World*, Jan. 25, 1890, 1:1–8, 2:1–8, 3:1–4.

p. 140 **Jarrett . . . accepted a wager** *NY World*, Nov. 14, 1889, 1:1–7.

p. 140 **Chambers set in motion** Chambers, *Newshunting on Three Continents*, p. 315.

p. 140 **to have the document ready** Interview, Irene Ravitch with Edward S. Van Zile, 1931, quoted in Ravitch, "NB: A Biographical Sketch," p. 25.

p. 141 **"If you want . . ."** NB, *Around the World*, p. 7.

p. 143 **"It will be seen . . ."** Ibid., p. 14.

p. 143 **"For almost a year . . ."** Ibid., p. 10.

p. 144 **She invited her colleague,** Ibid., p. 36.

p. 144 **"lures Mr. McCormick into a corner . . ."** *NY World*, Dec. 8, 1889, 1:1–2, 3:1–3.

p. 145 **The actual passport application** Postfiles Great Britain, Passport Vouchers, Vol. 5, No. 182, Record Group 84, State Department Files, U.S. National Archives.

p. 146 **"I know that cup of coffee . . ."** NB, *Around the World*, p. 38.

p. 146 **"It would make any American woman . . ."** Ibid., pp. 43–44.

p. 146 **"Why do you not go to Bombay . . ."** Ibid., p. 52.

p. 147 **"My mischievousness often plays havoc . . ."** Ibid., p. 57.

p. 147 **"the prettiest young girl . . ."** *NY World*, Dec. 26, 1889, 2:2.

p. 147 **"quite played out"** *NY World*, Jan. 9, 1890, 1:4.

p. 148 **"add one more to the many feathers . . ."** *NY World*, Nov. 14, 1889, 1:1–7.

p. 148 the two "Misses B" *NY World*, Nov. 15, 1889, 1:7, 2:1.

p. 148 "The practical value of the trip . . ." *The Journalist*, Nov. 16, 1889, 9:3.

p. 148 *The World* . . . conceded *NY World*, Nov. 14, 1889, 8:2–3.

p. 149 "Miss Nellie Bly and Miss Elizabeth Bisland . . ." *The Journalist*, Nov. 23, 1889, 8:2–3.

p. 149 "Miss Elizabeth Bisland is *not* on the *World* staff . . ." Ibid.

p. 149 "It will be much the same . . ." *NY World*, Dec. 8, 1889, 1:1–2, 3:1–3.

p. 150 the rail journey was "tedious and tiresome" *NY World*, Nov. 26, 1889, 1:5.

p. 150 profile of Elizabeth Bisland *The Journalist*, Nov. 30, 1889, 2:1–2.

p. 151 girls, "of the uncompromising kind" NB, *Around the World*, pp. 64–66.

p. 152 ". . . if the passengers then felt the scarcity . . ." Ibid., p. 66.

p. 152 "and their much-talked about prejudices" Ibid., p. 71.

p. 152 ". . . admiration for the free American woman . . ." Ibid., pp. 86–87.

p. 152 "The sailors were Lascars . . ." Ibid., p. 88.

p. 152 "an eccentric American heiress . . ." Ibid., p. 89.

p. 153 ". . . a stick beats more ugliness . . ." Ibid., p. 92.

p. 153 "I thought the conduct of the Arabs . . ." Ibid., p. 93.

p. 153 ". . . they would receive a stinging blow . . ." Ibid., p. 93.

p. 153 ". . . I wanted to see the juggler . . ." Ibid., p. 103.

pp. 153–154 "a few of the more reckless ones" Ibid., 109.

p. 154 favorably with . . . New York's night hackmen Ibid., p. 113.

p. 154 "I could not in honesty speak . . ." Ibid., p. 122.

p. 155 "Nellie Bly Delayed" *NY World*, Dec. 12, 1889, 2:3.

p. 155 "cooling lime squashes . . ." NB, *Around the World*, pp. 126–127.

p. 155 "deeply-dark emeralds . . ." Ibid., p. 127.

p. 155 "I felt a little sympathy . . ." Ibid., p. 134.

p. 156 "It was so comforting . . ." Ibid., p. 147.

p. 156 "When will we sail," she snapped Ibid., pp. 154–157.

p. 157 ". . . Tell papa what the moo-moo cow . . ." Ibid., pp. 164–165.

p. 157 wishing that some old-time pirates Ibid., p. 166.

p. 157 "While we might have been consuming our . . . stay . . ." Ibid., p. 167.

p. 158 " 'Why?' I demanded . . ." Ibid., p. 173.

p. 158 "I did resist the temptation . . ." Ibid., p. 175.

p. 158 "the most beautiful thing" Ibid., p. 176.

p. 158 "for the time a mad man" Ibid., p. 179.

p. 159 "the queerness of people" Ibid., p. 187.

p. 159 At the O. and O. office Ibid., pp. 191–196.

p. 160 Once in Hong Kong Ibid., p. 210.

p. 160 What a Christmas Ibid., p. 234.

p. 161 Her monkey . . . "showed his usefulness . . ." *San Francisco Chronicle*, Jan. 22, 1890, 8:1.

p. 161 "As the mercy has not been forthcoming" NB, *Around the World*, p. 262.

p. 161 number of papers sold was back up to 268,230 *NY World*, Dec. 16, 1889, p. 1.

p. 162 "Everybody . . . will be . . . improved . . ." *NY World*, Dec. 21, 1889, 2:4.

p. 162 "Nellie Bly is flying high . . ." Ibid.

p. 162 "total eclipse . . ." *NY World*, Dec. 23, 1889, p. 1.

p. 162 "Now that *The World* . . ." *The Journalist*, Jan. 4, 1890, 9:3.

p. 163 ". . . quite as much in favor of Miss Bisland . . ." *NY World*, Jan. 7, 1890, 2:5.

p. 163 "Her grit has been more . . ." *NY World*, Jan. 8, 1890, 2:5.

p. 163 "As recently as a year ago . . ." *Town Topics*, Jan. 16, 1890, 9:1.

p. 164 "The *Sun* might have commissioned . . ." *Town Topics*, Jan. 24, 1890, 7:2.

p. 165 *The World* began deploying staff *The Journalist*, Jan. 18, 1890, 5:1.

p. 165 ". . . the name of *The World*'s globe-girdler . . ." *NY World*, Jan. 15, 1890, 2:2.

p. 165 snowflakes the size of soda crackers *NY World*, Jan. 19, 1890, 1:8.

p. 165 expected to take a week *NY World*, Jan. 20, 1890, 2:3.

p. 165 7:42 A.M. *San Francisco Chronicle*, Jan. 22, 1890, 8:1.

p. 165 "with a hopefulness . . ." NB, *Around the World*, p. 267.

p. 166 threatened . . . to slit her throat NB, *Around the World*, p. 267.

p. 166 snow blockade in the Sierra Nevada Ibid., p. 267.

p. 166 A tug, called the *Millen Griffiths* NB, *Around the World*, p. 267; *San Francisco Chronicle*, Jan. 22, 1890, 8:1.

p. 166 examined her tongue NB, *Around the World*, p. 268.

p. 166 "the general hope seemed to be . . ." *San Francisco Chronicle*, Jan. 22, 1890, 8:1.

p. 166 "maze of happy greetings . . ." NB, *Around the World*, p. 269.

p. 167 ". . . It's not so very much for a woman to do . . ." *San Francisco Chronicle*, Jan. 22, 1890, 8:1.

p. 168 "the personal interest of every one . . ." NB, *Around the World*, p. 269.

p. 168 "violent rocking of the ship" *NY World*, Jan. 22, 1890, 2:1.

p. 168 "one of the fastest engines . . ." Ibid.

p. 168 held in place only by jackscrews *NY World*, Jan. 23, 1890, 1:8, 2:1–4.

p. 168 ". . . not much for Americans to see . . ." *Topeka Daily Capital*, Jan. 24, 1890, 4:1–4.

p. 169 train had broken the record for speed *State Journal* [Topeka], Jan. 24, 1890, 1:1–2.

p. 169 traveled in the Pullman car Ilion *NY World*, Jan. 25, 1890, 1:8, 2:1–3.

p. 169 "followed by three . . . cheers . . ." *NY World*, Jan. 25, 1890, 1:8, 2:1–3.

p. 169 declined . . . to confirm the rumors *Logansport Daily Journal*, Jan. 25, 1890.

p. 169 "Since Indiana furnished . . ." Ibid.

p. 169 William Pitt Kellogg *NY World*, Jan. 24, 1890, 1:8, 2:1–3.

p. 169 estimated the total number Ibid.

p. 170 had there been such pandemonium *Pittsburg Press*, Jan. 25, 1890, 1:1–3.

p. 170 The Pennsylvania Company presented her Ibid.

p. 170 "She was . . . Pittsburgh's own . . ." Ibid.

p. 170 "a present from the rajah . . ." Ibid.

p. 170 in his cage, chained *San Francisco Chronicle*, Jan. 22, 1890, 8:1.

p. 170 mandolin . . . a gift from a prince *Pittsburg Press*, Jan. 25, 1890, 1:1–3.

p. 170 "actually established a standard schedule . . ." Ibid.

p. 171 barreled on to Philadelphia *Pittsburg Press*, Jan. 26, 1890, 1:2.

p. 171 "She isn't much of a girl to talk . . ." *NY World*, Jan. 25, 1890, 2:1–8.

p. 171 Metcalfe would write a snotty parody "She's Home Again! Life's Greatest Enterprise/Our Peerless Sadie Beats the Record," *Life*, Jan. 23, 1890, Vol. 15, No. 369, p. 47 (courtesy of Time, Inc., Archives).

p. 171 Verne disagreed *NY World*, Jan. 26, 1890, 1:1–8.

p. 172 "Only when a goodly rate of speed . . ." *NY World*, Jan. 25, 1890, 1:1–8, 2:1–8, 3:1–4.

p. 173 ". . . about the brightness of the comment . . ." *NY World*, Jan. 26, 1890, 3:1–4.

p. 173 it would become a sensation *The Journalist*, Jan. 25, 1890, 5:3. The game was still featured in the McLoughlin Brothers catalog as late as 1911, when it was described as "an old-established favorite." McLoughlin Bros. Catalogue, 1911, p. 17.

p. 173 "combination of superb qualities . . ." *NY World*, Jan. 26, 1890, 4:3 (editorial).

p. 173 *Cosmopolitan*'s ill-fated challenge *NY World*, Jan. 26, 1890, 5:1–3.

p. 175 "the energetic and plucky little woman . . ." *San Francisco Chronicle*, Jan. 22, 1890, 8:1.

p. 176 "she would not have been able to beat . . ." *NY World*, Jan. 26, 1890, 5:1.

p. 176 "daintiness and distinction" *The Journalist*, Jan. 25, 1890, 5:3.

p. 176 "Nellie Bly has returned . . ." *The Journalist*, Feb. 1, 1890, 8:2–3.

p. 177 pandering tribute to . . . *Cosmopolitan* *The Journalist*, Apr. 30, 1892, p. 3.

p. 177 series of seven monthly articles *Cosmopolitan Magazine*, Vol. 8, Apr. 1890, No. 6, pp. 691–700; Vol. 9, May 1890, No. 1, pp. 51–60; June 1890, No. 2, pp. 173–184; July 1890, No. 3, pp. 273–284; Aug. 1890, No. 4, pp. 401–413; Sept. 1890, No. 5, pp. 533–545; Oct. 1890, No. 6, pp. 666–677.

p. 177 later compiled into a book Bisland, *In Seven Stages: A Flying Trip Around the World*, NY: Harper & Bros., 1891.

p. 177 "What Doth It Profit a Girl . . . ?" *Pittsburg Commercial Gazette*, Jan. 27, 1890, 4:3.

p. 177 considering donating him to the menagerie *NY World*, Jan. 26, 1890, 1:8, 2:1–2.

p. 178 "I expect to go back to work . . ." *Philadelphia Inquirer*, Jan. 26, 1890, 1:3–4.

p. 178 attributed to Logansport friends Ibid.

p. 178 Throughout that week *NY World* stories on Bly's adventure appeared daily from the time she left in Nov. to the end of Feb.

p. 179 "authentic biography" *NY World*, Feb. 2, 1890, 5:1. This is where the incorrect 1867 birth date for NB first appears in print.

p. 180 "Free from affectation or loudness . . ." *NY World*, Feb. 2, 1890, 5:1.

p. 181 Washington Memorial Arch *NY World*, Feb. 5, 1890, 5:2.

p. 182 first of many lectures *NY World*, Feb. 10, 1890, 3:3.

p. 182 filled the theater again *NY World*, Feb. 16, 1890, 5:1; Feb. 17, 1890, 5:1.

6

❧ ❧

Hiatus

p. 185 **Bly answered a letter** NB to Frank G. Carpenter, Aug. 12, 1890, Sophia Smith Collection, Smith College.

p. 186 **as much as Cockerill was earning** Forman, "The Chances in Journalism," p. 16. King, *Pulitzer's Prize Editor*, p. 243, put Cockerill's earnings at "up to $20,000."

p. 186 **lost her beloved brother Charles** Death certificate, Charles M. Cochrane, Mar. 30, 1890, Allegheny County Vital Records.

p. 187 **because of a libel suit** Letter, Mrs. J. M. Lynch to Irene Ravitch, Jan. 20, 1931, quoted in Ravitch, "NB: A Biographical Sketch," p. 44.

p. 187 **"Accuracy! Terseness! Accuracy!"** Swanberg, *Pulitzer*, p. 127. Dreiser, in *Newspaper Days*, p. 467, recalled placards in the *World* office with the words, "Accuracy, Accuracy, Accuracy! Who? What? Where? When? How? The Facts—The Color—The Facts!" Barrett, *Joseph Pulitzer and His World*, p. 11, quotes Pulitzer saying, "Accuracy is to a newspaper what virtue is to a woman."

p. 187 **tricky balance** Swanberg, *Pulitzer*, pp. 127–128.

p. 187 **demand "impeccable reliability"** Ibid., p. 111.

p. 188 **"Where is Nellie Bly? . . ."** *The Journalist*, Aug. 20, 1892, 14:1.

p. 188 **"What is Nellie Bly doing now?"** *The Journalist*, Oct. 8, 1892, 9:2.

p. 188 **she wrote again to Q.O.** Letter, NB to Erasmus Wilson, Aug. 22, 1890, Carnegie Library.

p. 188 **Henrietta Eliza Vaughan Stannard (John Strange Winter)** Stannard also used the pseudonym Violet Whyte. See Bainbridge, *John Strange Winter*. Re: *Bootles' Baby*, see pp. ix, 76, 79, and 89.

p. 188 **[Frances Hodgson] Burnett** Thwaite, *Waiting for the Party*, says Burnett's stories appeared in any number of popular magazines, starting with *Godey's Lady's Book* and excluding only *Harper's*, *Scribner's*, and the *Atlantic Monthly*, which she thought were too literary for her to approach.

p. 188 **"You did neglect me frightfully . . ."** Letter, NB to Erasmus Wilson, Jan. 26, 1891, Carnegie Library.

p. 189 **'Ras Wilson, I respect you 'cause . . .** *Pittsburgh Chronicle Telegraph*, Oct. 19, 1918.

p. 189 **"quite a favorite with the gentlemen"** Nevin, *The Social Mirror*, p. 29.

p. 190 **"the most frightful depression . . ."** Letter, NB to Erasmus Wilson, Mar. [no date], 1891, Carnegie Library.

p. 190 **"lively, interesting and instructive weekly"** *New York Family Story Paper*, Sept. 28, 1888, Vol. 13, No. 625.

p. 190 **Munro had begun the paper** *Dictionary of Literary Biography*, Detroit: American Literary Publishing Houses, 1638–1899, Pt. 1, Vol. 49.

p. 191 **"no plot, characters or ability . . ."** McDougall, *This Is the Life*, p. 189.

p. 191 **lease on a farm in White Plains** Lease to Mary Jane Cochrane by Joseph O. Carpenter, Nov. 12, 1890, Westchester County Deed Book, Liber 1249, p. 421, Westchester County Historical Society.

p. 191 **pleasure trip to Europe** *The Journalist*, Dec. 19, 1891, 9:4.

p. 191 **detractors had caused Bly "much unnecessary suffering"** Ibid.

p. 192 **to saddle the rest with a stereotype** Walker, in his 1934 *City Editor*, pp. 248–249, refers to "blanket indictments against women in journalism, some outrageously prejudiced and others based on sad experience." He cites slovenly habits of mind and workmanship; refusal to look up names and facts; impoliteness; tendency to regard the whole organization as having been created for their own convenience and whims. They "sulk at reproof, disdain well meant advice, either burst into tears or lament that a monster office political cabal has been formed against them. They plead that there is no sex in business . . . They depend, even the good ones, too much upon their male colleagues to help them over the tough places in their assignments. They accept these courtesies as a matter of course, and then, without thanking the man, double-cross him as often as possible . . . They do not understand honor and fair play and the code of human and professional conduct as men understand it . . . They are uniformly devoid of humor." Et cetera.

p. 193 **"Lapses in trifles like these . . ."** Twombly, "Women in Journalism," p. 170.

p. 193 **". . . she is an indispensable reality . . ."** Anderson, "The Individuality of the Reporter."

p. 194 **"A woman who comes into journalism . . ."** Stead, "Young Women in Journalism," p. 451.

p. 194 **"It [is] a fact based on experience . . ."** *The Journalist*, May 28, 1892, p. 6.

p. 194 **"It is admitted by everybody . . ."** *The Journalist*, June 15, 1892, p. 5.

p. 195 **". . . hundreds whose pay is $10 . . ."** *The Journalist*, Nov. 12, 1892, 5:1–2.

p. 195 **Albert Payson Terhune, for example** Churchill, *Park Row*, p. 55.

p. 195 **under scrutiny for "unfraternal" behavior** Twombly, "Women in Journalism," p. 170.

p. 196 **Eliza D. Keith** "What Is a Newspaper Woman?" *The Journalist*, Feb. 6, 1892, p. 10.

p. 196 **call for a second women's press club** *The Journalist*, Apr. 2, 1892, pp. 8–9.

p. 196 **As Jennie June, she effectively invented** Ross, *Ladies of the Press*, pp. 43–46.

p. 196 **Pulitzer kept his managers off balance** *The Journalist*, May 16, 1891; June 13, 1891; July 6, 1891. Also Swanberg, *Pulitzer*, pp. 164–165.

p. 197 **"The loss of their service . . ."** *Town Topics*, Nov. 26, 1891, 6:2.

p. 197 **His ouster came** *The Journalist*, Aug. 13, 1892, 9:1.

p. 197 **The positions kept changing** *The Journalist*, June 11, 1892; Aug. 20, 1892; Oct. 8, 1892; Nov. 5, 1892; Dec. 3, 1892; Dec. 10, 1892.

p. 197 **young Arthur Brisbane** *The Journalist*, Nov. 5, 1892. See also Carlson, *Brisbane*; McDougall, *This Is the Life*; and Swanberg, *Pulitzer* on Brisbane.

p. 198 **A published interview with John Roff** *The Journalist*, Sept. 3, 1892, 4.

p. 198 **Pulitzer dethroned . . . Ballard Smith** Swanberg, *Pulitzer*, pp. 173–174.

p. 198 ***The World* had fired twenty-five reporters** *The Journalist*, Oct. 22, 1892, 9:2.

p. 198 **"everybody in the *World* office . . ."** *The Journalist*, Dec. 3, 1892, 8:2–3.

p. 199 **"an exhibition of incomparable cheek"** *Town Topics*, May 11, 1893, 12:2.

p. 199 **It was, of course, Bly** *NY World*, May 7, 1893, pp. 51–60.

p. 199 **"reaching out for good men . . ."** *The Journalist*, Apr. 8, 1893, p. 9.

p. 200 **Ingram died of a heart attack** Obituary, *NY Times*, Mar. 19, 1893, 4:6.

p. 200 **hand over the editorship of *The World*** Swanberg, *Pulitzer*, pp. 184–188; Barrett, *Joseph Pulitzer and His World*, p. 153; Carlson, *Brisbane*, pp. 99 ff.

p. 200 **Pulitzer was forced to suspend Jones** Barrett, *Joseph Pulitzer and His World*, pp. 153–154; Swanberg, *Pulitzer*, pp. 184–185.

p. 200 **Morrill Goddard** Barrett, *Joseph Pulitzer and His World*, pp. 153–154; Swanberg, *Pulitzer*, p. 206.

p. 200 **She accepted** *The Journalist*, Oct. 7, 1893, 5.

7

❧ ☙

Comeback

p. 205 **"NELLIE BLY AGAIN"** *NY World*, Sept. 17, 1893, 1:1. The rest of the headline reads: "What Justus H. Schwab and Joh[an]n Most Say of Capital. Their Ideas of Marriage Do Away with All Ceremony. Schwab's Wedding Service Reads: "Here's To You."

p. 205 **"making the front page"** Ross, *Ladies of the Press*, pp. 1–13.

p. 206 **many continued to perform** Banks, "American Journalism," pp. 644–645. As late as 1898, stunt work was still being described as a popular newspaper form.

p. 206 **"low grade of sensationalism"** *The Journalist*, Oct. 15, 1892, 12:1.

p. 206 **"employing women to degrade . . . themselves . . ."** *Town Topics*, Oct. 5, 1893, 12:2.

p. 206 **Dolores Marbourg, had posed** *NY World*, Oct. 1, 1893, 25:1–4.

p. 206 **"There is only one more step . . ."** *Town Topics*, Oct. 5, 1893, 12:3.

p. 207 **discredited on ethical grounds** See Hulteng, *Playing It Straight*, a practical discussion of the ethical principles of the American Society of Newspaper Editors.

p. 207 **"Nelly [*sic*] Bly, of round-the-world fame . . ."** *The Journalist*, Sept. 30, 1893, p. 9.

p. 208 **its worst economic crisis** Smith, *The Rise of Industrial America*, Vol. 6, p. 491.

p. 208 **its own bread fund** *NY World*, Aug. 25, 1893, 1:8.

p. 208 **New York police . . . turned attention** *The New York Times* ran a front page series examining who the anarchists were and how much of a threat they represented (Aug. 22, 23, 24, and 26, 1893). *The World* also followed developments in their movement quite closely.

p. 208 **Arthur Brisbane wrote** *The Journalist*, Nov. 5, 1892; *NY World*, Sept. 16, 1893, 5:7–8.

p. 208 **Bly filled seven columns** *NY World*, Sept. 17, 1893, 1:1–2, 3:1–5.

p. 208 **She took her readers into The Tombs** Goldman, according to New York newspapers at the time, was arraigned Sept. 11, 1893, after which she walked to The Tombs to await her release on bail. It would have been during this time, probably on the eleventh, but perhaps as late as the twelfth, that NB's interview took place. The judge set bail at $2,000, according to *The World*.

p. 209 **a warrant was issued** Goldman's autobiography, *Living My Life*, written long after her deportation in 1919, makes no mention of waiting in The Tombs before her trial, nor does it mention the interview with NB. Goldman's recollection is that after her extradition she arrived at Penn Station from Philadelphia and was taken immediately to the Mulberry St. police station and locked up for the night. The next day, she appeared before the chief of police and later in the afternoon was brought before a judge to hear the indictment read. Dr. Julius Hoffmann then arranged for her release on $5,000 bail.

From the *NY World* and *NY Times* it appears that Goldman was arrested in Philadelphia on Aug. 31, 1893, a grand jury indictment was returned on Sept. 10, she was extradited to New York on Sept. 10 and arraigned on Monday, Sept. 11, before being taken to The Tombs to await arrangement of bail. Although NB's interview would have taken place at this time, it was not published until Sunday's paper, Sept. 17, 1893.

The trial began Oct. 4—not Sept. 28, as Goldman later recalled. At that time, Goldman was ordered back to The Tombs for the duration of the proceedings. Previous accounts of NB's interview say it took place while Goldman was in The Tombs "awaiting trial." To clarify, Goldman awaited trial free on bail. The interview took place, as NB reported, while Goldman was "waiting patiently in The Tombs until her friends could secure bail for her," probably a matter of hours.

Goldman biographer Alice Wexler, in an interview with the author in Mar. 1992, said Goldman had just started to become more widely known and feared when NB interviewed her, and that the interview's significance was in its sympathetic portrayal of the anarchist for a wide general readership.

p. 209 **"You have seen . . . pictures of her"** *NY World*, Sept. 17, 1893, 1:1, 3:6.

p. 209 **"fire-eating anarchist"** *NY Times*, Oct. 10, 1893, 5:1.

p. 210 **she still maintained her innocence** See Goldman, *Living My Life*, pp. 121–132, for her account of the Union Square rally, her arrest, indictment, and trial.

p. 211 **The embarrassed reporter** *NY World*, Oct. 10, 1893, 7:5–6.

p. 211 **sympathetic portrait implied no personal politics** A quarter of a century later, while Goldman served time in part for propounding the "glorious awakenment" of Bolshevism in America (see Wexler, *Emma Goldman in America*, pp. 226–244), NB, after four years in Austria, would go to Paris to implore President Woodrow Wilson to act against this ominous movement and save the West from its clutches.

p. 212 **"This is all my own"** *NY World*, Sept. 24, 1893, 31:1.

p. 213 **"Morrill Goddard . . . has been transferred . . ."** *The Journalist*, Oct. 7, 1893, 5.

p. 213 **Brisbane admired her** Detailed in subsequent chapters. NB–Brisbane correspondence, Brisbane Family Papers, Syracuse University Library.

p. 213 **"I have been devoting myself . . ."** *NY World*, Oct. 1, 1893, 17:1–2, 18:1–8.

p. 215 **Saratoga for the . . . Convention** *NY World*, Oct. 8, 1893, 17:1–4, 18:1.

p. 217 **"From its circumstances . . ."** *NY World*, Sept. 10, 1893, 10:4–8. Details of the Halliday case in the following paragraphs come from *NY World* reports of Sept. 6, 1893, 1:6–8; Sept. 7, 1893, 1:1–2; Sept. 8, 1893, 5:1–3; Sept. 10, 1893, 10:4–8; Sept. 13, 1893, 2:6.

p. 218 **" 'Did you or did you not kill' . . ."** *NY World*, Oct. 22, 1893, 17:1–4, 18:1–3.

p. 218 **Bly's interview appeared** *NY World*, Nov. 5, 1893, 25:1–8.

p. 219 **"The reporters of the New York papers . . ."** *Middletown Daily Press*, Oct. 23, 1893, p. 3.

p. 219 **Halliday was tried and convicted** Records of the Clerk of Sullivan County, New York, Indictment of Lizzie Halliday, Sept. Term, 1893; trial and conviction records, June Term, 1894. Special thanks to Dora Blume. The New York State Archives at Albany record no execution of Lizzie Halliday, nor any known record of where she was jailed. After trial, she was ordered to Dannemora Prison in Clinton County, but this facility, according to its present-day administrators, has never housed women.

p. 219 **visit to the Midway** *NY World*, Oct. 29, 1893, 17:1–3, 18:3–8.

p. 219 **" 'Will you go and play policy with me?' . . ."** *NY World*, Nov. 26, 1893, 25:1–7.

p. 220 **Mary Hooker . . . and . . . Dr. Robert H. M. Dawbarn** *NY World*, Dec. 3, 1893, 17:1–3.

p. 220 **The Reverend Dr. Charles Parkhurst** *NY World*, Dec. 10, 1893, 33:1–8. Parkhurst's crusade led to a state investigation that exposed systemic corruption, the sale of police jobs, widespread police brutality, and police compliance in election fixing. His disclosures brought the reform Fusion Party into City Hall in 1895. The subsequent Police Department reorganization instituted a merit system for appointments and promotions. Theodore Roosevelt was brought in to head up the department at that time. See Parkhurst, *My Forty Years in New York*. Also, Selwyn Raab, "Taking on Tammany, 100 Years Ago," *NY Times*, Feb. 14, 1992, B3:4–6.

p. 221 **mind reader, Maud Lancaster** *NY World*, Dec. 17, 1893, 25:1–8.

p. 221 **"The English woman says . . ."** *The Journalist*, May 26, 1894, p. 2.

p. 221 **120 West Thirty-fifth Street** New York City Directories, 1889–1894.

p. 221 **"The Midnight Band of Mercy"** *NY World*, Dec. 31, 1893, 25:1–6.

p. 222 **"Unfortunately, in the new division of labour . . ."** *The Spectator*, June 17, 1893, p. 800.

p. 222 **250 bona fide newspaperwomen** *The Journalist*, May 13, 1893, p. 11.

p. 222 **"She will be tired . . ."** Ibid.

p. 223 **five truly destitute families** *NY World*, Jan. 14, 1894, 29:1–5.

p. 223 **"Afraid of ghosts? . . ."** *NY World*, Feb. 4, 1894, 29:1–6.

p. 223 **expose a furniture swindler** *NY World*, Mar. 18, 1894, 25:1–4.

p. 223 **"The Siren of The Coleman House"** *NY World*, Feb. 18, 1894, 29:1–8.

p. 223 **to designate "Meg Merrilies"** *Town Topics*, Apr. 26, 1894, 11:2. Sample "Meg Merrilies" bylines: *NY World*, Feb. 11, 1894, 13:1–5; Mar. 4, 1894, 25:1–6; Apr. 22, 1894, 33:1–5; May 27, 1894, 17:1–4.

p. 224 **"As custodian of this article . . ."** *Town Topics*, Apr. 26, 1894, 11:2.

p. 225 **Sunday readership at *The World*** Circulation figures for the Sunday *World*, 1883–1898, in a private memo in the World (NY) Papers, Columbia University.

p. 225 **eleventh anniversary of Pulitzer's stewardship** *NY World*, Mar. 4, 1894, 1:1–8.

p. 225 **"Nell Nelson has made . . . bad breaks . . ."** *The Journalist*, Mar. 31, 1894, p. 9.

p. 225 visited the mysterious "Hindoo Idol" *NY World*, Mar. 25, 1894, 17:1–4.

p. 225 the Bloomingdale Insane Asylum *NY World*, Apr. 8, 1894, 25:1–5.

p. 226 *"The World* understands how to manipulate . . ." *The Journalist*, Apr. 28, 1894, p. 9.

p. 226 march of "Coxey's Army" *NY World*, May 6, 1894, 17:1–4, 8; 18:1.

p. 226 interviewed John Jacob Astor *NY World*, May 13, 1894, 25:1–8.

p. 227 "Newspaper women are here to hunt . . ." *The Journalist*, May 19, 1894, p. 2.

p. 227 exclusive interview with . . . Clarence Lexow *NY World*, July 1, 1894, 17:1–5.

p. 228 whipping and pillorying of eight men, *NY World*, May 20, 1894, 17:1–8, 18:1–2.

p. 228 critiquing the usefulness of a new . . . pawn shop *NY World*, June 3, 1894, 33:1–5.

p. 228 "gold cure" for alcoholism *NY World*, June 10, 1894, 17:1–4, 18:1–2.

p. 228 William Muldoon *NY World*, June 24, 1894, 17:1–4.

p. 228 "I always try to have a man . . ." *NY World*, July 1, 1894, 17:1–5.

p. 231 "Colonel Jones' ideas reflected . . ." Seitz, *Joseph Pulitzer, His Life and Letters*, p. 195.

p. 231 Tennant, had been forecasting repeal The act required the U.S. Treasury to purchase 4.5 million ounces of silver each month at prevailing prices and issue legal tender treasury notes redeemable in gold and silver. Smith, *Rise of Industrial America*, p. 464. It was repealed on Oct. 30, 1893, and considered a personal triumph for President Cleveland (p. 488).

p. 231 Jones dashed off a much-discussed editorial Swanberg, *Pulitzer*, pp. 187–188. Barrett, *Joseph Pulitzer and His World*, p. 153; Seitz, *Joseph Pulitzer*, pp. 195–196.

p. 232 "Mr. Pulitzer's position . . ." *Town Topics*, July 12, 1894, 15:1–2.

p. 233 "Can you tell me, please . . ." *NY World*, July 11, 1894, 5:1–4.

p. 234 "And you are all in the [Mrs. Astor's] 400 . . ." A reference to Mrs. Astor's ballroom, which held 400 people—those invited were considered New York's social elite.

p. 235 "I told them I came to Chicago . . ." *NY World*, July 15, 1894, 3:1–2.

p. 235 "I don't know which amuses me the more— . . ." *NY World*, July 13, 1894, 4:1.

p. 236 None of the other major New York newspapers Reviewed Pullman coverage July 1–15, 1894, *NY Sun, NY Herald, NY Times, NY Tribune*.

p. 236 to interview the controversial governor *NY World*, July 17, 1894, 5:2.

p. 239 **Leclaire, Illinois** LeClaire subsequently was absorbed into Edwardsville, Illinois. See "Leclaire, Illinois," *Gateway Heritage* (Quarterly Journal of the Missouri Historical Society), Spring 1988, pp. 20–31. Items from vertical file, Edwardsville, [Ill.], Library.

p. 239 *Profit-Sharing* Nelson, *Profit-Sharing*, St. Louis, 1887.

p. 239 **"the dissatisfaction of the unemployed . . ."** *NY World*, July 29, 1894, 21:1–7.

p. 240 **what it really takes to benefit the world** Actually (*Gateway Heritage*, p. 31), Nelson came to a sad end. By 1910, he was still calling Leclaire a qualified success, but nine years later, he looked upon it bitterly as a failure because, as his friend Upton Sinclair explained, the residents had "built themselves big houses and bought themselves pianos and dressed their daughters in silk stockings and high heeled fancy shoes, and are trying to outdo each other in snobbery." Nelson saw the struggle to attain such things as the road to ruin. An ill-fated venture in New Orleans started in 1911 forced Nelson into personal bankruptcy by 1918. He pledged his stock in the Leclaire company to pay his debts. In the process, he was forced to resign as president. Four years later, he died in Los Angeles, "broken in both health and finances."

p. 241 **"How I would like to see you! . . ."** Letter, NB to Erasmus Wilson, dated Tuesday, July [probably 24], 1894, Carnegie Library.

p. 241 **deflecting a silver bullet** *NY World*, July 22, 1894, 25:1–6.

p. 241 **silencing those "long-winded Sunday creatures"** *Town Topics*, July 26, 1894, 14:2.

p. 242 **Thomas F. Byrnes** *NY World*, Aug. 1, 1894, 5:1–3.

p. 242 **Byrnes's views on women** *NY World*, Aug. 1, 1894, 10:1–2.

p. 242 **advice of . . . William Muldoon** *NY World*, Aug. 3, 1894, 5:4.

p. 242 **the city's largest double-decker tenement** *NY World*, Aug. 5, 1894, 21:1–7.

p. 242 *How the Other Half Lives* Riis, *How the Other Half Lives*, 1890, reprint, 1957.

p. 242 **prizefighter James J. Corbett** *NY World*, Aug. 12, 1894, 13:1–6, 14:1–3.

p. 243 **"Crime is holding a convention there"** *NY World*, Aug. 19, 1894, 21:1–8.

p. 244 **"The element of unrestricted gambling . . ."** *NY World*, Aug. 26, 1894, 21:1–4.

p. 244 **"Governor Altgeld a Sick Man"** *NY World*, Sept. 15, 1894, 1:1–3.

p. 244 **another reporter was quickly assigned** Ibid.

p. 244 **"I have said that John Peter Altgeld . . ."** Ibid.

p. 245 **The only other major New York paper** *NY Herald*, Sept. 15, 1894, 3:5.

p. 245 **to the ill-kept Central Park menagerie** *NY World*, Sept. 16, 1894, 6:1–2.

p. 245 **Superintendent John P. Haines** *NY World*, Sept. 17, 1894, 9:1–2.

p. 245 **not even the most innocuous note** Letter to author, Mar. 31, 1992, from Cody Wright, archivist, Illinois State Archives, Office of the Secretary of State, Springfield, Ill.

p. 246 **"Miss Dashaway: . . ."** *Town Topics*, Aug. 30, 1894, 7:2.

p. 246 **"Darling Delia: . . ."** *Town Topics*, Sept. 20, 1894, 12:2.

p. 247 **purchase of a farm** Nov. 2, 1894, Westchester County Deed Book, Liber 1372, p. 272, Westchester County Historical Society.

p. 247 **"wonderful" piece** *The Journalist*, Nov. 17, 1894, p. 8.

p. 247 **"Fakirs! Fakirs! Fakirs! . . ."** *NY World*, Nov. 11, 1894, 25:1–8, 26:1–2.

p. 247 **the rival Meg Merrilies byline** *NY World*, Sept. 23, 1894, 25:1–8; Oct. 7, 1894, 25:1–5; Oct. 14, 1894, 17:1–7; Oct. 21, 1894, 33:1–6; Nov. 4, 1894, 33:1–5; Nov. 18, 1894, 18:1–4; Nov. 25, 1894, 33:1–4.

p. 248 **the "Astor Tramp"** *NY World*, Nov. 25, 1894, 25:1–6.

p. 248 **moral reformer Elizabeth Grannis** *NY World*, Dec. 3, 1894, 3:1.

p. 248 **Thomas C. Platt** *NY World*, Dec. 9, 1894, 41:1–6.

p. 248 **tenement homes owned by the Trinity Corporation** *NY World*, Dec. 17, 1894, 5:1.

p. 248 **Edith Kingdon Gould** *NY World*, Dec. 31, 1894, 12:1.

p. 250 **"people whose money is the sole thing . . ."** *NY World*, Sept. 1, 1889, 9:1.

p. 250 **"If Mrs. Gould ever does any literary slumming . . ."** *Town Topics*, Jan. 13, 1895, 9:2.

p. 251 **"In the world of modern wild-cat journalism . . ."** Cahoon, "Women in Gutter Journalism," pp. 568–569.

p. 251 **jailhouse interview with Eugene V. Debs** *NY World*, Jan. 20, 1895, 8:1.

p. 252 **datelined Valentine, Nebraska; Fairfax, South Dakota; and Butte, Nebraska** *NY World*, Jan. 28, 1895, 3:1–3; Feb. 4, 1895, 3:1–3; Feb. 11, 1895, 7:1–3; Feb. 13, 1895, 7:1–3.

p. 252 **"Imagine one broad and level stretch . . ."** *NY World*, Jan. 28, 1895, 3:1–3.

p. 253 **"Charity is a difficult matter . . ."** Ibid.

p. 253 **"Stay East! . . ."** *NY World*, Feb. 4, 1895, 3:1–3.

p. 253 **"I never realized before . . ."** *NY World*, Feb. 13, 1895, 7:1–3.

p. 254 **"Abdullah the Mind Reader"** *NY World*, Feb. 18, 1895, 3:1–3.

p. 255 **James W. Scott assumed control** *The Journalist*, Feb. 23, 1895.

p. 255 **Abbot recalled Scott** Abbot, *Watching the World Go By*, p. 131. Also, Scott's obituary, *NY Times*, Apr. 15, 1895, 1:3–4.

p. 255 **movement . . . to consolidate** Bleyer, *Main Currents in the History of American Journalism*, p. 415.

p. 255 **the lady reporter with "fire and flame"** McDougall, *This Is the Life*, p. 190.

p. 255 **"Nellie Bly in the County Jail"** *Chicago Times-Herald*, Mar. 10, 1895, 25:1–6.

p. 256 **"When Nellie Bly entered Chicago . . ."** *Town Topics*, Mar. 14, 1895, 8:1.

p. 257 **"Nellie Bly's story of the frightful conditions . . ."** *Chicago Times-Herald*, Mar. 13, 1895, 12:1–2.

p. 257 **". . . they are blessing Nellie Bly . . ."** *Chicago Times-Herald*, Mar. 24, 1895, 6:1–2.

p. 257 **Bly interviewed Frank Wenter** *Chicago Times-Herald*, Mar. 17, 1895, 25:1–6.

p. 257 **straight to the Bridewell Prison** *Chicago Times-Herald*, Apr. 7, 1895, 17:1–5.

p. 258 **Scott's unrelated . . . death** *NY Times*, Apr. 15, 1895, 1:3–4.

p. 258 **Chicago's Church of the Epiphany** Marriage License No. 231006, Robert L. Seaman–Elizabeth J. Cochrane, Apr. 5, 1895, Cook County Vital Records.

p. 258 **just turning seventy** Newspaper accounts of the marriage put Seaman's age at seventy-two, which was then repeated in references to him over the coming years. Testifying on Apr. 17, 1895, only days after the marriage, in a case before the Circuit Court of Cook County, Seaman replied when asked his age, "Well sir, I am nearly 70, approaching it quite rapidly." Seaman v. Bisbee, Superior Court of Cook County, Apr. 17, 1895. The couple's marriage license gives his age at sixty-eight. Seaman's birth, baptismal, death, and tombstone records are all inexact.

8

❧ ❧

Marriage

p. 261 **"owing to my business affairs . . ."** *Catskill Examiner*, Apr. 20, 1895, 1:1.

p. 261 **"no end of talk"** Ibid.

p. 261 **Bly had met Robert Seaman** *NY Advertiser*, quoted in ibid.

p. 262 **"metropolitan residence"** Ibid.

p. 262 **magnificent Victorian "cottage"** Interview, Melvin R. Van Loan with Mabel Parker Smith, Greene County Historian, undated 1955, quoted in Smith, June 20–24, 1977, *Catskill Daily Mail*.

p. 262 **so preposterous they dismissed it** *Catskill Examiner*, Apr. 20, 1895, 1:1.

p. 262 "Such is the degradation of the press . . ." *Town Topics*, Apr. 25, 1895, 12:1.

p. 262 "Nellie was deeply attached . . ." McDougall, *This Is the Life*, p. 189.

p. 262 to speak wistfully of a loan "to Life" *NY Journal and Advertiser*, Feb. 17, 1899, 3:6–7.

p. 263 "Mr. and Mrs. Nellie Bly" *NY World*, Apr. 21, 1895, 37:1–3.

p. 263 Metcalfe's marriage *Batavia* [NY] *Daily News*, Jan. 16, 1892; Aug. 12, 1896; and Aug. 27, 1896. *Buffalo Express*, Aug. 12, 1896, and Aug. 28, 1896. Mrs. Dowling's husband of two years died in the sanitarium at Goshen in 1892. Metcalfe's engagement to Mrs. Dowling was disclosed just two weeks before the ceremony at her parents' house in Batavia, the racetrack town not far from his native Buffalo.

p. 264 "I never knew, nor does anybody . . ." McDougall, *This Is the Life*, p. 189.

p. 264 "and, if so, Bly has accomplished . . ." *NY World*, Apr. 21, 1895, 37:1–3.

p. 264 Seaman's people were prominent Sprague, *The Metropolis*, p. 88.

pp. 264–265 saddle, trunk, and harness making Pinckney, *Reminiscences of Catskill, Local Sketches*, p. 54.

p. 265 "ardent and active" Democrat Ibid.

p. 265 born in 1825 Sprague, *The Metropolis*, p. 88. In this vanity profile written from information probably supplied by Seaman himself, he is said to have come to New York in 1843 at the age of eighteen, making his birth year 1825 and his age at the time of his marriage to NB nearly seventy, as he claimed in Chicago court testimony just days after the marriage. Baptismal records of the Athens Trinity Episcopal Church (Greene County Historical Society in Coxsackie, N.Y.) show no corresponding baptismal date for a Seaman child, although the records are somewhat haphazard. An unnamed Seaman child was, however, baptized July 25, 1821. To complicate matters further, Seaman's tombstone in Catskill reads, "Robert E. [*sic*] Seaman, 1817–1904." Census records from 1850 to 1900 all give different ages for him.

p. 265 wholesale grocery concern Sprague, *The Metropolis*, p. 88.

p. 266 Title was in the name Indenture, New York County Deed Book, Liber 51, p. 98, Block 839, No. 31, traced back to 1799, when the block passed from Samuel Nicol to William Ogden. When title passed to Ogden's widow and children, the property was divided into city lots, Dec. 18, 1840. New York County Real Estate Records.

p. 266 The neighborhood was the best *How to Know New York*, Boston: Rand Avery Co., May 15, 1887, p. 107.

p. 266 the Valentine G. Halls *The Metropolitan Directory*, New York: Trow Directory, Printing and Bookbinding Co., 1893, p. 346.

p. 266 "the fight of the iron clads" NB, "How I Was Robbed of Two Million Dollars," *Fair Play*, Jan. 20, 1912, pp. 27–29.

p. 266 "what was then called a beau . . ." *NY World*, Apr. 21, 1895, 37:1–3.

p. 267 "a clean-shaven face . . ." Ibid.

p. 267 ". . . Sir Roger [de] Coverly stamp . . ." A character described by Addison in *The Spectator*—a member of the Spectator Club, "a gentleman of Worcestershire, an ancient descendant, a baronet," *Oxford Companion to English Literature*, 3rd ed.

p. 267 **Ellen, Henry, and Edward . . . spent long periods** Ellen Seaman held title to the house from its purchase, Mar. 20, 1862, until her death, Mar. 9, 1888, when it passed to Henry. Henry, in turn, left the house to Robert when he died Nov. 4, 1891. Ellen's occupation in census records is given as "lady." Henry was in the saddlery importing business.

p. 267 **as evidenced by their wills** In her will, Ellen left a trust of $2,000 for Edward, from which he was to receive only interest at regular intervals. Robert at one point had made similar provisions for a regular allowance for Edward. Henry had very little to distribute. Clearly Edward was not considered trustworthy enough to hold any large sums of money. New York County Surrogate's Court records for the estates of Ellen (Mar. 9, 1888), Edward (June 29, 1902), and Robert (Mar. 11, 1904) Seaman.

p. 267 **"cumbersome and expensive carriage . . ."** *NY World*, Apr. 21, 1895, 37:1–3.

p. 267 **"He is today one of . . ."** Ibid.

p. 268 **she was probably braced** *Catskill Examiner*, Apr. 20, 1895, 1:1.

p. 268 **estimated value of $150,000** *NY World*, Apr. 21, 1895, 37:1–3.

p. 268 **"Bleak House"** *NY Journal and Advertiser*, Feb. 17, 1899, 3:6–7. This also includes details of the Seamans' early marital woes.

p. 268 **"Mr. Seaman is said to be worth . . ."** *NY Recorder*, Nov. 11, 1895, 1:3, 2:6. This also includes details of the Seamans' early marital woes.

p. 268 **"unaccountably jealous"** *NY Sun*, Nov. 11, 1895, 3:5. The *NY Recorder* story of the same date uses the term "exceedingly."

p. 269 **Saturday evening, November 9, 1895** The incident is reconstructed from accounts in *NY World*, Nov. 10, 1895, 2:7; *NY Sun*, Nov. 10, 1895, 4:6; Nov. 11, 1895, 3:5; *NY Recorder*, Nov. 11, 1895, 1:3, 2:6; *Catskill Examiner*, Nov. 16, 1895, 1:1; *NY Times*, Nov. 10, 1895, 7:2; *NY Tribune*, Nov. 10, 1895, 10:5. These articles also contain details of the Seamans' marital troubles.

p. 269 **"The prisoner, who was a short, . . ."** *NY Tribune*, Nov. 10, 1895, 10:5.

p. 270 **Seaman walked into the station house** *NY Sun*, Nov. 10, 1895, 4:6.

p. 270 **"Hansen should not have been arrested . . ."** *NY World*, Nov. 10, 1895, 2:7.

p. 270 **wandering peacocks** Smith, *Catskill Daily Mail*, June 20, 1977.

p. 270 **fistfight with . . . F. A. Titus** *Catskill Examiner*, Oct. 5, 1895, 5:1.

p. 270 **"feeble"** *NY Sun*, Nov. 10, 1895, 4:6. A very brief story that does not have the precision of one written by an eyewitness, putting the description of Seaman as "feeble" into question.

p. 270 "You will find a cab . . ." *NY Recorder*, Nov. 11, 1895, 1:3, 2:6.

p. 271 "Really there is nothing in it . . ." *NY Sun*, Nov. 11, 1895, 3:5.

p. 272 "The Mating of May and December" *NY Recorder*, Nov. 11, 1895, 2:6.

p. 273 turned out to be Seaman's niece *NY Sun*, Nov. 11, 1895, 3:5.

p. 273 "They are trying to make all the trouble possible . . ." *NY Recorder*, Nov. 11, 1895, 2:6.

p. 273 "My husband is in the house . . ." *NY Sun*, Nov. 11, 1895, 3:5.

p. 274 The man was John Hanley *NY Sun*, Nov. 29, 1898, 9:3.

p. 274 In court papers, Hanley charged Ibid.

p. 274 Chicago, Nov. 23—The litigation *NY Times*, Nov. 24, 1895, 6:3. A similar piece appeared the day before: *Chicago Evening Post*, Nov. 23, 1895, 2:4.

p. 275 "its extremely confidential character" Bisbee testimony, Nov. 1–30, 1895, Seaman v. Bisbee, Nov. 13, [*sic*] 1895, Case No. 136.002, Jeremiah Leaming, Master in Chancery, Circuit Court of Cook County, Illinois. Also, *Chicago Evening Post*, Nov. 23, 1895, 2:4.

p. 275 to fuel the "unfortunate gossip" *Chicago Evening Post*, Nov. 23, 1895, 2:4.

p. 276 "We sued for the recovery . . ." Ibid.

p. 276 The court ultimately found Seaman v. Bisbee, Case No. 136.002, 1894–95.

p. 276 Bisbee was vague and confused Ibid., Bisbee testimony, Nov. 1–30, 1895.

p. 277 He did acknowledge an acquaintanceship Ibid., Seaman deposition, Apr. 17 and May 15, 1895.

p. 277 Ernestine was born in France Death Certificate No. 13634, Ernestine Sanderson, Apr. 30, 1901, age 51, New York City Municipal Archives, Vital Records.

p. 277 Christmas Eve 1895 Robert Seaman drew up a will Estate of Robert L. Seaman, Probate Records, Clerk of the New York County Surrogate's Court.

p. 278 Hearst had purchased the . . . *New York Journal* Seitz, *Joseph Pulitzer*, p. 211.

p. 278 Hearst's behavior was tantamount Swanberg, *Pulitzer*, p. 206.

p. 278 "Please don't write in Delphic phrases . . ." World (NY) Papers, 1896, Columbia University.

p. 279 " 'What is your greatest ambition now?' . . ." *NY World*, Jan. 13, 1896, 9:1–4.

p. 281 John Daly, "The Gambler King" *NY World*, Jan. 20, 1896, 3:1–3.

p. 282 Hanley's suit against Seaman *NY Sun*, Nov. 29, 1898, 9:3.

p. 282 "The first thing I learned . . ." *NY World*, Jan. 26, 1896, 4:1–7.

p. 284 "Woman in the Pulpit" *NY World*, Jan. 27, 1896, 9:1–5.

p. 284 **never had she revealed more** Author conversation with Anthony biographer Kathleen Barry, Apr. 17, 1991. Barry also said NB's interview with Anthony was considered significant because the suffragist had never before revealed so many personal details in print.

p. 284 "Tell me about Cuba!" *NY World*, Feb. 2, 1896, 10:1–7.

p. 286 **homeless women's shelters** *NY World*, Feb. 9, 1896, 17:1–8.

p. 286 "Nellie Bly and Two Women Contrasts" *NY World*, Feb. 26, 1896, 32:1–7.

p. 288 **helping train the eight new elephants** *NY World*, Feb. 23, 1896, 17:1–7.

p. 288 "Nellie Bly Fin de Siecle Joan of Arc" *NY World*, Mar. 8, 1896, 25:1–6.

p. 291 **Seaman drew up yet another will** Estate of Robert L. Seaman (died Mar. 11, 1904), will dated Nov. 17, 1896, Paris, New York County Surrogate's Court.

p. 291 **The Iron Clad Manufacturing Company** NB, "How I Was Robbed," p. 27.

p. 292 **. . . plus stock in two banks . . .** *NY Herald*, Oct. 13, 1901, 4:2.

p. 292 "To Charlie. Merry Christmas . . ." Cards, Mary Jane Cochrane to grandchildren in Pittsburgh, Christmas 1896, personal collection of Peggy Cochrane Potts.

p. 292 **transferred title of the house at 15 West Thirty-seventh Street** Estate of Robert L. Seaman (died Mar. 11, 1904), will dated Dec. 24, 1896, Paris, New York County Surrogate's Court.

p. 293 **execution of a "warranty deed"** Title history of 15 W. 37th St., Liber 51, p. 98, Index Lot, No. 31, New York City Register's Office. Definition of warranty deed courtesy of New York real estate attorney Dennis Mandell.

p. 293 **put the Iron Clad in Bly's name** NB first appeared on the company's board of directors after an election was held Nov. 4, 1899. State of New York, County of New York, Certificate of Inspectors of Election, Nov. 1899, New York Superior Court. Seaman's will of Dec. 24, 1896, makes specific bequests to family members and grants everything else, which would include the Iron Clad, to NB.

p. 293 **Seaman's failing eyesight** Testimony of Rhein Hotel employees in documents relating to contest of Seaman's will. Estate of Robert L. Seaman.

p. 293 **Cleveland secured Seaman's power of attorney** *NY Herald*, Oct. 13, 1901, 4:2.

p. 293 **board of directors from three persons to five** July 13, 1897, Certificate of Increasing Number of Board of Directors, Iron Clad Manufacturing Co., New York County Superior Court.

p. 293 **Seaman gave Otis his power of attorney** Sept. 16, 1897, Designation under Sec. 430, Code of Civil Procedure, by Robert Seaman of David D. Otis as the person upon whom to serve a summons, etc. Miss R. Vol. 6, p. 606, filed and recorded Sept. 17, 1896, 9 H. 35 M.

p. 293 **Less than a month later, Seaman revoked Otis's power** Revocation filed and recorded Oct. 11, 1897.

p. 294 **filed a new certificate of election** New York County Superior Court records, Nov. 8, 1897, Iron Clad Manufacturing Co. Certificate of Election.

p. 294 **"I give and bequeath all my property . . ."** Estate of Robert L. Seaman (died Mar. 11, 1904), will dated Nov. 29, 1897, New York County Surrogate's Court.

p. 294 **"eyesight was greatly affected"** Ibid. Testimony of Karl Ebbighausen in support of the witnessed document, taken at Royal District Court at Wiesbaden, Jan. 23, 1909, in connection with the will contest over Robert Seaman's estate.

p. 294 **"TO WHOM IT MAY CONCERN . . ."** Ibid. Letter, appended to will of Robert L. Seaman dated Nov. 29, 1897.

p. 296 **help bail him out** NB, "How I Was Robbed," pp. 27–29.

p. 296 **Seaman, her latest dependent** Seaman had signed over all his property to NB but apparently still had some eyesight: One report of Seaman's death had him reading his newspaper when he collapsed, and NB's grandnephew, the late James Agey, recalled playing cards with Seaman in New York at around the time of his death. Notes of interview of Muriel Nussbaum with James Agey before his death in 1981.

p. 296 *Love Sonnets of Proteus* Volume is in the author's possession, gift of poet April Bernard from her personal collection.

p. 296 **thought to be in Vienna** Both the inscription in the Blunt book and NB's letter from Rome dated May 14, 1899, give rise to several possibilities: that the Seamans were in Rome for the entire period, that Robert Seaman remained in Vienna while NB was in Rome, or that they—or she alone—traveled back and forth.

p. 296 **put a series of questions to Seaman** The only surviving record of this case is contained in *NY Journal*, Feb. 17, 1899, 3:5–8.

p. 297 **"Did the plaintiff . . ."** The night in question, Valentine's Day 1896, fell between two of NB's last assignments for Brisbane. Her very last assignment, the elephant trainer story, ran the following week, Feb. 23, 1896.

p. 297 **management of her two homes** *NY Herald*, Oct. 13, 1901, 4:2.

p. 297 **fired Henry Hansen** Letter, NB to unidentified "Jennie" from Rome, May 14, 1899, Brisbane Family Papers, Syracuse University Library. Also, advertisement for Hansen floral business, *Catskill Examiner*, Apr. 7, 1899, 5:1.

p. 298 **"Affectionately, Pink"** Ibid. The signature and complimentary closing, as well as the contents, indicate the recipient of the letter was probably a family member. A detailed genealogy of the Cochrane family reveals no one named Jennie or Jennifer or any other variation. Albert's wife's name was Jane. The facts that they were all living at the house on West Thirty-seventh Street at this time and that the letter was found amidst letters to NB's mother strangely lodged in the Brisbane papers, indicate Jane was its most likely recipient.

p. 298 **Kate had remarried** Testimony, Estate of Michael Cochran, No. 2043, Armstrong County Courthouse.

p. 299 **Cleveland urged them to stay away** *NY Herald*, Oct. 13, 1901, 4:2.

p. 299 **Kate . . . contracted tuberculosis** *Catskill Weekly Examiner*, July 29, 1899, 5:3, did not include a cause of death. Greene County Historian Mabel Parker Smith, in her June 20–24, 1977, series for *The Catskill Daily Mail*, says Kate died of tuberculosis without citing her source. Greene County Vital Records was unable to locate a death certificate for Kate when requested by the author.

p. 299 **Seaman did not return until November** *NY Herald*, Oct. 13, 1901, 4:2.

p. 299 **installed a new general manager** Ibid.

p. 299 **asking them . . . to stop pestering her** *Catskill Daily Mail* series of 1977 mentions this, but the reported newspaper notice, which Mabel Parker Smith gleaned from interviews, could not be located. Mrs. Smith did not recall ever seeing it herself.

p. 299 **" 'Nellie Bly' who made herself famous . . ."** *Coxsackie Union*, Sept. 25, 1899.

p. 300 **to demand a retraction** *Catskill Daily Mail* series of 1977 quotes editor F. A. Gallt in a 1955 issue of *The Enterprise* recalling the incident. In Gallt's recollection, the funeral pyre was connected to Robert Seaman's death instead of Kate's, although this is unlikely since the house had burned down four years before Seaman died.

p. 300 **"There is hardly a doubt . . ."** *Catskill Weekly Examiner*, June 2, 1900, 1:6.

p. 300 **several new kerosene cans** Smith, *Catskill Daily Mail*, June 23, 1977.

p. 301 **Bly's two brothers and their wives** NY City Directory listings, 1899–1904.

p. 301 **Bly is known to have sent Charles** Author interviews with Peggy Cochrane Potts, 1991–92.

p. 301 **how beautiful the living room was** *New Kensington* (Pa.) *Dispatch*, Mar. 17, 1965, p. 12.

p. 301 **actress Beverly Sitgreaves** Letter, Beverly Sitgreaves to Irene Ravitch, Feb. 1, 1931, quoted in Ravitch, "NB: A Biographical Sketch."

p. 301 **Gertrude remembered a young butler** *New Kensington* (Pa.) *Dispatch*, Mar. 17, 1965, p. 12.

p. 301 **suspicious about her new maid** *NY American*, Feb. 27, 1904, 3:3.

p. 301 **struck by a horse and wagon rig** Obituaries: *NY Tribune*, Mar. 12, 1904, 5:4; *NY Times*, Mar. 13, 1904, 8:7.

p. 302 **died two hours after midnight** Death Certificate No. 9564, Robert L. Seaman, Mar. 11, 1904, 2:00 A.M., NY Municipal Archives. (Seaman's age is given as eighty-six.)

p. 302 **had the casket transported** *Catskill Weekly Examiner*, Mar. 19, 1904, p. 1.

p. 302 **buried in the . . . family plot** Catskill Village Cemetery. The gravestone of Edward Seaman gives his date of death as July 1, 1902, and his age at the time of death as seventy-six. Robert Seaman's headstone reads: "B. 1817, D. 1904." This would make Seaman nine years older than Edward, which is unlikely.

p. 302 **members of the Catskill community agreed** Smith, *Catskill Daily Mail*, June 20–24, 1977, quotes F. A. Gallt, editor and publisher of *The Catskill Enterprise*, in 1955, saying, "Nelly [*sic*] made a good wife and she loved and tenderly cared for her husband, so far as ever was known."

p. 302 **disinherited family members contested** Estate of Robert L. Seaman, document dated Nov. 19, 1904, filed by attorney David Otis, Clerk of the New York County Surrogate's Court.

p. 303 **case to drag on for five years** *NY Times*, May 18, 1909, 13:1.

p. 303 **Metcalfe became engaged** *NY Times*, June 25, 1904, 7:4.

9

Business

p. 305 **"purely as a mental distraction"** NB, "How I Was Robbed of Two Million Dollars," *Fair Play*, Jan. 20, 1912, pp. 27–29.

p. 305 **secured passage in the state legislature** Ibid. This could refer to a law passed Apr. 23, 1900, amending Chapter 4 of the Laws of 1899 entitled "An act to provide for rapid transit railways in cities of over 1 million inhabitants . . . ," which made it possible for the railway board to determine the necessity of railways, stations, and stops. Laws of New York, 1900, 123rd Session, Chap. 616, p. 1349.

p. 306 **"She discarded steam engines . . ."** *Brooklyn Daily Eagle*, Dec. 3, 1905, 3:1–5.

p. 306 **quadrupled the company's business** NB, "How I Was Robbed," pp. 27–29.

p. 306 **startling array of products** Iron Clad letterhead, dated 1906, Bella C. Landauer Collection, N-Y Historical Society.

p. 306 **"having no personal use for money . . ."** NB, "How I Was Robbed," p. 27.

p. 306 **"Mrs. Seaman's theory of life . . ."** *Brooklyn Daily Eagle*, Dec. 3, 1905, 3:1–5.

p. 307 **Bly eliminated piecework** Ibid.

p. 307 **Born in Thomaston, Maine** *Brooklyn Daily Eagle*, Obituary, Feb. 10, 1911, 3:8.

p. 308 **When Robert Seaman hired Gilman** NB, "How I Was Robbed," p. 27.

p. 308 **"They [steel barrels] are my own . . ."** *NY Times*, June 28, 1911, 7:1.

p. 309 *The Iron Clad factories are the Largest* Tin advertising card of the Iron Clad Manufacturing Co., 1901, author's collection.

p. 309 **conducting and expanding businesses they had inherited** Bird, *Enterprising Women*, pp. 130–138.

p. 309 **those women who ventured out on their own** Higgins, *Windows on Women*, p. 84.

p. 309 *Brooklyn Daily Eagle* **ran a five-column feature** *Brooklyn Daily Eagle*, Dec. 3, 1905, 3:1–5.

p. 309 **Both** *The Eagle* **and** *The New York Times* *Brooklyn Daily Eagle*, Dec. 24, 1905; *NY Times*, Dec. 24, 1905.

p. 309 *Pittsburgh Dispatch* **had also featured her** Letter, NB to Erasmus Wilson, Jan. 9, 1906, Carnegie Library. The article was not located in *Dispatch* files from Sept. 1906 through Jan. 1907.

p. 309 **Wilson had written about her** *Pittsburgh Gazette-Times*, May 16, 1906.

p. 310 **"Oh, she's all right . . ."** Ibid.

p. 310 **"It is just like your dear, good self . . ."** Letter, NB to Erasmus Wilson, May 19, 1906, Carnegie Library.

p. 310 **"Approximate Financial Statement"** Financial statement, Bella C. Landauer Collection, NY Historical Society.

p. 311 **Richards filed suit** New York Supreme Court archives have destroyed these records. Only the index card remains, confirming the case came to court Oct. 12, 1901.

p. 311 **Cleveland called the suit "malicious prosecution"** *NY Herald*, Oct. 13, 1901, 4:2; *NY Times*, Mar. 18, 1906, 22:2; *NY Tribune*, Mar. 18, 1906, 5:2.

p. 312 **threatened to cause** *NY American*, May 27, 1905, 1:3; *NY Herald*, June 12, 1905, 7:5–7; *NY Sun*, June 23, 1905, 3:2; *NY Times*, June 23, 1905, 5:3; July 29, 1905, 12:6.

p. 312 **Gilman had defrauded her of $50,000** NB, "How I Was Robbed," p. 27.

p. 312 **Arthur Brisbane had become** Letter, William Randolph Hearst to James Wright Brown of *Editor and Publisher*, Dec. 29, 1936, N-Y Historical Society.

p. 313 **"assumed war-time proportions"** Ibid.

p. 313 **Although he was rumored** Carlson, *Brisbane*, p. 137.

p. 313 **It is sure that he was a great admirer** The Brisbane Family Papers, Syracuse University Library, include a long correspondence with NB and also correspondence between NB and Brisbane's sister, Alice Thursby.

p. 313 **a would-be biographer of Bly** Evelyn Burke is quoted in Carlson's *Brisbane*, p. 137, as writing a "forthcoming biography" of NB, which apparently never was published. Burke apparently shared Brisbane's letter to her with Carlson, who excerpted it.

p. 313 "**I knew Nellie Bly . . .**" Ibid.

p. 314 **divorced her adulterous first husband** U.S. Census, New York City, 1910.

p. 314 **married Richard E. Brown** Marriage License, New York State, No. 11 84, Beatrice C. Kountze to Richard E. Brown, issued Feb. 2, 1907, New York Municipal Archives.

p. 314 **Albert and Jane** Bridgeport, Conn., City Directories, 1908–1913, Bridgeport Public Library Historical Collection.

p. 314 **Harry and Adele** Harry Cochrane does not appear in the NY City Directories for the years in question, nor was it possible to trace his name in directories for Milwaukee or the surrounding area in those years.

p. 314 **Bly asked Brisbane's advice** Letter, Brisbane to NB, Apr. 22, 1907, Brisbane Family Papers.

p. 314 "**The Gentle Sex**" Letter, Brisbane to NB, June 26, 1907, Brisbane Family Papers.

p. 314 **cartoon was something of a prophecy** *Brooklyn Daily Eagle*, Oct. 5, 1909, 2:7.

p. 315 "**My dear Law-suit Lucy**" Letter, Brisbane to NB, June 26, 1907, Brisbane Family Papers.

p. 316 "**With a kid's curiosity . . .**" *The Great Neck News*, Mar. 26, 1927, 7:1–4, 8:2–4.

p. 316 **Kerr and Fitzgerald were "buzzing"** Ibid.

p. 317 "**The part of what you told me . . .**" Letter, F. Scott Fitzgerald to Robert Kerr, undated, from collection of Kerr's daughter, Doris Kerr Brown, reprinted in Joseph Corso, Jr., for the *Fitzgerald-Hemingway Annual*, 1976, ed. Matthew Bruccoli. Corso is a Fitzgerald buff who happened upon Mrs. Brown at a Great Neck Library exhibition of Fitzgerald memorabilia.

p. 317 **Gilman rented what was known** Agreement, Louis Meyer and Edward R. Gilman, Oct. 31, 1907, recorded Mar. 12, 1908, Liber 3071, p. 194, Kings County Real Estate Records.

p. 317 **buy a more desirable property** Indenture, between Jacob Herrscher and Edward R. Gilman, dated July 9, 1908, recorded Apr. 30, 1909, Liber 3139, p. 356, Kings County Real Estate Records.

p. 317 **Bly was taking out a first mortgage** Mortgage, granted to Elizabeth C. Seaman by the Greenwich Savings Bank, July 14, 1908, for $62,500, Liber 180, p. 274, New York County Real Estate Records. Also NB, "How I Was Robbed," p. 27, in which NB said she put the proceeds of the mortgage "on my mother's house" into Iron Clad.

p. 317 "**. . . never seemed to be any money on hand**" NB, "How I Was Robbed," p. 27.

p. 317 **begun to suspect wrongdoing** Details of NB's version of the Iron Clad embezzlement scheme are from NB, "How I Was Robbed," unless otherwise stipulated.

p. 318 **Gilman was experiencing another . . . crisis** Indenture, Joseph Metzger, referee in bankruptcy to Grace McLaughlin, July 12, 1909, Liber 3153, p. 490, cites New York Supreme Court action of May 24, 1909, in case involving Edward R. Gilman, Kings County Real Estate Records.

p. 318 **Grace quietly transferred title** Title for the Sheepshead Bay property was in the name of Mary Jane Cochrane, July 22, 1913, Liber 3441, p. 267, Kings County Real Estate Records.

p. 319 **40 percent depreciation** 194 Federal Reporter, In re Iron Clad Manufacturing Co. (District Ct., E.D., N.Y., Mar. 15, 1912), p. 918.

p. 319 **securing loans using the real estate** Ibid.

p. 320 **case of stomach cancer** Gilman died Feb. 9, 1911.

p. 320 **"I felt myself . . . responsible . . ."** NB, "How I Was Robbed," p. 28.

p. 321 **"Mrs. Seaman said that she regretted . . ."** *NY Tribune*, Mar. 31, 1910, 4:5.

p. 321 **Bly led the firefighters** *NY Times*, Mar. 31, 1910, 4:2.

p. 321 **"also ventured into the building . . ."** *NY American*, Mar. 31, 1910, 3:2–3.

p. 321 **two very rare Antarctic gray geese** *NY American*, May 13, 1910, 3:3.

p. 321 **recollection of W. H. Hands** Letter, W. H. Hands to John Kouwenhoven, Apr. 14, 1964, Brown Brothers Collection, N-Y Historical Society. Kouwenhoven was writing a history of the Wall Street investment firm on its centennial when he received the letter from Hands. No other documentation from the company or the archive was available. At the time of his writing, Hands's recollections were a half century old and possibly confused. Some details of the episode he described could have been "telescoped" into similar events involving NB and Brown Brothers which occurred later. Or perhaps what Hands described was the reason for Brown Brothers' legal assault on the Iron Clad.

p. 323 **"His physician told me . . ."** NB, "How I Was Robbed," p. 27.

p. 323 **finally recording the 1899 deed** Deed, Elizabeth C. Seaman to Mary Jane Cochrane, dated Apr. 22, 1899, recorded Nov. 23, 1910, Liber 161, p. 238, New York County Real Estate Records.

p. 323 **Capt. Alexander Piper, reported** NB, "How I Was Robbed," p. 29.

p. 325 **"I went to Philadelphia . . ."** Ibid.

p. 325 **secure her ownership of the . . . brownstone** Title search, 15 W. 37th St., 173/150/31; 172/288/31; 176/415–416/31; 177/441–2/31, New York County Real Estate Records.

p. 325 **"I remembered that the major . . ."** NB, "How I Was Robbed," p. 29.

p. 326 **"The amounts . . . $100,000,"** Ibid.

p. 326 **"He came over that evening . . ."** Ibid.

p. 327 "While I do not believe . . ." Ibid., p. 28.

p. 327 a $5,000 political campaign contribution and a $25,000 yacht *Brooklyn Daily Eagle*, June 21, 1911, 4:1–3, quoting NB after independent auditors combed the books.

10

🍃 🍃

Bankruptcy

p. 329 "I cannot blame myself enough . . ." NB, "How I Was Robbed of Two Million Dollars," *Fair Play*, Jan. 20, 1912, p. 28.

p. 329 "make their harvest" Ibid.

p. 329 "Sorry to hear you are working . . ." Letter, Arthur Brisbane to NB, Chicago, Mar. 10, 1911, Brisbane Family Papers, Syracuse University Library.

p. 330 "We had asked him . . ." NB, "How I Was Robbed," p. 29.

p. 331 two cashiers were arraigned *NY Tribune*, Mar. 17, 1911, 1:4.

p. 331 Bly, her face layered in three veils *Brooklyn Daily Eagle*, Mar. 17, 1911, 2:6.

p. 331 When Caccia confessed to Bly NB, "How I Was Robbed," p. 28.

p. 331 Caccia and Gielnik claimed *NY Times*, Mar. 11, 1911, 1:5.

p. 331 had the indictments there dismissed *NY American*, June 27, 1911, 1:4–5, 4:2–3.

p. 332 as high as $400,000 *Brooklyn Daily Eagle*, May 11, 1911, 1:4; *NY Times*, May 12, 1911, 13:4; *NY Tribune*, May 12, 1911, 3:6.

p. 332 talk of a company reorganization *Brooklyn Daily Eagle*, May 2, 1911, 1:6.

p. 332 men she described as "dummies" *NY Times*, June 28, 1911, 7:2.

p. 332 first arraignment of her accused employees *NY Tribune*, May 5, 1911, 7:3; *NY Times*, May 5, 1911, 1:2; *Brooklyn Daily Eagle*, May 5, 1911, 5:3.

p. 333 "Now there was absolutely no cause . . ." *NY Times*, June 29, 1911, 2:2.

p. 333 petition of involuntary bankruptcy *NY Times*, May 25, 1911, 14:4.

p. 333 Brown Brothers was reported to have a claim *NY Times*, July 13, 1911, 7:3. This "purchase of tin" was probably the case Mr. Hands described in his Apr. 14, 1964, letter to John Kouwenhoven, Brown Brothers Collection, N-Y Historical Society.

p. 333 Seaboard Coal Company *NY Times*, May 25, 1911, 14:4.

p. 334 Bly sued Clark personally Elizabeth C. Seaman v. Appleton Clark, Supreme Court 230 U.S. 35, June 20, 1911, New York County Supreme Court Archives.

p. 334 whether the Iron Clad and American Steel Barrel Company were one and the same Ibid.

p. 334 "Some of the creditors are pointing . . ." *Brooklyn Daily Eagle*, June 21, 1911, 4:1–3.

p. 335 report of Bly's "obdurate" performance *Brooklyn Daily Eagle*, June 21, 1911, 2:2.

p. 336 Dressed in black satin *NY American*, June 27, 1911, 1:4–5, 4:2–3.

p. 336 Ross then confirmed Ibid.

p. 336 "I came here," she explained Ibid.

p. 337 "The checks of the Iron Clad Company . . ." *Brooklyn Daily Eagle*, June 27, 1911, 2:1.

p. 337 First National Bank of Jamaica stated *NY American*, June 30, 1911, 10:1–2.

p. 337 Van Tuyl advised Bly *Brooklyn Daily Eagle*, June 27, 1911, 2:1; *NY American*, June 28, 1911, 13:6.

p. 337 to meet with him the following week *NY Tribune*, June 28, 1911, 4:2.

p. 338 Assistant District Attorney Elder sent word *NY Times*, June 28, 1911, 7:2.

p. 338 "a fighting woman who has a fight . . ." Ibid.

p. 339 In June, she sent a raiding party Ibid.

p. 341 creditors were bankers, the receiver was a lawyer Ibid.

p. 341 By June 28, Bly had served notice *NY Times*, July 6, 1911, 11:1.

p. 341 "There may be some question . . ." *NY Times*, June 29, 1911, 2:2.

p. 341 informed Caccia that he could not see Ibid.

p. 341 coil on an electric generator snapped *Brooklyn Daily Eagle*, July 1, 1911, 16:3.

p. 342 she could do it in ten minutes *NY Times*, July 1, 1911, 8:3.

p. 342 Bly made the repair *NY Times*, July 6, 1911, 11:1.

p. 342 however many men he needed Ibid.

p. 342 "Her Royal Highness" *NY Times*, July 8, 1911, 5:3.

p. 342 "These vexatious problems . . ." *NY Times*, July 6, 1911, 11:1.

p. 343 "Authority to buy a paper of tacks . . ." *Brooklyn Daily Eagle*, July 1, 1911, 8:3.

p. 343 Chatfield delayed decision *NY Times*, July 1, 1911, 8:3.

p. 343 "Under this system of lawyer-receiverships . . ." *NY Times*, June 28, 1911, 2:2.

p. 343 largest balance on hand *NY Times*, July 1, 1911, 8:3.

p. 343 creditors putting their own men *NY Times*, July 6, 1911, 11:1.

p. 344 "I hope this all comes out" *NY Times*, June 28, 1911, 2:2.

p. 344 ". . . Clumsier forgeries have rarely been exhibited" *NY Times*, July 2, 1911, 1:3.

p. 345 Penton said it was "past belief" Ibid.

p. 345 Elder offered to postpone his vacation *NY Times*, July 1, 1911, 8:3.

p. 346 not all the money obtained . . . was stolen *NY Times*, July 2, 1911, 1:3.

p. 346 penchant for gambling Ibid.

p. 346 Hearst papers liked to support Letter, Arthur Brisbane to Speed, Mar. 10, 1913, Brisbane Family Papers. Also Carlson, *Brisbane*, p. 202.

p. 346 "Women Are Robbed About Nine Times Out of Ten . . ." *NY Evening Journal*, July 7, 1911, ed. page:1.

p. 347 "The difficulty of suspending judgment . . ." *NY Times*, July 10, 1911, 6:4, editorial.

p. 347 double-necked milk cans Charles R. Kroeger and Theodore Hogeman of Norwich, N.Y., retrieved newspaper files on this incident from the Utica Public Library.

p. 348 "The other companies kept on making cans . . ." *NY Times*, July 10, 1911, 3:1.

p. 348 "that it would be a fine thing . . ." *Utica Observer*, July 10, 1911, p. 6.

p. 349 "For more reasons than . . . my own welfare . . ." *NY Times*, July 9, 1911, 3:1.

p. 349 no attorney named William Grant Brown *Utica Observer*, July 10, 1911, p. 6.

p. 349 Risley was spared the prison term *Utica Observer*, Oct. 12, 1911, p. 3.

p. 350 "federal incorporation tax" It is not clear exactly what NB was referring to.

p. 350 "never been separated from the main company" 194, *Federal Reporter*, In re Iron Clad Manufacturing Co., Dist.Ct. E.D. N.Y., Mar 15, 1912, p. 921.

p. 350 "deal liberally with such questions . . ." *NY Times*, July 13, 1911, 7:3.

p. 350 Her "constant aim," she said Ibid.

p. 350 Veeder did allow the creditors *Brooklyn Daily Eagle*, July 12, 1911, 3:5.

p. 350 had hired . . . Moos, Prince and Nathan *Brooklyn Daily Eagle*, July 13, 1911, 2:6.

p. 351 withdrew a motion to hold Bly in contempt *Brooklyn Daily Eagle*, July 18, 1911, 9:5.

p. 351 "The petition might well have been disposed of . . ." Veeder's opinion as quoted in *Brooklyn Daily Eagle*, July 25, 1911, 1:3.

p. 351 "attitude of hostility" *NY Times*, July 26, 1911, 3:1.

p. 351 "Judge Veeder's ruling . . ." *NY Times*, July 29, 1911, 6:5.

p. 352 stop Bly from taking electrical power *NY Times*, Aug. 5, 1911, 7:4.

p. 352 several rulings against Bly's interests *Brooklyn Daily Eagle*, Aug. 8, 1911, 2:2.

p. 352 too ill to appear at trial *Brooklyn Daily Eagle*, Aug. 12, 1911, 2:4.

p. 352 avoided Clark's attorney Kiendl Ibid.

p. 353 she had resigned as president *Brooklyn Daily Eagle*, Aug. 11, 1911, 2:7.

p. 353 "Characterize them as you see fit . . ." *Brooklyn Daily Eagle*, Aug. 30, 1911, 2:7.

p. 354 The next day Bly was at the Iron Clad *Brooklyn Daily Eagle*, Sept. 1, 1911, 18:5.

p. 354 directors of the company included *NY Times*, Sept. 2, 1911, 3:2; *NY Tribune*, Sept. 2, 1911, 3:2.

p. 354 she would sue immediately *Brooklyn Daily Eagle*, Sept. 4, 1911, 2:4.

p. 354 Chatfield was back on the bench *Brooklyn Daily Eagle*, Oct. 21, 1911, 2:1; *NY Times*, Oct. 22, 1911, 9:5.

p. 355 take Bly into technical custody *Brooklyn Daily Eagle*, Oct. 26, 1911, 1:3.

p. 355 Metz . . . appeared with a surprising offer Undated article from the morgue of *The NY Evening Journal*, Ransom Humanities Research Center, University of Texas, circa Nov. 1911.

p. 355 funeral of . . . Joseph Pulitzer *NY World*, Nov. 2, 1911, 1:8, 2:1.

p. 355 jury sided with Bly's creditors *Brooklyn Daily Eagle*, Nov. 24, 1911, 5:1; *NY Times*, Nov. 24, 1911, 4:4; *NY Tribune*, Nov. 24, 1911, 4:3.

p. 355 Bly's attorneys moved at once *NY American*, Nov. 25, 1911, 13:2.

p. 355 Bly . . . commenced action against the banks *Brooklyn Daily Eagle*, Dec. 1, 1911, 2:5.

p. 355 "My dear N.B.: . . ." Letter, Arthur Brisbane to NB, Dec. 11, 1911, Brisbane Family Papers.

p. 356 had sought Brisbane's advice Letters, Arthur Brisbane to NB, Dec. 26, 1911; NB to Brisbane, Dec. 27, 1911, Brisbane Family Papers.

p. 356 Bly supported . . . Don Seitz *Brooklyn Daily Eagle*, Jan. 10, 1912, 5:9.

p. 356 "How I Was Robbed of Two Million Dollars" NB, *Fair Play*, Jan. 20, 1912, cover story. Also, *NY Times*, Jan. 20, 1912, pp. 27–29; *Brooklyn Daily Eagle*, Jan. 20, 1912, 2:6.

p. 356 Bly frantically contacted everyone Letter, Arthur Brisbane to NB, Jan. 30, 1912; NB to Brisbane, Jan. 30, 1912, Brisbane Family Papers.

p. 356 "... inextricable mess that I can do nothing with it" Letter, Samuel Untermyer to Arthur Brisbane, Jan. 30, 1912, Brisbane Family Papers.

p. 356 **Shearn begged off** Undated note from Shearn in Brisbane Family Papers.

p. 356 **"there is a great prejudice against you ..."** Letter, Arthur Brisbane to NB, Feb. 8, 1912, Brisbane Family Papers.

p. 357 **the creditors renewed their fight** 194, *Federal Reporter*, In re Iron Clad Mfg. Co. (Dist.Ct. E.D. N.Y. Mar. 15, 1912).

p. 357 **asked him to help ... sell the house** Letter, Arthur Brisbane to NB, Feb. 15, 1912, Brisbane Family Papers.

p. 357 **Robert J. Tilney** *Brooklyn Daily Eagle*, Feb. 16, 1912, 1:6.

p. 357 **pursuit of a friendly buyer** Letter, NB to Arthur Brisbane, Feb. 16, 1912, Brisbane Family Papers.

p. 357 **"I shall still fight ..."** Letter, NB to Arthur Brisbane, Feb. 20, 1912, Brisbane Family Papers.

p. 358 **"I know that the attorneys ... had gone ..."** Ibid.

p. 358 **Chatfield had ordered Bly to vacate** *NY Times*, Feb. 28, 1912, 12:6; *NY Tribune*, Feb. 28, 1912, 2:4.

p. 358 **invited Judge Charles M. Hough** *NY Times*, Mar. 9, 1912, 3:7; *NY Tribune*, Mar. 9, 1912, 13:4.

p. 358 **Chatfield charged with bias** The statute, which took effect in Jan. 1912, was from Sec. 21 of a new Judicial Code and considered applicable "in rare instances in which not merely adverse, but biased and prejudiced, rulings are shown and facts and reasons given. Section 21 of the Judicial Code is not intended as a means for a discontented litigant ousting a judge because of adverse rulings, or as a method of paralyzing the action of a judge who has heard the case by disqualifying him between the hearing and the determination of the matter heard." (Ex Parte American Steel Barrel Co. and Seaman, No. 14, Original, Supreme Court of the United States, 230 U.S. 35; 57 L.Ed. 1379; 33 S.Ct. 1007, Argued Apr. 21, 1913; June 16, 1913.)

p. 358 **taken off the case** Ibid.

p. 358 **new judge appointed** 194 *Federal Reporter*, p. 907; *Brooklyn Daily Eagle*, Mar. 30, 1912, 1:5; Also, 230 U.S. 35, 57 L.Ed. 1379; 33 S.Ct. 1007.

p. 359 **Chatfield said he regretted** *Brooklyn Daily Eagle*, Mar. 31, 1912, 12:3–5.

p. 359 **"I am told that my conduct ..."** *NY Times*, Mar. 17, 1912, 17:2.

p. 359 **declared Bly in contempt** *NY Times*, Mar. 27, 1912, 5:1.

p. 359 **"Perhaps I have done wrong ..."** Ibid.; *NY Tribune*, Mar. 27, 1912, 5:5.

p. 360 **Still, she did not pay the fine** *NY Times*, Apr. 2, 1912, 13:4; *NY Tribune*, Apr. 2, 1912, 4:5.

p. 360 "**Nobody wants to be mean**" *NY Tribune*, Apr. 2, 1912, 4:5.

p. 360 **this time on a bench warrant** The complete record of this case has not survived, so the reason for the bench warrant is not known. Details of the case come from People of the State of New York v. Charles W. Caccia and Stanley Gielnik, Supreme Court, Criminal term, Case No. 87846, New York County (1912–1915), New York Municipal Archives; NB, "How I Was Robbed."

p. 360 **Brisbane replied by return cable** Telegram, Arthur Brisbane to NB, Apr. 2, 1912, Brisbane Family Papers.

p. 360 **committing Bly to jail for contempt** *NY Tribune*, Apr. 3, 1912, 14:1; *NY Times*, Apr. 3, 1912, 1:6.

p. 360 **Bly . . . paid the fine** *NY Times*, Apr. 4, 1912, 4:4.

p. 360 **"The man in charge undoubtedly was honest . . ."** Letter, Arthur Brisbane to NB, Apr. 12, 1912, Brisbane Family Papers.

p. 361 **"energetic, progressive, capable lawyer . . ."** Letters, Arthur Brisbane to NB, Apr. 13, 1912; Apr. 15, 1912; and Apr. 17, 1912, Brisbane Family Papers.

p. 361 **"My dear N.B . . . I am on the train . . ."** Letter, Arthur Brisbane to NB, June 13, 1912, Brisbane Family Papers.

p. 363 **"and doing much more useful work . . ."** Letter, Arthur Brisbane to NB, June 13, 1912, Brisbane Family Papers.

p. 364 **"It was Teddy . . ."** *NY Evening Journal*, June 22, 1912, 3:1–5.

p. 364 **Mayer issued the second contempt . . . order** *NY Times*, June 27, 1912, 19:3; *NY Tribune*, June 27, 1912, 16:3; *NY American*, June 27, 1912, 1:7.

p. 365 **Mayer issued a stay** *NY Times*, July 2, 1912, 9:3.

p. 365 **"Nellie Bly Tells What She Saw at Baltimore"** *NY Evening Journal*, June 27, 1912, 1:1–2, 3:6–7.

p. 365 **" 'How are you getting on . . .' "** *NY Evening Journal*, June 27, 1912, 3:1–5. Frank Moss had served as counsel for the Society for the Prevention of Crime from 1891 to 1898 and had been president of the Board of Police Commissioners in 1897. King, *Notable New Yorkers*, 1896, p. 122.

p. 366 **carried her report on two columns** *NY Evening Journal*, June 28, 1912, 1:1–2, 3:1–7, 4:5.

p. 368 **"My vanity was piqued . . ."** *NY Evening Journal*, June 29, 1912, 1:1–2.

p. 369 **"And I never apologize . . ."** *NY Evening Journal*, July 1, 1912, 1:1–2.

p. 369 **case of . . . Caccia and Gielnik was postponed** People of the State of New York v. Charles W. Caccia and Stanley Gielnik.

p. 369 **"She writes a better story . . ."** Letter, Arthur Brisbane to Abe Erlanger, July 16, 1912, Brisbane Family Papers.

p. 369 **Bly and her mother had sent a painting** Letter, Arthur Brisbane to NB, Aug. 13, 1912, Brisbane Family Papers.

p. 369 **Alice Thursby . . . was moved to write** Letter, Alice Brisbane Thursby to NB, Aug. 19, 1912, Brisbane Family Papers.

p. 369 **Bly asked Brisbane if he would buy her home . . . He declined** Letter, Arthur Brisbane to NB, Aug. 23, 1912, Brisbane Family Papers.

p. 370 **a $10,000 mortgage** Mortgage, 15 W. 37th St., Liber 231, p. 172, New York County Real Estate Records.

p. 370 **two weeks later, the property was transferred** Deed, 15 W. 37th St., recorded and dated Sept. 13, 1912, Liber 176, pp. 415–416, New York County Real Estate Records.

p. 370 **Harry, in turn** Deed, 15 W. 37th St., Liber 177, pp. 441–442, New York County Real Estate Records.

p. 370 **"I do not know what they asked . . ."** Letter, NB to Arthur Brisbane, Dec. 11, 1912, Brisbane Family Papers.

p. 370 **"I do not know how it will end . . ."** Ibid.

p. 370 **"a man I believe to be the most honest . . ."** Ibid.

p. 371 **suggested some story ideas** Ibid.

p. 371 **"That isn't the kind of thing . . ."** Letter, Arthur Brisbane to NB, Dec. 14, 1912, Brisbane Family Papers.

p. 371 **"Be a good girl— . . ."** Handwritten note with letter, Arthur Brisbane to NB, Dec. 14, 1912, Brisbane Family Papers.

p. 371 **Chatfield suddenly came under investigation** *NY Times*, Jan. 3, 1913, 1:4.

p. 371 **"doing certain things . . ."** *NY Evening Journal*, Jan. 4, 1913, 5:1–2.

p. 372 **"Unless by 'adequate preparation' . . ."** *NY Times*, Feb. 2, 1913, 15:3.

p. 372 **"I believe it is only that . . ."** Letter, NB to Arthur Brisbane, Jan. 4, 1913, Brisbane Family Papers.

p. 372 **as a first-night theater critic** Metcalfe actually filed suit against the theater managers in 1906 for barring him from their theaters as a punishment for his negative reviews. Undaunted, he was said to have donned disguises or gone out of town to see plays in order to continue writing about them. He lost the suit on appeal. *NY Times*, Mar. 30, 1906, 9:3; Apr. 8, 1906, 9:2; July 13, 1906, 9:2.

p. 372 **"Are you the editor brave enough . . ."** Letter, NB to Arthur Brisbane, Feb. 14, 1913, Brisbane Family Papers.

p. 372 **"Thanks for your letter . . ."** Letter, Arthur Brisbane to NB, Feb. 17, 1913, Brisbane Family Papers. Carlson, in *Brisbane*, points out that *The Evening Journal* was criticized in this period for writing favorable editorials about certain plays that would then elicit full-page advertisements in the newspaper. Will Irwin in the June 1911 issue of *Collier's* said, "Every [theater] manager knew that the *Journal* offered a paid advertisement and a Brisbane editorial for a thousand dollars. It was remarked that Brisbane would not 'boost' under this arrangement any play he did not like—but his tastes are catholic. Just as well was it understood that for five hundred dollars *The Journal* would give a half-page advertisement and a 'special' with illustrations by Nell Brinkley, together with liberal 'news notices.' "

p. 373 **filed suit . . . to bring Judge Chatfield back** 230 U.S. 35 *46; 47, L.Ed. 1379, ** 1384; 33 S.Ct. 1007, ***1011.

p. 373 **a herald in the "greatest demonstration for women's suffrage . . ."** *NY Evening Journal*, Mar. 3, 1913, 3:5.

p. 373 **She had "stunning" riding togs** Ibid.

p. 373 **her beautiful jade beads** Bly's grandniece Peggy Cochrane Potts, who inherited the beads, as well as a turquoise strand, understood in the family to have been a gift to NB from Frederic Remington, the American artist. Nothing that would establish a relationship between them was uncovered in the course of this research.

p. 373 **"Some persons with a mistaken idea . . ."** *NY Evening Journal*, Mar. 3, 1913, 3:1–4.

p. 375 **"Can you imagine it? . . ."** *NY Evening Journal*, Mar. 4, 1913, 3:1–2.

p. 375 **"I stood alone on the platform . . ."** *NY Evening Journal*, Mar. 6, 1913, 3:1–3.

p. 377 **Battle contended that the defendants** *NY Times*, Mar. 7, 1913, 4:6.

p. 377 **"the most interesting contention involved"** *NY Tribune*, Mar. 7, 1913, 16:6.

p. 377 **"I don't know what point . . ."** Letter, NB to Arthur Brisbane, Mar. 7, 1913, Brisbane Family Papers.

p. 377 **"At the time that article was written . . ."** *NY Times*, Mar. 8, 1913, 7:2.

p. 377 **"Dear Mr. Speed: Please let us make . . ."** Letter, Arthur Brisbane to Speed, Mar. 10, 1913, Brisbane Family Papers.

p. 378 **"If I should prejudge your case . . ."** Letter, Arthur Brisbane to NB, Mar. 10, 1913, Brisbane Family Papers.

p. 378 **"Say Nellie Bly Was $1,680,000 Fraud Victim"** *NY Evening Journal*, Mar. 11, 1913, 1:2.

p. 379 **The case continued** People of the State of New York v. Charles W. Caccia and Stanley Gielnik.

p. 379 **"The story of her fight . . ."** *NY Evening Journal*, Mar. 13, 1913, 1:3, 3:5.

p. 380 **"In Business Men Usually ROB Women"** *NY Evening Journal*, Mar. 13, 1913, ed. page: 1.

p. 380 **they could not reach a verdict** People of the State of New York v. Charles W. Caccia and Stanley Gielnik.

pp. 380–381 **dismiss the indictments** Ibid.

p. 381 **prospects for winning the civil suits** New York Supreme Court Records. Elizabeth C. Seaman v. Guardian Trust Co.; Elizabeth C. Seaman v. Western National Bank; Elizabeth C. Seaman v. First National Bank of Jamaica; Elizabeth C. Seaman v. Broadway Bank of Brooklyn. In each case, the suits were lost because NB had not presented a clear enough case. She countered that this was because the records she needed to prove her case were held by the Iron Clad's receiver and had been seen by the banks. The fact that Caccia and Gielnik were never convicted weakened her case further.

p. 381 **yet another fire broke out** *Brooklyn Daily Eagle*, Apr. 23, 1913, 1:4.

p. 381 **Bly was aboard the *George Washington*** Letter, NB to Arthur Brisbane, May 16, 1913, reporting next day's departure aboard the *George Washington*, Brisbane Family Papers.

p. 381 **Gilman . . . left an estate of only** *Brooklyn Daily Eagle*, July 23, 1913, 1:4.

p. 382 **"the kind you can write . . ."** Letter, Arthur Brisbane to NB, May 16, 1913, Brisbane Family Papers.

p. 382 **"I have put it to better purpose . . ."** Letter, NB to Arthur Brisbane, May 19, 1913, Brisbane Family Papers.

p. 382 **She finally paid the $2,666 due** *Brooklyn Daily Eagle*, July 23, 1913, 1:4.

p. 382 **"I get away from one crook . . ."** Letter, NB to Arthur Brisbane, Aug. 4, 1913, Brisbane Family Papers.

p. 382 **"your lawyer said he didn't want you . . ."** Letter, Arthur Brisbane to NB, Nov. 28, 1913, Brisbane Family Papers.

p. 382 **Bly's mother had become seriously ill** Letter, Brisbane to NB, Dec. 16, 1913, Brisbane Family Papers.

p. 382 **Harry had been indicted** *Brooklyn Daily Eagle*, Dec. 17, 1913, 8:5.

p. 383 **"Will you do the Calumet strike NOW? . . ."** Note, Arthur Brisbane to NB, Jan. 9, 1914, Brisbane Family Papers.

p. 383 **she replied that she could not** No letter located, but evident from Brisbane's reply, which follows.

p. 383 **"About Calumet . . ."** Letter, Arthur Brisbane to NB, Jan. 13, 1914, Brisbane Family Papers.

p. 383 **a settlement . . . had been worked out** *NY Times*, Jan. 24, 1914, 3:8.

p. 383 **Mayer discontinued all proceedings** *NY Times*, Mar. 28, 1914, 18:1.

p. 383 **house in Sheepshead Bay had been foreclosed upon** Title, 3164 Emmons Ave, Referee Frank Cothren sells house to City Real Estate Co. Feb. 26, 1914, Liber 3482, p. 35, Brooklyn Real Estate Records.

p. 384 **Harry Cochrane's perjury case** *Brooklyn Daily Eagle*, Apr. 3, 1914, 2:3; Apr. 7, 1914, 18:5; Apr. 8, 1914, 20:2.

p. 384 **Van Doren had his chance to sue** *NY Times*, Apr. 25, 1914, 10:5; *NY Tribune*, Apr. 25, 1914, 7:2.

p. 384 **new indictment was returned** *Brooklyn Daily Eagle*, Mar. 4, 1919.

p. 384 **Bly arranged for . . .** Oscar Bondy Mortgage, 15 West 37th St., June 12, 1914, Liber 247, p. 191, New York County Real Estate Records.

p. 384 **Albert . . . , and Harry returned to New York** NY City Directories, 1915–16.

p. 384 **Bly quietly set out for Europe** Letter, NB to Mary Jane Cochrane, shipboard, dated Wednesday [Aug.] 5, 1914, Brisbane Family Papers.

11

❧ ☙

War

p. 389 **"Good bye, Miss Collins . . ."** Letter, Margaret Collins Carey to Mignon Rittenhouse, from Margaret Collins Carey, undated, circa Feb. 1955, quoted in letter, Rittenhouse to Legal Department, Metro-Goldwyn-Mayer Pictures, Feb. 14, 1959, Mignon Rittenhouse Collection, Wheaton College. Special thanks to David Malone.

p. 389 **"There is no telling where . . ."** Letter, NB to Mary Jane Cochrane, [Aug.] 5, 1914, Brisbane Family Papers, Syracuse University Library.

p. 390 **emergency passport** Passport Records, Emergency Passport Application No. 530, Nellie Bly, dated Aug. 11, 1914, Record Group 59, Paris, France, State Department Files, U.S. National Archives.

p. 390 **registering at the U.S. Embassy** Vienna Embassy registration, 1914, State Department Files, U.S. National Archives.

p. 390 **She wrote to C. A. Guibert** Letter, NB to Guibert, Sept. 18, 1914, Brisbane Family Papers.

p. 393 **last chance for battlefield initiation** Letter, War Department, 102967-331 9, from Office of M.I.D., Customhouse, N.Y., to Acting Director M.I.D., Washington, D.C., U.S., Mar. 6, 1919, Record Group 165, Military Intelligence Files, U.S. National Archives.

p. 393 **identified only as the U.S. assistant secretary of war** At the time this was Henry Breckinridge.

p. 393 **"as if he had all the time . . ."** Uncut version of NB's article for *Die Zeit* sent to Ritter Oskar von Montlong with her letter of Feb. 16, 1915, Haus-, Hof-und Staatsarchiv, Presse Leitung, 202/1915.

p. 394 **Baron Franz von Schönaich** (1844–1916), army general who served as Austrian defense minister (1905–1906) and Austro-Hungarian minister of war (1906–1911). From 1911 to 1914, he lived quietly with his family in a villa at the edge of Vienna. After the outbreak of war, he founded the Imperial and Royal Austrian Military Widows and Orphans Fund and served as its first president.

p. 394 **"There are so many motivations . . ."** Uncut version of NB's article for *Die Zeit*, sent to von Montlong with her letter of Feb. 16, 1915.

p. 394 **"exceptional graciousness and consideration"** Ibid.

p. 394 **"You have filed a request . . ."** Ibid.

p. 394 **"journalist of standing, who desires . . ."** Letter, Ambassador Frederic Penfield to Ritter Oskar von Montlong dated Oct. 8, 1914, Haus-, Hof-und Staatsarchiv, Presse Leitung, 202/1915.

p. 395 **"If I tell you now . . ."** Uncut version of NB's article for *Die Zeit* sent to von Montlong with her letter of Feb. 16, 1915.

p. 396 **correspondents who had been granted credentials** Letter, Giesl von Gieslingen to the foreign ministry, Oct. 22, 1914, Haus-, Hof-und Staatsarchiv, Presse Leitung, 202/1915.

p. 396 **"The expression of his eyes was frank . . ."** Uncut version of NB's article for *Die Zeit*, sent to von Montlong with her letter of Feb. 16, 1915.

p. 396 **She was en route to the battlefront** *NY Evening Journal* datelined the story "Banok." More likely the town was Sanok, also in Galicia, along the route from Alt Sandez to Przemyśl.

p. 396 **"Visiting on the penned-in garrison . . ."** Marshall, *World War I*, p. 114.

p. 396 **"I will send three articles . . ."** *NY Evening Journal*, Dec. 4, 1914, 3:4–6.

p. 397 **Kolowatring** is now the Schubertring.

p. 397 **Field Marshal Conrad's strategy** Marshall, *World War I*, pp. 110–117.

p. 398 **"I am," she wrote. "I write it . . ."** *NY Evening Journal*, Dec. 4, 1914, 3:4–6.

p. 398 **"I walked one block . . ."** Ibid.

p. 399 **"The burden was martyrdom . . ."** *NY Evening Journal*, Dec. 5, 1914, 3:3–4.

p. 400 **"On the ground was strewn straw . . ."** *NY Evening Journal*, Dec. 7, 1914, 3:5–6.

p. 400 **"baptism by fire"** *NY Evening Journal*, Dec. 8, 1914, 3:4–6.

p. 401 **"Colonel John yelled for us to fly . . ."** Ibid.

p. 401 **"Many of the men carry alcohol lamps . . ."** *NY Evening Journal*, Jan. 13, 1915, 3:4–5.

p. 404 "Everybody was excited except myself . . ." *NY Evening Journal*, Jan. 16, 1915, 2:4–5.

p. 406 illustrious Roda-Roda Pseudonym for Alexander Rosenfeld.

p. 406 Roda-Roda's story *Neue Freie Presse*, Nov. 7, 1914, p. 4.

p. 406 "—I shuddered . . ." *NY Evening Journal*, Jan. 19, 1915, 2:4–5.

p. 407 "real American cocktails" *NY Evening Journal*, Jan. 30, 1915, 2:4–5.

p. 407 the hotelier did not charge her *NY Evening Journal*, Jan. 26, 1915, 2:4–5.

p. 407 "Dr. MacDonald warned me . . ." Ibid.

p. 408 "I might have called this article . . ." Ibid.

p. 408 "Grand duchesses scrub floors . . ." Ibid.

p. 408 "I hope I don't have to walk . . ." *NY Evening Journal*, Jan. 27, 1915, 4:4–5.

p. 409 Two days later, in heavy snowfall *NY Evening Journal*, Feb. 6, 1915, 2:4–5.

p. 410 the magnificent loot *NY Evening Journal*, Feb. 5, 1915, 3:4–5.

p. 410 "There was not a man . . ." *NY Evening Journal*, Feb. 15, 1915, 3:4–5.

p. 410 no trip to the firing line Ibid.

p. 410 "I enter a ward where some 40 men . . ." *NY Evening Journal*, Feb. 19, 1915, 16:4–5.

p. 411 "a chronic invalid . . ." Marshall, *World War I*, p. 114.

p. 411 three creditors filed a bankruptcy petition *NY Times*, Nov. 17, 1914, 8:6; *NY Tribune*, Nov. 17, 1914, 6:6.

p. 411 Oscar Bondy's New York attorney *NY Times*, Dec. 22, 1914, 14:2; *NY Tribune*, Nov. 17, 1914, 6:6; Alien Property Custodian, U.S. National Archives.

p. 411 Greenwich Savings Bank repossessed the property Deed, 15 W. 37th St., Jan. 11, 1915, filed Feb. 2, 1915, cited foreclosure, Liber 195, p. 323, New York County Real Estate Records.

p. 411 332 East Sixteenth Street New York City Directories, 1915–1918.

p. 412 shifted her dependency Alien Property Custodian, U.S. National Archives.

p. 412 She did . . . instruct Mary Jane Letter, NB to Mary Jane Cochrane, Apr. 1, 1915, Brisbane Family Papers.

p. 412 huge excisions that seemed arbitrary *Die Zeit*, Vienna, Dec. 27, 1914, Nr. 4401, p. 5.

p. 412 "it being all the same to the censor" Postcard, George Schreiner to NB, Dec. 27, 1914, Haus-, Hof-und Staatsarchiv, Presse Leitung, 202/1915.

p. 413 **"Meanwhile, I would like to know . . ."** Second postcard, George Schreiner to NB, Dec. 28, 1914, Haus-, Hof-und Staatsarchiv, Presse Leitung, 202/1915.

p. 413 **"critical of the military's sanitary conditions . . ."** Cable, Austro-Hungarian Ambassador to Rome, Baron Karl von Macchio, to Vienna, containing complaints against NB and William Shepherd, Jan. 10, 1915, Haus-, Hof-und Staatsarchiv, Presse Leitung, 202/1915.

p. 414 **"I want to thank you again . . ."** Letter, NB to Ritter Oskar von Montlong, Feb. 6, 1915, Haus-, Hof-und Staatsarchiv.

p. 415 **one from D. Thomas Curtin** Postcard, D. Thomas Curtin to NB, Feb. 1, 1915, Haus-, Hof-und Staatsarchiv, Presse Leitung, 202/1915. Curtin's U.S. passport was withdrawn by U.S. Ambassador to London Walter Page in Oct. 1916 when he went into Germany as a reporter for Northcliff Press but was suspected of spying there for British interests. By Sept. 1917, he had been vindicated and his passport restored. He wrote a book about Germany called *Deepening Shadow*.

p. 415 **"What you tell me of the 'Zeit' . . ."** Letter, NB to Ritter Oskar von Montlong, Feb. 21, 1915, Haus-, Hof-und Staatsarchiv, Presse Leitung 202/1915.

p. 416 **Central Bohemian Sugar Enterprises** Jahr-und Adressbuch der österreichischen Zucker-Industrie, Rudolf Hand, ed. (Wien: Compassverlag, 1917), pp. 2211 and 2219–2220.

p. 416 **Bondy was an inveterate collector** Recollections of Ruth Blumka, owner of the Blumka Gallery, N.Y., in interview with the author, Apr. 11, 1991. Bondy's birth date was provided by a research librarian at the Österreichisches Staatsarchiv from a Vienna city birth registration file which he did not identify.

p. 416 **his nephew Norbert Rie** Letter to the author from Ivo P. Rie, July 1, 1991, with recollections of Bondy from his childhood. Mr. Rie is the son of the late Norbert Rie and Bondy's grandnephew.

p. 417 **As a family** Letter, Ivo P. Rie to author, July 1, 1991, and telephone conversation June 4, 1991.

p. 417 **Vienna's prestigious Musikverein** Formally known as the Gesellschaft der Musikfreunde, Benefactor Listing (Vienna City Library).

p. 417 **to entertain notions of emigrating** Bondy actually immigrated to the United States around 1942, according to Ruth Blumka, who knew him at the time. He died of stomach cancer Dec. 3, 1944.

p. 417 **It was a formidable committee** Jahrbuch 1917 des K.K. österreichischen Militär-Witwen und Waisenfondes, Wien, 1917.

p. 417 **worked only with the Austrian half . . .** Ibid.

p. 418 **her attitudes squared perfectly** Carlson, *Brisbane*, p. 215.

p. 418 **"Here are three articles . . ."** Letter, NB to Ritter Oskar von Montlong, Mar. 22, 1915, Haus-, Hof-und Staatsarchiv, Presse Leitung, 202/1915.

p. 418 collective cable to every major newspaper Ibid.

p. 419 "There are two major objections . . ." Letter, Ritter Oskar von Montlong to Austro-Hungarian Ambassador to Washington Konstantin Dumba, Mar. 24, 1915, Haus-, Hof-und Staatsarchiv, Presse Leitung, 202/1915.

p. 419 Von Montlong aired his concerns Ibid.

p. 419 "For your personal information . . ." Ibid.

p. 420 "no cause for a declaration of war" Carlson, *Brisbane*, p. 216.

p. 420 "I was motivated primarily by the concern . . ." Letter, Austro-Hungarian Ambassador to Washington Konstantin Dumba to Ritter Oskar von Montlong, May 12, 1915, Haus-, Hof-und Staatsarchiv, Presse Leitung, 202/1915.

p. 420 This time, they were sent through Telegram transmittal request from Austro-Hungarian Embassy, Berlin, May 13, 1915, Haus-, Hof-und Staatsarchiv, Presse Leitung, 202/1915.

p. 420 "Nellie Bly Pleads for Food . . ." *NY Evening Journal*, May 18, 1915, 3:5–6. *NY Sun* carried similar, same day.

p. 421 Dumba cabled back Cable, Austro-Hungarian Ambassador to Washington Konstantin Dumba to Foreign Ministry, Vienna, May 23, 1915, Haus-, Hof-und Staatsarchiv, Presse Leitung, 202/1915.

p. 421 "Gold Book and placed among the imperishable records . . ." *NY Evening Journal*, May 19, 1915, 6:2–3.

p. 421 *"Wehrmann in Eisen"* *NY Evening Journal*, May 24, 1915, 8:4–5.

p. 421 "He is a splendid man . . ." *NY Evening Journal*, May 19, 1915, 6:2–3.

p. 422 busy envisioning "nail-driving clubs" Ibid.

p. 422 her trunks had finally arrived Letter, NB to Mary Jane Cochrane, Vienna, Apr. 1, 1915, Brisbane Family Papers.

p. 423 "made many new friends, as usual" Excerpts from letter of Margaret Collins Carey to Mignon Rittenhouse, circa Feb. 1955, Wheaton College collection.

p. 423 she confided to her children Author interview with Ed Carey, son of Margaret Collins Carey, May 29, 1991, and Mar. 9, 1993. Mrs. Carey died in 1965.

p. 424 reporting a lost passport Index card only in the name of NB. Civil. 138.7/35, Aug. 11, 1915. Unfortunately, the actual file was not preserved. State Department Files, U.S. National Archives.

p. 424 "Dear Q.O. Thanks for the precious letter . . ." Postcard, NB to Erasmus Wilson, Aug. 21, 1915, Carnegie Library.

p. 424 "Are you still friends . . ." Letter, NB to Mary Jane Cochrane, Vienna, Oct. 21, 1914, Brisbane Family Papers.

p. 425 "For every American who has sent . . ." *NY Evening Journal*, May 24, 1916, 8:4–5.

p. 426 Brisbane and *The Journal* kept up Carlson, *Brisbane*, pp. 216–218.

p. 426 proposal for how the two countries Spanish Embassy transmittal of aide-mémoire of the Imperial and Royal Ministry of Foreign Affairs, Vienna, Apr. 6, 1917. The monarchy proposed: (1) That any American who wanted to leave the monarchy would be able to do so through Switzerland within four weeks of a break in diplomatic relations; (2) that those who elected to remain after the four-week period would only be allowed to leave in specific cases which authorities deemed justified; and (3) that Americans choosing to remain in the monarchy would be neither interned nor confined and would be "unmolested inasmuch as certain individuals do not personally render themselves guilty of a misdemeanor." The United States agreed to the proposal with the following amendments: In (1) elimination of the four-week limit; in (2) total elimination; and in (3), the addition of the words "or a menace to national safety" to the end. Agreement was reached May 21, 1917. Spanish Embassy Representation of U.S. 1917–1922, Vienna, 1917, State Department Files, U.S. National Archives.

p. 427 presidential proclamation Ibid., Proclamation, transmitted by State Department, Dec. 31, 1917, through Spanish Embassy in Washington to the Austro-Hungarian Foreign Ministry on Jan. 7, 1918. The proclamation further stated that no Austro-Hungarian citizens would be allowed to leave the United States except by special permit or court order, nor would they be allowed to enter the United States under restrictions.

p. 427 numerous Austro-Hungarian citizens were interned Both at the U.S. National Archives and the Haus-, Hof-und Staatsarchiv in Vienna, files concerning Spanish Embassy representation for the United States in 1917 show much correspondence between Vienna and Washington concerning the treatment, concerns, and eventual release of Austro-Hungarian citizens held in these U.S. military facilities. No comparable information on Americans held in Austria emerged from a review of these archives.

p. 427 The Austrians similarly maintained internment camps Cable, dated Dec. 3, 1918, to the U.S. consul in Genoa repeating advice to the U.S. Embassy in Vienna regarding "alleged American citizenship of civilians released from Austrian internment camps who arrive in Venice. Pending decision by Department relative to their citizenship and desirability of defraying expenses of their repatriation you are authorized to advance small sums necessary for their subsistence drawing upon Department therefore and taking usual agreement from them to reimburse the government." State Department Files, U.S. National Archives.

p. 427 Americans were free to move about Spanish Embassy response to query from Washington regarding treatment of internees, Feb. 22, 1918, Haus-, Hof-und Staatsarchiv, Administrative Registratur, F-36, 607–608.

p. 427 She traveled throughout the monarchy Document, MK/KM Nr. 17.562/1918, Kriegsarchiv, Vienna.

p. 427 "The American citizen Nelly [*sic*] Bly . . ." Document, Mar. 31, 1918, MK/ KM Pr Z.3445 Z. St. Kriegsarchiv, Vienna.

p. 428 The Hungarian Ministry of Interior echoed MK/KM Nr. 23.295/1918, Kriegsarchiv, Vienna.

p. 428 no indication she ever was subjected There have been suggestions that NB was subject to internment during the war, but nothing in the record bears this out. NB's name does not appear on various listings of Americans in special situations contained in the Kriegsarchiv or the Haus-, Hof-und Staatsarchiv in Vienna, or in the U.S. Embassy in Vienna files, or in those for Spanish representation during the war contained in the U.S. National Archives in Washington. No correspondence concerning NB's status in the monarchy was found in any of these repositories.

p. 428 American flag lapel pin Letter, NB to President Woodrow Wilson, Feb. 9, 1919, Woodrow Wilson Papers, Paris Peace Conference, Library of Congress.

p. 429 the new company was on solid footing Memo, to Mr. Garvan from Mr. Whitaker, Apr. 14, 1920, citing company valuation of $200,000. Alien Property Custodian, U.S. National Archives.

p. 429 Mary Jane . . . filed a bill of complaint Report of Examination of Corporation Management File No. 1923, Steel Barrel Company of America, Inc. Claim No. 4655, Trust No. 3574, Alien Property Custodian, U.S. National Archives.

p. 429 "flimsy" attempt to tie its hands Office Memorandum to Mr. Kenney from Mr. Baker, Nov. 12, 1918, re Steel Barrel Company, Mr. Cochran v. APC, Alien Property Custodian, U.S. National Archives.

p. 431 "I beseech you tell the President . . ." Cable, NB to William J. McCombs, Nov. 26, 1918, Archiv der Republik, Staatskanzlei No. 441-1919 and No. 1207/1-1919; the Allgemeines Verwaltungsarchiv, Ministerrats Praesidium, Presse Leitung Mixta and the Deutschösterreichisches Staatsamt für Ausseres No. 2054/4-1919.

p. 431 "long suffering newly liberated people" If NB meant the German-Austrians, she was mistaken. They suffered along with everyone else in the Habsburg monarchy, but the majority of the German-Austrians did not consider themselves "liberated." They identified with the Habsburg dynasty and empire and lamented the empire's disintegration. See Fellner, "The Dissolution of the Habsburg Monarchy," pp. 3–27, esp. pp. 12–13.

p. 431 "Have wired President Wilson an urgent appeal . . ." Cable, NB to Arthur Brisbane, Nov. 26, 1918, Archiv der Republik.

p. 432 published Bly's cable in full *NY Evening Journal*, Dec. 7, 1918, 2:3–4.

p. 432 Bly received a cable from her mother Index card, No. 130 B 6241, remains as record of a cable from Mary Jane Cochrane to Mrs. Nellie Bly, Vienna, Jan. 8, 1919, and re-sent to NB in New York at her request on May 17, 1919. Actual file was not preserved. State Department Files, U.S. National Archives.

p. 432 an exclusive interview with Renner Letter, State Chancellor Karl Renner to NB, of Jan. 18, 1919, enclosing answers to her interview questions, 441/1/St. K.—19,

Jan. 22, 1919, Archiv der Republik, Staatskanzlei No. 441-1919 and No. 1207/1-1919; the Allgemeines Verwaltungsarchiv, Ministerrats Praesidium, Presse Leitung Mixta, and the Deutschösterreichisches Staatsamt für Ausseres No. 2054/4-1919.

p. 432 **"It gives me great pleasure to confirm . . ."** Ibid.

p. 433 **In the interview, Renner laid out** Ibid.

p. 433 **The army . . . had fallen into confusion** Crankshaw, *The Fall of the House of Habsburg*, p. 419.

12

❧ ❧

Peace

p. 437 **"in the best possible way"** Letter, Chancellor Karl Renner's office to NB, Jan. 23, 1919, Archiv der Republik, Österreichisches Staatsarchiv.

p. 437 **proceeded immediately to Paris** Cable to Spanish Embassy, Berne, Switzerland, confirmed No. 4798, Jan. 28, 1919, with names of Americans, including NB, leaving on special train for Berne that night. Spanish Embassy representation of U.S. in Vienna, 1917–1922, State Department Files, U.S. National Archives.

p. 437 **Military Intelligence Division investigated** A long report of NB's appearance at the U.S. Passport Office in Paris was filed by 2nd Lt. John A. Chamberlain on Feb. 4, 1919. It was retransmitted on Feb. 24, 1919, by the Asst. Chief of Staff, G-2, S.O.S. to the Chief, Military Intelligence Branch, War Department, Washington, D.C., Military Intelligence Division, U.S. National Archives.

p. 438 **Rumplemayer's** A Paris brasserie at the time.

p. 439 **"I know all the different party leaders . . ."** Letter, NB to Wilson, Feb. 6, 1919, Woodrow Wilson Papers, Paris Peace Conference, Library of Congress.

p. 439 **interviews with Gen. John J. Pershing** Report, Asst. Chief of Staff, G-2, S.O.S. to the Chief, Military Intelligence Branch, Feb. 24, 1919.

p. 440 **"I asked her if she had ever been . . ."** Report, Pvt. John N. Moffitt, 700th Motor Transport Co., to Office of Chief of Staff, War Department, Military Intelligence Branch, Feb. 12, 1919, Military Intelligence Division, U.S. National Archives.

p. 440 **Bly received a reply** Letter, Wilson's Confidential Secretary to NB, Feb. 8, 1919, Woodrow Wilson Papers, Paris Peace Conference.

p. 441 **". . . Believe me, if my communications were not more important . . ."** Letter, NB to President Wilson, Feb. 9, 1919, Woodrow Wilson Papers, Paris Peace Conference.

p. 442 **sent inquiries back to Vienna** Name card index questioning NB's citizenship, Feb. 13, 1919, File No. 130 B 6241, not preserved. Vienna Embassy, 1919, State Department Files, U.S. National Archives.

p. 442 **"in order that our information . . ."** Letter, Lt. Col. Cabot Ward, Asst. Chief of Staff of the M.I.D., to Brig. Gen. D. E. Nolan, Asst. Chief of Staff, General Headquarters, Feb. 13, 1919, Military Intelligence Division, U.S. National Archives.

p. 442 **"She went to Austria in 1914 . . ."** Letter, Brig. Gen. D. E. Nolan, Asst. Chief of Staff, to Asst. Chief of Staff, G-2, S.O.S., A.E.F., Feb. 15, 1919, Military Intelligence Division, U.S. National Archives.

p. 443 **"The question of this lady . . ."** Letter, Lt. Col. Cabot Ward, Asst. Chief of Staff of the M.I.D., G-2, S.O.S., to Brig. Gen. D. E. Nolan, Asst. Chief of Staff, General Headquarters, Feb. 17, 1919, Military Intelligence Division, U.S. National Archives.

p. 443 **"Bohemians, Poles, Roumanians, Jugoslavs . . ."** Letter, NB to Oscar Bondy, Feb. 12, 1919, Archiv der Republik, Österreichisches Staatsarchiv.

p. 444 **Bauer gave a detailed description** Letter, Foreign Minister Otto Bauer to State Chancellery of German Austria, Mar. 1, 1919, Archiv der Republik, Österreichisches Staatsarchiv.

p. 445 **"Should it be possible . . ."** Letter, Baron [first name not determined] Löwenthal to Oscar Bondy, Mar. 8, 1919, Archiv der Republik, Österreichisches Staatsarchiv.

p. 445 **Military Intelligence in Paris cabled** Cable, signed "Armio," Bordeaux, to Washington, signaling NB's return to New York, Feb. 24, 1919, Military Intelligence Division, U.S. National Archives.

p. 445 **sent his office a copy of the earlier . . . reports** Letter, Lt. Col. Cabot Ward, General Staff, Military Intelligence Chief, A.E.F., to Chief, Military Intelligence Branch, War Department, Washington, D.C., Feb. 24, 1919, Military Intelligence Division, U.S. National Archives.

p. 445 **not been the view of Bly from headquarters** Letter, Asst. Chief of Staff D. E. Nolan, G-2, G.H.Q., A.E.F., to Acting Director of Military Intelligence, Washington, D.C., Feb. 22, 1919, Military Intelligence Division, U.S. National Archives. Nolan also sent copies of his exchange with Lt. Col. Cabot Ward regarding NB so that Washington would be aware of the opinion from headquarters, despite Ward's characterization of her.

p. 445 **Word of Bly's departure** Letter, Acting Director of Military Intelligence J. M. Dunn, Executive Branch, to Capt. J. B. Trevor, NYC, Feb. 25, 1919, quoting cable from Bordeaux (no further identification), Military Intelligence Division, U.S. National Archives.

p. 445 **"Although residents of New York . . ."** Ibid.

p. 446 **Two days later** Memo, Acting Director of Military Intelligence J. M. Dunn to Capt. J. B. Trevor, NYC, Feb. 28, 1919, quoting extract of cable from Bordeaux received in Washington, Feb. 26, 1919, Military Intelligence Division, U.S. National Archives.

p. 446 **dutifully filed a report** Letter, Capt. John B. Trevor, N.Y., to Acting Director Military Intelligence Division J. M. Dunn, Washington, Mar. 6, 1919, Military Intelligence Division, U.S. National Archives.

p. 447 **Egon Erwin Kisch** was a journalist in Prague before 1914 who was radicalized during the war. He served in the army during the war and became, in the early days of the Republic, a leader of the "Red Guard" in Vienna, an ineffective paramilitary group connected to an independent Communist Party organization. He also wrote for the party paper, *Der Weckruf.* See Pick, *The Last Days of Imperial Vienna,* pp. 106, 126, 160, 167.

p. 447 **". . . Bauer . . . is one of the ring leaders . . ."** The characterization of Bauer as a Bolshevik is misleading. He was the head of the left-wing faction within the Austrian Socialist Party but definitely not a Bolshevik. Along with other Socialist leaders, Bauer worked to prevent a transformation of the state and social order in the fall of 1918 and spring of 1919 in a manner similar to the Bolshevik Revolution in Russia. Furthermore, NB's view of him here is at odds with much of what she said of him elsewhere. As foreign minister, he was helpful and courteous to her. See Jelavich, *Modern Austria,* pp. 140, 151–153, 179.

p. 448 **seeking "all of the information . . ."** Letter, Asst. Chief of Staff, G.H.Q., A.E.F., D. E. Nolan, to M. Churchill, Director of Military Intelligence, Apr. 29, 1919, Military Intelligence Division, U.S. National Archives.

p. 448 **"It is our opinion . . ."** Letter, Brig. Gen. M. Churchill, to D. E. Nolan, Asst. Chief of Staff, G-2, G.H.Q., A.E.F., May 16, 1919, Military Intelligence Division, U.S. National Archives.

p. 449 **Bly was "just like her old self"** *Brooklyn Daily Eagle,* Mar. 4, 1919 (*Brooklyn Daily Eagle* morgue, Brooklyn Public Library). Also, Mar. 6, 1919, 12:3–4.

p. 449 **Jane had died** Death Certificate No. 5685, Jane Hartley Cochrane, Mar. 7, 1919, Brooklyn, at 332 E. 16th St., New York City Municipal Archives.

p. 449 **The McAlpin** Stern et al. *New York 1900,* p. 272.

p. 449 **a small two-room suite** Recollections of Dorothy Brauer, who lived with Bly, interviews with the author, Apr. 1991. Also, Bly published the room number several times in her columns for *The NY Evening Journal.*

p. 449 **Albert now felt he had full entitlement** Lawsuit, Oscar Bondy v. Harry C. Cochrane et al. as executors of the estate of Elizabeth C. Seaman, New York County Supreme Court, Special Term, Part III, No. 1354-1923.

p. 450 **"Dear Q.O. Thank you . . ."** Letter, NB to Erasmus Wilson, Mar. 29, 1919, Carnegie Library.

p. 451 **complaint against Albert** *Brooklyn Daily Eagle,* Apr. 8, 1919, 16:2.

p. 451 **Albert was arrested, formally charged** *Brooklyn Daily Eagle,* Apr. 15, 1919, 2:2.

p. 451 **Albert charged Bly** Ibid.

p. 451 **dropped the charges against Bly** *Brooklyn Daily Eagle*, May 23, 1919, 16:7.

p. 452 **trying to obtain . . . a copy of the cable** Index cards recording cables to NB from U.S. Embassy, Vienna, Apr. 7, 1919, 130 B 6241; May 17, 1919, 130 B 6241; June 4, 1919, 130 B 6241; June 13, 1919, 130 B 6241. Actual files not preserved, State Department files, U.S. National Archives.

p. 452 **case Mary Jane had brought** American Steel Barrel Co. of America, Entry 289, Box 4, Bureau of Law File No. 54, Alien Property Custodian, U.S. National Archives.

p. 452 **old perjury indictment was dismissed** *NY Times*, May 22, 1919, 7:5.

p. 452 **"A man may be down . . ."** *NY Evening Journal*, May 24, 1919, ed. page:3–8.

13

❦ ❧

The Journal

p. 455 **"*Nellie Bly, the famous woman writer . . .*"** *NY Evening Journal*, May 24, 1919, ed. page:3–8.

p. 455 **urging men whose hair had gone gray** *NY Evening Journal*, May 31, 1919, ed. page:3–6.

p. 455 **need for everyone . . . to have a home** *NY Evening Journal*, June 4, 1919, ed. page:7–8.

p. 455 **importance of constant fresh air** *NY Evening Journal*, May 30, 1919, ed. page:7–8.

p. 455 **upcoming heavyweight boxing championship match** *NY Evening Journal*, June 10, 1919, 1:4+++.

p. 455 **"giving her own impressions . . ."** Ibid.

p. 457 **"Would I hesitate and feel dumb . . ."** Ibid.

p. 457 **Willard, who caused a similar reaction** *NY Evening Journal*, June 11, 1919, 21:1–2.

p. 457 **increased opportunities in many fields** See Ross, *Ladies of the Press*, pp. 2–5.

p. 457 **Front page play was as significant** Ibid.

p. 458 **watched the fighters spar** *NY Evening Journal*, June 13, 1919, 23:1–3.

p. 458 **watched them train** *NY Evening Journal*, June 14, 1919, 7:1–2.

p. 458 **didn't faint when blood was drawn** *NY Evening Journal*, June 16, 1919, 14:6–8.

p. 458 **Willard's training quarters** *NY Evening Journal*, June 21, 1919, 7:3–5.

p. 458 **Willard's personal physician to attend her** Ibid.

p. 458 **TOLEDO, July 5—The king is dead** *NY Evening Journal*, July 5, 1919, 1:1–2.

p. 459 **obligatory victory interview with Dempsey** *NY Evening Journal*, July 8, 1919, 17:1–3.

p. 459 **gave birth to an advice column** The first ran under the headline "Nellie Bly Presents the True Picture of Human Nature," *NY Evening Journal*, July 18, 1919, ed. page:7–8.

p. 459 **Dix left the Hearst organization** Ross, *Ladies of the Press*, pp. 76–77.

p. 459 **Bly interviewed . . . Edward O'Brien** *NY Evening Journal*, July 21, 1919, 1:1, 3:1–5.

p. 461 **"Jack O'Hearts"** *NY Evening Journal*, July 26, 1919, ed. page:7–8.

p. 461 **"Can't you make up? . . ."** Ibid.

p. 461 **brought in scores of letters** *NY Evening Journal*, Aug. 1, 1919, ed. page:7–8.

p. 461 **"Dear Troubled Mother:"** Ibid.

p. 462 **plans to improve the subways** July 23, 1919, ed. page:7–8.

p. 462 **how to get a song . . . published** *NY Evening Journal*, Aug. 11, 1919, ed. page:7–8. Advice columns ran on Aug. 1, 5, 11, 12, 21, 22, 23, 25, 28, and 30.

p. 462 **"Am I my brother's keeper?"** *NY Evening Journal*, Aug. 25, 1919, ed. page:7–8.

p. 462 **". . . a story as old as the hills . . ."** Ibid.

p. 462 **Beatrice Alexander** Interview, Irene Ravitch with Beatrice Alexander, undated 1931, quoted in Ravitch, "NB: A Biographical Sketch," p. 53. Alexander told Ravitch that many people volunteered to help with the vast number of letters which arrived daily from people in need.

p. 463 **a makeshift nursery** *NY Evening Journal*, Nov. 29, 1919, 3:1–2.

p. 463 **no longer the object of . . . speculation** Ross, *Ladies of the Press*, pp. 58–59, made this assessment of NB in her *Journal* years. Although Ross did not attribute the information, the date of her book, 1936, means that it could represent the reflections of some of NB's *Journal* colleagues. Ross also said NB shared her two-room suite at the McAlpin with a woman friend, although there is no other source for this.

p. 463 **Mildred Gilman** Telephone interview with Mildred Gilman Wolfort from her home in Ridgefield, Conn., with author, Mar. 16, 1993.

p. 463 **no consequence to Bly** Ross, *Ladies of the Press*, pp. 58–59.

p. 463 **"IMPORTANT: Dear Friends— . . ."** *NY Evening Journal*, Sept. 20, 1919, ed. page:7–8.

p. 464 **backlog of letters awaiting replies** *NY Evening Journal*, Oct. 2, 1919, ed. page:7–8.

p. 464 **frame house at 1028 Beverly Road** Deed, Mary Jane Cochrane buys house at 1028 Beverly Road, Brooklyn, from Rose Fisher, Sept. 26, 1919, No. 86395, Brooklyn Real Estate Records.

p. 464 **still sprightly and in full command.** Order of U.S. District Court Judge Edwin L. Garvin in Mary Jane Cochrane v. Francis P. Garvan, Alien Property Custodian, U.S. District Court, Eastern District, Feb. 26, 1920, p. 6 (Alien Property Custodian, U.S. National Archives, Record Group 131, Entry 289, Box 4, Bureau of Law File No. 54).

p. 464 **"Nellie Bly Gives Day Out of Her Life"** *NY Evening Journal*, Oct. 14, 1919, ed. page:7–8.

p. 464 **salary by a stunning 50 percent** Letter, NB to Mr. Johnson of Bankers Trust, N.Y., Mar. 12, 1922, notes salary of $100 per week as of June 1, 1919, raised to $150 per week as of Oct. 15, 1919. Estate of Elizabeth Cochrane Seaman, Clerk of the New York Surrogate's Court.

p. 465 **"Know yourself"** *NY Evening Journal*, Nov. 6, 1919, ed. page:7–8.

p. 465 **"Nellie Bly Finds A Home . . ."** *NY Evening Journal*, Nov. 29, 1919, 3:1–2.

p. 466 **"My heart stood still . . ."** Ibid.

p. 466 **"The crippled girl sank . . ."** *NY Evening Journal*, Dec. 1, 1919, 3:1–2. Follow-up column, Dec. 2, 1919, 19:4–6.

p. 467 **"Disappointment is the state . . ."** *NY Evening Journal*, Dec. 5, 1919, ed. page:7–8.

p. 467 **staff at the McAlpin adjusted** Interview of Irene Ravitch with Austin Denniston of the McAlpin staff, Nov. 1930, quoted in Ravitch, "NB: A Biographical Sketch."

p. 468 **"One woman buoyed up . . ."** *NY Evening Journal*, Dec. 6, 1919, 3:2–4.

p. 468 **story of little "Ann Randolph"** Ibid.

p. 468 **"To Somebody—For the Love of Mike . . ."** *NY Evening Journal*, Dec. 10, 1919, 5:6–7.

p. 469 **child was given to the Wentzes** *NY Evening Journal*, Dec. 17, 1919, 1:1–8.

p. 469 **complaint of Lena Lisa** *NY Evening Journal*, Dec. 18, 1919, 1:4–8.

p. 470 **back to his natural mother** Ibid. and Dec. 18, 1919, 1:5–8, 3:1–5.

p. 470 **Love of Mike was back at Bellevue** *NY Evening Journal*, Dec. 20, 1919, 3:1–3.

p. 470 **offering to sell their third child** *NY Evening Journal*, Dec. 22, 1914, 1:4.

p. 472 **"A man who offers his child for sale . . ."** *NY Evening Journal*, Dec. 23, 1919, 1:3, 2:4.

p. 472 **"The greatest crime . . ."** Ibid.

p. 472 **"open their hearts and homes . . ."** *NY Evening Journal*, Dec. 24, 1919, ed. page:7–8.

p. 473 **given Oscar Bondy her power of attorney** Lawsuit, Oscar Bondy v. Harry C. Cochrane et al. as executors of the estate of Elizabeth C. Seaman, New York County Supreme Court, Special Term, Part III, No. 1354-1923, including excerpts from Bondy–NB correspondence, 1919–1921.

p. 473 **"I have just returned from Bohemia . . ."** Letter, Oscar Bondy to NB, July 8, 1919, Oscar Bondy v. Harry C. Cochrane et al.

p. 474 **". . . You know I have all that sugar dividends . . ."** Letter, NB to Oscar Bondy, Jan. 26, 1920, Oscar Bondy v. Harry C. Cochrane et al.

p. 474 **"It's *terrible* that you underwent hardships . . ."** Letter, Oscar Bondy to NB, Aug. 20, 1919, Oscar Bondy v. Harry C. Cochrane et al.

pp. 474–475 **"Pray don't be foolish . . ."** Letter, Oscar Bondy to NB, Feb. 7, 1920, Oscar Bondy v. Harry C. Cochrane et al.

p. 475 **judgment in Bly's favor** Opinion, U.S. District Court Judge Edwin L. Garvin in Mary Jane Cochrane v. Francis P. Garvan, Alien Property Custodian, Feb. 26, 1920, pp. 1–9. Also, *NY Evening Journal*, Feb. 22, 1920, 22:3.

p. 476 **"Salary from *NY Journal* began . . ."** Letter, NB to "Mr. Johnson, Bankers Trust Co." Mar. 15, 1920, File of Estate Probate of Elizabeth Cochrane Seaman, Clerk of the New York County Surrogate's Court.

p. 477 **the story of a fifteen-year-old girl** *NY Evening Journal*, Jan. 8, 1920, 1:4, 3:5.

p. 477 **follow-up in the Love of Mike case** *NY Evening Journal*, Jan. 9, 1920, 1:4, 3:2–5.

p. 478 **Love of Mike never lived to leave** *NY Evening Journal*, Feb. 25, 1920, ed. page:7–8.

pp. 478–479 **descriptions of adorable infants** *NY Evening Journal*, Jan. 24, 1920, ed. page:7–8; Jan. 26, 1920, ed. page:7–8.

p. 479 **Brisbane, witnessing the first electrocution** Carlson, *Brisbane*, p. 97, says Charles Edward Russell looked over at Brisbane "and noticed that as the convicted man was being strapped to his seat, Arthur's usually ruddy face turned greenish white. He was visibly shaking. He remained through the electrocution but he became so sick he couldn't stay for the official autopsy."

p. 479 **"Horrible! Horrible! Horrible! . . ."** *NY Evening Journal*, Jan. 30, 1920, 1:3, 3:4–6.

p. 479 **"January 29, 1920. A slight remembrance . . ."** Ibid.

p. 479 **"I shall never forget . . ."** *NY Evening Journal*, Feb. 5, 1920, ed. page:7–8.

p. 480 **Bly urged support for the measure** *NY Evening Journal*, Mar. 13, 1920, ed. page:7–8; Mar. 15, 1920, ed. page:7–8; Mar. 16, 1920, ed. page:7–8.

p. 480 **"If the death penalty is abolished . . ."** *NY Evening Journal*. The Boylan-Pellet Bill had been submitted for several sessions before and after Bly's brief anti–capital punishment campaign. On Apr. 20, 1920, the state senate defeated Boylan's motion to get his bill out of committee by a vote of 28–18. Capital punishment was not abolished in New York State until 1965.

p. 480 **the evils of gambling** *NY Evening Journal*, Feb. 28, 1920, ed. page:7–8.

p. 480 **real jobs to the blind** *NY Evening Journal*, Mar. 30, 1920, ed. page:3–6.

p. 480 **"And as so many of you have written . . ."** *NY Evening Journal*, Apr. 1, 1920, ed. page:3–6.

p. 481 **"I have never written a word . . ."** *NY Evening Journal*, Apr. 6, 1920, ed. page:7–8.

p. 481 **cured a lonely wife** Ibid.

p. 481 **give first offenders a second chance** *NY Evening Journal*, Apr. 20, 1920, ed. page:7–8.

p. 481 **society to help men released from prison** *NY Evening Journal*, Apr. 22, 1920, ed. page:7–8.

p. 481 **when he came . . . to thank her** Interview of Irene Ravitch with Beatrice Alexander, undated 1931, quoted in Ravitch, "NB: A Biographical Sketch," p. 55.

p. 481 **what she would do with a spare million** *NY Evening Journal*, Apr. 26, 1920, ed. page:7–8.

p. 482 **"arch Bluebeard and slayer"** *NY Evening Journal*, May 3, 1920, 1:5.

p. 482 **Henrietta Bulte . . .** NB coverage of Bulte vanishing: *NY Evening Journal*, May 7, 1920, 1:3, 2:4–5; May 8, 1920, 1:3, 3:6–7; May 10, 1920, 1:6, 2:6–7; May 11, 1920, 1:4, 2:3–6; May 12, 1920, 1:7–8, 2:1–4; May 13, 1920, 1:6, 2:3–4; May 14, 1920, 1:3, 1:7, 2:4–5; May 15, 1920, 1:4, 3:3–6; May 17, 1920, 3:1–2; May 18, 1920, 1:5, 1:2–3, 2:4–7; May 19, 1920, 1:6, 3:5–6; May 20, 1920, 15:4.

p. 482 **an all-expense-paid picnic** *NY Evening Journal*, June 1, 1920, 7:4–5.

p. 483 **Republican National Convention in Chicago** *NY Evening Journal*, June 7, 1920, 3:1–2.

p. 483 **"They have all arrived . . ."** Ibid.

p. 483 **women would have taken over politics** Ibid. Also, *NY Evening Journal*, June 8, 1920, 3:1–2; June 9, 1920, 3:1; June 10, 1920, 3:1–2; June 11, 1920, 3:1; June 12, 1920, 3:1–2.

p. 483 **slaying of Joseph B. Elwell** *NY Evening Journal*, June 19, 1920, 1:6–7, 2:4–7; June 21, 1920, 1:6–7, 2:2–4; June 23, 1920, 3:1–2; June 24, 1920, 1:6–7, 2:4–7; **turfman**: a devotee of horse racing; **whist**: a card game of four players in two partnerships played with one deck of cards; one point is scored for every trick in excess of six.

p. 484 **"If it weren't an insult to brutes . . ."** *NY Evening Journal*, July 12, 1920, ed. page:3–6.

p. 484 **Sir Thomas Johnstone Lipton** *NY Evening Journal*, July 21, 1920, 1:6–7, 2:2–4.

p. 484 **a hint of a British accent** Interview of Irene Ravitch with Beatrice Alexander, undated 1931, quoted in Ravitch, "NB: A Biographical Sketch," p. 55.

p. 484 **Her assistants . . . recalled** Ibid., pp. 54–56.

p. 485 **wonders of plastic surgery** *NY Evening Journal*, Oct. 26, 1920, ed. page:7–8.

p. 485 **importance of women dressing well** *NY Evening Journal*, Sept. 27, 1920, ed. page:3–6.

p. 485 **buying American goods** *NY Evening Journal*, Sept. 24, 1920, ed. page:3–6.

p. 485 **deporting foreigners who commit crimes** *NY Evening Journal*, July 29, 1920, ed. page:3–6.

p. 485 **"Like belongs to like . . ."** *NY Evening Journal*, Nov. 27, 1920, ed. page:3–6.

p. 485 **"My dear young man. MARRY THE GIRL . . ."** *NY Evening Journal*, Nov. 26, 1920, ed. page:3–6.

p. 485 **the worthy but sickly electrician** *NY Evening Journal*, Dec. 11, 1920, ed. page:3–6; Dec. 20, 1920, ed. page:3–6; Dec. 21, 1920, ed. page:3–6; Dec. 24, 1920, ed. page:3–6.

p. 485 **"I have never yet written . . ."** *NY Evening Journal*, Dec. 10, 1920, ed. page: 7–8.

p. 486 **story of Zita** *NY Evening Journal*, Apr. 11, 1921, ed. page:3–6.

p. 487 **"To be happy . . ."** *NY Evening Journal*, June 30, 1921, ed. page:3–6.

p. 487 **"Like a streetcar, it takes in . . ."** *NY Evening Journal*, June 27, 1921, ed. page:3–6.

p. 488 **"No home can be a home . . ."** *NY Evening Journal*, Sept. 12, 1921, ed. page:3–6.

p. 488 **plight of the nation's seamen** *NY Evening Journal*, Mar. 5, 1921, ed. page:3–6.

p. 488 **from late February until the middle of October** *NY Evening Journal*, Feb. 28, 1921, ed. page:7–8; Mar. 16, 1921, ed. page:3–6; Mar. 18, 1921, ed. page:3–6; Mar. 23, 1921, ed. page:3–6; Mar. 31, 1921, ed. page:3–6; Apr. 7, 1921, ed. page:3–6; Apr. 13, 1921, ed. page:3–6; Apr. 20, 1921, ed. page:3–6; Apr. 27, 1921, ed. page:3–6; May 9, 1921, ed. page:3–6; May 14, 1921, ed. page:3–6; May 20, 1921, ed. page:3–6; May 26, 1921, ed. page:3–6; June 1, 1921, ed. page:3–6; June 6, 1921, ed. page:3–6; June 14, 1921, ed. page:3–6; June 20, 1921, ed. page:3–6; June 28, 1921, ed. page:3–6; July 8, 1921, ed. page:3–6; July 12, 1921, ed. page:3–6; July 19, 1921, ed. page:3–6; July 23, 1921, ed. page:3–6; Aug. 2, 1921, ed. page:3–6; Aug. 9, 1921, ed. page:3–6; Aug. 15, 1921, ed. page:3–6; Aug. 26, 1921, ed. page:3–6; Sept. 1, 1921, ed. page:3–6; Sept. 9, 1921, ed. page:3–6; Sept. 24, 1921, ed. page:3–6; Oct. 4, 1921, ed. page:3–6; Oct. 7, 1921, ed. page:3–6; Oct. 14, 1921, ed. page:3–6.

p. 490 **the American Seamen's Association** *NY Evening Journal*, May 14, 1921, ed. page:3–6.

p. 490 **Bly's mother died** Death Certificate No. 4025, Mary Jane Cochrane, Feb. 26, 1921, Brooklyn, New York City Municipal Archives.

p. 490 **"Life is a mask of uncertainties . . ."** *NY Evening Journal*, Sept. 26, 1921, ed. page:3–6.

p. 490 **"Death, which leaves no opportunity . . ."** *NY Evening Journal*, Oct. 12, 1921, ed. page:3–6.

p. 491 **Albert had spent the preceding two days** *NY Times*, Oct. 16, 1921, 13:2.

p. 492 **Margery Rex** started in journalism in 1917 in Chicago and came to work for Brisbane at *The Journal* in 1918. Ross, *Ladies of the Press*, pp. 194–202.

p. 492 **"taste of the bliss of heaven"** *NY Evening Journal*, Nov. 19, 1921, ed. page:3–6.

p. 493 **"saved their names and spared their families . . ."** *NY Evening Journal*, Nov. 18, 1921, ed. page:3–6.

p. 494 **"I have now given strict orders . . ."** *NY Evening Journal*, Nov. 19, 1921, ed. page:3–6.

p. 495 **the heartrending story** *NY Evening Journal*, Dec. 15, 1919, ed. page:3–6.

p. 496 **Dorothy had come into the care** All details of Dorothy's appearances before Children's Court, her time as a ward of the New York Society for the Prevention of Cruelty to Children, notations, memos, and correspondence concerning her case come from confidential files of the NYSPCC. Access was granted with Dorothy's permission and the kind cooperation of the society.

p. 497 **"I would never leave her . . ."** Letter, Clarence Coulter to NYSPCC's Ernest Coulter, June (possibly Jan.) 20, 1920.

p. 497 **"She [Grace] was addicted . . ."** Letter, Helen Love-Beauregard to NYSPCC's Ernest Coulter, Feb. 10, 1920.

p. 498 **"Mrs. Seaman said she was not willing . . ."** Memo of NYSPCC's Ernest Coulter's conversation with NB, Feb. 3, 1920.

p. 499 **In a lengthy two-part story** *NY Evening Journal*, Oct. 19, 1920, ed. page:3–6; Oct. 20, 1920, ed. page:7–8.

p. 501 **"Dear Miss Bly . . ."** Ibid.

p. 502 **Bly again appeared** Notation, Confidential Case File of Dorothy Coulter, NYSPCC.

p. 502 **Leake and Watts Orphan Asylum** All information concerning Dorothy's stay at the Leake and Watts Orphan Asylum is from her confidential file at the facility, now called the Leake and Watts Home. Access was granted by Dorothy and with the kind cooperation of Leake and Watts.

p. 502 "**My dear Mrs. Seaman: I understand . . .**" Letter from A. S. McClain to NB, Jan. 3, 1921.

p. 503 "**She isn't really a princess . . .**" *NY Evening Journal*, May 6, 1921, ed. page: 7–8.

p. 504 "**. . . I may be able to do something with Nellie Bly . . .**" Letter, Joseph Applegate to A. S. McClain, Leake and Watts Superintendent, May 15, 1921.

p. 504 **she had made other plans** Letter, NB to A. S. McClain, May 23, 1921.

p. 505 "**Are we not governed by destiny . . .**" *NY Evening Journal*, Jan. 9, 1922, ed. page:3–6.

p. 505 **Bly entered St. Mark's Hospital** Death Certificate no. 2759, Elizabeth C. Seaman, Jan. 27, 1922, New York City, New York City Municipal Archives.

p. 506 **she gave . . . Harry and . . . Beatrice $800** Suit, Beatrice K. Brown et al. v. Harry C. Cochrane individually and as executor of estate of Elizabeth C. Seaman, File No. 5207, 1923, filed Nov. 8, 1922, New York County Supreme Court.

p. 506 **signed her will on January 11** Will of Elizabeth C. Seaman, also known as Nellie Bly, Jan. 11, 1922, Probate of Estate of Elizabeth C. Seaman, died Jan. 27, 1922, File Clerk's No. P. 758-1922, Clerk of New York County Surrogate's Court.

p. 506 **accumulated debt to the Internal Revenue Service** Probate of Estate of Elizabeth C. Seaman.

p. 507 **the estate's net value** *NY Times*, Aug. 30, 1924, 3:8.

p. 507 **Bondy's share had claimed the bulk** (Death Certificate No. 26302, Oct. 26, 1923, New York City, New York City Municipal Archives). Probate of Estate of Elizabeth C. Seaman. Also File No. 5207, New York County Supreme Court, 1923. Albert Cochrane, NB's estranged brother, died Mar. 1, 1926, in Brooklyn (Death Certificate No. 4950, New York City Municipal Archives). Beatrice could not be traced after 1926.

p. 507 **Dorothy Coulter . . . would never benefit** Author interviews with Dorothy Watson Brauer and family members, April–May 1991.

p. 507 **it was attended by newspaper workers** *NY Evening Journal*, Jan. 30, 1922, 6:6.

p. 507 **for half a century "unmarked by loving hands"** The New York Press Club, at the behest of Woodlawn Cemetery, arranged to have a headstone placed over NB's grave at a ceremony held June 22, 1978. Each year, the club presents a Nellie Bly/Thomas D. Zumbo Cub Reporter of the Year award to a deserving journalist with no more than three years' experience in print or electronic media.

p. 507 **ran over the wires of the Associated Press** *St. Louis Post-Dispatch* (AP logo), Jan. 27, 1922.

p. 507 "**Luck turned against her . . .**" *NY Times*, Jan. 28, 1922, 13:4.

p. 508 *The New York World* **reported her death** *NY World*, Jan. 28, 1922, 11:4.

p. 509 **"Nellie Bly, whose work and character . . ."** *NY Evening Journal*, Jan. 28, 1922, ed. page:1–2. Brisbane's column was entitled "The Death of Nellie Bly." In Feb. 1931, Brisbane friend Eleanor "Cissy" Patterson, editor of *The Washington Herald*, wrote a column about her failed attempt to interview Albert Einstein. Patterson had walked uninvited onto the Untermyer estate in Palm Springs, Calif., where Einstein was known to be visiting, and found the renowned scientist dressed only in a small white handkerchief knotted at each corner and resting on his unruly gray locks. In embarrassment, she fled (*NY American*, Feb. 11, 1931, 2:5–7). Brisbane told Patterson through his front page column the next day how a "regular determined go-getter she reporter" would have handled the situation: "Under such circumstances, Nelly [*sic*] Bly, best American woman reporter, with the possible exception of Dorothy Dix, would have got a blanket, put it over Dr. Einstein and got the interview, if necessary, sitting on the blanket and Einstein to keep him from getting away" (*NY American*, Feb. 12, 1931, 1:1).

Epilogue

p. 513 **"Dorothy," she remembered Bly saying** All recollections of Dorothy Coulter/Harris/Watson/Brauer come from author interviews with her at her home in Black Mountain, N.C., Apr. 1991.

p. 515 **"Helen," "a dainty princess,"** *NY Evening Journal*, July 2, 1921, ed. page:3–6.

p. 515 **"I am very anxious indeed . . ."** Letter, A. S. McClain, Superintendent of Leake and Watts Orphan Asylum, to NB, Aug. 19, 1921, confidential case file of Dorothy Coulter.

p. 515 **"I would be pleased to see you . . ."** Letter, NB to A. S. McClain, Superintendent of Leake and Watts Orphan Asylum, Aug. 22, 1921.

p. 516 **"The mother did her best . . ."** *NY Evening Journal*, Dec. 22, 1921, ed. page: 3–6.

p. 516 **a cashier for H. Black and Company** Cleveland City Directories, 1922–1926; genealogy records, Ohio Surname Index, Ohio Necrology File, Ohio Census for 1910, housed at the Western Reserve Historical Society in Cleveland Heights, all yielded details of the Watson family and enabled the tracing of Dorothy, who had never before been located, from Cleveland to St. Petersburg, Fla. Jack Payton, former foreign editor of the *St. Petersburg Times*, and his assistant, Natalie Watson (no relation), helped trace Dorothy, through *The Times* obituary file and St. Petersburg criss-cross directory, from St. Petersburg to Black Mountain, N.C., where she had gone to live with her granddaughter. In Black Mountain, she was listed in the telephone directory.

p. 517 **Dorothy arrived at the Watson home** Adoption of Dorothy Harris by Harry and Clara Belle Watson, Dec. 4, 1923, Adoption Records, Cuyahoga County Probate, State of Ohio. Record obtained from Dorothy Coulter/Harris/Watson/Brauer.

p. 517 **Lee Elementary School** Ibid.

p. 517 **entered Miss Kate Phillips's** Cleveland Heights Board of Education student records for Dorothy Watson. Lisa Goodell of that office retrieved the information from school archives.

p. 517 **The Watsons left Cleveland** Genealogical records of the Western Reserve Historical Society. Necrology (newspaper obituary) files for the Bosworth and Watson families enabled the tracing of the family to St. Petersburg, Fla. Cleveland City Directories, 1918–1927, indicated the 1926 departure, later confirmed by family members.

p. 518 **no birth certificate could ever be found** Author interviews with Anita Scheublein, Dorothy's daughter, Apr. 1991 and subsequently.

p. 518 **"big and wide and blue . . ."** *NY Evening Journal*, Dec. 1, 1921, ed. page:7–8.

BIBLIOGRAPHY

❦ ❧

Newspapers

The Albany Argus, The Albany Morning Express, The Albany Times, The Albany Times-Union, The Apollo News-Record, The Apollo Sentinel, The Armstrong Democrat and Farmer's and Mechanic's Advertiser, The Batavia Daily News, The Brooklyn Daily Eagle, The Buffalo Courier, The Buffalo Evening News, The Buffalo Express, The Catskill Daily Mail, The Catskill Messenger, The Catskill Recorder, The Catskill Weekly Examiner, The Chicago Evening Post, The Chicago Times-Herald, The Chicago Tribune, The Coxsackie Union, The Daytona Beach News-Journal, The Greensburg Tribune, The Herald (Omaha, Nebr.), The Indiana County Gazette, The Indiana Evening Gazette, The Indiana Tribune Review, The Kiski Weekend, The Kittanning Daily Times, The Kittanning Leader-Times, The Kittanning Times, The Logansport Daily Journal, The Middletown Daily Press, The New Kensington (Pa.) Dispatch, The New York American, The New York Assembly Journal, The New York Evening Journal, The New York Herald, The New York Mail and Express, The New York Recorder, The New York Sun, The New York Times, The New York Tribune, The New York World, The New York World Telegram, The Philadelphia Inquirer, The Pittsburgh Chronicle Telegraph, The Pittsburgh Commercial Gazette, The Pittsburgh Dispatch, The Pittsburg Gazette, The Pittsburgh Gazette-Times, The Pittsburgh Post, The Pittsburgh Post-Gazette, The Pittsburgh Press, The Pittsburgh Sun-Telegraph, The St. Louis Post-Dispatch, The San Francisco Chronicle, The San Francisco Examiner, Staats-Zeitung, The (Topeka) State Journal, The Topeka Daily Capital, The Utica (N.Y.) Observer, The Vandergrift Citizen, The Vandergrift New Citizen, The Vandergrift News, Die Zeit (Vienna).

Magazine Articles

"The Decay of American Journalism." *The Dial*, Vol. 22, No. 260, Apr. 16, 1897.

"Echoes of Early Hazelwood and Glenwood, Pittsburgh." *Western Pennsylvania Historical Magazine*, Vol. 7, 1924.

"Emancipated Woman." *The Spectator*, Vol. 57, No. 2948, Dec. 27, 1884.

"An Indictment and a Remedy." *Harpers Weekly*, Vol. 36, No. 1872, Nov. 5, 1892.

"Journalism in New York." *The Nation*, Vol. 57, No. 466, Aug. 3, 1893.

"Journalistic Dementia." *The Nation*, Vol. 60, No. 1550, Mar. 14, 1895.

"Lady Travelers." *The Living Age*, Vol. 210, No. 2717, Aug. 1, 1896.

"Some Methods of Modern Journalism." *Chamber Journal*, Vol. 68, No. 385, May 16, 1891.

"Woman Journalists." *The Spectator*, Vol. 70, No. 3390, June 17, 1893.

"Youth and Age in Industry." *The Spectator*, Vol. 81, No. 3667, Oct. 8, 1898.

Ainsworth-White, Marian. "Women in Journalism." *The Arena*, Vol. 25, No. 6, June 1900.

Anderson, Thomas F. "The Individuality of the Reporter." *The Journalist*, Dec. 13, 1890.

Andrews, J. Cutler. "The Gilded Age in Pennsylvania." *Pennsylvania History*, Vol. 34, No. 1, Jan. 1967.

Banks, Elizabeth L. "American Journalism." *The Living Age*, Vol. 215, 1895, pp. 640–649.

Brown, Ira V. "The Woman's Rights Movement in Pennsylvania, 1848–1873." *Quarterly Journal of the Pennsylvania Historical Association*, Apr. 1965.

Burke, Evelyn. "Nellie Bly Started This Globe-Girdling." *Pittsburgh Press Magazine*, Oct. 31, 1936.

Cahoon, Haryot Holt. "Women in Gutter Journalism." *The Arena*, Vol. 17, No. 88, Mar. 1897.

Cockerill, John A. "The Newspaper of the Future." *Lippincott's Magazine*, Vol. 50, Aug. 1892.

———. "Same Phases in Contemporary Journalism." *Cosmopolitan*, Vol. 13, No. 6, Oct. 1892.

Cutler, Andrew J. "The Gilded Age in Pennsylvania." *Pennsylvania History*, Vol. 34, No. 1, 1967.

Fellner, Fritz. "The Dissolution of the Habsburg Monarchy and Its Significance for the New Order in Central Europe: A Reappraisal." *Austrian History Yearbook*, 4–5 (1968–69), pp. 3–27.

Forman, Allan. "The Chances in Journalism." *The Author*, Vol. 3, No. 2, Feb. 15, 1891.

Fowler, William J. "Character in Journalism." *The Writer*, Vol. 2, No. 1, Jan. 1888.

Gribayédoff, Valerian. "Pictorial Journalism." *Cosmopolitan*, Vol. 11, No. 4, Aug. 1891.

Hamm, Margherita Arlina. "Among the Newspaper Women." *The Journalist*, recurring article, 1891–1893.

King, Henry. "The Pay and Rank of Journalism." *The Forum*, Vol. 18, No. 1, Jan. 1895.

Lilly, W. S. "The Ethics of Journalism." *The Forum*, Vol. 7, No. 5, July 1889.

Lloyd, W. H. S. "English and American Journalism." *The Writer*, Vol. 3, No. 1, Jan. 1889.

Marcosson, Isaac F. "The Millionaire Yield of Pittsburgh." *Munsey's Magazine*, Vol. 46, Mar. 1912.

Bibliography

Mathews, Fannie Aymar. "The Women's Press Club of New York." *Cosmopolitan*, Vol. 11, No. 4, Aug. 1891.

Moulder, Priscilla E. "The Industrial Position of Women." *The Westminster Review*, Vol. 151, No. 3, 1899.

O'Rell, Max. "Lively Journalism." *North American Review*, Vol. 150, No. 3, Mar. 1890.

Rawford, Emily. "Journalism as a Professional Woman." *Eclectic Magazine*, Vol. 58, No. 6, Dec. 1893.

Sears, Elizabeth. "Business Women and Women in Business." *Harper's Magazine*, Vol. 134, Jan. 1917.

Sprague, J. F. *The Metropolis.* New York: New York Recorder, 1891.

Stanley, Olga. "Personalities of Literary and Journalistic Women." *Outlook*, Vol. 57, No. 7, Oct. 16, 1897.

Stead, W. T. "Young Women in Journalism." *The Review of Reviews*, Vol. 6, No. 34, Nov. 1892.

Stille, Werner A. "Newspaper Reading; To the Editor of the Nation." *The Nation*, Vol. 60, No. 1551, Mar. 21, 1895.

Tarbell, Ida M. "Women in Journalism." *The Chautauquan*, Vol. 7, No. 7, Apr. 1887.

Thomas, August. "Recollection of Frederic Remington." *Century Magazine*, Vol. 86, May–Oct. 1913.

Twombly, Mary. "Women in Journalism." *The Writer*, Vol. 3, No. 8, Aug. 1889.

White, Z. L. "A Decade of American Journalism." *The Westminster Review*, Vol. 128, No. 7, Oct. 1887.

Unpublished Essays

Henry, T. J. "Memories of Apollo." family collection, undated.

Merryman, John Edward. "Indiana University at Pennsylvania: From Private Normal School to Public University." University of Pittsburgh, 1972.

Myers, Alfred Frantz. "Nellie Bly: Fact or Fiction, The Life and Legend of Elizabeth Jane Cochrane." Stapleton Library, Indiana University of Pennsylvania, 1970.

Ravitch, Irene. "Nellie Bly: A Biographical Sketch." Arthur Hays Sulzberger Library, Graduate School of Journalism, Columbia University, 1931.

Reference Works

Armstrong County, Pa.: Her People, Past and Present. Chicago: J. H. Beers, 1914.

Atlas of Armstrong County, Pa. Philadelphia: Pomeroy Whitman, 1876.

Barnard's Estates. 351 Pa. 313 41 A 2nd 578. Supreme Court, Pa., Mar. 1945.

History of Allegheny County. Chicago: A. Warner, 1889.

State of Pennsylvania Constitution of 1838.

Standard Pennsylvania Practice. Rochester, N.Y.: Lawyers Co-operative Publishing, 1960.

Violin Iconography of Antonio Stradivari, 1644–1737. Larchmont, NY: Herbert K. Goodkind, 1972.

Women in Industry. New York: Alexander Hamilton Institute, 1918.

Bibliography

Ashley, Perry J., ed. *American Newspaper Journalists, 1873–1900, Dictionary of American Biography*, Vol. 23. Detroit: Bruccoli Clark, 1983.

Bleyer, Willard Grosvenor. *Main Currents in the History of American Journalism.* Cambridge, Mass.: Houghton Mifflin, Riverside Press, 1927.

Caldwell, J. A. *History of Indiana County, Pennsylvania.* Newark, Ohio, 1880.

Canfield, Leon H., and Howard B. Wilder. *The United States in the Making.* Cambridge, Mass.: Houghton Mifflin, Riverside Press, 1939.

Cassady, John C. *The Somerset County Outline.* 1932.

Cornell, William Mason. *History of Pennsylvania.* Boston: Quaker City, 1876.

Dickey, Luther S. *The History of the 103d Regiment Pennsylvania Veteran Volunteer Infantry, 1861–1865.* Chicago, 1910.

Eastman, Frank M. *Courts and Lawyers of Pennsylvania, 1623–1923,* Vol. 2. New York: American Historical Society, 1922.

Emery, Edwin. *The Press and America: An Interpretative History of Mass Media,* 3rd ed. Englewood Cliffs: Prentice-Hall, 1972.

Estes, Glenn E., ed. *American Writers for Children Before 1900, Dictionary of Literary Biography*, Vol. 42. Detroit: Bruccoli Clark, 1983.

Goodkind, *Iconography of Stradivarius Violins.* 1972.

Harvey, Paul, ed. *The Oxford Companion to English Literature,* 3rd ed., 1964.

Hudson, Frederic. *Journalism in the United States, 1690–1872.*

Hulteng, John L. *Playing It Straight: A Practical Discussion of the Ethical Principles of the American Society of Newspaper Editors.* Chester, Conn.: Globe Pequot, 1981.

Jackson, Joseph. *Encyclopedia of Philadelphia,* Vol. 2. Harrisburg: National Historical Association, 1931.

Juliette, Ron, and Dale E. Landon. *Indiana University of Pennsylvania: Our Homage and Our Love.* Virginia Beach: Downing, 1991.

King, Moses. *King's Handbook of New York City, 1893.* New York: Benjamin Bloom, 1972.

———. *Notable New Yorkers, 1896–1899.* New York: Bartlet, 1899.

Kunitz, Stanley, and Howard Haycraft, eds. *American Authors, 1600–1900.* New York: Wilson, 1938.

Livermore, Mary A., and Frances Willard, eds. *American Women.* New York and Chicago: Mast, Crowell and Kirkpatrick, 1897.

———. *A Woman of the Century.* Detroit: Gale, 1893.

Malone, Dumas, ed. *Dictionary of American Biography,* Vol. 16. New York: Scribner's, 1935.

Mott, Frank Luther. *American Journalism: A History of Newspapers in the United States Through 250 Years, 1690–1940.* New York: Macmillan, 1941.

———. *A History of American Magazines.* Cambridge, Mass.: Harvard University Press, Belknap Press, 1957.

Pinckney, James D. *Reminiscences of Catskill, Local Sketches.* Catskill: J. B. Hall, 1868.

Riley, Sam G., ed. *American Magazine Journalists, 1850–1900, Dictionary of Literary Biography*, Vol. 79. Detroit: Bruccoli Clark, 1983.

Ross, Ishbel. *Ladies of the Press: The Story of Women in Journalism by an Insider.* New York: Harper, 1936.

Smith, Page. *America Enters the World: A People's History of the Progressive Era and World War I.* New York: Penguin, 1985.

Bibliography

———. *The Rise of Industrial America: A People's History of the Post-Reconstruction Era.* New York: Penguin, 1984.

Smith, Robert Walter. *History of Armstrong County.* Chicago: Waterman, Watkins, 1883.

Stokesbury, James L. *A Short History of World War I.* New York: Morrow, 1981.

Symonds, Craig L. *A Battlefield Atlas of the Civil War.* Baltimore: Nautical and Aviation Publishing, 1985.

Walker, Evelyn H., W. Fletcher Johnson, John Rusk, and Allen E. Fowler. *Leaders of the Nineteenth Century.* Springfield, Mass.: Hampden, 1990.

Welfley, William H. *History of Bedford and Somerset Counties, Pa.*, Vol. 2.

Wiley, Samuel T. *Biographical and Historical Cyclopedia of Indiana and Armstrong Counties, Pa.* Philadelphia: John M. Gresham, 1891.

Wilson, Erasmus. *Standard History of Pittsburgh, Pennsylvania.* Chicago: Goodspeed, 1898.

Other Selected Books

Abbot, Willis J. *Watching the World Go By.* Boston: Little, Brown, 1933.

Abbott, Edith. *Women in Industry.* New York: Appleton, 1910.

Anthony, Carl Sferrazza. *First Ladies: The Saga of the Presidents' Wives and Their Power, 1789–1961.* New York: Morrow, 1990.

Appignanesi, Lisa, and John Forrester. *Freud's Women.* New York: Basic, 1992.

Bainbridge, Oliver. *John Strange Winter.* London: East and West, 1916.

Baker, Nina Brown. *Nellie Bly.* New York: Holt, 1956.

Baldwin, Leland D. *Pittsburgh: The Story of a City.* Pittsburgh: University of Pittsburgh Press, 1938.

Bardes, Barbara, and Suzanne Gossett. *Declarations of Independence: Women and Political Power in Nineteenth Century American Fiction.* New Brunswick: Rutgers University Press, 1990.

Barrett, James Wyman. *The End of the World.* New York: Harper, 1931.

———. *Joseph Pulitzer and His World.* New York: Vanguard, 1941.

———. *The World, the Flesh and Messrs. Pulitzer.* New York: Vanguard, 1931.

Barry, Kathleen. *Susan B. Anthony: The Story of a Singular Figure.* New York: New York University Press, 1988.

Beller, Stern. *Vienna and the Jews, 1867–1938: A Cultural History.* Cambridge: Cambridge University Press, 1989.

Berger, Meyer. *Meyer Berger's New York.* New York: Random House, 1953.

———. *The Story of The New York Times.* New York: Simon and Schuster, 1951.

Bird, Caroline. *Enterprising Women.* New York: W. W. Norton, 1976.

Bisland, Elizabeth. *In Seven Stages: A Flying Trip Around the World.* New York: Harper, 1891.

Blain, Bob. *The Historic Cooperative Village of Leclaire, Edwardsville, Illinois: A Centennial Collection.* Edwardsville, Ill.: Words Worth, 1990.

Bly, Nellie. *The Mystery of Central Park.* New York: G. W. Dillingham, 1889.

———. *Nellie Bly's Book: Around the World in Seventy-Two Days.* New York: Pictorial Weekly, 1890.

———. *Six Months in Mexico.* New York: John W. Lovell, 1886.

————. *Ten Days in a Mad-House.* New York: Norman L. Munro, 1887.

Boucher, John Newton. *A Century and a Half of Pittsburgh and Her People.* Vol. 2. Pittsburgh: Lewis, 1908.

Burgoyne, A. *All Sorts of Pittsburgers.* Pittsburgh: Leader All Sorts, 1892.

Campbell, Helen Stuart. *Women Wage Earners: Their Past, Their Present and Their Future.* Boston: Robert, 1893.

Carlson, Oliver. *Brisbane: A Candid Biography.* New York: Stackpole, 1937.

Chambers, Julius. *Newshunting on Three Continents.* New York: Mitchell Kennerly, 1921.

Chevigny, Bell Gale. *The Woman and the Myth: Margaret Fuller's Life and Writings.* Old Westbury, N.Y.: Feminist Press, 1976.

Churchill, Allen. *Park Row.* New York: Rinehart, 1958.

Clarke, Donald Henderson. *Man of the World.* New York: Vanguard, 1950.

Conway, Jill K. *The Female Experience in Eighteenth and Nineteenth Century America: A Guide to the History of American Women.* Princeton: Princeton University Press, 1985.

Cook, Blanche Wiesen. *Eleanor Roosevelt, Vol. 1, 1884–1933.* New York: Viking, 1992.

Crankshaw, Edward. *The Fall of the House of Habsburg.* New York: Penguin, 1983.

Deák, István. *Beyond Nationalism: A Social and Political History of the Habsburg Officers Corps, 1848–1918.* New York: Oxford University Press, 1990.

Dickens, Charles. *American Notes and Picture from Italy.* 1842. Reprint. London and New York: Macmillan, 1893.

Dreiser, Theodore. *Newspaper Days.* 1931. Reprint. New York: Beekman, 1974.

Drinnon, Richard. *Rebel in Paradise: A Biography of Emma Goldman.* Chicago: University of Chicago Press, 1961.

Ehrlich, Elizabeth. *Nellie Bly.* New York: Chelsea House, 1989.

Emerson, Kathy Lynn. *Making Headlines: A Biography of Nellie Bly.* Minneapolis: Dillion, 1981.

Ferro, Marc. *The Great War, 1914–1918.* London: Routledge and Kegan Paul, 1973.

Fitzgerald, F. Scott. *The Great Gatsby.* New York: Scribner's, 1925.

Fussell, Paul. *The Great War and Modern Memory.* New York: Oxford University Press, 1975.

Gilbert, Felix. *The End of the European Era: 1890 to the Present.* New York: Norton, 1984.

Golding, Louis Thorn. *Memories of Old Park Row, 1887–1897.* New York: Printed for Private Circulation, 1946.

Goldman, Emma. *Living My Life: An Autobiography.* New York: Knopf, 1931.

Granberg, William. *The World of Joseph Pulitzer.* London: Abelard Schuman, 1965.

Harper, Ida Husted. *Life and Work of Susan B. Anthony,* Vol. 2. Boston: Beacon, 1959.

Haughton, Ida Cochran. *Chronicles of the Cochrans.* Columbus, Ohio: Stoneman, 1915.

————. *Chronicles of the Cochrans, Volume Second.* Columbus, Ohio: F. J. Heer, 1925.

Hearst, William Randolph, Jr. *The Hearsts: Father and Son.* Niwot: Roberts Rinehart, 1991.

Henry, T. J. *1816–1916: The History of Apollo, Pennsylvania.* Apollo: News-Record, 1916.

Higgins, Ardis O. *Windows on Women.* North Hollywood, Calif.: Halls of Ivy Press, 1975.

Howard, John Tasker. *Stephen Foster, America's Troubadour.* New York: Crowell, 1934.

Howard, Robert P. *Most Good and Competent Men, Illinois Governors, 1818–1988.* Springfield: Sangamon State University and Illinois State Historical Society, 1988.

Ireland, Alleyne. *Joseph Pulitzer: Reminiscences of a Secretary.* New York: Dutton, 1914.

Jelavich, Barbara. *Modern Austria: Empire to Republic, 1800–1986.* New York: Cambridge University Press, 1987.

Kessler-Harris, Alice. *Out to Work: A History of Wage-Earning in the United States.* New York: Oxford University Press, 1982.

King, Homer W. *Pulitzer's Prize Editor: A Biography of John A. Cockerill, 1845–1896.* Durham, N.C.: Duke University Press, 1965.

Kluger, Richard. *The Paper: The Life and Death of the New York Herald Tribune.* New York: Knopf, 1986.

Lafore, Laurence. *The Long Fuse: An Interpretation of the Origins of World War I.* New York: Lippincott, 1971.

Lancaster, Paul. *Gentlemen of the Press: The Life and Times of an Early Reporter, Julian Ralph of the Sun.* Syracuse: Syracuse University Press, 1992.

Lorant, Stephan. *Pittsburgh: The Story of an American City.* New York: Doubleday, 1964.

Lubow, Arthur. *The Reporter Who Would Be King: A Biography of Richard Harding Davis.* New York: Scribner's, 1992.

McDougall, Walt. *This Is the Life.* New York: Knopf, 1926.

[Marks, Jason]. *The Story of Nellie Bly.* New York: American Flange and Manufacturing Co., 1951.

Marks, Jason. *Around the World in Seventy-two Days: The Race Between Pulitzer's Nellie Bly and Cosmopolitan's Elizabeth Bisland.* New York: Gemittarius, 1993.

Marshall, S. L. A. *World War I.* Boston: Houghton Mifflin, 1964.

Meyer, Michael, and William L. Sherman. *The Course of Mexican History.* New York: Oxford University Press, 1979.

Milton, Joyce. *The Yellow Kids: Foreign Correspondents in the Heyday of Yellow Journalism.* New York: Harper and Row, 1989.

Monk, Ray. *Ludwig Wittgenstein: The Duty of Genius.* New York: Free Press, 1990.

Nelson, N. O. *Profit-Sharing.* St. Louis, 1887.

Nevin, Adelaide Mellier. *The Social Mirror.* Pittsburgh: T. W. Nevin, 1888.

Noble, Iris. *Nellie Bly: First Woman Reporter.* Detroit: Messner, 1956.

Nye, Edgar Wilson. *Bill Nye: His Own Life Story.* New York: Century, 1926.

Parkhurst, C. H. *My Forty Years in New York.* New York: Macmillan, 1923.

Pick, Robert. *The Last Days of Imperial Vienna.* London: Weidenfeld and Nicolson, 1975.

Pletcher, David M. *Rails, Mines and Progress: Seven American Promoters in Mexico, 1867–1911.* Ithaca: Cornell University Press, 1958.

Riis, Jacob A. *How the Other Half Lives: Studies Among the Tenements of New York.* 1890. Reprint. New York: Hill and Wang, 1957.

Rittenhouse, Mignon. *The Amazing Nellie Bly.* Freeport, N.Y.: Books for Libraries Press, 1956.

Rodman, Selden. *A Short History of Mexico.* New York: Stein and Day, 1982.

Ross, Ishbel. *Charmers and Cranks.* New York: Harper and Row, 1965.

Sante, Luc. *Low Life: Lures and Snares of Old New York.* New York: Farrar, Straus and Giroux, 1991.

Schneider, Dorothy, and Carl J. Schneider. *Into the Breach: American Women Overseas in World War I.* New York: Viking Penguin, 1991.

Schorske, Carl E. *Fin-de-Siècle Vienna: Politics and Culture.* New York: Vintage, 1981.

Schudson, Michael. *Discovering the News: A Social History of American Newspapers.* New York: Basic, 1978.

Seitz, Don D. *Joseph Pulitzer: His Life and Letters.* New York: Simon and Schuster, 1924.

Sipes, William B. *The Pennsylvania Railroad: Its Origin, Construction, Conditions and Connection.* Philadelphia: Passenger Dept., 1875.

Stephens, Mitchell. *A History of News: From the Drum to the Satellite.* New York: Penguin, 1989.

Stern, Robert A. M., Gregory Gilmartin, and John Messengale. *New York 1900.* New York: Rizzoli, 1983.

Swanberg, W. A. *Citizen Hearst.* New York: Collier, 1961.

———. *Dreiser.* New York: Scribner's, 1965.

———. *Pulitzer.* New York: Scribner's, 1967.

Tebbel, John. *The Compact History of the American Newspaper.* New York: Hawthorn, 1963.

Thwaite, Ann. *Waiting for the Party: The Life of Frances Hodgson Burnett.* New York: Scribner's, 1974.

Trudeau, Noah Andre. *Bloody Roads South: The Wilderness to Cold Harbor, May–June 1864.* New York: Fawcett Columbine, 1989.

Verne, Jules. *Around the World in Eighty Days.* 1873. Reprint. New York: Bantam, 1984.

Walker, Stanley. *City Editor.* New York: Stokes, 1934.

Waltz, George H. *Jules Verne.* New York: Holt, 1943.

Wendt, Lloyd. *Chicago Tribune: The Rise of a Great American Newspaper.* Chicago: Rand McNally, 1979.

Wexler, Alice. *Emma Goldman in America.* Boston: Beacon, 1984.

Wilson, Erasmus. *Quiet Observations on the Ways of the World.* New York: Cassell, 1886.

Zurosky, Ann. *The First One Hundred Years, 1891–1991.* Pittsburgh: Women's Press Club, 1992.

INDEX

❦ ❦